The Psychology of Musical Development

The Psychology of Musical Development provide＿＿up-to-date and comprehensive account of the latest theory, empirical research and applications in the study of musical development, an important and emerging field of music psychology. After considering how people now engage with music in the digital world, and reviewing current advances in developmental and music psychology, Hargreaves and Lamont compare ten major theoretical approaches in this field – including cognitive stage models and neuroscientific, ecological and social cognitive approaches – and assess how successfully each of these deals with five critical theoretical issues. Individual chapters deal next with cognition, perception and learning; social development; environmental influences on ability, achievement and motivation; identity, personality and lifestyle; affect and emotion; and wellbeing and health. With an emphasis on practical applications throughout, this book will be essential reading for students and scholars of music psychology, developmental psychology, music education and music therapy.

David Hargreaves is Professor of Education at the University of Roehampton, London, and a chartered psychologist and fellow of the British Psychological Society.

Alexandra Lamont is Senior Lecturer in Psychology of Music at Keele University and recent editor of the journal *Psychology of Music*.

The Psychology of Musical Development

David Hargreaves
University of Roehampton, London

Alexandra Lamont
Keele University

CAMBRIDGE
UNIVERSITY PRESS

CAMBRIDGE
UNIVERSITY PRESS

University Printing House, Cambridge CB2 8BS, United Kingdom

One Liberty Plaza, 20th Floor, New York, NY 10006, USA

477 Williamstown Road, Port Melbourne, VIC 3207, Australia

4843/24, 2nd Floor, Ansari Road, Daryaganj, Delhi – 110002, India

79 Anson Road, #06-04/06, Singapore 079906

Cambridge University Press is part of the University of Cambridge.

It furthers the University's mission by disseminating knowledge in the pursuit of
education, learning, and research at the highest international levels of excellence.

www.cambridge.org
Information on this title: www.cambridge.org/9781107686397
DOI: 10.1017/9781107281868

First published 2017

Printed in the United Kingdom by Clays, St Ives plc

A catalogue record for this publication is available from the British Library.

Library of Congress Cataloging-in-Publication Data
Names: Hargreaves, David, 1948– | Lamont, Alexandra.
Title: The psychology of musical development / David Hargreaves & Alexandra Lamont.
Description: New York: Cambridge University Press, 2017. |
Includes bibliographical references and index.
Identifiers: LCCN 2017004384 | ISBN 9781107052963 (hardback) | ISBN 9781107686397 (paperback)
Subjects: LCSH: Music – Psychological aspects. | Developmental psychology. | Musical ability.
Classification: LCC ML3830.H24 2017 | DDC 781.1/1–dc23
LC record available at https://lccn.loc.gov/2017004384

ISBN 978-1-107-05296-3 Hardback
ISBN 978-1-107-68639-7 Paperback

This book is dedicated to the memory of
Mollie Hargreaves (née Metcalfe), 1923–2016

Contents

Figures

Tables

Tables

Preface

All the world's a stage,
And all the men and women merely players;
They have their exits and their entrances,
And one man in his time plays many parts,
His acts being seven ages. At first, the infant,
Mewling and puking in the nurse's arms.
Then the whining schoolboy, with his satchel
And shining morning face, creeping like snail
Unwillingly to school. And then the lover,
Sighing like furnace, with a woeful ballad
Made to his mistress' eyebrow. Then a soldier,
Full of strange oaths and bearded like the pard,
Jealous in honour, sudden and quick in quarrel,
Seeking the bubble reputation
Even in the cannon's mouth. And then the justice,
In fair round belly with good capon lined,
With eyes severe and beard of formal cut,
Full of wise saws and modern instances;
And so he plays his part. The sixth age shifts
Into the lean and slippered pantaloon,
With spectacles on nose and pouch on side;
His youthful hose, well saved, a world too wide
For his shrunk shank, and his big manly voice,
Turning again toward childish treble, pipes
And whistles in his sound. Last scene of all,
That ends this strange eventful history,
Is second childishness and mere oblivion,
Sans teeth, sans eyes, sans taste, sans everything.

From *As You Like It*, spoken by Jaques to Duke Senior, act II, scene 7
William Shakespeare, 1564–1616

Shakespeare's famous and often-quoted poem is remarkably insightful, especially in that it was written at least 300 years before the advent of the discipline of psychology. His idea of seven ages of man is not essentially dissimilar from the view that some developmental psychologists might have of lifespan development today, and his central analogy between life and the stage also has a great deal in common with some contemporary ideas in social theory, including role theory, the notion of identities, and the importance of narrative in explaining human development. In *Acts of Meaning* (1990), for example, Jerome Bruner suggests that 'People narrativize their experience of the world and of their own role in it' (p. 115), and adds that 'The fact that the historian's "empirical" account and the novelist's imaginative story *share* the narrative form is, on reflection, rather startling' (p. 45). The poem is also of more specific interest here because Shakespeare makes four different references to music, or at least to vocalisation: to the infant's mewling, the schoolboy's whining, the lover's ballad, and the 'childish treble' voice of old age.

The basic questions we answer in this book are how and to what extent people engage with music in different ways across the lifespan, from infancy to old age, and what effects these engagements have on different aspects of their behaviour and experience. Developmental psychologists still have not reached agreement about the possible existence, nature, and number of developmental stages today, and we could say a lot more about the possible validity of Shakespeare's seven proposed stages – although doing so may not add a great deal of insight. This is partly because our emphasis here is less on the details of age-related changes in musical development and more on how different musical competencies develop at different ages, and how these manifest themselves in different aspects of behaviour. As we shall see, music has a role to play in our physical development and our neural functioning; in the development of our perception, thinking, and learning; of our motivation and emotion; of our personality, social development, and sense of identity; and of our health and wellbeing. The ways in which it does so form the essence of this book.

If our main task is to investigate how music can influence these many different areas of our lives as well as the converse – i.e. how these different aspects of behaviour form different parts of our musical lives – then we need to be more precise about what we mean by 'engagement with music'. In the past, the distinctions between musicians, composers, improvisers, performers, and listeners were fairly straightforward, and most members of all five groups would probably have been clear about which group, or groups, they belonged to. Recent changes in our understanding of these concepts, many of which derive from psychological insights, mean that these distinctions have now become much more blurred. For example, it would previously have been widely agreed that the term 'musician' meant someone who was actively involved in producing music: composers, improvisers, and performers would all have been included and listeners or audience members took a more passive and reactive role. However, Nikki Rickard and TanChyuan Chin (2017) have recently argued that it is possible to define musicianship in terms of listening with just as much validity as it is in terms of production skills. They suggest that a 'musicianship of listening' exists alongside the more conventional 'musicianship of production', and that the widespread use of the term 'non-musician' should therefore decline: we wholeheartedly agree with this perspective.

Another related view is that 'we are all musical': that 'every human being has a biological and social guarantee of musicianship ... and that the technical and expressive aspects of musical performance demand skills that everyone is capable of learning given the appropriate environmental intervention' (Hargreaves,

MacDonald, & Miell, 2012a, pp. 129–130). This view is gaining support from a growing number of researchers exploring the foundations of musical behaviour. In particular, Colwyn Trevarthen's research (e.g. Trevarthen, 2002, 2012) has shown how the earliest communication between caregiver and child is essentially musical. This communication, which consists of vocal, visual, and gestural interplay, has more in common with musical interaction than with spoken language, and research evidence has demonstrated this to be the case by means of detailed microanalyses of communicative interactions.

Although we all have the potential for musicianship, the problem is that many of us do not fulfil this potential because musical talent and ability tend to be defined in terms of high-level performing skills. Although provision is made in schools and other institutions for children who show promise to develop their musical skills, many others start to see themselves as being 'unmusical', fail to develop their early potential and follow a downward spiral in which lack of musical self-esteem and motivation leads to lower levels of performance, which leads to still lower self-esteem, and so on. In Pablo Picasso's words, 'Every child is an artist. The problem is how to remain an artist once he grows up.'

This book has its origins in *The Developmental Psychology of Music*, by one of us (David Hargreaves, 1986a): this book was published more than thirty years ago, and was intended at the time to be a first attempt to delineate the field as such. At that time the scope of music psychology in the UK was very limited in comparison to today, and a major role in its development was played by the Society for Education, Music and Psychology Research (SEMPRE). The changes that have taken place since then have been expertly documented by Gordon Cox, Leon Crickmore, Charles Plummeridge, and Desmond Sergeant, all early stalwarts of the Society, in their article 'SEMPRE: 40 years on', which was published in the special issue of the Society's journal *Psychology of Music* to celebrate its fortieth anniversary. Cox et al. (2012) identify one of the central concerns in the 1980s as being the debate about the relationship between theory and practice, and John Sloboda, in his second issue as editor of the journal, raised this question in an open letter to members of the Society about 'achieving our aims in music education' (Sloboda, 1986). This produced a number of responses, including an article by David (Hargreaves, 1986b) on 'developmental psychology and music education', which summarised many of the concerns and issues set out in the earlier book.

Cox et al. describe the rapid growth and diversification of music psychology and music education which has occurred since then, and we have both played our parts in this, as editors of *Psychology of Music* (David between 1989 and 1996 and Alexandra between 2012 and 2016), and as members of the Music Development Task Group of the Qualifications and Curriculum Authority in England in the 1990s, a 'think tank' whose aim was to translate ideas and methods from music psychology and other fields into practical applications for the classroom. David had also begun to introduce musical content into his teaching of developmental psychology in the Department of Psychology at the University of Leicester, and when he left that post in 1998 for Durham, the Open University, and eventually the University of Roehampton, Alexandra was appointed as his replacement in the Leicester Music Research Group, working alongside Adrian North and Mark Tarrant. Alexandra and Mark both moved to lectureships in psychology at Keele University in 2001 to join John Sloboda in the Unit for the Study of Musical Skill and Development, and we both collaborated on research described later in this book on children's musical engagement along with Mark and a new colleague of David's, Nigel Marshall, at Roehampton. Our somewhat intertwined careers have thus spanned some of the major centres of music psychology research in the UK.

Our own personal stories of musical development have also had an inevitable effect on the contents of this book. David studied the piano from a very early age, and soon became more interested in improvising and playing by ear than in playing the pieces he was set, and was never entered for any of the ABRSM grade examinations. He went on to study the oboe at secondary school (including performing in the school's wind quintet, at the school's 450th anniversary, for an audience including Queen Elizabeth II), playing in many orchestral concerts, but it was not until his arrival as a student at Durham University in 1966 that his future activity as a semi-professional jazz musician began to crystallise: this new direction was given a fortuitous boost by the appointment of John Booth Davies as David's first psychology tutor, and also as his first bandleader, in the Durham University jazz quintet. Alexandra, on the other hand, had a rather more traditional career in classical music beginning with recorder at school, piano lessons (and many grades) from the age of six, and picking up (and putting down) the violin from the age of nine, sticking with it when she joined Trinity College of Music's junior department at the age of thirteen. After a degree in academic music which was accompanied by many classical performance opportunities, she left the world of practical music behind for many years. However, like many adults, she subsequently returned to performing, and now spends much of her spare time playing the violin in classical symphony and chamber orchestras and in a small band accompanying a range of indie pop musicians.

Over the years we have been fortunate to work with and alongside a number of different colleagues and research students who have helped shape our thinking about musical development, many of whom are cited in the bibliography of the present book. It is of course invidious to pick out individuals, but those whose input has been most influential for one or both of us include Adrian North, Mark Tarrant, John Sloboda, Jane Davidson, Raymond MacDonald, Dorothy Miell, Ian Cross, Graça Boal-Palheiros, Patrik Juslin, Göran Folkestad, Ambjörn Hugardt, Gary McPherson, Bengt Olsson, Sandra Trehub, Glenn Schellenberg, Frances Rauscher, Allan Hewitt, Karl Maton, Alinka Greasley, Adam Ockelford, Emery Schubert, and Arielle Bonneville-Roussy. We should like to acknowledge our debt and gratitude to all these collaborators, as well as to Steven Caldwell Brown, Gary McPherson, Adam Ockelford, Arielle Bonneville-Roussy, Jon Hargreaves, and an anonymous reviewer, who have kindly given us their constructive comments on drafts of the book. Due to our own artistic and technical limitations, sincere thanks to Niall King for help with illustrations. Our thanks also go to the staff at

Cambridge University Press, especially Hetty Marx and Janka Romero, for their wisdom and support from beginning to end. Any errors that remain are of course our responsibility.

On a more personal note, David would like to acknowledge the unstinting support and help of Linda, Jon, and Tom Hargreaves, who have contributed to his thinking about and experiences of music, psychology, and education over many years, and who are now joined by two more formidable family members, Ruth Newton and Holly Mathieson. Jon and Tom's songs and drawings formed a memorable part of the 1986 book, and David's practical knowledge of musical development in the early years has been given a vigorous recent update by his grandchildren, Sam and Rowan, who have their own powerful and distinctive views on many issues! Alexandra is hugely grateful to Niall King for his sustained support, encouragement, and motivation. Thanks are also due to her friends, many of whom are actively involved in music, for their constant questioning: first about the progress of the book, and second about ensuring important issues are addressed particularly in the realm of music education – a discipline and an activity under considerable threat in the UK throughout the time of writing. 'I hope you've put in something about . . .' has become a familiar refrain over the past few years, and, at the end of this endeavour, we hope we have.

1 Introduction

This book presents our view of the current state of the study of musical development. As researchers and writers who have studied, worked, and researched in the fields of development, education, and music, we have gathered together the current state of knowledge and given our perspectives on what has become a diverse and wide-ranging field of enquiry which is of importance and interest to musicians, educators, psychologists, students, and all those concerned with the effects and impact of music in our lives.

The forerunner of this book – *The Developmental Psychology of Music*, by David Hargreaves (1986a) – was published more than thirty years ago, and was intended to be a first attempt to delineate this field as such. One reviewer of the original book proposal pointed out at the time that 'the book is more about what the developmental psychology of music might become than about what it is', and this was a fair comment which reflected the original aim of mapping out the field for the first time. In the intervening years, development has become well established as one of the main sub-disciplines of contemporary music psychology along with the cognitive psychology of music and the social psychology of music. So many developments and changes have occurred since 1986 that there is a clear need for a completely new account of what the field has become. These changes are so wide-ranging and profound, covering not only basic theoretical perspectives but also different areas of content and new methodologies, that this is considerably more than just a second edition of the earlier book: we have wiped the slate clean, and started as if from scratch. In this first chapter, our primary aim is to set out the key developments which have characterised the past thirty years of research and investigation on musical development, but before we can do that we need to look more generally at the recent history of people's engagement with music, and indeed with the changes that have taken place in music itself.

Developments in Music and Musical Engagement

The nature of music itself has changed dramatically, particularly over the twentieth century: the pace of change has accelerated, and is still accelerating right up to the present day. In Western classical music, musicologists have documented many revolutions and dramatic changes: the 'new' music of Beethoven, Wagner, Debussy, Stravinsky, Schoenberg, and Messiaen, to name just a few, revolutionised the ways in which future composers worked. After World War II, developments in electronic sound production opened up entirely new musical territory for composers such as Stockhausen, whose vigorous discussions with other iconoclastic composers including Pierre Boulez and John Cage became part of the post-war modernist movement in the arts. The subsequent postmodern turn in classical music included what has become the minimalist tradition, notably the work of composers such as John Adams, Philip Glass, Michael Nyman, Steve Reich, and Terry Riley, who reacted against the perceived elitism, intellectual complexity, and dissonance of atonal modernism by producing music with simple textures and relatively consonant harmonies.

Alongside the increasing pace of change, it is the move away from modernist ideals in music that characterises the changes that have taken place since 1986. Composers in classical music have been openly influenced by popular music, jazz, and world ethnic musical traditions, while others, most notably John Cage, challenged the prevailing standards of beauty and objectivity that were a fundamental part of modernism. Within popular music, the powerful influences of the blues, rock'n'roll, the Beatles, punk rock, and many subsequent styles have diversified, cross-fertilised, and reached a point at which the plethora of available genres and styles have become increasingly difficult to distinguish: similarly, in jazz, the succession from bebop to hard bop to fusion music and 'free jazz' has led to a point at which European free improvisation and folk music are all potential parts of a much richer tapestry than in the past. In this context it is easy to see that the distinction between 'serious' and 'popular' music, and the relative evaluation of them, has blurred considerably within the last few decades. It is widely recognised today that the use of the former term to refer largely to Western classical music is an anachronism, and that musics from many other cultures and continents should be given equal status.

Technological Developments and Their Effects

Going back to 1586, probably about when William Shakespeare wrote the famous poem in the Preface, the only way to hear music would have been by attending live performances. The range of musical styles and instruments to be heard would have been very limited: listening to music would have occurred much less often, and most people would have heard particular pieces only a few times in their lives. This situation persisted through to the late nineteenth century, when a seismic revolution occurred in music listening with the invention of sound recording. Pioneered by Thomas Edison, this was quickly followed by the mass production of recordings which were sufficiently inexpensive as to be accessible to a wide range of listeners. These developments had a profound influence on the nature of music listening, which was changed still further by the advent of radio and television, and the growth of the mass media.

In a children's Ladybird book *The Story of Music*, published in 1968, Geoffrey Brace wrote that

'[T]oday, by means of the radio or a record player, we can hear any music we choose from any period, in any style, played by the finest musicians in the world. What is more, with a record we can hear it as often as we are like, and this has completely changed the part music has taken in our daily lives. Perhaps we have too much music now – and because it is so easily obtained, we make too little effort to listen to it. An enormous amount of music on radio and records is often regarded as just a background to talking, eating or housework. This may make us forget that there is a great deal of music that is meant to be really listened to with all our attention.' (p. 50)

Brace's view of music listening reflected the enormous changes that had occurred, as well as expressed a tinge of sadness about the disappearance of some of the qualities of what has now become known as 'live' (as distinct from recorded) musical experience.

The pace of change accelerated still more sharply with the digital revolution of the 1980s. This has had profound effects on many aspects of people's lives, including not only music listening but also the ways in which music is produced, recorded, and transmitted. Due to technological developments that derive from the digitisation of music and its transmission via the internet, 'being a musician' today involves far more skills than it did only twenty or thirty years ago: it might now be considered by some to include some arranging or improvising skills, and/or a working knowledge of music hardware and software. However, technology has also facilitated involvement and engagement with these processes: a single composer can 'perform' an entire symphony or 'play' all the parts in a band with relative ease, and without thousands of hours of practice at the instruments. The introduction and rapid growth of personal computing and the growth of the internet means that digital music files are easily accessible and transferable within the music business, as well as for members of the general public.

In addition to recording, two more recent technological changes have been very influential. One is the development of relatively inexpensive but high-capacity portable digital music players, the best known of which is probably Apple's iPod: these enable individuals to carry their entire music library with them wherever they go, and to listen to different selections from it in many everyday situations. The second change concerns how people obtain their music. The traditional practice of purchasing vinyl or CD records is rapidly being overtaken by downloading and streaming of digital music from internet sites, such as Apple's iTunes, onto personal music players. Furthermore, the ways in which music is distributed and shared between people have also been powerfully influenced by the growth of YouTube, Spotify, and other such music websites, and by the sudden and massive growth of social networking sites including Facebook and Twitter. Technological change has contributed to the ubiquity and portability of music, as well as to its demystification and globalisation. Another effect, as we shall see later in the book, is that people's music listening is becoming more functional, chosen to meet their particular needs in particular situations.

Table 1.1. Brown's (2016) 'meaningful creative engagement matrix', with exemplary musical activities in each cell

	Appreciating	Evaluating	Directing	Exploring	Embodying
Personal	Listen, Read, Watch	Analyse, Select	Compose, Produce	Improvise, Experiment	Practice, Play
Social	Share files	Discuss, Share playlists	Conduct, Lead	Jam	Rehearse, Record
Cultural	Attend events, Patronage	Curate, Publish reviews	Promote, Manage	Publish research	Perform

Source: Table 11.2 (p. 212) in Brown, A. R. (2016). Engaging in a sound musicianship. In G. E McPherson (Ed.), *The child as musician: A handbook of musical development* (2nd edition, pp. 208–220). © Oxford University Press. By permission of Oxford University Press.

Andrew Brown (2016) has summarised the general effects of these changes in terms of what he calls the 'technoculture': children can now access the internet via touch-screen mobile devices, and use them to play games and make video calls to their distant family members all around the world at a very early age. Given these changes, Brown suggests that we should reinterpret the nature of musical experience, and he uses his own three-dimensional framework in order to do this. First, he proposes that there are five 'modes of creative engagement' which can describe present-day musical activities: these are 'Attending – paying careful attention to creative works and analyzing their representations; Evaluating – judging aesthetic value and cultural appropriateness; Directing – crafting creative outcomes and leading creative activities; Exploring – searching through artistic possibilities; and Embodying – being engrossed in fluent creative expression' (p. 210). Each of these five modes of creative engagement is seen by Brown as taking place in three different types of context, namely the Personal (the intrinsic enjoyment of creative activities), the Social (the development of artistic relationships with others), and the Cultural (the feeling that one's creative actions are valued by the community).

By combining the five modes of creative engagement with the three contexts, Brown emerges with what he calls a 'meaningful engagement matrix', which is shown in Table 1.1: he has populated the cells of this matrix with illustrative examples of typical activities in each case. Brown then goes further in using this framework to broaden the definition of musicianship along the lines that we suggested earlier. Brown's suggestion is that what he calls 'sound musicianship', which is broadened to cover all the facets demanded in the technocultural age, has four main components. These are: the sonic component, which concerns the exploration of sound from an acoustic point of view; the psychological component, which deals with people's cognitive and emotional engagement with music, which is the main focus of this book as a whole; the embodied component, which concerns the inextricable inter-relationships between music and human movements, such as physical gestures and motor synchronisation with aspects of music, and with other aspects of the performance environment; and the cultural component, which includes the social, political, and economic contexts in which music-making occurs, and all the ideas, customs, and habits which are associated with them.

Personal Music Listening and Control

An important consequence of these recent technological advances is that people now actively *use* music in everyday listening contexts. They cannot avoid their exposure to it in shops, restaurants, and other everyday environments, but they actively *control* its use in the home, in the car, on public transport, and in many other everyday situations in order to create certain mood states or to moderate their levels of arousal (see North & Hargreaves, 2008). Data from experience sampling studies, in which people's everyday experiences are randomly sampled over a particular time period (Csikszentmihalyi & Lefèvre, 1989), have shown that adults are exposed to music around 37–53 per cent of the time (Greasley & Lamont, 2011; Juslin, Liljeström, Västfjäll, Barradas, & Silva 2008; North, Hargreaves, & Hargreaves, 2004; Sloboda, O'Neill, & Ivaldi, 2001), and children, as we shall see later, experience over 80 per cent of their waking hours with music (Lamont, 2008).

The critical factor in personal music listening, absent in public listening, is the degree of control that the listener has over the listening situation, and the rapid and recent rise in personal music listening is changing the ways in which people do it. Mehrabian and Russell's (1974) model of environmental psychology (M-R) suggests that people respond to particular environments by showing approach and avoidance behaviours. Environmental factors affect their emotional states, such as their levels of pleasure or arousal, which lead them either to approach or avoid particular environments. There are four aspects of approach/avoidance behaviour, namely (a) the desire to physically stay in (approach) or to leave (avoid) the environment, (b) the willingness to explore (approach) the environment or to avoid interacting with it, (c) the willingness to communicate with others in the environment (approach) or to avoid them, and (d) the increase (approach) or decline (avoidance) in satisfaction with behaviour in the environment. Individuals' tendency to decide to approach or avoid the environment depends on their emotional response to it, and this is determined by three different dimensions, namely pleasure, arousal, and dominance.

We deal with pleasure and arousal in much more depth in Chapter 7, but attention has shifted towards the notion of *dominance* in some recent research. Following the M-R model, Amanda Krause argues that dominance (i.e. control) should lead to more positive listening experiences. Devices that offer more control over listening (e.g. MP3 players or personal computers) seem to promote contentment and further motivation to listen (Krause, North, & Hewitt, 2015), and selection methods with more control (e.g. choosing a specific album or a personal preselected playlist) have similar positive effects (Krause, North, & Hewitt, 2014). Confirming many other findings, Krause, North, & Hewitt (2016) found that music heard in private spaces and locations was liked more and given more attention than that heard in public spaces and locations, in which people felt less in control (or were less dominant, in terms of the M-R model).

In summary, the choice of listening device is important in public, as people's use of mobile devices allows them to exert control. This means that the listening context includes location and also the device through which music is played, which supports the M-R contention that dominance can be important, and that listener control may well be an index of this. Listeners can be seen as active consumers rather than as passive ones (which, incidentally, coincides with the view of listening as a creative musical activity proposed by Hargreaves, Hargreaves, & North, 2012). These results overall provide support for the notion that individual choice of music exerts a strong influence over the ways in which it is perceived. This is in line with other findings from the field of music, health, and wellbeing, in which it is now well established that control of music affects feelings of wellbeing and health, and in particular people's reactions to stressors and physical pain (see further in Chapter 8).

Advances in Developmental Psychology and Music Psychology

Alongside these changes in music and technology, there have been corresponding changes in the academic disciplines on which we need to draw in explaining musical development, which now go well beyond psychology to include sociology, neuroscience, music theory, education, marketing, and communication. In 1986, the developmental psychology of music was an emerging sub-discipline, alongside cognitive and social music psychology. The subsequent growth of all of these, as in other areas of music psychology, has been phenomenal, such that the multidisciplinary connections of music psychology are now very extensive. We can identify another emerging field which might be called applied music psychology, in which the findings of the discipline are applied in the areas such as broadcasting and the media, education, health and wellbeing, consumer behaviour, social inclusion, and musicianship itself.

The Current State of Research in Developmental Psychology and Education

Towards the end of the last century, Western developmental psychology was characterised by the 'grand theories' of human development proposed by Jean Piaget and Sigmund Freud, the twin influences of behavioural and cognitive psychology, and the ecological or perceptual–development theory of James Gibson (1979/2015). Since then, three further theoretical approaches have had a profound influence on the explanation of human development. The first derives from the work of Lev Vygotsky (1966, 1978), whose work was translated and made available in the West from the 1980s onwards. Vygotsky emphasised the fundamentally social nature of learning and development, along with the basic idea that children's learning is mediated by what he called 'cultural tools', the most prominent of which is language. He emphasised the powerful influence of the social and cultural context in which development takes place; recent developments of these increasingly influential ideas have collectively become known as the *sociocultural* approach. The second approach comes from the rapid growth of cognitive neuroscience over the last decade or two, aided by the relatively recent development of brain imaging techniques. Developmental neuroscientists have developed two different but complementary approaches in trying to explain the mechanisms of cognitive development and learning. These are *neuroconstructivism*, which investigates how neural structures become increasingly specialised in response to children's choice of activities, and *connectionism*, which uses computer modelling to predict the effects of the repeated activation of neural networks. The third is a recent upsurge of interest in the self, and self-theories: this has taken the form of investigations of self-regulation and metacognition, as well as of identity and the self-concept.

In addition to these approaches, three further ideas originally identified by Hargreaves (1986a) are still important today. The first of these is the idea that the child is an active agent in its own socialisation: in parent–child relationships, for example, the child is seen to influence the parent to at least the same extent as vice versa. The notions of *reciprocity* and *intersubjectivity* in adult–child relationships are now very well established in developmental thinking. The second feature, closely related to the first, is the emphasis on what might be called a cognitive approach. The 'cognitive revolution' of the 1980s (see e.g. Gardner, 1987) was specifically interested in the processes going on within the 'black box' of the mind: phenomena such as attention, memory, planning, and creative thinking represented the essence of this approach. This perspective has now been taken in a different direction to incorporate the study of emotional development, and the social and emotional aspects of learning, including Harris's (1989) research on children's understanding of the emotional and mental states of others and Gardner's (1999) identification of inter- and intra-personal intelligences. This is particularly significant for the study of musical development, since emotional communication and expression is one of the central functions of music, as will become evident later in the book.

The third feature is the significant increase in methodological sophistication. Sophisticated sequential methods (see e.g. Schaie, 1965, 1983, 1996) have enabled the traditional strengths and weaknesses of longitudinal and cross-sectional approaches to be overcome by incorporating aspects of both, taking account of the differences between age effects, cohort effects, and time-of-measurement effects. Ongoing advances in technology have also expanded opportunities to collect and analyse different types of data, and in the areas of infant research, everyday engagement with music, and in neuroscience, technology has continued to help advance the fields of research that apply to musical development.

We shall return to these theoretical perspectives and different features of developmental research in more detail in Chapter 2, along with two further features of the contemporary study of musical development: its interdisciplinarity, and its applicability to real-life practical issues. Music psychology as a whole has many applications in a wide range of areas, as we shall see, but perhaps the most obvious area of application of the developmental study of music is in its influence upon education. In the Preface we mentioned the concern about the relationship between theory and practice which existed in the 1980s: in the intervening years, the links between theory and practice in music education have strengthened considerably, to the extent that it is worth considering how current developments in educational research might have influenced the study of musical development.

It turns out, perhaps not surprisingly, that the main new directions in educational research have a great deal in common with those in developmental psychology, which illustrates how theory and practice have come together. All three of the important new theoretical directions identified above have clear parallels in educational research. To take them in order, the current predominance of sociocultural approaches is apparent in educational research as well as in psychological studies of development: one very interesting example of this, which may derive directly from Vygotsky's emphasis on language and social 'talk', is the rise of interest in classroom dialogue (see e.g. Howe and Abedin's 2013 review of the past 40 years of research in this area).

Egalitarian dialogue is that in which each participant's contribution is considered according to its quality and validity rather than by the status or power of that participant. This principle has been used in *dialogical education* by Ramón Flecha (2000); Mercer (1995) and Alexander (2008) have also emphasised the importance and educational benefits of dialogic teaching and learning. Some of the techniques that have been developed in this approach, such as *dialogic literary gatherings* (DLGs), involve discussions between teachers and pupils, in this case about classic works of literature, in which the views of each individual are given equal status, thereby removing the usual power differential between teacher and learner. Such techniques have been shown to exert powerful positive effects on pupils' literacy acquisition as well as on their emotional and social development, and it is interesting that they also have some features in in common with the use of informal methods in music education, as we shall see in Chapter 5.

It is also very clear that the rapid growth of cognitive neuroscience, our second important new approach, now exerts a powerful influence on educational theory and research. In Chapter 2 we will describe how developmental neuroscientists are constructing new approaches to the explanation of cognitive development and learning, and that these have important practical implications for teaching and learning. We identified the third important new direction as the recent upsurge of interest in the self and self-theories, which has led to new investigations of self-regulation and metacognition. These also form an important new direction in educational research, and one particular area of interest is in studies of children's wellbeing. In the UK, these arose in part from the UNICEF (2007) Report *Child poverty in perspective: An overview of child well-being in rich countries*. This report, which received considerable publicity, placed British children at the bottom of the league table of rich nations with respect to their emotional wellbeing and happiness. Similarly, Layard and Dunn's (2009) *A good childhood* – the report of The Good Childhood Enquiry – stimulated a national debate about the possibility that 'toxic childhood' could be an unfortunate aspect of contemporary life: that the pressures on young children from educational institutions, from their parents, from their peers, and in particular from the images and concepts they gain from the media have become intolerable, such that children cannot cope and either drop out or turn away from this pressure. It is also worth noting here that one important new direction in music psychology is in the positive effects of music on stress, coping, health, and wellbeing (see e.g. MacDonald, Kreutz, & Mitchell, 2012a, and Chapter 8).

The Growth and Diversification of Music Psychology

There has been an explosion of interest in the psychological basis of musical thinking, behaviour, and development over the last two decades or so which shows no sign of abating. The specialist journals in the discipline such as *Psychology of Music*, *Music Perception*, *Psychomusicology*, and *Musicae Scientiae* are healthier than ever before.

Before the 1980s, music psychology had been characterised by a preponderance of psychometric and acoustical studies. This approach was very clearly represented by Seashore's (1938) book *The Psychology of Music*, which placed a strong emphasis upon the objective measurement of auditory sensory abilities, with very little interest in the investigation of musical behaviour as such. A new era was ushered in by the publication of two more books entitled *The Psychology of Music*, by John Booth Davies (1978) and Diana Deutsch (1982, 1999, 2013): although these adopted very different styles and approaches, they both broadened the horizons of the discipline, and had a strong grounding in cognitive psychology. The cognitive psychology of music deals with the internalised rules, strategies, and operations which people employ in musical behaviour, and early research in this field included studies of the effects on listeners of tones, intervals, and scales; of the perception of and memory for melody; and of the internal representation of harmony and larger-scale aspects of musical structure.

The cognitive psychology of music was cemented by John Sloboda's (1985) *The Musical Mind* (see also Sloboda, 2005), representing psychologists' first attempt to deal with problems and issues of real musical concern. Although the cognitive tradition continues in contemporary music psychology research, and indeed provides the foundation for many other specialisms, some of its early research was subsequently criticised for the artificiality of some of its experimental tasks and 'laboratory' testing situations, for the unrepresentativeness of its participant groups, and because many of the experimental stimuli employed bore very little relation to actual musical materials. Some challenges came from musicology, which provided a counter-perspective of understanding structural relationships within and between different musical works (see e.g. Clarke, 1989) and often claimed more subtleties in interpretation (e.g. Margulis, 2005; Temperley, 2003).

A new approach, zygonic theory (Ockelford, 2006), attempts to combine the concerns of musicology and cognitive music psychology, and this has recently been applied to developmental issues; we discuss this more fully in Chapter 2. Empirical musicology (Clarke & Cook, 2004) and systematic musicology (e.g. Honing, 2004) are both recent brands of more inclusive and broader adaptations of traditional music theory. Correspondingly, the psychology of music has now developed to include much more complex and ecologically valid questions about musical behaviour and understanding, such as the nature of musical expressiveness in performance; the effects of music on listeners' emotions and aesthetic responses; the creative processes involved in composing and improvising; and practical issues for musicians such as sight reading and practice techniques.

The social psychology of music has also become much more influential, particularly in the European tradition (Hargreaves & North, 1997, 1999; North & Hargreaves, 2008). Research has begun to explore the social functions of music for individuals, for small and large social groups, and for society and culture as a whole. The social functions of music seem to be manifested in three main ways for both musicians and non-musicians alike. Firstly, music plays a clear part in the growth and expression of *self-identity*, as we shall see in much more detail in Chapter 6. Historiometric research suggests that composers express their distinctive identities and world views through their music. Furthermore, research on adolescence shows that young people join some musical subcultures, and reject others, as a means of defining themselves. The second social function of music concerns establishment and maintenance of *interpersonal relationships*. Musical preference judgements in adults as well as in teenagers reflect a desire for acceptance into particular social groups: they can provide a means of defining ethnic identity, for example, and the affiliation with one style or genre rather than another can even mediate the perceived characteristics of others, such as physical attractiveness or personality (see Chapter 7). Thirdly, there is clear evidence that music can provide a means of *mood management* in everyday life. Research shows that musical taste is mediated by the immediate listening environment, and so reflects situationally determined and situation-specific goals. Adolescents use music to adapt their mood to specific situations: and 'applied' research shows that music can be used to alleviate pain, or to influence customers' behaviour in shops and stores (Chapter 8).

Finally, the developmental psychology of music, the main topic of this book, is another sub-discipline which has expanded considerably in recent years. Some of this development stems from the impetus within developmental psychology to explain the emergence of different processes in more depth. Experimental researchers might carry out studies which compare infants' musical and speech perception skills, for instance, or which shed light on important genetic and environmental influences in early development. Researchers also make comparisons across developmental stages, such as between infancy, childhood, and adulthood, to establish the skills and abilities that result from experience in general and from training in particular, and to understand more, for example, about how the damaged brain might process music.

The range and diversity of the topics covered in this book give another clear indication of the way in which the study of musical development has expanded almost beyond recognition in the last few decades. The breadth and depth of current research on perceptual and cognitive aspects of musical development in Chapter 3, for example, vastly exceeds what was known in 1986. The same is true of the range of theoretical models of musical development which are reviewed in Chapter 2, of our detailed knowledge of different aspects of the social, emotional, and affective aspects of musical development which are covered in Chapters 4, 6, and 7, and of our current understanding of the complex of interacting environmental factors at play (Chapter 5).

In summary, music psychology is currently flourishing as never before: many new books have been published and several new journals launched in the last two decades. A growing number of music departments in British universities are beginning to take a serious interest in music psychology, and the music conservatoires of the UK all now engage with research and educational issues. We might plausibly argue that the status of music psychology in the 2010s resembles that of psycholinguistics in the 1960s: conceptual and methodological advances mean that it can now deal with theoretical and conceptual issues previously regarded as intractably abstract, complex, and difficult to subject to empirical enquiry. Topics such as music and emotion, the relationship between music and language, creativity, composition and improvisation, and the development of psychologically based strategies and interventions for the enhancement of performing musicians are now within our grasp because the sophistication of the discipline has reached a new level.

Aims and Plan of the Book

Our basic questions, to quote from the Preface, are 'how and to what extent people engage with music in different ways across the lifespan, from infancy to old age, and what effects these engagements have on different aspects of their behaviour and experience'. This book, unlike its predecessor, follows a topic-based approach, focusing on specific areas of musical behaviour such as cognition, perception, emotion, and so on. We pursue the question of specific developmental changes and milestones within each of those areas: this has allowed us greater flexibility to adopt different strategies in each chapter, depending on the issues under investigation, as well as to present musical development in a more detailed and nuanced manner.

Mirroring developmental psychology more broadly, the lifespan approach is given prominence in this book. We cover development from infancy through to old age, reflecting the recent growth of theory and research in these areas. Our approach is also necessarily multidisciplinary, due to the multidisciplinary nature of the research evidence on musical development, ranging from neuroscience, through cognitive, social, and developmental psychology, to sociology, musicology, and education. The psychology of musical development is the central discipline represented here, but the contents of the book make it clear that this overlaps with many other disciplines which have affected both our theoretical perspectives and our methodological approaches, so that our approach is essentially an eclectic one. Throughout, but especially in areas where research is less extensive with children, we draw on evidence from adults differing in terms of experience (e.g. comparisons between musically trained and untrained participants) in order to extrapolate developmental concerns.

The study of development in general, and musical development more specifically, can cast a great deal of light on some key questions in music education, and throughout the book we consider another key question: what are the best conditions and teaching approaches for helping children (and adults) to learn different musical skills most effectively? Reflecting the collaboration between music teachers on the one hand, and music education researchers on the other (see Hargreaves, Marshall, & North, 2003), we consider music educational applications, where appropriate, in each of the chapters individually. Our intention is to weave theory, research, and applications together in as integral a fashion as possible, and at as detailed a level as possible.

In Chapter 2 we outline what we consider to be the ten main theoretical approaches, from different disciplines, which are currently being used to explain musical development. Here we deal with the different theoretical models in developmental psychology and their applications to theories and models of musical development. We then evaluate all of these models and emerging models with respect to how they deal with five critical questions, namely the relationship between the biological and social; the different modalities of musical development, i.e. production, perception, performance, and representation; developmental progression; domain-specificity; and finally, the distinction between normative and expert musical development.

Chapter 3 considers the details of development in music perception and cognition, comprising a lengthy review of research on the effects of genetics, early musical training and experience on various aspects of development. We first consider how skills and understanding develop in isolated elements of music (pitch, rhythm, timbre, tonality) and then explore how these elements of music combine to shape children's and adults' perception of musical structure and form. This chapter includes material on creativity and on assessment in music across childhood. Chapter 4 looks in depth at the social aspects of musical development, and is divided into two main parts. The first part covers main theoretical approaches from sociology and developmental theory, while the second part reviews developmental research which focuses on social development across the lifespan.

In Chapter 5 we consider environmental influences on musical development and the question of motivation, dealing with the definition of musical ability and talent, with research on the effects of practice on its development, and with the role of motivation. We then focus on two large-scale studies of the development of musical ability and achievement which were carried out by related teams of researchers: the Keele-Exeter study of biographical determinants of musical excellence, based in the UK, and a longitudinal study based in Sydney, Australia whose results have recently been summarised in book form. This chapter goes on to consider the relationship between musical development and music education, looking specifically at recent changes in music education in the UK, at the effects of international, national, and local contexts on the nature of music education, variations in the aims and objectives of different music education systems, and at the issue of formal and informal music teaching and learning.

Chapter 6 deals with the questions of identity, personality, and lifestyle in musical development. We look first at the concept and definition of musical identity, which underlies the whole chapter: what does this term mean, and how do our musical identities influence our musical development? We go on to review how our musical identities develop, how they differ between individuals, in particular in relation to personality and lifestyle, and look finally at how they might be influential in education: do pupils form musical identities which are antithetical to those which education tries to foster, how do the musical identities of pupils and their teachers relate to each other, and how are these influenced by the new technology?

In Chapter 7 we explore emotional responses to music, moving from the origins of emotional reactions in the communicative musicality between infant and caregiver and tracing these through to adult engagement with music for mood regulation and other psychological functions. We use a recent framework from Patrik Juslin to organise this material, applying a new developmental perspective to this. Chapter 8 considers the ways in which music makes a difference for children, young people, and adults of all ages. We firstly consider this from the perspective of music listening, looking at how music can affect children's concentration and learning, how music tastes bring people together, and how sharing music can create social bonds. Secondly, we explore the impact of music performance and instrumental training on aspects of cognition and social interaction, including the social and emotional benefits of learning an instrument in childhood through to old age.

Chapter 9 is an Afterword in which we reflect on the current state of the study of musical development. We reflect on the effectiveness of our priorities in organising and synthesising the wealth of empirical data and theoretical development, and we identify five broad themes that have emerged, namely the social nature of musical development; the powerful influence of digital technology; the importance of the lifespan approach to musical development; the importance of the self-concept and self-identity; and the applications of music psychology. Finally, we look forward to the future, considering whether the pace of change in both musical development and its investigation is likely to accelerate still further in the years to come, and if so, what form this is likely to take.

2 Musical Development: Theoretical Models, Approaches, and Issues

It has become clear that music psychology has important overlaps with a number of related disciplines such as cognitive science and computing, sociology, cultural studies, anthropology, education, medicine and health studies, acoustics, broadcasting, marketing and communication studies, as well as with music and musicology. Each of these fields has its own theoretical models, approaches, and issues, and our challenge is to identify those that have been successfully applied to the explanation of musical development. In Chapter 1 we contextualised and summarised the main current trends and concerns in the fields of developmental psychology and music psychology, and in this chapter we focus on the important theoretical trends in development and the explanation of musical development in particular.

We begin with some of the more traditional and well-known approaches to development by looking at stage/phase models and models based on learning and cognition, drawing on developmental theories from the latter part of the twentieth century. We move on to two newer approaches: the symbol systems theory, and one deriving from music theory. We then review two further theoretical approaches – the first of which we have labelled, very broadly, as social approaches to musical development: these include the sociocultural, the ecological and transactional, and the social cognitive approaches. We feel that more formal models are likely to emerge from the first two of these at least within the next few years, and we indicate what form we think these models might take. Finally, we describe neuroscientific studies of music: these provide a unique perspective on musical development, but need further development before they are likely to give rise to specific theoretical models.

To clarify, we have identified six general theoretical approaches which can be further subdivided into ten distinct approaches, namely those based on developmental stages (x2), learning and cognition (x2), symbol systems, music theory, social factors (x3), and neuroscientific methods respectively. We have also suggested that the first six of these ten have given rise to specific models of musical development. It is true to say that a certain amount of overlap exists among all these approaches, such that our division into ten different types is somewhat arbitrary – but it serves, nevertheless, to focus attention on the criteria required for a valid and useful model by drawing attention to the advantages and disadvantages of each one. This leads us to a final section in which we review and evaluate these models and approaches in relation to five specific theoretical issues: the operation of biological and social factors in musical development; the relationships between musical production, perception, performance, and representation; developmental progression; domain-specificity; and the distinction between normative and expert musical development.

Theoretical Models of Musical Development

Three key questions which we need to bear in mind when looking at theories and models of musical development are as follows: (a) how does each deal with musical production, perception, performance, and representation? (b) how does each deal specifically with developmental progression? and (c) how does each deal specifically with music? In so doing we also need to consider the overall theoretical orientation of the approach or model, and we link these to traditions in mainstream developmental psychology wherever possible.

Developmental Stage/Phase Models

The archetypal and by far the best known stage model of child development is that of Jean Piaget (e.g. Piaget & Inhelder, 1969), who proposed that children go through four main stages of development as result of their changing levels of cognitive maturity. Piaget saw logic as an essential part of the organisation of thinking, and the concept of an *operation* was central to this. Piaget proposed that the intrinsic features of logic have their origin in the activities of the subject. Thought operations are derived from the actions we perform upon objects in the outside world, and so thought is an internalised form of action. This view led him to propose that development tends towards increasingly abstract and logical forms of thinking, such that similar sets of logical rules develop in all children.

Piaget also proposed that *equilibration* is the mechanism by which the acquisition of logical thinking occurs: he saw cognitive structures as being 'unstable' in relation to new objects and experiences, and so the tendency to equilibrate towards more stable states is a kind of intrinsic 'cognitive drive' which motivates exploration. The environment is a constant source of feedback, which guides the tendency to explore: and the developmental stages represent successive levels of stabilisation, or adjustment to it. Piaget's theory is based on the biological idea of *adaptation* to the environment: adaptation is seen as taking place via the twin processes of *assimilation* and *accommodation*. We assimilate new objects and events that we encounter in our environment; we accommodate to these objects and events by changing our ways of thinking about them; and our thinking moves to a new level of equilibrium as a result. Assimilation and accommodation are indissociable aspects of any developmental acquisition: as in biological nutrition, that which is taken in (Piaget used the analogy of cognitive 'food', or 'aliment') becomes part of that which takes it in.

One of the best-known aspects of Piaget's theory is his proposal that there are four major, qualitatively different *stages* of cognitive development through which all children pass. The sensori-motor stage (ages 0–2) is divided into six substages, which move from the primitive use of reflexes in early infancy through to the beginnings of internal representation, or symbolism. Symbolic development provides the essence of the second, pre-operational stage (ages 2–7): this is sometimes divided into the preconceptual (ages 2–4) and the intuitive (ages 4–7) sub-periods. A major revolution in the child's thinking occurs at the age of about 7, with the transition into the concrete operational stage; and the acquisition of abstract formal operational thinking, which represents the final stage, occurs around the age of eleven. The central tenet of Piaget's theory, therefore, was that the child's thinking gradually moves through these stages towards more idealised forms of scientific thought, based on his own underlying theory of logical operations; as such, it is often referred to as a cognitive-developmental theory.

Much has been written about the merits and limitations of Piaget's approach, and we will come to those arguments and debates when we present alternative perspectives that have challenged them, both below and later in the book. First, though, we consider musical theories broadly based on Piaget's approach.

The two best known Piagetian-style models of musical development – Swanwick and Tillman's (1986) 'spiral' model of musical development, and Hargreaves and Galton's (1992) 'phase' theory of artistic development – differ in certain important respects. Neither of these adopts Piaget's view of the importance of logical operations, but both nevertheless postulate age-based developmental stages or phases which are based on cognitive maturation and development, and which also take account of social and cultural influences on the acquisition of new ways of understanding.

Swanwick and Tillman's 'Spiral' Model

Swanwick and Tillman (1986) based their well-known model on the analysis of a collection of 745 musical compositions produced by 48 3- to 9-year-old British schoolchildren over a period of several years. June Tillman was the class music teacher for many of the children, and analysed the compositions produced in her lessons for her doctoral thesis. Ten different types of composition which varied in complexity were collected in total: these ranged from playing rhythm patterns on a pair of maracas and a tambour through to instrumental improvisations based on short phases and sentences. The analysis suggested that there were some distinct changes with age in the nature of the compositions: three judges' independent ratings of three items from each of seven children revealed that their composer's age could be judged fairly accurately, and this was used as the basis for a general model of musical development which has subsequently been applied to music listening and improvisation (Swanwick, 1998). Swanwick and Tillman claimed that the model also received support from Piaget's (1951) theory of play and from the work of Ross (1984), Moog (1976), and Bunting (1977), and it also has some obvious affinities with Bruner's (1960) spiral curriculum in the sense that material is revisited at different levels of understanding.

The model (see Figure 2.1) has three main organising principles. The first is that the spiral is organised into four ascending loops according to the child's basic

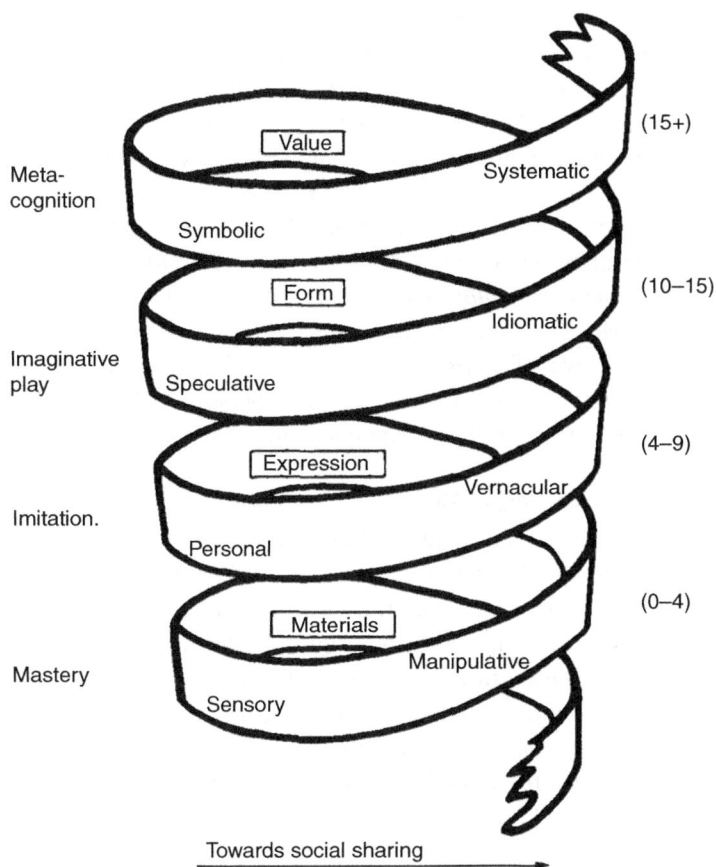

Figure 2.1.   Swanwick and Tillman's spiral model of the development of children's compositions.
Source: Figure 3 (p. 331) in Swanwick, K., & Tillman, J. (1986). The sequence of musical
development: A study of children's composition. *British Journal of Music Education*, 6,
305–339. By permission of Cambridge University Press.

mode of engagement with music. The first three are based on an analogy with
three aspects of children's play, namely *mastery*, *imitation*, and *imaginative play*.
Mastery involves the simple sensory response to and the control of sound: imitation describes how children attempt to represent the world about them by musical
means: and imaginative play involves a creative musical contribution on the part
of the child, over and above simple imitation. Although Swanwick and Tillman
claim that these three levels are based on Piaget's theory of play, Piaget (1951) did
not view imaginative play as representing a higher level of thinking than 'simple'
imitative play. The fourth loop is labelled 'metacognition', and describes the child's
awareness of her own musical thinking and experience.

The second organising principle is based on those aspects of musical experience which are salient at each of the four levels, namely *materials*, *expression*, *form*,
and *value*, and the third is the shift between the personal, individual aspects of

composition which are represented on the left-hand side of the spiral, towards those which focus more on 'social sharing' on each level, which are shown on the right-hand side. This gives rise to eight distinct 'developmental modes' which appear as the spiral ascends. At the level of *mastery*, there is a developmental shift from 'sensory' to 'manipulative' musical behaviour, which arises from a gradual increase in the control of sound production. At the level of *imitation*, the equivalent shift is from personal expressiveness to the vernacular, which reflects the gradual incorporation of musical conventions such as short melodic and rhythmic sequences. At the level of *imaginative play*, the shift is from speculative to idiomatic composition, during which a coherent, conventional musical style is established: and finally, at the fourth level of *metacognition*, Swanwick and Tillman proposed a shift from symbolic to systematic expression, in which personal, idiosyncratic expression gradually incorporates the stylistic principles underlying a given musical idiom.

Hargreaves and Galton's 'Phase' Model

An original model of five age-related phases in artistic development proposed by Hargreaves and Galton (1992) was later revised by David (Hargreaves, 1996), who renamed them the sensori-motor, figural, schematic, rule systems, and professional phases. Two important points about the origins of this model are that (a) we deliberately used the term *phase* rather than *stage* to avoid the Piagetian connotations of logical-scientific thinking, which may well be quite inappropriate in the arts, and (b) the model was based on a detailed analysis of the empirical literature across the arts, which had been reviewed by acknowledged experts in each of the main art forms, and published in *Children and the Arts* (Hargreaves, 1989). The clear implication is that cross-modal generalities can be made across different art forms, and these are based on observed regularities in the research literature rather than on a specific theoretical point of view. We shall return to the issues of cross-modality and domain-specificity in the final section of this chapter.

We shall provide only the briefest summary of this phase model in the rest of this section, which is not intended to be comprehensive: we focus on the musical aspects of the model only, which are shown in Table 2.1. In the *sensori-motor* phase (approximately 0–2 years), most of the major developments involve the practice and development of physical skills and co-ordinations. The link with physical action is most obvious in rhythmic dancing: early singing is also characterised by a good deal of vocal play and babbling which forms the basis for recognisable 'musical' singing. Sensori-motor activity can also be seen in the scribbling movements which infants make on paper: these are present in their attempts at drawings as such, as well as in their 'story-writing', which is essentially scribbling with verbal commentary, and also in their attempts to represent musical stimuli by graphic means. When they do this, their actions with the pencil on the paper may match the timing of the pattern of sounds, but what emerges on the paper bears little resemblance to it. In this phase, most musical activities are largely pre-symbolic in the sense that abstract symbolism – the capacity to mentally conceive of or represent an object in its physical absence – is not yet present.

The next, *figural* phase is characterised by the profound developmental change which occurs when children become able to *symbolise* at the age of 18 months or so – to

Table 2.1. Hargreaves and Galton's (1992) phase model of artistic development

Phase	Singing	Graphic representation	Melodic perception	Composition
Professional (15+ years)				enactive and reflective strategies
Rule systems (8–15 years)	intervals, scales	formal-metric	analytic recognition of intervals, key stability	'idiomatic' conventions
Schematic (5–8 years)	'first draft' songs	figural-metric: more than one dimension	conservation of melodic properties	'vernacular' conventions
Figural (2–5 years)	'outline' songs: coalescences between spontaneous and cultural songs	figural: single dimension	global features: pitch, contour	assimilation of cultural music
Sensori-motor (0–2 years)	babbling, rhythmic dancing	scribbling: 'action equivalents'	recognition of melodic contours	sensory, manipulative

Source: Adapted from Table 6.1 (p. 156) in Hargreaves, D. J. (1996). The development of musical and artistic competence. In: I. Deliège & J. A. Sloboda (Eds.), *Musical beginnings: Origins and development of musical competence* (pp. 145–170). © Oxford University Press. By permission of Oxford University Press.

conceive of objects, people, or situations which are not physically present. Piaget (1951) proposed a detailed account of what he called the symbolic or semiotic function, and elaborated upon the different areas of behaviour in which it is manifested, which include *deferred imitation, symbolic play*, graphic representation in *drawings*, and *verbal evocation*. The third of these is directly relevant here: one central characteristic of pre-school drawings is that they are *figural* – they depict the overall shapes or outlines of their subjects, but the details within them are not yet accurate. A good example of this is the familiar 'tadpole figure', in which children appear to attach limbs to the head of the drawn person and omit the trunk. Children typically produce these up to the age of three or so, and there have been numerous explanations of the phenomenon. Similar 'figures' are found in young children's drawings of musical sequences (Bamberger, 1982, 1991, 2006), in which the shapes and patterns are prioritised over the details and precise relationships between notes or beats (see further Chapter 3).

Children's command of the conventions which are used by adult artists and musicians has increased considerably by the age of 5 years or so, and they may well also have invented some of their own conventions. This leads to the production of what might be called 'schematic' art works in which adult conventions are present, but not yet fully developed: and these characterise the next, *schematic* phase. One good example of this is in the 'air gap' drawing which children typically produce up to the age of 10 years or so: an example is shown in Figure 2.2. Their landscape drawings often include a 'ground line' along the bottom of the page and a 'sky line' along the top in order to give some overall spatial organisation, but the resulting 'gap'

Figure 2.2. An 'air gap stereotype' drawing.
Source: Original drawing by Fraser van Amerongen.

which persistently remains, and which children typically identify as 'air', means that the drawing is still not visually realistic (see Hargreaves, Jones, & Martin, 1981). Artistic conventions are beginning to develop, but these are still not yet integrated into a coherent sense of style.

In the next *rule systems* phase, approximately between the ages of 8 and 15 years, the accurate use of artistic conventions becomes established: works can be produced and perceived with full adherence to adult conventions of style and idiom in literary, graphic, musical, and other domains. In their spiral model of musical composition, Swanwick and Tillman (1986) proposed a shift in their spiral model from 'speculative' composition, which involves experimenting with different conventions, to 'idiomatic' composition, which shows a firm grasp of some of those conventions, during this phase. The acquisition of adult conventions and styles is perhaps most clearly and explicitly shown in studies of the development of aesthetic appreciation in the arts.

In Hargreaves and Galton's (1992) original description of the developmental model of artistic development, the term 'cognitive aesthetic appreciation' was used to refer to the body of work that has investigated age-related changes in artistic perception in a number of domains, but largely the visual arts (e.g. Winner, Rosenblatt, Windmueller, Davidson, & Gardner, 1986). Parsons' (1987) theory of the development of aesthetic appreciation, for example, was specifically based on visual art. Parsons suggested that up to the age of 5 years or so, children tend to focus on the concrete properties of art works, and the means of producing them: they are equally likely to be as concerned about who is allowed to play a musical instrument, for example, as they are about what is being played on it. Works in the visual arts are judged primarily in terms of their relevance to children's own lives, such as whether the objects portrayed are familiar to and liked by them. These might be described, in the figural phase, as 'egocentric' reactions to art.

In the *schematic* phase, visual art works become judged primarily in terms of their subject matter, and their degree of realism: pictures or drawings are considered to be successful if they accurately represent what they are supposed to, and this is much more important than any stylistic considerations. The small body of research on the development of style sensitivity in music has produced much less clear-cut findings with respect to the effects of age. Gardner (1973a) found 11-year-olds to be more sensitive to similarities and differences between extracts of classical music drawn from different styles than 14- and 18-year-olds, for example, and a partial replication of this study by Castell (1982) using popular music styles found that 8- to 9-year-olds appeared to be more stylistically sensitive than 11-year-olds. The cultural salience of the specific styles which are played to particular age/subject groups in these investigations probably gave rise to these counter-intuitive results (discussed further in Chapter 3).

Having mastered the conventions of particular art forms, some individuals are able to transcend them, producing works which display independence from conventional styles, and the capacity of self-reflection in relation to them. This degree of expertise is probably only achieved at the level of the professional artist, and so we describe this as characterising the final, *professional* phase of the model. The highest level of Swanwick and Tillman's (1986) spiral model of musical development is what they called the *metacognitive* mode: this term refers to the capacity to 'think about thinking', i.e. to reflect upon one's own thought processes. Preschool children have been shown to display metacognition and self-regulation in their behaviour, but here we are dealing with the ability to show these attributes at high levels of artistic perception and performance: self-reflection is guided by universal understandings about music rather than through personal experience alone.

This level of thinking acknowledges that there are no absolute standards in art: that there is a sense in which rules exist in order to be broken. Many of the great composers, such as Igor Stravinsky or Claude Debussy, or the great innovators in jazz, such as Charlie Parker or John Coltrane, achieved their greatness by breaking the rules of the time rather than by following them, and created new styles or genres as a result. However, each of these figures had achieved mastery of the existing conventions before going beyond them, and this is an important part of real-life creativity. These great names represent only a tiny proportion of the population of musicians, of course: many professional artists, composers and improvisers have the capacity to work in a variety of styles, even if the effects of their innovations upon their peers are not as profound as those of acknowledged innovators.

Our decision to group Swanwick and Tillman's and Hargreaves and Galton's models together as 'phase/stage models' is partly because a central feature of both is their description of age-related changes in behaviour which form the basis of stages/phases. We suggested earlier that Hargreaves and Galton's view of developmental change is based essentially on the underlying cognitive operations, although as noted previously we described these as phases rather than stages to avoid the logical connotations of the Piagetian model. Swanwick and Tillman's description is based on the characteristics of a collection of musical compositions, and also incorporates other theoretical ideas, including some from Piaget. The underlying basis of their phases, or 'modes' as they are called in the model, is still essentially based on their generalisations about observed age-related changes. What the authors consider to be evidence in support of the model is their demonstration that independent observers can identify the age-appropriateness of children's compositions which are chosen so as to represent the different developmental modes: this does not, of course, demonstrate the theoretical or conceptual validity of those modes, nor of the constructs on which they are based.

Swanwick and Tillman's model deals explicitly with musical composition, and also generalises about aspects of musical perception, performance, and representation on this basis, whereas Hargreaves and Galton's model is explicitly based on a review of research on artistic behaviour across these modalities, and indeed across other art forms as well. It is perhaps most useful to regard the latter as a broad framework which can deal with a wide range of phenomena of artistic development, and Swanwick and Tillman's spiral as forming a more specialised account of musical development within it.

Music Learning and Cognition

Two different cognitive models of musical development have been proposed that look at the rules and representations of specifically *musical* understanding in children. Serafine's 'music as cognition' model (1988) and Gordon's music learning theory (1997) both focused on the role of both experience and training in shaping children's thinking about music, and both present a relatively complex and domain-specific view of what musical development is.

Serafine's Model of 'Music as Cognition'

Mary-Louise Serafine (1988) proposed a radical theory of music as cognition, based on a set of core cognitive processes that she argued were present in musical composing, performing, and listening. She claimed that the critical interaction in musical communication was between a person (e.g. the performer, or the listener) and the piece of music: this was more important than any interpersonal communication. She believed in essence that music itself was the result of cognitive processing, rather than being an organised set of physical sounds, or an abstract concept or construct. She proposed two basic types of general cognitive process which cut across all styles and idioms – *temporal* processes (dealing with relationships among musical events in time) and *non-temporal* processes (dealing with more general, formal properties of pieces of music). Two distinct types of temporal process were identified, based on succession and simultaneity (e.g. counterpoint and harmony in Western classical music), and within this, four basic types of successive processes (idiomatic construction, motivic chaining, patterning, and phrasing). Four types of non-temporal process were also proposed concerned with the overall properties of the musical material, namely closure, transformation, abstraction, and hierarchic levels.

Quite clearly, Serafine's radical view diverged not only from the presumptions of a good deal of music theory but also from many of the main approaches in music psychology such as psychometric testing, philosophical views of musical communication, behaviouristic accounts of music learning, and psychophysical explanations of musical perception: she felt that all of these missed the point of what is distinctly musical about music, which she saw as these constructive mechanisms in the listener.

From this starting point she developed an account of musical development based on a complex set of musical tasks designed to operationalise and assess the operation of these processes, and administered them to a large sample of children aged between 5 and 11, a smaller sample of 4- to 11-year-olds with Suzuki training, and a group of adults, along with a pitch discrimination task, a Piagetian number conservation task, and a human figure-drawing task as comparison measures. In short, Serafine found a gradual developmental acquisition of these temporal and non-temporal processes across childhood. Children aged between 5 and 6 did not possess any of the processes, although there were some early signs of emerging abilities, including the ability to identify phrase boundaries, to recognise differences between textures, and to identify some transformations. Children aged 8 possessed some but not all of the processes, and the majority of the processes had been acquired by the age of 10 or 11. The Suzuki-trained children performed at a comparable level to same-age children unless they had experienced intensive long-term training specifically relevant to the specific tasks, so training only influenced development in a very narrow way. We can conclude that Serafine provides some evidence for age-related changes in the generic musical processes which she puts forward, but this does not equate to proposing a specifically developmental theory.

Gordon's Music Learning Theory
Edwin Gordon developed his own brand of music learning theory over the course of many years, closely linked with his work on developing psychometric tests of musical ability. A central concept in Gordon's theory is audiation:

'[T]he process of assimilating and comprehending (not simply rehearing) music we have just heard performed or have heard performed sometime in the past. We also audiate when we assimilate and comprehend in our minds music we may or may not have heard, but are reading in notation or composing or improvising. In contrast, aural perception takes place when we are actually hearing sound the moment it is being produced. We audiate actual sound only after we have aurally perceived it. In aural perception we are dealing with immediate sound events, whereas in audiation, we are dealing with delayed musical events.' (Gordon, 2007, pp. 3–4)

Gordon claimed that 'audiation is to music what thought is to language' (Gordon, 2007, p. ix). He identified four 'vocabularies of music', namely listening, speaking, reading, and writing, and suggested that individuals' aptitudes and progress determined the extent to which these vocabularies are acquired and employed. In young children, Gordon proposed three types of *preparatory audiation*, namely acculturation, imitation, and assimilation, which were held to prepare them for more formal music instruction, developing their audiation. He put forward eight types and six stages of audiation: the six stages follow a developmental sequence, whereas the eight types do not, though some types serve as preparation for others. Gordon cautioned that

'The six stages of audiation and the mental processes occurring within each stage can only be presumed. However, logic and reason suggest when learning conditions for a given type of audiation are ideal in terms of music learning theory, all relevant stages are included in one form or another and interact in a complex circular sequence of mental activity. Moving forward and backward in this complex circular sequence is preparation for audiation required in other stages.' (ibid., pp. 18–19)

Gordon (1976) constructed a complex and detailed account of music learning sequences on the basis of these foundations, which fall into three interrelated and elaborate sequences dealing with skills, tonal content, and rhythm content respectively. A great deal of Gordon's own empirical research was devoted to the development of psychometric tests designed to describe, measure and evaluate musical aptitude and achievement: his Musical Aptitude Profile (1965), for example, is still one of the most widely used tests of musical aptitude internationally, and in his later years he was increasingly concerned with the development of tests and measurements for young children. Although he saw this as being closely related to the development and assessment of his music learning theory, it may well be that Gordon's contributions to musical aptitude testing are of greater significance and have had more impact than those of his music learning theory.

In a review, Swanwick and Runfola (2002) noted that there was some divergence of opinion about the extent to which Gordon's theory was securely based on the available evidence from research in music psychology, as his supporters (e.g. Holahan, 1986) claimed. Other critics, including Colwell and Abrahams (1991), argued that there was little support from research other than that which had been collected by Gordon's own students and co-workers. Swanwick and Runfola also pointed out that the theory may be regarded as somewhat ethnocentric in that all of the learning sequences in the taxonomy are specifically based on Western classical music. They also noted the strong emphasis in Gordon's approach on music literacy and pedagogy rather than on the abilities involved in activities such as improvising and composing. To these criticisms we would add that Gordon's use of psychological terminology is somewhat idiosyncratic: the terms 'learning theories' and 'acculturation', for example, have quite specific connotations in psychology (see e.g. Eysenck, 1998), and terms like 'assimilation' and 'imitation' also have quite specific and longstanding meanings in Piagetian theory, but Gordon used these terms in quite different ways.

Both Serafine's and Gordon's theories, which we group together because of their joint focus on music learning and cognition, deal specifically with developmental progression in that they are based on the psychological processes underlying age-related changes in musical behaviour, although as noted earlier the developmental implications of Serafine's research are unclear. Her results show that children of different ages, and adults, process music in qualitatively different ways, but as Huron (1990) pointed out, this raises fundamental difficulties for a theory that starts from the premise that 'music' resides in cognitive constructions rather than in the notes themselves. If children and adults construct different representations of the same piece, then presumably the essence or identity of the piece does not reside in those notes as such. Serafine's results do suggest that children and adults employ qualitatively different modes of processing, and this is more consistent with a Piagetian-style stage model: we could say that this theory claims to deal with developmental processes, but does not include a specifically developmental account of age-related changes in music processing.

Both theories are also undoubtedly specific to music. Where both are less successful, however, is in their applicability to the different modalities of production, perception, performance, and representation. Both are concerned more with the receptive processes of auditory perception and internal representation, and in particular with the detailed processes underlying the latter, than they are with musical production and performance, and especially about the generative aspects of musical behaviour such as composing and improvising. There is something of a disconnect between the scope and diversity of real-life musical behaviour and the relatively narrow range of phenomena that is covered by each theory: both may be too complex and inflexible to be widely applicable to music learning in different social and cultural environments.

Symbol Systems: Gardner and Harvard Project Zero

The 'symbol systems' approach largely stems from the work of the Harvard Project Zero group, founded by the philosopher Nelson Goodman in 1967 to study and improve education in the arts. Goodman was a resident scholar at Jerome Bruner's Harvard Center for Cognitive Studies in the early 1960s, and Bruner's influence runs throughout the work at Harvard that continues to this day. Bruner provided a counterpoint to Piagetian models of cognitive development with a far simpler developmental model (1966). He argued that there were three modes of understanding which might apply to a child's, or adult's, engagement with a particular domain of thinking. These were the enactive, the iconic, and the symbolic. *Enactive* representations focused on actions and can be seen to be related to the sensori-motor stage in Piaget's approach. *Iconic* representations are where understanding is at the level of close mappings – for instance, a picture of a tree which resembles the tree in physical appearance, while *symbolic* representations are more abstract and removed from direct experience – such as the word for tree in relation to the object of a tree. Bruner diverged from Piaget in that he argued that while these modes of understanding might emerge in turn, the earlier modes were not lost and all three could co-exist (Bruner, 1966).

Bruner is not best known as a developmental psychologist, as his major contributions were in the fields of cognitive psychology and education, and his concerns were far broader than the arts (as we shall see later on in this chapter). However, he set the groundwork and the intellectual foundations for Project Zero, so-called because Goodman felt that 'zero' had at that time been firmly established about the important topic of artistic learning. The group was co-directed by David Perkins and Howard Gardner between 1972 and 2000, and served as a focus for research on development in the arts in the Boston region, with researchers and collaborators including Jeanne Bamberger, Lyle Davidson, and Ellen Winner. Many of the early investigations of the group were psychologically oriented studies of developmental change within a variety of art forms, including experimental, cross-sectional, and longitudinal studies, and their research gradually expanded to include the nature of intelligence, creativity, cross-disciplinary and cross-cultural thinking, problem solving, critical thinking, and brain organisation. In the mid-1980s the general focus became more applied, with a greater emphasis on educational issues.

In *The Arts and Human Development*, Gardner (1973b) suggested that the arts transcend the distinction between affect and cognition: aesthetic objects simultaneously produce patterns of thought and of feelings in the observer. Gardner built this idea into his proposal of three interacting 'systems' in development. The *making* system produces acts or actions, and this is seen most clearly in the creator or performer; the *perceiving* system deals with discriminations or distinctions: and the *feeling* system gives rise to affects, which are most clearly seen in the audience member. The three systems are held to be present in all animal and human life, and development is conceived as a process in which the degree of interaction between them gradually increases, eventually reaching a point at which no single system can be considered in isolation from the other two.

Gardner's account of development centred on the child's acquisition and use of *symbols*. Symbols are organised into different systems, which can either be primarily *denotational* (e.g. numerical notation, where each number has a precise referential meaning) or *expressive* (e.g. abstract art, which has no precise reference to other aspects of experience). Some symbol systems can encompass works which display one, or the other, of both of these properties (e.g. language, dance, drama, drawing, sculpture, and of course music): systems also vary widely in the precision with which they can be mapped on to behaviour and experience, i.e. in their 'notationality'. Gardner felt that an important task of developmental psychology was to identify the nature of adult competences in specific symbol systems, to study the developmental changes which culminate in these, and to explain the relationship of these changes to cognitive development as a whole.

Gardner saw the preschooler's acquisition and use of words, drawings, make-believe, and other symbols as 'the major developmental event in the early years of childhood, one decisive for the evolution of the artistic process' (1973b, p. 129). Accordingly, his account of aesthetic development had just two broad stages: a presymbolic period of sensorimotor development in the first year of life, during which the three systems unfold and differentiate, followed by a period of symbol use from ages 2 to 7 in which the arbitrary elements of symbol systems become linked to specific artistic activities, i.e. to the 'code' of the culture. Towards the end of this period, children's work acquires a sense of competence, balance, and integration within symbol systems, and by the age of seven, most children have achieved the essential characteristics of the audience member, artist and performer, such that they can be considered to be more or less fully fledged participants in the artistic process. In a later publication Wolf and Gardner (1981) suggested a developmental sequence whereby children pass through a series of waves of symbolisation. From 'enactive representation' in infancy, that is, infants' ability to organise their actions into symbolic sequences, a 'mapping wave' of symbolisation occurs at around the age of 3 years, in which spatial relationships can be represented in media such as drawing or clay. This is followed by a third wave of 'digital mapping' at around the age of four, which involves increasing precision – for example in counting, or in singing pitch intervals – and by the age of 5 or 6 years, children become able to use cultural symbol systems such as musical notation or written language.

In comparing his own approach with the dominant view of Piaget, Gardner claimed that 'the groupings, groups and operations described by Piaget do not seem essential for mastery or understanding of human language, music, or plastic arts' (1973b, p. 45). Gardner (1979) argued that mature cognition involves a good deal more than logical-rational thinking, and that Piaget consequently had little to say about development outside the logic of science in fields such as music and the arts, and areas such as intuition, creativity, and novel thinking. Gardner also argued that Piaget had paid insufficient attention to the specific content of children's thinking.

The Project Zero group's early investigations included empirical studies of style sensitivity in visual art (Gardner, 1970) and literature (Gardner & Gardner, 1971) as well as in music (Gardner, 1973a). They also investigated children's use of and preference for metaphor (Winner, Rosenstiel, & Gardner, 1976); the development of song (Davidson, McKernon, & Gardner, 1981); numerical symbolism and children's counting (Shotwell, 1979): and the ability to distinguish fantasy from reality (Morison & Gardner, 1978). This substantial body of research on children's artistic development includes some important studies of musical development, including work on composing, song acquisition, and aesthetic appreciation. One area of research that illustrates the symbol system approach well is that on graphic representations of music, and the pioneer of research in this area was undoubtedly Jeanne Bamberger, who collaborated with Project Zero while working at MIT.

Bamberger (1982) made an important distinction between *intuitive* and *formal* types of musical knowledge. The former is the unschooled, 'natural' response to music which might manifest itself in unorthodox forms of musical representation, and the latter is that which provides the basis of most traditional music education. Central to this, Bamberger developed a distinction between *figural* and *metric* modes – broadly related to Bruner's iconic and symbolic modes – in her studies of children's graphic representations of clapped rhythmic sequences. Figural drawings focus on the function of claps within the figure: they represent the way in which an individual subjectively 'chunks' the rhythm such that the immediate context of an event affects the way in which it is heard. This is not true in metric drawings; in these, beats are perceived in a context-independent fashion, since attention is paid to the exact duration of the claps. We discuss this and other Project Zero research on music by Davidson and Scripp (1988, 1989) further in Chapter 3. It is nevertheless worth mentioning here that Bamberger (2013) has considered the application of her work on notation to wider investigations of children's strategies in musical thinking, including the distinction between 'path-making' and 'map-making', and the use of *reflective conversation* in developing these strategies.

We have designated the symbol system approach as a specific model of musical development because it has a distinctive set of theoretical foundations as well as a specific account of the progress of musical development. It makes a very strong case for viewing developments in music, and indeed in any art form, from a general cognitive perspective. Bamberger (1991) argues

'[T]hat the changing mental organising structures that guide hearings, constructions, and descriptions at various ages and stages of musical development do not constitute a unidirectional progression in which earlier mental structures are replaced by later ones ... the goal of musical development is to have access to multiple dimensions of musical structure, to be able to choose selectively among them, to change focus at will.' (pp. 3–4)

It is also clear that the interaction between development (in the broad sense of 'enculturation') and musical training is an integral part of the symbol system research, and this is an important issue for practitioners.

Music Theory: Ockelford's 'Sounds of Intent' Model

Adam Ockelford's *zygonic theory* is a new approach in music theory which starts from the premise that most musical structures demonstrate *repetition with variation*: their elements are repeated in a similar but not identical fashion in a great deal of music (see e.g. Ockelford, 2006). Zygonic theory is based on the principle of *derivation through imitation*: the Greek word *zygon* means 'yoke', so that 'zygonic relationships' exist in the theory between similar but non-identical musical events. This deceptively simple starting point has enabled Ockelford (2013) to develop an entirely new interdisciplinary approach which he calls *applied musicology*. This applies analytical methods derived from zygonic theory to musical interactions in teacher-learner pairs, therapist-client therapeutic sessions, and other real-life musical situations, thereby enabling the investigation of phenomena including the *intentionality* of musicians, and their *mutual influence* upon each other, via the structure of their real musical interactions.

Ockelford's theory and his 'Sounds of Intent' (SoI) model of musical development (see e.g. Ockelford, Welch, Jewell-Gore, Cheng, Vogiatzoglu, & Himonides, 2011, Ockelford, 2013) has developed from his work with children on the autistic spectrum and those with profound learning difficulties, for whom music provides a means of communication often not available through conventional verbal and other behavioural channels (see Ockelford, 2008). More recently, he has taken this approach further by proposing that the increasingly complex musical structures that are proposed in zygonic theory (*events*, *groups*, and *frameworks*) can be seen to arise naturally in the musical development of neurotypical children in their early years as well as in those with special needs. Ockelford and Voyajolu (2017) have set out this new development in relation to the SoI model, and also provide new empirical research evidence in support of the model, which is shown in Figure 2.3: it includes six proposed levels of musical development, represented by the six concentric circles, along with three domains of musical engagement, represented by the three segments of the circle, giving rise to eighteen cells. The three domains of musical engagement are what Ockelford calls Reactive (listening and responding to sounds): Proactive (causing, creating, or controlling sounds): and Interactive (engaging in sound-making activity with other people) (R, P, and I).

The six levels of the model start, at the lowest level 1, with 'Confusion and chaos' (no awareness of sound), followed by 'Awareness and intentionality' at level 2, which demonstrates 'an emerging awareness of sound and of the variety that is possible within the domain of sound'. Each of the next three levels 3, 4, and 5 directly represents the acquisition of the recognition of one of the musical structures whose increasing complexity is proposed in zygonic theory, namely events, groups, and frameworks. Thus, level 3, 'Relationships, repetition and regularity' represents a growing awareness of the possibility and significance of relationships between sonic events, level 4, 'Sounds forming clusters', includes the evolving perception of groups of sounds and the relationships that may exist between them; and level 5, 'Deeper structural links', demonstrates a growing recognition of whole pieces, and the frameworks of pitch and perceived time that lie behind them. Finally at level 6, 'Mature artistic expression', the child demonstrates a developing awareness of the culturally determined 'emotional syntax' of performance that articulates the 'narrative metaphor' of pieces.

Ockelford cites several examples of psychological research on musical development which support his contention that the phenomena of events, groups, and frameworks can be seen to emerge in that order, and Ockelford and Voyajolu (2017) also describe a new study in which the SoI model was investigated in an early years setting for neurotypical children, thereby departing from a good deal of their previous research. This was an observational study of 58 children at an inclusive children's centre in south west London, in which 125 discrete episodes were videotaped, including the children's musical interactions with peers and with adults as well as self-directed play. Ockelford and Voyajolu then described the main features of each episode, and coded them in terms of the potential components of the SoI framework. They conclude, broadly speaking, that the SoI framework has made a promising start on modelling musical development in the early years.

In comparing the SoI model with the other models of musical development that are described in this chapter, its clearest and most outstanding advantage is its unique basis in music theory. By working with the substance of music itself, there can be no doubt of its ecological validity: all of the other models we have considered use

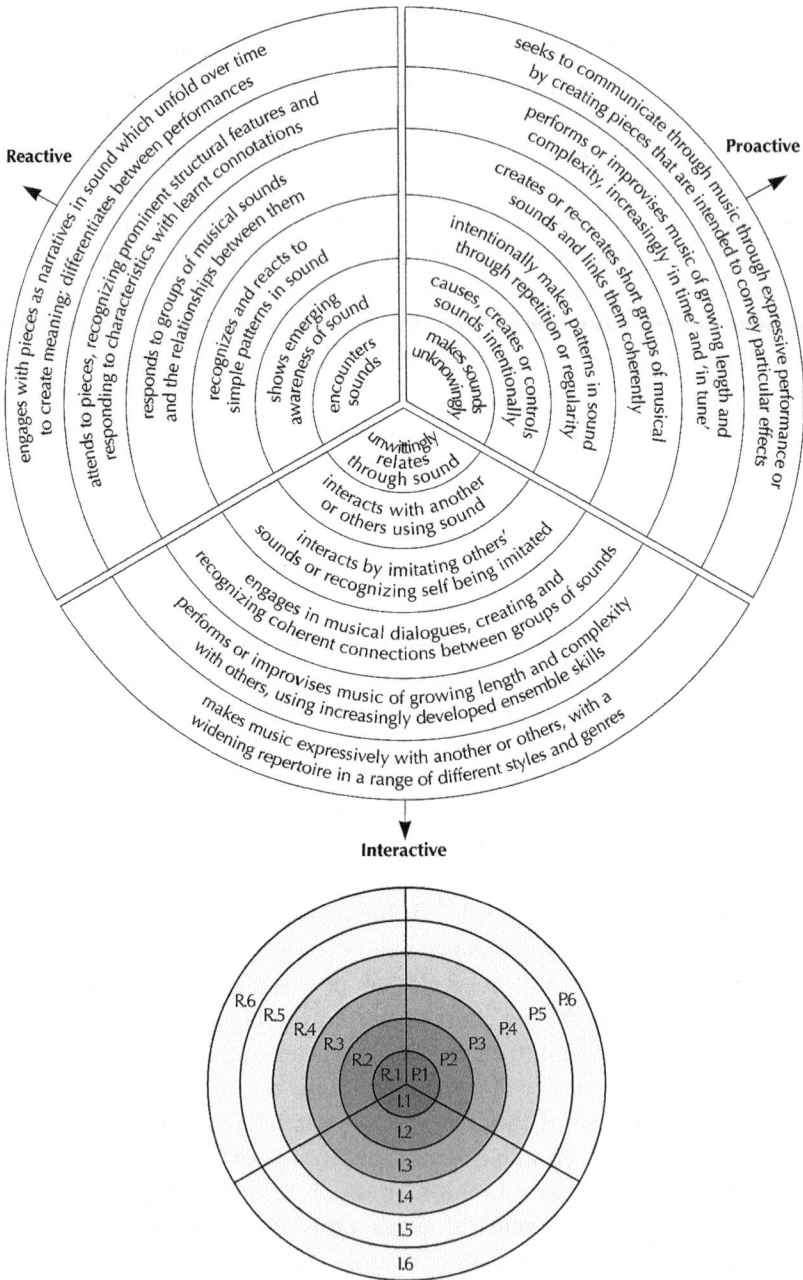

Figure 2.3.   Ockelford's Sounds of Intent model of musical development.
Source: Figure 5.26 (p. 165) in Ockelford, A. (2013), *Applied musicology: Using zygonic theory to inform music education, therapy, and psychology research.* © Oxford University Press. By permission of Oxford University Press.

indirect measures of musical development, many of which are based on cognition and other psychological and behavioural indices. Because of this uniqueness as well as its relative newness, there is as yet little evidence to support SoI theory other than that gathered by Ockelford himself. Nevertheless, there is scope for the SoI model to be supported by neuroscientific evidence of the neural origins of the three different levels of structural hearing, and of how these emerge and develop in childhood and beyond. Another potentially very powerful aspect of Ockelford and Voyajolu's discussion of the nature of developmental change is their use of Vygotskian-type 'zones of proximal development' in their description of the role of interaction with others in musical development. Unlike any other model, this also has the potential to explain and predict the nature of the declines in or diminutions of children's powers of musical engagement which might occur as a result of neurodegenerative disease or other physical trauma. In summary, there is a great deal to commend not only the SoI model, but also the possibilities which are offered by zygonic theory and applied musicology: both of these deserve to play a central role in the study of musical development.

Social Approaches to Musical Development and Some Emerging Models

Sociocultural Approaches

As mentioned in Chapter 1, the sociocultural approach originates from the work of the Russian psychologist Lev Vygotsky (1896–1934). Vygotsky rejected Piaget's view of the child as an adult in miniature working in isolation to try to understand the world, and proposed instead that we are initially social beings: we interact with others by observing what they say and do, and gradually internalise those elements so that they become part of our own thinking. In this sense, our social environment – parents, other family members, peers, teachers, and so on – provides the basic content of our own individual development, and Vygotsky (1966) went further in suggesting that the relations between our own higher mental functions were at one time real relations among people.

Vygotsky's idea that 'we become ourselves through others' was formulated as a 'general genetic law of cultural development' as follows: 'any function in the child's cultural development appears on the stage twice, on two planes, first on the social plane and then on the psychological, first among people as an *intermental* category and then within the child as an *intramental* category' (p. 40). This central idea led on to various other important concepts in Vygotskian theory, including people's use of *cultural tools*. When children encounter new objects in their environments, they act upon and interpret these through the mediation of cultural tools. These can be either internal (e.g. symbolic systems such as language or concepts) or external (e.g. books or computers). The concept of tool mediation means that we do not respond to objects directly, but with reference to the cultural norms that are involved in other people's use of the same tools.

The most prominent internal cultural tools are those involved in language: Vygotsky believed that the development of speech and thought were independent in young children, such that thinking is 'preverbal' and language is devoid of thought, and that these come together only gradually. Another important Vygotskian view was that the interactions between teacher and learner are much more important, such that the notion of *instruction* is much more carefully formulated. *The capacity to learn from instruction* is at the heart of Vygotsky's theory of development, unlike that of Piaget, who viewed children as 'mini-scientists' exploring and attempting to explain the world logically and in a solitary manner, as we saw earlier.

Several more recent developments of Vygotsky's approach have been widely adopted, and we consider three particularly influential ideas and show how they have been applied in the study of musical development. The first is Rogoff's (1990) suggestion that *guided participation* might provide a very useful way of describing the process of instruction. She proposed that teachers act as a bridge between the knowledge and understanding of the learner and the demands of the task: they provide an overall context or structure in which the learner is encouraged to seek a solution, rather than to give up on the task. They do this by enabling learners to become active participants in the task, such that the responsibility for its successful completion gradually transfers from the teacher to the learner. In this way learners become able to employ the resources around them much more effectively: they build on the collective knowledge and experience that has been developed within the learning community.

Guided participation is probably exemplified most clearly in the process of *scaffolding*. In a well-known study Wood, Bruner, and Ross (1976) observed individual preschoolers working together with their mothers on the task of building a wooden pyramid made up of small pieces. They were able to show that the mothers monitored the children's levels of thinking in relation to the task, and were then able to change their own behaviour so as to give the child the optimum chance of completing it. In other words, the mothers seemed to create behavioural 'scaffolds' on which the children could build their learning, and they did so by working with an 'implicit theory of the learner's acts'. Wood et al. identified five distinct tutorial strategies which varied in the level of specific guidance provided, namely *recruiting attention, making the task limits manageable, maintaining direction, controlling frustration*, and *modelling the solution*.

Adachi (1994) was able to demonstrate a kind of musical scaffolding when she investigated adult–child partners playing musical duets: the adults demonstrated the same kind of 'contingent teaching' as seen in Wood et al.'s study by acting as 'transmitters of musical signs', as 'practice partners', or as 'co-players': and once again these varied in the level of guidance and structure provided for the child. The idea that learners build on the collective knowledge and experience that has been developed within the learning community is the foundation of the second influential idea deriving from Vygotsky, namely that of *communities of practice*. Rogoff (2003) suggested that this term can be used to describe the skills, practices, and ways of doing things that have been developed within particular communities, so that these practices are essentially social and culturally specific. Children learn by acting as 'apprentices' to those already experienced in a particular area: to use a musical example, we might think of the ways in which a novice musician might be introduced to a community band or orchestra by observing and following the example of their more experienced and expert peers. Communities of practice share three features: a *domain* of knowledge, such as a particular musical style, or set of skills that the band wants to cultivate: a *community* of people who have a commitment to this domain of knowledge (such as their friends, and other fans of that musical style, who come to see the band play); and a shared set of *practices* that are developed within the domain.

Abrahams and Abrahams (2016) have elaborated upon the apprenticeship idea as it applies to music learning in a chapter entitled 'The child as musical apprentice'. They note the historical antecedents of this idea in the work of Paulo Freire, Jerome Bruner, and Howard Gardner, among others: Bruner (1986) wrote, for example, 'I have come increasingly to recognise that most learning in most settings is a communal activity, a sharing of the culture. It is not just that the child must make his knowledge his own, but that he must make it his own in the community of those who share his sense of belonging to a culture' (p. 127). Abrahams and Abrahams also suggest that there are three forms of musical apprenticeship: traditional apprenticeship, in which the pupil learns alongside an experienced and expert mentor; cognitive apprenticeship, in which pupils learn skills and concepts by watching and imitating their mentor within the context of real-world experiences and issues, such as discussing why the composer set a particular piece in a particular key, or why a particular section of the orchestra has problems in playing a particular passage correctly; and the third form is what they call socio-transformative apprenticeship.

Socio-transformative apprenticeship not only involves learning new skills and concepts, but also the experience of change in the learner's perceptions of the musical experience, and of its broader context and significance. This is something like what Paolo Freire (1973) called 'critical consciousness', which can transform how the learner approaches new musical tasks. Abrahams and Abrahams also provide further details of the different processes involved in socio-transformative apprenticeship, as well as of four ways in which mentors might categorise different learner styles ('imaginative', 'analytic', 'common sense', and 'dynamic'), and use these to change the learner's perceptions of new tasks.

These ideas have a great deal in common with those in the work of Lave and Wenger (1991; Wenger, McDermott, & Snyder, 2002), who introduced the third influential idea deriving from Vygotsky, namely that of *legitimate peripheral participation*. This is how newcomers to the community of practice are introduced to it and engage with its three main dimensions, namely its processes of mutual engagement, of joint enterprise, and of adoption of a shared repertoire (Wenger, 1998). This is a more formal statement of the idea of apprenticeship, in that children become legitimate peripheral participants in the mature cultural practices of their communities, including their musical practices. North and Hargreaves (2008) quote the example of Everett's (2001) analysis of the shared practices and developing compositional skills of a young group from Liverpool who were inspired by the

British skiffle craze of the 1950s, and by American rock'n'roll. They started out as a skiffle duo called the Black Jacks, comprising John Lennon on guitar and vocals and his friend Pete Shotton on washboard and thimbles: they soon became the Quarrymen, named after the Liverpool secondary school that they attended: more talented musicians joined and undertook legitimate peripheral participation in the group, and the rest is history.

The most recent and elaborate development of Vygotskian theory takes the form of what has become known as *cultural-historical activity theory* (CHAT), which has been developed by Yrjö Engeström and his colleagues (see e.g. Engeström, 1987; Engeström & Miettinen, 1999). We describe this approach in more detail in Chapter 4, but in brief, Engeström's theory takes Vygotsky's approach further by moving beyond the analysis of the actions of individuals to the collective analysis of groups, and then further still by dealing with dialogue and interactions within those groups in relation to those of other groups, i.e. within larger communities.

Musical learning is an obvious domain in which the principles of CHAT could be applied, although relatively few people have yet attempted to do so. Perhaps the most sustained attempt is that by Welch and Ockelford (2016), looking at how institutions and teachers support music learning. They do so by carrying out CHAT analyses of four different examples of music learning that come from their own empirical research. The first of these is the musical tuition provided for the prodigious musical savant Derek Paravicini, whose case has been widely discussed in the literature and in the media, and who is now, as a young adult, able to exhibit prodigious feats of musical memory and improvisation. The CHAT analysis enables progress to be described in Derek's musical aims at different points in his learning career, and the ways in which his 'communities of practice' changed as his career developed. The analysis also enables us to appreciate the key role played by Derek's teacher, Adam Ockelford, which changed as this development occurred.

Welch and Ockelford also discuss teaching methods in higher music education, in conservatories and universities, in classical, popular, jazz, and Scottish traditional genres: needless to say the skills, expertise, and experience required in these genres differ considerably, such that a detailed comparative analysis of the elements of music learning is very helpful. The other two examples described by Welch and Ockelford are, first, the introduction of female choristers into a UK cathedral choir, a world which had hitherto been dominated by males: this is a clear instance of legitimate peripheral participation, to use Lave and Wenger's (1991) term, and activity theory enables its developmental course to be charted with clarity. The second example is that of music learning in the lower secondary school, looking at the social practices and learning systems involved, once again, in the teaching of different genres.

A key feature of all four analyses is that they are concerned with processes which take place outside the individual: the teacher and the learner all form part of an interacting activity system, which in itself forms part of a broader community which is subject to specific social and cultural rules. Another important area of musical learning in which sociocultural explanations have been adopted is that of collaborative learning in music, in particular in creative tasks such as composing and improvising: this is particularly pertinent in the UK, where primary school music teaching often involves a good deal of collaborative group work. A number of different studies have been carried out in this area at all levels of the education system, and we shall consider these in more depth in Chapter 4 when looking at the social aspects of musical learning and development.

Finally, we should mention another theoretical approach which is closely allied to but not identical to sociocultural theory, namely *cultural psychology*. This also has a strong emphasis on the ways in which the cultural environment has a direct and formative influence on the development of thinking and behaviour, as well as on the significance of cross-cultural comparisons, which are closely related to the concerns of sociology and anthropology (or in this case, ethnomusicology). Cultural psychology also has a strong emphasis on individuals' *experiences* of their lives, particularly in their connection to local cultural traditions, as well as on the notion that people display *agency* in dealing with their environments.

In Chapter 4 we shall describe Miranda, Blaise-Rochette, Vaugon, Osman, and Arias-Velanzuela's (2015, p. 198) recent attempt 'to define, ground, and situate a new perspective towards a cultural-developmental psychology of music in adolescence': this represents one possible emerging model of musical development from socio-cultural theory, and we have already touched on two others, namely those based on musical scaffolding and apprenticeship, and those deriving from CHAT. While none of these as yet has the status of a formal model, it does not seem too fanciful to imagine that one or more such might emerge in the not-too-distant future.

Ecological and Transactional Approaches

Ecology is the study of living forms and systems, and in particular of the relation-ships that exist between organisms and their physical and biological environments (Capra, 1996). Capra suggests that in more recent years the ecological paradigm has been applied in the number of different fields, perhaps in a desire to move beyond Western individualistic (mechanistic, reductionist, and atomistic) explanations of thought and activity to the recognition of more diverse and pluralistic factors. This general focus has been extended to ways in which social and cultural factors shape the interactions and relationships between people, such as in cultural psychology (e.g. Cole, 1996): probably the most prominent representative of the ecological approach within developmental psychology has been Urie Bronfenbrenner, whose *bioecological systems theory* (1979, 2001, 2005) has been very influential. This dis-tinguishes between four levels of system, which are nested within each other, and which range from the lowest, most specific level of social influence to the highest and most abstract. In Bronfenbrenner's (1979) original formulation, *microsystems* refer to the immediate settings of children's lives in their families, peer groups, and schools, for example; and the links between these form *mesosystems*, in which dif-ferent microsystems interact with one another (events at school might influence what children do at home, for example). *Exosystems* are the broader social settings which exert more indirect influences on children's behaviour, such as community

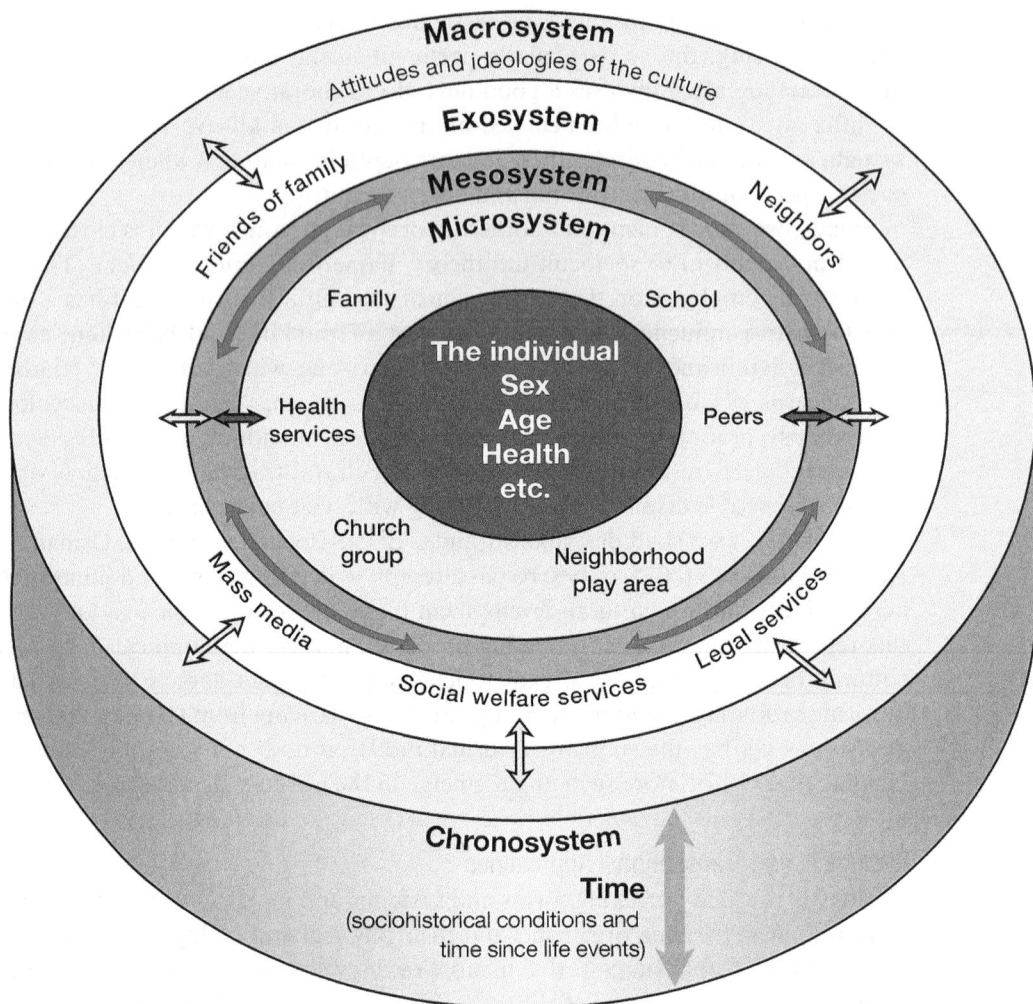

The individual
Sex
Age
Health
etc.

Microsystem

Family   School

Health services   Peers

Church group   Neighborhood play area

Mesosystem

Friends of family   Neighbors

Mass media   Legal services

Social welfare services

Exosystem

Macrosystem
Attitudes and ideologies of the culture

Chronosystem

Time
(sociohistorical conditions and
time since life events)

Figure 2.4.   Bronfenbrenner's (1986) revised ecological model, incorporating the chronosystem.
Source: Redrawn from Santrock, J. W. (2010), *Topical Approaches to Lifespan Development*, New York: McGraw-Hill. Figure 15, p. 23, reproduced with permission of McGraw Hill Education.

groups or parents' associations, and *macrosystems* exert the most indirect and abstract influences, such as government policies or social class-based institutions.

Several years later, Bronfenbrenner (1986) expanded this model to take account of the very dimension along which development occurs – i.e. the dimension of time, as illustrated in Figure 2.4. He incorporated what he called chronosystem models into his earlier formulations, which had focused largely on different aspects of the social and cultural environment, so that the system as a whole could be seen as a 'process-person-context-time' model of human development. The development of interest in the social context, and its increasing importance in the study of musical development, is an integral part of several of the other theoretical approaches with which we are dealing in this chapter alongside the ecological approach. These include the sociocultural perspective, that of cultural psychology, social cognitive approaches, and those which take a broader sociological and/or anthropological approach. We endeavour to disentangle these strands, and to compare their specific contributions to the study of musical development, at the end of this chapter.

Two main directions have been followed in the application of the ecological approach to music. In the first of these, the ideas of James Gibson have been applied to musical perception: the main protagonist of this approach is Eric Clarke, set out in his book *Ways of Listening* (2005). The second is more specifically developmental, in applying Eleanor Gibson's conceptions of ecological development to musical development.

Clarke (2005) starts from another fairly radical point of view, as far as 'mainstream' music psychology is concerned, that there are serious problems with applying an information-processing cognitive approach to musical behaviour: in particular, that the mental representations which are typically proposed in cognitive psychology are essentially conjectural, and are therefore fundamentally inferior to 'direct' perceptions of the auditory environment, given that the auditory environment does contain real and discernible structures. This fundamental point of view derives from James Gibson's ecological approach to visual perception (see e.g. Gibson, 2015). Both James and his wife Eleanor Gibson were strong proponents of the view that objects are perceived directly, such that there is no need to postulate internal cognitive constructs such as the processing mechanisms of cognitive psychology.

On the face of it, the simple idea that people perceive the structure that is present in the environment in a fairly accurate manner seems straightforward and plausible, but does not get us very far, and Clarke proposes that there are three factors which make this process much more psychologically significant and interesting. The first is the close relationship between *perception* and *action*: people are actively involved in perceiving different objects, and these actions may indeed determine which perceptual fields they choose to approach. The second is the idea of *adaptation*: that there is a continual interaction between the organism and its environment which is reminiscent of Piaget's ideas of assimilation and accommodation: we adapt our behaviour to meet the demands and possibilities offered by the environment, and this can involve corresponding changes in that environment. The third is that *perceptual learning* is seen as being passive in certain respects. This is not to imply a behavioural view of a passive learner who is completely shaped by the environment, but that no explicit training is involved in determining the best direction of learning: in this sense the organism is active, and learning is self-organised, in that the person becomes attuned to the environment.

This leads on to another feature of Clarke's approach: internal cognitive representations are rejected, but Clarke moves instead to connectionist models of learning, which have been linked with the neuroscientific approach (cf. Goswami, 2008). The child's developing networks of neural connections become increasingly adapted to the environment, and a gradual process of something like 'shaping' occurs which is under the control of the self, but which becomes increasingly attuned to the characteristics of the environment. This whole approach implies that the structure of stimulus objects in the environment is critically important, and the idea of the 'affordances' of objects takes its place here in explaining musical meaning. Affordances are the 'action consequences' of objects: the actions that are capable of being performed on them given their characteristics, and this leads to a new set of considerations when these are 'sound objects' rather than physical ones. It means that the physical location and source of sounds, their structure and function, and their cultural and ideological value all form part of their 'information content', and cannot be detached from one another. This conception is very important in the explanation of musical meaning, and Clarke elaborates the point in a number of different examples from different musical genres.

Our main concern here is in the explanation of children's musical development, and it is Eleanor Gibson's work (see e.g. Gibson, 1969) that is most directly relevant. Like her husband, she saw no need to postulate internal cognitive processing mechanisms, but instead saw perceptual development as the process of learning to extract information that is in the stimulus, i.e. 'what is already there', rather than as one in which the child supplies additional meanings, or constructions. Children can only take in a limited amount of information at any one time, and must therefore use certain strategies in order to reduce the amount of information that they take in: these strategies become increasingly efficient with age. A melody within a given piece of music might not be perceived as such on first hearing, for example, as children may not initially be able to recognise the difference between its variant and invariant features. This ability gradually develops as they become able to realise that the sequence of pitches (contour) is what remains characteristic of the melody; that other features such as key signature, tempo, instrumentation, and so on can be varied without any change in the essential character of the melody.

Gibson proposes three specific mechanisms by which these developmental changes occur, namely increasing correspondence between what children perceive and the information that is present in the stimulus; improvements in their attentional strategies, such that they are increasingly able to focus on the essential features of stimulus arrays and ignore the relevant ones; and thirdly, children's 'information pickup' becomes more efficient, or economical: this is accomplished by identifying distinctive features in the stimulus array by extracting invariants from it, and by recognising progressively larger units of perceptual structure. Gibson's approach emphasises that humans are active perceivers of information, and stresses the importance of the particular and specific environments, that is, the ecological context, in which perceptual development occurs. In this respect it is well suited to the explanation of musical perception and development.

We conclude this section by looking very briefly at three more 'ecological' suggestions that have been made about how the social and cultural environment might influence the developing child's musical thinking and behaviour, all three of which are pursued later in this book. First, Alexandra (Lamont, 1998, 1999, 2002) attempted to build the sociocultural context into the description of musical development by incorporating aspects of Bronfenbrenner's (1979) bioecological systems theory into a developmental model of musical pitch perception in children, suggesting that musical development can be seen as 'a constant and ongoing process of mediation between the social and cultural domain – which embodies the values of a particular culture and leads to particular kinds of activities – and the personal and individual domain, within which individual representations are formed' (Lamont, 1999, p. 5). Alexandra proposed a specific model of the development of pitch perception which involves mapping five developmental phases in the personal and individual domain onto four contexts in the social and cultural domain. She suggests that progress in developmental theories needs to take account of both systemic and individual influences at the same time, as well as concluding that longitudinal designs and a variety of methods are required (Lamont, 2016).

These suggestions represent the first of three possible ways forward in this field. A second is David's (Hargreaves, MacDonald, & Miell, 2012a) proposal that children's musical identities provide a way in which sociocultural factors can be built into the exploration of individual development, since individuals' views of themselves can actually determine their motivation and subsequent performance in music. We pursue this suggestion later in this chapter. The third approach is that taken by Gary McPherson, Jane Davidson, and Robert Faulkner (2012), in explaining the wealth of data which they collected on the musical development of a sample of 157 young Australians over a 14-year period, between the ages of 7 and 22. They adopt Sameroff's (2000) transactional approach to their participants' interactions with significant others (such as family members, teachers, peers, and other members of the community) in their environments, taking these interactions as predictors of the participants' own self-perceptions and musical development, proposing a very elaborate taxonomy of the regulatory sites at which the nature of the musical transactions with significant others are negotiated. McPherson, Davidson, and Faulkner describe their account as a taxonomy rather than as a 'model' of musical development, but it deserves at the very least to be considered as an emerging model alongside Alexandra's contextual model of the development of pitch perception. We look in more detail at the Australian study in Chapter 5.

Social Cognitive Approaches

The renowned psychologist Albert Bandura first became known in the 1960s when he formulated *social learning theory* (e.g. Bandura, 1969, 1977): this emerged from the behaviourist tradition, and focused on the role of *imitation* in human learning, and in particular the imitation of aggression in both children and adults. One feature of this approach which distinguished it from traditional behaviourist thinking was its emphasis on cognitive functions in social learning, including the concept of *identification* with powerful others. The cognitive aspects of the theory became increasingly important in Bandura's thinking, and led in 1986 to his formulation of *social cognitive theory*, in which he re-conceptualised people as being self-organising, self-reflective, and self-regulating.

Bandura's triadic view of the nature of human agency envisages reciprocally influencing processes stemming from three major classes of determinant of the self: behaviour, internal personal factors such as cognitive, affective, and biological events, and factors in the environment. The 'reciprocal determinism' of this system gives rise to three different forms of *self-regulation*, namely *behavioural self-regulation*, which involves self-observation in making adjustments to one's performance on a given task; *environmental self-regulation* the adjustment of one's own behaviour to environmental conditions, such as finding an appropriate environment for task completion; and *covert self-regulation*, which involves adapting cognitive and affective internal states to the environment and to one's behaviour. These ideas led eventually to a strong emphasis on the concept of *self-efficacy*, i.e. the 'beliefs in one's capabilities to organise and execute the courses of action required to produce given attainments' (Bandura, 1997, p. 3). Self-efficacy is not grounded in general, non-specific beliefs, but in specific contexts and domains, and the domain of music is what concerns us here.

Jackie Wiggins (2016) has applied the concept of human agency specifically to music education, taking a broad interdisciplinary view: she sees 'musical agency' as describing children's ability to initiate and develop their own musical ideas, i.e. to 'act musically', without necessarily needing the help of adults. She distinguishes between what she calls *learner agency* – learners' constructions of their own understanding within social contexts – which derives from the theoretical views of Vygotsky, Rogoff, and Wenger, and *personal agency* – belief that one has the capacity to engage, initiate, and intentionally influence one's own life circumstances – for which she invokes the views of Bandura, as well as the sociological concepts of Giddens (1991), and Ryan and Deci's (2002) self-determination theory: personal agency may also form the basis, in groups, of *collective efficacy* (Bandura, 2000). Finally, *musical agency*, in which the concept is specifically applied to music learning, involves aspects of learner as well as of personal agency. Wiggins also reviews a number of different theoretical approaches to and empirical investigations of musical agency, including psychological research on musical identities (e.g. by Hargreaves, MacDonald, & Miell, 2002); the sociological work of DeNora (e.g. 2001) and Karlsen (2011; see also Westerlund, Partii, & Karlsen, 2017); and that of early years and ethnomusicological researchers who have studied children's musical play, including Margaret Barrett (2011), Patricia Shehan Campbell (2011), Kathy Marsh, and Susan Young (2016). She concludes that fostering and enabling agency and independence are at the heart of learning and development.

Piaget and Vygotsky were both interested in the extent to which children are able to regulate their own development and learning, and how this ability develops, but the study of self-regulation and the associated topic of metacognition (in brief, thinking about one's own thinking) were given new impetus by the work of Flavell (1977, 1979). Self-regulation, the associated construct of self-regulated learning, and metacognition are all now seen to be part of the domain of executive function (EF), which Drayton, Turley-Ames, and Guajardo (2011) defined as a strategic 'cognitive system that controls and manages other cognitive processes, including flexibility of thought, planning, inhibition, and coordination and integration of information' (p. 534). EF has a planning and monitoring role in intelligent activity, whereas IQ represents the overall resources and strategies on which EF can draw in the service of different tasks.

There is a great deal of current interest in executive function, which is seen to involve three main cognitive abilities: cognitive flexibility, inhibitory control, and working memory. Recent research in neuroscience suggests that these cognitive abilities may be interrelated (e.g. Goswami, 2008), and there is also seen to be a close relationship between EF, self-regulation, self-regulated learning, metacognition, and the concept of effortful control and theory of mind. Whereas EF derives from the cognitive tradition, and from cognitive neuroscience in particular, effortful control is a construct deriving from research on socio-emotional development and temperament, and has been defined as 'the ability to inhibit a dominant or prepotent response in favour of a subdominant or less salient response' (Blair & Razza, 2007, p. 647). Theory of mind research, which has also proliferated in recent years, concerns children's abilities to predict the states of mind and feelings of others, and as such is closely related to metacognition.

There are two main theoretical traditions in this field: the first derives from Flavell's work, and is mainly concerned with mental processes and capacities, in particular metacognition, which Flavell (1976) defined as 'one's knowledge concerning one's own cognitive processes and products or anything related to them, e.g. the learning-relevant properties of information or data' (p. 57). The second tradition stems from the sociocultural approach and the theories of Vygotsky (1978), which sees self-regulation as a phenomenon which contrasts with other-regulation, in which the child's learning is guided or 'scaffolded' by an adult or more experienced tutor, and which is thereby deeply embedded in the social context, incorporating the emotional, social, and motivational aspects of cognition (Whitebread, 2013).

The distinction between self-regulation and metacognition is clarified in the model proposed by Nelson and Narens (1994), which suggests that two levels of mental operation are involved in any cognitive activity, namely an object-level and a meta-level. The former refers simply to the cognitive processes involved in the task being undertaken, whereas the latter refers to the strategies which are adopted to regulate this cognitive activity. Metacognition occurs at the meta-level, and includes knowledge about people's mental abilities and cognitive strategies. Nelson and Narens' model has been extended by Whitebread et al. (2009), whose conceptualisation incorporates all of these different aspects of self-regulation: it suggests that the three main areas of self-regulation are metacognitive knowledge, metacognitive regulation, and emotional/motivational regulation, and subdivides each of these further into specific self-regulatory behaviours.

Another issue of great interest in this field is the development of self-regulation in children: one of the main research questions has been whether this occurs in a domain-specific fashion, such that self-regulation occurs more efficiently in one domain than another, and then gradually becomes more general, or whether the acquisition of self-regulation is general, following a pattern of age-related maturational changes. One description of this development which adopts the latter, domain-general point of view, and which is modelled on Piagetian theory, is that of Kopp (1982). In brief, Kopp proposes a sequence of distinct phases in the development of emotional and behavioural control which parallel the general growth of cognitive skills. The first phase of neurophysiological modulation refers to the biological mechanisms which protect babies from overstimulation, and this is followed by a phase of sensorimotor modulation between about 3 and 9–12 months: it involves the baby's ability to engage in voluntary motor action such as grasping or sucking, and in moderating these actions in response to social and environmental stimuli. In the third 'control' phase, between approximately 12 and 24 months, the infant starts to show awareness of the social aspects of situations, and is responsive to external signals and commands as well as engaging in a certain amount of self-monitoring. This develops into the fourth 'self-control' phase which occurs at around the age of 2 years, and which involves the ability to control impulses, to respond to requests to delay responses, and to behave according to social expectations without direct instruction. This develops into fully blown self-regulation when children internalise adult-based regulatory strategies and are able to adapt to all the demands of different social situations.

The importance of the social context is emphasised by many scholars, as is the social nature of a great deal of self-regulation. A good deal of current research is devoted to co-regulated learning, i.e. socially shared learning, which takes place in collaborative social activity with one or more others, such that motivation is shared and co-regulated. Co-regulated learning can sometimes involve unequal partnerships in which one member is skilled in some key aspect of the task but the other is not, and the goal here is to make the transition either towards self-regulated learning, or to coordinate independent self-regulated learning among the members of the group. Hadwin, Järvalä, and Miller (2011) make the important distinction between self- regulated (individual) learning, co-regulated learning, which occurs when there is coordination between the self-regulation of the self and any other partners who are collaborating on the task, and socially shared regulation of learning, which occurs when the task is shared by more than two collaborators in which a shared outcome is sought, when peers regulate their activity collectively, and their regulatory behaviours are co-constructed within the group.

It is quite possible for self-regulation, co-regulation, and socially shared regulation to occur within the same collaborative task, in that control can gradually shift from one form of learning to another: for this reason collaborative learning, including group work and peer tutoring, can promote self-regulation in educational contexts. This has led to the development of educational strategies for the promotion of self-regulation: educators have considered the optimum teaching strategies and classroom environments for the development of self-regulation, and have looked in particular at pretend play and talk, both of which are seen as key activities in this respect. The ability to pretend that one object can represent another, which occurs during the child's second year of life is seen as the origin of meta-representation, and make-believe play is seen as an important arena for the provision of the origins of advanced forms of thinking. Closely related to this is the incidence of private speech, which is most often seen in pretend play and in 'functional' play (that involving simple motor actions), and which is seen to play a key role in the development of metacognition. One particular area in which research has proliferated is that of collaborative musical composition, and we will return to this in Chapter 4.

Thus the study of self-regulation and metacognition has become an active area of developmental research, and their promotion in young children has become an important educational goal. Educators have considered the optimal teaching strategies and classroom environments for the development of self-regulation, and pretend play and talk are both seen as key activities in this respect. It seems therefore to follow that musical play could be an important area in which these developments could take place, since it provides a prime arena for children's communication and collaboration. There has been very little empirical research on this topic, however, with the exception of a recent doctoral study by Antonia Zachariou (2014). Zachariou's project included a quantitative cross-sectional study of 36 6- and 8-year-olds in primary schools in Cyprus, who were observed during musical play sessions which were implemented in their music classes. She also conducted four qualitative case studies of individual children who varied widely in their levels of self-regulation.

Zachariou adapted an established coding framework to observe self-regulation in musical play systematically, and also assessed the children's general self-regulatory ability and their levels of musicality. Her results clearly showed that various forms of regulatory behaviour could be observed in the children's musical play, and that this occurred more frequently in the 8-year-old children than in the play of the 6-year-olds. She also found that several contextual variables, including the type of musical play (e.g. clapping games, movement play, instrumental play, circle games, or singing play), the extent to which the teacher was involved, whether the activities were child- or teacher-initiated and led, and whether the musical play occurred individually, in pairs, or in groups ('self- regulation', 'co-regulation', and 'social regulation' respectively), all had a significant influence on the extent to which self-regulatory behaviour occurred. General self-regulatory ability was positively related to self-regulation during musical play, and this relationship was stronger for the younger than for the older children.

The qualitative case studies were able to illustrate how self-regulation occurred in practice: this was this was manifested in actions such as getting musical instruments ready, planning musical activities, monitoring mistakes in the lyrics of a song, and guiding peers with gestures or by moving to the beat. Metacognitive knowledge was manifested in the form of talking about one's own or another's abilities, and comparing musical tasks and their features. The case studies also identified several factors which mediated between musical play and self-regulation, namely musicality, friendship, finding the task interesting, and peer tutoring. High levels of musicality, for example were typically (but not always) associated with high levels of regulatory behaviour. Zachariou's research represents a very promising start on the study of self-regulatory behaviour in musical play, and no doubt will be followed by other studies, since it provides novel insights which inform psychological theory as well as educational practice, and which confirm the importance of the domain of music in the development of children's learning.

Hargreaves, MacDonald, and Miell (2012a) argue that *musical identities mediate musical development*: that people's developing self-concepts tell us a great deal about why they develop in the ways they do. The main theoretical underpinning of this view comes from Vygotsky's (1966) basic idea that 'we become ourselves through others', which we elaborated earlier in this chapter. Our social relationships with others form the basis of our own individual development, and this leads to an emphasis on the importance of individual *identity* in musical development: Hargreaves et al. discuss this proposal in three representative areas, namely the cognitive, the social, and the affective (emotional) aspects of musical development. This approach in effect represents an explanation of development 'from the inside': understanding how individuals perceive and conceptualise their own musical development may be important in shaping that development.

This argument conceives of musical identities as ubiquitous, constantly evolving aspects of the self-concept that are negotiated across a range of social situations. They influence not only the development of specific musical skills, but also the rate at which that development occurs. Furthermore, this link is *reciprocal*: the development of specific musical skills influences developing musical identities just as much as vice versa. For example, a young child who learns to play a demanding new piece of piano music may experience a boost in confidence about her own musical abilities more generally.

The ways in which we view ourselves, and evaluate our own skills and competencies, form a key part of the development of our identities, and these self-assessments influence our development in general (Bandura, 1986) as well as in musical terms (Hargreaves et al., 2002). Individuals with low self-efficacy (i.e. with a low estimate of their capability to complete a specific task) in a musical context may regard their musical potential as minimal, perhaps arguing that 'my family is not musical and so I cannot learn to play the guitar'. This is a very common misconception about the development of musical skills, and it is often low levels of expectancy such as this, rather than the family's lack of musicality, that can lead to the potential for musical skills remaining undeveloped. Developing a positive musical identity, on the other hand, can increase the extent to which individuals will engage in musical practice, which can in turn promote the development of specific musical skills (Lamont et al., 2003; McPherson & O'Neill, 2010).

This section of the chapter has taken a fairly broad view of what we have called social cognitive approaches, ranging over a number of different interdisciplinary points of view. We have focused mainly on the developmental aspects of self-regulation and self-perception, and we also looked in particular at the development of self-regulated learning and metacognition in young children.

We should also point out, however, that there exists a substantial research literature on self-regulation in adults with high levels of musical experience and expertise. Varela, Abrami, and Upitis (2016) have recently published a very thorough review of this literature, pointing out that good deal of it stems from Zimmerman's (2000) theory of self-regulation, and in particular from the application of that theory to music learning and practice in empirical studies by Gary McPherson and his associates (e.g. McPherson & McCormick, 2006; McPherson & Renwick, 2001).

Varela et al. carefully selected 25 empirical studies of the relationships between self-regulation and aspects of music learning according to a number of selection criteria for their meta-analysis, and the variables of interest included level of expertise, performance scores, amount of practice, persistence, content of informal and formal practice, efficiency, general music instruction, and self-regulation instruction. The results, perhaps somewhat disappointingly, were that most of these showed weak positive relationships with self-regulatory behaviour, and that by far the strongest positive association was with self-regulation instruction. We shall also see in Chapter 5, in looking at musicians' practice strategies, that Bonneville-Roussy and Bouffard (2015) have recently proposed a framework that includes self-regulation, deliberate practice strategies, and overall practice time to predict achievement – they emphasise the importance of self-regulation alongside practice strategies.

It is clear that theory and research which adopts the social cognitive approach has a great deal of promise and potential, although this has not yet reached the point at which we can identify any specific models or emerging models of musical development as such.

Neuroscientific Studies of Music

The field of cognitive neuroscience has become very rapidly established over the last two decades or so: it investigates the networks of neurons that are active in the brain when specific cognitive representations are occurring in the mind. The activation of mental representations is associated with the firing of many neurons simultaneously, such that thinking can be studied directly in terms of brain structure and function. This has become possible because of the development of brain imaging techniques which have become available relatively recently, and there are currently three main techniques. These are electroencephalography (EEG), which records the low voltage changes caused by the 'firing' (activation) of cells during cognitive activity; functional magnetic resonance imaging (fMRI), which measures changes in blood flow in the brain; and functional near-infrared spectroscopy (fNIRS), which measures the level of oxygenation of blood in the brain by optical means. These have relative advantages and disadvantages for different uses, but all are suitable for use with children.

In trying to explain the processes of cognitive development and learning, neuroscientists have used two different but complementary approaches. The first is *neuroconstructivism*, which investigates how neural structures become increasingly specialised in response to children's choice of activities. This explains cognitive development in terms of the biological constraints on the neural activation networks that form mental representations. New experiences in children's environments change the 'wiring' of the brain, and this leads on to the discovery of new experiences and thus still further changes to the neural systems. A key feature of this approach is the interaction between the environment and the growing brain: neuroconstructivism could thus be said to offer a biological perspective on cognitive development (see Goswami, 2008).

Connectionism, on the other hand, uses computer modelling to predict the effects of the repeated activation of neural networks, and offers a biological perspective on *learning*. It is concerned with the ways in which networks of neural connections develop as the child encounters new experiences. Cognitive constructs such as mental representations or aspects of language are represented by patterns of activation across these neural networks, and these are distributed across various regions of the brain. It is important to note here that neuroscience considers that infants have the same learning mechanisms as adults: gradual exposure to different patterns of sensory events give rise to the development of neural networks that enable infants to learn in different ways. The difference between child and adult learning is not in the structure of their brains, but in children's relative lack of experience, metacognition, and self-regulation: we will return to these in the following sections.

Children are capable of recognising similarities between different situations, and thus of constructing causal explanations of why different things happen. Goswami and Bryant (2010) have suggested that four main kinds of learning mechanism can be seen in infants. The first of these is statistical learning by neural networks, which represents the application of neuroconstructivism. This is unconscious learning, which continues throughout life, and in which the brain learns the statistical structure of events perceived by the infant and builds neural networks to represent this information. For example, babies can distinguish between simple visual forms (e.g. crosses and circles) from birth, and can also recognise the correspondence between the same stimulus when it is experienced in different modalities, such as in vision and hearing. During the first year of life, infants learn the statistical patterns which govern the sequences of sounds that are mainly used to make words in their home language (Saffran, Aslin, & Newport, 1996).

The other three mechanisms of learning identified by Goswami and Bryant are learning by *imitation*, in that babies can imitate adult facial expressions from birth, for example; learning by *analogy*, which involves noticing similarities between one situation and another and then applying analogous solutions to the problem; and *causal* learning, in which they are able to develop causal explanations of physical effects such as objects falling down, blocking out the view of one another, supporting one other and containing one another. The fact that children appear to understand the principles according to which these transformations take place, i.e. that they are able work out the explanations for why things happen, means that this learning involves more than just simple contingencies or associations between different events.

Two further features of the neuroscientific approach to development have emerged in recent research involving the social abilities of infants and young children, which have been seriously underestimated in previous developmental research. The first of these is in studies of theory of mind. As this concerns children's abilities to predict the behaviour of others on the basis of their perceived beliefs and desires, it is closely related to metacognition, which we reviewed in the previous section. Metacognition and metarepresentation are important concepts within the social cognitive approach: they were reviewed in the previous section, as was the application of this approach to music. Imitation is one of the ways in which knowledge about the feelings of others can be gained, and pretend play and language also form important sources of insight into the attitudes and feelings of others. Recent research shows that the earlier belief that theory of mind does not develop until around the age of 4 years is no longer valid, and that it develops perhaps as early as in the second year of life (e.g. Baron-Cohen, Leslie, & Frith, 1985; Onishi & Baillargeon, 2005).

Blakemore (2010) has also strongly emphasised the importance of 'mentalising' and of social interaction with others in neurocognitive development, and points out that 'a large number of independent studies have shown remarkable consistency in identifying brain regions that are involved in theory of mind or mentalising. These studies have employed a wide range of stimuli including stories, sentences, words, cartoons, and animations' (p. 745). She also points out that a number of developmental fMRI studies have shown that cortical activity during mentalising tasks decreases between adolescence and adulthood: in other words, the operation of theory of mind is not only demonstrated in young children at much earlier ages than was previously thought, but is also active and still undergoing development at the relatively late stage of mid-adolescence, and then declines with the entry into adulthood.

These developments run parallel to that of a growing area of developmental neuroscience which has emerged with the discovery of a neural system called the 'mirror neuron system'. Mirror neurons were discovered in research with monkeys in which when one animal carried out actions such as tearing, holding, grasping, and manipulating objects, the same neurons were found to be activated as when the animal observed another performing the same actions (Rizzolati & Craighero, 2004). In humans, the mirror neuron system seems to be activated when people imitate the actions of another person, or imitate their facial expressions: this is thought to be at the heart of children's perceptions of the intentions, desires, and feelings of others, such that 'theory of mind' includes emotion as well as cognition. Molnar-Szakacs, Assuied, and Overy (2012) have emphasised the importance of the idea that when we observe the emotional states of others, we empathetically feel the same emotions, and they have reviewed the use of this 'shared affective motion experience' (SAME) in creative interactive music therapy.

Neuroscientific studies have rapidly become one of the most promising new directions in developmental psychology, and one of the leading edges of neuroscience is the study of music. Neuroscientific studies of musical development would therefore appear to be a very fruitful area of potential investigation: and as it turns out, this area of studies is more than fulfilling its potential. This is because there is now a substantial and increasing body of evidence which shows that early musical training can lead to many different cognitive, social, emotional, and motivational benefits in children, as we shall see in more detail in Chapter 8.

Before looking at the wide range of studies of the effects of music on psychological development, however, it is worth putting them in context by describing three more general neuroscientific findings with music. The first is that music has extremely powerful effects at the neural level, as demonstrated in a widely quoted study by Blood and Zatorre (2001). They used positron emission tomography (PET) to study the neural mechanisms underlying intensely pleasant emotional responses to music, i.e. those involving physiological responses such as 'shivers-down-the-spine' or 'chills'. Blood and Zatorre found that their listeners' reports of these effects were accompanied by changes in heart rate, electromyogram responses, and respiration, and that as the intensity of these chills increased, cerebral blood flow increases and decreases were observed in the brain regions thought to be involved in reward/motivation, emotion, and arousal and also activated by food, sex, and other euphoria-inducing stimuli. They suggest that this link between music and the neural pleasure centres highlights the biological and survival-related importance of music.

The second general finding is that music activates many different areas of the brain due to its complexity and the wide range of multimodal responses which result from this. In their review of this field, Miranda and Overy (2009) point out that from the neuroscientist's point of view, the investigation of musical behaviour can give insights into a number of other different types of processing including auditory processing, motor skills, short-term memory, emotional responses, and other aspects of cognitive and social behaviour. For this reason, music can also be used in the study of the ways in which the different parts of the brain communicate and interact with one another. Miranda and Overy also suggest that because the neural mechanisms engaged by music also play an important role in other aspects of human intelligence, such as in speech, motor control, and emotion, research in this field might eventually lead to medical and other social benefits (see further Chapter 8).

Alluri, Toiviainen, Jääskeläinen, Glerean, Sams, and Brattico (2012) demonstrated these wide-ranging neural effects of music empirically by making fMRI scans of adult listeners' brains while they were listening to a modern tango – a stimulus with a rich musical structure. Through a combination of neuroimaging, acoustic feature extraction, and behavioural methods they were able to identify the large-scale cognitive, motor and limbic brain circuitry used for acoustic feature processing during listening to a rich stimulus. They examined the timbral, tonal, and rhythmic features of the music, and found that the processing of its *timbral* features was associated with activations in cognitive areas of the cerebellum, and sensory and default mode network cerebrocortical areas, whereas the processing of musical *pulse* and *tonality* recruited cortical and subcortical cognitive, motor, and emotion-related circuits.

The third general finding in this broad research is that the brain structures of musicians have consistently been found to be different from those of non-musicians. They have higher levels of auditory cortical representation (Pantev, Oostenveld, Engelien, Ross, Roberts, & Hoke, 1998), and the corpus callosum, the structure that joins the two hemispheres of the brain, was found by Schlaug, Jancke, Huang, Staiger, and Steinmetz (1995) to be consistently thicker in the brains of musicians than in non-musicians. Furthermore, the extent of these differences seems to be correlated with the age at which musicians began to practise. Gaser and Schlaug (2003) found differences in motor, auditory, and visual–spatial brain regions when comparing professional musicians (keyboard players) with a matched group of amateur musicians and non-musicians, and conclude that this is evidence for structural adaptation in response to skill acquisition and rehearsal. A further study comparing 5–7-year-old children who practised a lot or a little (Hyde, Lerch, Norton, Forgeard, Winner, Evans, & Schlaug, 2009) revealed that after twenty-nine months of learning and practice, those who practised more showed greater functional differences, so that intense levels of musical experience/practice could produce these neural effects.

These are clear demonstrations of the phenomenon of *neuroplasticity*, which refers to the changes in neural pathways and synapses which occur as a result of changes in behaviour, environment, and other psychological processes. This idea has superseded the commonly held twentieth-century view that brain structures remain relatively immutable after an initial critical period in early childhood. The brain is now seen to change throughout life, and the role of neuroplasticity is now widely recognised in development, learning, memory, and in particular in recovery from brain damage: functions which are affected by such damage are seen to recover through the large-scale changes which are involved in *cortical remapping* in response to injury. Although theory and research in this rapidly developing area has not yet reached the point at which we can identify any specific models or emerging models of musical development as such, progress is such that this seems very likely to occur sooner rather than later.

One potentially important theoretical advance which is supported by the growth of neuroscientific evidence is the concept of *imagination* as being the cognitive basis of musical perception and production. Imagination is the essence of the creative perception of music, and we shall see in Chapters 3 and 7 that there is a great deal of new research on the emotion-arousing properties of music, as well as on the determinants and development of musical likes and dislikes. In particular, David (Hargreaves, 2012) proposed a revised and simplified view of the reciprocal feedback model of musical communication originally put forward by Hargreaves, MacDonald, and Miell (2005). This revised model, which appears later in this in chapter (see Figure 2.5) is based on the view that musical imagination, which consists of internal cognitive representations, is at the core of both musical perception and musical production, and the model now consequently deals with music processing rather than with communication.

The idea that common mental structures underlie the three main activities of musical invention, namely composing/improvising, performing, and listening, is supported by some growing evidence that these mental processes have identifiable neural correlates. Imagining music, for instance, activates similar parts of the brain to experiencing it (Zatorre & Halpern, 2005). Based on fMRI studies, Olivetti

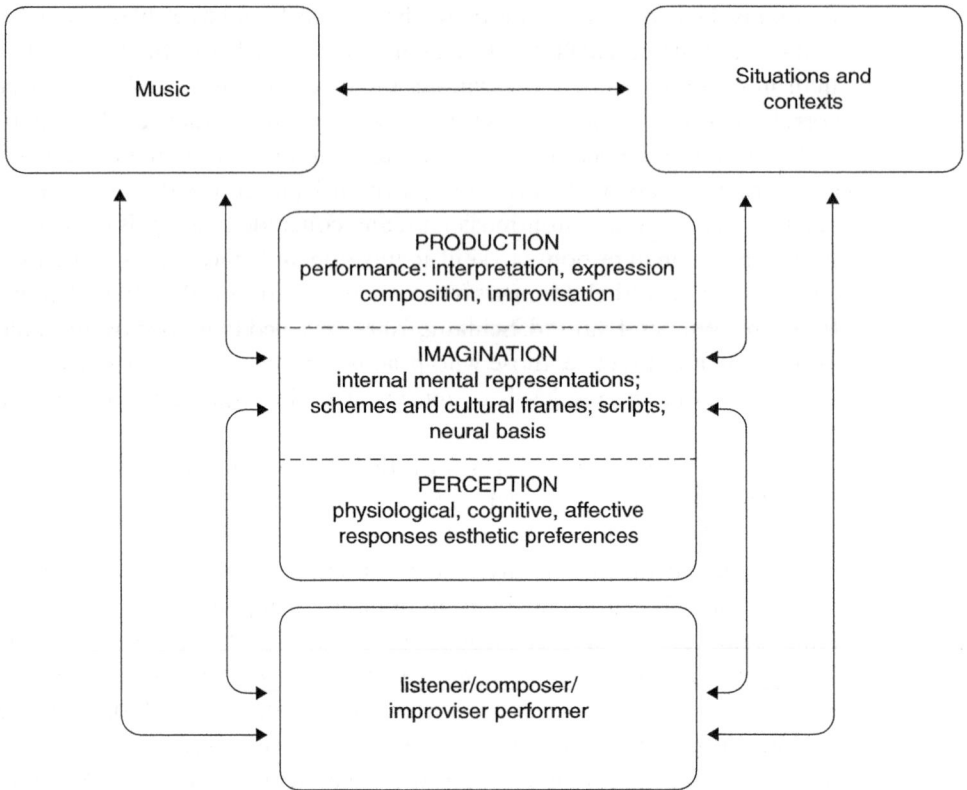

Figure 2.5.   Hargreaves' (2012) revised reciprocal–feedback model of music processing.
Source: Figure 16.1 (p. 305) in Hargreaves, D. J., North, A. C., & Tarrant, M. (2016),
How and why do musical preferences change during childhood and adolescence? In: G.
McPherson (Ed.), *The child as musician: A handbook of musical development* (pp. 303–322).
© Oxford University Press. By permission of Oxford University Press.

Belardinelli et al. (2004) found a great deal of overlap between mental imagination shown in the different modalities of composing, performing, and listening, as
well as overlap between all of them and visual representation. 'The results indicate
either the involvement of amodal functional circuits of mental imagination or the
presence of a visual imagination component in different types of mental images'
(Olivetti Belardinelli, 2006, p. 330). Developmental research is likely to provide one
of the best ways of testing and advancing these ideas.

Theoretical Issues

As noted at the start of this chapter, we have identified six general theoretical
approaches which can be further subdivided into ten distinct approaches, namely
those based on developmental stages (x2), learning and cognition (x2), symbol systems, music theory, social factors (x3), and neuroscientific methods respectively. We
have also suggested that the first six have given rise to specific models of musical

development. The remaining four approaches have not yet led to any comparable models, but have the potential to do so. One area of potential confusion is in clarifying the precise differences between the seventh, eighth, and ninth of these. The sociocultural approaches, ecological approaches, social cognitive approaches and that of cultural psychology, not to mention sociological and anthropological approaches, are all concerned in one way or another with the effects of the social and cultural environment on individual and group behaviour – how do they differ?

A brief summary might be as follows: the sociocultural approaches, given their basis in Vygotsky's theory, are essentially concerned with the social interaction between children and those around them, notably other family members, and peers; and Vygotsky emphasised the importance of talk and language in providing the vehicle for this. Ecological and transactional approaches, on the other hand, are more centrally concerned with the characteristics of different environments and contexts, and with their *affordances*, for example, and with the ways in which these form part of the child's active perceptual learning. The approach of cultural psychology takes this still further, looking in particular at cross-cultural differences between environments, and the comparative effects that these have on the individuals growing up in those environments. This is probably nearest to the broader disciplinary approaches of sociology, anthropology (and specifically ethnomusicology), which focus on the global diversity of different social and cultural rule systems and structures, and the ways in which they influence individual and group behaviour. Finally, social cognitive approaches focus on individuals and their self-perceptions, and with the ways in which these perceptions shape individuals' actual development.

To conclude this lengthy chapter, we look at five key theoretical issues in terms of the ten new theoretical perspectives that we have set out, and we refer to earlier debates evaluating different theoretical approaches (Hargreaves & Zimmerman, 1992; Swanwick & Runfola, 2002) only where these can make a useful new contribution. Our underlying question is the extent to which the ten different theoretical models/approaches are capable of dealing with each of these issues, namely *the biological and the social; the relationships between musical production, perception, performance, and representation; developmental progression; domain-specificity;* and *the distinction between normative and expert development.*

The Biological and the Social

Recent studies of infant socialisation (see Chapter 3) show that the interaction between the biological predispositions of infants and caregivers, and the social environment, are at the heart of human development. Mothers behave towards their babies in ways that are biologically pre-determined, such as in their facial expressions, gaze, and speech: and babies take the lead in many early interactions – usually by means of crying or smiling – and mothers respond accordingly. Mothers construct meaning in these cries and smiles, and in turn the babies begin to attribute different meanings to their mothers' different reactions: and so increasingly complex chains or patterns of interaction gradually develop which involve mutual constructions of meaning. This process represents the interaction between the biological and the social.

We shall see in Chapter 3 and elsewhere how Colwyn Trevarthen and Stephen Malloch (e.g. Trevarthen, 1999; Trevarthen & Malloch, 2017) have proposed that these interactions are themselves inherently musical in character, and that what they call 'communicative musicality' characterises them: their studies of mutual talk, singing, and other rhythmic games with infants show these features. We will also see in Chapter 3 how Sandra Trehub and her colleagues at the University of Toronto (see e.g. Trehub & Degé, 2016) have shown that caregivers' infant-directed speech is effectively 'slowed down' and exaggerated in relation to their adult-directed speech: once again, musical meaning is co-constructed, and we have already seen that early musical play can be an important arena for the development of young children's self-regulation.

This brief characterisation of early development shows that social cognitive theories have a part to play in describing the interaction between the biological and the social: Trevarthen and Malloch's conception of communicative musicality draws not only on sociocultural and ecological approaches in that the social and cultural environment is seen to form an integral part of musical development, but also, explicitly, on neuroscientific developments which suggest that certain neural events underlie children's perceptions of the intentions of others. We also saw in this chapter that children's perceptions of the intentions of others and of others' 'theories of mind' may have their origins in the mirror neuron system. Although this area of research is in its infancy, and although its role in the domain of music remains to be explored, both social cognitive and neuroscientific approaches may have important contributions to make to the explanation of musical development.

Musical Production, Perception, Performance, and Representation

The relative effectiveness of different theoretical models in accounting for all of these musical modalities was raised originally by Hargreaves and Zimmerman (1992), and in that discussion we considered the idea that there may exist general cognitive structures that underlie the processes involved in more than one modality. We also saw earlier in this chapter that Gardner (1973b) proposed the existence of three interacting systems in development, which he called the *making* system, the *perceiving* system, and the *feeling* system. More than thirty years later, these notions have received clear support from the neuroscientific literature: there is a clear consensus that common mental structures underlie the three main activities of invention (composing and improvising), performance, and listening; that these structures are constantly changing, revealing imagination and creativity; and there is also increasing evidence that these mental processes have identifiable neural correlates. Taking this further, Hargreaves, Miell, and MacDonald (2012b) have recently argued that the active process of cognitive construction in which new sensory input is interpreted in the light of the perceiver's accumulated schemata, or mental representations, lead to a view of *imagination* as the cognitive basis of musical perception and production, and this idea is developed in the next section.

Creativity and Imagination in Music Listening

Imagination is the essence of the creative perception of music, and imagination in music is underpinned by internal cognitive representations. In the revised version of the reciprocal feedback model of musical communication (Hargreaves, 2012: see Figure 2.5), musical imagination is seen as the core of both perception and production. There is clear evidence that the brain processes underlying auditory imagery are similar to those involved in real-life music listening. Halpern and Zatorre (1999) asked participants to imagine melodic continuations after being given a few notes or to listen to them and then imagine the sequences. Using PET, they found that the auditory cortical areas were activated even in the absence of sound, and the real-tune imagery task showed primarily right-sided activation in particular areas of the cortex (the frontal and superior temporal regions, and the supplementary motor area: see also Zatorre & Halpern, 2005). Herholz, Halpern, and Zatorre (2012) have further shown that imagery activates more areas of the brain than real listening, with an extended network including the prefrontal cortex, supplementary motor area, intraparietal sulcus, and cerebellum.

As well as listening and imagination, other musical processes also seem to share a great deal of neural resources, and Olivetti Belardinelli (2006) has proposed a systemic cognitive perspective on creativity such that composing, performing, and enjoyment of music all share a set of multimodal activations in the brain. This suggests imagination is a more fundamental construct than creativity, as the latter refers mainly to aspects of musical performance (see Hargreaves, Hargreaves, & North, 2012). The notion that creativity is underpinned by perception and reflection is not a new idea (cf. Davis & Gardner, 1992), but what is new is the neuropsychological support for this idea. We can conclude that the neuroscientific approach stands out from all the others as uniquely having the potential to deal with this issue of the range of coverage of different modalities.

Developmental Progression

The central theoretical issue here is whether developmental change is *continuous*, with skills and knowledge increasing in a smooth, accumulative fashion with age, or whether it is *discontinuous*, proceeding in a series of qualitatively different steps. Piaget's stage theory is by far the best-known version of the latter view, although it is not now generally accepted by many researchers in its original form: the reasons for this are discussed in detail by North and Hargreaves (2008, pp. 327–330). One fundamental problem is Piaget's view of the child as a 'mini-scientist', whose main developmental goal is to achieve logical thinking: we described Gardner's (1973b) explicit rejection of this view earlier in this chapter.

North and Hargreaves (2008) emphasised this point by suggesting that the 'consensus of opinion ... is that development has *multiple* endpoints: individuals build up a repertoire of behaviours whose heterogeneity precludes any idea of a general direction' (p. 328). This point of view resonates strongly with the neuroscientific view of development and learning, discussed earlier, that babies use the same learning mechanisms as adults in which gradual exposure to different patterns of sensory events leads to the development of neural networks which give rise to different forms of learning. The differences between child and adult learning result from children's relative lack of experience, metacognition, and self-regulation, which strongly implies that learning is a continuous process, and that there is no need to propose the existence of developmental stages.

Having said that, empirical research on development in the arts clearly shows that regular age-related changes in artistic behaviour do occur: older children are generally more advanced than younger ones in the ways in which they engage with the arts, and in their potential range of achievements (see Hargreaves & Galton, 1992; Hargreaves, 1996). However, this does not imply that any such age-related regularities are the result of underlying cognitive maturation, as is the case with Piagetian stages, which is why we use the term 'phases' rather than 'stages' to describe them. As we pointed out earlier, many of Piaget's critics have drawn attention to his relative lack of attention to social and cultural diversity in cognitive development, and some theorists have tried to build sociocultural contexts into their developmental models. As we saw earlier, Alexandra (Lamont, 1998, 1999), for example, incorporated some aspects of Bronfenbrenner's (1979) ecological systems theory into her developmental model of musical pitch representation in children. However, stage theories, as generalised descriptions, typically preclude any specification of social circumstances and cultural contexts. The implication is that the sociocultural, ecological, and neuroscientific approaches all have contributions to make to the explanation of developmental progression, and Hargreaves et al.'s (2012a) argument that 'musical identities mediate musical development' suggest that the social cognitive approach, and the concept of identity in particular, also has its part to play.

Domain-Specificity

This issue is closely linked to the foregoing discussion: does our view of developmental progression apply to musical development, to development across the arts, or to cognitive development in general? Piaget's view was that the same underlying processes of reasoning and learning apply across all cognitive domains, i.e. that learning is 'domain-general'. However, different cognitive domains (such as the understanding of physical causality or that of social relationships) almost certainly involve different levels of knowledge, and so it may well be that certain types of learning process are domain-specific, and proceed in different ways and at different speeds. This has become a central issue in neuroscientific research, in which one suggestion is that different cognitive domains involve different levels of knowledge, such that some learning processes are domain-specific and others are domain-general: processes such as learning by analogy and the learning of causality may be domain-general and apply to various aspects of physical causality, for example, but may be of little use in the domain of moral reasoning, and so are domain-specific with respect to the latter.

The complex domain of music draws on a very wide range of different skills and abilities, which is probably why it is one of the most active areas of neuroscience. The central question then becomes whether artistic developments are or are not domain-specific: does musical development have anything in common with that in the other arts? The current consensus seems to be that development is more diverse and culture-specific than Piaget proposed, such that many theorists would argue for some degree of domain-specificity: this view is perhaps expressed most clearly in Gardner's well-known theory of multiple intelligences (see e.g. Gardner, 1983, 2003). Within the domain of artistic development, Gardner and his colleagues proposed that developments which occur within particular symbol systems, or artistic domains, demand different skills and techniques than those required in other domains. However, some developments do seem to exist at a broader level of description, as in Wolf and Gardner's (1981) notion of 'waves of symbolisation', for example, and this concurs with our own view that 'although medium-specific aspects of musical development clearly do exist, most notably at very high levels of skill and expertise, it is nevertheless possible to delineate general features of the course of artistic development which do exist across domains, and which do display regular changes with age' (Hargreaves, 1996, p. 153).

Normative and Expert Development

'Development' refers to any overall changes in the patterning of behaviour which follow an invariant sequence with age, and these changes are the result of two quite distinct influences, namely *maturation* and *learning*. Maturational changes take place in the absence of specific environmental experience, and tend to be physiologically based (e.g. physical development), whereas *learning* refers to those changes which do result from specific environmental experiences, and this leads us on to the distinction between *enculturation* (or acculturation) and *training*. Enculturation refers to age-related changes that occur in a given culture without any conscious effort or direction, and which could be described as *normative* development, whereas training refers to changes that arise from conscious, directed intervention, and which might therefore be called specialist, or *expert* development (Sloboda, 1985).

Most of the developmental research to be described in this book is concerned with normative musical development, investigating advances in the ability to deal with pitch and melody, tonality and harmony, rhythm, and so on, which occur without specific training. However, another body of research has grown on the development of specialist or expert musical skill, and on the environmental conditions which best promote it (see e.g. Parncutt and McPherson, 2002; Williamon, 2004; and Chapter 5). The study of expert musical development has largely drawn on the cognitive psychology of skill learning rather than on developmental theory, and Sloboda (1994) suggested that four general conclusions can be drawn from this literature, namely that expert musical skills are dependent on the ability of the performer to detect pattern and structure in the musical material; that the level of skill exhibited depends much more on the amount of relevant practice undertaken than on any other factor; that skills tend to become automatic, or unconscious, as they are practised; and that they tend to be specific to certain domains of activity, and therefore not to be susceptible to transfer to others.

Most research in this area has adopted one of two main methodological approaches. The first has been to make comparisons between experts and novices so as to illuminate some of the processes underlying complex activities such as composing and performing (see e.g. Ericsson & Smith, 1991), or jazz improvisation (see e.g. Hargreaves, Cork, & Setton, 1991). The second has been to carry out biographical studies of high achievers in music: several studies have undertaken detailed analyses of the environmental determinants of excellence in expert musicians. Aside from cognitive psychology, sociocultural approaches probably have the most obvious direct applicability in this area. Earlier in this chapter we showed how Welch and Ockelford (2016) used cultural-historical activity theory to show how 'activity systems' – the detailed sociocultural networks surrounding specific areas of musical learning, involving institutions, teachers, informal peer groups, and audiences – might be used to explain the sociocultural basis of different types of music learning in their own research. We also cited McPherson, Davidson, and Faulkner's (2012) extensive study of the musical development of 157 young Australians between the ages of 7 and 22, highlighting their adoption of Sameroff's (2000) transactional approach in explaining their interactions with significant others, including family members, teachers, and peers, in explaining their own self-perceptions and musical development. This provides another excellent example of the application of sociocultural and social cognitive theory to musical development and learning, and is probably the most elaborate account of the ways in which specific aspects of young people's environments, i.e. of their social and cultural contexts, affect their musical development.

To summarise, we can see that all of the theoretical approaches reviewed in this chapter have different contributions to make in explaining the differences between normative and expert musical development. This may have important practical implications, as it parallels the distinction between specialist and generalist methods of music education. Specialist tuition (usually of instrumental skills) is typically carried out in conservatories and at specialist music schools, whereas generalist music education is that which all pupils encounter in their regular schooling. This division is blurring rapidly as a result of social and technological changes, however, as we shall see in Chapter 5, and we shall comment on related issues in music education throughout the book.

Conclusion

This chapter has focused on the explanation of development in general and musical development in particular, both of which have seen a great deal of recent change. We have reviewed six specific theoretical models from four different theoretical perspectives, as well as two theoretical approaches from which we feel that more formal models are likely to emerge within the next few years (the sociocultural, and the ecological and transactional approaches), and have indicated what form we think that these models might take. We have also described two further approaches – the social cognitive and the neuroscientific – which have not as yet given rise to specific theoretical models, but whose unique perspectives on musical development also hold great promise. Finally, we have evaluated all of these models and approaches in relation to five specific theoretical issues, namely the operation of biological and social factors in musical development; the relationships between musical production, perception, performance, and representation; developmental progression; domain-specificity; and the distinction between normative and expert musical development.

This conclusion represents a 'state of the art' snapshot of a field of study which is changing very rapidly in response to new thinking and methodologies that are emerging simultaneously in several related disciplines: it is likely to remain in a state of transition for some time yet. This is not only an exciting but also an important picture, since theoretical developments provide the foundations of the new ideas which will drive future research.

3 Cognition, Perception, and Learning

The earliest approaches to developmental psychology of music were cognitive in nature and this field has grown considerably in recent years. This chapter provides an overview of the large body of literature studying responses to music and the development of musical understanding (cognition, perception, and learning). Throughout we consider how the various theories of development might be applied to these domains of musical understanding.

The Origins of Music Perception

Responses to music begin long before birth. The foetus is first responsive to sound at around 20–25 weeks gestational age (Chelli & Chanoufi, 2008), and initially shows motor responses to a narrow band of frequencies around 300 Hz when the cochlea begins to become active. Physical development of the auditory system continues gradually throughout the remainder of the foetal period, reaching almost adult-like levels by birth (Joseph, 2000). At around 33 weeks, foetuses show relatively consistent heart rate and movement changes in response to a musical stimulus (Kisilevsky, Hains, Jacquet, Granier-Deferre, & Lecanuet, 2004). Shahidullah and Hepper (1994) found a change from 27 weeks to 35 weeks in terms of the foetus's ability to discriminate both pitch and speech sounds, which suggests this process of development is rapid but steady. Thus before birth foetuses are able to experience something of the auditory environment around them.

Memory for auditory sequences also develops early and can be studied in the womb. Studies *in utero* can be carried out using paradigms such as habituation, looking for behavioural changes such as changes in motion patterns or heart rate in response to changes in the auditory stimulus. After repeated exposure to a complex auditory stream, like speech or music, in the later stages of pregnancy, heart rate changes are found in the foetus (DeCasper, Lecanuet, Maugeais, Granier-Deferre, & Busnel, 1994; Krueger, Holditch-Davis, Quint, & DeCasper, 2004). While heart rate is relatively variable in foetuses (DeCasper, Granier-Deferre, Fifer, & Moon, 2011), if research is carefully controlled it is possible to discover whether changes in stimulation are being detected, and heart rate seems to accelerate in response to familiar auditory sequences such as music.

Considering the longer-term effects of prenatal exposure to auditory patterns, there is clear evidence for *transnatal memory* – memory shown after birth for experiences taking place before birth. This explains why infants prefer their mother's voice to that of a stranger (DeCasper & Fifer, 1980; Kisilevsky, Hains, Lee, Xie, & Huang, 2003), and even at 4 months infants still prefer their mother's voice to their father's due to far greater quantities of prenatal exposure (Ward & Cooper, 1999). Peter Hepper's groundbreaking work showed that mothers who watched the popular television show *Neighbours* during pregnancy had infants who immediately after birth would show alert concentration to the theme tune, while other infants whose mothers had not watched the programme showed no similar reaction, although this familiarity appeared to be short-lived and had disappeared by 21 days after birth (Shahidullah & Hepper, 1994). Using more controlled materials, three weeks of exposure at the end of pregnancy led 1-month-old infants to show twice as much cardiac deceleration to a familiar version of a simple highly controlled piano melody compared with an unfamiliar version which was identical in amplitude (Granier-Deferre, Bassereau, Ribeiro, Jacquet, & DeCasper, 2011). Some of these musical memories can be long-lasting. Partanen, Kujala, Tervaniemi, and Houtilainen (2013) found that very small within-key changes in *Twinkle Twinkle Little Star* could be detected by both neonates and 4-month-old infants who had been familiarised with the melody in the last trimester of pregnancy, as shown through brain event-related potentials. We return to this issue later in this chapter when considering musical form, and again in Chapter 7 when considering how music preferences might develop.

Parncutt (2016a) has argued that the prenatal period is perhaps the most important for exploring development of responses to music, as it allows some disentangling of the effects of processing predispositions and those of experience or enculturation. He also suggests that it is challenging and perhaps mistaken to use the term music when referring to this period and proposes 'protomusic' as an alternative to refer to the combination of music, singing, and infant-directed speech that the foetus and then infant experiences. There are some suggestions based on fMRI data that speech and music might be processed differently even in the prenatal period (Dunn, Reissland, & Reid, 2015), with left temporal activation bias being seen in responses to speech but not music. However, Parncutt's suggestions chime well with the work on early infant socialisation through infant-directed speech and singing, which we discuss in more depth in Chapters 4 and 7.

Development of Perceptual and Cognitive Skills

Perception and cognition together represent one of the largest and fastest-moving areas in the field of musical development, aided partly by the advances in neuroscience and, in parallel, innovative and ingenious research techniques for working with infants and young children. Techniques and theories are in a state of constant flux, with many areas of debate and avenues for future work to be followed. We present the current state of play and identify as many directions for future development as possible, covering techniques and findings interwoven with theory and developmental implications.

Measurement and Assessment of Early Perception and Cognition

There are a number of different ways that perceptual and cognitive skills can be studied in development, and the remainder of this chapter covers a broad range of these. Most researchers have followed the experimental method, whereby carefully identified musical materials (the stimuli) are presented to the listener (the participant) and some kind of response (electrophysiological, physical, perceptual, or cognitive) is measured. Much of this research uses carefully controlled experimental stimuli which may sound little like real everyday music, but which enable the researchers to manipulate them in order to carefully test hypotheses about listeners' reactions. Electrophysiological and physical studies often simply involve playing music to the listener without requiring their conscious attention, while behavioural research usually involves some kind of task for the listener, whether this be choosing between two different sequences, detecting the goodness of fit of various patterns, or noticing changes. Behavioural responses range from simple looking behaviours through to awarding prizes for puppets giving musical performances, depending on the requirements of the study and the ingenuity of the researchers. Finding creative ways to work with pre-verbal and linguistically less able children, in particular, is often challenging. Researchers tend to borrow extensively from mainstream developmental psychology in the preschool and primary school years to find innovative games that will enable children to demonstrate their understanding without being limited by tasks that are too challenging or complex in themselves, so as to give an accurate picture of their abilities.

Historically, discrimination has been one of the most popular experimental techniques used in perception and cognition of music. Different kinds of musical stimuli, usually in pairs, are played to infants or children and their responses can be used to indicate whether they can tell the difference between one and the other. In infancy, discrimination techniques include the head-turning procedure first used for music by Sandra Trehub and colleagues in Toronto. In this paradigm (which is also used with speech and other auditory stimuli) the infant is seated on its mother's lap facing forward, and an experimenter attracts and then maintains the infant's attention forwards, typically by use of a soft toy and some verbal encouragement. A speaker is located 45° to one side and a musical stimulus is played repeatedly. The music used in these studies is typically very short and simple, such as a melody of a few notes in length: for instance, Trehub, Thorpe, and Trainor (1990) used a five-note diatonic melody. The infant will often look at the source of the sound initially, but once it has become used to the repeating sequence its attention will move back to, and be held by, the experimenter directly in front of it. A small change is then introduced to the repeating sequence, such as a mistuned note, a transposition, or a change in rhythmic position of a note: Trehub et al. (1990) moved the fourth note of their melody down one semitone. If the infant correctly detects the change, it

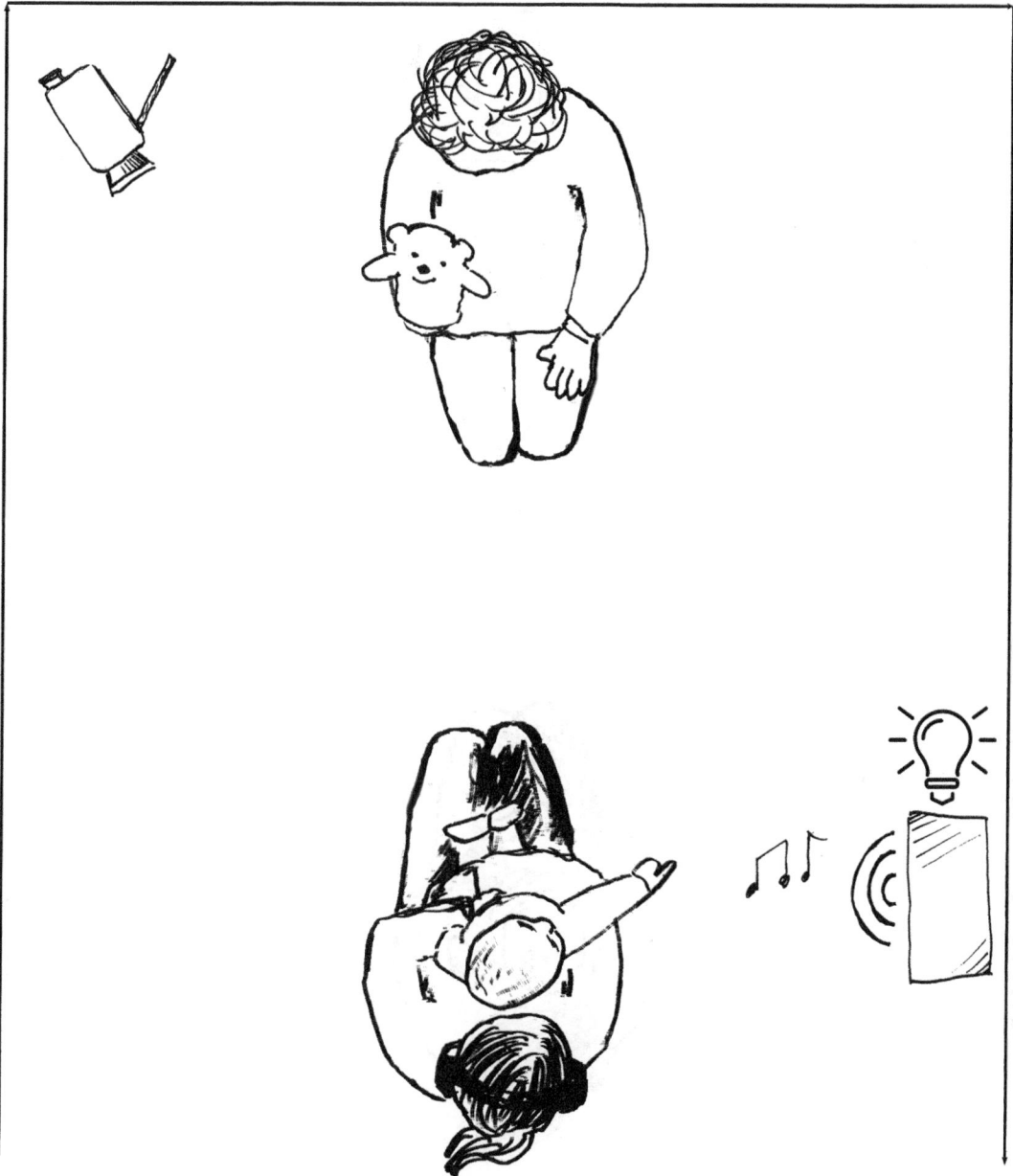

Figure 3.1.   Conditioned head-turn procedure used with infants.
Source: Original drawing by Niall King.

will look again towards the source of the sound, and be rewarded by a visual display of some kind (see Figure 3.1). In the 1970s and 80s these tended to be large
Plexiglas boxes with mechanical toys that lit up and moved around, although more
recently this kind of reinforcement has been provided in video or digital forms.
Being rewarded for detecting correct changes in the stimulus is highly motivating

Figure 3.2.   Head-turn preference procedure used with infants.
Source: Original drawing by Niall King.

for the infants, and the procedure enables the researchers to identify which kinds of features of the musical stimuli infants are able to discriminate.

A similar procedure also used with infants over the age of about 6 months is preferential looking/listening. This technique involves comparing two different musical stimuli (which come from different locations and are supported by a visual reinforcer, as illustrated in Figure 3.2), presented in an alternating or random pattern, and measuring the amount of time the infant spends looking at one or the other. Looking times are taken as a proxy for listening, and if there are differences found in looking times to one stimulus compared with the other, this indicates that the infants can discriminate between the two. Simple variations of this present just two stimuli and measure comparisons: for instance, Conrad, Walsh, Allen, and Tsang (2011) compared 6- to 7-month-old infants' responses to fast and slow versions of unfamiliar playsongs and lullabies. Their findings showed the infants listened longer to the faster tempo versions of playsongs but not lullabies. More complex versions might involve some additional familiarisation prior to the study. In another study, 6-month-old infants listened to one of two English folk songs for 3 minutes a day for 7 days, and were then tested on their discrimination of the two songs in the laboratory (Trainor, Wu, & Tsang, 2004). The findings were that the infants looked longer to listen to the novel melody, which is taken as evidence that they remembered the familiar melody.

Preferential looking/listening is also a contingent procedure where the infant is in control of the stimulus, although as Trehub notes (2012), attrition rates are lower in such studies as the contingency is very much simpler than in conditioned head-turning. In both paradigms, a short learning phase precedes a testing phase: in the learning phase the infants are presented with more marked changes in the discrimination head-turn procedure (such as a three-semitone note change in Trehub et al., 1990) or without the visual reinforcer in the preference procedure, so that the contingency between their own behaviour and the musical materials they get to experience is firmly established. Most infants at the age of 6 months and older are able to grasp these contingencies very rapidly and thus can demonstrate their preferences for music, speech, and other auditory stimuli in a relatively clear and robust manner. Problems arise if null results are found (cf. Trehub, 2012). For instance, in Conrad et al.'s (2011) study, no difference was found in looking times for the fast or slow versions of the lullabies. Various explanations were proposed in the paper for this, including the fact that developmental sensitivity to faster tempi might occur earlier than that to slower tempi, but an absence of difference does not necessarily mean an absence of discrimination. Trehub (2012) also notes that although these studies use the term 'preference', since they rarely include any assessment of positive or negative affect, it is difficult to draw parallels between infant preference and adult aesthetic judgement (see further Chapter 7).

In addition to behavioural and physical responses to music, brain scans can be used to explore the areas of the brain that are activated by music, and as we outlined in Chapter 2, this area has seen much recent growth in research output. Scanning does not require any explicit language or instructions, and so can be used with infants and children of all ages to measure their responses to different kinds of musical stimuli. The technique is non-invasive and comfortable for the participants, as well as generating useful data on brain activity. The findings of some of these studies are remarkable. For instance, using evoked response potentials (ERPs), Winkler, Háden, Ladinig, Sziller, and Honing (2009) found newborns were able to detect the beat in drum patterns while asleep, as shown by changing brain responses when the pattern changed to violate the beat. One of the challenges of using ERP as a technique is that any movement by the participant interferes with the data, and thus data can only be gathered when infants are either asleep or awake but not moving; this may be one reason why ERP is less frequently used with older infants and children. Another challenge is that interpretation of the data is complex. While differences in brain patterns indicate some kind of receptivity or discrimination, the meaning of this response is far from being understood, and the neonate's response to a simple musical sequence is far removed from a conscious aesthetic response to music (cf. Trehub, 2012). In speech perception there is some evidence that while speech patterns – for instance, the mother or an unfamiliar woman saying the word 'baby' – can be detected from ERP data, the familiar sequence is not sufficiently interesting to motivate newborns to suck on a pacifier to activate more of the familiar stimulus (Moon, Zernzach, & Kuhl, 2015). Hence some caution must be exercised in the interpretations drawn from this kind of data. Nonetheless, data that has been gathered using these techniques provides important new evidence on the beginnings of music perception and cognition, to which we return under the relevant headings later in this chapter.

Pitch, Tonality, Melody, and Harmony

Due perhaps to the dominance of pitch in Western musical systems, pitch relationships have been the most studied aspects of children's musical understanding. Pitch includes tone chroma (individual notes), contour (high/low and patterns), and melodic and harmonic relationships between tones (key membership and a sense of harmonic relationships or tonality), although in many studies these different aspects of pitch relationships are often studied together and sometimes conflated.

Given the aforementioned caveats about over-interpreting evidence from very young infants, it seems that brain responses to pitch as a musical parameter go through rapid development after birth and become adult-like at the age of 3–4 months (He, Hotson, & Trainor, 2007; 2009). He and colleagues have shown that 2-month-old infants seem to be using different mechanisms for processing pitch in the auditory cortex, but between 2 and 4 months infants develop the ability to show increased mismatch negativity (MMN) responses, indicating that they have detected a difference, to greater pitch changes using single notes. Tew, Fujioka, He, and Trainor (2009) found that 6-month-old infants showed a different brain activation pattern to adults in response to more complex melodic processing. From repetitions of a four-note melody with the final note either the same or changed, transposed between trials, Tew et al. found an extended right frontally positive wave response from the infants, compared to a right frontally negative MMN response from adults. They concluded that infants are also sensitive to the changes in melodic structure but are using a different neural pathway to process this. This could suggest that early processing is focusing on different features, such as absolute pitch cues or simple up and down responses, rather than more complex ways of understanding such as treating a melodic pattern as a Gestalt and comparing it with other similar or different patterns. With more complex musical stimuli, development in brain responses to sound sequences continues more gradually throughout childhood (see further in the following section).

Absolute and Relative Pitch

Infants show responses to changes in relative pitch patterns from early in development. The sequence of intervals between notes of a melody is one of the first musical elements to be discriminated, and melodic contour dominates responses from infants and children alike (e.g. Trehub, Thorpe, & Morrongiello, 1987). In the experimental paradigm established for studying pitch development with infants and children in the 1980s, using conditioned head-turning, the simple, typically melodic stimuli used would be repeated from trial to trial, with changes then introduced to the melodic pattern for the infant or child to detect. For instance, Trehub, Thorpe, and Morrongiello (1985) played very simple 6-tone sequences to 6- to 8-month-old infants, and changed one of the notes in the melody. The infants were able to correctly detect single-note changes wherever in the sequence they occurred. Infants are able to treat melodies as the same under transposition in a range of contexts. Within a single session, they can ignore transpositions of a short melodic or harmonic sequence and focus attention instead on the changes within the melody or harmonic progression (Trehub, Schellenberg, & Kamenetsky, 1999). At 6 months, infants can also remember the relative pitch patterns in a short melody after short-term repeated exposure. Plantinga and Trainor (2005) found longer listening times in 6-month-olds to novel melodies compared to melodies they had listened to over the previous seven days, and equivalent listening times to the original melody at its original pitch level or in transposition.

Pitch discrimination skills increase in acuity as children get older. Most studies with infants and children have used a range of pitch differences in testing in order to guarantee that the listeners will be able to detect some change. Stalinski, Schellenberg, and Trehub (2008) found 5-year-olds were able to distinguish and identify upward and downward shifts of up to 0.3 semitones correctly, while 8 years old, children were also able to identify shifts of 0.1 semitone. This very small pitch difference appears to be at the limit of adults' pitch perception abilities, so children have reached adult levels of discrimination by this age. However, pitch abilities are subject to further development, most notably due to musical training. 8- to 10-year-old children with 12 months of music training were found to have larger MMN responses for speech sounds, suggesting that training affects the auditory pathway (Chobert et al., 2014). Hutka, Bidelman, and Moreno (2015) found musically trained adults had higher perceptual acuity for pitch and language as well as larger MMN responses in response to music and speech sounds, which suggests that training has the capacity to further enhance these skills throughout life (see further discussion in Chapter 8). Zatorre and Baum (2012) have suggested that the basic pitch acuity shown in contour processing may be a separate system from a more fine-grained pitch acuity required for music, with the former developing early on and the latter taking many years of expertise to refine.

Absolute pitch processing abilities are also found in infancy, although this has little to do with the explicit absolute pitch labelling and identification abilities found in children and adults with extensive musical training (which we return to later). Trehub, Cohen, Thorpe, and Morrongiello (1986) had identified that infants were able to detect a semitone pitch change in a melody composed of notes of the augmented triad, a so-called dissonant and unstable pattern, when the trials were not transposed, meaning they must have been using absolute pitch cues as the basis for their responses. Saffran and Griepentrog (2001) compared 8-month-old infants' responses to absolute and relative pitch changes in a statistical learning task. They constructed tone 'words' out of three-note melodic fragments which were played in a continuous stream of 45 'words' to familiarise infants with the 'grammar' of the materials. All sequences were played at the same absolute pitch levels. After this process of statistical learning, the infants were then tested on three-note words used in familiarisation and three-note part-words, created by joining the final tone of one word to the first two of another, which were in fact transpositions of some of the words used in familiarisation but heard less frequently. Infants were more interested in what they perceived as novel sequences in the testing phase, meaning their bias was to process absolute pitch. In a second study, with a modification to the design so that only relative pitch cues could be used to discriminate words from part-words, infants showed no differences in listening to the two types of sequence. These results contrast with those from adults in the same study, who were only able to discriminate unfamiliar sequences based on relative pitch information.

Whether absolute or relative pitch is used by listeners to process pitch sequences thus varies from study to study, and different designs seem to emphasise and prioritise different responses. One reason infants 'fail' to detect transpositions from trial to trial in contingent head-turning is that they are trained to do so: they are not given a reward for turning their head on each successive transposition, but are rewarded when they detect a change within a relative pitch pattern (e.g. Trehub et al., 1999; cf. Stalinski & Schellenberg, 2010). Conversely, in tasks that reward a focus on absolute pitch, infants at similar ages are found to be able to use that skill (Saffran & Griepentrog, 2001). Stalinski and Schellenberg (2010) explicitly tested the difference between the two processing types with children and adults, finding that while 5- to 12-year-olds and adults were both sensitive to both absolute and relative pitch information, older children and adults were more influenced by melodic features, and that the 'difference' of a transposed version of a piece became less important. There are thus some arguments that absolute pitch skills become less important in development.

Nonetheless, for some listeners, absolute pitch may be the driver of continued musical engagement. Ockelford (2013) has argued that children on the autism spectrum who have absolute pitch abilities will develop this into an enthusiasm or obsession with music. He suggests that this is partly because they can encode music more readily and directly, having a processing advantage which helps them remember melodies and pitch structure and which may guide them in playing by ear (see also Ockelford, 2016). Heaton (2009) further suggests that many children on the autism spectrum have over-developed pitch sensitivity, which could be developed into savantism. Adult listeners can also demonstrate excellent absolute pitch memory for highly overlearned sequences, such as television jingles or familiar favourite recorded songs (Levitin, 1994; Schellenberg & Trehub, 2003). We return to this in considering the processing of melodies later in this chapter, along with the more rarefied skill of absolute pitch identification.

Consonance and Dissonance

A hotly debated area of perceptual ability in infancy concerns consonance and dissonance. These are somewhat contested concepts in musicology, and the definition of consonant sounds varies in different musical cultures around the world, changes over time, and is highly context-specific. A somewhat simplistic definition of consonance in a Western setting concerns the relationships between the individual elements (simple frequency ratios) or the harmonic components (harmonicity) of the complex tones making up a musical interval or chord (Terhardt, 1984). In support of this definition, early evidence suggested that infants showed a preference for (Western) consonant tone combinations, and for simple integer ratios, by about the age of 6 months (Schellenberg & Trehub, 1996). Zentner and Kagan (1998) created consonant and dissonant versions of the same melody, consonant versions being a sequence of major and minor thirds and dissonant versions created using semitones. Both types were played to adults who reported that the dissonant version was 'hurting their ears' (Zentner & Kagan, 1998, p. 487). They found that 4-month-old infants looked longer at their consonant versions of melodies than the dissonant ones, with less motor movement and fretting during listening. Zentner and Kagan concluded that this early preference for consonance must be innate, and several other studies appeared to confirm this by finding similar preferences at similar and even earlier ages (e.g. Masataka, 2006; Trainor & Heinmiller, 1998).

More recently, however, Plantinga and Trehub (2014) have challenged this interpretation, proposing that the preferences for consonance seen in earlier studies may simply be a familiarity response. First, they played 6-month-old infants pairs of either consonant or dissonant musical stimuli which varied in complexity. These included a simple ten-note melody used in many other developmental studies (Trainor & Trehub, 1992, 1994): the melody itself and its accompaniment were either consonant or dissonant, and with varying degrees of richness. They also included consonant and dissonant stimuli from the two earlier studies on consonance in infancy (Trainor & Heinmiller, 1998 and Zentner & Kagan, 1998), and real pieces of tonal and atonal music from the classical repertoire (by Clementi and Berio). Their data indicated that looking times were actually greater in response to the dissonant stimuli, although did not differ significantly; there was no preference for consonant stimuli as found in the earlier studies. In a final experiment Plantinga and Trehub familiarised the infants with the musical sequences at the start of the study, half with the consonant stimuli and half with the dissonant ones. The infants chose to listen longer to familiar than novel stimuli regardless of consonance or dissonance, leading to the conclusion that familiarity influenced preferences for consonance or dissonance. A similar suggestion arose from the results of Trainor, Tsang, and Cheung (2002) with 2- and 4-month-old infants, who listened longer to a dissonant block of trials when it preceded a consonant series and vice versa. Plantinga and Trehub conclude that there is no support for innate preferences for consonance, and propose that processing fluency might be a more plausible explanation for the preferences shown in their study. This underlines the importance of experience in developing responses to music, although evidently more research on this topic is needed.

Pitch Relationships: Scales, Key Membership, and Harmony

Considering the more complex elements of pitch, scales, and tonality, the role of exposure and experience in shaping infants' and children's implicit and explicit understanding is more accepted and better understood. However, arguments are still put forward for inherent processing biases to try to explain the sometimes remarkable processing capacities of young infants. These include the relationships between notes (the simple frequency ratio mentioned earlier), and the uniqueness of the interval steps within a scale (Balzano, 1982). In a developmental sequence which closely mirrors that of language (Werker & Lalonde, 1988), infants at 6 months of age are able to detect very small changes to pitch patterns that conform to the scale structure of their own culture as well as those of other cultures and even invented musical scales. Lynch, Eilers, Oller, and Urbano (1990) compared infants' performance on mistunings in sequences of Western diatonic major scales or Javanese *pelog* scales, finding that 6-month-old infants could easily detect changes in both whereas Western adults performed more poorly in detecting changes to the Javanese scale. Trehub et al. (1999) compared 9-month-old infants and adults presented with melodies based on Western diatonic scales (which are themselves unequal in interval steps) and on equal and unequal-step scales that were artificially created by subdivisions not found in any musical cultures. They found some support for the notion of uniqueness proposed by Balzano (1982), in that infants were equally able to detect changes to melodies using both kinds of unequal step scales while adults were better with the Western scale, familiar to them through many years of repeated exposure. In addition, infants below the age of 12 months are also able to detect changes to tonal melodies that remain within the same key, while adults fail to spot those within-key differences (Trainor & Trehub, 1992).

By around 12 months, the ability to process music or sounds from unfamiliar cultures or invented musical structures becomes 'lost', but at the same time perception and cognition of patterns from the native culture becomes better established and more efficient (Lynch & Eilers, 1992). In one study, Trehub et al. (1990) constructed three different melodies: a 'good' Western melody from the diatonic scale (based around a major triad), a 'bad' Western melody using notes from the chromatic scale but not a single diatonic scale, and a 'bad' non-Western melody consisting of intervals that do not exist in Western tonality, including two intervals smaller than a semitone. They

Figure 3.3.   Examples of expected and unexpected chord sequences. (A) Chord sequence ending with a regular tonic. (B) Chord sequence ending with an irregular supertonic. (C) Chord sequence ending with an irregular Neapolitan sixth chord.
Source: From Jentschke, S., Friederici, A.D. & Koelsch, S. (2014). Neural correlates of music-syntactic processing in two-year old children. *Developmental Cognitive Neuroscience*, 9, 200–208. Figure 1, p. 203. Reprinted in accordance with the Creative Commons Attribution (CC BY) license.

presented these to 7- to 10-month-old infants in a conditioned head-turning paradigm, with five different transpositions. Test trials consisted of a semitone change to the fourth of the five notes in each melody, which were correctly detected by the infants only in the well-structured Western diatonic melody. This illustrates that diatonic scale structure was being used by these infants to guide detection of melodic changes across transpositions. From this point onwards, processing of pitch relationships appears to continue to develop in a broadly linear fashion. The precise rate of development seems to be dependent on the type of data gathered, as well as the specific materials used. Overall, implicit tasks show earlier evidence for firstly discrimination and secondly detection of change, while explicit tasks have a slower rate of progress.

In relation to key membership and harmony, sensitivity can be found as early as 6 months, as shown by Tew et al. (2009), and two studies with children below the age of 5 provide evidence for an 'immature' brain response that shows sensitivity to both key membership and harmony but in a different way to older children and adults. Listeners are presented with musical stimuli ending conventionally or less conventionally in these studies, such as the phrases shown in Figure 3.3. Listening to these kinds of sequences, adults consistently show two types of brain response to unexpected musical events that violate the syntax of tonality: early right anterior negativity (ERAN) and N5 (Koelsch, Gunter, Friederici, & Schröger, 2000). These responses characterise both the location and the timing of response, and comparing them across different kinds of stimuli (such as language and speech) can reveal the responses evoked under various conditions. Both ERAN and N5 responses have been assumed to be responses to musical syntax. Jentschke, Friederici, and Koelsch (2014) found similar ERAN responses to unexpected harmonies in 2.5-year-old children to the same sequences, although the N5 response was absent. They did however find the ERAN more broadly distributed over the scalp in the younger children than in adults, with slightly different positioning depending on whether it was a supertonic (mildly unexpected; bilateral slightly leftward fronto-central distribution) or Neapolitan sixth (more unexpected; right-centro-temporal electrodes).

Corrigall and Trainor (2014) found that 4-year-old children showed sensitivity to violations to both Western key membership and harmony, although instead of an ERAN they observed an early *positivity* in frontal regions in response to unexpected chords. By the age of 5, however, ERP data illustrates that these types of unexpected chords are responded to with the same ERAN and N5 responses found in 9-year-olds and adults (Koelsch, Grossman, Gunter, Hahne, Schröger, & Friederici, 2003). Koelsch et al. also found that boys showed a greater left lateralisation of the early anterior negativity than girls in this response, something not found in other music studies but sometimes apparent in language processing (e.g. Dennis, 1980). This may relate to the syntactic nature of the processing required and the ways in which girls and boys process language.

The evidence from neuroscience for a gradually developing sensitivity to pitch relationships, key membership, and harmony is supported by findings from implicit experimental tasks such as detection of change. Key membership was not found to be relevant for 8-month-old infants, who correctly detected within-key mistunings that adults failed to detect (Trainor & Trehub, 1992). Similarly, 9- to 11-month-old infants could detect semitone changes easily in both diatonic and non-diatonic contexts (Trehub et al., 1986). Key structure was found to be relevant for 4- to 6-year-olds by Trehub et al. (1986), as they were better able to detect semitone changes in a diatonic context than in a non-diatonic one. Trainor and Trehub (1994) also found 5-year-olds able to detect out-of-key changes to melodic sequences, but they failed to notice changes that remained within the key or the harmony. Both adults and 7-year-olds were able to detect both out-of-key and out-of-harmony changes, but both struggled with changes that were within both the key and the implied harmony. In a priming study, both 6- and 11-year-olds made faster judgements about which vowel or instrument sound occurred on a target tone, and whether it was consonant or dissonant, when the target was a tonic and thus an expected chord (Schellenberg, Bigand, Poulin-Charronat, Garnier, & Stevens, 2005).

With explicit judgement tasks that require conscious attention, a slower progression of sensitivity is seen. In several studies, children have been asked to make explicit judgements about the goodness of fit or completion of a tone with a pattern of other notes. In one of the first such studies, Krumhansl and Keil (1982) presented short melodic sequences based around a tonic triad and asked 6- to 12-year-old children to judge the suitability of a range of pairs of completion note. Results showed that by age 12, pairs of tones that come from the tonic triad (including the tonic itself) were the most preferred choices, and any non-triad notes (particularly in the second position of the pair) became less preferred with age. The pattern of preferences shown by the 12-year-olds differed from that of adults, with still further decreases in non-triad tones and increased preferences for triad and tonic tones. Similar evidence of gradual development in sophistication was found by Lamont and Cross (1994), using both structured and unstructured sequences. Their patterns of preference illustrated the importance of the tonic, subdominant, and dominant notes as completions of either triadic or randomised melodies, suggesting an influence of implied harmony in judgements from older children.

The type of materials used in these tasks seems to be important. Cuddy and Badertscher (1987) found that simple triads were only sufficient to evoke a tonal hierarchy in school-aged children if they had a clear tonic, as a diminished triad failed to generate the appropriate tonic responses. Their results indicated children were more influenced by pitch proximity and only afterwards by tonal function, as also found by Schellenberg and McKinnon (1996) in melodic expectancies with 10- to 12-year-old children. Using familiar materials, however, performance on this kind of task can be enhanced at an earlier age. In an ingenious study, Corrigall and Trainor (2010) asked children to choose the best performance of familiar songs from two versions played by puppets, and found that 4- and 5-year-olds were able to judge the song's ending as better when it ended in the appropriate key or expected harmony. Four-year-olds did not rate out-of-key endings as any worse than in-key endings in melodic or chord sequences, while 5-year-olds rated all the out-of-key differences as worse. Both age groups found the task easier with complete melodies and accompaniments than with reduced chord sequences, highlighting the importance of using realistic musical stimuli in experimental studies. Using the same judgement task but with unfamiliar melodies consisting of either chords or single tones, Corrigall and Trainor (2014) found that while 4-year-olds could not distinguish any of the sequences based on key membership or harmony, 5-year-olds were able to identify 'best' performances based on key membership and out-of-key harmony changes for both melodies and chords, although did not differentiate based on within-key harmonic variations.

These results combine to show that harmonic relatedness is something that begins to emerge with experience of listening to conventional tonal music relatively early in childhood, and continues to develop. Age-related enculturation in terms of understanding pitch relationships takes place for all listeners, with a broad progression from simpler to more complex elements of pitch relationships (height, intervals, melodies, key structure) across childhood. As we show later in this chapter, this progression is also affected by additional musical experience resulting from training, which accelerates the course of development (Lamont, 1998; Morrongiello, Roes, & Donnelly, 1989).

Effects of Music Training on Pitch Representations

Even at the age of 12 months, music training can make a difference to infants' understandings of tonality. Gerry, Unrau, and Trainor (2012) found that 6 months of active musical experience was enough to result in changes in perceptual abilities. They gave 6-month-old infants 6 months of either active or passive music experience, with a control group; the active music experience involved Suzuki-based classes involving movement, singing, playing percussion, and learning lullabies and action songs, supported by at-home musical activities led by parents, while infants in the 'passive' group were exposed to 'Baby Einstein' CDs. At the conclusion of the study a number of tests were conducted, including a head-turn preference procedure to two versions of a Sonatina by Thomas Atwood: a tonal version and an atonal version where every second and fourth beat of the bar was transposed down a semitone. As illustrated in Figure 3.4, infants in the active training group were the only ones to show a clear and significant preference for the tonal version of

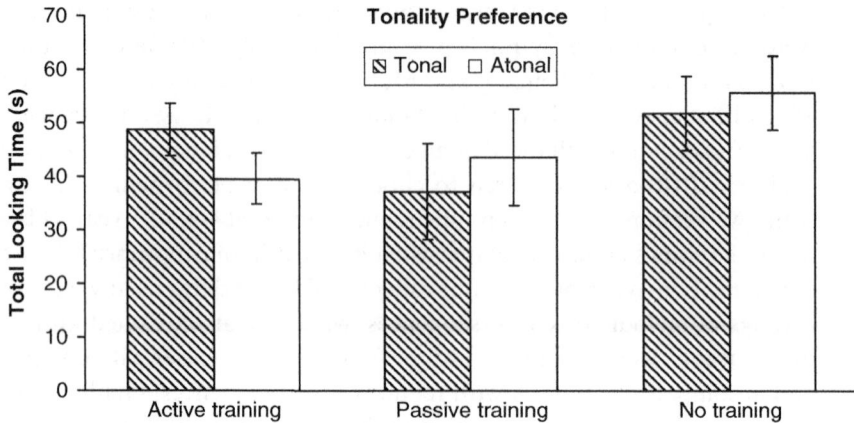

Figure 3.4. Infants' preferences for tonal and atonal versions of an exceprt from Atwood's Sonatina in G major.
Source: From Gerry, D. W., Unrau, A. & Trainor, L. J. (2012). Active music classes in infancy enhance musical, communicative and social development. *Developmental Science*, 15(3), 398–407. Figure 2, p. 402. John Wiley and Sons. Reprinted with permission © 2012 Blackwell Publishing Ltd, 9600 Garsington Road, Oxford OX4 2DQ, UK and 350 Main Street, Malden, MA 02148, USA.

the Atwood Sonatina, which is taken to assume that they have the beginnings of sensitivity to tonality.

Later in development, musical training appears to accelerate sensitivities to different aspects of pitch perception. While Corrigall and Trainor (2009) found no difference in 3- to 6-year-old children's abilities to detect out-of-key and out-of-harmony endings of a familiar melody (*Twinkle Twinkle Little Star*) after a year of music lessons, those with training were better able to detect out-of-key and out-of-harmony changes in a simplified chordal version consisting of the underlying harmony of the familiar piece (which can be thought of as a simplified but also unfamiliar musical sequence). Moreno, Marques, Santos, Santos, Castro, and Besson (2009) found that six months of training at age 8 was enough for children to be better able to detect what they termed weak incongruities – modifications of one-fifth of a tone to the final note of familiar melodies – although training did not make a difference for stronger incongruities – modifications of a semitone. This study used both behavioural and ERP data from the same participants, finding that music training also led to a higher amplitude N300 component when correctly discriminating weak incongruities, which begins to point to some links between brain changes and explicit processing abilities. In response to violations to pitch structure, Jentschke and Koelsch (2009) found a larger early right anterior negativity (ERAN) in 11-year-olds who had musical training, similar to that found in adults. As noted earlier, ERAN reflects syntactic processing and involves long-term syntactic knowledge of music which seems to be enhanced by training. In an experimental study, Alexandra (Lamont, 1998) studied a large sample of children aged 6 to 16 using diatonic test sequences and probe-tone judgements, finding that those children undergoing music training were more affected by the nature of the sequences and thus able to make more analytic judgements reflecting the characteristics of tonality. The development of sophistication in judgements continued beyond the age of 11, and it would be important for future work to include these later stages of development in order to understand how higher-order cognitive development, such as the development of formal operational thinking and abstract concepts, might influence the understanding of music.

Absolute Pitch as a Cognitive Capacity?

Absolute pitch (AP), known colloquially as 'perfect pitch', is a rare phenomenon, estimated at around 1 to 5 in every 10,000 individuals (Brown et al., 2003). AP is more likely to occur in those who began music training at a very young age (Miyazaki, 1988). It may be understood as a two-step process, requiring firstly enhanced tonal memory, or fixed pitch-chroma categories, and secondly cultural labels (note names) that can be retrieved and assigned to the categories. Most researchers agree that 'true' AP – the ability to effortlessly identify and label pitches in isolation – is dependent on early learning which should occur during a critical period before the age of 6 (e.g. Takeuchi & Hulse, 1993), based on evidence that AP was more likely to occur in those who began training very young.

Considering enhanced tonal memory, as shown previously, infants possess AP skills in that they are able to detect notes that change in a repeated sequence that stays constant (Trehub et al., 1986) and use absolute pitch as a cue for learning (Saffran & Griepentrog, 2001). The absolute-to-relative shift which had been commonly found in other areas of pitch perception might explain why young children are more readily able to acquire AP (Takeuchi & Hulse, 1993). Crozier (1997) suggested that music training, emphasising relative pitch skills, made many children 'unlearn' their earlier absolute skills in favour of the more relevant relative pitch processing. AP is also more common in children on the autism spectrum, and Heaton, Hermelin, and Pring (1998) found it easier to teach absolute pitch capacities to children with autism than those without. This suggests some genetic component to the ability (Trainor, 2005). More recently, it has been suggested that auditory working memory capacity (WMC) might also be linked to AP. Adults with AP were found to have unusually large auditory memory spans (Deutsch & Dooley, 2013), and adults with higher WMC were better able to learn absolute pitch note categories (Van Hedger, Heald, Koch, & Nusbaum, 2015).

The ability to label a pitch explicitly requires other declarative abilities which children sometimes find difficult. One of these is labelling the dimension of pitch height. While pitch changes are highly detectable from early infancy, young children often find difficulties in labelling pitch as 'high' and 'low' because of problems in analogical mapping between the musical and verbal concepts (Costa-Giomi & Descombes, 1996). Sergeant and Boyle (1980) found that 11- to 12-year-old children's ability to identify whether two pitches (from 5 to 100 cents difference) were the same or different was extremely accurate at 95 per cent correct, but when identifying which one was higher or lower performance dropped to 75 per cent accuracy due to the additional task demands. Spatial verticality, or 'high' and 'low' mapping of pitch, is far from common in non-Western cultures and other metaphors for pitch include 'light' and 'heavy', 'small' and 'large', 'young' and 'old', 'weak' and strong', and even in the Shona mbira in Zimbabwe, 'crocodile' (low pitch) and 'those who follow crocodiles' (high pitch) (Eitan & Timmers, 2010). This illustrates how terminology for various features of music can be confusing for young children: the labels for the dimension of pitch height must be learned and take time to stabilise.

Soderquist and Moore (1970) managed to train 5- to 9-year-old children to identify the direction of two pure tones over the course of six days, although whether this information could be retained over longer time periods is unknown. Crozier (1997) found that six weeks of training helped preschool children in their reference tone identification and reproduction skills, although similar improvements were not found for 13- to 15-year-olds. Stalinski, Schellenberg, and Trehub (2008) found that within-study feedback was enough to help 5-year-olds improve their pitch direction identification skills, although again the durability of this kind of training is unknown. The fact that AP seems to be somewhat 'learnable' or 'trainable' is somewhat at odds with its early categorisation as a dichotomous state and the self-reports of those with AP that it is effortless. However, there is plenty of evidence that there are elements of AP such as the detection of overlearned pitch patterns at the same pitch intervals (Levitin, 1994; Schellenberg & Trehub, 2003), and even among 'true' AP possessors there is some variability in accuracy and latency of identification (Miyazaki, 1990). AP can thus be considered as a skill which could be improved with extensive training, if desired, and particularly if musical training had been experienced during the critical period before the age of about 6.

While the ability to label pitches in the absence of a reference tone might seem a rather arcane skill, for many years pitch discrimination was a central part of tests of musical abilities or aptitudes which could have considerable consequences for children's future engagement with music. This followed assumptions that pitch discrimination abilities were central for making progress with a musical instrument (e.g. Mawbey, 1973). The Bentley *Measures of Musical Abilities*, for instance, includes 20 pitch test items. Pairs of tones are presented sequentially with differences from one semitone down to around one-tenth of a semitone, and children have to identify whether one of the pitches is higher or lower or both are the same. These kinds of test are still in use in some parts of the United Kingdom (Moscardini, Barron, & Wilson, 2013) and also probably elsewhere in the world, as means of selecting children for extracurricular music training.

It has been suggested that a lack of pitch discrimination ability might be at the root of congenital amusia (Hyde & Peretz, 2004), a hereditary condition which involves reduced neural connectivity between the auditory cortex and inferior frontal gyrus on the right side of the brain (Loui, Alsop, & Schlaug, 2009). Isabelle Peretz and colleagues have devoted considerable efforts to developing the Montreal Battery of Evaluation of Amusia, a screening tool to detect amusia in adults (e.g. Peretz et al., 2008), and more recently generated a version suitable for use with children below the age of 10 (Peretz et al., 2013). This test and the condition itself are held to rely on pitch (contour, key, intervals) as well as rhythm, metre, and musical memory. Collecting data with 6- to-8-year olds, Peretz et al. found task performance on the pitch tasks to be highly variable with the youngest and least musically experienced children, and this chimes with the evidence reviewed earlier that pitch sensitivity is a skill which improves with age and which can be improved through training. We return to issues concerning testing and aptitude in Chapter 5.

Pitch and Pitch Relationships in Adulthood

Looking at adult responses to music of their own and other cultures can also shed some light on the understanding of pitch representations. In one of the first studies to explore this, Castellano, Bharucha, and Krumhansl (1984) found that while Western listeners were able to respond to the most important tones in a North Indian *rāg*, the tonic and fifth scale degree, only Indian listeners were able to show responses based on the underlying scales, the *thāts*. This suggests that extensive experience over many years is necessary to internalise the scale structure of a given musical culture. Castellano et al.'s data did not suggest that the Western listeners used their own internal representations of Western tonality to make judgements of North Indian classical music, however. Learning mechanisms are implicit in the research on understanding tonality in adulthood, with the general consensus being that the properties of music that listeners are exposed to in individual pieces (the event hierarchy) collate to lead to a stable representation of pitch (the tonal hierarchy) (Bharucha, 1984). These properties include the frequency of occurrence, duration, positioning, metric emphasis, and patterning or contours. However, studies often found that responses change depending on the precise content and structure of the experimental materials presented to participants (e.g. Brown, Butler, & Jones, 1994), suggesting that the stability implicit in the more abstract types of responses is not always present. Implicit understanding of tonal relationships has been demonstrated in adults without musical training; for instance, Koelsch, Gunter, Schröger, and Friederici (2003) found ERAN responses for chords that violated musical regularities and late frontal negativity (N5) in response to harmonic integration. The same kinds of problems exist in research with adults as with children, however, in terms of the influence of the context on the response. Bigand, Delbé, Poulin-Charronnat, Leman, and Tillmann (2014) have recently suggested that it is equally important to use materials that avoid the influence of the psychoacoustic properties of sounds.

Looking at pitch perception as a perceptual ability across the lifespan, many older adults experience difficulties with pitch as part of the ageing process. There is evidence that frequency discrimination and frequency modulation declines with age, particularly for lower frequencies (He, Mills, & Dubno, 2007). Harris, Mills, He, and Dubno (2008) found older participants (aged 65–80) to be less sensitive to frequency changes than younger participants (aged 18–30), particularly at lower frequencies, as shown by slower response latencies and differences in P1-N1-P2 responses. These ERP data suggest that frequency discrimination difficulties in older adults could be partly a result of pre-attentive levels of auditory processing as well as of age-related changes in the central auditory system.

Very little research has explored how features such as tonality might be perceived through adulthood (cf. Halpern & Bartlett, 2002). However, Andrea Halpern and her colleagues have explored age- and experience-related change across adulthood. In a series of experiments, Halpern, Bartlett, and Dowling (1995) asked younger (18–30) and older (60–80) participants with and without musical training to judge variations of a melody which was transposed, either changing or preserving the contour, in tonal and atonal forms as same or different. Their findings in relation to age and experience are complex, but suggest that elements of the task that require musical encoding were more affected by experience while elements that required general cognitive processes and working memory were more affected by age. Overall, experience seemed to be a more important predictor of performance than age.

In a second study, Halpern, Kwak, Bartlett, and Dowling (1996) studied younger (age 15–20) and older (age 60–80) trained and untrained adults using the probe-tone technique, with a triadic pattern followed by a probe tone to be rated for goodness of fit. Adults with training responded more closely according to the principles of the tonal hierarchy than those without, but older adults and untrained participants were more likely to use pitch height when the stimuli encouraged this (i.e. using sine waves, which give strong clues to pitch height, rather than Shepard tones, which are indeterminate in terms of pitch height). Halpern et al.'s overall conclusions are that music training serves to maintain the ability to use tonal relations into older age, but that some aspects of music processing are impaired by age if they depend on more general cognitive processes. This pattern is the inverse of that observed with absolute pitch discussed earlier, and serves to again highlight the complexity of researching complex musical tasks.

Pitch Relations: Summary

We have seen that very young children exhibit certain fundamental pitch processing capacities, including responsiveness to absolute and relative pitch, which become more refined and culturally specified with age. Between 4 and 7 years (depending on tasks), children growing up in a Western culture begin to exhibit an implicit understanding of Western key membership and tonality as revealed by their brain responses, listening judgements, and song productions. A shift from context-dependence to context-independence in pitch relationships seems to occur between 6 and 11 years of age, at least in explicit tasks (Lamont & Cross, 1994; Paananen, 2006). Musical training accelerates the development of understanding of pitch and tonality, although often does not change it radically. There has been very little research on development in the areas of pitch and tonality beyond the age of 11, despite the evidence from some studies that children's representations of tonality at age 11–12 differ from adults (Cuddy & Badertscher, 1987), some evidence for continued development past 11 (Lamont, 1998), and evidence that adults with and without musical training process music of their own and other cultures in different ways (Castellano et al., 1984). Long-term representations of pitch seem to be relatively stable and overwhelmingly a product of experience through listening to music in a particular cultural idiom, with some age-related decline in older adulthood related to general cognitive processing.

Tempo, Timing, Rhythm, and Metre

While pitch has had the most research attention, the development of understanding temporal aspects of music is an area that has been receiving more recent research interest. Tempo changes can be detected by 6-month-olds, who treated 25 per cent faster and slower versions of a familiarised melody as unfamiliar (Trainor, Wu, & Tsang, 2004, Experiment 2). As highlighted earlier, ERP data reveals that newborns are sensitive to the beat in simple metric sequences, as they notice when downbeats are removed (Winkler et al., 2009). Using habituation techniques, tempo changes to simple isochronous tone sequences can be detected by 2- and 4-month-old infants in the same way that adults do (Barucha & Drake, 1997), and 5-month-olds can differentiate contrasting rhythmic groupings (Chang & Trehub, 1977). At 6 months, infants are found to encode melodies in terms of tempo as well as melodic structure and timbre (Trainor et al., 2004). At 9 months, infants are able to detect changes in strongly metric frameworks and in duple metre (Bergeson & Trehub, 2006), although they do not notice changes in weaker frameworks or patterns in triple metre.

To explore potential perceptual bias for simple ratios further, Hannon and Trehub (2005a) explored 6-month-old infants' and North American, Bulgarian, and Macedonian adults' responses to metrical patterns consisting of simple ratios (common in Western music) and complex ratios (drawn from Bulgarian and Macedonian folk music, and common in many folk musical cultures). The 6-month-old infants were able to detect changes to the sequences that violated or preserved the metrical structure in both types of sequence, but adults were only able to do this for the complex ratios if they had prolonged experience of the musical culture using those ratios. This suggests a very similar developmental sequence affected by enculturation to that found for pitch and key relationships, with infants below the age of 12 months able to detect changes to tonal systems they are unfamiliar with but adults unable to do so.

Hannon and Trehub (2005b, Experiment 1) found that by 12 months, infants were responding to these kinds of rhythmic patterns in a very similar way to adults, not detecting the structure-violating alterations to sequences which were culturally unfamiliar to them. How much exposure and of what kind is necessary to turn a young listener into a culturally sensitive listener? Drawing on evidence from language exposure, where only 5 hours of listening experience with Mandarin gave North American 12-month-olds the ability to show sensitivity to Mandarin speech contrasts (Kuhl, Tsao, & Liu, 2003), Hannon and Trehub (2005b, Experiment 2) gave parents short 10-minute CDs containing Eastern European folk music recordings and asked them to play the music to their infants twice daily for two weeks. This relatively short exposure period prior to the study was enough to help

the infants distinguish between structure-preserving and structure-violating alterations to the folk music. However, adults with similar amounts of exposure to the
unfamiliar music (Experiment 3) showed more tendency to assimilate the unfamiliar rhythms into a Western simple-ratio metrical framework, and did not show the
exposure effect found in the 12-month-old infants.

Hannon and Trehub's (2005b) findings suggest that listening alone appears to be
sufficient to generate learning of metrical patterns, and that relatively short durations
of exposure are necessary. More active types of intervention are also effective. Phillips-
Silver and Trainor (2005) familiarised 7-month-old infants with ambiguous auditory
rhythms, either emphasising a duple (every second beat) or triple (every third beat)
by means of bouncing the infants. Afterwards, infants preferred to listen to the pattern they had been familiarised with, showing that they had encoded the pattern into
either duple or triple metre. There was no preference found in a group of infants who
simply watched the experimenter bouncing, highlighting the importance of movement. In a follow-up study, Gerry, Faux, and Trainor (2010) found that 7-month-old
infants who were attending Kindermusik sessions showed a bias towards the patterns
in duple metre. The Kindermusik training was not tailored for this particular study, so
was implicitly prioritising the simple 2:1 metrical ratios found in much Western music
(London, 2004) and thereby shaping infants' responses to that metrical structure.

Very similar effects of experience have been obtained for 7- and 15-month-old infants
by Cirelli, Spinelli, Nozaradan, and Trainor (2016) using EEG. In a more controlled
study Zhao and Kuhl (2016) found that twelve sessions of music intervention sessions
which deliberately targeted triple metre patterns led to 9-month-olds being better able
to detect structure violations to such patterns, as shown by mismatch responses using
magnetoencephalography (MEG). Learning after the age of 12 months appears to be
more difficult: Cirelli et al. (2016) found that 20 weeks of music training made no difference to 14 - to 16-month-old infants' brain responses to different metrical patterns.
This evidence converges to support the importance of a critical period for enculturative
learning in music (cf. Trainor, 2005), during which infants have enhanced learning skills.

This critical period may explain why there is little developmental change in the
field of temporal processing later in childhood. Several different studies show
remarkable stability in 4- to 12-year-olds' abilities to detect temporal irregularities
and to segment according to changes in tone duration or pause duration (Drake,
1993; Drake, Jones, & Baruch, 2000). What tends to emerge from these tasks is
that children become better able to process faster and more complex materials
with age, but that there are no qualitative shifts in understanding. For instance,
Trehub, Schneider, and Henderson (1995) found 6.5-month-old infants could not
discriminate gap durations of 8 milliseconds (ms) but were able to do so for gaps of
12ms and above, and 5-year-old children were poorer than adults on the gap durations of 12ms and 16ms. Trehub et al. traced a developmental curve in gap detection thresholds from 11ms for infants to 5.6ms for children and 5.2ms for adults,
showing a more rapid progression between infancy and childhood than between
childhood and adulthood. Similar linear changes with age and task complexity are
observed in other temporal processing skills such as the ability to detect synchrony.

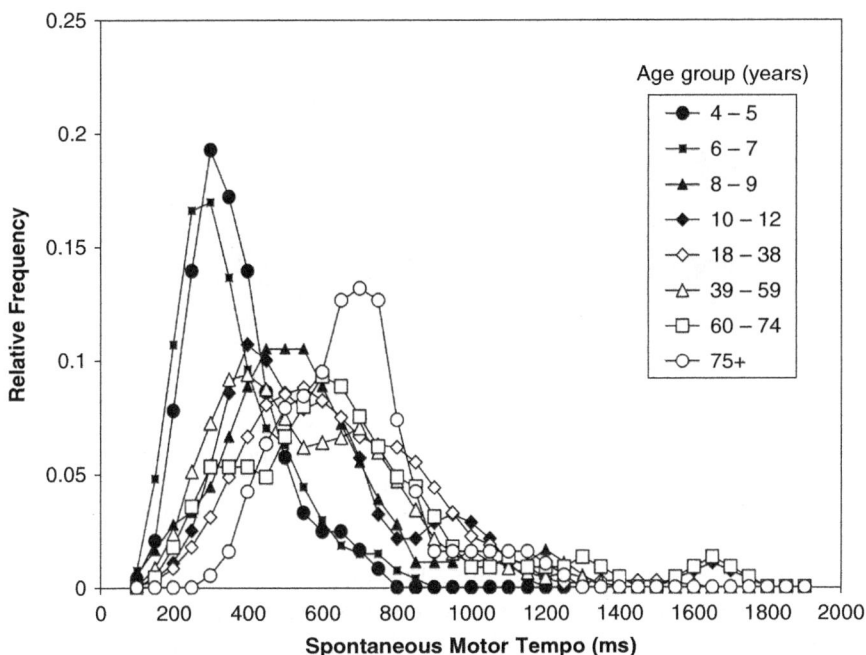

Figure 3.5. Spontaneous motor tempi for different age groups.
Source: Figure 4 (p. 355) in McAuley, J. D., Jones, M. R., Holub, S., Johnston, H. M. & Miller, N. S. (2006). The time of our lives: Life span development of timing and event tracking. *Journal of Experimental Psychology: General*, 135(3), 348–367. American Psychological Association, reprinted with permission.

For instance, EEG data showed that 7-year-olds were able to extract regularities to predict beats as well as adults at slower tempi (390 and 585ms) as well as adults, but not at faster tempo (780ms) (Cirelli et al., 2014).

In terms of production tasks, synchronising is a skill which requires practice and also gradually develops during childhood. McAuley, Jones, Holub, Johnston, and Miller (2006) tracked the ability to synchronise across a wide age range. They measured spontaneous motor tempo (SMT), fastest and slowest motor tempo, preferred perceptual tempo (PPT), and cognitive ability, and then asked participants to complete a synchronise-continue tapping task in which they synchronised along with a pacing stimulus (at varied speeds from trial to trial) and then continued tapping as accurately as possible. Spontaneous motor tapping was fastest in the 4- to 5-year olds at 300ms and fairly slow for the older participants (aged over 75 years). Closer analysis of their data, as shown in Figure 3.5, showed that SMT slows at two stages, in middle childhood and in late adulthood, but is relatively constant in between.

Faster motor tempi were distributed in a U-shaped profile, with slower performance in the very youngest and oldest age-groups, and slowest motor tempi showed the opposite inverted U-shaped profile. McAuley et al. (2006) also found a reduced range of stable period matching at the ends of the age spectrum, and concluded that the entrainment region widens throughout childhood, stays relatively stable

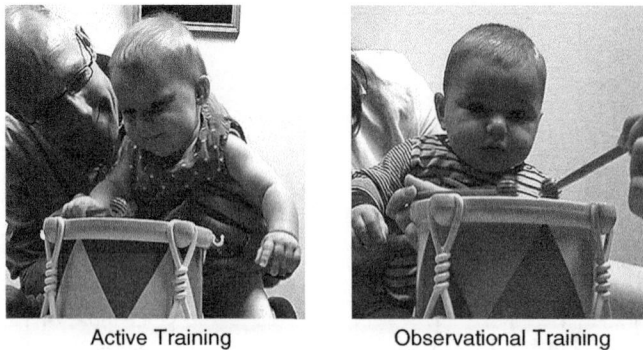

Active Training   Observational Training

Figure 3.6.   Active versus observational training of synchronisation with infants.
Source: Figure 1 (p. 5) in Gerson, S. A., Schiavio, A., Timmers, R., & Hunnius, S. (2015).
Active drumming experience increases infants' sensitivity to audiovisual synchrony during
observed drumming actions. *PLoS One*, 10(6), e0130960, doi:10.1371/journal.pone.0130960.
Reprinted in accordance with the Creative Commons Attribution (CC BY) license.

throughout later childhood and adulthood, and then narrows late in life. Younger
and older participants are less accurate at slower tempi, and they note that the error
patterns were strikingly similar at 6–7 years and at over 75 years of age.

McAuley et al.'s study used a simple tapping task where participants had to
keep the beat going on their own, and they did not test children younger than
4. Kirschner and Tomasello (2009) found that younger children were better able to
learn to synchronise accurately if their beat identification was done with a human
partner. They asked 2.5-, 3.5-, and 4.5-year-olds to drum with a human partner, a
drum machine, or a drum sound from a speaker. The youngest children were able
to adjust their tempo to match the human partner outside their spontaneous motor
tempo range, and all children were more accurate when drumming with a human.

Another way of measuring synchrony to the beat is to test the ability to match
auditory and visual information. Evidence from other areas of infancy suggests
that multisensory information is more useful for early learning (Gogate, Walker-
Andrews, & Bahrick, 2001). Gerson, Schiavio, Timmers, and Hunnius (2015) gave
6-month-old infants the opportunity to actively engage with a drum or to watch
an adult playing the drum (Figure 3.6), and found that after active engagement the
infants were better able to detect a video of an adult drumming where the auditory sequence was out of synchrony with the video presentation. The infants in the
active engagement condition looked longer at a video where the adult was in synchrony by 600ms compared to infants in the observational condition or controls,
although there were no differences in condition for 300ms offset events, suggesting
that finer synchronisation abilities take more time to develop.

In a more explicit judgement task, Einarson and Trainor (2015, 2016) found
that 5-year-old children were able to make some sophisticated timing judgements.
They were asked to select the better drummer in pairs of stimuli where a puppet
was performing a drumming sequence, heard as a woodblock sound, along with a
short musical sequence. In one of the pair the puppet/woodblock was in synchrony

with the sequence, and in the other it was either out of phase or at an incorrect tempo. The 5-year-olds were able to correctly identify synchrony from either static or dynamic visual stimuli (still pictures or videos) in simple 4/4 metres, but were unable to do so for more complex 5/4 or 7/4 metres.

Two developmental implications arise from these findings on temporal and metrical perception with children. The first is that development of timing abilities seems to have a gradual progression throughout childhood, a long period of stability through later childhood and adulthood, and some older-age-related declines in perceptual sensitivity. The second is that observation is insufficient to generate learning, and that active involvement, embodiment, and movement is important (and, as we shall see in Chapter 8, has important consequences when considering the effects of music performing). This corresponds to findings with adults that highlight visual cues to timing as being less efficient than auditory ones (Repp & Penel, 2004) and that tactile metronomes, where adults 'feel' the beat from vibrations across their backs, can be as good as auditory metronomes in facilitating synchronisation in tapping for untrained adults (Ammirante, Patel, & Russo, 2016). As discussed further in Chapter 7, entrainment is a powerful mechanism by which emotion can be evoked in music, from performers and listeners alike, and understanding the development of these fundamental skills is likely to receive more research attention in the coming years.

Timbre

While timbre is a complex musical property, representing a combination of spectral envelope, temporal envelope, and spectral flux, it has no hierarchical or complex structure to be learned, and while it may affect other aspects of response to music such as emotion (Hailston et al., 2009), acquiring a sense of timbre for children is primarily focused at the level of being able to distinguish different instruments from one another. There is, however, some evidence that timbre is perceived and implicitly encoded in infancy. Trehub (1990) found 7- to 8-month-old infants were able to detect small changes in spectral structure, and Thorpe and Trehub (1989) found infants could discriminate sine- from sawtooth-wave tones. Trainor et al. (2004, Experiment 3) found that familiarising 6-month-old infants with a melody for a week using either piano or harp timbres was sufficient for the infants to encode the pitch, tempo, and timbre. If the melody was presented using a different timbre in the test phase the infants treated it as novel, indicating that context-specific features are important in early memorisation of music. Timbre is also at the root of infants' demonstrated preferences for familiar and overlearned sequences such as their mother's voice (DeCasper & Fifer, 1980). The importance of experience continues throughout childhood. Shahin, Roberts, and Trainor (2004) found larger auditory evoked potentials in 4- to 5-year-olds with Suzuki musical training in response to isolated tones of all kinds, and also larger P2 responses for the instrument the children were learning (piano or violin).

One direct investigation of timbral sensitivity (Lowther, 2004) found rapid development between the ages of 3 and 8. Children were given pairs of sounds and asked to verbally identify whether the sounds were the same or different. Younger children made easy discriminations very accurately (e.g. comparing a triangle sound to a ratchet, or tuba to celeste), but were much less successful on more difficult comparisons (e.g. flute to clarinet, or cello to violin). Overall accuracy improved linearly from 3 to 8 years of age, but by 8 years of age children were still having some difficulty with the more challenging pairs, and performance overall was worse at higher pitch levels. Lowther repeated the task a week later, finding high levels of correspondence in children's responses. The study was well matched to children's verbal abilities in that no labelling was required, and helped children demonstrate discrimination without worrying about what the sounds actually were. From children's qualitative responses, she concluded that although accuracy increased with age, specific experiences with particular sounds were responsible for helping children make sense of timbral information. For instance, one 4-year-old boy talked about the drum sound being similar, but not the same, to one he had played at nursery. As with much research with children at this age, there was also a degree of imagination in their answers: a 3-year-old girl talked about the woodblock sound as sounding like a horse, and then identified the following sound as a rabbit.

In another direct investigation involving timbre, Creel (2016, Experiment 3) studied preschool children's musical representations with discrimination tasks and sound-picture associations. She played 3- to 5-year-olds two melodies, one on a muted trumpet and the other on a vibraphone, in a training phase in which associations were learned between the melodies and two different cartoon characters. Children had to identify whether the two melodies were the same or different (a discrimination task) and also identify which of the two characters was playing its favourite tune (an identification task). Creel found high levels of timbre discrimination and identification. In this short-term learning environment, children were more accurate in identifying timbre associations than melody associations (Experiments 1 and 2).

Older children are more readily able to identify the differences between different musical instrument sounds. Indirect information comes from research on tonality. Schellenberg et al. (2005, Experiment 2) showed that 8- to 11-year-old children could correctly identify whether a third chord in a sequence was played by a piano or a trumpet, after hearing two previous chords generated using Shepard tones (synthesised complex tones with no discernible pitch height). The children in this study responded at ceiling levels in identifying the instruments, and were quicker in responding to the piano than the trumpet, due to its more rapid onset time. Their results were further influenced by the nature of the chords, as discussed earlier. Easy discrimination of piano and trumpet tones was also found by Gudmundsdottir (1999). In her study, children became more accurate at identifying simultaneous melodies between the ages of 6 and 12, and identified the trumpet melody most frequently: this may be due to the spectral envelope rather than onset characteristics of the two timbres.

Other indirect evidence for timbre perception comes from the growing field of research into the music perception experiences of children and adults with cochlear implants (CI). Vongpaisal, Trehub, and Schellenberg (2009) found both normal hearing and CI children performed better on identifying the original versions of familiar television theme tunes than specially created melodic or instrumental versions using different timbres, and although all the children performed more poorly on the variations of the theme tunes with different instruments their responses were still above chance (although, as expected, far better for the normal hearing children). Similar results were found with younger children by Volkova, Trehub, Schellenberg, Papsin, and Gordon (2014). In their study 4- to 7-year-olds were able to identify familiar theme songs played on different instruments, although the CI users were poorer when given reduced sequences with only timing cues and at chance when given only relative pitch cues. With the growing use of cochlear implants and the desire to make these work effectively for music as well as speech, the nature of timbre perception is likely to become a popular topic in future years and the importance of understanding how timbre is perceived and affected by experience in childhood will surely be heightened.

In the only controlled study to explore timbre across the lifespan (Hailston et al., 2009), while timbre affected perception of emotion among listeners aged 18–30 and 58–75, there were no differences in responses for the two age groups and no differences for timbre according to years of musical training. This suggests that while it might be an important aspect of music perception, in the absence of other musical features it is less likely to be significant. However, it has been suggested that timbre can be important in helping identify familiar music. Studies have shown that adults are able to recognise familiar music from real recordings as short as 400ms duration (e.g. Krumhansl, 2010), and timbre may be implicated in these rapid judgements since little other information is available.

Despite the paucity of empirical evidence about its development and its implications, timbre identification has often been used as an indicator of exceptional musical ability in children, being presumed to indicate a high level of auditory discrimination (Shuter-Dyson, 1999) and potential for learning (see Chapter 5). It is also one of the elements of music identified by the National Curriculum for Music to be taught to all primary school children in England and Wales, with the underlying assumption that it is an important musical feature.

Combining Musical Elements

Much important developmental evidence comes from exploring individual and isolated features of music, such as isochronous tones which change in pitch but maintain equivalent rhythmic intervals or patterns of beats that have temporal structure without pitch structure. However, real music typically consists of combinations of features, and the understanding of how these features combine to generate understanding of real music cannot be simply generated from the sum of their parts. Musical structure and form operate in cognition in a more complex way than combining what is known about scale/tonality and rhythm/metre, and as we shall see, attention to different features of music is also subject to change across development.

Combinations of Elements: Musical Structure and Form

Understanding musical structure depends on the ability to detect and remember similarity and difference in the individual structural components of music. Musical structure can be understood at a local and a more global level in terms of memory and processing: the first concerns melodic patterns (which more typically also contain rhythmic and metric information), and the second concerns combinations of musical sequences that may invoke structural features such as tonality, metric structure, choice of instruments, and style over longer time periods. In terms of research, most of the work with children has focused on melodies and on memory and processing of real pieces of music, and we address these separately.

Melody in Combination with Other Musical Elements

Six-month-old infants are able to process melodies in very similar ways to adults, suggesting that this might be a fairly fundamental musical skill. As seen in the Pitch section, infants are able to discriminate pitch and contour changes (Trainor & Trehub, 1992) and recognise melodies when they are transposed (Plantinga & Trainor, 2005). At 6 months infants are also able to detect changes in rhythm and pitch in conventional rhythmic patterns as well as adults, suggesting that there are some temporal constraints early in life (Trehub & Hannon, 2009). Sensitivity to the tonal structure of a melody, in terms of key membership, develops between 6 and 12 months, and harmonic relationships develop more gradually up to the age of around 11 years. Plantinga and Trainor (2009) showed that 2-month-old infants discriminate familiar from unfamiliar melodies after limited exposure. Using eye movements rather than head turning, due to the age of their participants, infants were able to demonstrate preferences for one of two folk songs with which they had just been familiarised by fifteen repetitions. A preference for the familiar melody was found in the first half of their test period, although not in the second; their suggestion is that infants had habituated to the 'novel' melody by this time as they heard it repeatedly during the first half of the test period. At 6 months, infants showed a preference for a novel melody compared with the same original folk songs after a week of at-home familiarisation (Trainor et al., 2004), representing a switch from familiarity to novelty preference.

Looking at melodies as patterns and shapes rather than as exemplars of particular pitch and tonal relations provides a different perspective on how development might progress. Krumhansl and Jusczyk (1990) found that 4.5- to 6-month-old infants preferred to listen to Mozart minuets that had pauses occurring at the end of each phrase rather than variations on these that had pauses inserted within the phrases. As they had used real musical examples in this study, Krumhansl and Jusczyk were able to carefully analyse musical features to see if there were cues in the musical structure guiding this discrimination and preference behaviour. They found that overall pitch height dropped towards the end of the phrase, notes became longer, and octave intervals occurred more frequently, as compared with the pauses they had inserted within the phrases. They suggest that these acoustic markers might help guide the infants to recognise more appropriate phrase endings.

It has been suggested that the structure of melody is involved in how readily listeners are able to process and recall it. Melodic expectancy, first formulated by Narmour (1990), refers to relationships between different pitches and how these may shape future expected events or expectancies. Narmour's implication-realisation theory breaks the melody down into sequential intervals, and considers how likely notes might be to continue a given pattern. These follow the principles of registral direction (smaller intervals are likely to continue in the same pitch direction while larger ones are more likely to be followed by a change) and intervallic difference (the idea that small intervals lead to expectations for similarly small ones while large ones are more likely to be followed by small ones). Through elaboration, these basic ideas lead to three further principles: registral return (build from three-note symmetrical melodic archetypes), pitch proximity, and closure, which are achieved through combinations of the first two. Narmour's theory has provided some general rules which he argued were innate and are similar to Gestalt grouping principles. Schellenberg (1997) simplified this to two factors, pitch proximity and pitch reversal, which summarise the general approach in a more parsimonious and non-overlapping manner. With children, there is supporting evidence for Schellenberg's two-factor model. Pitch proximity was the overriding feature that characterised 5-, 8-, and 11-year-olds' responses, but pitch reversal also became important in older children's judgements on both perception (listening) and production (singing) tasks. Schellenberg's data casts doubt on Narmour's argument that these principles can be entirely innate, although they may reflect predispositions in music which are readily acquired through experience.

Considering evidence from production tasks, Davidson, McKernon, and Gardner (1981) taught a group of five 4- to 5-year-olds an unfamiliar song over the period of a year. They found four phases in the way the children learned the song which can tell us about their musical understanding. The first was overall topology: the words of the song were learned, phrases and phrase boundaries were present, and children sang with an underlying pulse and consistent pace. Next, the rhythmic surface was mastered, but while melodic contour was present there was no key stability across phrases and intervals might vary from one version to the next. The next phase was where pitch contour was mastered, although tonality was still inaccurate, and finally key stability was achieved. More recent research shows that young children take some time to master accuracy when it comes to pitch and memory in singing (Demorest & Pfordresher, 2015; Leighton & Lamont, 2006), so some caution should be applied in assuming that singing production skill is a good match for perception skills: indeed, Rutkowski (2015) found no relationship between children's singing accuracy and their pitch perception as assessed using Gordon's Intermediate Measures of Music Audiation. However, the progression outlined by Davidson et al. (1981) provides additional support for the idea that various musical features are acquired at different stages in early childhood through trial and error. Similarly, Brand (2000) explored children's errors in learning to sing a new and unfamiliar song between the ages of 6 and 12. While older children learned the song more rapidly, all children, irrespective of age or musical training, made plausible errors in terms of song organisation (e.g. more symmetrical phrases). Thus children attempt to organise the music they encounter into meaningful sections and familiar gestures, as is also found in their invented songs (which we discuss further in Chapter 4). Oura and Hatano (1988) found that 9- to 10-year-olds with around five years of musical experience could reproduce a novel melody as rapidly and accurately as trained adults (and more so than inexperienced adults). Thus internalised organising principles such as tonality or repetition are used to make sense of unfamiliar music and to guide internal representations of melodic structure, and while this skill is tied to the development of tonal sensitivity, it is not very much influenced by any other effects of training or enculturation.

A small body of research has explored children's similarity judgements, which also sheds light on how they process combinations of musical elements. This work draws on the concepts of object and relational similarity (Ratterman & Gentner, 1998). Object similarity is the process of comparing two single values, while relational similarity involves comparing binary relationships in the form A:B::C:D, or, put more simply, listening to pairs of sequences and deciding whether they have the same relationship to each other. Stevens and Gallagher (2004) applied these concepts to children's judgements of similarity relations between the ages of 5 and 11, using pitch and duration as the deciding features but separately. Children either listened to two notes and decided if they were the same in pitch or duration or to four note patterns and judged if the first two were same in pitch or duration to the second two. Children were better in their study at pitch judgements, with 5-year-olds performing above chance and 8- and 11-year-olds performing relatively well, while duration was more difficult for the youngest children.

These results show support for the absolute-to-relative shift in understanding, which was also found in Schwarzer's (1997) study. Younger children organised musical stimuli using melody-independent features such as loudness (5- to 6-year-olds), tempo, and timbre (6- to 7-year-olds), while adults used more melody-specific features like contour. Stalinski and Schellenberg (2010) found a shift from an emphasis on absolute pitch changes in early childhood to one on melodic variations in middle childhood when 5- to 12-year-olds were rating the similarity of melodic pairs. Children categorised short melodies analytically (using one musical element) rather than holistically (using combinations), and none of the younger children used pitch or contour relations. However, when real musical stimuli were used in a sorting task, surface features such as dynamics and contour as well as underlying features such as tonal structure were commonly employed by 10- to 11-year-olds (Koniari, Predazzer, & Mélen, 2001).

Considering the interaction between melody and timbre, Trainor et al. (2004, Experiment 3) found that 6-month-old infants familiarised with a version of a melody in one timbre treated the same melody with a change in timbre as if it was a novel melody. They listened just as long to the supposedly familiar melody as to a novel melody also played on the same instrument (the comparison being harp and piano). Gudmundsdottir (1999) asked 6- to 12-year-old children to listen to simultaneous melodies played in different registers and timbral combinations, and to identify which songs they could hear (two of the melodies were familiar while the third was unfamiliar). Older children were better able to identify two simultaneous melodies, and usually the upper register dominated, but if the two melodies were played with contrasting timbres (piano and trumpet), the trumpet melody was usually identified (alone) or identified first (in a pair), regardless of register. Performance was better for familiar melodies. The effect of age suggests that decoding a complex auditory signal is an ability which is affected by experience, but which can also be assisted by surface features such as timbre: here the trumpet sound clearly provided a more engaging stimulus that attracted attention to its melody even if it was the lower in pitch. Galvin, Fu, and Oba (2008) found adult CI users to be better at identifying melodic contour with certain timbres than others (organ being best and piano poorest), but there were also effects of music experience. The adults with more musical experience were better able to extract pitch and were less influenced by timbre, which again emphasises the importance of experience in recognising similarity in structure across differences in acoustic cues. There is little research on the development of this interaction, however, so more needs to be known about the interactive role of timbre in melodic processing. It is interesting to note that the piano timbre turns out to be particularly poor in helping focus auditory attention for infants, children, and CI users, given its prevalence in a wide range of educational settings.

This research paints a somewhat complex picture, and results vary depending on the nature of the tasks employed. If explicit judgements are being made to artificial and simplified materials, young children seem to be very capable of focusing on isolated musical elements, prioritising different features of the music at different ages (Stalinski & Schellenberg, 2010; Stevens & Gallagher, 2004). With more complex materials and real music (e.g. Koniari et al., 2001), it is more likely that musical elements are processed in combination, but this ability develops with age throughout childhood. Although children aged 5–6 can recognise different musical elements and structures in complex tasks, older children are better able to process more complex underlying structures of music, and this is also sometimes dependent on formal training. It may take until adulthood to fully integrate different musical features in perception (Schwarzer, 1997), but again research has not explored this in adolescence.

Looking at memory for melodies into adulthood, very little research has engaged with this topic. Using simple melodies, Dowling, Bartlett, Halpern, and Andrews (2008) asked young, middle-aged, and older adults with different amounts of musical experience to detect alterations in familiar and unfamiliar melodies at different tempos. A modest decline in performance was found in the oldest group, reflecting general cognitive slowing in older age, but tempo did not make any difference. Familiar melodies were harder to process when tempo was altered and adults with more experience performed better, but there was no combined influence of age and experience. Deffler and Halpern (2011) explored how older adults might learn new melodies in a rich real-world setting. They provided young and older adults (mean ages 19 and 70 years) with a series of melodies and a range of snippets of information: (random) category only, and category with either neutral or positive or negative emotional facts. For instance, a melody might be said to be played by a soldier during military exercises (neutral fact), an awards ceremony (positive fact), or a military funeral (negative fact). Deffler and Halpern predicted that the category information and associations might hinder older adults by placing too much memory load on them, and their results broadly confirmed this, providing more evidence for a mild age-related decline in music processing skills. However, older adults were able to increase their learning of new melodies through repetition, which illustrates that it is possible to teach older adults new tunes, as we will explore further in Chapter 8. These studies confirm the idea that age might slow general cognitive abilities but that musical experience helps maintain music-specific skills.

In an intriguing study with a large number of twins, Seesjärvi et al. (2016) have recently proposed different contributions of genetics and environment on the development of different elements of musical understanding. They studied the genetic and environmental effects on melody perception in 384 young adult twins, including monozygotic and dizygotic twin pairs and individuals, using three different tasks from the Montreal Battery of Evaluation of Amusia (Peretz et al., 2008). In a two-melody comparison task listeners had to detect pitch changes: most similarity was due to genetic effects. Detecting incongruities in a single melody due to key (for instance, including tones outside the musical key but preserving contour) was explained primarily by shared environmental effects, and detecting beat incongruity (where, for instance, pauses were inserted within phrases) was explained most by non-shared environmental effects. Their results clearly support many of the findings reviewed earlier to suggest that pitch discrimination is largely genetically or biologically determined while implicit perception of both tonal and metric structures is mediated by environmental factors.

Memory for Real Music: Melody, Harmony, Structure

The perception and cognition of extended pieces of music is also dependent on musical memory, indicated by the ability to encode sequences as the same, similar, or different. Memory for music begins before birth and as we saw earlier in the chapter, extended prenatal exposure to particular pieces of music can result in postnatal preferences or discrimination responses (Granier-Deferre et al., 2011; Partanen et al., 2013). Transnatal memories do not seem to depend exclusively on any kind of structure to the auditory material, as they occur for environmental auditory stimuli like aeroplane noise. Ando and Hattori (1970) compared responses to aircraft noise among infants who had prior experience of the noise in the foetal period and those who had not, finding that almost half the infants with prior experience slept soundly through aircraft noise and less than 13 per cent awakened and cried, while the reverse pattern was found for those without experience to the noise. This and a wealth of other findings on preference for maternal voice compared to the same utterances made at the same pitch levels by other female speakers discussed earlier (e.g. Kisilevsky et al., 2003) suggest that timbre and acoustic properties play a role in early memories for sound and music.

In addition to memory for broader acoustic features such as spectral envelope and pitch height, the ability to focus on the absolute pitch properties of a musical sequence as illustrated by Saffran and Griepentrog (2001) can become firmly associated with specific musical sequences. This seems to be a function of extensive repetition, as it was not found with short exposure periods in infants. Latent absolute pitch memory – the ability to recall absolute pitch levels of familiar music – is found in children and in adults with and without musical training. Trehub, Schellenberg, and Nakata (2008) found 9- to 10-year-olds were able to perform above chance at identifying the correct version of familiar songs compared to those shifted up or down by one semitone, in a similar manner to adults (Schellenberg & Trehub, 2003). Jakubowski, Müllensiefen, and Stewart (2017) used 5-second clips from well-known children's television theme music in its original format and shifted by one or two semitones, and tested children aged 4–12 years, finding similarly above-chance levels of performance and no effects of age or experience. This suggests that while regular exposure is required (Jakubowski et al. identify this as at least once a month, but found no effects of increased recognition with increased familiarity), attention and training are not necessary for latent absolute pitch.

However, in some cases, structure does make a difference. The ability to encode specific pitch patterns explains why small pitch changes can be detected in familiar melodies (Partanen et al., 2013). Saffran, Loman, and Robertson (2000) gave recordings of Mozart piano sonatas to parents of 7-month-old infants and asked them to familiarise the infants with the music by playing these once daily for two weeks. In a first experiment excerpts were taken from the middle of the original pieces and compared with segments from other, unfamiliar sonatas in a preferential listening task. The infants preferred to listen to the novel pieces, while infants in the control group (with no familiarisation) showed no preference for either piece. In a second experiment a simple comparison was made between passages from the beginnings and the middles of the original familiar pieces, and results showed a clear preference for passages taken from the beginnings of the piece for the infants who had been familiarised with it. This highlights the importance of both musical context and structure: in the first experiment the middle passages were taken out of context and less preferred than entirely novel beginnings from unfamiliar music, while in the second, familiar beginnings were preferred over familiar middles.

Representations of Music

Studies directly testing the relevance of Swanwick and Tillman's (1986) developmental spiral for listening by Liane Hentschke (e.g. Hentschke & Del Ben, 1999) have found some broad correspondence between the ways children talk about music and the levels of the spiral model. Between the ages of 6 and 10, there is a growth in the number of descriptions of real music which rely on personal expressiveness along with a decline in the number of sensory descriptions. By the age of 14, children are beginning to use vernacular expressions to describe the music played to them (which

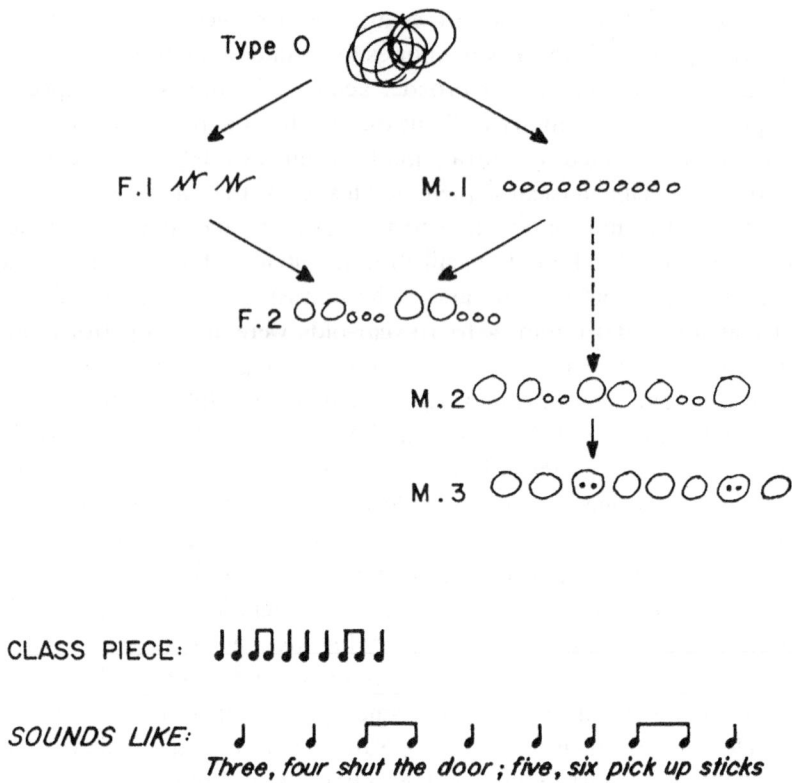

Figure 3.7. Typology of drawings.
Source: Figure 8.1 (p. 194), reprinted from Bamberger, J. (1982), Revisiting children's drawings of simple rhythms: A function for reflection-in-action, *U-shaped behavioral growth*, S. Strauss & R. Stavy (Eds.), New York: Academic Press, with permission from Elsevier.

consisted of conventional Western music such as Schumann's Album for the Young). However, these studies were relatively constrained in that the children were given tools (picture cards) which reflected the elements in the spiral with the aim being to determine at which ages which types of descriptions were more commonly used.

Taking a more open-ended approach to understanding children's representations of music is a key feature of the symbol-system approach discussed in Chapter 2. For instance, in a series of in-depth investigations using game-playing techniques with young children over time, Bamberger (1991, 2006) uncovered different ways in which children understood the elements of music separately and in combination. Interactive data from extensive game-playing sequences with young children revealed a general shift from the concrete to the more abstract. Bamberger (1991) asked a range of children aged between 4 and 12 to draw a rhythm they had been clapping in their music class so that they would remember what they had done or someone else could see what to do next time around. She classified their drawings into three main types, shown in Figure 3.7. The first, produced by the youngest children, were scribbles, dots, or outlines of hands (Type O). While these give some idea of the action of clapping, either by illustrating the instrument (hands) or 'performing' the music on the page which left a trace of dots or scribbles, these gave no information as to the content or structure of the rhythm.

The other two types of drawing reflect the number of items but prioritise different aspects of the rhythm in so doing. These were typically generated by children aged 6–11. Children without training (and adults, as found in other tasks by Smith, Cuddy, & Upitis, 1994) were more likely to produce what Bamberger termed figural drawings (F1 and F2), which correspond closely to Bruner's (1966) iconic mode of understanding. The drawings represent a close mapping of the actual materials, just like a picture of a tree resembles the tree shape. These patterns show the repeated sequence of the rhythm, with larger (longer) and smaller (smaller) circles in the more advanced version of this (F2). However, clapped rhythm has no actual duration, and it is the inter-onset-interval between the claps that is important for identifying precise timing. Children with musical training were more likely to produce formal, or in Bruner's terms, abstract, drawings (M1-M3). Here there is an abstract mapping between elements of the drawing and the sequence (the corresponding analogy would be the word 'tree' to describe the tree). In Bamberger's data the trained children accurately represented the formal element of the rhythm by identifying the intervals between claps as long (larger) or short (smaller), but in so doing the formal drawings do not clearly show the repeating pattern which is illustrated by the figural drawings.

Bamberger suggested from this work that all types of representation are important, but that music training appears to bias children's responses towards the more abstract formal representations (Bamberger, 1986). From a Piagetian perspective one might assume this means children's understandings are more developed, but from a Brunerian viewpoint it means they have lost something of the earlier ways of understanding. Very similar developmental trajectories were found for pitch in melodic context, with studies using familiar melodies like *Twinkle Twinkle Little Star* giving children the chance to demonstrate their understanding of the pitches in the melody and out of context. In these studies, children actively construct melodies using Montessori bells, so there is a physical tool (in the Vygotskian sense) to help them demonstrate their representations. In general, children without training tended to construct melodies in what Bamberger (1986) termed 'felt paths' or purpose-built melody-specific organisations of notes. Children with training were more likely to construct more abstract schemes which, rather than following the course of a given melody in a linear fashion, explicitly showed awareness of repeated notes at different temporal positions. Bamberger (1991, 2006) mapped this sequence of development both cross-sectionally and through studying individual children in detail over extended time periods. Her conclusions were that *multiple hearings* should be the ultimate end-point of this sequence of understanding, and the ability to represent different elements of music at different times and for different purposes is what ought to be emphasised by music education (Bamberger, 2006).

The idea of focusing on invented notations has been developed by other researchers in larger cross-sectional studies. Barrett (1997) studied 4- and 5-year-old children's drawings of their own invented compositions, finding different categories

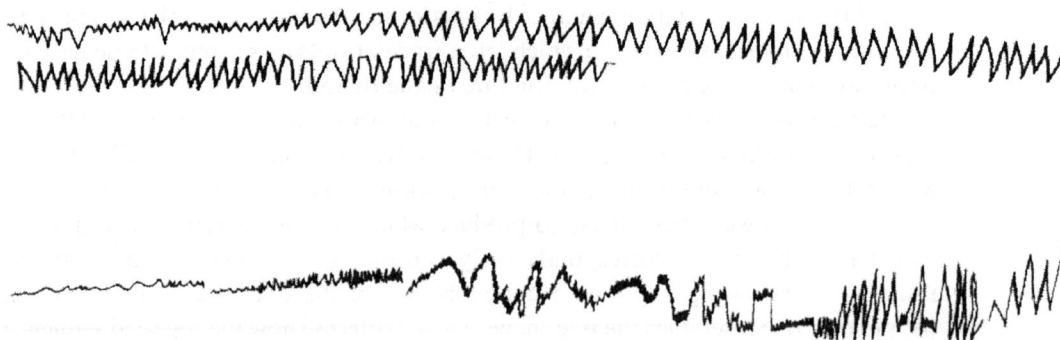

Figure 3.8.   Invented notations by passive (top) and active (bottom) listeners of the same unfamiliar Korean piece Sa Mul Nor I.
Source: Image republished with the permission of SAGE Publications. Originally published as Figures 1 and 2 (p. 136) in Fung, C. V., & Gromko, J. E. (2001). Effects of active *versus* passive listening on the quality of children's invented notations and preferences for two pieces from an unfamiliar culture. *Psychology of Music*, 29(2), 128–138.

of symbolisation. These included exploration (somewhat random drawings), representations of the instrument or the shape of it, instruments along with some reference to musical elements, representations of gesture, and symbolic representations (the latter two very similar to Bamberger's rhythm drawings shown earlier). Barrett used the drawing categories to infer what was important for the children about the musical performance, whether that be the sound of the instrument itself (drawings of instruments) or particular musical elements. In her sample, type of drawing was not linked to age, and none of the drawings bore close resemblance to conventional music notation, as the children from kindergartens had not experienced any formal training. Looking later in development, Fung and Gromko (2001) explored the effects of brief musical experiences on the kinds of representations children generated. They divided children aged 7 to 12 years into two groups: an 'active' group moved while listening to the music with props and sand, while a 'passive' group simply sat quietly and listened to the music (two highly unfamiliar Korean pieces); afterwards both groups were asked to draw how the music went. Drawings were subsequently scored for evidence of musical parameters such as pitch, rhythm, and grouping. The passive group showed less evidence of rhythm/beat and grouping/phrasing in their drawings, which suggests that the movement allowed in the active group helped to emphasise those features of the music: responses from two children from one of the pieces are shown in Figure 3.8.

Although it is clear that larger-scale musical structure in Western tonal music is premised on a range of structural features such as tonality, it appears that listeners are not very responsive to this. Cook (1987) found that highly trained adult listeners were unable to differentiate between the original compositions of tonal pieces from 30 seconds to 6 minutes in length and variations on them which resulted in them ending in the 'wrong' key. Very similar findings were obtained by West Marvin and Brinkman (1999), suggesting that the stylistic expectations such as patterning that occurs towards the end of phrases and larger sections dominated over tonal structure in shaping listeners' judgements. To date nobody has tested children's capacities to retain tonal structure during extended pieces of music, but it seems likely that they would respond in a similar manner, if not being more influenced by the more local features of the music.

Musical Style

Style discrimination is another area of research which brings together a range of musical elements, although the focus tends to be at a more global level and often compares dramatically different styles. However, a study by Ilari and Polka (2006) showed that 8-month-old infants were able to discriminate two very similar examples of music by the same composer: in their Experiment 1, infants listened longer to orchestral recordings of Ravel's Prelude compared with his Pavane, both taken from the same overall piece (*Le tombeau de Couperin*) and both with similar metre and tonal centre. This discrimination did not arise when both pieces were played in a piano version, although infants listened to the piano version for longer than the orchestral version. As their design was between-subjects, different infants listened to the two different instrumental versions so it is not possible to assess whether full orchestral versions were actually more preferred. Ilari and Polka's starting point was the idea that young children do not need to only hear 'simple' 'children's' music, and their findings support the idea that rich materials can lead to richer responses in listeners of any age. This is important evidence to counter the notion of young listeners as somehow limited in capabilities, or as they put it, 'the implicit assumption … is that the musical processing abilities of infants are limited to repetitive music with intervals, contours, rhythms, timbres, and structured forms' (Ilari & Polka, 2006, p. 9).

More research is needed to establish whether this preference has to do with richness and how it might work across different timbres, as Ilari and Sundara (2009) found 5-, 8-, and 11-month olds preferred to listen to an unaccompanied vocal melody than to a variation of it with an instrumental and percussive accompaniment. Ilari and Sundara suggested that the preference shown here, but not in the earlier study, could be due to the dominance of the voice and predispositions for attending to voices in infancy, in addition to the preference for higher pitch which we have seen is typically found in infants. In any case it is clear that fine style sensitivities can be shown early in infancy.

These sensitivities carry forward into childhood, and early work by Gardner (1973a) showed 6-year-old children were able to detect whether pairs of extracts came from the same or different pieces of music drawn from different styles of classical music from 1680 through to 1960. For instance, a Baroque extract would be paired with a Classical, a Romantic, and a Modern extract, and children were able to correctly judge style. This ability did not seem to change from 6 years up to 18 years of age. Addessi, Baroni, Luzzi, and Tafuri (1995) found only gradual improvements in children's abilities to make style discrimination judgements between the ages of 8 and

13, using the same kinds of music in both a pair-matching and an odd-one-out choice of three pieces. Marshall and Hargreaves (2007) modified this procedure for younger children with a cassette tape matching game, asking children to choose a tape to listen to and then find another tape that matched the music. Four classical styles were used as in Gardner's original work, and in a second step of the study four popular styles were chosen to provide sufficient instrumental music to generate 4 minutes of music (Vanessa Mae, David Arkenstone, Ultravox, and Yanni). The popular styles were perhaps less style-representative, and arguably more similar to one another in the use of synthesisers, drums, and elements of folk and classical cross-over. However, Marshall and Hargreaves argued that they reflected different types of music, and their results from children aged 3–5 showed that matching for the popular music was more accurate (81 per cent) than the classical music (69 per cent). In an extension of this designed to help young children focus on style and potential connections to real people, Marshall and Shibazaki (2011) asked 3- and 4-year-olds to match pieces of music (grunge/rock, jazz, blues, classical, and baroque) with their ideal and preferred listeners, choosing from pre-existing person types (teachers, old people, business people, sportspeople, and bikers). Two examples of each musical style were included to see if they would be 'correctly' matched to the same person, and children were able to do this above chance. Stylistic competence, however, was not the same across all musical styles and again children were better able to judge popular styles. We explore the development of preference for different musical styles more fully in Chapter 7.

Creativity and Music-Making

Another body of work has explored the ways in which children represent the structures of music by analysing their creative music-making, looking at their outputs and the ways in which they achieve these. Creativity can be seen to underpin the activities of both composing and improvising, and arguably composing begins from, and also involves, improvising. Thus the dividing line between improvising and composing is by no means clear, particularly when considering the musical outputs of young children. Many of the studies of children's compositions we are about to consider involve a good deal of improvisation as well. Listening can also be considered to be creative (Hargreaves, Miell, & MacDonald, 2012b). According to this view, *imagination* might form the core of music perception and production, as we discussed in Chapter 2; we shall consider creativity in more detail in Chapter 4. Treating music as a multifaceted activity, we shall consider these interacting elements of musical creativity as they intertwine and unfold in development, with a particular focus on the social dimensions of creative music-making and on the value placed on it by society.

The Roots of Musical Creativity

In his study of collaboration in student jazz musicians, Seddon (2005) re-introduced the concepts of attunement and mirroring as essential components of improvisation, linking back to early infant socialisation through music and communicative musicality (Malloch, 1999; Trevarthen, 1999). Neuroscience has begun to examine the neural bases of musical improvisation and creativity. Beaty's (2015) review of this field includes fMRI studies of vocal and instrumental improvisers including jazz pianists, classical musicians, freestyle rap artists, and untrained adults, and these suggest that their performances promote neural activity in a network of prefrontal brain regions including the pre-supplementary motor area, medial prefrontal cortex, inferior frontal gyrus, dorsolateral prefrontal cortex, and dorsal premotor cortex. Beaty suggests that improvisation involves large-scale brain networks which are associated with spontaneous and unconstrained thinking as well as those involved in motor planning and cognitive control. For instance, in a study of professional jazz pianists by Limb and Braun (2008), neocortical sensorimotor areas that mediate the organisation and execution of musical performance saw widespread activation during improvisation, while limbic structures that regulate motivation and emotional tone were deactivated. Similarly, Bashwiner, Wertz, Flores, and Jung's (2016) brain imaging studies of people who self-report as being musically creative suggest that their creative activity involves not only highly intricate, domain-specific knowledge and skill which draw on the dorsal premotor cortex, supplementary and pre-supplementary motor areas, and planum temporale, but also domain-general cognitive processing styles associated with the default mode network (dorsomedial prefrontal cortex, middle temporal gyrus, and temporal pole), and emotion-related regions (orbitofrontal cortex, temporal pole, and amygdala), which give rise to a strong affective drive to create music.

The neuropsychological approach emphasises a cognitive approach to understanding creativity through an analysis of the process, decision-making, and problem-solving skills, and there are many cognitive models of creativity in terms of both composition (such as Sloboda's analyses of composers' manuscripts which focus on the planning stages, 1985) and improvisation (such as Johnson-Laird's theoretical analysis of how jazz improvisers negotiate between predetermined musical structures such as chord sequences and their own semi-arbitrary inventions, 1988a). Clarke (2005, 2012) has noted that cognitive models of creativity are limited as they ignore the social nature of the activity, particularly with reference to improvisation. Sociocultural approaches to understanding creativity focus very much more on the nature of the social interactions between those involved (e.g. John-Steiner, 2000; Miell & Littleton, 2004). This view, with which we have much sympathy (see Chapter 2), implies that to understand and characterise creativity we need to study the culture which supports and sustains it. Collaborative composition and improvisation provide ideal vehicles for the exploration of the communication, interaction and 'identity work' associated with musical creativity, discussed more fully in Chapters 4 and 6.

Development of Music-Making: Composing

Vocalisation begins very early in development, with infants at about 6 months generating babbling that sounds musical, and this forms part of young infants' communicative musicality (Malloch, 1999). Moog (1976) was one of the earliest to systematically observe preschool children's musical expressions and responses, and as part of his research he recorded examples of infants' and young children's singing. He found that between 3 and 6 months of age, infants began to respond actively to music, turning towards the source of the sound, expressing emotional responses to it, and beginning to use bodily movements such as swaying or bouncing in response to the sounds. Vocalisation occurred by 12 months, with evidence for two types: non-musical and musical babbling. Non-musical babbling emerged first, was believed to be the precursor of speech, and initially did not seem to relate to anything in the child's environment. Musical babbling, on the other hand, was a specific response to music heard by the child, although Moog suggested these early songs bore little resemblance to any other music heard by the child. Structure can be discerned in babbling songs, although caution must be applied in reading too much into infants' spontaneous vocalisations.

Moog observed rhythmic actions in response to music at the age of 2, which declined later in 3- to 5-year-olds, and this was taken to assume that children were gradually internalising their responses to music. Moorhead and Pond (1978) undertook a descriptive study of young children's creative singing at the Pillsbury Foundation School, which was set up specifically to study the spontaneous expression and development of music and equipped with relevant instruments and a musically intensive curriculum. From their observations of children's vocalisations, they distinguished between chants (evolved from speech, rhythmic, simple, repetitive, and social) and songs (typically more complex and individual). Lyle Davidson (1985, 1994) has explored different types of song in children's vocal productions. Outline songs develop over the second and third years of life: these have a basic form but often lack precise details of pitch relationships and rhythm. Before 2 years of age, brief phrases tend to be repeated, consisting of discrete pitches with relatively constant melodic contours and rhythmic patterns. Small intervals dominate, but there is no tonal centre to children's singing at this stage. Later on, existing musical schemes are incorporated into children's original songs. In the preschool period, between the ages of about 3 and 5, children start to borrow from the learned repertoire of words, melodies, and rhythms from other songs to generate their own 'pot pourri' songs (Moog, 1976). 'First draft' songs appear around the age of 5, which are recognisable models of the songs of their own culture, of which they are trying to fill in the details (see Hargreaves, 1986a for more detail on invented songs).

Music-making forms an important part of young children's lives at home, in educational settings, and in the spaces in between (see Burnard & Kuo, 2016; Ilari & Young, 2016). Research has recently begun to explore the kinds of musical cultures that exist in these different in-between contexts. The home is obviously the first and most important of these, and an entire volume has been devoted to children's music-making at home around the world (Ilari & Young, 2016). This work is informed by the communities of practice approach to developmental theorising and fits clearly with sociocultural notions such as guided participation discussed in Chapter 2. The rich ethnographic data reported from the MyPlace MyMusic project in this book show how important the home is for providing access to music and providing links, particularly through digital technology, to popular culture as well as children's music. In relation to creative music making, children chose to sing different songs depending on who was listening, with a particular influence of their own parents' expectations about music. However, interestingly, at the age of 7 a great deal of the home musical culture that was captured was relatively solitary and individual, in contrast with the more 'sociable' environments that exist beyond the home.

Campbell (2010, 2011) has captured rich data on children's music-making in a range of different places, such as preschool, primary school playgrounds, the school cafeteria, and the school bus. Campbell highlights the near-constant nature of children's music-making, with a focus on songs. She also describes the complexity of the songs and musical utterances the young children in her study created as being both melodically and rhythmically rich. Marsh (1995, 1999) has focused on the school playground as a place for musical creation, showing how children draw on many different social and cultural influences in their developing music-making. Custodero, Calì, and Diaz-Donoso (2016) recently conducted some ethnographic observations of children's music-making on the New York subway. Their observations include very young children entertaining themselves through musical utterances and movements which are sparked by environmental noises such as the train itself, and friendship groups of children singing invented songs to one another. Custodero et al. conclude that music is brought to a range of situations such as the subway as a 'security blanket' by children, to bring familiarity into less familiar spaces, often through singing. They also note that most singing and musical behaviours occurred when adults did not intervene, highlighting the importance of children's own musical cultures (see also Campbell, 2010; Young, 2008; Chapter 4).

In addition to the everyday contexts of informal music-making, children learn or engage in music-making and composing at school. In the UK, composing is one of the basic skills in music and children are required to create music in many different ways throughout the compulsory period of study (currently age 5–14). A large body of research has explored composing abilities in a more formal setting, beginning from the seminal work of Swanwick and Tillman (1986) discussed in Chapter 2. The highly formal stage theory they proposed suggested that children's abilities to manipulate musical elements progressed in a strict sequence from a focus on materials, expression, and form to reach aesthetic value. This progression, loosely tied to age, implies that aesthetic creativity through the use of formal structures is not seen until later in development around the age of about 9 or 10. Kratus's (1994) work supports this, with a high incidence of repetition found in 9- and 11-year-olds' compositions (but not in 7-year-olds).

However, the evidence from children's invented songs shows that repetition, structure, and form are present at a much earlier age. Barrett (1996) analysed 137 compositions from children in Australia aged between 5 and 12. From the compositions themselves she was able to highlight the importance of repetition as a structural device across this age span, and through analysis of the process she showed how children were able to develop their own musical ideas through processes such as abstraction, transferral, and inversion, and to achieve closure in their compositions. Glover (2000) studied the development of children's composition at school in the primary years in the UK (between 4 and 14), exploring the purposes of what compositional decisions were made in their composing activity and why. Children at this age relished the opportunities to think about their own compositional experiences, and the process they go through involves intentional activity around the issues of form and structure, confirming that complex musical structures are found earlier in development. Burnard (2006) explored 12-year-old children's compositions at a lunchtime club as well as the meanings they gave to the activity. She identified a multidimensional and multi-layered set of meanings around composition, including the elements of time, the composer as a knowing body, playing out relations within compositions in a lived space. This provides an understanding of composing within context.

This research suggests that there is much sophistication but little change in the ways in which children go about composing in the primary years between about 4 and 11. Musical experience also does not appear to play a significant role. Barrett (1996) illustrated two different compositions produced by children of the same age. The first, by an 8-year-old untrained boy named Anthony (Example 3), was for bass metallophone and is described as including a clear pulse and metre, a tonal centre of C major/Aeolian mode, a range of melodic intervals, modified in sequences that transform the order of the rhythmic units, with changing metre and harmony, performance effects, tempo changes to mark structural features such as ritardando to mark closure, and repetition and development of both rhythmic and melodic patterns – an impressive set of musical features! The second by an unnamed peer of the same age with some musical training was described as 'repetitive with little evidence of experimentation with, or development of musical ideas' (Barrett, 1996, p. 56), which suggests that creativity is not simply or linearly dependent on musical training.

Barrett and Tafuri (2012), in a valuable review of the literature on children's creative music-making, describe 'children's creative meaning-making in music' rather than composing as such, and this stems from the early interactions between infants and caregivers which we introduced in Chapter 2 and discuss further in Chapter 7. Summarising the main findings of a wide range of research, Barrett and Tafuri (2012) provide seven 'emergent principles' which help to sum up this field. First, children's lives begin in what they call 'aural and kinaesthetic interaction' with the culture of the adults around them, and the beginnings of musical creativity occur in this context; second, the social institutions and cultural traditions within which children grow up provide the cultural tools, to use Vygotsky's term, which shape that creativity. Third, as we have emphasised elsewhere, children's learning is active and not passive: infant–adult interaction is a two-way process based on the mutual construction of meanings, within which infants often take the lead; and fourth, 'repetition and variation are fundamental features of children's early creative engagement'. The fifth principle is that creative work occurs both in interaction with others as well as with other tools and artefacts in the environment. Sixth, they suggest that 'young children display strongly musical preferences in both listening and performing', indicating that the early years music educator should therefore strive to provide many different ways of engaging with music as well as examples of different genres and styles. If this is achieved successfully, seventh, children's capacity to use musical materials for creative purposes is likely to thrive such that 'the development of cultural knowledge and creative thought and activity are mutually constitutive' (p. 310). We return to these issues in Chapter 4 when considering the social nature of music-making.

In adulthood there are also well-documented changes in creative productivity. An increase in creativity in early adulthood, rising to a peak at around the age of 30–40, is typically followed by a decline. This varies depending on domain: creative individuals in the arts (composers, poets, and architects) and the sciences (biologists, chemists, and mathematicians) typically peak in their forties, whereas those in history and philosophy do not show any appreciable decline in their fifties and sixties (Lehman, 1953). In music, based on historical data, Simonton (1984) suggested different ages depending on what kind of music is being written: instrumental selections peak at 25–29, symphonies at 30–34, chamber music at 35–39 and light opera or musical comedy at 40–44. Simonton also noted that quality is usually at a peak before quantity in most fields. One needs to consider environmental and career constraints alongside any age-related changes in abilities, as circumstances can prevent people fulfilling their potential (see Romaniuk & Romaniuk, 1981). Looking at the quality of the product, Simonton also identified an inverted backwards-J function of originality with age. To do this he analysed the melodic originality of 5,046 themes by ten eminent composers (Simonton, 1980a), finding a gradual increase in originality over the lifespan with a slight decline in older age. The fame of different melodies was also found to be a positive function of the composer's creative productivity, with more famous melodies generated at composers' most productive periods (Simonton, 1980b).

Development of Music-Making: Improvising

Improvisation provides more or less direct access to creative musical processes as they happen 'live', and many musical cultures outside the Western classical tradition have improvisation at their heart. As a playful type of sociable musical activity improvisation has the potential to draw in children of all ages, and it sits alongside composition in many generalist school curricula, yet formal music training in the West typically prioritises other more formal skills such as notation and sight-reading, and many highly qualified conservatoire graduates have been found in the past to be unable to compose or improvise (see Campbell, 1991): whether or not this is still the case is an interesting empirical question. Improvisation requires the individual to relinquish control and trust other musicians, but it also needs input from existing musical knowledge to complement the entirely spontaneous musical utterances, some of which is necessarily gained through practice and expertise (Berliner, 1994; Monson, 1996).

The literature on the development of songs discussed earlier gives us the starting point for understanding children's improvisation skills, as many of the songs recorded and analysed were true 'one-off' improvisations which might later become elaborated through repetition and rehearsal into compositions. A few studies have looked directly at developmental aspects of children's musical improvisation. Flohr (1985) studied 2- to 6-year-olds' improvisations on a xylophone, finding that their ability to use musical structure developed across the age range in accordance with their levels of musical understanding. He proposed three stages in improvisation: motor energy (2–4 years, notes of roughly equal duration and repeated pitches), experimentation (4–6 years), and formal properties (6–8 years, using structural characteristics like tonality and repetition). This model has many similarities with Swanwick and Tillman's (1986) compositional spiral discussed earlier, and fits with a rather rigid stage-based approach. Brophy (2005) investigated the melodic improvisations of 62 children over a 3-year period, between the ages of 7 and 9. Each child improvised three melodies per year on a pentatonic xylophone, which were analysed in terms of their phrase and motivic (melodic and rhythmic) structure, and their metre. Brophy found increasing use of antecedent-consequent phrases, sense of pulse, and of repeated melodic and rhythmic motives between the ages of 7 and 8, but not between the ages of 8 and 9. Paananen (2007) investigated the keyboard melodic improvisations of 36 6–11-year-olds, and found that the hierarchical structures of tonal music developed sequentially in three stages. In the first, children focused either on the melodic-rhythmic surface or on deep structures (tonality or metre); in the second, surface and deep structures started to become coordinated, and in the third and final stage, they were fully integrated. These findings all correspond with the progression towards integration seen in the development of children's perceptual abilities with elements of music discussed earlier.

Research with adults on improvisation skills, including those studies in the neuroscientific literature which were reviewed in Chapter 2, has mostly focused on the skilled performances of expert musicians (see Pressing, 1988), which often tell us little about the processes of development. A different methodological approach has been to compare the performances of experts and novices on different tasks, and Hargreaves, Cork, and Setton (1991) adopted this technique in comparing the jazz improvisational strategies of novice and expert improvisers. Novices were found to use one of three strategies: filling in the time with no organisational plan; rigidly emphasising a single musical element such as rhythm or harmony; or focusing on one element while being open to change as the improvisation progressed. Experts, however, all had a strategy from the outset (confirming the relevance of the cognitive approach to understanding their improvisations) which organised and unified the improvisation, and which could be modified during the course of the improvisation if necessary.

Another adult study which sheds light on development is Sudnow's (2001) phenomenological account of his learning jazz piano improvisation over several years at around the age of 30. Sudnow describes the three broad stages through which he progressed in mastering fluent jazz piano improvisation skills. The first involved the mastery of individual notes, phrases, and scales: Sudnow describes how his original jerky attempts were gradually 'smoothed', but that they still did not fit into an identifiable 'jazz' style. His emergence into the second stage, which he calls 'going for the sounds', involved the realisation that he was consciously trying to make up melodies, and after he had gained some fluency in doing so, his next problem was to integrate them into coherent wholes. His emergence into the third stage, which occurred in his fourth year of study, was inspired by his watching the pianist Jimmy Rowles, and in particular by observing Rowles's relaxed posture at the piano. Absorbing this insight led him into the third stage, in which he became able to improvise with fluency, with some degree of originality, and within a recognisable idiom.

Conclusion

This chapter has covered a large number of different elements of music and uncovered many different developmental trajectories. The clearest summary is that there are some broad perceptual predispositions which operate easily and early in development, and other aspects of musical enculturation that are acquired relatively early and provide the building blocks for future development. Following this a slow process of gradual enculturative development takes place throughout childhood whereby children become better able to detect tonal relationships, tap along with rhythms, and use musical form and structure to express themselves through music. As Seesjärvi et al. (2016, p. 514) note, 'music perception or musical skills should not be regarded as a single, unitary domain driven mainly by genetic influence, but a complex, multifaceted phenomenon affected by both genetic and environmental factors'. This chapter has emphasised the importance of learning experiences in music, whether these are informal, through engagement with the music of a given culture, or more formal, such as feedback from an adult or interaction with others. Kirschner and Tomasello's (2009) ingenious study of children's abilities to synchronise provide fascinating insights into how learning can be scaffolded by interactions with others. These kinds of paradigms have not yet been applied to other domains of musical understanding, but it would be interesting to see how our understanding of early training and learning of pitch and harmonic relationships, for instance, might change if such evidence were available. We would underline the point raised by Seesjärvi et al. (2016) about the importance of including context and looking for a richer understanding of cultural and environmental influences on development, in order to gain a fuller picture of how this complex multifaceted phenomenon is shaped by interactions with others: we continue with this theme in Chapter 4.

Development in perceptual and cognitive skills in music certainly continues across the lifespan. Creativity in particular is an area which is subject to development in adulthood, and despite some well-cited evidence for musical prodigies and the foundations of creativity in music and the arts being present early in life, the vast majority of composers produce their greatest works in adulthood and later in life. Most areas we have reviewed here show a pattern of slight age-related decline – the inverted backwards-J – in older adulthood, which in many cases is ascribed to general cognitive decline rather than a specific impairment for music. On a more positive note, this is a relatively small decline, and the evidence shows that adults retain memories and processing skills for memory into older age, which enables them to experience the many benefits that sustained musical engagement can bring, as we will see in Chapter 8.

4 Social Development

Music is an inherently social activity, and in this chapter we consider the aspects of musical experience, development, and learning that are influenced and shaped by others. To explore how children's musical development takes place from a social perspective we need to draw on a number of different approaches. We start with a brief consideration of sociological approaches, which provide a way of thinking about the social structures underpinning the world of music, which in turn has implications for how children and young people find their place in that world. We then move on to the social-psychological perspective, building on the theories and concepts of sociocultural development. We explore how researchers define creativity, how children work with others in being creative, and how others respond to and evaluate that creativity. We also consider the influences of social identity theory and cultural psychology, which can explain questions including how adolescents form allegiances with particular styles of music, and the wider effects that these allegiances might have.

Sociological Approaches

The sociology of music has a longer history than the psychology of musical development, and has generally been concerned with larger-scale questions of the production of musical culture and its relationship to social organisations. Tia DeNora (2001) acknowledges the central importance of Theodor Adorno's (1976) work in the growth of the discipline, which was 'dedicated to exploring the hypothesis that musical organisation is a simulacrum for social organisation' (DeNora, 2001, p. 2). Adorno, who was also a classically trained pianist in the Second Viennese School tradition, argued that different musical forms and languages are a direct product of existing social divisions and structures. This line of argument was pursued by the Marxist sociologist Pierre Bourdieu (e.g. Bourdieu, 1971) who proposed that social forces impose and shape norms of cultural taste, and that dominant social groups 'legitimate' their standards of taste in relation to those of other groups, such as in the definition of what constitutes 'serious' as distinct from 'popular' art or music. Bourdieu argued that 'nothing more clearly affirms one's "class", nothing more infallibly classifies, than tastes in music. This is of course because ... there is no more "classificatory" practice than concert-going or playing a "noble" instrument' (Bourdieu, 1984, p. 10). He saw the musical establishment as legitimating the seriousness of classical music as compared with pop music, and linked this with the preferences of different social class groups. He suggested that there existed a *homology* between taste and social position: taste was seen as being a significant indicator of social class, and indeed vice versa, in that that people's preferences and aversions were seen to contribute significantly to the perpetuation of social hierarchies.

The competition between different social class groups for dominance and control over resources is closely related to the idea of the legitimation of different musical forms. DiMaggio and Useem (1978) proposed that the dominant upper and middle class groups want to defend and advance their relative standing in society, and that they do so by regulating people's access to artistic training, their familiarity with the context within which different varieties of art works are presented, and so on. Their review of the empirical literature on the social stratification of audiences clearly showed that 'high culture' (e.g. fine art, opera, classical music) tended overwhelmingly to be 'consumed' by upper- and middle-class audiences, and that education was the best predictor of this. This leads to the sociological viewpoint that 'cultural capital' (i.e. control over resources) is highest in upper class groups, which may also possess a relative lack of economic capital.

At the time, these theories provided a relatively clear explanation of 'taste publics' in music (e.g. Fox & Wince, 1975), but the evidence for the relationship between taste and social position was by no means clear-cut, and today the relationship between taste and social class is very much more difficult to define. Hierarchies of social stratification and patterns of legitimation are increasingly blurring and constantly changing, and the constant and rapid evolution of new styles and genres in popular music makes this relationship even more complex. De Boise (2016) points out that there exists something like a move towards what he calls a 'post-Bourdieu moment' in the sociology of music, although he also feels that 'few have attempted to outline empirical strategies which are critically sensitive to social inequalities, whilst addressing questions of aesthetics, value, resistance and social change' (p. 1). De Boise argues for a broader focus on the nature of musical engagement, and on greater methodological flexibility: sociologists should try to update Bourdieu's approach without losing its key insights into the relationships between musical taste and social structure.

Alongside the Bourdieusian *homology* argument of a direct relationship between social status and the possession of cultural capital, Chan and Goldthorpe (2007) present two alternative perspectives: (1) the *individualisation* argument, which places greater emphasis on individual characteristics such as age, gender, or musical training than on social status in the formation of musical taste, and (2) the *omnivore-univore* argument, in which so-called 'highbrow', 'middle-brow', and 'low-brow' taste patterns are defined in terms of cultural consumption rather than of social status, as originally conceived by Bourdieu (see also Beck, 1992; Parzer, 2013). This latter argument is supported by Elvers, Omigie, Fuhrmann, and Fischinger's (2015) empirical demonstration that musical 'omnivorousness' – the tendency to appreciate a wide range of musical styles, including those regarded as 'highbrow' or 'sophisticated' – tends to be positively related to musical training/sophistication.

Parzer (2013) explains this phenomenon in terms of what he calls 'cultural variety' in musical taste, and suggests that cultural variety may have replaced Bourdieu's view that preferences for either one group of genres or another are what distinguish between members of different social class groups. In this sense, Parzer does not suggest that the notion of 'cultural variety' completely invalidates Bourdieu's original views, but that it may instead have taken the place of the idea of 'cultural capital', which sees preference for 'serious' or 'popular' culture as legitimating patterns of social stratification; in other words, it may be that musical omnivorousness is now what is seen as demonstrating cultural and social superiority. His conclusion is that although Bourdieu's original analysis may be limited and based on outdated views of musical taste, the mechanisms of transmission of social distinction may still be the same.

We return to some of this work elsewhere in the book when it has a bearing on specifically developmental issues: but two more recent scholars of music sociology have also made significant contributions which bear on our central topic here. The first is Simon Frith (e.g. Frith, 1996) who has a strong interest in pop music and its role in society, and who pointed out that the aesthetics of pop music are dependent on the language and the social situations in which value judgements are made, whether that be (for example) criticism in the popular music press, or in the serious daily broadsheets. Frith primarily saw music as a commodity which was shaped by the industrialisation of culture, and which was therefore conceived within three quite distinct discourses: that of the world of the arts, that of folk art, and that of commerce. He saw musical genre as being critical to the discussion of pop music in each of these discourses.

Frith's analysis of the role of technology in these social processes also foresaw some of the subsequent developments which we reviewed in Chapter 1. He pointed out that the vast quantity of music available to many listeners meant that some of it would be perceived as being for 'everyday' consumption rather than as being high art, and that because this vast musical resource is available in many different situations, some music would be seen as more situationally appropriate than others in different situations and contexts. He also predicted that the development of individualised listening, which was already then present in the form of the Sony Walkman and its derivatives, would lead to a distinction between individualised and social listening, and that this would influence the ways in which people create and organise their own music collections (see also Krause & Hargreaves, 2013). Frith was right on all three counts, as we saw in Chapter 1, as well as in his prediction that all of these phenomena, essentially through technology, would exert a clear influence on the development of personal identity: that pop music could be seen as a means of creating identity rather than merely of expressing it.

This is a topic that we will develop much further in Chapter 6, but we also need to consider the second important sociological explanation of the role of music in the development of personal identity at this point. DeNora (2000) proposed that the ways in which people use music, including for mood change, gaining pleasure, accompanying activities such as exercise, working, eating, reading, and so on, may be 're-viewed as part of a fundamentally social process of self-structuration, the constitution and maintenance of the self. In this sense then, the ostensibly "private" sphere of music use is part and parcel of the cultural constitution of subjectivity, part of how individuals are involved in constituting themselves as social agents' (p. 47).

DeNora (2017) has developed this argument further by identifying five main properties of identities. Firstly, identities are developed through social interaction, which involves negotiation, and so DeNora sees them as being exchangeable, trade-able, and steal-able: one person in a given interaction may take on some of the characteristics of the other, on a temporary or permanent basis. Second, identities are seen as resources which have differing levels of status: one's identity can be raised ('promoted') or lowered ('demoted') in relation to others. Third, identities are plastic and malleable, and can be changed at any time. Fourth, this malleability of identities can involve *hybridisation*: different aspects of different identities can be combined to form new ones; and fifth, hybridisation indicates how identities are created *relationally*, i.e. by reference to social and environmental artefacts and conditions which are outside individuals, such as other people, landscapes, buildings, or furnishings.

This kind of analysis is very helpful in explaining the development of musical identities in specific geographical communities. For example, Ilari (2017) has investigated ethnic identity, which can be defined in terms of the cultural values and traditions of the society into which one is born. She was interested in the role of ethnic identity in the perceptions and interactions of minority groups living among other ethnic and racial groups, such as Mexicans in the USA, or South-Eastern Asians and Eastern Europeans in the UK, and the corresponding development of their self-perceptions. Ilari argues that an important aspect of the ability to deal with the immigrant and refugee experience is to be able to negotiate multiple identities, the basic mechanisms for which have been proposed in DeNora's analysis: and one valuable domain of activity in which this can take place is that of music.

Similarly, Zapata Restrepo and Hargreaves (2017) have investigated the important role of music upon the developing identities of displaced families in Colombia. A complex of factors including drug dealing, weak social and judicial systems, and the presence of the paramilitary and of guerillas in the rural areas, leads to the violence which results in the displacement of many people from the country to the big cities, like Bogotá. This has an adverse effect on personal identity, stemming from a distrust of others and feelings of anger and powerlessness against their environment. The children who feel this loss of their relationship to the places in which they grew up can be seen in terms of DeNora's analysis: these children's identities are in effect 'demoted', so that they rely on hybridisation to provide psychological strength which can counter their conditions of deprivation. Hybrid identities can provide a wider family in which people feel welcome and fully human, and one of the main ways in which this can occur is through music: children's cultural musical heritage is one thing that cannot be taken away from them as a result of external circumstances. We discuss research relating to the effects on wellbeing of music for displaced and culturally diverse communities further in Chapter 8.

In covering the sociological approach in this opening section we have looked at some phenomena of social development which apply to all age groups: some of these may have a particularly powerful effect on young people, yet may not be specifically developmental in character. In the rest of the chapter we cover the main contributions of developmental psychology to the study of social development. We look first at the predominant theoretical approaches in the field, and specifically at sociocultural theories: we next take a lifespan approach to the research literature on social development and music, working through from infancy to adolescence and old age; and the chapter concludes with a consideration of some current issues in music education which are closely bound up with social and developmental issues.

Theories of Social Development in Music: Social and Sociocultural Approaches

The sociocultural perspective and the study of self-regulation and metacognition are both intrinsically concerned with social processes. We gave a general overview of these, looking specifically at musical development, and covering sociocultural, ecological, and social cognitive approaches, in Chapter 2: each of these is concerned with a different aspect of the influence of social factors on musical development. In this chapter, our specific focus is social development in music, and so we return to the sociocultural approach in more detail. This has become the dominant approach in many areas of developmental and educational psychology, and we need to understand some of the reasons for this: we therefore look next at the pioneering contributions of (and the divergence between) Piaget and Vygotsky, two of the founding fathers of the discipline, and go on to look at some more recent developments, and in particular at cultural-historical activity theory (CHAT).

Piaget, Vygotsky, and Social Interaction

Piaget's monumental stage theory of development (see e.g. Piaget & Inhelder, 1969; Chapter 2) remains influential today, but some of its basic tenets have been rejected by contemporary scholars. As we saw in Chapter 2, two points in particular have been roundly rejected, namely (a) the view that children can be thought of as 'mini-scientists' whose developmental goal is to reach increasingly advanced states of logical thinking, and (b) that they achieve this goal by following a common developmental sequence regardless of the specific cultural events, situations, and groups which they experience. This was the main point of difference between Piaget and Vygotsky, elaborated earlier. Vygotsky's opposing view was that we start out as social beings: we interact with others, observing what they say and do, and gradually internalise those actions so that they become a part of our own thinking.

One of the most important of Vygotsky's concepts was the view that 'the relations between the higher mental functions were at one time real relations among people' (Vygotsky, 1966, p. 37): in other words, his suggestion was that 'we become ourselves through others'. Vygotsky's view was that language and actions (i.e. practical activity) converge in early childhood, and that this convergence represents the origins of practical and abstract intelligence. This contrasts with Piaget's view, in which individuals assimilate the social world around them to their own thinking, and this divergence between the two theorists leads to different views of the relationships between language, thought, and action. Piaget proposed that language is a medium of representation through which thinking expresses itself, and which plays no major formative role: he saw thinking as being derived from actions, so that actions and speech serve quite different functions.

Vygotsky's view that social relationships form the basis of the development of thought itself means that the interactions between teacher and learner assume far more prominence than in Piagetian theory; and these are explained in terms of the *zone of proximal development* (ZPD): this is probably Vygotsky's best-known concept, and has profound educational implications. Vygotsky defined the ZPD as the discrepancy between children's level of performance on a task at a given point in time, and their potential level of performance on that task given appropriate instruction. This is quite different from Piaget's view that thinking is derived from the child's own actions because it places *the capacity to learn from instruction* at the heart of development, and implies that social and cognitive development are interdependent. Vygotsky's point of view has been investigated in numerous recent research studies on how children learn from their peers, as well as from their teachers and other instructors, and scaffolding and guided participation have been discussed in Chapter 2.

This leads to another theoretical divergence between Piaget and Vygotsky about the role of social relationships in children's learning. Piaget's view was that children's peer interactions represent negotiations between partners of equal status, and that because, in his view, children were 'egocentric' below the age of 7, the discussion and negotiation which leads to learning involves *conflict*, so that conflict forms the basis of collaborative learning. This is quite the opposite of Vygotsky's view, since the idea of the ZPD is that *co-operative* interaction is what leads to learning: learning arises from co-operation rather than conflict. Since a great deal of children's music-making is carried out with others, and in groups, these ideas have an important bearing on the explanation of musical development: we will return to the growing body of research on collaborative composition later in this chapter.

Rogoff (1990) pointed out another difference between Piaget's and Vygotsky's views of the relationship between social interaction and cognitive development, which concerns the nature of intersubjectivity. Piaget held that young children's egocentricity in the preoperational stage declined when they entered the concrete operational stage, and therefore became able to demonstrate reciprocity in their social relationships and to appreciate other people's points of view. For this reason, their ability to learn from cognitive conflict only took place around middle childhood. For Vygotsky, however, social interaction had a different function, namely the transfer of knowledge and skills from the more to the less experienced partner, such that it could result in learning at any age. It is also important to point out here that Vygotsky saw this transfer as being a fundamentally creative process, rather than as a re-learning of existing rules and facts. The teacher in this relationship was seen to take an active role in promoting guided social participation in the learner, such that creativity fundamentally occurred within a social community of thinkers.

Tharp and Gallimore (1991) also explored the nature of the teacher–learner relationship in Vygotsky's concept of the ZPD: in essence, the discrepancy between the child's unassisted and teacher-assisted performance on a given task is the basis of that individual's ZPD, and the overall level of that performance in relation to others is also related to the child's level of development. Vygotsky (1956) brought these two issues together in seeing good teaching as that which 'awakens and rouses to life those functions which are in the state of maturing, which lie in the zone of proximal development' (p. 278), and Tharp and Gallimore used this as the basis for their own definition of teaching, namely that 'Teaching consists in assisting performance through the ZPD. Teaching can be said to occur when assistance is offered at points in the ZPD at which performance requires assistance' (Tharp and Gallimore, 1991, p. 46). They went on from this to identify four different stages of the ZPD, in which there is a general shift from self- to social control.

In the first stage, in which 'performance is assisted by more capable others', children need to rely on adults in order to regulate their task performance, and the notion of scaffolding, discussed in Chapter 2, is an important aspect of this. In the second stage, 'where performance is assisted by the self', the child is able to carry out tasks without assistance from others, but this performance is still not fully developed or automatised. This can be seen in the use of self-directed speech, in which children direct their behaviour through their own speech. In the third stage, 'where performance is developed, automatised, and "fossilised"', task performance is smooth and integrated, and no external assistance is needed: however, Vygotsky also described it as being 'fossilized' in the sense of being fixed, rigid, and incapable of adaptation or change. This ability to adapt and change is finally acquired in the fourth stage, 'where de-automatization of performance leads to recursion back through the ZPD'. By this stage the child has the developed the flexibility to use a variety of resources including other-regulation, self-regulation, and also previously learnt automatised processes, in order to give solve a given new task.

Tharp and Gallimore's analysis puts some flesh on the bones of the notion of the zone of proximal development, explaining some of the processes which underlie it which show how it might operate in complex real-life social situations. The next development of Vygotsky's theory, which we discuss in the next section, achieves this same aim even more systematically.

Cultural-Historical Activity Theory

At the heart of Vygotsky's theory, as we saw in Chapter 2, is the idea that when people encounter an object in their environment, they interpret and act upon it through

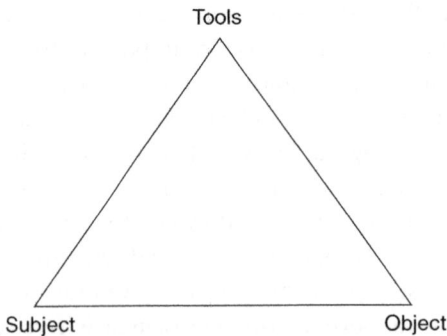

Figure 4.1.   Vygotsky's basic mediational model.
Source: Figure 6.1 (p. 323) in North, A. C., & Hargreaves, D. J. (2008), *The social and applied psychology of music*. © Oxford University Press. By permission of Oxford University Press.

the mediation of 'cultural tools', which can either be internal (e.g. the symbols which exist in systems such as language, concepts, or behavioural scripts) or external (e.g. books or computers). For example, a preschooler might use a tambourine or drum at her playgroup, and use it to beat out a regular rhythm for the other children to jump or dance to, and this could be the basis for the development of a symbolic system such as naming different types of jumps or dances: in this case, the tambourine is the 'cultural tool'. The idea of *tool mediation* is that we do not respond to the object directly, but by referring to the cultural norms that are involved in other people's use of those same tools: any further naming of jumps or dances in our example is very likely to be influenced by the other children's previous experiences and understanding of jumping or dancing games. This is Vygotsky's basic mediational model, which is shown in Figure 4.1, and it is considered by Engeström (2001) to be the first of three generations of research in what has become known as cultural-historical activity theory (CHAT). This is the most prominent current theoretical formulation of the social-cultural approach, and has been led by Yrjö Engeström and his associates in Helsinki (e.g. Engeström, 1987; Engeström & Miettinen, 1999).

The second generation of research went beyond individuals acting alone to the analysis of how they function in groups, and this important distinction was developed by one of Vygotsky's two main collaborators, Leont'ev (1981). Leont'ev's view that individual activities were located within 'collective practice' enabled him to develop the concept of 'distributed cognition'. This is the idea that individual learning is influenced by others in their collective activity, which could include the history of community-wide social and political relationships as well as the activity of the individuals actually present. In the example of our young tambourinist, the dancing and jumping games that she develops with her peers may also incorporate elements of nursery rhymes, folk songs, or songs/activities which they have seen and heard in the media.

The third generation of research on activity theory extended the analysis of how people talk to one another and interact in social groups of any size. In this expanded view of activity systems, it is the system as a whole, rather than the individual,

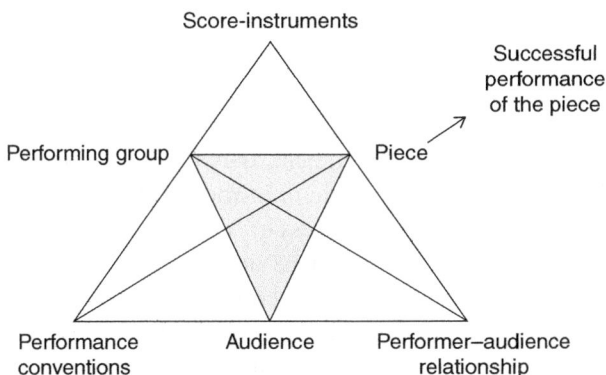

Figure 4.2.   Rehearsing a new piece as an activity system in CHAT.
Source: Figure 6.2 (p. 324) in North, A. C., & Hargreaves, D. J. (2008), *The social and applied psychology of music*. © Oxford University Press. By permission of Oxford University Press.

which forms the basic unit of analysis for understanding human learning and development. Children's musical learning, for example, should be considered within the context of the musical activities of the groups of which they are part, including their families, peer groups, school classes, community institutions, and national groups. Figure 4.2 shows Engeström's view of an activity system. The top triangle is Vygotsky's original, as in Figure 4.1, in which the *subject*(s) can be an individual or a group and the *object* is the intended learning outcome (i.e. the *objective*, rather than the actual object which is being studied). If we take the hypothetical example of a newly formed Western classical string quartet comprising students in a music conservatoire who are rehearsing a new piece for a concert performance, then the subject is the quartet itself, and the object is the piece of music to be performed. The object has an *outcome*, i.e. a successful performance of the piece, and as in Vygotsky's original model, the relationship between subject and object is mediated by the cultural tools involved (e.g. the score, the musical instruments).

Vygotsky's original model is represented by the top triangle in Engeström's model, the lower section of which adds three new components to it. The activity system is seen as part of a *community* of people who are also engaged in that activity: in our example, this could be the students' peers in the conservatory, the audience present at the concert performance, the radio audience for a broadcast of the performance, or even the wider community of musical performers and listeners, all of whom might have an interest in or a view about that particular performance. This community is regulated by certain *rules* – the norms and values which shape the activity, which may be explicit and formal or implicit and informal, such as the conventions regarding the performance itself (e.g. the piece is divided into three movements, which are divided by silent intervals), and the relationship with the audience (e.g. they should remain silent during the performance, and applaud only when it is finished). There is also a *division of labour* within the community: different tasks are undertaken by its different members (e.g. the performers, their tutors, and the audience all have distinctive roles to play).

In this view, the individual's learning can only be understood in the context of the activity system as a whole: and this learning results from the internal tensions and contradictions which occur within the activity system. Engeström explained this by introducing the notion of the 'expansive cycle': as novices begin to acquire competence and expertise in the domain of the object, they begin to internalise some of its elements: and when this occurs, they begin to introduce innovations and changes which lead to expansion outwards, by a process of 'creative externalisation'. In our example, the members of the quartet could be described as novices at their first rehearsal of the piece, even though they may be competent on their instruments. As they begin to rehearse, they learn not only the piece, but also something about each other's abilities, attitudes, and musical personalities. They gradually get to know the piece, and to adapt to each other's playing styles and idiosyncrasies: and after a while, they may work on their ways of playing together, and to introduce innovation and change ('expansion'). These changes occur in activity systems as a result of the opposition between internalisation and externalisation, and so the systems evolve.

Musical learning is an obvious domain in which these ideas could be applied, and we described Welch and Ockelford's (2016) attempt to do so in Chapter 2, drawing on four different examples of their own empirical research on music learning. Other than that, very few attempts have been made to explain music learning or collaborative composition in terms of activity theory, and this is an obvious area for further exploration.

Developmental Research across the Lifespan

Since social development starts at (if not before) birth, and continues right through to old age, and since engagement with music is a significant part of most people's lives at all ages, the task of describing people's social development with respect to music is a weighty undertaking. Lifespan developmental research, which was established at the end of the 1960s by Paul Baltes and Warner Schaie, has its own distinctive issues and methodologies, one of which is a commitment to contextual effects (see e.g. Baltes, 1987; Nesselroade & Baltes, 1974). A new approach in this area which claims to look at variations between individuals, as well as between cohorts and historical contexts, is that of life course research (e.g. Elder & Giele, 2009). This approach identifies 'four paradigmatic factors that affect the diverse ways the life course and human development are influenced: *historical and geographical location*, *social ties* to others, *human agency* in the construction of one's life course, and *variations in timing* of events and social roles. Each factor applies to the full life span, consistent with the principle of lifespan development – that human development and ageing are lifelong processes' (Elder & Giele, 2009, p. 9).

The first of these principles, which encapsulates the other three, could be rephrased as 'historical time and place', or cultural background: we have seen very clearly in previous chapters that the musical environment which surrounds individuals has changed remarkably quickly in recent years, and such that the musical experiences and attitudes which are salient for different historical cohorts are likely to lead in profoundly different developmental directions, given their powerful influence. The second principle is that of social ties to others, or social integration: and once again we have seen that the effect of family members, peers, and other influential figures in the child's immediate social environment have can have a profound influence on their musical development. Considering the nature of musical *identity* and its development, as we shall see in Chapter 6, introduces the third of Elder and Giele's life course principles, namely that of human agency, or individual goal orientation. It is very clear from the identity literature that one of the key determinants of musical development is the child's own view of that development, which is mediated by self-identity and self-esteem. Finally, the fourth principle of timing, i.e. the strategic adaptation to and the timing of key life events, such as learning an instrument, having a life-changing musical experience, or changing educational institutions, is influenced by individuals' ability to adapt to the events and situations that they experience at different times in life, and this can also exert a profound influence on musical development (see Chapter 5).

Although this area of study has made immense strides in recent decades, it is still a long way from being able to fulfil the criteria of lifespan or life course research for any kind of a consistent or even coherent explanation of individual musical development. The social and contextual factors which affect people's musical behaviour are so numerous and diverse, as indeed is the nature of musical behaviour, that it is difficult to work out what the limits of a lifespan developmental explanation of musical behaviour would constitute. We do have one or two leads elsewhere in this book: Trevarthen and Malloch's (2017) suggestion that their concept of communicative musicality might extend across the lifespan in different ways at different ages, for example, and our own developmental account of musical identity (Chapter 6) might provide possible ways of working towards conceptual unity, for example. But achieving these ideals will have to be left to future scholars, and we will restrict ourselves here to looking at those aspects of social development in music which are salient at each of the main periods of the lifespan.

Infancy and Early Childhood

In newborn babies' first few days of life, they show spontaneous vocal behaviour, including crying and babbling, which gradually comes under greater control as the infants start to produce sounds of their own: they do this partly for the simple pleasure of practising the sensori-motor activity of vocalisation, but also because of the effects that those sounds have on other people, notably their caregivers. Initially, they signal discomfort, hunger, or pain by crying or screaming, and make other sounds such as gurgling, and babbling to signify pleasure, and these sounds gradually become more diverse and varied. Very early on, newborns are sensitive to adults' reactions to their sounds: the 'other' starts to be present to them and the foundations of the self–other relationship are laid. Infants begin to vocalise to attract adults' attention, or when the adult talking to them stops. If this situation occurs again several times, infants start to be involved in a 'conversation' (Boysson-Bardies, 1999).

Elsewhere, we cover how these interactions form the basis of later development in terms of understanding the main elements of music separately and in combination, looking at research that isolates and explores these elements experimentally as well as at evidence from more ecologically valid tasks such as singing and composing (Chapter 3). Our particular focus here is on how these interactions represent the beginnings of social interaction, and the study of musicality as a social phenomenon. One of the most obvious manifestations of this is the way in which music is central to many aspects of child care from early infancy onwards in most parts of the world. The vast majority of Western mothers report singing to their infants, for example: Street, Young, Tafuri, and Ilari (2003) found that everyone in their sample of 100 mothers sang to their infants at one time or another. They also identified one of the main purposes of singing as being early communication: for example, one mother explained that 'I sing to my baby at home because … it makes him smile … it's easier than finding things to say and I don't like to not communicate with him' (Street et al., 2003, p. 628). Other early musical interactions between caregiver and infant (or even between infants), such as co-ordinated rhythmic movements, take place in a highly intuitive way, and seem to stem from the powerful positive affect that joint interaction and attention provides (see e.g. Bradley, 2009; Zentner & Eerola, 2010). As Bannan and Woodward point out, 'children acquire musical culture as naturally as they learn to walk and talk' (2009, p. 467), and they are constantly learning from others.

In a recent special issue of *Research Studies in Music Education* which is devoted to early childhood music education, Young (2016) offers a thoughtful commentary upon the state of play in this field, drawing attention to two major paradigm shifts in recent years. The first is a transformation of the earlier behaviouristic view of an 'incompetent' infant as a 'blank slate' who passively responds to her environment, to one of a competent person who is skilful, competent, and actively responsive to her environment: and the second is a corresponding move away from the formulation of universal or normative models of musical development towards an emphasis on the individual social and cultural contexts of this development. Like ourselves, Young also draws attention to the increasing influence of digital technology on young children's musical lives, as well as to the increasing importance of the application of research findings e.g. in designing pedagogical interventions. A more detailed formulation of the second of Young's paradigm shifts appears in a paper by Ilari (2016) in the same special issue, which proposes that there exist three basic 'building blocks' of social cognition in early childhood, namely *social referencing* (how humans reference their own behaviour in relation to that of others): *joint attention*, in which individual intentionality becomes shared with others in collaborative interactions: and *joint action*, which Ilari defines as 'social interactions in which two or more individuals coordinate their actions in time and space' (p. 27).

Probably the most influential theoretical account of how social development occurs in musical activities is Trevarthen and Malloch's (2017) view of the development of communicative musicality. This characterises the ways in which child and caregiver interact together in an essentially musical fashion, implying intersubjective communication as well as precise synchronisation of activity, and gives rise to the construction of cultural meaning between them. Soon after birth, they see babies as engaging in time and in tune with skillful intention and feelings of another human being, intimately sharing movement. The way infants participate in the rituals of action songs with age-related changes as the body and brain grow has made it clear that their play with someone they love is constructive of a cultural social awareness (Trevarthen, 2012). 'This is the essential process of "attunement" by which affective relations or "attachments" are established and nurtured in living with emotions in musical time – a musical "companionship" of selves within which language and other cultural skills may be learned' (Trevarthen & Malloch, 2017, p. 159).

Trevarthen and Malloch (2017) have developed their view of communicative musicality beyond the arena of parent–infant interaction in order to describe the development of musical identity across the whole life span, speaking of 'communicative musicality as the human way of life' (p. 169). They suggest that the traditional idea of an 'inner self' as only being accessible to the person experiencing it is being broadened in recent neuroscientific research to incorporate the idea that the emotions and identities involved actually take place *between* people: this occurs in research which focuses on the concept of mirror neurons, those cells which appear to 'mirror' intentions in the movements of other individuals (see e.g. Goswami, 2008; Chapter 2).

Starting with this view of the infant as an innately social creature, Trevarthen and Malloch extend their view of communicative musicality to include the whole of human identity and development, with music as the communication system which mediates this, and they go on to plot the course of communicative musicality across the life span, as we describe in more detail in Chapter 6. Another important aspect of their view, like that of Elliott and Silverman (2017), is that an integral feature of this social-musical development should be an ethical and moral dimension, as in Aristotle's view of eudaimonia and wellbeing: they suggest that infants have 'uniquely human talents to make or detect the *aesthetic* value of melodic stories, and *moral* feelings of the relationship, both of which may be sustained with a respectful and sympathetic Other in expressive body movements and song' (Trevarthen and Malloch, 2017, p. 158). It is interesting to note in this respect that parents and educators in Eastern countries such as Korea, Japan, and China, which have a foundation in Confucian philosophy, place much more emphasis on the moral and spiritual value of the arts than do their Western counterparts. Their primary aim is to develop the character of children and to lay the foundations for a 'virtuous and joyful life', whereas our aims in the West tend to focus more on achievement and competition.

Looking at early social behaviour with music, the *inCanto* project was a six-year longitudinal study of the developing musical behaviour of infants which was carried out in Italy by Johannella Tafuri (e.g. Tafuri, 2008). Tafuri noted those studies (e.g. Parncutt, 2016b) which have shown that the foetus hears and reacts to sounds present in the external environment and in the womb, including the mother's heartbeat and external regular sounds: the reactions are shown by variations in heart rate as well as by different movements in the eyelids, the head, limbs, and the trunk, for example. There is then a diversity of responses to sounds and music at birth, as we saw in Chapter 3, and Tafuri collected some detailed information about these from her study of 119 pregnant mothers. Some of these, effectively an experimental group, attended weekly meetings with the researchers during pregnancy and after birth in which they were invited to sing together and invent songs, to dance and listen to music, and to play percussion instruments along with music. They were also encouraged to conduct similar musical activities at home as part of everyday family life, and to record any sung dialogues with their babies, as well as to complete diaries with questions prepared by the researchers.

Tafuri compared the developing behaviour of this group with a comparable (control) group of infants who did not receive the extra musical instruction, and found that those in the music group were more likely to sing in tune, that they were more likely to develop certain musical skills earlier than those who did not receive the instruction, and that their vocalisations were generally more complex. Some of the music group's mothers also took up the researchers' suggestion of choosing a special song and singing it daily, especially in the last month of pregnancy. Tafuri's video recordings of thirteen of these children as newborns showed that all of them reacted to it: five of them opened their eyes wide and gazed attentively, four moved their eyes from side to side, and the others turned their head towards the source of the music. Tafuri concluded that singing these familiar songs as well as others was very effective in calming down children when they were restless or crying, some of them even falling asleep at that point. The diary studies show that as time progressed, mothers increased the diversity of their singing songs and games with different gestures and movements like clapping hands, jumping, and dancing. From 6 months to 1 year or so, many of the mothers played singing games which included very clear interactions with babies, especially physically – including rocking, bouncing, clapping hands, and dancing, and this was always associated with pleasure.

Tafuri goes on to describe the ways in which musical babbling and singing develop, as well as playing instruments. This was also investigated in the *Nido sonoro* project, in which Delalande (2009) explored the musical dimensions of the first sounds produced by children through the exploration of objects/instruments, and tried to establish whether this exploration and organisation of sounds could be considered as an embryonic form of creative music-making. Our main focus here, however, is on how music is an integral part of the developing network of the infant's social relationships, and this is a prime function of *musical play*. It has become a commonplace in early childhood education to say that children learn through play, and many psychological theories have been advanced to explain how this might work in different aspects of behaviour such as cognition, emotion, and social development (see e.g. Sutton-Smith, 1997). Play can be defined in many different ways, and we follow Marsh and Young (2016), who deal specifically with musical play, in suggesting that play is activity that children initiate for themselves and in which they choose to participate voluntarily, often with others. This kind of activity is enjoyable, intrinsically motivated, and under the control of the players: it is generally free of externally imposed rules, but could nevertheless involve rules developed by the players.

Marsh and Young provide a review of different forms of musical play at different ages: preschool musical play, for example, is characterised by spontaneous vocalisations and by two distinctly different kinds of singing – one repetitive, chant-like singing of short phases and ideas, which Sundin (1998) suggested tends to be produced in groups, and another more free-floating, personal and 'improvisatory' singing which can include the child's own take on different familiar elements, and which Sundin suggested are more likely to be solo performances. Preschoolers also engage in play with instruments and movement play, and Marsh and Young point out that musical play has three important characteristics. The first is *multimodality*: singing brings together physical movements and making sound with objects or instruments – it is therefore visual and kinaesthetic as well as aural. Second, musical play is *spontaneous*: it is typically made upon the spot, and although it might include elements drawn from oral traditions, it is nevertheless unplanned. Third, musical play is essentially *social*, which is our main focus here: through it, children form relationships with other children, and learn to follow social rules such as turn-taking, and to develop friendships.

Interestingly, Marsh and Young's characterisation of children's musical play is very similar to the features of improvisation as set out by MacDonald, Wilson, and Miell (2012). In their chapter on 'Improvisation as a creative process within contemporary music', they cite four key features of improvisation: it is *creative*, *spontaneous*, *social*, and *accessible*. Two of these terms are identical to those in our description of children's musical play, and it is self-evident that musical play is accessible to all children, requiring no special training or expertise. MacDonald et al.'s first contention, that improvisation is essentially creative, is also a characteristic that has been attributed to children's musical play, and we shall return to this shortly.

Middle and Later Childhood

As children get older and enter school, their play becomes more stylised and is increasingly drawn from the oral traditions of the culture such as in singing games, dance routines, or sports/games activities. Their play includes games involving handclapping, skipping, counting, and ball-bouncing, and takes place in more 'rule-based' social formations. Spontaneous play thus becomes more socially organised, and play with adults is also used in the development of learning. Young (2005) pursued the developing complexity of the musical communication between children and adults as the former get older, conducting a detailed analysis of a video-recording of a long musical dialogue between an adult community musician and a 4-year-old played on wooden pipes. Her description of the background to this session, and of the way in which it developed over time, enabled her to show how the processes of *imitation*, *elaboration*, and *organisation* were all observable in this episode of shared musical play, and that the adult was able to combine the roles of pedagogue and of play partner within it.

Young (2012) has also more recently undertaken an international study of music in the home among 7-year-olds, which showed a wide variety of musical activities (see also Ilari & Young, 2016). These now include not only musical toys and instruments but also video games, and activities based on radio, CD players, and digital internet-based players. As we suggested in Chapter 2, the rapid recent advances of digital technology have had an immense impact on musical engagement in general, and this applies just as much, if not more so, to the activities of young children. Marsh and Young (2016) have also described some of the structural characteristics of the musical play of middle childhood, commenting on its complex rhythmic properties, and its use of elements like syncopation, and the use of repeated ostinati. They also review studies of musical play in countries including Norway, Russia, Japan, Sweden, the USA, Australia, Ghana, and South Africa, among others, including some ethnomusicological studies which clearly demonstrate that the characteristics of musical play are subject to specific influences within given cultures.

Musical Creativity and Peer Collaboration

The capacity to adapt to new situations and to produce new innovations in ever-changing conditions is fundamental to our existence. At the same time, creativity is associated with the arts in many people's minds: acknowledged artistic geniuses such as Mozart, Dylan Thomas, or Van Gogh all displayed extremely high levels of creativity. There is an inherent difficulty in trying to define creativity, because its essence is to go beyond the bounds of what is already given. Plato put it like this: 'How will you set about looking for that thing, the nature of which is totally unknown to you? Which among the things you do not know is the one you propose to look for? And if by chance you should stumble upon it, how will you know that it is indeed that thing, since you are in ignorance of it?' (Merleau-Ponty, 1962, p. 371). It seems to follow from this that definitions of creativity should be context-specific: to refer to specific problems, in specific situations, and in specific social and cultural contexts. This firmly identifies creativity as a social phenomenon which can only be understood in context.

We commented earlier on MacDonald et al.'s (2012) view that musical improvisation is creative and also essentially social, and the link between creativity and social collaboration has been pursued in a substantial amount of psychological research. A good deal of musical composition work in primary schools is currently done in small groups, such that peer collaboration is a central determinant of compositional creativity within it. Music educators are increasingly concerned with fostering the creative processes involved in musical performance and composition, and collaborative creativity has emerged as a distinctive field of study its own right: not only in music, but also in other fields including online student project work, business teams, and children's collaborative writing (see Miell & Littleton, 2004).

The social nature of creativity in music has been emphasised by many researchers over the past few years. Miell, Littleton, and Rojas-Drummond (2008) argued that to take 'a view of creativity in general, and of music making in particular, as fundamentally and necessarily social, and in many cases as an explicitly collaborative endeavour … can bring new and important insights to our understanding of both the processes and outcomes of creative activities' (p. 1). This social agenda means that it is important to consider the cultural and interpersonal contexts of creative music-making even though this activity, by definition, is inevitably unconstrained and unpredictable. Sawyer (2008) outlines a general model of group creativity which is derived from the sociocultural tradition, and which draws on the notion of scaffolding, both described in Chapter 2. When children are first performing music in a group, the teacher must provide them with appropriate levels of structure, and different levels are appropriate for different age groups and levels of skill. Each child adopts the collective practice at his or her own pace, and effective scaffolds enable them to make easier transitions from peripheral participation to playing a more central role (Lave & Wenger, 1991). Effective scaffolding activities allow all learners to engage meaningfully regardless of their level, and are structured so that successive levels of participation involve them in increasing appropriation, mastery, and central participation.

Sawyer (2003) had also previously proposed that group creativity, as seen in particular in improvisation, has five distinct characteristics, namely *process*, *unpredictability*, *intersubjectivity*, *complex communication*, and *emergence*. This has a good deal in common with MacDonald et al.'s (2012) description of improvisation as described previously, namely that it is creative, spontaneous, social, and accessible, but it also has some of its own distinctive features. By *process*, for example, Sawyer is referring to the idea that creativity is displayed in the process of interaction rather than necessarily in its *product*. *Unpredictability* can more or less be equated with spontaneity, and *intersubjectivity* and *complex communication* are both features of the social aspects of creative improvisation; the meaning of an improvisation, whether in theatre or in music, is constantly negotiated and renegotiated from moment to moment during its course. Sawyer's use of the concept of *emergence* is based on the idea that the whole is greater than the sum of the parts: that in group creativity, the individual members of the group are performing at a higher level than they would have achieved if working by themselves. Group creativity is therefore seen as a complex dynamic system in which the behaviour of the system as a whole emerges from interactions among its individual parts: Sawyer has also used the term *collaborative emergence* to refer to the outcomes of small group improvisation.

Given the unpredictability of creative music-making, it is hardly surprising that many empirical studies in this field tend to be exploratory, typically involving detailed, naturalistic accounts of small samples of participants, and using qualitative, open-ended research methods rather than experimental interventions. For instance, Burnard and Younker (2008) reported some empirical data collection directed towards a specific attempt to apply a particular theoretical model, namely

Engeström's CHAT model (discussed earlier). They conducted a micro-analysis of the social and language processes involved in children's collaborative music-making in two settings: a group composing task with 10-year-olds in the USA, and a group arranging task with 13-year-olds in the UK. Their analysis involved coding the talk and action sequences which occurred in the groups, using Miell and MacDonald's (2000) scheme for the content analysis of children's talk and music-making in collaborative musical groups. This scheme, which builds on the work of Berkowitz and Kruger, is based on the distinction between *transactive* communications, which involve interpersonal dialogue and mutual decision-making, and *non-transactive* ones, which do not.

The analysis of talk, a central tenet of Vygotsky's theory and the sociocultural approach, features strongly in research in collaboration and music-making with children. For instance, Miell and Littleton's (2008) conception of 'the band as a learning community' is based on their analysis of the talk during rehearsals of a band of five 15- to 16- year-olds, who regularly performed at school and other gigs. They demonstrate how the band members 'continually construct, negotiate and re-negotiate a shared understanding of the qualities of their sound – a kind of "musical common knowledge"' (p. 47), such that they develop their range of skills, as well as their sense of identity, through music. Littleton and Mercer (2012) followed this up in their study of three bands of musicians: the same group originally studied by Miell and Littleton, a group of three male adult musicians preparing to accompany the staging of a musical play, and a group of adult male and female musicians playing country/roots music. Littleton and Mercer also used sociocultural discourse analysis, in this case of field notes and audio recordings, to investigate the talk of these musicians in joint activity, with an interest in how they negotiated 'musical common knowledge', resolved disputes and conflicts, and how different influences emerging from the musicians were used and combined to produce a distinctive and unique sound.

Young's (2008) analysis of collaborative music-making play in preschoolers led her to the conclusion that their collaboration was largely carried out through non-verbal means – 'through gestures, direction of gaze and eye contact, facial expression, bodily movement, posture and body alignment in relation to one another' (p. 3) rather than by verbal means. She also argued that 'a tendency to import language-derived versions of collaboration as templates for understanding children's collaboration has obscured processes intrinsic to the act of making music' (p. 3). This may represent a divergence of opinion about the relative importance of verbal and non-verbal aspects of communication, or it may simply arise because preschoolers rely more on non-verbal aspects since their language is less well developed.

From a Vygotskian perspective, collaboration and learning can involve more capable others and also tools: some research has explored the role of technology in children's creative music-making. From a more individual perspective, Folkestad (see e.g. Folkestad, Lindström, & Hargreaves, 1997; Folkestad, Hargreaves, & Lindström, 1998) used a music software package which enabled 15- to 16-year-olds to compose pieces of music. Using the 'save as' command to explore the process of composition provided a step-by-step sequence of the compositional processes involved, which was supplemented with interviews and observations. Folkestad identified two main approaches to the compositional process. *Horizontal* strategies included creating the melodic, harmonic, and other structural aspects of the piece first, before elaborating and adding instrumentation. Conversely, *vertical* strategies involved creating the piece in sections with all the details added at once. Mellor (2008) similarly employed a computer-based music composition system, Dance eJay, with 13- to 15-year-old adolescents. She found her participants only used a vertical composing strategy (in part determined by the visual presentation of the software), but that within this homogeneity, creativity – defined as divergent thinking skills in response to challenge – in individual response was found.

From a more social perspective, Hewitt's (2008) study of 10- to 11- year-olds composing in pairs on the computer also drew on the distinction between transactive and non-transactive communication raised by Burnard and Younker (2008), showing that factors such as musical experience and friendship among the pairs apparently had no influence on the nature of transactive communications, even though an earlier study by Miell and MacDonald (2000) had found that transactive communications occurred more often among pairs of friends than non-friends in the musical and verbal interactions that occurred in collaborative compositions. There are many possible reasons why this divergence could have occurred, of course, including differences between the musical tasks, the ages and characteristics of the participants, and so on, which really serve to emphasise that research in this area is still at a very early stage. Gall and Breeze (2008) emphasised the role of the teachers in guiding and 'orchestrating' the process of collaboration in 10- to 11-year-olds who were using Dance eJay software. These studies suggest that technology may be a fruitful way of encouraging children and adults without formal music training to engage in creative acts of composition.

Considering specific models of sociocultural development more closely, as discussed above Burnard and Younker (2008) used Engeström's CHAT model to analyse data sets drawn from two different projects which are based on a group composition task with 10- to 11-year-old pupils in a school in the USA, and a group arranging task with 12- to 13-year-olds in a British secondary school. They concluded that CHAT provides a useful framework for the analysis of peer collaboration in composition, but this can be challenged as the basic unit of analysis is the activity system, rather than the individual. As the individual's development and learning can only be understood in the context of the system as a whole, this implies that if children were put in different groups their learning might proceed in different directions (Hargreaves, 2008). Questions like this, and the relative emphasis that researchers place on cognitive, verbal, emotional, social, and indeed musical aspects of learning, mean that the jury must remain out on whether CHAT will provide adequate answers to the main issues of collaborative composition: for now, however, it seems to provide a promising start.

There are some obvious areas for further research in this field of study, including the development of the distinctions among musical, verbal, and non-verbal communication; the investigation of wider ranges of participant groups, and of individual difference factors within them; the investigation of a wider range of musical tasks, and of their structures and settings; and of the role of the teacher. In terms of research approaches it will be important eventually to develop more controlled, experimental studies using quantitative methods alongside these exploratory, qualitative ones.

There are also some important theoretical questions which remain to be explored and developed. Folkestad (2012) has pointed out that taking a broad view of the social and cultural context in musical composition, as in Engeström's CHAT model, leads to two distinct notions of peer or collective communication: the first is simply the *interpersonal* communication between the members of the working group working together at a given time, and the second is the notion of the *intrapersonal* or internal psychological dialogue between an individual composer and the collective experiences and knowledge base of previous composers, i.e. the canon of work within a particular genre, idiom, or style which goes back historically: Folkestad draws on this distinction, previously drawn by Wertsch (1997), in labelling this the 'double dimension of collectivity'. One excellent example of the latter, intrapsychological type of communication is to be found in the tradition of organ improvisation, the history and characteristics of which are traced in fascinating detail by Johansson (2012). Johansson describes the different styles and levels of creativity which are displayed in different types of organ improvisation, which vary the degree to which they depart from the written score.

Assessment of Creativity and Musicianship

What makes a piece of music creative, and how is it valued? In Chapter 3 we touched on the notions of eminence and analyses of the creative product, but assessment is a key issue which intertwines the individual with his or her social context: other people's judgements about one's own work are inherently social. Despite long-standing arguments about whether assessment is possible or desirable in the arts (e.g. Ross, 1986), assessment is a fact of life in twenty-first century educational settings, and children's own opinions of assessment may guide their involvement in creative endeavours in formal education (Lamont & Maton, 2008). The emphasis on assessment has increased in the UK as parents and other 'consumers' of education place increasing emphasis on the transparency of the 'service' they receive. Developments such as the National Curriculum in the UK involved the clear specification of attainment targets and objectives in teaching, as well as of the means by which these would be assessed. This means that in the arts, as for other curriculum subjects, assessment of progress has been seen as an integral part of teaching, and it has been argued that feedback from assessment benefits pupils as well as providing a yardstick for the effectiveness of teaching.

Educational assessments take place in two main ways. Firstly standardised testing is used to administer large-scale tests to all school pupils (such as Standardised Assessment Tests or SATs in the UK, and National Assessment of Educational Progress or NAEP state achievement tests in the USA). These are most commonly administered for core curriculum subjects like mathematics, literacy, and science. The graded examinations of the Associated Board of the Royal Schools of Music (ABRSM) and similar organisations, taken by many instrumentalists of all ages, can be seen as equivalents of standardised testing for instrumental performance.

The second type of testing is classroom assessment, and in the UK this is the only formal evaluation that occurs for music (in the USA, NAEP tests are only periodically conducted for arts subjects). With the introduction of the National Curriculum for Music in the early 1990s in England, a Qualifications and Curriculum Authority working group was set up, and as mentioned in the Preface both of us were part of this group in its formative years. We guided the QCA on aspects of assessment and helped shape a series of attainment targets which attempted to identify the levels of attainment expected from children at different ages in response to the curriculum materials. Teachers assessed their pupils on these outcomes (e.g. 'be able to hold a tune with others', 'express yourself confidently in original composition') to try to map progress, although the attainment targets have recently been dropped from the curriculum (along with the mandatory teaching of music education between 5 and 14, to make room for subjects perceived as more important). Nonetheless, creativity is at the heart of assessment in music and may even be one of the reasons its formal academic study is not very popular among schoolchildren (Lamont & Maton, 2010). The notion of teachers assessing their own pupils is one which also emerged from an initiative from Harvard's Project Zero research in the 1980s. *Project Spectrum* proposed methods of assessing children in their familiar classroom settings, including unobtrusive observations and recordings of semi-structured assessment activities which are interesting and attractive to the children, such as using Montessori bells to measure musical perception in preschoolers (Wexler-Sherman, Gardner, & Feldman, 1988).

Creativity can be defined and assessed in terms of what we might call the 4 Ps: person, product, process, and place. Trends in assessment have shifted between these over time, in particular as highlighted by Arts Propel from Project Zero (described later) in shifting the emphasis from the product to the process. In the next section we consider each of the key definitions of creativity and how they have been used in assessment.

A focus on the *person* being creative stems from Boden's (1994) definition that creativity is 'the ability to come up with ideas or artefacts that are new, surprising, and valuable'. Research has linked these to individual factors such as personality factors (including independence, non-conformity, and confidence – Kemp, 1996; MacKinnon, 1962; Roe, 1953) and cognitive style (chiefly convergent and divergent thinking). Convergent thinking involves the logical, deductive thinking skills needed to come up with the one correct answer to a problem such as 'what is the next number in the sequence 2, 4, 7, 11', whereas divergent thinking is concerned with the generation of many different solutions to an open-ended problem, such as 'how many uses can you think of for a melon?'. Creativity in the arts and sciences involves both convergent *and* divergent abilities. Musical composers and improvisers at all levels need to be able not only to generate new ideas, but also to display the skill and discipline which can translate these ideas into a coherent musical product.

As far as assessing the person is concerned, the development of tests of divergent thinking has included adaptations with musical content. These measures have quite a long history, with two early tests being developed in Germany by Vidor (1931) and Vater (1934), who asked their participants to perform tasks such as building tunes upon tapped rhythmic patterns, and other short-term improvisations. In the forerunner to this book, Hargreaves (1986a) summarised the details of three further tests of musical creativity, namely those devised by Vaughan (1977), Webster (1979), and Gorder (1980). Of these, by far the best known and most widely used today is Webster's (1994) *Measurement of Creative Thinking in Music* (MCTM), which is based on the *Torrance Tests of Creative Thinking* (Torrance, 1974), the most widely used standardised tests of creativity: this sees divergent thinking as comprising the four variables of fluency, flexibility, originality, and elaboration. In the MCTM, participants are asked to perform improvisations based on imaginative scenes, such as a rocket launching into space, and respond by using a foam ball on a keyboard, their voice on a microphone, or temple blocks. The resulting improvisations are recorded and scored for extensiveness, flexibility, originality, and syntax, as well as for overall musical creativity. While undoubtedly useful as a research tool, these tests are rarely used in educational settings.

Emphasis on the *product* of composition adopts a different approach in valuing the creative response to a problem. In studying teachers' assessments of children's creativity in the classroom, for example, Hargreaves, Galton, and Robinson (1996) investigated primary schoolchildren's work on classroom activities in writing, drawing, and music. The research discussed in Chapter 3 by Swanwick and Tillman (1986) and others is an assessment of the end products of composing, and this definition can be incorporated into assessments of creativity. The best known example of the assessment of creativity in context is Amabile's (1983) consensual assessment technique. This requires 'appropriate observers' to agree on the creativity of a product. In 1996, Amabile reported on 53 different studies using this technique for artistic domains including music, noting high levels of inter-rater reliability and construct validity. An example of this applied to music is Hickey's (2001) study of different expert judges' ratings of the creativity of eleven musical compositions produced by 9- and 10-year-old schoolchildren. Five groups of judges (music teachers, composers, theorists, 12-year-old children, and 7-year-old children) rated the same compositions, and the mean interjudge reliabilities within each group were as follows: composers – 0.04; music teachers – 0.64; music theorists – 0.73; 12-year-old children – 0.61; and 7-year-old children – 0.50. Significant correlations were also found between the music teachers and the music theorists, and between the two groups of children, and the composers' ratings had very weak or negative correlations with those of the other groups. These results suggest that those best suited to judging creativity are not necessarily professionals, but those who are closest to the students in creating the works, including teachers and peers. Webster and Hickey (1995) compared the reliability of consensual assessment approaches with those using more standardised, criterion-based scales for rating creativity in children's musical compositions, and found that consensual assessment was at least as reliable as criterion-based items. Hickey and Lipscomb (2006) have provided a useful review of different kinds of assessment of children's creative musical thinking.

The effects of teaching and input from more capable others on children's creativity in music have also been assessed using this product-based approach. For instance, Azzara (1993) was interested in the potential effects of using improvisation as part of a music curriculum designed for elementary school instrumental music students, and found that fifth-grade students who received training with an emphasis on improvisation performed at significantly higher achievement levels than students who received training without such emphasis. Koutsoupidou and Hargreaves (2009) carried out a quasi-experimental study of the effects of improvisation on the development of children's creative thinking in music. One group of 6-year-old children were given music lessons over a six-month period which included a variety of improvisatory activities through their voices, bodies, and musical instruments, while those in a matched control group had music lessons over the same period which were didactic and teacher-centred, and which did not include any improvisation. Webster's (1987, 1994) *Measure of Creative Thinking in Music* was administered before and after the six-month teaching programmes, and the results revealed that improvisation had a significant positive effect on the development of creative thinking on all four of the Webster subscales, namely musical flexibility, originality, and syntax.

One fairly recent study has suggested a new approach to the assessment of musical creativity which combines person-based and product-based approaches. Barbot and Lubart (2012)'s Musical Expression Test (MET) includes a systematic observational approach and a focus on musical exploratory behaviours and product-based assessment of musical pieces resulting from musical activities, involving a sound-production set and a computer-based recording system. Barbot and Lubart report a high level reliability and convergence between behavioural and product-based assessments, and claim this is particularly useful for people without musical training. They use this to present a typology of product-based 'creative styles', along with the behavioural correlates of these styles. This appears to be a novel and powerful new technique with a great deal of potential: it deserves further research attention and empirical testing in comparison with other person and product-based approaches.

Prioritising the *process* has been a recent turn in a great deal of music education, following Johnson-Laird's (1988b) definition of creativity as 'mental processes that lead to solutions, ideas, conceptualisations, artistic forms, theories or products that are unique and novel', and Robinson et al.'s (1999) focus on 'imaginative activity fashioned so as to produce outcomes that are both original and of value'. Considering the ways musicians work, there is a diversity in approach, as shown from introspective reports. Some composers, including Haydn, Schumann, and Mozart, seemed to be able to compose with relatively little effort, whereas Beethoven and Bach expended a great deal of toil and sweat on the details of successive revisions (see further Ghiselin, 1952). A distinction has been made between 'small c' and 'big C' creativity (see e.g. Gardner, 1993). The former refers to most people's 'everyday creativity' (Richards, 2010) which appears in daily life. Weisberg's (1993) case studies of well-known scientific discoveries and works of artistic creation suggest that the 'breakthroughs' that take place do not involve some kind of extraordinary thought process, but rather the repeated and persistent use of the methods by which ordinary people solve problems, such as reformulations, new interpretations of existing facts, and drawing on inspiration and ideas from other people or situations around them. Mozart's reports on his own composition also suggest that his new musical discoveries arose from extensions and elaborations of his ordinary thinking processes rather than from special or extraordinary thinking. In contrast, Creativity refers to the kinds of breakthrough which only occur in great thinkers such as Einstein, Picasso, or Stravinsky. Boden (1999) makes a similar distinction between what she calls P(sychological) creativity – e.g. the formulation of an idea that might be new to a particular person, but which many others may have had before, and H(istorical) creativity, which applies to ideas which are novel with respect to the whole of human history.

Another Project Zero piece of research, *Arts Propel*, with older secondary (high school) children, proposed including qualitative evaluations of children's creative abilities, and emphasised the importance of evaluating process and reflection as well as product (Gardner, 1989; Wolf, 1988a, 1988b). Byrne and colleagues (Byrne, MacDonald, & Carlton, 2003; MacDonald, Byrne, & Carlton, 2006) attempted to assess creativity in musical composition using the concept of flow, which is usually seen as an aspect of creative process. Csikszentmihalyi's (1990, 2002) theory of flow attempts to describe the optimal experience which is experienced by creative people when they are engaged in their favourite activity: its crucial elements are excitement, surprise, and the gradual transformation of the activity into one that becomes completely self-motivated, such that the creator's sense of time disappears, and an ideal balance is struck between skills and challenges. According to Csikszentmihalyi, the state of flow involves focused attention, ease of concentration, clear-cut feedback, control of the situation, intrinsic motivation, excitement, change in the perception of time and speed, and clear goals. Group compositions from 45 university students were rated on creativity and other standard criteria by the students themselves and 24 music education experts, and flow ratings were also included. A significant positive correlation was found between students' flow levels and the quality of their group compositions as measured by creativity ratings. Byrne et al. have suggested the notion of 'flow' may be able to provide a means of obtaining formative assessments of creativity, and Pachet (2006) has begun to explore this with children's computer-based compositions.

Finally, considering the *places* – contexts and environments – in which creativity takes place, and the explanation of the ways in which cultural, social, and situational contexts affect individual thinking is the main focus of the sociocultural approach we have been discussing in this chapter. This approach enables us to explain the broad effects of interpersonal and environmental influences on many aspects of creative and other behaviour, as well as the ways in which members of small groups interact with one another in collaborative creativity (see e.g. Miell & Littleton, 2004 discussed earlier in this chapter). There is a great deal of cultural diversity in the many possible manifestations of creativity (see Kaufman & Sternberg, 2006).

The effects of social and environmental factors on the development of musical creativity can also be explored (Burnard & Kuo, 2016). Odena and Welch (2009) proposed a generative model of teachers' thinking about musical creativity based on qualitative data from in-depth interviews with six music teachers from different backgrounds. These teachers mentioned two main categories of features of the pupils' environments which they felt would be important influences on their creativity: emotional environment (motivation, school culture, teachers' role, teaching methods, and time requirements) and physical environment (complaints and proposals for improvement, and classroom settings). The generative model that these authors propose seems to hinge on the interactions between the teachers' experiences, their perceptions of creativity, and their classroom teaching experiences, and these are seen as being in constant interaction and consequently as evolving continuously over time. These studies of environmental influences on musical creativity have not been used in its assessment as such, and indeed it would be difficult to imagine how this could possibly be done given that every individual's environment is unique. This does not mean, of course, that the findings of this research are not useful for teachers, parents, and indeed pupils themselves in trying to explain musical creativity.

Indirect evidence on assessing outputs in relation to context come from a range of studies in the USA and UK which show that after a steady increase in children's creativity in mid-childhood, it 'slumps' around age 9–10. This phenomenon was first identified by Torrance (1967) in his analysis of the figural and verbal divergent thinking test scores of groups of 6- to 11-year-olds in ten different cultures, and empirical confirmation in a British sample comes from our own research (Hargreaves, 1982). Slumps have also been found at the same age in more general aspects of behaviour such as school self-concept and school motivation, but not for general self-concept (Williams, 1976), suggesting that it is the context of school that is responsible for this change in creative output. The changing nature of the school environment was held to be responsible, as children were affected by the pressures to succeed, although in our own data from the early 1980s pressures on British schoolchildren were believed to be less intense. Changes in school structure do affect the ways in which children view themselves as capable of success in music, however, and the requirement to maintain high levels of creative individual output alongside high levels of technical skill and knowledge has been proposed as one reason why children may find academic study of music relatively unpopular in the later stages of formal education (Lamont & Maton, 2008).

Adolescence

One very long-standing idea about adolescence is that it is a time of 'crisis', which occurs as the individual discards the role of child and takes on that of the adult: that it can involve 'storm and stress', difficult and rebellious behaviour, extreme clothing styles, and arguments within the family. Although prominent theorists in this area (e.g. Coleman & Hagell, 2007; Coleman & Hendry, 1999) have played down this view, pointing out that many teenagers go through the transition into adolescence without any of these problems or difficulties, it still persists in a great deal of the literature. The clearest psychological explanation of it has been in terms of identity, in that the adolescent is seen to experience an 'identity crisis' which involves the exploration of several possible identities, and which is then resolved through the adoption of one of them. Another well-known finding from developmental research which has been apparent since the emergence of pop music as we now know it in the 1950s and 1960s is that listening to pop music is by far the most frequent leisure activity of teenagers, including sport (see e.g. Bjurström & Wennhall, 1991; North, Hargreaves, & O'Neill, 2000), such that pop music preferences have become critical aspects of their identities. Pop stars provide role models for many aspects of teenagers' lifestyles, including patterns of friendship, other leisure interests, clothing and hair styles, and many other aspects of their behaviour and attitudes. Simon Frith (1981) encapsulated this in his suggestion that music becomes a 'badge of identity' in adolescence.

One of the most prominent psychological explanations of the development of identity is Erikson's (1950, 1968) model of eight stages of psychosocial development, and Marcia's (1980) elaboration of the ways in which this can be applied to the issues of adolescent identity has become very well known: we deal with this in more detail in Chapter 6 and return to it in Chapter 8. In brief, Erikson proposed that adolescence and early adulthood were critical and key periods in the development of identity: many people experience an 'identity crisis' in adolescence in which they are neither child nor adult, but in an awkward transitional period which needs to be resolved. This process is mediated by *identification* with others: by *individuation*, in which we develop a stable individual identity across different contexts; and by *integration*, in which we organise our newly adopted characteristics into the new stable identity.

Marcia's (1980) extension of this model gave rise to the prediction that one of four possible outcomes can result from the extent to which the identity crisis is successfully resolved, namely *achievement*, in which a coherent identity is successfully achieved; *moratorium*, in which individuals are still trying to explore the possibilities for their own identities; *foreclosure*, which occurs in those who have adopted a particular adult identity but have not fully explored the possible alternatives: and *diffusion*, in those who have not successfully resolved the crisis. In Chapter 6 we will look in more detail at how Evans and McPherson (2017) draw on Marcia's ideas, as well as on Ryan and Deci's (2000) self-determination theory (SDT), in explaining the development of musical identity during adolescence, investigating the importance of different kinds of music learning in individuals' lives, and the extent to which they express commitment to life-long engagement with music.

Investigations of the role of music in adolescent identity have followed one of two distinct theoretical traditions: those of social identity theory, and of cultural psychology. We next consider each of these in turn.

Social Identity Theory

Perhaps the most sustained psychological attempt to study musical identity in adolescence was carried out by Mark Tarrant and colleagues (see e.g. Tarrant, North, & Hargreaves, 2002; Hargreaves, North, & Tarrant, 2016). This research was based on social identity theory (SIT – see e.g. Tajfel, 1978; Tajfel & Turner, 1986), which had its origins in research on inter-group relations. SIT proposes that people tend to categorise themselves as members of certain groups, which become 'ingroups' for them, and that this automatically excludes other people who are members of corresponding 'outgroups'. This categorisation provides a sense of self, or social identity, which serves to guide future behaviour. In particular, SIT predicts that group membership leads its members to discriminate in favour of ingroup and against outgroup members, and this was confirmed empirically in several well-known studies which involved distributing money between ingroup and outgroup members (e.g. Tajfel, Billig, Bundy, & Flament, 1971; Billig & Tajfel, 1973).

Tarrant et al.'s research investigated the extent to which teenage musical likes and dislikes could be used as the basis for in- and outgroup discriminations. Tarrant, Hargreaves, and North (2001), for example, found that adolescents believed that pupils at their own school (representing the ingroup) should like what they regarded as prestigious musical styles more than pupils at a different school (the outgroup), and also that pupils at their own school would like non-prestigious music less than would those at the different school. This confirmed North and Hargreaves's (1999) earlier finding that teenagers responded more positively to an individual when s/he was described as a fan of a prestigious (e.g. pop) rather than a non-prestigious (e.g. country) musical style. These studies show that musical preference can be used as the *basis* of discrimination in favour of an ingroup and against an outgroup, and also that it can form a *measure* of group discrimination, and Tarrant et al. (2002) proposed a formal statement of this relationship as follows:

1. through the affiliation of their peer groups with certain styles of music, adolescents associate those groups with the meta-information which such affiliation activates;
2. through intergroup comparison, this affiliation can be exaggerated or diminished according to the value connotation of that meta-information, and in response to social identity needs (p. 140).

Tarrant et al. (2001) also found that these discriminations were influenced by individuals' self-esteem: those with lower levels of self-esteem were more likely to believe that pupils at a different school should like non-prestigious music and that pupils at their own school should like prestigious music than were those with higher levels of self-esteem. It appeared that pupils used these estimates of in and outgroup musical preference as a way of gaining self-esteem. Furthermore, Tarrant et al. (2001) found that music preferences were more important in social identity processes than were other activities, such as in media interests and sport: adolescents relied mainly on statements about music in order to distinguish ingroups from outgroups, and this may reflect the reduction in 'open-earedness' which is seen to occur in late childhood and early adolescence (i.e. the ability to accept and listen to a wide range of musical styles, which we will cover in more detail in Chapter 7). This confirms the view that liking for specific styles of music in adolescence may form a key defining feature of social identity, and may enable the prediction of many other aspects of teenagers' values and attitudes (see also Rentfrow & Gosling, 2003).

One interesting potential outcome of the establishment of these group norms is that some members may violate the norms by deviating from accepted ingroup attitudes, and this has become known as the 'black sheep effect' (Marques, Yzerbyt, & Leyens, 1988). Research on this phenomenon has shown that the presence of a deviant group member can threaten the distinctiveness of a group, and that a common response is for the group to devalue the 'black sheep' (see e.g. Castano, Paladino, Coull, & Yzerbyt, 2002). When the black sheep's deviant behaviour can be attributed to factors outside of that individual's personal control, however (e.g. to a difficult social situation), that member's deviance can be overlooked.

Developmental research on the 'black sheep' effect may well have a useful contribution to make to the study of adolescent musical identity. Hargreaves et al. (2016) point out that although children as young as 4 or 5 years are found to hold consistent preferences for their own social groups (e.g. Bennett, Lyons, Sani, & Barrett, 1998; Nesdale, Maas, Griffiths, & Durkin, 2003), their ability to determine when a group norm has been violated does not seem to emerge until later in childhood, and this may enable us to explain the decline in 'open-earedness' which occurs at that time. As we saw earlier, younger children seem to be willing to listen to and accept a wider range of musical styles of music than do older ones (they are more 'open-eared'). This may be because specific musical styles have not yet acquired normative values within particular ingroups, or because the group members have not yet developed the ability to recognise when preference norms have been violated. In either case, 'black sheep' can only be identified when children become more sensitive to norm violation in later childhood, explaining the corresponding decline in 'open-earedness'.

Other research on young people's uses of music to express their group affiliations and values has shown that they recognise clear and distinct stereotypes about the fans of different types of music, which may be shared by people across different cultural contexts (e.g. Rentfrow, McDonald, & Oldmeadow, 2009). It seems clear that adolescents' expressions of their own music preferences and their views about the preferences of others enable them to derive psychological benefits from group memberships: and while these are usually positive, there are other contexts in which they can they can underlie negative feelings of group-based prejudice, such as in racial attitudes (see Rentfrow & Gosling, 2007; Reyna, Brandt, & Viki, 2009). Fortunately, this can also work in reverse: one line of research is beginning to show that the power of music can also be used in the construction of new social relationships, and to promote positive relations between different social groups (see further Chapter 7).

This line of research is based on the common ingroup identity model (Gaertner, Dovidio, Anastasio, Bachman, & Rust, 1993), which proposes that intergroup conflict can be reduced by encouraging members to re-think ingroup and outgroup membership in terms of an inclusive social identity: by changing their perceptions from 'us' and 'them' to 'we'. Bakagiannis and Tarrant (2006) assigned adolescent participants to social groups created for the purpose of the experiment (cf. Tajfel et al., 1971), and then led them to believe that two of the groups either had very similar or very different music preferences, while a third (control) group was not told anything about the groups' music preferences. When all the participants then rated each group on along a series of personality traits, those who believed that the groups had very similar music preferences were significantly less likely to perceive that the groups differed in their personality traits than did those who were not told anything about the groups' music preferences, which suggests that they came to view these two groups in terms of a new common social identity

This study seems to represent a promising new means of investigating whether music can be used to improve relationships between social groups by changing members' group-based perceptions, although the groups were of course artificially created in this study rather than based on real life. Having said this, we might mention the West-Eastern Divan Orchestra, which was formed by Daniel Barenboim in the late 1990s and which involves musicians from across Middle Eastern countries including Israel and Palestine. This is intended to help break down some of the cultural and political barriers at the heart of the Arab–Israel conflict, which has a long history of mutual distrust and hatred. Such initiatives are unlikely to be straightforward, and there is some research which shows that group members can sometimes react against interventions which promote the formation of a common ingroup identity (Crisp, Stone, & Hall, 2006): when they are strongly attached to their existing (subgroup) identities, such interventions can even make intergroup relations worse (Tarrant, Calitri, & Weston, 2012). Nevertheless, in reviewing this area, Hargreaves et al. (2016) conclude that 'we are greatly encouraged that researchers and practitioners are starting to acknowledge and explore music's potential in this regard' (p. 318).

There are also some ways in which membership of what North and Hargreaves (2008) call 'problem music subcultures' could be particularly helpful to vulnerable teenagers. We saw earlier that membership of ingroups could contribute to self-esteem, so that membership of a strong problem music subculture might allow its members to define themselves in terms of a positive collective identity: the existence of this identity outside the framework of 'normal' social acceptability may well serve to make it even more attractive and desirable, and to enhance self-esteem. This may explain why 'problem music' styles are associated with 'tribal' subcultures with members drawn from vulnerable backgrounds, as in the case of rap and hip-hop music, which is preoccupied with urban strife within the African-American community. North and Hargreaves (2008) point out that this 'could be interpreted in the light of SIT as a self-esteem boosting assertion of ingroup identity in reaction to the perceived threat to an undervalued social group from a white, conservative

outgroup that is believed to possess disproportionate economic and political clout'
(p. 222). We shall return to these issues in Chapter 8.

Cultural Psychology

In Chapter 2 we looked in some detail at the sociocultural approach within developmental psychology, which clearly has its origins in Vygotsky's theory, including some more recent concepts which have been introduced by theorists including Rogoff, Lave, and Wenger, and Engeström's development of CHAT. Another closely related field of study is that of cultural psychology, first introduced by Michael Cole (1996), which emphasises the ways in which the cultural environment has a direct and formative influence on the development of identity and behaviour. Cole starts by pointing out that most psychologists fail to establish the cross-cultural generality of their findings and principles before they consider them to be established, and that although cross-cultural research is being carried out, 'general psychology does not know what to make of a good deal of the data that cross-cultural psychologists produce because the research does not live up to the methodological requirements of the discipline' (p. 3). Cole argues that culture cannot be treated as a variable or an addition to existing approaches but rather that a whole new discipline of cultural psychology should be pursued, following Shweder's (1990) assertion that the mind is 'content-driven, domain-specific, and constructively stimulus-bound; and it cannot be extricated from the historically variable and culturally diverse intentional worlds in which it plays a co-constitutive part' (Shweder, 1990, p. 13).

The specific application of cultural psychology to the study of aspects of musical development and music education has become sufficiently distinctive to characterise this as a second theoretical approach which can stand alongside SIT. Although their approaches are distinctively different, they emphasise different aspects of social behaviour rather than opposing one another. SIT emerged from a strong tradition of European experimental social psychology and intergroup relations, partly as a result of the influence of Henri Tajfel, focusing on what makes people belong to different groups, and what effect their membership of those groups has upon them. Cultural psychology is more concerned with the explanation of human development, learning, communication, and social behaviour in terms of people's specific social and cultural environments: in doing so, it also draws on some of the traditions of sociology and anthropology. We next identify five features of this approach, and then discuss one recent and very promising attempt to apply it to the study of adolescent music preferences.

The first and main feature of cultural psychology, as indeed of the sociocultural approach, is that the social and cultural environment is considered to be an inescapable central foundation of individual thinking and behaviour to the extent that it shapes people's ways of thinking and the different concepts that they form: in discussing the sociocultural approach in earlier chapters we used the term situated cognition to encapsulate this idea. We also saw how the concepts of communities of practice and legitimate peripheral participation have been used to explain how children and adolescents become cultural apprentices, in that they learn by taking part in cultural activities alongside more experienced members of those communities. This is closely related to the ecological approach to development, discussed earlier in the book, looking in particular at Bronfenbrenner's (2001) well-known bioecological systems theory.

This leads to the second feature of the cultural psychological approach, which is its strong cross-cultural (in this case, ethnomusicological) tradition: it is very important to identify the specific features of individual musical cultures, and their effects on local musical behaviour and experience, all around the world. This aspect is apparent in Barrett's (2010) edited book, *A cultural psychology of music education*, which includes chapters on the learning of music and dance in Bali, musical play in playgrounds all over the world, the history of music listening in schools, performance and songwriting using technology, cultural diversity in musical performance, and the specific experiences of choral singers in cathedrals: there is a strong ethnomusicological emphasis in this collection.

The third, fourth, and fifth features of the cultural psychological approach as they apply to music are all related to individuals' *experiences* of music. O'Neill (2017) has drawn on Habermas's (1987) notion of 'life worlds', as well as on other phenomenological theories (e.g. Husserl, 1936/1970) in order to focus on young people's subjective experiences of *connectedness* in their everyday musical lives, suggesting that they inhabit what she calls 'learning ecologies' which are a combination of their 'life worlds' and the ecological systems which surround their musical activities. We will say more about her study in Chapter 5 but suggest, for now, that the third feature of the cultural psychological approach is its ability to specify the young person's level of connectedness, or engagement, with the surrounding musical world. Closely related to this is the fourth feature, common in sociological thinking, is that individuals display *agency* in dealing with their environments (see Chapter 2, and Westerlund, Partii, & Karlsen, 2017). Westerlund et al.'s analysis of the interactions and networks of relationships which exist within the school classroom suggests that 'the concept of agency refers to aspects related to one's perceived and actual ability to act in the world, and hence concerns matters such as self-esteem, experience purpose of life, ego strength, internal locus of control' (p. 495).

The fifth distinguishable feature of the approach of cultural psychology essentially concerns the means, or mechanisms, by which engagement and agency are expressed, and that is simply through talk. This emphasis on language originated with Vygotsky, who saw language as one of the most fundamental and central cultural tools that people use in forming social relationships, and which has developed in recent years into an extensive body of theory and research on communication, teaching and learning, and dialogic thinking which seems to have immense power as a practical tool in education, especially for children from disadvantaged groups (see e.g. Alexander, 2001, 2008; Flecha, 2000; Mercer, 2000). Psychologists, educators, and linguists have investigated the discourses through which children communicate with teachers inside and outside classrooms, and have identified distinctive patterns of dialogue which can convey underlying power relationships and other interpersonal negotiations. One specific way in which this has been applied to adolescent musical identity has been in research on how teenagers talk about pop music; MacKinlay and McVittie (2017) have investigated how young people talk about different genres and styles of pop music, thereby showing their identifications with different genres and styles, and maintaining social identity and self-esteem in the ways that we discussed in the previous section on SIT. This example confirms the point we made earlier that findings from SIT and cultural psychology, although having different starting points and overall aims, can nevertheless converge in other respects.

Having set out at the main features of the cultural psychological approach, we next consider Miranda, Blaise-Rochette, Vaugon, Osman, and Arias-Velanzuela's (2015) ambitious recent attempts '(1) to define, ground, and situate a new perspective towards a cultural-developmental psychology of music in adolescence; and (2) to offer a critical outlook on the slowly growing but fragmented literature that can pertain to culture, psychology, and music in adolescence' (p. 198). As argued earlier, it has been widely accepted for some time that the study of pop music in adolescents is very important not only because they spend so much time on it, but also because it plays an essential role in their identity formation. Miranda et al. nevertheless point out that not only is music psychology dominated by Western musical and sociocultural perspectives, but also that the study of cultural difference in music psychology is neglected almost to the same extent that music is neglected in research in cultural psychology, and this reflects Cole's (1996) view of psychological research more generally. Miranda et al. propose that a cultural-developmental psychology of music in adolescence should consider 'how the biopsychological development of adolescents can have reciprocal relationships with their musical behaviors, cognitions, emotions, motives, and functions within and across sociocultural contexts that can evolve during the course of the lifespan and across generations' (pp. 198–199).

Miranda and colleagues adopt a transactional model of cultural psychology based on the idea that 'culture consists of explicit and implicit patterns of historically derived and selected ideas and their embodiment in institutions, practices, and artifacts; cultural patterns may, on the one hand, be considered as products of action, and on the other as conditioning elements of further action' (from Adams & Markus, 2004, p. 341). This comprehensive and inclusive approach to the cultural perspectives includes both elements that are 'in the world', such as cultural products and objects, as well as those which are 'in the mind', such as aspects of identity and other internal cognitions. Miranda et al.'s conception also covers *emic* and *etic* perspectives, i.e. those which are culture-specific, or local, and those which are culture-comparative, or global, respectively, as well as taking a wide-ranging view of the evolution and fundamentals of music and its diverse uses and functions in different societies, as exemplified in ethnomusicological research.

Having established these fundamental features of their cultural-developmental approach to music in adolescence, these authors review what they consider to be the seven main areas of research in the field. The first are studies of music preferences, in which they consider the extent to which the main psychological dimensions underlying preferences (a) have been successfully identified, and (b) might apply within different cultures, questions which are fraught with problems of the definition and hybridisation of styles and genres. Second are studies of musical motivation and functions, in which they emphasise the paucity of genuinely cross-cultural studies; third and fourth are studies of dance, which are often integrally related with music in different societies (see Gregory, 1997), and those of language and music, which includes the social aspects of song lyrics which are part of youth culture, as shown by their appearance in the current pop media and video. This leads on, fifth, to studies of the use of social networking and multitasking, which are becoming an essential feature of the ways in which many young people listen to music; and sixth, to studies of ethnicity and cultural diversity, which are important in the lives of many present day adolescents, especially those with disturbed or hybrid identities (see Chapter 6, and Miranda & Claes, 2008). Seventh, and finally, are studies of music-based interventions, which can include psychotherapeutic treatments, and social inclusion projects which are based on pop music programs designed for adolescent immigrants.

There can be little doubt of the importance of research in these areas, given the immense power of music on adolescent development (see further Chapter 8), and Miranda et al. are right to point out the surprisingly low level of cultural diversity in the research that has been carried out to date, and to stress the importance of addressing this in future research. As a more general point, in spite of the phenomenal increase in research in music psychology as a whole in recent years, the extent to which the musical materials used in many empirical studies are representative of the wide range of the world's musics is woefully inadequate, and Miranda and his colleagues have performed a valuable service in pointing this out.

Adulthood and Later Life

We have seen in the earlier sections of this chapter that distinctive aspects of social development in music can be identified in infancy, in later childhood, and in adolescence: in fact it is arguable that musical developments in infancy and in adolescence are critical aspects of development as a whole. In adulthood and later life, however, which covers a much wider age span, it is much more difficult to identify specific social phenomena that are defined by music. Although this age range is arbitrarily defined, it could be seen as lasting from say 18 to 85 years, with the upper limit continually increasing as medical science advances, such that older and older people are able to participate in work, leisure and other activities just as effectively as the young. The difficulty is compounded by a far greater range and diversity of musical activities, ranging from the lives of full-time professional musicians, through highly skilled 'semi-professionals' whose main focus may be in other professions and areas of work, through varying levels of amateur musicians, whose levels of skill and expertise may match that of professionals in some cases, to those who identify themselves as 'non-musicians', even though this can sometimes hide musical expertise, as Alexandra's (Lamont, 2002) research has shown.

There is an interesting parallel with sport here in that music and sport are both very wide-ranging sets of activities that can be enjoyed at many different levels of expertise, and at all age levels. At the higher levels they can both form the basis of competition at local, national, and international levels, such that top level and elite exponents can earn vast sums of money relatively early in life: this applies to professional footballers in the UK, for example, as well as to eminent conductors and instrumental soloists. At lower levels, both sporting and musical activities involve social interaction and identity formation of many different kinds in groups and communities, which can also exist at local, national, and international levels. Many long-term personal friendships are based in early bonds formed through musical groups or sporting teams that originated in childhood activities.

One way of trying to make sense of adults' social development in music is in terms of the concept of musical identity, with which we shall deal in depth in Chapter 6. We argue that there is little doubt that the ways in which people see their own musical activities, which is one definition of musical identity, are a powerful influence on the actual development of those activities: this is true in children, and lifespan developments have also been investigated (see Lamont, 2017). It is not yet possible to chart anything like a coherent lifespan pattern for the adult years however, partly for the aforementioned reasons, and also partly because very little research has been done on adults in relation to the volume of research on the first 18 years.

Furthermore, we shall also see in Chapter 6 that Rickard and Chin (2017) have suggested that the definition of 'musician' needs to be broadened considerably: that in today's digital age it is possible to conceive of musicianship in terms of the perception as well as of the production of music, and that it is possible to be a 'musician' without necessarily needing to have undertaken many years of rigorous instrumental practice. Is also undoubtedly the case that diversity of genres in which musicians now work gives rise to many different learning and professional practices: popular and folk musicians are likely to learn aurally, for example, whereas jazz and classical musicians are more likely to need to learn notation and sight reading as well as needing aural skills (for a review of contemporary practice which takes this diversity on board, see Stakelum, 2013).

Having said this, it is useful to refer back to Hargreaves, Miell, and MacDonald's (2002) distinction between 'identities in music' (IIM) and 'music in identities' (MII). As far as the former are concerned there are some specific areas of research on adults and IIM, and we shall mention two of them in this section. Our main aim in this chapter, however, is in looking at MII as part of music and social development, and we are suggesting that the range of possible activities which might fall under this label is very much broader, and therefore more difficult to pin down. The two broad areas of research within IIM are those on the lives and activities of professional and other expert musicians, and on the study of people in music-related professions, and in particular in music education.

First, research on musicians and musicianship is now well established: one sign of this is that while nearly all of the major music conservatories in the UK showed little interest in activities outside instrumental performance until the past twenty years or so, every single one of them now has a research department and employs staff who research and promote the learning, teaching, and performance of music, often from a psychological point of view. One excellent example is the Centre for Performance Science at the Royal College of Music in London, which specialises in research on performance, and whose director has edited one of the key textbooks in the field (Williamon, 2004). This has become an international field of study, and other notable texts in the field include those by Hallam (1998), Parncutt and McPherson (2002), and Lehmann, Sloboda, and Woody (2007). The coverage of these books includes, to give a few examples, the acquisition of high-level musical skill and expertise (Eriksson, Krampe, and Tesch-Romer, 1993); the role of practice (Jørgensen & Lehmann, 1997); body movement and expressiveness (Clarke, 2004; Davidson, 2004); sight reading (Sloboda, 1985); performance anxiety (Kenny, 2011); musical memory (Chaffin, Imreh, & Crawford, 2002); and improvisation and composition (Hargreaves, MacDonald, & Miell, 2012).

The second area of 'research on IIM' is in music education, which is of course well established and has a long history, and we cover research in music education with children and adolescents in various chapters of this book. When it comes to adults, however, we can identify the field of higher music education as one which is currently receiving more research attention than it has done for some time: Gaunt and Westerlund (2013), for example, recently published an edited volume on *Collaborative learning in higher music education* which in some ways runs parallel to the work on peer collaboration and musical creativity in childhood and adolescence which we reported earlier in this chapter. They point out that higher music education has traditionally seen teaching and learning in terms of the one-way transmission of knowledge from the 'master' (teacher) to the apprentice, such that the concepts of collaborative learning which have been found to be so powerful in other areas of education have been neglected. Their book attempts to rectify this imbalance by providing case studies examples of activities including peer learning, co-teaching, self-directed learning, new approaches to assessment, informal learning, and other forms of innovative practice in higher music education.

There is also a growing body of research on the education and working lives of school music teachers, important 'more capable others' in children's musical development, and an important focus of this has been upon their identities, which has taken two forms: first, on their self-perceptions as musicians and/or teachers, and second, on the inter-relationships between their musical identities and those of their pupils. We shall see in Chapters 5 and 6 that one of the key issues in British music education in recent years has concerned the *authenticity* of secondary school music: many secondary school music teachers have been and still are trained in the Western classical tradition, and may be relatively inexperienced in other genres, as was shown in a study by York (2000). In the Teacher Identities in Music Education (TIME) project (see e.g. Hargreaves, Purves, Welch, & Marshall, 2007), we investigated how student music teachers' identities as musicians and/or as teachers changed over the course of their training, and suggested that the interaction between these and the musical identities of their pupils was an important factor in this authenticity. Westerlund et al. (2017) adopt a similar point of view in their focus on *agency* in identity formation, which they see as 'one's perceived and actual ability to act in the world', which involves self-esteem and intrinsic motivation. They also suggest that a simple transmission model in which teachers pass on knowledge to their pupils is inadequate, because the social networks and inter-relationships that exist outside classrooms are just as if not more important in explaining the effectiveness of music lessons: they also feel that what they call 'the perceived hegemony of Western classical music' can intensify pupils' views of the inauthenticity of secondary school music education. We shall return to these issues in Chapter 5, and consider in particular whether the introduction of informal teaching methods, as proposed by Lucy Green (2008), might provide at least one viable solution.

Conclusion

The first half of this chapter has reviewed the field of music sociology, which has a much longer history than that of the psychology of musical development: broadly speaking it has dealt with questions of the production of musical culture and its relationship with social institutions. The well-known early work of Theodor Adorno and Pierre Bourdieu has been followed more recently by equally well-known work by contemporary sociologists, notably Simon Frith and Tia DeNora. One central issue is the relative amount of emphasis that should be placed on social and cultural as compared with psychological and individual factors in musical behaviour, and this is encapsulated in the recent discussion concerning 'univorous' and 'omnivorous' musical tastes and their respective origins. One possible solution to this this apparent dichotomy is to adopt a socio-cultural approach, to which we have referred in various parts of this book, and which has distinguished antecedents in the work of Vygotsky and subsequent theorists including Rogoff, Lave & Wenger, and Engeström. We have set out some of the ways in which this might approach might be applied to the study of musical development.

The second half of the chapter consists of a review of the social aspects of musical development across the lifespan, including infancy and early childhood, middle and later childhood, adolescence, and adulthood and later life. Because it is impossible to separate the age-related changes that occur in the cognitive determinants of musical behaviour from the social influences upon them, there is overlap between this review and some of the research reviewed in Chapter 3, in particular in the areas of singing, social and collaborative musical games, and peer collaboration and creativity. The period of adolescence turns out to be a critical arena for debate about social and cultural influences on musical development and several theoretical strands can be distinguished. Two of the main influences within this are social identity theory, which derives from the social psychological work of Henri Tajfel and his associates, and that of cultural psychology, whose main features we have identified. One recent attempt 'to define, ground, and situate a new perspective towards a cultural developmental psychology of music in adolescence' has been made by Miranda et al. (2015), and this typifies some of the central theoretical questions in this area. The concept of identity, and more specifically musical identity, is one which is useful in various contexts, and we shall devote the whole of Chapter 6 to its investigation.

5 Environmental Influences on Ability, Achievement, and Motivation

In the earlier chapters of this book, we have laid strong emphasis on social and environmental influences on musical development from various points of view. We have covered sociocultural approaches, which try to specify the mechanisms by which the social environment influences the developing individual; sociological approaches, which deal with the ways in which broader societal structures exert their effects upon the individual; and ecological approaches, which try to specify the different types and levels of environmental influence which are involved. The latter also includes cultural psychology, which we discussed in Chapter 4, and which focuses on the specific features of different musical cultures across the world, and the ways in which these exert differential effects.

In this chapter we look specifically at those factors which constitute 'environmental influences', and at research which has tried to demonstrate their effects on musical development. The focus of this has broadly been upon how specific environmental influences such as peers, the family, and schools, affect young people's motivation to engage in musical activity, and their developing abilities, as well as the musical achievements that might result. Some of this research deals with *normative* musical development, i.e. that which occurs naturally through simply growing up in a particular culture, but there is also a substantial body of research which deals with specialist or *expert* musical development. This involves the backgrounds and life histories of those who eventually become musicians, either as amateurs or professionals.

We look first at some of the conceptual issues which surround the question of developing musical ability, and what is sometimes called 'musicality': is it the case that 'everyone is musical', or are some people more naturally 'gifted' than others? To what extent can people's levels of musicality be influenced by practice and training, and what is the role of motivation in promoting musical achievement? The answers to some of these questions are gradually being revealed by empirical research, and we focus in particular on two large-scale studies of the development of musicality: one British study which was carried out in the 1990s by a research team from the Universities of Keele and Exeter (see e.g. Sloboda, Davidson, Howe, & Moore, 1996) and an Australian longitudinal study, linked to the first, whose results have been brought together in the book *Music in Our Lives* (McPherson, Davidson, and Faulkner, 2012). These studies throw a great deal of light on the effects of specific environmental influences, and on the roles of family, schools, and peers in particular: we shall try to summarise the current state of knowledge about these influences, and ways in which they might exert their effects. We then go on to look in more detail at the complex question of the effects of music education on musical development, a question which has very clear and obvious practical implications.

Musical Ability and Its Development

What Is Musical Ability, and Can It Be Measured?

In the 1960s and 1970s, music psychology was dominated by psychometric and acoustic studies. Textbooks such as Lundin's (1967) *An Objective Psychology of Music* and Shuter-Dyson and Gabriel's (1968, 1981) *The Psychology of Musical Ability* illustrate this well, and this approach can probably be traced back to Seashore's (1938) *Psychology of Music*, which placed a strong emphasis on the measurement of acoustic abilities. Among Seashore's many chapters on 'Duration', 'Sonance', 'Volume', 'Violin', and 'Voice', for example, there are also chapters on 'Imagining in Music' and on 'Nature of Musical Feeling', for example, but these are also grounded in a strong emphasis on sensory and physical capacities rather than on psychological phenomena as we would understand them today.

Along with this approach came a strong interest in the development of tests of different musical capacities, and Shuter-Dyson and Gabriel's (1981) book gives a comprehensive account of all such tests up to the early 1980s. There are three main types: tests of *ability* (aptitude), which are designed to assess an individual's potential for skilled musical behaviour regardless of previous musical learning experience; tests of musical *achievement*, which are used to assess the individual's knowledge of or attainments in music such as performance skills, or knowledge of music theory or history; and tests of *attitudes* towards music, which include those concerned with people's interest in music, and with individuals' preferences. Susan Hallam (2016) has discussed the use of the term 'musicality', which is often used interchangeably with some of these other terms, although she points out that 'there are no universally agreed definitions of these terms. Meanings are socially constructed and reflect cultural, political, economic, and social factors pertaining in the time and place that they are adopted (Blacking, 1973)' (p. 67).

The development of these psychometric tests was associated with the rise of a field of psychology known as individual differences, or sometimes as differential psychology: this refers to the study of the ways in which large groups of people, who have certain specific characteristics, vary systematically in terms of their test scores in relation to other groups with different characteristics. In the field of music, the main individual difference factors which have been investigated are age, for which distinctive age-related patterns or trends in test scores can reliably be identified; gender, for which documented differences seem to depend on the extent to which the capacity in question is subject to social and cultural influences; musical training and experience, which unsurprisingly relates strongly and usually predictably to individuals' musical abilities; and personality, which received some research attention in the 1970s and which has seen a revival of interest in the last decade or so. Another individual difference factor which appeared in some of the early literature but which has now dropped out of favour is that of social class, in which interest has declined probably because of the difficulties of definition, and also because of changes in society which have rendered the concept less useful than hitherto (see Chapter 4).

Is Everyone Musical?

Although there can be little doubt that individual differences exist in musical talent and abilities, and that different people's musical development proceeds at different rates, it is nevertheless indisputable that all children have the potential to express themselves through music. Many scholars have suggested that 'we are all musical': that every human being has a biological and social guarantee of musicianship (see e.g. MacDonald, 2008; Welch, 2005). We have already seen in Chapter 2 from the work of Colwyn Trevarthen (e.g. Trevarthen, 2017) that the earliest communication between a parent and a child is essentially musical. The notion of communicative musicality encapsulates the principle that the cooing and babbling interplay that takes place between a parent and a child is a form of communication that has more in common with musical interaction than with spoken language, and the chains or patterns of interaction involve mutual constructions of meaning. In other words, music plays a vital role in the earliest and most important social relationships with adults.

Given this powerful evidence to suggest that 'we are all musical' to differing degrees, as well as widespread anthropological and ethnomusicological evidence that young children communicate via music in many different cultures (e.g. Nettl, 2012), it is rather surprising to find that many people regard themselves as 'unmusical', or as being 'tone-deaf'. Some may attribute this to not having been raised as part of a 'musical family': received wisdom, or what Sloboda, Davidson, and Howe (1994) call 'folk psychology', tends to suggest that in order to develop advanced musical skills, individuals' genetic inheritance must be favourable, and that this should coincide with a history of music-making within the family.

Hargreaves, MacDonald, and Miell (2012a) have referred to people's views of themselves as unmusical or as lacking in talent as partly arising from what they call the 'fundamental mastery misconception': this is the idea that even though everyone is capable of learning the technical and expressive aspects of musical performance skills, given an appropriate environment and upbringing, the overemphasis that is placed upon the technical aspects of performance in music education in many countries could be a primary reason why many people feel 'unmusical'. The misconception is that in order to be an authentic musician, one must possess an exceptionally high level of technical skill on a given instrument, and that these high levels of technical skill are what define the professional musician (Johansson, 2012; MacDonald, Kreutz, & Mitchell, 2012b). It is also worth pointing out here that technical performance skill is by no means the only relevant aspect of musical performance: McPherson (1995a, b), for example, has emphasised that musical performance skills encompass *aural* and *creative* orientations alongside *visual* ones: being able to play by ear and from memory, and to improvise, are just as important for overall musical growth as being able to sight read and perform a written score with speed and accuracy.

This misconception persists despite the evidence that many other personal characteristics such as intelligence, creativity, and athletic prowess are normally distributed throughout the population, such that there is no reason to suppose that this does not also apply to musical skills. Another widespread view is that some people have a 'natural talent' for music, and that this is an essential prerequisite of the very high levels of success achieved by prodigies and virtuoso musicians: research on the latter has been given a significant recent boost by the publication of McPherson's (2016) edited collection *Musical Prodigies*. McPherson takes an interdisciplinary view, including perspectives from psychology, education, musicology, and ethnomusicology, and the book includes various potential theoretical explanations, descriptions of the development of musical prodigies, as well as numerous case studies of individual prodigies, ranging from Mozart and Beethoven through to Stevie Wonder and Michael Jackson. It is impossible to do justice to McPherson's substantial volume here, but we might nevertheless mention one or two key ideas.

McPherson points out that the term prodigy, for most people, suggests three defining characteristics: an extraordinarily fast pace of learning; an outstanding level of competence; and the attainment of this level of competence at a very early age, usually before adolescence. Winner's (1997) definition of giftedness in children, of which she sees prodigiousness as an extreme case, includes three characteristics which complement these, namely precocious mastery of a particular domain; what she calls an 'insistence on marching to one's own drummer', i.e. a strong sense of independence and self-determination; and what she calls a 'rage to master' (i.e. intense interest and focus). One prominent idea about the developmental mechanisms through which prodigies emerge is that various sets of favourable biological and environmental circumstances – which might include physical characteristics, personal qualities and talents, family support systems, and wider social, political, and historical contexts – all happen to coincide, and this is the essence of the *coincidence framework* (Feldman with Goldsmith, 1986). This has a lot in common with what Davidson and Faulkner (2013) call *syzygies*: these refer to 'the alignment and complex permutations of physical characteristics, personality traits, general intelligence, domain-specific abilities, and a wide range of social, cultural, and other environmental factors that lead to emergence of exceptional achievements in a particular domain' (p. 134), and we shall return to this idea later in this chapter.

Syzygies can occur not only in gifted pupils and prodigies, but at all levels of ability, and this is congruent with Hargreaves et al.'s (2012a) suggestion 'that we are all musical, but that musical ability is still normally distributed within the population. To put it simply: we are all musical, but some people have more natural potential to develop musical skills than others' (p. 130). Hargreaves et al. also suggest that musical talent may be normally distributed within the general population around a mean that is much higher than received wisdom suggests. Some of MacDonald's work, for example, has shown how individuals with learning difficulties or mental health problems can learn to play a musical instrument, and that psychological benefits often result from musical engagement of this kind (e.g. MacDonald, Davies, & O'Donnell, 1999; MacDonald & Miell, 2002).

'Natural Talent' or Practice?

Sloboda, Davidson, and Howe (1994; henceforth SDH) wrote a target article entitled 'Is everyone musical?' as the focus of a debate in a peer commentary review issue of *The Psychologist*. Their approach was to look much more carefully at the nature of musical ability, and in particular at the age-old question of whether it is innate or acquired – in effect, they revisited the nature-nurture question in relation to musical ability. They were keen to challenge the folk psychology view mentioned earlier that talented 'musicians are born, not made' – or at least, that high levels of musical achievement rely largely on an innate gift, or 'natural talent' for music. They suggest, instead, that it makes much more sense to regard musical ability as a learnt cognitive skill – an approach which renders it much more amenable to empirical investigation, and the investigation of the most important environmental determinants of higher than average levels of musical achievement was the basis of the joint study of the 'Biographical determinants of musical excellence' by the Universities of Keele and Exeter, which we describe in more detail later in this chapter.

SDH also referred to the 'folk psychology' viewpoint as the 'talent' approach, as it sees high achieving musicians as possessing a higher level of innate talent than the rest of the population. In trying to evaluate the relative effectiveness of the talent and the environmental explanations of musical ability it is important at the outset to settle on an adequate definition of talent: to avoid a definition which places too much emphasis on innate ability on one hand, or on levels of achievement on the other. Howe, Davidson, and Sloboda (1998) suggested a five-fold definition: '(1) It originates in genetically transmitted structures and hence is at least partly innate. (2) Its full effects may not be evident at an early stage, but there will be some advance indications, allowing people to identify the presence of talent before exceptional levels of mature performance have been demonstrated. (3) These early indications of talent provide a basis for predicting who is likely to excel. (4) Only a minority are talented, for if all children were, then there would be no way to predict or explain differential success. Finally, (5) talents are relatively domain specific' (p. 400).

Howe et al. provide examples of other researchers' explanations of talent: Gardner (1993), for example, defines it as a sign of precocious biopsychological potential in a particular domain, and when this potential coincides with a set of positive environmental factors, high levels of achievement will emerge. Gagné (2009) teases out this distinction further by distinguishing between giftedness and talent: in essence, he sees giftedness as a measure of ability, or potential, and talent as a measure of actual performance, in which specific skills are demonstrated. In his model, Gagné specifies six domains of 'natural abilities' (*gifts*), four of which are mental (intellectual, creative, social, perceptual) and two of which are physical (muscular, motor control); three varieties of what he calls 'environmental catalysts' (milieu, individuals, and provisions) as well as five 'interpersonal catalysts' (physical, mental, awareness, motivation, and volition), and these exert their effects, in interactions which are partly determined by chance, through three types of developmental process (activities, progress, and investment).

The results of these interacting factors give rise to eight talents or competencies which McPherson and Williamon (2016), in applying this model to music, identify as performing, improvising, composing, arranging, analysing, appraising, conducting, and music teaching, and McPherson and Gagné (2016) have taken this further in a very lengthy chapter which applies Gagné's integrative model of talent development to the analysis of musical prodigiousness. The extent to which the myriad of different possible pathways through this model enables us to predict how particular musical talents might arise from particular environmental or personal circumstances may be too complex to trace, but at the very least this model gives a clear and comprehensive account of the many influences on musical talent.

SDH put forward seven different arguments in favour of their own view that environmental determinants are more important in musical achievement than are genetic ones. First, they point out that musical accomplishments are much more widespread in certain non-Western societies than they are in Western ones. They quote from the ethnomusicologist Messenger's (1958) account of the musical activities of the Anang Ibobo tribe in Nigeria:

'We were constantly amazed at the musical abilities displayed by these people, especially by the children who, before the age of five, can sing hundreds of songs, both individually and in choral groups, and, in addition, are able to play several percussion instruments and have learned dozens of intricate dance movements calling for incredible muscular control. We searched in vain for the "non-musical" person, finding it difficult to make enquiries about tone-deafness and its assumed effects because the Anang language possesses no comparable concept.' (pp. 349–350)

This suggests that the Western conception of musical talent is more restricted than it is in some other parts of the globe, and a wider conception of talent means that everyone can be considered to be 'musical' to a much greater extent. A second related argument is that people who are thought to be 'non-musical' nevertheless possess many musical skills. Studies of *normative* rather than *expert* musical development, or what has been called *acculturation* rather than *training* (Sloboda, 1985), show that many musical skills are learnt simply by growing up in a particular culture (see e.g. Mito, 2004, 2007). The problem seems to be that engaging in musical performance is an unfamiliar and relatively uncommon activity in Western society; it is regarded as specialised and even as requiring special gifts or talents, and this is not the case in many other societies.

SDH's third argument is based on the extent to which early signs of promise are identifiable in exceptionally talented musicians. There are many reports in the literature of the feats of child prodigies, especially in music, who demonstrated precocious achievements in their early years. Igor Stravinsky is reported as having been able to generate realistic imitations of the performances of local singers at the age of 2, for example, and violinist Yehudi Menuhin was performing with symphony orchestras by the age of 7. There are also many stories about Mozart's abilities as a composer, performer, and improviser by the age of 5, as mentioned in Chapter 4. SDH are sceptical about this, pointing out that a great deal of this evidence is based on the reports of parents or other observers rather than on direct observations by the investigator, and that these reports have often been made many years after the occurrence of the events in question, or are autobiographical accounts by the prodigies themselves.

SDH also point out that documented studies provide little support for the idea of early signs of musical talent. For example, Howe, Davidson, Moore, and Sloboda's (1995) interview study of the parents of 257 children who had studied a musical instrument but who differed in their levels of expertise investigated whether those with high levels of expertise had shown earlier signs of this ability than those with lower levels, and found that the age of appearance of these behaviours showed very few differences between the most and the least competent groups: the only significant difference was that the higher achieving children were reported as tending to sing on average six months earlier than all the other children, at a mean age of 1.7 years. At a much higher level of expertise, Sosniak (1985, 1990) interviewed twenty-one outstanding American pianists in their mid-thirties who were on course to become concert pianists, and also talked to their parents. It turned out that very few of them had shown signs of future excellence when they were still very young: it was more often the case that they made extremely fast progress after a combination of good opportunities and strong encouragement from their parents and teachers.

Simonton (2016) followed up this argument by providing some empirical evidence from two separate studies: the first investigated the length of time taken to acquire sufficient expertise to begin to make lasting contributions to the classical repertoire (Hayes, 1989), and the second was his own investigation of how classical composers vary in their acquisition of this level of expertise (Simonton, 1991). In summary, Hayes' study of 76 classical composers showed that all but three of them did not produce their first masterpiece until at least a decade after starting intensive study and that their early compositions, even those of Mozart, were unlikely to receive widespread recognition.

However, Simonton points out that Hayes' study took no account of individual differences between composers with respect to factors such as their level of achieved eminence, their lifetime contributions, and their career trajectories. His own study of 120 classical composers, much larger than that of Hayes, was based on six measures of their productivity, namely 'age at first hit', 'age at best hit', 'age at last hit', 'age at maximum output', 'maximum annual output', and 'lifetime output', based on data from the thematic dictionary of Barlow and Morgenstern (1948, 1976) and the catalogue of Gilder and Port (1978). With this much more detailed database and sophisticated statistical analysis, Simonton found generally positive correlations between the 'age at first hit' – i.e. at which the composer made his first contribution to the standard repertoire, and the age which they started training: this, and various other intercorrelations among his six measures, led him to the general conclusion that the most eminent and prolific classical composers seem to exhibit greater creative productivity as a result of their early precocious development: that 'the most eminent composers get better faster and attain more bang for the buck – more creative outputs with less time allotted to deliberate practice' (p. 195). This conflicting evidence suggests that the extent to which early signs of promise are identifiable in exceptionally talented musicians remains unclear.

The fourth argument, to which we return later in this chapter, is that a well-established result from several studies is that highly 'talented' musicians have typically carried out far more 'deliberate practice' on their instruments than those with lesser levels of achievement. One well-known study by Ericsson, Krampe, and Tesch-Romer (1993) obtained specific information about the amount of formal practice carried out by student violinists in a conservatoire, and discovered a clear positive relationship between proficiency and accumulated practice. They found that the best students in the performance class of the conservatoire had accumulated about 10,000 hours of practice by the age of 21, i.e. before they embarked on their professional careers of musicians, whereas the less accomplished students had only accumulated about half of that amount of practice.

Sloboda et al. (1996) provided further evidence of the importance of practice in their study of 257 young people between 8 and 18 years old who had undertaken individual instrumental tuition. Evidence from in-depth interviews and practice diaries kept by 94 of them over a 42-week period showed a strong relationship between level of musical achievement and the amount of formal practice undertaken. In particular, there was no evidence that high achievers were able to gain a given level of examination success with low levels of practice than were lower achievers. This evidence supports the argument that formal effortful practice is a principal determinant of musical achievement, and indeed that it might be just as important as 'natural ability'. However, it must be remembered practice clearly is insufficient alone; a recent meta-analysis across the domains of music, sport and games (Macnamara, Hambrick, & Oswald, 2014) found practice was responsible for only 21 per cent of the variance in excellence in music, and less so in other domains such as sport and education. Some further studies and theoretical interpretations of the effects of different practice regimes have been undertaken more recently, and we return to these in the next section.

SDH's fifth argument is that pupils from families with no obvious musical background or experience are capable of rapid musical learning and progress. Sloboda and Howe's (1991) study found that 30 per cent of the pupils at a highly selective specialist music school had parents without any musical interest, skill, or specialist experience. This proportion rose to 40 per cent in the group with the highest levels of musical achievement. This seems to disprove the idea that genetically transmitted talent is related to musical achievement, and Howe, Davidson, and Sloboda (1998) further point out that there is a certain amount of circularity in the argument that talent contributes to exceptional abilities, for example: 'She plays so well because she has a talent. How do I know she has a talent? That's obvious, she plays so well!' (p. 405).

Sixth, as we outlined in Chapter 3, it has been well established that musical learning can take place before the child is born, and that infants and young children can benefit from rich early musical environments. SDH suggest that 'Our current research is beginning to indicate higher levels of such early musical stimulation in families whose children make the most subsequent progress with music ... early differences, possibly incidental and unintended, in exposure to music can lead to substantial variability in children's ability to take advantage of later formal learning opportunities such as instrumental lessons' (1994a, p. 350).

The seventh and final argument is that the talent explanation seems to suggest that there exists an identifiable set of intercorrelated skills which differentiate between the talented and the untalented. This is not borne out by the evidence, which suggests instead that the wide range of skills and subskills such as memory, sight reading, improvisation, playing by ear, and so on which make up what we understand as musical ability seem to be independent of one another, rather than being positively intercorrelated (see e.g. Hallam, 2016).

Given this fairly strong case against the 'folk psychology' or 'talent' viewpoint, and the numerous examples of the power of environmental factors on the development of musical excellence, it is rather surprising that the folk psychology review remains so widely accepted. SDH suggest that one prominent reason for this is that this view is held by many members of the music profession, since it reinforces the idea that music teachers and other professionals require special talents, thereby maintaining their own exclusivity.

Another argument which is sometimes used to bolster this position is that while SDH's approach may apply to the development of musical skills, it may nevertheless fail to account for differences in more complex attributes such as expressivity or creativity, and that 'natural talent' or 'gifts' are needed for the attainment of these more abstract, elusive qualities. However, SDH cite studies of expressive variations in performance by authors including Shaffer (1981) and Clarke (1988), which have investigated these phenomena by measuring microvariations in musicians' timing, and these show that features of 'expressiveness' such as rhythmic variation, articulation, and rubato are actually highly systematic both within individual performers and across different performers within a given musical culture. In other words, expressiveness can be explained in terms of the application of specific component skills, and there is no need to postulate the existence of special talents.

SDH's rejection of the talent model in favour of one based on environmental factors created controversy and received a good deal of criticism. The commentators on their article raised a number of different objections: in summary, Davies (1994) suggested that the environmental view partly derives from a middle class, liberal, and what might now be called 'politically correct' position which may not take adequate account of the scientific evidence from genetics and biology, and that SDH had overemphasised the dichotomous nature of the relationship between nature and nurture; Hargreaves (1994) was concerned with the narrowness of SDH's definition of musical achievement; Radford (1994) suggested that their definitions of musical ability and achievement were so wide-ranging that they must necessarily involve cultural factors, since genetics can only convey the *potential* for different activities, and cannot be manifested directly in specific behaviours; and Torff and Winner (1994) argued that SDH had gone too far in denying the importance of inherited differences in musical aptitude, and thus had effectively thrown out the baby with the bathwater.

SDH gave a considered response to all these criticisms, but in the end the arguments and counter-arguments, like all those in the 'nature-nature' debate, ultimately boil down to the degrees of emphasis which are placed on one side or the other, and which cannot be resolved either way as the effects of each are impossible to disentangle from the interactions between them.

One fascinating new piece of evidence comes from a recent study by Eriksson, Harmat, Theorell, and Ullén (2016), who interviewed ten Swedish monozygotic twin pairs who were what they call 'highly discordant' for piano practising: i.e. in which one member of the pair played actively, but the other showed little interest in doing so. Although there was some predictable evidence that the playing members of the pairs found music more interesting and enjoyable from an early age than their co-twins, and also gave richer and more elaborate descriptions of the meaning of music in their lives and identities, and had a significantly higher openness to experience and tendency to experience flow in their musical activities, there were nevertheless no apparent within-pair differences in important factors such as the musical engagement of their peers, parental support, music teachers, ensemble playing, public performances, or their interest in and aptitude for languages. In other words, there was no clear evidence that the differences in musical engagement between members of the pairs were caused by systematic environmental influences: and the authors suggest that the reasons for the discordance in practising may be highly individual and idiosyncratic in each case.

Further evidence for evolutionary and genetic influences on musical achievement and ability is provided by Vandervert (2016a, b) and by Mosing and Ullén (2016) in the context of explaining of musical prodigiousness, so that the age-old nature-nurture question remains under contemporary investigation in relation to musical ability. One possible way around the problem of disentangling some of the effects and interactions involved is to conduct longitudinal research, and we will look later in this chapter at an Australian longitudinal study which followed on from the Keele-Exeter University biographical study, and which informed many of these arguments.

Practice

The effects of the variety of different forms of practice on musical achievement have been the topic of various studies in the research literature, and also have obvious practical significance for music education. Following Ericsson et al. (1993) and

SDH, most scholars in this field now regard the development of musical ability and expertise as a process of cognitive skill acquisition, as this approach renders it much more amenable to empirical investigation, and indeed has given rise to a body of new theory and research over the last two decades (see e.g. Barry & Hallam, 2002; Lehmann, 1997; Lehmann & Davidson, 2002; Lehmann, Sloboda, & Woody, 2007). 'Formal effortful practice', sometimes also described as 'deliberate practice', might include technical skills, pieces, and exercises which are systematically set by the teacher, whereas 'informal practice' refers to more spontaneous and autonomous playing which is not set by the teacher and might include improvisation with others, playing tunes by ear, or simply 'messing about' on the instrument.

Barry and Hallam (2002) identified the range of different types of practice that can exist, and incorporated suggestions as to how learners might best manage their practice in terms of task division, timetabling and so on, as well as what teaching strategies might be adopted to optimise its effectiveness. Hallam (1997) suggested that different kinds of practice are effective for different levels of expertise of performer: the needs of beginners are different from those of more advanced players, for example. Hallam identified seven aspects of the processes of effective practice: that teachers need to demonstrate and model how to obtain an overview of the work; identify difficulties; select appropriate strategies; work on sections and integrate them into a whole; monitor progress; set personal goals; and self-evaluate progress.

The *Investigating Musical Performance* project, led by Graham Welch, found that students' patterns of practice and general musical activity were distinctly different in different musical genres (e.g. Welch, 2012). Whereas traditional classical musicians regarded practising alone, and mastering accurate sight reading and playing from notation as being particularly important, for example, those who were working in jazz, popular music, and Scottish traditional music put far more emphasis on skills such as improvisation, memorisation, and playing by ear, and this casts doubt upon the view of a simple positive relationship between deliberate practice and achievement.

Even though the positive correlation between the amount of deliberate practice that students undertake and their levels of musical achievement is well established, there is nevertheless no simple *causal* relationship, as a recent study by Bonneville-Roussy and Bouffard (2015) points out. They cite more recent research, such as that collated and re-evaluated by Hambrick et al. (2014), which shows that a substantial proportion of the variance in the positive relationship between performance and deliberate practice in some studies could be explained by other factors: they also draw attention to the considerable interest that is currently being shown in the effects of self-regulation (which we reviewed in Chapter 2) on musical achievement. As a result of these more recent developments, Bonneville-Roussy and Bouffard propose 'an integrative framework in which self-regulation, deliberate practice strategies and practice time are simultaneously taken into account in the prediction of musical achievement. In this framework, we propose that formal practice should be defined as a goal-directed and focused period of practice that includes both self-regulation and deliberate practice strategies. We further posit that practice time will predict musical achievement only if associated with formal practice' (p. 686). This is

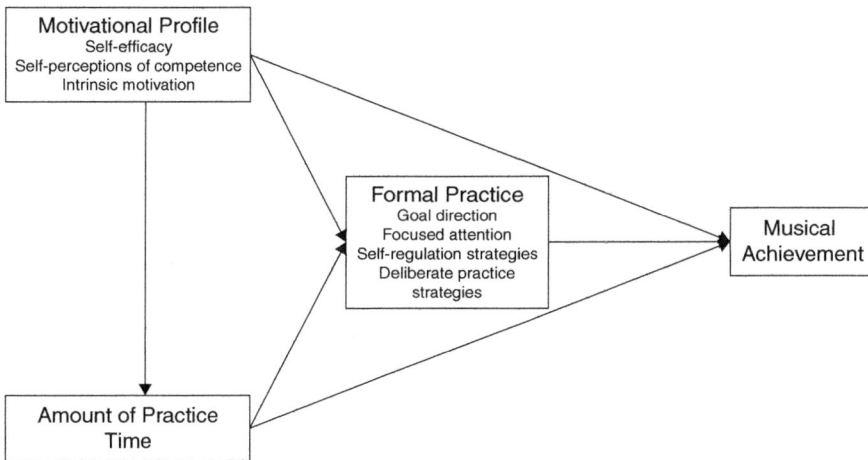

Figure 5.1. Proposed framework of the links between practice time, formal practice strategies and
musical achievement.
Source: Image republished with the permission of SAGE Publications. Originally published
as Figure 1 (p. 690) in Bonneville-Roussy, A., & Bouffard T. (2015). When quantity is not
enough: Disentangling the roles of practice time, deliberate practice and self-regulation in
musical achievement. *Psychology of Music*, *43*(5), 686–704.

shown in Figure 5.1, in which we can see that aspects of what they call the learner's
'motivational profile', in particular those involving self-perceptions and self-efficacy, give rise to the total amount of practice time undertaken: and that both of
these determinants then contribute towards the amount of formal practice which
is undertaken, which in turn can predict the level of musical achievement attained.
Bonneville-Roussy and Bouffard go on to test this framework in a prospective study
of 235 music students using structural equation modelling, and their results confirm that it provides better predictions of musical achievement than do traditional
approaches which rely only on either deliberate practice or self-regulation.

In a related study, Evans and Bonneville-Roussy (2016) adopted Ryan and Deci's
(2000) self-determination theory in order to explain the motivation of university
music students: this suggests that the three psychological needs of competence,
relatedness, and autonomy must be fulfilled in order to maintain psychological
wellbeing, which in turn motivates successful practice and performance. They surveyed 392 students from schools of music in nine universities in Australia and New
Zealand in order to examine whether needs fulfilment and autonomous motivation
within the university music learning context would explain context-specific affect
and behaviour, testing the hypothesised relationships using structural equation
modelling. They found that a number of behaviours, including more frequent practice, more frequent quality practice, and greater preference for challenging tasks
were explained by psychological needs fulfilment and autonomous motivation.

Araújo (2016) also carried out a study of self-regulated practice behaviour in
advanced musicians using a specially designed online questionnaire which was completed by 212 musicians with varying levels of skill and expertise. Factor analysis

of the results led Araújo to identify three types of self-regulated behaviour in his sample, namely self-regulation through practice organisation, through personal resources, and through external resources. He found that self-regulation through personal resources was the most predominant strategy for advanced musicians, that self-regulation through external resources decreased with experience, and that practice time was negatively related to age and positively related to practice organisation and self-regulation through external resources: this suggests that younger and less experienced musicians rely more heavily on time, organisation, and external resources.

These studies provide a rather more nuanced and sophisticated account of the different factors involved in formal practice than has hitherto been available, and lead to some clear implications for the advice that should be given to music educators. Self-regulation and personal autonomy are now seen to play a much more important part in music learning than was recognised hitherto, and three recommendations for music educators have been proposed by Renwick and Reeve (2012). These are that teachers should nurture students' inner motivational resources by appealing to their intrinsic interest in the music itself, and create a sense of challenge by providing material that is difficult but within their reach; that they should use informational, rather than controlling language to communicate with students, explaining *why* particular challenges and learning goals are being set; and that they should acknowledge and accept students' affect and behaviour rather than seeing them as being problematic.

Some further insight into this comes from a recent interview study of the origins of maladaptive perfectionism and performance anxiety in 14 classically trained musicians (aged between 21 and 54 years) by Hruska, Hargreaves, and Ockelford (submitted). They also used SDT to explain their results, concluding that optimal function and growth involves

'[N]ot forcing movements and ideas, but doing the task in a way that is possible at a given moment: not over-analysing or giving up, but trying new approaches. Participants also mentioned not taking music or life too seriously, being more open and curious, welcoming mistakes, trusting themselves and their knowledge (self-confidence, self-efficacy), listening to their instincts about what is right or wrong, and focusing on music that is already known internally rather than relying on notes or technique as being helpful approaches to the achievement of success in preparation and practice. By minimising the importance of goals (e.g. reducing pressure from the self), technical/musical skills are recontexualised and anxiety level drops.'

Motivation

We pointed out earlier that one of the key factors which determines whether or not specific environmental influences such as the family, schools, and peers might exert a positive effect on young people's musical abilities and achievements is the extent to which they promote their *motivation* to engage in musical activity: motivation is a key mediating factor. MacDonald, Hargreaves, and Miell (2009) have also argued that another important part of this mechanism is that the positive feedback that young people get from others in their social world. This fosters their motivation by developing their positive *identities* as musicians: their self-perceptions as 'being good at music' can motivate them to achieve higher levels of practice and achievement, which in turn can lead to further reinforcement of the 'myself as musician' role, so that a 'virtuous cycle' can develop in which increasing levels of musical achievement motivation and musical identity are interdependent.

In other words, children's motivation to succeed in music is linked with aspects of their musical identities: the ways in which they think about their own abilities have a direct influence upon their motivation to engage in activities which develop those abilities, and vice versa. To achieve a high level of success in musical performance in many Western countries is notoriously difficult, of course, given the high number of young people who aspire to musical careers in relation to the relative dearth of openings and opportunities available to them: to achieve success demands immensely high levels of motivation, hard work, ability, and persistence as well, probably, as other personal qualities such as competitiveness: Bonneville-Roussy, Lavigne, and Vallerand (2011) use the term *passion* to describe what may well be involved at this level.

There is an extensive body of theory and research on motivation for educational attainment more generally – in subjects such as mathematics and reading, for example – and this has been applied to specifically to motivation in music learning by authors including O'Neill and McPherson (2002), Hallam (2002), Austin, Renwick, and McPherson (2006), Lehmann, Sloboda, and Woody (2007), and Evans (2016) has recently contributed an insightful review. Evans draws on Schunk, Meece, and Pintrich's (2014) definition of motivation as 'the process by which goal directed behaviour is instigated and sustained', pointing out that this definition contains four important contemporary psychological views about motivation. These are (a) that motivation includes not only the observed behaviour and its own direct cause, but also the relevant choices, beliefs, thoughts, and social influences which lead to it; (b) that motivated behaviour is thought of in terms of the attainment of goals; (c) that it involves all physical and mental activity, including the cognitive processes of planning, evaluating, and strategising goal-directed behaviour as well as the behaviour itself; and (d) that it is concerned not only with the instigation of this behaviour, but also with its longer-term maintenance and sustainability.

Several main theoretical points of view can be distinguished in this field, and we shall mention several of them in the review that follows. First of all, following our earlier suggestions concerning musical identity, *self-theories* form a central part of the theoretical models of educational and musical motivation which have emerged in recent decades, and Austin, Renwick, and McPherson (2006) demonstrate this in proposing a *process* model of motivation which is based on the work of Connell (1990). The model has four components – the *self-system* (e.g. perceptions, beliefs, thoughts, emotions); the *social system* (e.g. teachers, peers, siblings); *actions* (e.g. motivated behaviours including learning and self-regulation); and *outcomes* (e.g. learning, achievements). Each of these four components is seen to have a reciprocal causal relationship with each of the others, and so the motivational system develops and changes as learning proceeds, and as new challenges are sought by the learner.

Many scholars seem to agree that *expectancy-value* theory (e.g. Eccles et al., 1983; Fishbein & Azjen, 1975; Pintrich & Schunk, 2002) is the most well-established and useful theoretical approach, and explanations of motivation based on this approach have three main components. These are the *value* component – the extent to which learners see a particular task, activity or domain as being important, and as being of value to them: the *expectancy* component – learners' beliefs about their abilities to succeed in the activity: and the *affective* component, namely how learners feel about themselves in relation to the activity. In other words, young musicians' motivation to progress to higher levels will depend on the extent to which they see playing their instrument as being important in their lives, and in having future benefits and payoffs: on whether or not they perceive that they are capable of achieving higher levels of success; and on whether or not they simply enjoy playing their instrument in relation to all their other interests and activities.

Eccles et al. (1983) proposed that there are four main aspects of the value component, namely its *attainment value* (the importance to the individual of success in the task); its *utility value* (its perceived usefulness to the individual); its *intrinsic interest* (the absorption in and enjoyment of the activity for its own sake); and its *perceived cost* (the loss of time spent on other activities as a result of engagement in the activity, and the consequent loss of interest in them). The third of these aspects raises the important distinction between *intrinsic* and *extrinsic* motivation: the former is evident when interest in an activity is natural, unforced, and high, and the latter occurs when external rewards and punishments (such as praise and criticism) are involved. Some research by McPherson (2000a) showed that these aspects were well understood by children as young as 7–9 years old, who were only just beginning to play music: they could differentiate between the four components, and make clear statements in relation to each concerning the value and expectations they associated with musicianship.

Amabile's (1996) social psychological theory of creativity, discussed in Chapter 4, emphasises the importance of intrinsic motivation, proposing that 'the intrinsically motivated state is conducive to creativity, whereas the extrinsically motivated state is detrimental' (p. 107). The *perceived cost* of engaging in an activity may involve both intrinsic and extrinsic motivation: children may decide that the time and work involved in practising an instrument is not worth the effort, for example, and consciously decide to give up in favour of other pursuits (e.g. Eccles, Wigfield, & Schiefele, 1998). Amabile points out that external rewards do not always lead to improvements in performance: if intrinsic motivation is already high, rewards can have the effect of undermining performance rather than of improving it.

The decision as to whether to persist in music or to give up relates to the second, *expectancy* component of the expectancy-value model, which refers to learners' beliefs in their own ability to succeed on the task. This may be related to Bandura's (1997) self-efficacy, which plays an important role in the explanation of educational motivation, but it may also be more directly related to longer-term predictions (expectancies) that students have about their likelihood of future success in music. McPherson (2000b), for example, sees different levels of commitment to music (short, medium and long-term) as interacting with practice to determine achievement.

Dweck (2000) suggests that people differ in the extent to which they display *mastery-oriented* as distinct from *helpless* behaviour, which in turn relates to their *locus of control*. Learners with an *internal* locus of control are likely to display mastery-oriented behaviour, for example in trying to persist with the task when they come up against difficulties, whereas those in this situation with an *external* locus of control are likely to feel that the circumstances are beyond their own control, and to display helpless behaviour. O'Neill (1997) investigated the longer-term effects of these motivational patterns in children who were about to begin instrumental tuition, by giving them problem-solving tasks which were arranged such that all of them were bound to fail. She found that those who displayed mastery-oriented behaviour after failing on the task made more progress after one year of instrumental music lessons than those who initially displayed helpless behaviour.

This result leads us to a more general consideration of the third component of expectancy-value theory, namely the *affective* component: people's beliefs about and reactions to success and failure can be explained in terms of *attribution theory* (e.g. Heider, 1958; Kelley, 1973; Weiner, 1985, 1992). According to this, people attribute their success or failure on a task to four main factors: *ability* ('I am good/poor at this task'): *effort* ('I practised hard/insufficiently'); *task difficulty* ('this particular task was easy/difficult'); and *luck* ('I had a lucky/unlucky day'). The first and second of these are internal in the sense that they are under the control of the learner, and the third and fourth are subject to external influences. This approach argues that these attributions are more important in determining expectations of success in future attempts than are previous successes or failures, and this has clear implications for motivation: if you believe that future attempts are likely to be successful you will persevere, even in the face of failure.

These theoretical analyses of educational motivation reveal some of the ways in which musical achievement and development can be related to musical identities. We referred at the beginning of this section to a hypothetical 'virtuous cycle' according to which increasing levels of musical achievement give rise to higher levels of musical self-esteem, and vice versa; children who feel that they are competent musicians are likely to achieve higher levels of success than those who do not, as are those who find music intrinsically interesting, and value it positively (Eccles et al., 1983). This can work in both directions, of course: some children may get the idea that they are 'unmusical', perhaps because of an unwitting remark by a teacher, parent, or another pupil, and this perception could correspondingly lead on to a negative spiral of not trying, therefore becoming less able, therefore trying even less, and so on. It is clearly important in music education that teachers and parents should foster 'virtuous cycles' and do their best to avoid negative ones, and we shall look at some of the factors involved in the last part of this chapter.

Early on in this section we suggested that several main theoretical points of view can be distinguished in this field, and it is clear from our review that various different perspectives, including self-theories, expectancy-value theory, social psychological theories, and attribution theory, along with concepts which are associated with some of these, including intrinsic–extrinsic motivation and internal–external locus of control, simply coexist in their explanations of different motivational phenomena rather than necessarily bearing any similarities between or relationships with one another. In his recent review of this complex theoretical field, Evans (2016) attempts to cut through the terminological confusion by focusing on some of the key behavioural components of motivation, including 'beliefs', 'values', 'identity', and 'needs' and he also makes a valiant attempt to integrate the different theoretical approaches by drawing on Martin's (2007) construct validation approach.

Perhaps more successful than this, however, is his recent attempt (Evans, 2015) to introduce some degree of theoretical integration into this field in terms of self-determination theory (SDT: Ryan & Deci 2000; Deci & Ryan 2002). This approach is gaining increasing prominence in the field of positive psychology, and is already being applied in several different areas of music psychology. As we shall see later, for example, the Sydney longitudinal study uses concepts from SDT in explaining the transactional regulation that occurs in musical development, which we shall describe later in this chapter, and it is also being used in research on music, health, and wellbeing (see e.g. Ockelford, 2012).

Evans identifies two fundamental tenets of self-determination theory which are adopted in applying it to music. The first is in identifying the concept of basic psychological needs. This is the idea that humans have an innate set of psychological needs which need to be fulfilled through interactions with the social environment: and that if this occurs, it will lead to positive growth and wellbeing. Furthermore, as outlined earlier, SDT proposes the three basic needs of competence, relatedness, and autonomy. Evans describes the ways in which these three needs apply to children's musical development: to what extent does music enable children to feel competent, e.g. to be effective in basic skills, to feel related, i.e. in their relationships with significant others such as peers, parents, and teachers, and to fulfil their feelings of personal autonomy? It turns out that music is a particularly fruitful medium for the fulfilment of all three of these, and can clearly be seen to promote personal growth and self-identity in each case.

The second fundamental tenet of SDT is what Evans describes as 'the process by which externally regulated behaviours are aligned with the self' (p. 67): he suggests that 'behaviour is more enjoyable and contributes more to personal wellbeing when motivation is internalised and more closely aligned with the self' . . . and also that . . . These two features of self-determination theory are related, such that motivation is internalised to the extent that basic psychological needs are fulfilled' (p. 65). In practice, the implications of this relate to the distinction between intrinsic and extrinsic motivation: some learners are intrinsically motivated to succeed in music because they value the activity for its own sake, whereas others see it as a means of achieving rewards such as parental approval or social prestige, for example. We referred earlier to Amabile's notion that intrinsic motivation is a vital part of creative ability in music, and that extrinsic motivation can even be detrimental towards it.

Evans goes on to review the limited amount of research which has been carried out which has adopted a basic psychological needs approach, and specifically that using SDT, as well as research on motivation from other theoretical perspectives. This convinces him that the SDT approach is generally supported by the evidence, and so he goes on to develop an integrated model of motivation in music education based on SDT principles which draws on the hierarchical model of motivation proposed by Vallerand (1997) and Vallerand and Ratelle (2002). These propose that three basic levels of motivation exist: the global, the contextual, and the situational. *Global* motivation reflects people's overall motivational disposition, which can involve different levels of competence, autonomy, and relatedness, and these can be seen in the domains of cognition, affect, and behaviour. *Contextual* motivation refers to that in specific domains of activity, such as sport, music, or academic activity, or other domains: people can be motivated to greater or lesser extents in these different domains. Finally, *situational* motivation refers to specific situations in which motivation becomes important such as in the family, in academic work, or in musical activities.

The ultimate usefulness of Evans' theoretical integration awaits further investigation: he suggests that the application of concepts drawn from SDT to practical issues like how parents and teachers should best motivate their learners might show that a good deal of current practice is misguided, for example, and might in fact be demotivating if it relies on extrinsic rewards, for example. Whether or not this turns out to be the case, the increasing prominence of SDT in various areas of applied psychology suggest that it is likely to represent a promising advance in the promotion of psychological wellbeing through the use of music.

Two Large-Scale Studies

The two studies which we mentioned earlier are interlinked, and both have their origins in the early 1990s. At that time, Jane Davidson was beginning a three year post-doctoral fellowship at the University of Keele, UK, working with John Sloboda and Michael Howe of Exeter University on a Leverhulme Trust-funded study of 'The biographical determinants of musical excellence in learning of Western classical music', and Gary McPherson was carrying out his doctoral research in Australia on the skills involved in the successful learning and performance of music. We shall look first at the Keele-Exeter study, which has made a considerable contribution to the understanding of the effects of environmental factors on musical development. The aims of this study and those of McPherson were to a considerable extent complementary, and this led to the planning of a new joint research project by McPherson and Davidson which was eventually funded by two large grants from the Australian Research Council and which we will go on to describe. Although there are inevitable differences between the two original studies, given their different contexts and timing, they nevertheless produced some clear mutual findings about the effects of specific environmental influences, and in particular about those of family, peers, and schools.

The Keele-Exeter Study: Biographical Determinants of Musical Excellence

The first enquiry had its origins in an interview study of forty-two young (10- to 18-year-old) people who were pupils at one of the UK's specialist musical schools, and who had consequently achieved very high levels of musical skill and achievement (Sloboda & Howe, 1991). As noted earlier, Sloboda and Howe were interested in the important *environmental* determinants of these higher than average levels of achievement, as they were frustrated by the widely held folk belief that 'musicians are born, not made'. They focused on comparisons between those who were particularly musically successful and those who were less so, but who were nevertheless working at a high level as compared with the population norm: they found that the more successful students tended to come from *less* musically active families, and to have had *fewer* early lessons than the less highly accomplished students. The most able students had not devoted more time to practice than the others, but their practice time was more evenly distributed between a number of instruments.

This preliminary study led to a successful application for a large-scale study which ran between 1991 and 1997. This involved interviews with 257 children divided into five levels of ability/experience and matched for socio-economic status, sex, age, and musical instrument studied, as follows: (1) those who had received a minimum of one year of lessons and had then given up playing; (2) those who had carried on learning music, but who considered it to be no more interesting than other hobbies, such as dancing or sports; (3) those who considered themselves to be serious musicians and regarded music as an important part of their lives, and who had considered entering a specialist music school; (4) those who had auditioned for but failed to achieve entry to a specialist music school, but who nevertheless had high achievement levels in music; and (5) those who attended one of the leading specialist music schools in the UK.

The results of this study were reported widely in a number of different journals and books, as well as creating a good deal of media interest: and some of its main findings were as follows. First, the interview data revealed that students attending specialist music schools, i.e. those in group 5, had sung spontaneously as infants about six months earlier than had members of all of the other groups, although this was the only one of five different early signs of exceptional musical ability to which this applied – the other four signs being moving to music, showing a liking for musical sounds, being attentive to music, and making requests to be involved in musical activities (Howe et al., 1995). Second, it was clear that there were large differences between the amounts of practice undertaken by the students in the five groups: those in group 5 did approximately four times as much practice as those in the non-specialist groups (Sloboda et al., 1996). This is congruent with Ericsson et al.'s (1993) earlier finding that music conservatoire students aiming for professional performing careers had achieved approximately 10,000 hours of formal practice by 21 years of age. This was one of the most striking of Sloboda et al.'s findings, and led to their conclusion that the amount of 'formal effortful practice' undertaken was just as important as possessing talent, which resulted in newspaper headlines along the lines of 'Even Mozart had to put the hours in'.

Third, the students in group 5 progressed rapidly through their music performance graded examinations, and it appeared to be the total amount of practice time that determined one's chances of passing the exam rather than the ability/ experience group that they were in, such that someone doing far more practice would progress through the grades much more quickly. Fourth, the students in the specialist groups had parents who were much more closely involved in their lessons and practice than those in the less specialist groups: the parents' level of involvement, and levels of support for their children's musical activities, were more important than whether or not they themselves were musical (Davidson, Howe, Moore, & Sloboda, 1996). Fifth, the students who were in the specialist groups tended to have siblings who were supportive of their musical activities, in some cases taking up the same instrument. For example, six members of the more specialist groups reported having peers who were supportive of their musical activities, perhaps because they too were attending specialist music schools, and this may have helped to overcome the prejudice against music performance that may have occurred at another school. Sixth, those in the specialist groups rated their first teacher higher than did those in the less successful groups on personal dimensions such as friendliness, and they also rated their current teachers as being higher than other learners on task-oriented professional dimensions such as 'pushiness'. On average, the highly successful students had studied with more teachers than the other learners, and had also generally received more individual training than the children who eventually ceased lessons (Davidson, Moore, Sloboda, & Howe, 1998).

What is clear from these last few sets of findings is that social support networks from the family, from teachers and schools, and from peers are all important in maintaining the focus upon and motivation for musical activity in the more successful students. The interviews revealed that the students in group 1, who had given up playing their instruments, reported having some family members, teachers, and friends who were unsupportive, uninterested in, and not involved in their musical activities. Students in the specialist groups tended to have more one to one lessons with their teacher than those in another groups, and they were less likely to change their teacher over a given period of time. It seemed that most of these students reported having warm, friendly, and supportive teachers, although they were able to distinguish between personal support and warmth on the one hand, and musical talent and expertise on the other, and to realise that these different characteristics might take on greater or lesser importance at different points of their learning careers.

The Sydney Longitudinal Study

As we said earlier, McPherson had been focusing his research on relationships between the visual, aural, and creative aspects of performance skills. A great deal of instrumental training at that time was based on visual orientation, i.e. on performing rehearsed music from scores, and on developing sight-reading skills, with relatively little emphasis upon playing by ear and from memory (i.e. aural aspects) and on improvisation (creative aspects). On the basis of critical path analyses of his empirical data, McPherson (1993) developed a theoretical model of the relationships between these different musical skills and different conditions of study (such as its length and quality) which is shown in Figure 5.2. As we can see, this gives equal importance to performing rehearsed music and sight-reading on the one hand, and to playing by ear and improvisation on the other, with playing from memory occupying a middle ground between the two. This broader view of the nature of musical skill ran counter to the attitudes of many instrumental teachers at the time, but is widely accepted today.

As McPherson, Davidson, and Faulkner (2012) (henceforth McPDF) point out, it is also congruent with Sloboda and Davidson's (1996) delineation of five essential characteristics of high-level expressive music performance which had emerged from the Keele-Exeter research, namely *automaticity, systematicity, communicability, stability*, and *flexibility*. Significantly, this research indicated that these qualities were learnt whether or not the pupils had been taught formally, and they revealed 'a high level of domain-specific structural knowledge and significant memory span increases' (McPDF, p. 9) on the part of the musicians. McPDF suggest that the importance of this analysis of high-level performance has still not been fully recognised, even in current discussions about the relative efficacy of informal and formal teaching methods in music education.

Their mutual interest in the nature of early instrumental learning and teaching and its development from childhood to the secondary school and into adulthood formed the basis for McPherson and Davidson's longitudinal study, which attempted to disentangle some of the main influences on musical development. This was the first award by the Australian Research Council for a project in music education. The study initially investigated young musicians in eight primary school instrumental music programmes in Sydney, with an initial sample of 157 students (87 girls and 70 boys) between 7 and 9 years old. In the weeks before the students began their school instrumental programmes, they were all interviewed to gather information about their beliefs about and attitudes towards music learning, any previous experiences they may have had of it, why they wanted to learn an instrument, why they had chosen the particular instrument they had, and their expectations of and attitudes towards learning an instrument. All the parents were also interviewed, and this gathered information about their child's early experiences of and interests in music, the reasons why they were interested in their child learning an instrument, other family members we were also learning music, and their beliefs about music as an area of learning, as well as their expectations of their child's likely progress.

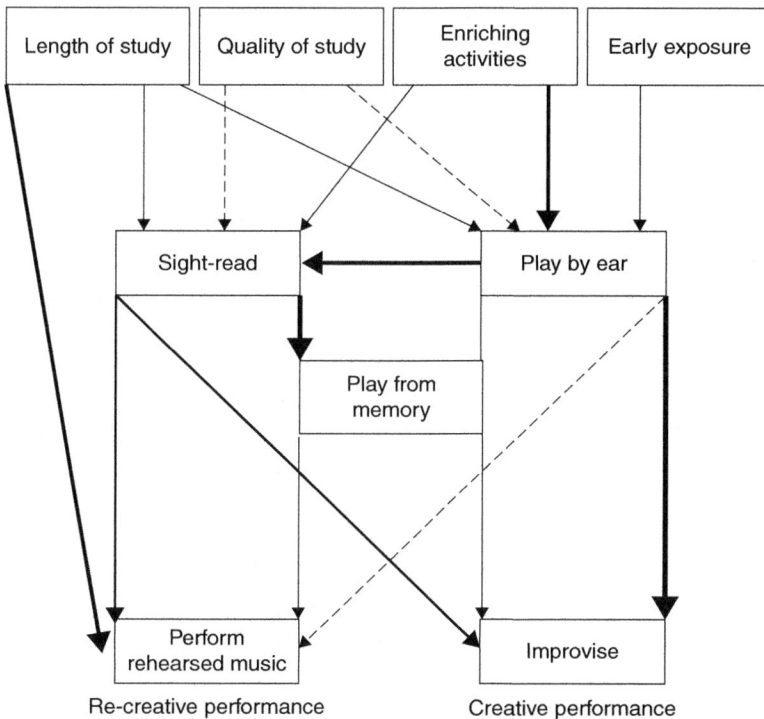

Figure 5.2. McPherson's (1993) theoretical model of relationships between musical skills and conditions of study.
Source: Figure 1.2 (p. 8) in McPherson, G. E., Davidson, J. W., & Faulkner, R. (2012). *Music in our lives*. © Oxford University Press. By permission of Oxford University Press.

After this initial phase of data gathering, further data of various kinds were subsequently collected over a fourteen-year period, such that the age range of the participants across the study ranged between 7 and 22 years. All of the children were interviewed again at the end of each of the first three years of study, and were also given a range of tasks which were designed to assess different aspects of their instrumental progress – sight reading, performing rehearsed music, playing from memory and by ear, and creative improvisation. Many of the students also had their home practice sessions videotaped regularly, and this information was triangulated with parents' interviews, some of which were conducted by telephone. These dealt with how much practice the children were doing, their general attitude and level of motivation towards their instrumental learning, and any relevant family circumstances. Information was also gathered during this first three-year period from interviews with the children's classroom teachers, from their instrumental teachers, and from their ensemble directors. The children's music grade test information was also collected, such that a wide variety of information was available about each participant in the study over the first three years of their instrumental programme.

After these children had made the transition to secondary school, data continued to be collected about their musical activities, albeit at a less intensive level, from themselves and from their parents. This was done between the ages of 14 and 15 years, i.e. at the point at which they were making choices about their specialist subjects for their final school examinations. Some time later, Davidson and McPherson were awarded a second Australian Research Council Discovery Project grant to follow up as many of the original participants as possible: they conducted an online survey and telephone interviews with the ex-students and their parents immediately after they had left school and gone either into taking a gap year, employment, or going to university. In this way it was possible to contact over two-thirds of the original sample, and Evans, McPherson, and Davidson (2013) suggest that there was no reason to believe that the students with whom they had lost contact were fundamentally any different in terms of their musical achievement and ability than those who remained in the sample: in other words, there was no reason to suspect any selective dropout.

Overall, the research team collected a large body of data which included quantitative information about musical practice, scores on musical ability tests, and a great deal of qualitative information from students, parents, and teachers concerning their beliefs about and attitudes towards musical learning. Further information was also collected through informal contacts when particular developments or changes occurred, such as moving house, or success in a particular examination. Over a fourteen-year period, this wealth of data from an overall sample of 157 students makes this almost certainly the largest longitudinal study of musical development ever undertaken. The detailed results are presented in a series of journal articles by McPherson and Davidson, who were joined in some of these by Robert Faulkner and Paul Evans on different aspects of the data analysis and publication.

In their book *Music in our Lives*, McPDF (2012) not only provide a very useful overview of the project as a whole, but also weave different theoretical models into the wide range of their empirical findings throughout the book. Among others, they draw on theoretical constructs from positive psychology (e.g. Deci & Ryan's 2002 self-determination theory), from sports psychology (e.g. Abbott & Collins' 2004 model of the development of sporting expertise), from educational psychology (e.g. Trautwein and colleagues' multilevel modelling of the processes involved when children and teenagers complete their school homework – Trautwein, Kastens, & Köller, 2006a; Trautwein, Ludtke, Schnyder, & Niggli, 2006b), and on McPherson and Williamon's (2016) adaptation of Gagné's (2009) differentiated model of giftedness and talent to music. The theoretical model on which they draw most generally and centrally, however, is Sameroff's (2009, 2010) transactional regulation approach, which they apply in detail to their participants' interactions with significant family members, teachers, peers, and other members of the community, and we shall finish this section by summarising the broad findings from the study, as well as by explaining some of the ways in which they employ Sameroff's approach.

McPDF begin the discussion in 1997, at the outset of the study, when most of the participants were 7 years old. At this early stage, the focus was on describing the young learners' previous musical experiences up to that point, and their opportunities for music performance and practice at home. The authors report that 'the significance of the school instrumental program in terms of shaping the child's musical future cannot be underestimated. The schools regarded the engagement as serious, with parent–child evenings being organized by all participating schools where an ensemble performed for parents and their children, staff explained how the instrumental program was organized, and children were encouraged to sign up for learning an instrument following year' (p. 19). There was a good deal of variation among different families in the extent of their songs and singing at home, as well as in early instrumental training: 52 per cent of the sample had never learnt an instrument previously, 27 per cent had done so but had stopped, and 21 per cent were continuing on a second instrument as well as their new instrument. Most of the students with previous experience had played piano or keyboard, and a small number had played strings or woodwind instruments.

One critical decision to be made at about this point was what choice of instrument should be made for or by the child, and some parents expressed strong views on this topic. This was because they wanted to be confident that their child would be likely to continue with the instrument, that it would provide future opportunities to play in ensembles, and that family finances would eventually be able to cover the cost of a good instrument. The children, on the other hand, were more interested in an instrument that would be exciting or enjoyable. They were often influenced by performances by their school ensembles and also by significant siblings or close friends. Some were influenced by gender stereotypes, others by the recommendations of their teachers, and still others by the practical availability of particular instruments at their school. McPDF describe the process of choosing an instrument in terms of Sameroff's concept of transactional regulation: different balances are struck between the child's desire to self-regulate their learning, and the influences of other powerful individuals such as parents, peers, and teachers, and this balance changes as they get older. Many factors may influence the final decision: to give a personal example, David's older son settled on the oboe largely because an instrument was available at home (previously learnt by David himself), whereas his younger brother was determined from the start to play the trumpet, to such an enthusiastic extent that he persuaded several of his friends to learn that instrument also!

The issue which has been investigated perhaps more than any other about instrumental learning in younger children concerns *practice*: how much time do individuals spend on this, and what is the nature of their practice? This had earlier been investigated in the Keele-Exeter study, which made the distinction between formal and informal practice. As we saw earlier, Sloboda et al. (1996) found that their high achievers tended to undertake significantly greater amounts of formal practice than members of their lower achieving groups, supporting Ericsson et al.'s (1993) finding that most professional musicians have accumulated approximately 10,000 hours of practice by the age of 20.

McPDF collected extensive video evidence on students' practice habits, and found that practice was often carried out in their own bedroom or in the family lounge after returning from school or just before going to bed. They also found that conditions were often much less than ideal – instrument cases or other objects served as music stands, posture was often inappropriate, and there were many distractions.

As far as the content of practice was concerned, this tended to be highly standardised: students mostly played through a small number of scales or other technical exercises, as well as some recommended pieces, with the main aim of achieving a high standard of fluency: this turned out to mean little more than playing the right notes at the right time. Video recordings strongly suggested that most students typically had no practice strategy other than playing pieces through from start to finish, without any attempts to focus on particularly difficult passages or important sections. They found that students typically practised about five times a week for about 20 minutes in each session, as well as engaging in twice-weekly instrumental sessions at school which lasted between 30 minutes and 2 hours, according to the type of ensemble.

It is interesting to compare these findings with those of Hallam (1997), who compared beginner and expert performance practice strategies in relation to interpretation, practice, memorisation, and performance. Hallam found that beginners made very few attempts to take account of dynamic markings, and were largely unconcerned about the musical aspects of interpretation: the main aim of practice was to play the notes correctly, and McPDF's results confirm this interpretation. Another phenomenon that was observed in further research by Hallam (e.g. Creech & Hallam, 2003) is the importance of collaborative relationship between students, parents, and teachers: the interactions between these can be critical in supporting successful practice. Creech and Hallam proposed a systems-based model to examine these interactions in relation specifically to instrumental music lessons, whereas McPDF chose to look more broadly at other areas of school homework in their own theoretical interpretation of instrumental practice, which they based on the work of Trautwein and colleagues mentioned earlier.

Trautwein and colleagues (e.g. Trautwein et al., 2006a,b) emphasise the importance and great complexity of the interactions between many different influences in fostering effective homework, and also stress the importance of avoiding negative emotions in relation to it. McPDF point out that this complexity is likely to be even greater in the case of instrumental practice, partly because some parents may themselves lack musical skills, and may therefore feel incompetent and frustrated about their lack of knowledge as the children's learning increases. McPDF's videos of practice sessions showed that parents were in close proximity to their child's practice sessions about 65 per cent of the time during the first nine months of the study, with 81 per cent of that time spent listening, and 12 per cent guiding the sessions: only 6 per cent of the time was spent in any active teaching role.

Starting at the left-hand side of Figure 5.3, we can see that the three main influences on pupils' practice are the teachers' characteristics, the students' own characteristics, and the role of parents. Different aspects of these give rise to what Trautwein et al. term the *expectancy* and *value* components of motivation to practice, which we discussed earlier in this chapter. The model shows that these two main aspects of motivational factors give rise to different characteristics of practice behaviour, which include aspects of effort, time, and learning strategies, and that different aspects of these give rise to different music learning outcomes. In this brief summary we have not attempted to detail the many different factors involved

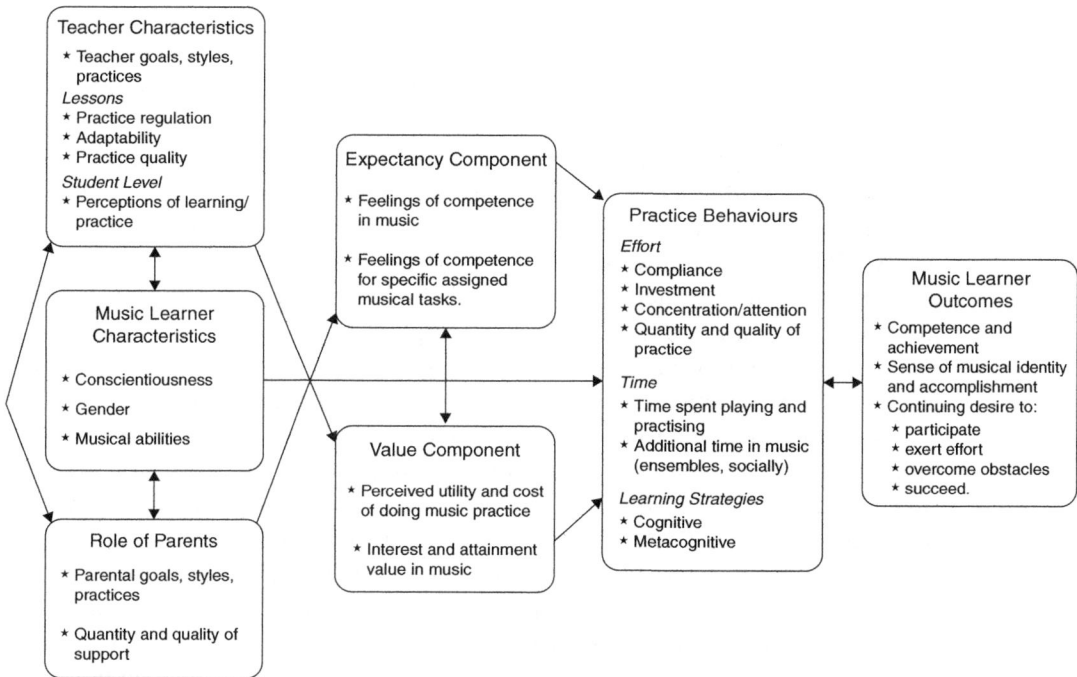

Figure 5.3. Schematic depiction of Trautwein et al.'s practice process factors.
Source: Figure 2.1 (p. 36) in McPherson, G. E., Davidson, J. W., & Faulkner, R. (2012).
Music in our lives. © Oxford University Press. By permission of Oxford University
Press. Originally adapted from Figure 1 (p. 440) in Trautwein, U., Ludtke, O., Schnyder,
I., & Niggli, A. (2006b). Predicting homework effort: support for a domain-specific,
multilevel homework model. *Journal of Educational Psychology*, 98(2), 438–56. American
Psychological Association, reprinted with permission.

in these main components of the model, although it is clear to see that this follows
the general transactional conception of musical learning which McPDF espouse.

In the next phase of their longitudinal study, McPDF tracked members of their
sample's early progress in terms of what they see as the five key areas of performing music, namely performing rehearsed music, sight reading, playing by ear, playing from memory, and improvising. They provide a wealth of detailed information
about their participants' progress in each of these five areas, and their general summary of these results as a whole is that progression occurs relatively smoothly, with
most learners improving across the initial years of their music learning. This was
true for all five of the key areas of performance between the ages of 6 and 7, and
also for all five areas except improvising between the ages of 7 and 8: this latter result
is probably because relatively little time is spent on teaching improvisation in relation to performing test pieces in many schools. The general impression of smooth
and steady progress masked a great deal of individual variation among individuals'
results, however. By the end of the third year of the study some students had still
not attained the average standard of the whole sample's results in year one, and this
was also dependent on the area of musical skill under consideration.

McPDF emphasise the significance of these individual differences, suggesting that it is important to recognise and take account of individuals' readiness for instrumental learning at different stages. They also emphasise the importance of mental strategies in practice in predicting pupils' abilities to sight read, play from memory, and play by ear. The more advanced players were characterised by the more sophisticated practice strategies they adopted throughout their development. This finding tallied with the results of the earlier studies by McPherson (2005) and McPherson and Renwick (2011), who found that students who used musically appropriate mental strategies early in their learning were more likely to succeed as compared with those who did not: this applied for all five musical skills, which emphasises the importance of developing appropriate practice habits at an early stage, and of the particular problems that can arise from not doing so.

This last point relates to another issue which was investigated in McPDF's study, namely the causes of dropout from instrumental learning. Several of these are identified, in particular (a) parental expectations: in some cases these were simply too high, leading to inevitable disappointment with their child's rate of progress. In other cases parents believed, correctly or not, that their child was not coping emotionally and/or practically with the rigours of learning their new instrument, and so began to discourage them or steer them into some other kind of activity in which they might be more successful. (b) Another common cause was the inappropriate selection of an instrument. For example, 20 per cent of the sample of students had instruments assigned to them rather than selecting them themselves, and this was a common cause of early discontent and demotivation: interestingly, this was most often true of the selection of the French horn!

Other causes of dropout included (c) what parents perceived as teachers' failure to take adequate care of individual pupils' special needs, such as medical conditions: (d) unrealistic expectations on the part of the children, such as in over-estimating the amount of time that they would be able to devote to practice, or in anticipating whether they would play they instrument for a relatively short period (e.g. a year or two) or whether they would continue until much later in life: (e) other significant family issues such as parental separation or other sudden, traumatic events: (f) negative feedback to the child, e.g. when parents were not as enthusiastic about their children about learning to play an instrument: (g) incompatibility between pupil and teacher, such as when the teaching style adopted by a particular teacher was perceived as inappropriate by the pupil, which could lead to disillusionment and disengagement.

Finally, in the latter stages of the project, McPDF were able to contact 104 of their original 157 pupils, and were interested in the ways in which, now as young adults, they had developed some eleven years later. Their analysis showed that more than 80 per cent of these pupils were still playing their instruments in year 8, i.e. at the age of 13–14 years, but that this dropped dramatically to 37 per cent in the years 9–10, and then down to 23 per cent in years 11–12, i.e., at the end of their school careers. The nature of these students' musical engagement was analysed in more detail by Paul Evans, at that time a PhD student who joined the project from the University of Western Australia. Evans looked at the types of musical activities in which these 104 students were engaged at different stages of their high school careers, and found that they were very diverse, falling into seventeen categories in all, including playing in rock bands, in community bands and orchestras, in competitions such as eisteddfods, as well as more conventional activities such as playing in school bands and orchestras, and studying for performance examinations. This range of activities led the researchers to conclude that musical participation fulfilled three main specific functions, namely '(a) formal, competitive, skills-based for external incentives; (b) creative, peer-based and social for both external and internal (self) satisfaction: (c) personal, self-regulating function (changing mood, relaxing, being in one's own company).' (p. 77)

We have only had space here to attempt a very brief summary of the findings of this large and important study, and McPDF's account in their book is itself only a summary of their much more detailed analysis of the databases, which are to be found in more detailed journal publications. In rest of their book they carry out a number of case studies which adopt an idiographic approach, such that the project as a whole used mixed methods. Some of the case studies used interpretive phenomenological analysis (IPA), which looks in depth at the underlying ways in which participants conceptualise and try to explain their motivation and rationale for learning an instrument. Space does not allow us to attempt to convey the essence of any of these here, and we will confine ourselves instead to a description of McPDF's transactional approach to explaining their data, which points the way forward for subsequent research.

Summary: Explaining the Effects of Specific Environmental Influences

We have devoted a lot of attention to the Sydney study partly because it follows naturally from the Keele-Exeter project, partly because of its size and scale (not only in terms of participant numbers, but also its 14-year longitudinal span), and also because of the wealth of theoretical insights which it brings. We have already mentioned McPDF's use of several specific theoretical models, including those of Trautwein, Gagné, Deci and Ryan, and Abbott and Collins. These models all complement McPDF's central use of the concept of *transactional regulation*, which is based on Sameroff's theoretical ideas, and which they use in conjunction with self-determination theory (SDT, which we encountered earlier in this chapter).

Transactional regulation can be used in the explanation of many different findings: in essence, it is concerned with the balance between the interacting influences of the external guidance provided by teachers, family, and peers, and the young learner's own self-regulation, which in turn influences their motivation and subsequent achievement level. This can be a delicate balance: it is important that teachers, for example, should provide some basic guidance but that they should not be over-controlling, and allow the pupil some autonomy, so as to encourage the development of self-regulation. McPDF express this as follows: 'From our study, a key component of effective instrumental music teaching appears to be the sensitive and flexible negotiation of transpersonal regulation to deliver develop individual interest and musical autonomy as the basis for sustainable musical development. The strategy for doing so may be found in appropriate teacher support for self-regulation at every opportunity, in every lesson' (p. 41).

Another related and central idea which McPDF introduce is that of the *syzygy*, which is perhaps best described as a 'favourable alignment of circumstances'. Sameroff's view is that the social, biological, and psychological experiences involved in music learning all 'foster and transform each other' (Sameroff & Fiese, 2000). This means that the delicate balance between self- and other-regulation involved in successful musical development – which involves complex interactions between caregivers, parents, teachers, and the learners themselves – need to be such that musical development is promoted rather than inhibited: syzygies represent the positive combinations of circumstances when this does occur, and when the learner's current needs, ambitions, and aspirations are aligned with present provision and resources.

McPDF go on to outline how these different combinations of circumstances may ultimately give rise to positive, no, or indeed negative musical development, and they do so by drawing a distinction between *promotive* and *demotive* environmental factors in musical development. If syzygies exist with respect to a pupil's positive circumstances (having a sympathetic family background, a good teacher, the time and motivation to practice, friends who sympathise, and so on), they can be seen as promotive factors in musical development. If any of them are negative, however (e.g. having an unsympathetic or overambitious parent, or having a competing interest such as sport), such factors could be described as demotive, and progress would be much slower. It is also possible, of course, to have a combination of promotive and demotive factors, in which case syzygy would not be present. Another term which McPDF use to describe a positive syzygy of promotive factors for musical development is 'musical matching', in which the learner's biological, social, and psychological background is aligned with a positive set of learning circumstances, parental expectations, and so on.

Having established this basic theoretical background, McPDF apply it to what they see as the three key interacting systems in musical development, namely those relating to the family, to teachers, and to peers, and they do so by proposing what they call a taxonomy of regulatory sites, which are described on pages 193–200 of their book. The five key factors which are identified for the transactional regulation within the family are *physical resources, practice and performance, child competence and autonomy, musical works,* and *teachers and schools*; there are four key factors for teachers, namely *physical resources, child competence and autonomy, music teaching content, style and strategy,* and *general teacher behaviour*. There is only effectively one factor for peers, namely *social groups*, which can give rise to transactional regulation.

This taxonomy enables us to pin down exactly where self-regulatory transactional behaviour can be used to support the three psychological needs specified by self-determination theory, i.e. those of competence, relatedness, and autonomy, and McPDF have worked out decision trees for each of these that could be used by parents and teachers in planning their young learners' musical training and experience. They see the ways in which musical activity can meet the needs of relatedness as being those which are likely to be able to sustain musical activity in the long term, and that this occurs on both the interpersonal and intrapersonal levels. In order to achieve this, competency needs have to be met in order to provide the basic skills necessary for achieving inter- and intra-relatedness; and autonomy gives individuals a clear role in determining what are the appropriate courses of musical action to adopt at different parts of their developing lives.

In summary, the results of this study as well as those of the Keele-Exeter study emphasise the overwhelming importance of analysing the interactions between family, schools, and peers. Musical activity has a unique capacity to satisfy people's need for relatedness, and this involves not only social networking and collaboration, but also the fulfilment of their striving for personal meaning and aesthetic experience: it can meet emotional needs, along with social and cognitive ones.

Music Education and Musical Development

We dealt in the previous sections of this chapter with the effects of schools on their pupils' musical development in the context of other 'environmental influences', but this of course raises the distinction between normative and expert development, which closely parallels that between acculturation and training, which we discussed in Chapter 2. Normative development and acculturation both refer to what happens to members of a particular community or society as a result of simply growing up within that community, whereas expert development and training imply specific attempts to guide development in a certain direction. The latter raises the question of the concept of education, and the aims and objectives of education are a weighty subject of great philosophical discussion and interest, of course. The idea that 'education is what survives after all that was taught has been forgotten' is an attractive one to those, like ourselves, who have passed through the intensive and highly specialised British secondary education system. Defining the aims of music education raises equally interesting and difficult issues, and many different attempts to do so have been made in different parts of the world, as we shall see in this final section of the chapter.

Our strategy in this section is to look in detail, first, at music education in England, partly because a lot of important general issues have recently come to the fore, with several fundamental changes occurring very rapidly over the last two decades, and partly because this is the system that we know best. This will provide the depth of coverage for our analysis, and we shall go on to consider some broader international and comparative issues in global music education, which should provide our coverage with complementary breadth. Some of this ground has already been covered by North and Hargreaves (2008), and we refer back to more detailed coverage there where this seems appropriate.

Music Education in England, 2000–

Music and arts education more generally have traditionally been regarded as the 'Cinderella' of education policy in English schools: for many years this subject area has been among the first to suffer when financial cuts are proposed, and one which has lower status and resources devoted to it than other curriculum subjects which are seen as more important in pupils' future careers, such as English, science, or mathematics. Perhaps because education has been such a highly politicised domain in the UK in recent years, however, there has been unprecedented investment in and support for music education on the part of different governments over the last decade or two, although it is important to point out that there are widespread variations in music education policy between the education systems in England, Scotland, Ireland, and Wales.

In England, the government's *Music Manifesto* (DfES, 2004) proposed that the traditionally narrow and elitist view of musical expertise, against which we argued in the early part of this chapter, should be broadened and 'joined up' with other parts of the musical world to a much greater extent than had traditionally been the case. The basic philosophy was that musical activity should be accessible to and participated in by everyone, and should not be the territory of a small number of 'experts' with highly specialised and cultivated skills. The idea was, and still is, that teachers and pupils in schools should collaborate with those working in other areas of musical life such as in broadcasting and the media, in therapeutic and clinical settings, in communities, in bands and orchestras, and in commercial businesses based on music. In this way, it is argued, music educators ought to be able to capitalise on the power of music to promote the emotional, social, and cognitive development of pupils of all ages.

The *Music Manifesto* provided the policy platform for the government to make major investments in three further significant initiatives in music education, namely Sing Up (2012), a national singing programme which ran between 2007 and 2011; the *Wider Opportunities* (Whole Class Instrumental and Vocal Teaching) programme, which ran between 2005 and 2011, and *In Harmony*, an orchestral education programme which ran in Lambeth, Leeds, Liverpool, Gateshead/Newcastle, Nottingham, and Telford/ Stoke-on-Trent, and which was inspired by the Sistema programme in South America (see Lewis, 2011). The latter also inspired the formation of 'Sistema Scotland' in 2008, which was launched in order to start a pilot social transformation programme, the Big Noise, teaching children from the Raploch estate near Stirling to play instruments within the context of an orchestra (see Jourdan & Holloway, 2017). Along with these specific performance-based programmes came some significant innovations in school-based music education as a result of two initiatives from the Paul Hamlyn Foundation, namely *Musical Futures*, which looked specifically at the potential role of informal teaching methods in schools and at 'out-of-school-hours' music-making, and *Musical Bridges*, which was concerned with the effects of school transition, in particular the transition between primary and secondary school.

All of these innovations were accepted by most music teachers in England, successfully changing the attitudes and working practices of many of them, and this led to a rise in the perceived and actual importance of informal music-making and listening, which usually (but not always) takes place outside school. We describe

Lucy Green's research on introducing informal methods in the secondary music classroom in more detail later in this chapter, and it is no exaggeration to say that informal methods are now seen by some as being as important as the formal music-making that takes place in schools, universities, and conservatoires. One consequence of this is that some of the traditional distinctions which have formed the basis of music education curricula and pedagogy for many years are being rethought. These include the distinction between 'specialist' and 'general' (or 'curriculum') music at school; that between institutional and community music making; and even that between the teacher and the learner of music.

All of these emerging strands were brought together in Darren Henley's *Review of Music Education in England*, commissioned by the Department of Education and the Department for Culture, Media and Sport (Henley, 2011), which made a series of 36 recommendations about all aspects of the structure, delivery, and funding of music education in England. This was soon followed by the publication of the *National Plan for Music Education* (NPME: DfE, 2011), which indicates an unprecedented level of government interest in and support for music education. One of the key features of the NPME is that schools should draw on newly formed organisations called Music Education Hubs, which were designed to take forward the work of local authority music services from September 2012, thereby helping to improve the quality and consistency of music education across England both in and out of school.

The rationale for these Hubs is that the different organisations involved in music education in different parts of England, which include schools, local education authorities, music services, arts organisations, and private teachers, with their different sets of skills and leaderships, should come together in partnership: the Hubs should represent a unified music education sector which includes all of these organisations, rather than just being a loose collective body of music-making organisations. Central government funding will be channelled through one lead organisation, usually a Local Authority Music Service, and as part of an open bidding process for these funds, intending Hubs need to show that they are able to cater for the music education of all children in their particular area. After the launch of these initiatives, the Paul Hamlyn Foundation commissioned a review of schools-based music education in the UK in 2014, and this has resulted in the formation of a time-limited Expert Commission, *Inspire Music*, which has the task of producing clear, comprehensive guidance for teachers and music leaders in making choices about curriculum and pedagogy, and in collating examples of best practice and innovation in this sector (see Zeserson, Welch, Burn, Saunders, & Himonides, 2014).

Having looked in depth at the issues which are currently salient in music education in England, some of which are likely to apply also in many other countries, the rest of this section is devoted to a review of the ways in which the social, cultural, and ideological influences which shape the nature of music education all over the world affect the musical development of children and adults, and we do so from three different points of view. First, we consider the *contexts* of music education: how does music teaching and learning in school relate to that which takes place out of school, for example, and what are the role of institutions such as conservatories, universities, and community organisations in different countries? In answering this last question we draw on an international study of music education and learning carried out by Hargreaves and North (2001), which revealed that different countries have quite different *aims and objectives* for music education, and the definition of these constitutes our second question. For example, should music education largely be concerned with fostering and developing musical performance skills, or should it go beyond this in developing pupils' personal qualities and attitudes? How important is instrumental tuition in relation to what is involved in being a musician in the digital era? Thirdly, and finally, we consider the processes of *learning and teaching* in music: can musical skills be self-taught rather than learnt from others, for example, and how do the different contexts of music-making influence the ways in which we learn? Given the changing view of what is involved in being a musician, what is the present-day role of the music teacher?

Contexts

There are striking differences between the contexts, aims and objectives, and processes of music teaching and learning in different countries, and international comparisons provide a valuable means of describing these. Campbell (2016) and Walker (2006) have both addressed some important conceptual issues involved in making such comparisons: Campbell explores 'global practices' of children's learning of music, demonstrating the similarities between the ways in which this occurs across all cultures even though it is based on the specific cultural values and practices of local homes, families, and communities. Walker emphasises the importance of specific cultural traditions, citing Merriam's (1997) view that ethnomusicologists consider music to be one of the most stable elements of culture, and suggesting that 'music is one of the most important elements through which a child maintains a stable cultural identity, even when cultural traditions and associated life-styles have all but disappeared' (p. 439). The ways in which children develop and maintain their cultural identities, and the important role that music education can play in this process, are elaborated by Ilari (2017) and by Zapata Restrepo and Hargreaves (2017).

Hargreaves and North (2001) undertook a comparative review of fifteen different countries from around the world by asking eminent music educators in each country to review three main aspects of their national provision, namely 'aims and objectives', 'contents and methods', and 'student issues'. Although this provision varied widely, it was nevertheless possible to identify several issues of common concern, in particular (a) the tension between the Western classical tradition, Western pop music, and traditional local musics; (b) the role of general and specialist provision in the curriculum; (c) the aims and objectives of music education; and (d) the question of music learning in and out of school. The detailed findings of our review are described by North and Hargreaves (2008), and so we will restrict ourselves to the main conclusions here.

The countries covered by our review varied considerably with respect to factors such as their geographical size, cultural diversity, population, and economic wealth. China and India incorporate numerous nationalities and different languages and a wide range of political, cultural, and musical traditions, for example, and both countries have ancient philosophical traditions which deal with questions of moral and personal development, and which influence their views of the arts and the role of arts education. Recent technological developments mean that Western (largely Anglo-American) pop music is available to an increasingly large proportion of the world's population, and this is having a powerful effect not only on people's musical experience and consumption, but also upon more general aspects of popular culture, including leisure interests, clothing styles, and social attitudes.

In China, the world's most populated country, Western pop culture appears as yet to have had relatively little impact upon music education, although Western pop music is making rapid inroads into the vast new entertainment market of China. It was only a decade or two ago that China was closed to foreign music, but cultural restrictions have gradually been loosened, and China is now a very important new market, especially at a time when record sales in the West continue to plunge. Primos's (2001) account of music education in South Africa revealed a similar tension between the Western classical tradition, which has been a prominent influence in the past, African music, and the influx of pop culture.

The second issue of common international concern stems from the distinction between 'general' and 'specialist' music education: most countries offer both of these, but vary in the ways in which each is provided in and out of school, and in the balance that is struck between them. Specialist music education is typically offered as an optional subject for older pupils in different school systems, and those intending to go on to a career in music typically seek additional tuition from outside the school alongside that they receive within it. General music is typically part of the general curriculum for younger pupils, and is usually taught either by specialist musicians or by general class teachers with extra training in general music; the question of which of these types is best qualified to do so can be a controversial issue. We shall return to the other two issues which emerged from the international review later in the chapter.

In response to the concerns of the Music Development Task Group of the Qualifications and Curriculum Authority, the body that was responsible for music education policy in English schools in the early years of the new millennium, but now disbanded, we formulated a 'globe' model of the range of *opportunities* available to pupils within music education, conceived as widely as possible (see e.g. Hargreaves, Marshall, & North, 2003). This was designed to meet the Group's concern that school music should forge important links between the home, the school, and the wider world (QCA, 2002). The model is shown in Figure 5.4, and is organised around three bipolar dimensions. The vertical dimension distinguishes between formal, institutional contexts that lead to qualifications and careers (the 'northern hemisphere' of the model), and informal contexts which do not. The horizontal dimension distinguishes between statutory and elective provision: the

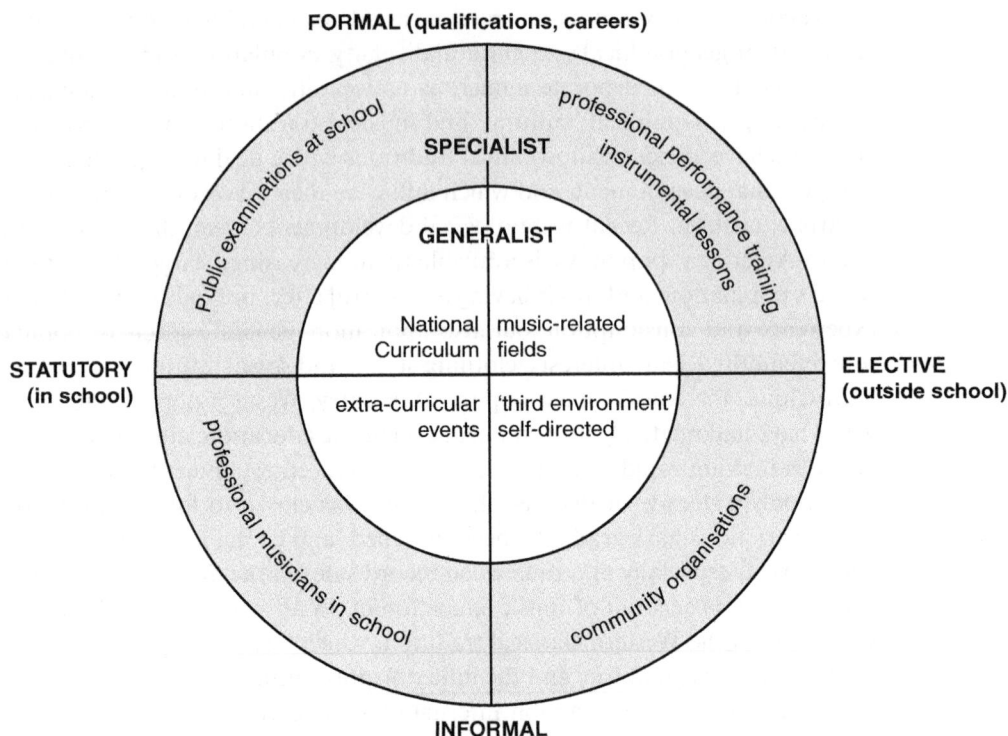

Figure 5.4.   Globe model of pupil opportunities in music education.
Source: Redrawn from Figure 1 (p. 158) in Hargreaves, D. J., Marshall, N., & North, A. C. (2003). Music education in the 21st century: a psychological perspective. *British Journal of Music Education*, 20(2), 147–163. By permission of Cambridge University Press.

'western hemisphere' includes in-school music provision in all its forms, and the 'eastern hemisphere' includes all of those opportunities that are optional, voluntary, and self-selected by pupils. The third dimension, 'specialist-generalist', derives from an earlier model of teaching methods in music education (Hargreaves, 1996), and shows that opportunities at both of these levels exist in all four quadrants of the model.

North and Hargreaves (2008) have described the model in detail, but in brief, its 'north-eastern' quadrant refers to the traditional 'specialist musician' route, usually involving instrumental grade examinations, ensembles and orchestras provided by local education and music agencies, which can lead on to the conservatoire, and to careers in professional music, its 'south-eastern' quadrant incorporates what has been called the 'third environment', i.e. those contexts in which musical learning takes place in the absence of parents or teachers, to which we will return to in Chapter 6; its 'north-western' quadrant includes the different kinds of provision that take place in schools; and its 'south-western' quadrant includes the informal music education provision that is available in schools.

The balance between musical learning in and out of school varies widely across different countries. In many parts of South America and Africa, for example, music is an integral part of everyday life: it is a natural part of work, play, rituals, ceremonies, and religious and family occasions. In countries in which the provision of school music is relatively scarce, informal music-making assumes prominence: but in the UK and other European countries there is a clear distinction between music inside and outside school, particularly at the secondary school level.

Aims and Objectives

We suggested earlier that one of the four key issues to emerge from Hargreaves and North's (2001) international comparison of music education concerned its aims and objectives: respondents from different countries gave different responses to the question 'What are arts and music education for?' Our review revealed two main underlying issues: the first is whether the development of musical experience and expertise is an end in itself, such that music education serves mainly to promote musical and artistic skills, or whether it should have broader personal and cultural aims. As we noted earlier, there were clear differences between Eastern and Western countries in this respect. Arts and music educators from Eastern countries placed much more emphasis on the moral and spiritual role of the arts than their Western counterparts: their primary aim was to develop the character of pupils. In Japan, for example, the emphasis is on 'educating the student through music' rather than on 'teaching music to students'.

In the West, on the other hand, there is much more interest in the non-musical benefits of music education, and in the so-called 'transfer' effects of participation (see e.g. Hetland & Winner, 2000). Perhaps the best-known example of this is in the research carried out since the mid-1990s on the so-called 'Mozart Effect', originally stimulated by an article by Frances Rauscher and her colleagues (Rauscher, Shaw, & Ky, 1993), which showed that a group of undergraduates who listened to ten minutes of Mozart's music performed better on a subsequent test of spatial ability than matched groups who received either relaxation instructions or silence. This study provoked a wealth of replication attempts and further studies, which are reviewed and evaluated in Chapter 8, but the general level of disagreement about the results of this research means that we are a long way from being able to formulate educational recommendations based upon them.

The second main issue concerning aims and objectives is the extent to which music education should be teacher- or pupil-centred. The Indian *guru-shishya* system, for example, epitomises the teacher-centred approach (see Farrell, 2001): in this system the pupil (literally) sits at the feet of the teacher (the guru), and learns the philosophy, traditions, and techniques of the music over a long period of months and years. This contrasts sharply with the highly pupil-centred 'creativity' movements which predominate in Australia, in the UK, and in North and South America, in which pupils' self-expression and originality are seen as far more important in the early stages of learning than technique or tradition.

Figure 5.5 shows a conceptual model of the potential outcomes of music education, which was developed along with the model of opportunities in music education (Figure 5.4). It is based on a broad division between three main types of

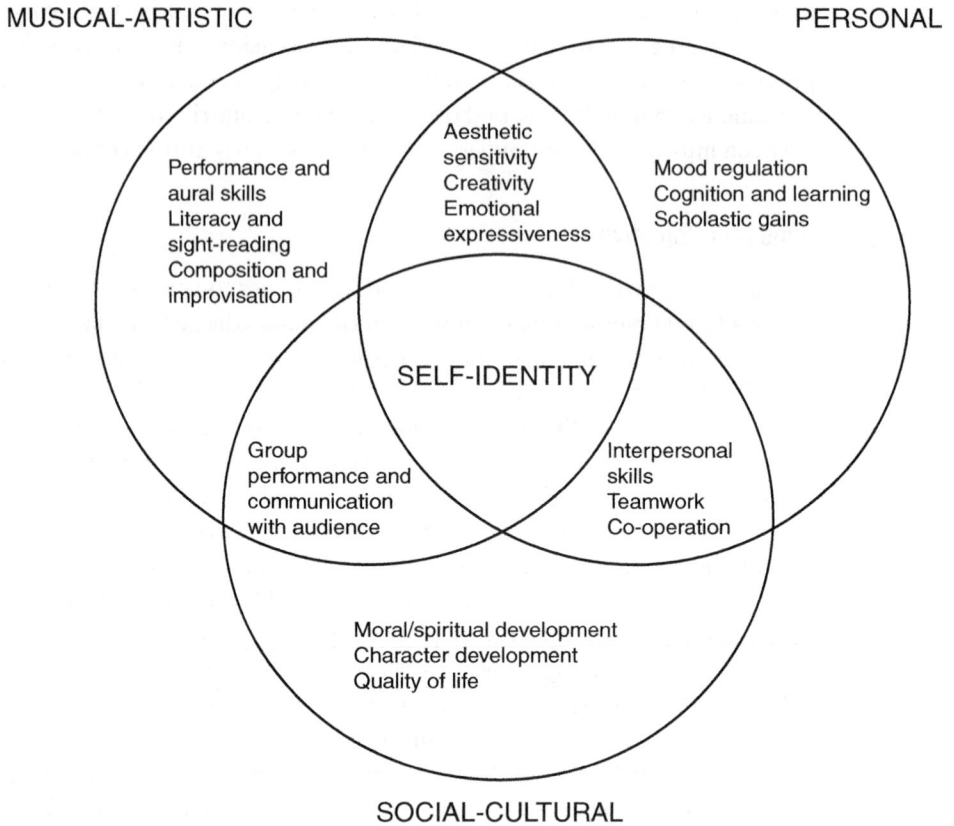

Figure 5.5.   Potential outcomes of music education.
Source: Redrawn from Figure 2 (p. 160) in Hargreaves, D. J., Marshall, N., & North, A. C. (2003). Music education in the 21st century: a psychological perspective. *British Journal of Music Education*, 20(2), 147–163. By permission of Cambridge University Press.

outcome, namely the *musical-artistic*, the *personal*, and the *social-cultural*. Expert musical skills such as performing, sight-reading, singing, aural skills, literacy, composing, and improvising are the basis of specialist conservatoire training, and these are closely associated with broader *musical-artistic* skills such as emotional expression in performance, musicological understanding, aesthetic appreciation and discrimination, and creativity in improvisation and composition: these latter skills are shown in the intersection between 'musical-artistic' and 'personal' in the model.

There are two main types of *personal* outcome in the model, which relate to cognition, learning, and scholastic gains on the one hand, and emotional development or mood regulation on the other. The aims of the national curriculum framework for the arts in Australia have a similar emphasis on a holistic view of the 'core goals' of arts education, which include the promotion of confident self-expression, creative and innovative thinking, being involved, and 'having a go'.

The third broad group of *social-cultural* outcomes include the development of moral character, spiritual values, and the 'quality of life': music and the arts are seen as a means of transmitting these cultural ideals and values from one generation to the next. These outcomes clearly overlap with those *personal* outcomes which are based on social skills and cultural development. Most musical activity is carried out either with or for other people, and therefore plays an important part in promoting interpersonal skills, teamwork, and co-operation. Social-cultural outcomes also overlap with *musical-artistic* ones, since musical expressiveness involves communication with the audience, as well as between co-performers within a group.

The centre of the model brings us back to the notion of identity that we explored earlier in this chapter, and to which we will return in Chapter 6: this represents the view that the ultimate outcome of music education is the development of individual self-identity in certain specific directions. In this sense, the model could be said to simultaneously represent a mapping of the different aims and objectives of music education, as well as of the ways in which these might be internalised within the individual.

Teaching and Formal-Informal Learning

The co-existence of the three dimensions of formal-informal contexts, statutory and elective provision, and specialist-generalist education in the model of opportunities in Figure 5.4 means that they are conceived as being independent of one another, which has the important implication that formal and informal music learning can take place, at generalist or specialist levels, in school-based as well as out of school contexts.

Our focus in this final section of the chapter is on the nature of the distinction between formal and informal music learning, and on the ways in which this is related to different teaching styles. Campbell (2016) made a further distinction between informal learning which is 'only partly guided, occurring outside institutionalized settings through the prompting of non-consecutive directives, frequently by expert musicians to novices', and that which is 'enculturative, occurring naturally, non-consciously, and without direct instructional activity of any sort' (pp. 556–7).

Earlier attempts to identify the main features of the distinction between formal and informal learning were made by Folkestad (2005, 2006), Green (2005), and Hargreaves and Marshall (2003), and four main dimensions emerge from these analyses. The first refers to the *contexts* of learning, such as the home, the school, and the third environment, which we have discussed already. The second is that of *autonomy* and *ownership*: school music usually involves the teacher's control of the curriculum, as well as of the selection and direction of the activities taking place, whereas music out of school is typically self-directed: the learners set their own agenda and adopt their own ways of working, and this can engender high levels of motivation and commitment.

The third dimension is what Folkestad (2005) called *learning style*. This is 'the nature and quality of the learning process' (p. 283), and several different aspects of learning styles can be identified. Green (2005) specified four of these, pointing out that informal music learning typically (a) involves playing and copying recordings by ear, rather than working from notation or from spoken or written instructions;

(b) takes place in groups rather than individually, such that peer learning occurs through discussion, observation, and imitation; (c) proceeds in 'top-down' rather than in 'bottom-up' fashion in the sense that informal learners usually work with 'real-life' pieces of music in their own idiosyncratic ways, whereas formal music education typically involves a planned progression from simple to more complex skills and achievements; and (d) tends to involve the integration of listening, performing, improvising, and composing activities rather than their differentiation and increasing specialisation, as in formal learning.

The fourth dimension of learning content refers to the content of the particular pieces of music which are being studied, and in particular the selection of different styles and genres. Folkestad (2005) has pointed out that 'popular music is already present in school, brought there by the students, and in many cases also by the teachers, as part of their musical experience and knowledge' (p. 280). In spite of the inclusion of a wide range of musical styles in many music curricula around the world and in many people's everyday music listening, school music is still nevertheless typically associated with 'serious' genres, most notably Western 'classical' music, whereas music out of school is typically associated with pop and rock. This was clearly spelt out in two of our own studies, namely North, Hargreaves, and O'Neill's (2000) survey of 2,465 British 13–14-year-olds, which showed that they perceived the benefits of playing and listening to pop music (including 'enjoyment') as being very different to those for classical music ('to please parents and teachers'); and Boal-Palheiros and Hargreaves' (2001) study of 9- to 10- and 13- to 14-year-old school pupils in the UK and Portugal, which found that they associated school music listening with motivation for learning, being active, and the content of particular lessons, but associated home music listening with enjoyment, emotional mood, and social relationships.

The inter-relationships among these four dimensions of formal and informal learning – *contexts, autonomy and ownership, learning style, and learning content* – determine the *authenticity* of secondary school music for pupils, and thereby its likely success. The challenge for secondary school music teachers is somehow to be able to capitalise on the high levels of motivation and commitment that informal music learning can engender, but to do so within the school environment. Lucy Green's (2002, 2008) studies of how young musicians learn to play in pop bands out of school encouraged her to attempt to introduce the same informal learning methods inside school in some studies which have generated widespread interest in the UK as well as internationally.

In her book *How popular musicians learn: A way ahead for music education*, Green (2002) describes her interview study of fourteen pop musicians aged between 15 and 50 who were living in or near London, UK. Her interviews covered topics including the nature of their skills and knowledge, how they had gone about acquiring it, how they had developed as musicians, what attitudes and values they had about their music, and what experiences they had had as pupils and students in formal music education. Their responses suggested that the use of informal learning methods, which encompass the four dimensions which we described earlier, might be able to increase pupils' levels of motivation, to widen the range of musical skills that they might gain, to make music education more inclusive for pupils of all abilities and backgrounds, and also to broaden their appreciation and respect for a range of musical styles going well beyond the usual boundaries of the school curriculum. The final chapter of the book puts forward a number of suggestions for introducing informal learning practices into formal music education settings, 'not as a substitute, but as a complement, running side by side with existing approaches' (Green, 2002, p. 4).

In her later book *Music, informal learning and the school: A new classroom pedagogy*, Green (2008) describes how the informal methods investigated in the first book can be applied in the music classroom, and describes her own empirical study of this in 21 secondary schools, which involved 32 classroom teachers and over 1,500 pupils, and which received funding as part of the Paul Hamlyn Foundation's *Musical Futures* project. The research methods and detailed results, which are largely qualitative and based on copious quotations from the teachers and pupils taking part, are reported in this book in terms of the seven main stages of the project. Each stage consisted of between three and six lessons of about an hour, once a week, in normal curriculum time.

In brief, stage 1 consisted of pupils bringing in their own choice of music, listening to it in small friendship groups, and choosing one song, which they then attempted to copy by ear, selecting their own instruments and directing their own learning. In stage 2 they were provided with recordings of a funk track plus 15 of its riffs played separately and in combination, and once again listened, discussed, and attempted to play it through by ear, creating their own version of the song. Stage 3 was a repetition of stage 1, designed to consolidate the skills acquired during the first two stages, and in stage 4, pupils were asked to compose, rehearse, and perform their own music by self-direction in friendship groups. In stage 5 they were introduced to a 'musical model' of songwriting by 'a band of peer musicians or community musicians' (Green, 2008, p. 193), and then continued to work on their own self-directed music in friendship groups.

Green's discussion of the interview transcripts suggests that the use of informal learning methods can enable the recognition and promotion of a range of musical skills and knowledge that have long been overlooked, but which give a new perspective on music learning which may encourage pupils to take part, and possibly thereby to address the 'problem of secondary school music' we mentioned earlier. These musical skills and knowledge, which emerge without intentional guidance from teachers, include what Green calls 'purposive listening' to and copying music from CD recordings, thereby developing 'critical musicality' and appreciation; the development of motivation and personal autonomy in music-making; confidence and enjoyment; and the growth of group co-operation.

Green also describes the initial reticence of some of the music teachers to take part, partly because of the challenges involved in introducing informal learning: this can conflict with their notions of professionalism, and can appear to run counter to many official discourses, and statements of curricular aims and objectives. However, she argues that these possible tensions turned out to be more apparent than real, and that they were more than compensated for by the new perspectives and insights offered by the new methods. Another significant issue is that of genre: informal learning always starts with music which the learners have chosen themselves, and this tends to be music which they know, understand and like, which is almost always pop music in some form. The studies we cited above clearly link pop music with enjoyment, the pupils' autonomy, and out of school locations, whereas classical music is correspondingly linked with learning, teacher control, and being inside school.

Green addressed the genre issue directly in stages 6 and 7 of the project by attempting to apply the same informal learning techniques to classical music: pupils were asked to listen to classical music and then to copy it in their own instrumental performances. This poses different problems from pop music, of course, in that the musical material cannot be chosen by the children, and in that classical music is not usually taught or learnt by informal methods. Nevertheless, there were two main tasks: in stage 6, pupils were provided with recordings of five pieces of classical music drawn from TV advertisements, and were asked, in friendship groups, to 'listen, discuss, select, copy, arrange, rehearse, and perform the music as an ensemble' (p. 194). The link with TV advertisements was to place the music in a familiar context and to make it seem less alien and unfamiliar: but in stage 7, pupils were provided with five recordings of classical pieces which were mostly unfamiliar, as well as with recordings of the individual melodies and bass lines of the pieces, simplified in some cases. Once again they were asked, in friendship groups, to produce a performance with exactly the same instructions as mentioned earlier.

Green reports that the teachers were particularly apprehensive and nervous about these final two stages, since the pupils' initial views of classical music were often very negative, hostile, and frequently rude. Nevertheless, she reports that most of the teachers reluctantly 'took it on board', and that as the pupils themselves became more familiar with the detailed content of the music through having to analyse it, that their attitudes towards it became less negative. In analysing the pupils' products, Green reports that the children introduced a certain amount of variation and interpretation, and that somewhat to their own surprise, the teachers judged many of the performances to be better than they expected.

Generally speaking, Green concludes that the pupils' attitudes towards classical music did change, and that their preconceptions of its 'difficulty' and/or strangeness tended to change after they had had some direct experience of it. More children thought that classical music should be included in the curriculum after they had experienced stages 6 and 7, and the teachers were generally surprised that their pupils were willing to take part. She concludes that 'when pupils' listening experiences are meaningfully connected to some amount of social action, which is both autonomous and co-operative, and when these experiences also involve the direct production of musical inter-sonic meanings in a way which can "flow" and which can be playful, and when pupils are stimulated by whole pieces of "real" music, then their musical awareness and response, or "critical musicality", seem to open up' (p.180).

Green's project was independently evaluated as part of a broader survey of the Paul Hamlyn Foundation's Musical Futures initiative by the Institute of Education, University of London (Hallam, Creech, Sandford, Rinta, & Shave, 2008), and the responses of 691 teachers along with 1,079 pupils suggest that over 50 per cent of the teachers had adopted the informal teaching approach, and reported that their own teaching had become more confident, effective and enjoyable as a result; and that the pupils had experienced many benefits, including enhanced motivation, better behaviour, enhanced musical skills, and more confidence. The majority of the pupils correspondingly reported that they preferred Musical Futures to other types of music lessons, benefitting most in terms of enhanced self- confidence, motivation, and enjoyment of music. Hallam et al. conclude that 'Musical Futures has the potential to enhance pupil motivation in relation to music and enhance the quality of teaching and learning' (p. 8), and the associated gains in musical development and achievement, as well as in other areas of these young people's lives suggest that this initiative deserves to be developed and extended. We might sound a small note of caution, however: we have argued elsewhere (Lamont & Maton, 2010) that while encouraging motivation and enthusiasm, the programme could ultimately be difficult to reconcile with the formal assessments embedded in secondary education, and it may be that some pupils find it difficult to transfer what they learn to different contexts.

Conclusion

In this chapter we have considered a wide range of environmental influences on musical ability, achievement, and motivation. This has meant tackling some of the difficult conceptual issues which surround the definition as well as the development of musical ability and 'musicality', as well as evaluating the evidence for the commonly held current view that 'everyone is musical', to some degree at least. This led us to the related questions of whether some people are more naturally musically gifted than others, of the extent to which children's levels of musicality can be influenced by practice and training, and of the role of motivation in promoting musical achievement. We focused next on two large-scale and inter-related studies of the development of musicality: one British study which was carried out in the 1990s by a research team from the Universities of Keele and Exeter, and a more recent Australian longitudinal study based in Sydney. Both of these studies throw a great deal of light on the roles of family, schools, and peers in particular: we have tried to summarise the main findings of these important studies, and to focus in particular on the theoretical concepts and models on which they have drawn in explaining musical development in its real-life complexity.

We went on to look at the complex and important question of the effects of music education on musical development, which has very obvious practical implications.

Partly because a great deal of government attention has been paid to music education in England in recent years, partly because this is the system we know best, and partly because the underlying issues are of universal importance, we next reviewed the main developments in English music education since 2000, and this highlighted some of the main current issues in music education, including the effects of different contexts (including international variations, and the differences between music inside and outside school); the aims and objectives of music education, and international variations in them; and at formal and informal music learning, including some research on the use of informal teaching methods in formal contexts, which seem to hold a great deal of future promise.

6 Identity, Personality, and Lifestyle

In Chapter 5 we noted the shift from research on individual differences in musicality (as measured by tests of ability, achievement, and attitudes) to the current focus on how an individual's capacities with respect to these different factors determine that individual's self-perception. This brings in the important concept of *identity*, which forms the main focus of this chapter. Whereas the field of individual differences was based on a *nomothetic* approach, in which the main aim is to map the profiles of different groups of individuals according to these different characteristics, the study of identity adopts an *ideographic* approach to the same phenomena, looking at how these individual difference characteristics lead to certain distinctive self-concepts.

How do people see themselves in relation to other people around them, and in particular in relation to the different social groups of which they are and are not apart? When Accrington Stanley Football Club is playing against their Lancashire near-neighbour rivals Bury F.C. in the English Football League Division Two, for example, David is a Stanley supporter; when Lancashire plays against Yorkshire in the County Cricket championship, however, he becomes a Lancastrian. When Manchester United plays against Arsenal, Chelsea, or any of the other London-based teams in the Football Association Premier league, his partisanship becomes that of a Northerner, and therefore a rival of any team from the South of England; but when England plays in the UEFA World Cup against any European or South American team, he becomes an Englishman. When the Europe golf squad beats the American side in the Ryder Cup, as happened in September 2014, he becomes a European. In other words, our identities are always defined in terms of specific social reference groups, and within particular contexts that have meaning for us.

The nature of our identities, and their relationship to other similar concepts such as the self-concept, self-esteem, self-image, and so on have been studied in many disciplines, in particular in philosophy and sociology, and have been of interest in psychology from the work of William James onwards. In *The principles of psychology*, James (1890) made what was probably the first attempt to understand the self from the point of view of psychology – which he called 'the most puzzling puzzle with which psychology has to deal' (p. 330). We return to some of James' prescient ideas in the next section.

We begin with some definitions of the different terms that have been used in relation to self and identity, which in itself involves the introduction of some central theoretical ideas. We then go on to look at the question of identities in music, and consider some of the more recent developments in their investigation. There follows a section on the development of musical identities, which looks at different theoretical approaches and introduces some of the stage-type models of development which have been put forward, and then go on to consider the question of individual differences in musical identities. We look in particular at the relationship between musical identity and people's personalities and their lifestyle choices, reviewing some recent research on these topics. Finally, we consider the question of musical identities in education, as this raises many of the developmental issues with which we are concerned in this book. This involves the question of whether there are inherent problems in secondary school music, and if so how these might arise, which leads to the questions of musical identities in pupils in relation to those of teachers; the concept of agency and its application in this field; and the powerful role of digital technology in accentuating and accelerating some of these developments.

Defining and Explaining Self and Identity

There is a great deal of terminological confusion in this field, and so we start by defining some of the main terms that are used. First of all, the *self-system* is made up of a number of different *self-concepts* (or *self-images*), which are the ways in which we see ourselves in different situations or contexts. These might be specific to those situations and contexts (such as how you behave with other people, how you are able to cope with stress, or how you see yourself as a mother, or as a teacher). Thus, at different times of the day, you might see yourself as a wife, as a mother, as a motorist, as a commuter, as a trade union member, or as a business executive: and your *self-identity*, or global self-concept, is the view that you have of yourself in which all of these different aspects are integrated (although the extent to which different individuals are able to achieve this integration is still an unresolved question).

Another central concept is that of *self-esteem*: this is the evaluative component of the self, and has both cognitive and emotional components – it deals with how worthy we *think* we are and how worthy we *feel* that we are: the implications of having high or low self-esteem are widespread, and have been widely investigated. James (1890) suggested that our self-esteem, or what he called 'our self-feeling in this world depends entirely on what we *back* ourselves to be and do. It is determined by the ratio of our actualities to our supposed potentialities … thus, Self-esteem = Success / Pretensions' (p. 310). To put this in more contemporary language, James is suggesting that our self-esteem can be expressed by the ratio between our evaluations of our actual selves and of our ideal selves: people who have high opinions of themselves which are not based on their actual capabilities will have higher levels of self-esteem than those who have low opinions of themselves which are unwarranted.

The implication is that the most satisfactory state of affairs is when we have a realistic impression of our own abilities, even though we might strive to improve some of them in various ways. To jump ahead to music for a moment, James suggested another solution to the optimisation of our own levels of self-esteem in proposing, no doubt somewhat tongue in cheek, that 'to give up pretensions is as blessed a relief as to get them gratified ... Many Bostonians, *crede experto* (and inhabitants of other cities, too, I fear), would be happier women and men to-day, if they could once for all abandon the notion of keeping up a Musical Self, and without shame let people hear them call a symphony a nuisance' (p. 311).

More recently, psychometric scales have been devised for the assessment of many other different aspects of self-esteem. Perhaps the most widely used is the Rosenberg Self-Esteem Scale (1965), and there is also a Single Item Self-Esteem Scale (Robins, Hendin, & Trzesniewski (2001), which, as its title suggests, consists of a single item: 'I have high self-esteem', which respondents are asked to rate on a five-point scale ranging from 'not very true of me' to 'very true of me'. Other measures, some of which have been collated by Lonsdale and North (2011), include scales for the assessment of Collective Self-Esteem (CSE) (Luhtanen & Crocker, 1992); Intolerance for Uncertainty (IUC) (Freeston, Rhéaume, Letarte, Dugas, & Ladouceur, 1994); Self-Concept Clarity (SCC) (Campbell et al., 1996); Self-Monitoring (SM) (Snyder, 1974); social Desirability (Crowne & Marlowe, 1960); self-Consciousness (Fenigstein, Scheier, & Buss, 1975); Identity Style (Berzonsky, 1989); and openness to Experience (Costa & McCrae, 1985).

The development of different aspects of the self-concept and self-esteem in childhood and adolescence has received a great deal of research attention, particularly because having low self-esteem can lead to poor developmental outcomes in certain circumstances. The development of self-esteem occurs through a process of monitoring our own behaviour and making comparisons with others. We constantly compare ourselves with others: particular social groups exert powerful influences on what we do, what we say, and how we see ourselves. The most obvious influences on most children and adolescents are those of their parents, siblings, other members of their family, peer groups, and influences at school, which can be critical.

One of the principal theoretical accounts of this process is that of social identity theory, which we discussed in Chapter 4, developed by Henri Tajfel and his colleagues (e.g. Tajfel, 1978). This proposes that individuals have a fundamental drive to develop and maintain a high level of self-esteem, and that they do so by *identifying* with groups of people of whom they have a positive image, since social identity and personal identity are closely linked with one another. They attempt to maximise the differences between their own groups (the ingroups) and others (the outgroups) by changing their attitudes accordingly, and this can be seen to have its effects in clothing styles, friendship patterns, leisure activities, and so on. Since music is one of the principal leisure activities of adolescents, it is easy to see how musical identity plays a powerful role in shaping the self-concepts of young people – and this is a theme to which we will return.

This social identity theory account of the self stems from a psychological perspective which emphasises the individual: we experience our selves as being self-contained, internally coherent, and as being relatively stable and consistent over our lifetimes, as well as being different in important ways from others around us. There is another point of view which conflicts with this, however: social constructionist approaches within psychology suggest, instead, that the self cannot be characterised in this somewhat static way (e.g. Gergen & Davis, 1985). Instead, their view is that the self is in constant transition, and is being formed, re-formed, and continuously developed through conversation and interactions with others. In other words, in this view, our selves are in effect based on the substance of our interactions with other people, so that the distinction between personal and social aspects of the self is differentiated to a much lesser extent than in the theories of James or Tajfel (as well as in that of Erik Erikson, 1968, whose stage theory of the development of the self-concept will be covered later in this chapter).

A third point of view derives from social cognitive theory, and in particular from Albert Bandura's (1986) view of the self. Bandura's view of the nature of human agency – of 'how people exercise influence over what they do' – is based on the principle of *triadic reciprocal causation*. This is a transactional view of the relationship between self and society, and is based on three major classes of determinants of the self: *behaviour*, *internal personal factors* (cognitive, affective, and biological events), and the *external environment*. Bandura's view is that each of these three determinants exerts a mutual influence on each of the others such that the whole system is 'reciprocally deterministic', and in a constant state of dynamic change. People create social systems, but are themselves influenced by those systems, so that human behaviour is a product of both the social influences and the internal psychological factors.

As far as the self is concerned, Bandura (1997) developed a strong emphasis on the concept of self-efficacy, which refers to 'beliefs in one's capabilities to organise and execute the courses of action required to produce given attainments' (p. 3). Self-efficacy beliefs are based in social and contextual factors: different individuals view different areas and situations as varying in the levels of skill and effort required to succeed. Teachers and social workers place a high value on social empathy and interpersonal skills, for example, whereas business executives might emphasise their entrepreneurial or bargaining skills to a much greater extent. This example shows that self-efficacy is not grounded in general or non-specific beliefs, but in specific contexts and domains. Furthermore, Bandura suggests that since self-efficacy is dependent on our self-evaluation of a given activity, it is likely to be a much better predictor of behaviour in that activity than is self-esteem.

The domain of activity of interest here is that of music, of course. Musical identity has been a relatively new topic of interest in music psychology, with the first major collection (to which we both contributed) in 2002 (MacDonald, Hargreaves, & Miell, 2002). This field has grown in recent years, as illustrated by the much larger follow-up *Handbook of musical identities* (MacDonald, Hargreaves, & Miell, 2017). The concept of musical identity has become broader and more diversified, with many more empirical studies of musical identity, which we consider next.

Musical Identities

When we come to consider the nature of musical identities, i.e. the ways in which we perceive ourselves in relation to our musical achievements, aspirations, and abilities, many questions immediately arise such as 'What are musical identities?'; 'Does everyone have them, or only musicians?'; 'Do negative musical identities exist as well as positive ones?'; 'Are our musical identities related to our musical development, and if so, how might this process be affected by powerful environmental influences such as the family, peer groups or school?'

Hargreaves, Miell, and MacDonald (2002) proposed a fundamental distinction between *identities in music* (IIM), and *music in identities* (MII). IIM refers to those aspects of our musical identities that are defined within existing cultural roles and categories, such as composer, performer, improviser, pianist, or critic, and these roles are defined and maintained by musical institutions such as schools, universities, and conservatoires. MII, on the other hand, refers to how we use the domain of music as a reference point in other aspects of our own individual identities: for example, in relation to the main dimensions of individual differences which we mentioned at the start of this chapter. How does our interest in and participation in music relate to our self-perception as male or female, as older, middle-aged or younger, as musically trained or untrained, as extravert or introvert, as able-bodied or disabled, or as a member of one nationality rather than another? In the last few years, some striking new ideas about the nature of musical identity have arisen (MacDonald et al., 2017). Here we identify just three of these, namely the precise definition of 'music' and 'musicians'; the idea of musical identities being performative and social; and that of musical identities having an ethical and moral dimension.

What Is Music, and Who Are Musicians?

As pointed out earlier in this book and in various earlier publications, the recent rapid technological developments in the music industry have had some powerful effects on people's experience of music in everyday life. The widespread availability and relatively low expense of devices such as MP3 players, smartphones, and tablet computers, and the increasing use of social media and other related technology means that a vast diversity of music is available to an increasingly wide population of listeners in many parts of the world, and that the ways in which people engage with music – as composers, performers, critics, or merely as fans – is far more diverse than at any time in the past.

One of the effects of this is that musical styles and genres have become what might be called 'democratised' in the sense that the automatic linkages between the notion of 'serious' music with styles including Western classical music, jazz, and opera, and the corresponding association between 'popular music' and styles such as rhythm and blues, chart pop, progressive rock, hip-hop, and so on, no longer exist for most people. It is perfectly possible to hear 'serious' classical music played in shopping malls, cafes, or other commercial settings, as well as to hear pop music played in concert halls and other traditional bastions of serious music. As far as the study of musical identity is concerned, this means it has become vital to incorporate all forms of musical expression: this includes not only the performances of expert and highly trained musicians, but also those of children, or of people with disabilities. In other words, our definition of music must be much broader than that which would hold in the field of musicology, for example.

Closely associated with this expansion of the idea of what constitutes 'music' is a corresponding broadening of the definition of the 'musician', and the blurring of the distinctions between different practitioners. Cook (1998) suggested that the traditional view of the composer as being at the apex of a kind of musical hierarchy in which (almost always) he passes on the 'core product' to the performer, who then interprets this from a written score and transmits the composer's intentions to the audience, whose members might react in a variety of ways, is inauthentic: it is based on outmoded hierarchical value systems which derive from nineteenth-century European classical music, and can be traced back to the time of Beethoven. In today's technological world in which music is recorded, transmitted, and mixed digitally, the divisions between the composer, the arranger, the studio recording engineer, the performer, and even the audience, are much more blurred than hitherto. This means that 'musicians' can be regarded as such without necessarily having had to undertake many years of rigorous instrumental practice; some knowledge of studio techniques and computing might be equally valuable in certain musical contexts.

There is a second, equally important way in which Rickard and Chin (2017) suggest that the broadening of the concept of 'musician' needs to occur. Their argument is that the definition of a musician as someone who *produces* music, whether as a composer, improviser, or performer, is also inappropriate in the sense that many aspects of the *perception* of music can provide definitions of musicianship which are just as valid. They draw on recent evidence from cognitive neuroscience which suggests that there is a great deal of overlap between the neural mechanisms underlying musical processing in composing, performing, and listening, and this reinforces the point of view which has been put forward by David (Hargreaves, 2012; Hargreaves, Hargreaves, & North, 2012) in arguing for a new interpretation of the concept of musical imagination.

Rickard and Chin also support the now widely accepted view that everyone has the capacity to be musical, as well as the notion (see the foregoing) that high levels of musical creativity can be achieved by those with little traditional instrumental skill, given the technology that is currently available. They also go on to consider the definition of the 'non-musician', suggesting that there might also exist a 'musicianship of listening' which is based on evidence that a great deal of detailed knowledge about music is acquired through everyday exposure to it, as well as a 'musicianship of engagement' based on community activities which are primarily intended to build relationships between people, or to create group identity. In short, they suggest that this 'musicianship of engagement' may have a great deal of overlap with the traditional 'musicianship of production', and that both of these can be equally advantageous from a developmental and health point of view. This implies, of course, that the notion of the 'non-musician' also needs to be considerably broader than it currently is.

Musical Identities as Social and Performative

Trevarthen and Malloch (2017) suggest that

'Music is an expression of the human need for synchrony and . . . sympathy of self-expression with that of others. Our innate musical powers and sensibilities grow with the body and the company we keep. Within a few months a baby is an active and inventive musical companion, and soon can learn to be a co-performer in ritual action games and songs, beating time with arms and banging sonorous objects. This musicality of performance needs the affectionate company of a person who feels happy with 'belonging' in a musical community and remembering their own childish confidence in discovery.' (p. 169)

This quotation illustrates the idea that the origins of musical identities in very young children are very clearly both *social* and *performative*. One of the main functions of music is to communicate with others, and musical play between children, as well as that between children and adults, provides many demonstrations of the intrinsically social nature of musical activity: music is something that they do with others. At the same time this musical play is also quite clearly behavioural, or *performative*: Tafuri (2017) describes some of her own research in the *inCanto* project, discussed in Chapter 4, which shows that infants make different kinds of sounds such as wailing, whimpering, whining, and gurgling, and produce them in a progressively richer and more varied ways. Very early on, newborns are sensitive to adults' reactions to their sounds: the 'other' starts to be present to them and the foundations of the self–other relationship are laid. These developing interactions form what Tafuri calls the 'building blocks' of communicative musicality: in other words, they demonstrate the performative nature of musical identity at this early age.

As children get older, their musical sophistication increases to include singing with words and repeating phrases, rhyming, copying elements of the music and songs that they hear around them, and inventing new musical expressions with other children (see further Chapters 4 and 5). It is easy to see that these developments can lead to the development of healthy musical identities in children, and Tafuri traces these back to the musical prototypes and utterances of infants. The social and performative dimensions of musical identity are also present in later childhood and adulthood, and this argument has been adopted by Elliott and Silverman (2017) in outlining their concept of *personhood*. They regard the *self* and *identity* as being the primary components of personhood, which they see as having two dimensions – *embodied* and *enactive*. The enactive self is what is seen in early musical activity as we have just described it, and adults, just as children, are seen as being able to *perform* their identities. This contrasts with the more widely used embodied sense of the term identity, which refers to the ways in which we see ourselves. In this way we can see identities, and indeed musical identities, as being performative and dynamic, and as not having narrative: they refer to things that we *do* just as much as to those that we *have*.

Elliott and Silverman see music-making as a very important social, interactive context in which people help to construct each other's musical and personal identities, and they point out that this draws on the Aristotelian concept of *praxis*, which refers to the ways in which people engage practically with music, i.e. put it into practice, together. Elliott and Silverman (2017) have proposed that what they call a praxial philosophy of music education (see Elliott & Silverman, 2015) 'has the potential to provide logical foundations and pragmatic principles for ensuring that the facilitation of people's musical and personal identity development is ethical and beneficial in many ways' (Elliott & Silverman, 2017, p. 42).

It might be useful at this point to consider Aristotle's notion of praxis in relation to some of his other concepts. In brief, Aristotle held that there were three basic activities of man: *theoria, poiesis*, and *praxis*, and that each of these dealt with three different types of knowledge respectively: the theoretical, which strives towards truth; the poietical, which is dedicated to the pursuit of production; and the practical, of which the end goal is action. Whereas poiesis means 'to make', referring to the moment at which something/s become another, praxis is a practice which involves the application of skill, and if done well, can lead to the universal and public acknowledgement of excellence. Praxis also involves critical thinking and self-reflection: the combination of acting, reflecting on the impact of that action, and then planning future actions with a revised plan or conception is a common iterative cycle in education.

An Ethical Dimension of Musical Identities

Another important part of Elliott and Silverman's (2015) conception of praxis is that the process of identity construction involves a strong ethical and moral dimension. Aristotle saw praxis as being guided by a moral disposition to act truly and rightly, with a concern to foster the wellbeing and healthiness of others: this involves joy, respect for others, fellowship, virtue, and the pursuit of happiness for oneself and others. This 'life of flourishing' was summarised in the word *eudaimonia*. Aristotle's ethical philosophy was directed towards the pursuit of eudaimonia, which he saw as 'an activity of the soul in accordance with excellence'. In other words, eudaimonia is an activity, i.e. that of flourishing, rather than a state of mind like 'happiness', although though the former is very likely to be associated with the latter. We return to this in Chapter 8 when discussing music and wellbeing.

Elliott and Silverman's (2015) praxial philosophy of music education, correspondingly, invokes ethical ideals and the development of empathy between individuals, as well as of 'moral communities', in the construction of personhood and identities. They draw on humanistic philosophers such as Chappell (2011) in arguing that 'when a person consciously or non-consciously interprets an-other as a person ... he or she understands consciously and/or nonconsciously that as a person herself, she is a member of a moral community of persons and, therefore, that she has (or she feels) an ethical responsibility to treat the other with some degree of respect, consideration, and *empathy*. In return, when she acknowledges the other as a person, it is reasonable for her to expect a certain degree of consideration in return' (p. 34).

This involves the music mentor's desire and disposition to 'act truly and rightly', with continuous concern for protecting and advancing human wellbeing. From this viewpoint, musical mentors who are *only* concerned with teaching music-making techniques, or organising community music groups, or teaching information about music (and so forth) are not engaged in praxis and praxial musical identity formation. To promote socially constructive and ethical musical and personal identity formation, musical mentors of all kinds must harness musical affordances with a conscious commitment to an '*ethic of care*' and 'care-guided actions' (Elliott & Silverman, 2017, p. 43).

As we noted in Chapter 4, this ethical and moral dimension is also an important part of Trevarthen and Malloch's (2017) view of the ways in which infants develop their musical selves, and with the way in which their well-known concept of communicative musicality discussed throughout the book operates. Trevarthen and Malloch suggest that infants' innate musical intersubjectivity gives rise to their personal identities within the social, interactive context described by Elliott and Silverman, and that an ethical and moral dimension should be an integral part of this in civilised human development.

Development of Musical Identities

To explain the many phenomena of musical development we have presented a variety of different theoretical perspectives in this book. The sociocultural approach has been shown to be particularly useful in explaining how music-making operates at a social and interactive level, such as looking at children making music together (see Chapter 4). Sociocultural approaches are also prominent in the study of the development of musical identities (Hargreaves, MacDonald, & Miell, 2012a). As we have suggested, 'People's developing self-concepts tell us a great deal about why they develop in the ways they do' (p. 125). Considering how identity develops, a broad trajectory can be traced out: young children (a) have fairly generalised self-concepts which become increasingly differentiated with age, (b) they emphasise physical characteristics and activities, and their identities gradually move more towards psychological judgements involving feelings and emotions as they get older, and (c) they have self-concepts which become increasingly based on comparisons with others in late childhood through to adolescence (Hargreaves, MacDonald, & Miell, 2002; Harter, 1999).

More specific accounts of the development of musical identity have emerged more recently, and we shall look at three main approaches here. All draw to varying degrees on Erik Erikson's (1968) model of eight stages of psychosocial development, and on Marcia's (1980) well-known elaboration of this. Erikson (1950, 1968) proposed that adolescence and early adulthood were critical periods in the development of identity, and that many people experience an 'identity crisis' in adolescence in which they are neither child nor adult, but in an awkward transitional period which needs to be resolved: failure to do this adequately could have negative effects on subsequent development. Erikson also proposed that three key processes mediate this development, namely *identification* (taking on some of the characteristics of individuals or groups with whom we a have strong relationship); *individuation* (developing a consistent and continuous individual identity across different contexts and over time); and *integration* (organising these newly adopted characteristics into a continuous sense of personal identity).

Marcia (1980) extended this model by proposing two main processes of identity development: *exploration* (the extent to which individuals try to discover different activities and attitudes while searching for a new sense of self), and *commitment* (taking on a particular set of beliefs and values). Marcia suggested that individuals display these two processes at varying levels, and that it is possible to distinguish between combinations of high and low levels of each. This gives rise to four possible identity outcomes arranged in 2×2 form, with either high or low levels of exploration and commitment. High levels of both exploration and commitment are seen to give rise to what Marcia called *achievement* (clearly attaining a coherent identity), high exploration with low commitment was identified as *moratorium* (in individuals who are still trying to explore the possible range of their own identities), low exploration with high commitment was seen as *foreclosure* (in those who had taken on a particular identity but had not fully explored the alternative possible identities in advance), and low levels of both exploration and commitment were characterised as *diffusion* (in those who have not taken on an identity, nor explored the possibilities).

Trevarthen and Malloch (2017) have recently developed their well-known notion of communicative musicality well beyond the arena of parent–infant interaction, in describing the development of musical identity across the whole life span. In doing so they draw on a number of different concepts from other disciplines, most notably philosophy, in looking at the question of the self versus the other, and the nature of embodied cognition and personal experience. They also draw on aspects of sociocultural psychology and other areas of developmental psychology, as well as 'applied' areas of music psychology, in particular music education and music therapy, in an ambitious attempt to integrate all these different aspects of human development into a broad theory of 'communicative musicality as the human way of life'. The extent to which they have to date been successful in integrating all of these different aspects of human development in terms of a single concept is debatable, and works better for some aspects than for others, but their attempt to do so is to be applauded, and may well prove to be an important starting point for other theorists and researchers.

Trevarthen and Malloch suggest that the traditional idea of an 'inner self' as only being accessible to the person experiencing it is gradually being replaced by the idea of emotions and identities occurring *between* people: this is demonstrated with particular clarity in some recent developments in neuroscience which focus on the concept of mirror neurons, namely the identification of neural events which appear to 'mirror' intentions in the movements of other individuals. Starting with the notion of the infant as an innately social creature, Trevarthen and Malloch extend their previous view of communicative musicality to include the whole of human identity and development, with music as the communication system which mediates this. They set out their 'radical conclusion ... that an infant is born a humanly social creature, an artful person or Self, with a motor intelligence equipped with uniquely human talents to make or detect the *aesthetic* value of melodic stories, and *moral* feelings of the relationship, both of which may be sustained with a respectful and sympathetic Other in expressive body movements and song' (p. 158).

They go on to plot the course of musical identity across the four main stages of human development, relying on Erikson's psychosocial stage theory to form the basic framework of this. In infancy (Erikson's first stage of trust versus mistrust), children develop their physical and motor skills and self-expression, and develop their interactions with adults in stories and play with their bodies. In early childhood (Erikson's second, third, and fourth stages of autonomy versus shame, initiative versus guilt, and industry versus inferiority), young children develop their own musical culture, which is a fascinating combination of their own musical creations and the songs and rhymes they hear all around them (see Chapter 4). With increasing age, these self-created songs gradually approximate more and more to the musical conventions of the culture, and songs and performing abilities are refined and developed until adolescence (Erikson's fifth stage of identity versus role confusion), when music preference and taste becomes a much more central aspect of musical identity.

As we shall see later in this chapter, popular music preferences in adolescents are critical aspects of their identities, and Frith (1981) has encapsulated this in his suggestion that music is a 'badge of identity' in adolescence. As noted earlier, research studies from the UK, Scandinavia, and elsewhere (e.g. Bjurström & Wennhall, 1991; Davis, 2016; North, Hargreaves, & O'Neill, 2000) clearly show that teenagers spend more time per day listening to pop music than in doing any other kind of activity, including sport, and that pop music preferences are strongly related to their clothing styles, leisure interests, patterns of friendship, and many other aspects of their values and attitudes. We will consider this topic in much more detail, including the idea that there are consistent age-related changes in 'open-earedness' across the life span, in Chapter 7. The idea that 'open-earedness' gradually declines in later adulthood and old age is consistent with Erikson's eighth stage of ego integrity versus despair, in that older people become increasingly aware of their increasing limitations and infirmity, and so develop a more contemplative relationship with music.

Looking at the development of identities in music more specifically, two similar projects have explored transitions in musical careers. As part of a series of longitudinal studies carried out by Jane Davidson and colleagues, Davidson and Burland (2006) compared the responses of half of a group of 20 adults who had been highly successful childhood musicians and who were working in performing careers with the other half, who were working in non-performance careers, including primary school teaching, as solicitors, or in sales, and asked them to reflect on the reasons that affected their career decisions during adolescence. They found that the two groups seemed to have different sets of beliefs about their relationship with the music itself. Those who had not gone into music said that their adolescent experiences had made them feel pressurised and overwhelmed by competition and criticism from teachers and peers, whereas those who had become performers regarded these experiences as positive, and as helping them towards their future careers. Davidson and Burland explained this difference in terms of external attributions that the participants made about the attitudes and behaviour of influential others.

Another concept that they used was that of 'provisional selves', describing the process by which individuals try out different identities in eventually arriving at their chosen career (see also Creech et al., 2014a). This can occur either because the individual adopts the characteristics of a particular role model, such as someone who is successful in that field, or because they adopt a number of different characteristics from different role models. In so doing, Davidson and Burland drew specifically on Marcia's (1980) ideas of *exploration* and *commitment* in adolescents' developing identities. In another study, Evans and McPherson (2017) also used Marcia's concepts of exploration and commitment in an investigation of the extent to which adolescents explore different identities within music, and how this might affect their future careers. In an empirical study with 157 children who were learning to play musical instruments, they asked the children at an early stage (i.e. before they began formal training on their instruments) how long they thought they would continue to play the instrument. Evans and McPherson found that those who took a longer-term view said that they were likely to continue playing until adulthood and were more likely to continue their involvement with the instrument than those who expressed a short-term view, and that this relationship and seem to be mediated by the amount of practice that they did.

Evans and McPherson also drew on self-determination theory (SDT) in explaining their results. As discussed in Chapter 5, SDT holds that people's wellbeing thrives most when their behaviour is regulated by themselves rather than by others – and that this self-regulation is directed towards three basic psychological needs, namely competence, the desire for mastery and effectiveness in one's activities; relatedness, the need to feel a part of and to be accepted by other individuals and groups; and autonomy, the need to feel that one is in control of one's own activities rather than being directed by someone else (such as a schoolteacher or parent). Evans and McPherson applied these ideas to the development of adolescents' musical identities by asking them questions about the ways in which their musical practice was determined by themselves or by others, and the extent to which they saw different kinds of music learning as being important parts of their lives: they also provide four detailed case studies of musicians which illustrate Marcia's four hypothetical combinations of high and low levels of exploration and commitment respectively.

Finally, Alexandra (Lamont, 2017) emphasises the importance of considering the specific social and cultural contexts which shape people's behaviour in describing the development of musical identities, and takes a lifespan developmental approach with this notion at the core. She draws a clear distinction between the social constructionist idea that identities are fragmented, multiple and in a state of constant transition on the one hand, and phase/stage approaches, such as those we have mentioned earlier in this section, on the other. She adopts a theoretical framework for the analysis of contexts and environments by drawing on Bronfenbrenner's (1979) ecological systems theory of development, which distinguishes between four different levels of social influence. These are the *microsystems* within which children develop, which exert the most direct influences upon them, the *mesosystem*, the *exosystem*, and the *macrosystem*, whose influences becomes progressively more abstract and indirect. Focusing on specific microsystems like school or family but addressing the relationships between them and the higher-level forces that influence them is extremely important if we are to understand how identity is shaped by the complex concept of 'context'.

Looking at the later development of adult musical identity, it is clear that music can assume greater and lesser importance at different stages of life according to the pressures of family, career, or other external demands, and some of Alexandra's (Lamont, 2011a, b) research has attempted to do this. She suggests that

Many older adults seem to find new enthusiasm for different forms of music-making which are not typically taught in formal education, such as folk bands or new styles like jazz, and ... many of them go on to take up different instruments to the ones they devoted so many hours to as child learners ... adult beginners often talked about going through various life crises and wanting something more through music, such as impressing others or achieving something for themselves. (Lamont, 2017, p. 186)

In terms of Erikson's model, people in 'middle age' may re-engage with music as a way of achieving generativity rather than stagnation, and this may fulfil social needs just as much as the achievement of high levels of skill or musicianship. Erikson suggests that many people at this stage and in the next stage of 'older adulthood' carry out an 'end of life review', and Alexandra (Lamont, 2011a) suggests that their engagement in musical activities can provide a means of achieving what Erikson calls 'integrity' as distinct from 'despair'. At the time of writing, the post-war 'baby boom' generation, in the UK at least, have either retired or are approaching retirement, and the social and political changes that have occurred since the 1950s mean that this generation has much higher levels of good health and spending power than had most previous generations – which is unfortunately not the case for their children's generation. Their 'end of life reviews' can lead them to re-evaluate their post-employment priorities, which can include opportunities to re-engage with other activities including music, perhaps learning alongside their children or grandchildren. Recent research highlights that music has a great deal to offer to many people in later life, and that activities such as going to concerts, taking part in choirs, bands, and orchestras can promote cognitive, social, and emotional benefits in many older people. This provides an interesting contrast with Erikson's view of a general decline in the relationship with music in old age, which perhaps adds weight to the social constructionist idea that musical identities can be modified and adapted to circumstances at any point across the lifespan.

It is perhaps these social changes that have led to a noticeable increase in research on music, health, and wellbeing in older people (see e.g. Creech et al., 2014b; Hays & Minichiello, 2005; MacDonald, Kreutz, & Mitchell, 2012a), and there has been a corresponding increase in interest in the whole field of positive psychology (see e.g. Seligman & Csikszentmihalyi, 2000), which is devoted to the promotion of positive aspects of physical and mental health, rather than maintaining a focus on mental illness and the psychotherapies, as in a great deal of clinical psychology and psychiatry. We return specifically to the role of music in these new developments in Chapter 8, where we look in more detail at the relationship between music and wellbeing.

Thus, the beginnings of identity in infancy can be seen in research on mothers singing to their infants, which largely adopts the idea that musical interactions between caregiver and child are an early part of human socialisation and communicative musicality. In childhood, Bronfenbrenner's ecological approach leads to a focus on the effects of the home, school, and peer groups in the development of musical identity: this system is dealt with in more detail later in this chapter, as are the complex changes which take place in self-identity in adolescence. Erikson and Marcia provide a framework within which much research on lifespan and transitions can be contextualised. It is clear from the range of theory and research that we have reviewed in this section that there is still a great deal to be learnt about the development of musical identities across the lifespan, but also that is very important to do so. Age-related regularities in the self-regulation of musical activities clearly do exist, but they are capable of being changed by particular contextual and environmental influences.

Another important point in trying to draw conclusions about this topic is to be very clear about defining our terms. The development of musical identities, i.e. of the ways in which we perceive ourselves in relation to music, is not the same as the development of musical activity in general (the main subject of this book), although we are making the claim that musical identities are a key factor mediating musical development as a whole (see Hargreaves et al., 2012a). A related point, which arose earlier, is that music preferences are not the same as musical identities, although they are likely to overlap to a considerable extent. We shall pursue this issue later in this chapter.

Individual Differences in Musical Identities

As noted earlier, the main individual difference factors which have been investigated in the field of music are gender, age, musical training and experience, and aspects of personality: groups of females and males, or representative samples of people from different age groups, with varying levels of musical training and experience, or with different personality characteristics are compared on whatever aspect of musical behaviour is of particular interest. This approach to research, which is primarily based on psychometric tests, was very prominent in music psychology in the 1960s, as it provided a means of studying systematic variations among people in a relatively consistent manner.

Studies of individual differences in musical identities are much less common, and rely on the extent to which musical self-perceptions can be identified or assessed in measures of musical ability, interest, or attitude. The factor which has received the most attention is that of age, and indeed the whole of the previous section on the development of musical identities could be seen as being devoted to that. There is also a substantial body of research on gender differences, for example in music preferences, in levels of expressed interest in music, and in the selection of particular instruments for boys and girls, although it is often very difficult to disentangle the behavioural differences that are being investigated in these studies with the self-perceptions that give rise to them. As we said at the end of the last section, it is critically important to be very precise about our definition of terms here.

In the next two subsections we review some studies which use musical preference and taste as indications or manifestations of musical identity and which relate these to two specific individual difference factors, namely personality, and aspects of lifestyle. Because of this subject matter, the lifespan focus here is largely on adolescent and adult development rather than on children.

Musical Identity and Personality

Setting the scene for later identity research, some pioneering work on personality and musical behaviour was carried out in the 1980s by Kemp (e.g. 1981a, 1982), who was concerned with mapping out the personality structure of the musician. He administered various personality questionnaires, notably Cattell's 16 PF questionnaire, to large groups of musicians including performers, composers, students, and teachers as well as to non-musician control groups. Kemp's main broad finding was these musicians of all kinds are characterised by a common core of personality traits, namely *introversion*, *pathemia* (sensitivity and imagination), and *intelligence*.

Kemp also suggested that the performers of different instruments had distinct personality styles: one of his studies (Kemp, 1981b) found that string and woodwind players had higher levels of introversion than brass and keyboard players and singers, for example. This theme was also developed by Davies (1978), who investigated the personality stereotypes about musicians held by the players of different instruments. Davies organised a series of unstructured group discussions with musicians from a Glasgow-based symphony orchestra, and found that they held some quite clear stereotypes. Perhaps the clearest of these was the distinction between their views of brass and string players. The brass players describe the strings as 'precious', 'oversensitive and touchy', 'humourless', and 'wet', whereas the strings regarded the brass players as 'oafish and uncouth', 'heavy boozers', 'loudmouthed and coarse', and so on. There is a rich vein of material here which could still be developed, combining the two approaches to explore how objective assessments of musicians' personalities relate to their self-concepts and their views of the personalities of others (cf. Hargreaves, 1986a).

A great deal of research has followed up on the links between preference and personality, which we discuss in Chapter 7. Two studies have explicitly addressed the concept of identity, however, and we consider these next. First, Greenberg and Rentfrow's (2017) approach was to regard personality and general aspects of self-identity as some of the 'psychological underpinnings' of musical identities; they were also interested in the relationships between music preferences and aspects of social relationships and group processes, especially in teenagers and young adults. They describe the development of their own factor analytic model of music preferences, which has five dimensions summarised in the acronym MUSIC, which comprises Mellow (e.g. soft rock and adult contemporary music, which is seen as romantic relaxing, and slow); Unpretentious (e.g. country and western or folk music which is uncomplicated and relaxing); Sophisticated (e.g. classical, opera, and jazz, which is seen as aspiring, intelligent, and complex); Intense (e.g. punk and heavy metal, which is characterised by distorted, loud, and aggressive sounds, and Contemporary (e.g. pop, rap, and dance) which are associated with social recognition, permissive attitudes, and extraversion.

Greenberg and Rentfrow (2017) describe an original empirical research project which looks at the relationship between the preferences of over 3,500 participants with an overall mean age in the category of between 31 and 35 years, measured in terms of the MUSIC model, and their interpersonal relationships, as well as the normative beliefs that they hold about the characteristics of fans of different styles. Their findings generally confirmed the view that there are strong relationships between social attitudes and the personality characteristics which are linked with preferences for different styles (see also Tarrant, North, & Hargreaves, 2002).

Dys, Schellenberg, and McLean (2017) explicitly address the relationship between musical identities, music preferences, and individual differences. Since music plays such an important part of the lives of adolescents and emerging adults, it is also likely to play an important role in their efforts to establish a consistent identity. But Dys et al. point put that 'whereas music preferences are concerned with how much someone likes specific genres of music, musical identity – based on psychological theories of identity development in general – reflects the degree to which someone is *committed* to liking *any* specific genre or genres, shifting the focus away from the actual genres' (p. 248). They try to explain the extent to which musical identities are related to general aspects of their self-identities, and whether or not these are affected by music preferences. They tackle these ambitious questions by drawing primarily on Erikson's (1968) theory of the development of identity, and Marcia's (1980) extension of it, which we have already covered in this chapter, as well as on Berzonsky's (1989, 1990) model of individual differences in processing styles, which makes a distinction between three different cognitive orientations, or 'identity styles'. These are an *informational* style (giving attention to decision making, and having high levels of self-esteem and conscientiousness), a *normative* style (conforming to the expectations of friends and family), and a *diffuse-avoidant* style (characterised by delaying and putting off decisions which affect the development of identity).

Dys et al. (2017) describe an original empirical study of 330 undergraduate students from two university campuses, who were asked to complete a measure of ego identity status which was adapted to quantify *musical* identity on four different scales (Marcia's achieved, moratorium, foreclosed, and diffuse states); one of Berzonsky's measures of processing styles related to *non*-musical identity; the Big Five Inventory (John & Srivastava, 1999), a widely used measure of the five main dimensions of personality; a measure of self-concept clarity; and an extended version of the Short Test Of Music Preferences (STOMP; Rentfrow & Gosling, 2003). This data was used to answer four specific research questions, namely (a) are musical identities linked with preferences for specific musical genres? (b) do musical identities reflect more than just music preferences? (c) what is the relationship between personality, identity style, music preferences, and musical identities?, and (d) are there consistent differences between trained performers and non-performers with respect to these questions?

This is an ambitious set of research questions to be asked of a specific dataset, and perhaps it is not too surprising that many of the detailed results which emerged from their analysis are unclear. However, the broad findings which did emerge were that (a) preferences for different musical genres varied according to culture and environment, and ethnic background; (b) participants' musical identities were related to their identities in other non-musical domains only to a small degree; (c) there were some significant relationships between music preferences and musical identities, but that this relationship was different for different genres; (d) there were some significant associations between musical identities, personality characteristics, self-concept clarity, and musical training; and (e) there were some significant relationships between musical identities and other aspects of self-identity.

Musical Identity and Lifestyle

There is a great deal of anecdotal evidence to show that stereotypes exist about the characteristics of the fans of different musical genres and styles. North and Hargreaves (1999) provided some evidence for this idea in undergraduates' and 9- to 10-year-old children's views about the fans of chart pop music, alternative pop music, and classical music. They found that being a fan of either chart pop or rap was associated with making positive evaluations of another hypothetical person who shared that fan's musical preference, and with making negative evaluations of a hypothetical person who did not share that fan's musical preference.

Such effects have been explained in terms of social identity theory, which we met earlier on in this chapter, and which argues that people tend to make positive judgements about members of their own ingroups, and to derive positive self-esteem from this (see Tarrant, Hargreaves, & North, 2001): this leads them to make lifestyle choices which increase their similarity with those of their ingroups. North and Hargreaves (2007a, b, c) carried out a large-scale study of these effects, which investigated how fans of different types of music might also make consistently different lifestyle choices. While being a 'fan' of a particular musical style or genre is strictly speaking an index of musical preference or taste rather than of *identity* as such (which we return to later), it is nevertheless the case that many young people's preferred styles of pop music are deeply ingrained in their attitudes, preferred clothing styles, leisure interests, and so on, such that these inter-relationships could have important commercial and marketing implications, for example. It is therefore worth looking in some detail at the results of this study.

In order to obtain a cross-section of the general population, 2,532 participants with a mean age of 37 years were recruited from a variety of locations (a university campus, a city centre shopping mall, a railway station, several office complexes, a gas supply company, and an employment bureau) in a city in the Midlands of the UK. Participants completed a specially devised questionnaire with 13 sections, covering 'General information', 'Travel', 'Relationships', 'Living', 'Money', 'Education', 'Employment', 'Health', 'Drinking and Smoking', 'Media', 'Beliefs', 'Crime', and 'Music' respectively. The final 'Music' section consisted of a list of 35 different musical styles, each with examples of typical composers/performers, and participants were asked to 'tick one that best describes your current taste in music'. Sixteen of the 35 musical styles were selected by fewer than 50 of the respondents, and so were excluded from further analyses. The remaining 19 musical styles selected by more than 50 respondents were opera, country and western, jazz, rock, current chart pop, R&B, soul, classical, disco, dance/house, hip-hop/rap, musicals, blues, 1960s pop, indie, adult pop/MOR, DJ-based music, other pop music styles, and 'other' musical styles.

The findings were reported in three separate journal articles focusing on different elements of the data. The first (North & Hargreaves, 2007a) reported findings concerning *relationships* (whether or not participants had two parents, were in a relationship, and if so had a different sex partner); *living arrangements* (whether or not home owner, living in terraced, semi-detached, or detached house); *beliefs* (political party membership, religious affiliation, and attitude to recycling), and *crime* (whether arrested for driving offence, or whether tried drugs). The many significant inter-relationships between these lifestyle factors and musical preference were explained in terms of a 'liberal-conservative' dimension, and the music preferences were conceived in terms of membership of 'high' and 'low culture' groups respectively. Generally speaking, the results were consistent with the idea that participants at the liberal end of the dimension were more likely to be members of 'high' than 'low culture' preference groups, and that those in 'low culture' groups tended to have more conservative preferences.

The second paper (North & Hargreaves, 2007b) reported findings concerning *media usage* (whether a regular newspaper reader, whether had a preferred radio station, preferred TV programmes, books, and magazines); *leisure time preferences* (whether intellectually undemanding/domestic, open air, cerebral, creative activities, or activities involving pets), and *patterns of music usage* (listening preferences and location). Once again, there were many significant inter-relationships between these lifestyle measures and those of musical preference, and these were once again interpreted in terms of the distinction between 'high culture' and 'low culture' preferences: members of the former tended to prefer 'high art' leisure activities. In the third paper (North & Hargreaves, 2007c) findings were reported concerning *travel* (frequency of holidays); *money* (whether share owner, bank account holder, credit card user, and whether charity donor); *education* (school type, degree level); *employment* (employed/unemployed); and *health* (visits to doctor, alcohol use, smoking). Once again numerous significant inter-relationships were found between lifestyle choices and music preferences, which indicated that liking for 'high art' music was associated with the lifestyle choices of the upper-middle and middle classes, whereas liking for 'low art' music was associated with lifestyle choices of the lower-middle and lower social classes.

How might these numerous associations between musical taste and lifestyle choices be explained? As outlined in Chapter 4, sociological research has suggested that the 'real world' status of music might be used as a means of discriminating social groups (see e.g. DeNora, 2000; Frith, 1978, 1981). Research on 'taste publics' categorised fans of particular musical styles in terms of sociodemographic variables, identifying a number of clearly definable groups, or 'taste publics', comprised of groups of people who subscribe to a particular taste culture (see Shepherd, 2003). Gans (1974) identified five major American taste cultures associated with corresponding taste publics, which ranged along a social class continuum from 'high culture' through 'upper-middle culture', 'lower-middle culture', and 'low culture' to 'quasi-folk low culture'. This proposed an explicit link between different taste cultures and social structure, and emphasised the importance of the educational attitudes and values of different socioeconomic groups. Similarly, Fox and Wince (1975) identified five taste cultures in the demographic data they collected on 767 sociology undergraduates, including a 'jazz-blues' taste public associated with an urban background; a 'popular hits' taste public related most strongly to religious preference (its members were predominantly Catholics rather than atheists, agnostics, or Jews); a 'folk music' taste public most strongly associated with sex (women rather than men); a 'rock-protest' taste public negatively associated with age; and a 'country and western' taste public related to sex (mostly men) and age (positively related to membership). Fox and Wince regarded these results as support for Gans' concepts of taste cultures and taste publics.

In Chapter 4 we also reviewed Adorno's (1941) argument that different musical forms and languages are a direct product of existing social divisions and structures, and Bourdieu's (1971, 1984) views: Bourdieu contended that an adequate sociology of art requires an understanding of the relations between a piece of art, its producer, and the various institutions in the 'field of production' in which cultural goods are created (e.g. conservatories, museum curators, learned societies, other artists, etc.). These institutions legitimise certain art works but not others, thus creating two respective tiers of 'high' and 'low' art. The former gains its status through endorsement by (supposedly) discerning connoisseurs with access to the field of cultural production, whereas the latter is intended for consumption by a large proportion of the population, leading to financial profit. Bourdieu argued that listeners' individual tastes depend on the extent to which they are members of those groups which legitimise art and form the field of cultural production; and in this respect he argued that artistic tastes are determined by social background.

Bourdieu's distinction between 'high' and 'low' art is reflected in Frith's (1990) work on music: Frith made the distinction between a bourgeois taste public whose musical appreciation is dependent on certain specialised knowledge and interpretative skills, and a commercial audience who listen to music that is designed to be financially profitable. It is also important to point out that an adequate understanding of people's music listening must also account for the relationship between the music itself, the consumers of that music, and also, critically, the situation in which it is heard (see e.g. North, Hargreaves, & Hargreaves, 2004). In others words, research should address not only the means by which art is produced and legitimised, but also the specific means by which this process manifests itself.

Although a few studies have investigated the detailed cultural and lifestyle backgrounds of individual musical movements (e.g. Crafts, Cavicchi, & Keil, 1993; Finnegan, 1989; Weinstein, 1991), we are not aware of many other attempts to date to compare these micro-social variables between the fans of different musical styles. This is particularly interesting in the present day context, given the prevalence of music in everyday life (e.g. North et al., 2004). It is of course possible that clearly identifiable taste publics no longer exist in the postmodern digital world, and that the concept is now outdated. But if music really is a means of identifying different social groups in the 'real world', then the correlations between particular music preferences and lifestyle choices may well have genuine significance.

Alongside the dimensions of individual differences reviewed in this section, Hargreaves, MacDonald, and Miell (2017) review four of the main real-life domains in which musical identities have been investigated, namely in music and musicianship itself; in education; in specific geographical communities; and in the field of health and wellbeing, to which music psychology is beginning to make an increasingly significant contribution. The area most relevant to our developmental concerns in this chapter is that of education: teachers and schools can have profound effects on their pupils' developing identities, and so we will conclude the chapter by considering some of the ways in which this might work.

Musical Identities in Education

A 'Problem of Secondary School Music'?

About fifteen years ago, around the dawn of the new millennium, there was a great deal of animated debate about what had become known as the 'problem of secondary school music' in English schools. Although music in the primary school (age 5–11) seemed to be reasonably well integrated with other curriculum subjects, and accepted by pupils, there appeared to be a sudden decline of interest in music in the secondary school (age 11–16). Evidence from examination entry statistics, school inspection reports, and independent research studies (e.g. Harland et al., 2000; Ryan, Boulton, O'Neill, & Sloboda, 2000) suggested that a good deal of secondary school music teaching was unimaginative, unsuccessful, and out of touch with many pupils' interests. The study by Harland and colleagues at the National Foundation for Educational Research examined four different sources of qualitative and quantitative evidence about art, music, and drama from 152 secondary schools in England, and concluded that music was 'the most problematic and vulnerable art form' at GCSE level, and that 'pupil enjoyment, relevance, skill development, creativity and expressive dimensions were often absent' (Harland et al., 2000, p. 568).

One obvious reason for this is the importance of pop music in the lives of teenagers outside school. Listening to pop music is easily the most common leisure activity of most teenagers: surveys in the UK, Scandinavia, and elsewhere consistently show that the typical 13-year-old listens for approximately two to three hours per day, far longer than time spent on any other leisure activity (e.g. Bjurström & Wennhall, 1991; North, Hargreaves, & O'Neill, 2000). We pointed out earlier in this chapter that this music plays a central role in the lives of most teenagers, and constitutes a 'badge of identity' for many of them (see e.g. Tarrant, North, & Hargreaves, 2000): the distinction between music at school and at home is consequently much more pronounced for secondary than for primary school pupils. Davis (2016) has written an account of her own experiences as a music teacher in the USA which shows how musical identity construction forms an essential part of engagement with popular music, as children start to perceive themselves in socially defined roles such as singer or songwriter, and become recognised as such among their families and peers.

Another influential idea is that of the 'third environment', which exists outside the school *and* the home. As mentioned in Chapter 5, this refers to contexts in which musical learning takes place in the absence of parents or teachers (e.g. Heath, 2001). These could be places such as garages, youth clubs, or public places: but they could also be one's bedroom, or even a school classroom, if no formal activity or adult supervision is involved. The *contexts* of music-making – school, home, or third environment – may well determine its *authenticity* for young people, and the key factor which is closely associated with these different contexts is the level of autonomy and control which they possess. Musical activities in the third environment are self-directed, and thereby engender high levels of motivation and commitment. John Lennon and Paul McCartney's groundbreaking compositions emerged from just such an environment, namely in Paul's bedroom when they both skipped school lessons, and had very little to do with school music education.

There are three interrelated issues here. First, school music tends to involve the teacher's control of the curriculum, and of the direction of activity, whereas music out of school usually involves far more autonomy and *ownership* on the part of the learner (cf. Green's 2001 study of the ways in which young pop musicians learn from each other in the 'third environment'). Second, Boal-Palheiros and Hargreaves (2001) showed that 9–10- and 13–14-year-old pupils in the UK and Portugal associated school music listening with motivation for learning, being active, and the content of particular lessons, and home music listening with enjoyment, emotional mood, and social relationships. Third, it may also be the case that school music is associated with 'serious' genres, typified by 'classical' music, and music out of school with pop and rock.

Musical Identities in Pupils and Teachers

The previous point leads on to another key issue, namely the authenticity of secondary school music. Many secondary school music teachers are products of the Western classical tradition, which is still largely based on the conservatory, and which still seems to predominate in a good deal of secondary school music. An analysis of the qualifications of seventy-four postgraduate secondary music teaching students in the Teacher Identities in Music Education (TIME) project, which represented approximately 20 per cent of all such students in the UK at the time, showed that the overwhelming majority of them had advanced school examination passes in music, advanced classical performance qualifications, and undergraduate music degrees: very few came from non-classical backgrounds involving pop, jazz, or rock music (Hargreaves, Welch, Purves, & Marshall, 2003). This background may be inappropriate for the demands of the contemporary secondary school classroom if teachers trained in classical music are relatively inexperienced in other genres. York (2000) carried out a survey of 750 heads of secondary school music which showed that although they had a good knowledge of Western classical music, of musicals and opera, and of the pop music of their own era (25+ years old), their knowledge of and engagement with current pop music and modern jazz was 'patchy and in many cases inadequate' (p. 1).

The main focus of the TIME project was the developing identities of classroom music teachers, and in particular the ways in which student teachers' identities as musicians and/or as teachers changed over the course of their training: we investigated these issues by tracing the development of the attitudes and identities of intending specialist secondary music teachers during the transition into their first teaching post, and comparing them with music students from university and conservatory backgrounds. The project had two main strands: the Longitudinal Questionnaire Study (LQS), carried out in two phases, and a series of case studies. Twenty-nine members of our sample of 74 postgraduate secondary music teaching students were followed from the first phase of the LQS into its second alongside 29 members of a sample of 54 undergraduate music students, and we selected 6of these for more detailed case studies. We designed and adapted a series of quantitative measures for the LQS which included assessments of musical and educational backgrounds and experiences; self-efficacy in music and in teaching; identification with professional groups in these two domains; and attitudes towards the aims of music education, and towards important skills for musicians and teachers.

To summarise, the main findings were that (a) as expected, the vast majority of music teaching students had similar qualifications in the 'classical performance' tradition; (b) their views of their own general effectiveness as teachers and as musicians changed very little over this period, but (c) their perceptions of the required skills for successful music teaching did change, towards an emphasis on communication and interpersonal skills rather than musical performance skills; (d) many music undergraduates were put off teaching careers because of fear of pupil behaviour and disinterest, and concerns about their lack of piano skills. In spite of the wide-ranging demands of contemporary music teaching, we concluded that the profession is still largely judged in terms of musical performance skills, and that this public perception needed to be broadened.

The extent of this problem may have declined over the last decade or two, however: some of our own research, which was commissioned by the Music Development Task Group of the Qualifications and Curriculum Authority in England (now disbanded), on which both of us served, showed some signs of change. Lamont, Hargreaves, Marshall, and Tarrant (2003) designed and administered a Pupils' Music Questionnaire to 758 girls and 721 boys at different age levels between 8 and 14 years, and carried out interviews with head teachers and teachers responsible for music in the same schools, as well as conducting focus group discussions with 134 of the same pupils. The questionnaire results showed that 67 per cent of pupils overall reported enjoying their class music lessons: the enjoyment stemmed in particular from playing musical instruments and singing. Approximately 25 per cent of pupils were learning an instrument at school, and of those who were not, approximately 40 per cent said that they would like to. Over half of the pupils said that they created or played music outside school regularly, and of those who did not, almost half said that they would like to. These are just the headlines from a wide range of different results, but they show quite clearly that there was no evidence for a 'problem of secondary school music' in this sample at least. In follow-up work, we have also highlighted the different views held by parents, teachers, and pupils themselves on what 'success' in music is. While teachers value engagement and parents are more eager to prioritise publicly visible elements of music such as school performances, pupils themselves are aware of these differences in value and thus the provisional nature of what counts (Lamont, 2017).

The interaction between the musical identities of music teachers and their pupils may well be critical to the success of music lessons. Teachers' own preferences and identities inevitably influence the ways in which they plan and deliver their lessons, and so the musical identities of teachers and pupils are interdependent. There is an implicit paradox here, however: if school teachers and other adults attempt to become involved in pupils' autonomous music-making in the third environment, it ceases to be such, so that any music that is played or taught in school is automatically unpopular by association. The challenge for music teachers is to create learning structures and situations which are sufficiently integrated with the third environment so as to provide knowledge and skills which can support activity within it, and yet to remain sufficiently distant from it themselves.

Agency and Technology

Westerlund, Partti, and Karlsen (2017) see *agency* as a key aspect of identity formation, which refers to 'one's perceived and actual ability to act in the world, and hence concerns matters such as self-esteem, experienced purpose of life, ego strength, and internal locus of control' (p. 495). They suggest that the social interactions and relational networks that exist inside and outside classrooms provide a much better account of what goes on in them than does a simple transmission model in which teachers pass on knowledge to their pupils. They also bring the perceived hegemony of Western classical music in a good deal of music education into their argument, and consider some of the issues that we discussed earlier about the use of popular music, as well as some issues concerning nationalism and gender. Agency enables pupils to reach beyond their current identities and to predict what they might like to become in the future: this means taking a sense of responsibility about their futures and developing the confidence to pursue these ambitions. Music provides an important area in which this might be made possible, and so educational institutions play a key role in the developing musical identities of their pupils.

As far as nationalism is concerned, Westerlund et al. point out that music in schools still tends to be regulated by national laws, educational policy, and curriculum documents in many countries, so that it is perhaps unsurprising that music is often used to express national identity (see also Folkestad, 2002). However, they also warn that nationalism and patriotism may reflect outdated beliefs of national superiority, based as they often are on historic memories and political goals rather than on the contemporary features of territories and populations themselves. Some developmental insight into this topic is to be found in Winstone and Witherspoon's (2016) study of the relationship between responses to the British National Anthem, and the sense of national identity in a sample of 8- to 10-year-old schoolchildren from the South of England.

In the first of two studies, Winstone and Witherspoon established that the majority of a group of 30 9–10 year olds were able to recognise the British National Anthem as such, and that they were able to generate national associations to it in their writing and drawings (which were categorised into 'royal', 'sport', 'military', 'religious ceremonies', 'music', and 'other'). In the second study, roughly equal groups of 8-, 9-, and 10-year-olds were played the British national anthem alongside two other pieces which varied in their national salience (Parry's *Jerusalem*, and Jeremiah Clarke's *The Prince of Denmark's March* ('The Trumpet Voluntary'): they generated national associations to these as well as completing the *Strength of Identification Scale* (Barrett, 2007), which is a measure of national identity. The authors found that 'The 10-year-old children generated more national associations to the National Anthem than younger children', and that 'More national associations were generated to the National Anthem by children with high, as opposed to low, national identity, but only for the 9- and 10-year-old children' (p. 263). We can conclude that the concept of national identity does indeed play a part in the development of musical identities, and that this topic is worthy of further investigation from both the psychological and the sociological points of view.

O'Neill (2017) also supports the idea that young people display agency in creating their identities by drawing on what they see as the most important influences in their social and cultural worlds. She develops this idea by investigating what she calls young people's 'learning ecologies', as well as the *connectedness* between young people and the world around them: and she bases her account on two main theoretical approaches. Habermas's (1987) conception of life worlds, which is based in phenomenology, provides an overall framework for thinking about the many structures, processes, and layers which make up young people's musical worlds: and ecological systems theory, represented by the approach of Bronfenbrenner (e.g. 1979), as well as Engeström's (1987) cultural-historical activity theory, emphasise the influence on young people of social and environmental factors at different levels, from the individual, through the institutional, to the cultural.

O'Neill uses this theoretical background to explain the results of 'Mapping young people's musical lives', her own empirical study of over 90 Canadian 10- to 19-year-olds, based on one-to-one interviews with young people about their musical engagement in everyday life, which were used to map all of the musical activities in which they were involved inside and outside school. O'Neill's analysis of her data led her to propose three distinct musical lifestyles which vary in the degree of their connectedness. *Segmented* musical lifestyles are comprised of different episodes not necessarily linked to one another, and O'Neill linked this with Giddens' (1991) concept of segmentation in twentieth-century life. What she calls *situated* musical lifestyles are based on the places or spaces in which interaction occurs, rather than on the musical activities themselves, and *agentive* styles are those in which all of the aspects of identity work with clearly connected, such that musical activity provides a clear-cut arena for it.

The rapid recent development of digital technology in music has had many widespread effects; we suggested in Chapter 1 that two of the most important have been the democratisation of musical styles and genres, which clearly works against the idea of a hegemony of Western classical music, and the blurring of the traditional distinctions between musical roles such as the composer, performer, improviser, arranger, studio engineer, and listener. We also discussed the third phenomenon, which is very important in our discussion of self-identity, namely the rapid rise of personal music listening on MP3 players and other devices. Many young people now use music downloading, and more recently music streaming, to access any music that they desire, and this has made music listening very much more flexible and personalised than hitherto, as well as enabling listeners to choose music to suit any particular listening situation.

Another phenomenon has been the rapid recent rise of smartphones with integrated music players: Randall and Rickard (2013) point out that over a fifth of the 5 billion mobile phones in the world are smartphones, and that smartphone penetration has risen to 52 per cent, 51 per cent, and 44 per cent of the populations of Australia, the UK, and the USA respectively. Randall, Rickard, and Vella-Brodrick's (2014) study used a mobile experience sampling methodology incorporated in their MuPsych app, which was developed in their previous study in order to provide a real-time and ecologically valid measurement of music listening, to investigate the ways in which 327 young people with a mean age of 21.02 years used personal music listening to regulate their emotional states. They confirmed that personal music listening did allow their participants to reach specific emotional goals and hedonic outcomes. It is not a long step from these results to suggest that personal music listening over a period of time is very likely to have a profound influence on musical identities: that the rapid advances in digital music technology are also directly affecting young people's agency and identities.

Even more important may be the most recent phenomenon of the widespread use of social media as a primary means of communication among many young people (as well as some older ones): the use of Twitter, Facebook, and YouTube has largely replaced email in certain groups, and these changes in the nature of social interaction are also likely to influence the development of identity. Auh and Walker (2017) looked specifically at the effects of social media in creating some new musical identities, comparing this phenomenon in Australia and South Korea. They comment that 'the emergence of new and more powerful digital technology over the last two decades has gradually changed the whole field of music perception and reception, especially in the popular music field ... the new technology has allowed individuals from anywhere in the world to become linked through interest, similar allegiances, and shared musical tastes' (p. 803) rather than doing this via localised peer or interest groups. The most striking example of this, from South Korea, is the artist Psy's *Gangnam Style*, a song which was posted on YouTube on 15 July 2012 and which had been viewed by 170 million people two months later, and by over 2000 million people in 2012 as a whole, which was an unprecedented global phenomenon.

Conclusion

There can be no doubt that the study of personal identity is increasingly important in psychology. It is a difficult concept to pin down, which is why the problem of definition is so important: but the opposite side of this coin is that this difficulty arises from the permeation of identity into just about every area of human life. The study of *musical* identities is of vital current significance because of the increasing ubiquity and availability of all forms of music as a result of the digital revolution, and we have seen in this chapter how this has had a direct effect on the perception of genres and styles, on mood regulation, and on social relationships and friendships, for example.

Two characteristics of identities which have emerged in recent years, which we have discussed in this chapter, are (a) that they are social and performative – we *do* identities just as much as *having* them – and (b) that they have an ethical and moral dimension – this has its roots in some of Aristotle's original ideas. When we look specifically at identities in music, three important questions arise. The first of these is the definition of music and musicians: some of the issues investigated in music psychology demand that our view of who is a 'musician' and what constitutes 'music' must be much broader than hitherto: the idea of a musician being someone with a high level of experience and training on instrument is far too narrow, and no longer appropriate. The second question concerns the relationship between musical identities and preferences for different genres, styles, or pieces, and this leads to the third issue, namely the extent to which identities and preferences are themselves linked to individual difference factors such as personality and lifestyle.

In summarising the scope and status of the concept of musical identities in 2002, Hargreaves, Miell, and MacDonald suggested that 'the concept of identity is important because it enables us to understand individuals' musical development 'from the inside' while clearly locating identity as an emergent feature of our fundamentally social worlds. It provides us with a way of conceptualising the interaction between biological and social influences, and provides continuity between our explanations of infant, adult and child behaviour. Studying the ways in people perceive themselves in relation to music has the potential to explain some phenomena of musical behaviour and experience that otherwise might be accessible' (p. 18).

Looking back at this field over a decade later, it seems even more clear that the study of people's musical identities is an essential part of the explanation of their musical development as a whole: that people's developing self-concepts tell us a great deal about why they develop in the ways they do, and enable us to see how the social environment is incorporated into the development of musical thinking at the individual level. As digital technology develops further and more quickly, and as its latest features become the province of younger and younger members of society, we can expect musical identities to develop and diversify still further.

7 Affect and Emotion

Introduction to Affect and Emotion

Before considering how affect and emotion might develop, it is helpful to consider some of the theoretical underpinnings of affect and emotion in music, which has been one of the most-studied areas in music psychology, dating back to the publication of Meyer's *Emotion and meaning in music* in 1956. At the start of the modern discipline, Meyer first noted that:

> Any discussion of the emotional response to music is faced at the very outset with the fact that very little is known about this response and its relation to the stimulus. Evidence that it exists at all is based largely upon the introspective reports of listeners and the testimony of composers, performers, and critics. Other evidence of the existence of emotional responses to music is based upon the behaviour of performers and audiences and upon the physiological changes that accompany musical perception. (Meyer, 1956, p. 6)

Meyer went on to define emotional responses to music as being evoked by expectation in one way or another: expectations are fulfilled, extended, or denied. This definition of emotion in music focuses primarily on the musical content and suggests that this is the best way of understanding the emotional impact a given piece or sequence will have on the listener. Although Meyer acknowledges the importance of learning, culture, and the mind of the listener in shaping such emotional responses; he argues that embodied meaning is the most important determinant (see further 'Expectancy' later in this chapter).

Meyer's work sparked an interest in understanding emotions which has grown over the past sixty years, and happily researchers now know a lot more about emotional responses to music, although the developmental evidence is still somewhat lacking (cf. Schubert & McPherson, 2016). This research, spanning a wide range of perspectives and methods, has illustrated that emotional responses to music are far more complex. As we have set out earlier, understanding musical responses seems to require a focus not only on the stimulus itself but also on the listener and the situation, in a pattern of reciprocal feedback over time (cf. Schubert, Hargreaves, & North, 2014). Based on extensive research in the realms of both performance and listening, Juslin (2013) has recently theorised emotional and affective response to music as being determined by eight different factors, many of which are held to operate in conjunction with one another and which span these three aspects.

Theorising Affect from an Ontological Perspective: Juslin's BRECVEMA Framework

Juslin's BRECVEMA framework is based on the acronym for its eight components, as follows: the most primitive response is the *Brain stem response* to any kind of sound, which is held to be an evolutionary response concerning arousal. We return to the notion of arousal throughout this chapter as it forms the underpinning of much research on emotional response. *Rhythmic entrainment* refers to the way the listener co-ordinates to or with a common periodicity in the music, through physical features such as heart rate, breathing, or actions. *Evaluative conditioning* explains how the musical stimulus becomes paired, at a relatively general level, with particular emotions, such as the use of trumpets in Western classical music to evoke ceremonies. The mechanism of *emotional contagion* relates to the relatively automatic mimicking of the emotion perceived in the music by the listener. *Visual imagery* concerns shapes in the music and visual patterns in the listener's mind which are stimulated by the music. Next, *musical expectancy* refers to patterns embodied within the music which evoke tension and release, such as harmonic prolongations (bringing in Meyer's 1956 notion of expectancy), and finally, *episodic memory* refers to the 'Darling They're Playing Our Tune' theory (Davies, 1978) according to which particular pieces of music become associated with specific moments in listeners' lives, which tend to evoke emotions such as nostalgia. These combine, most likely in varying proportions depending on the circumstances, to produce the final component, the *aesthetic response*, which goes some way to explain the power of music. The mechanisms in Juslin's BRECVEMA approach thus serve to identify different levels of specificity in terms of musical response and provide us with a useful way of considering the literature on development. We discuss these in the order in which they relate to developmental issues in this section.

Brain Stem Response

At the outset, the brain stem response to sound explains why music in general is pleasurable, and a wealth of evidence supports this. The (very) simple notion underpinning this is that sound evokes arousal. The arousal-based approach is best associated with Berlyne (1971), who suggested that arousal potential explained a great deal of responses to a range of stimuli. Arousal potential refers to the autonomic nervous system being activated by informational properties of the stimulus such as complexity and familiarity. We return to familiarity and a more detailed consideration of how experience shapes listening separately later on, but Berlyne's underpinning notion from an experimental aesthetics approach was that intermediate levels of arousal potential are supposed to be liked most.

Infants are able to show their levels of arousal and attention to liked stimuli or discrimination between stimuli through a number of behavioural outcomes, including deceleration of heart rate, maintenance of visual attention, and – somewhat paradoxically when thinking about physical responses to music later in development – a reduction in physical movements (Bacher & Robertson, 2001). Music is well known to be intrinsically pleasurable, and infants are attracted to musical sounds, particularly singing, from birth. When presented with speech and singing, infants are either equally interested in both kinds of stimuli (Costa-Giomi & Ilari, 2014) or sometimes show preferences for music over speech, from the newborn period onwards (Shenfield, Trehub, & Nakata, 2003). In addition to the well-known preferences that infants show for their own mother's voice (e.g. DeCasper & Fifer, 1980) and for infant-directed singing (Trainor, 1996), infants also seem to prefer video recordings of their own mother singing rather than talking (Nakata & Trehub, 2004). This preference forms the basis for engagement and interaction through music (see 'Emotional Contagion' in this section).

There are also fairly direct unmediated effects of listening to music on arousal levels which are evoked by the qualities of the sounds and which begin in the early infant period (Granier-Deferre, Bassereau, Ribeiro, Jacquet, & DeCasper, 2011; Shenfield et al., 2003). Infants at 1 month of age showed heart rate decelerations after listening to familiar or unfamiliar melodic lines (Granier-Deferre et al., 2011). Similarly, after listening to infant-directed singing, 6-month-olds' cortisol levels reached a mean level (either increasing from below or decreasing from above), showing that pleasurable music serves an emotion-modulation function (Shenfield et al., 2003). This builds on earlier findings that simpler stimuli, in this case continuous pure tones, soothed aroused infants while arousing soothed infants (Birns, 1965; Birns, Blank, Bridger, & Escalona, 1965). One of Juslin's definitions of brain stem response relates to the attraction of interest generated by high pitched and fast sounds, which is held to be important from an evolutionary perspective. Infants show more interest in music at higher pitch levels (Trainor & Zacharias, 1998; O'Neill, Trainor, & Trehub, 2001) and in faster tempi, at least for playsongs (Conrad, Walsh, Allen, & Tsang, 2011; Tsang & Conrad, 2010). This emphasis on arousal as evoked through faster tempi is also found in preference studies: Hunter, Schellenberg, and Stalinski (2011) found 5- and 8-year old children preferred music excerpts high in arousal potential, as well as being better able to identify the high-arousal emotions. Manipulation of tempo, a basic feature of arousal, led 4-year-olds to be able to distinguish between happy and sad versions of the same piece (Mote, 2011). This evidence suggests that the basic properties of sound are responsible for evoking some kind of reaction and emotion or affect.

It may be that the regularity and repetitiveness of maternal singing evokes more moderate arousal levels than speech, with its greater variability, and that these patterns help to sustain infants' attention and engagement (Nakata & Trehub, 2004). This is probably enhanced by the communicative intention of such singing. This introduces us to the social dimensions of emotional responses to music, which leads to the next two key mechanisms from Juslin's framework: both rhythmic entrainment and emotional contagion encompass the fact that music is inherently social and shared.

Rhythmic Entrainment

Rhythmic entrainment refers to the emotions generated through synchronising with others, – music is 'the ideal synchronisation device' (Brown, 2003, p. 16).

Newborns are sensitive to the beat in simple metric sequences (Winkler, Háden, Ladinig, Sziller, & Honing, 2009), showing different brain activation patterns when downbeats in a repetitive sequence are omitted, and infants also show beat detection skills at 6 months (Hannon & Trehub, 2005a).

Matching movement patterns to different kinds of music is another skill that begins in early childhood and takes its roots from early caregiver–infant interactions (which are discussed in the next subsection on emotional contagion). As we saw in Chapter 4, Zentner and Eerola (2010) captured infants' physical responses to a wide range of musical and rhythmic stimuli and also to adult- and infant-directed speech. Analysing video recordings and using motion-capture technology, they found more rhythmic movement from the infants in response to music and other rhythmically regular sounds such as isochronous drumbeats than to speech. Moreover, the better the infants were able to co-ordinate their movements rhythmically with the sound sequences the more likely they were to show positive affect through smiles, which can be taken to suggest that movement in time with the pulse actually generates positive affect. However, they describe their findings that infants moved faster to faster auditory patterns as more to do with 'tempo flexibility' than true entrainment (Zentner & Eerola, 2010, p. 5799). One important element of this study is that the infants' responses, found broadly across the age range 5 to 24 months, were completely spontaneous and unsolicited. Another is the importance of more than just arousal in the infants' movements: faster tempi did not result in more vigorous movements, only faster ones.

Building on this early skill, synchronisation abilities develop more slowly. Although spontaneous motor tapping is found from an early age in response to regular rhythmic stimuli, children's skills in synchronisation to a beat become more accurate and children are better able to anticipate the patterns at the age of 4 than 2.5 (Provasi & Bobin-Bègue, 2003). Initially children are only able to entrain to a beat if it falls around their preferred spontaneous motor tempo (McAuley, Jones, Holub, Johnston, & Miller, 2006; van Noorden, 2014). By about the age of 4, children have developed the ability to synchronise in tapping exercises (McAuley et al., 2006), and in an intriguing study, similar skills were found in 2.5-year-olds when the drumming partner was a real human rather than a drum machine or synthesised sound (Kirschner & Tomasello, 2009). Being able to predict beats depends on the ability to extract regularities in the temporal patterning of music, and as discussed in Chapter 3, an EEG study showed that while 7-year-olds were able to do this accurately at slower tempi (390 and 585ms), faster tempi (780ms) were still difficult at that age, so evidently this skill develops and is refined throughout childhood (Cirelli et al., 2014). The ability to consistently tap along with a beat improves all the way through into adulthood, with improvements seen between the ages of 8 to 18, although in older adulthood tapping performance becomes more variable (Thompson, White-Schwoch, Tierney, & Kraus, 2015). The ability to synchronise is also greater in both children and adults with some formal musical experience (Braun Janzen, Thompson, & Ranvaud, 2014; Slater, Tierney, & Kraus, 2014; Thompson et al., 2015).

Reflecting the emotions in different kinds of music (typically characterised by different tempi) through sympathetic movement is something that 4- and 5-year-olds can also do, given an appropriate experimental setting. Boone and Cunningham (2001) asked 4- and 5-year-olds to move a teddy bear to music to indicate the emotions of happiness, sadness, anger, or fear to match musical segments, finding that adults were able to accurately categorise the emotions the children were expressing through their movements. Children aged 5 and 8 are also able to match their motion features to musical stimuli, with close correlations between musical parameters such as increasing loudness and motion changes such as increased speed and muscular energy (Kohn & Eitan, 2016). Children are thus able to recognise and respond to emotional tone through features such as rhythm and tempo effectively relatively early in life, with refinement in accuracy with more complex tasks developing more gradually. Entrainment has been shown to be responsible in evoking emotions in music listening for adults (Labbé & Grandjean, 2014), and this may also be the case in development.

Emotional Contagion

Emotional contagion provides an explanation for how musical affect is perceived so early, and this can be related to Trevarthen and Malloch's notion of communicative musicality (Malloch, 1999; Trevarthen, 1999), which we have discussed in earlier chapters. Trevarthen and Malloch argue that music communicates with an 'intrinsic motive pulse' in the brain through the listener's ability to detect regularities in musical sounds, the qualities of the human voice, and the 'narrative' structures in vocalisation and music that form much of the intuitive way in which adults sing and speak to infants. Through detailed analysis of the melodic and rhythmic 'co-creativity' that mother-infant musical communication exhibits, Malloch (1999) was able to derive these three components from spectrographs and pitch plots of those interactions and measurements of onset and offset of vocalisations. The narratives, formed by combinations of pulse and quality, illustrate a poetic form of proto-conversation. For instance, an upward moving vocalisation from the 6-week-old infant Laura is reprised by her mother in a rising pitch swoop, and her mother's subsequent descending pitch pattern is then echoed by Laura's own vocalisation. This fine-grained matching of pitches shows the beginnings of situated meaning, communication, and musicality first identified by Papoušek and Papoušek (1981), which set the foundations of emotional responses to music, and showed evidence of contagion through musical expression and communication.

From a Vygotskian perspective, such adult–infant interaction would be seen as necessary in order to stimulate this kind of development and learning about the world. Indeed, Dissanayake (2000) suggests that this intimate communication between infant and adult through music may be both the origin of musicality in human development and the starting point for developing other social forms of co-operative behaviour. The more capable other, whether a parent or child, is certainly aware of the emotional tone of infants' own vocalisations and thus able to respond appropriately. Papoušek (1992) found that a range of 'others', including parents, speech therapists, and 8-year-old children, were all able to accurately match the emotional content of vocalisations produced by 2-month-old infants who were expressing comfort, discomfort, or pleasure, and that mothers were able to adjust their own vocal responses accordingly.

Infants' earliest preferences for emotional stimuli in a laboratory setting but using real materials also confirm the importance of social interaction underpinning and enhancing musical communication of emotion. Very young infants prefer to listen to the far more exaggerated patterns of infant-directed (ID) compared to adult-directed (AD) speech (Cooper & Aslin, 1990; Pegg, Werker, & McLeod, 1992). While the differences in singing are more subtle (for example, the exaggerated pitch contours which characterise ID speech are not always possible in singing as they would alter the structure of the music), there are clear acoustic differences between ID and AD singing which are similar to those found in speech (Papoušek, 1992). Trainor, Clark, Huntley, and Adams (1997) found that mothers sang more slowly and with more jitter (variation in the fundamental frequency) when singing to an infant as compared with singing the same songs in the absence of the infant. When singing playsongs, mothers also used more variability in overall pitch and more exaggerated rhythms and patterns of stress, although this was not found from lullaby singing. Sensitivity to the 'tone' of communication expressed through music is present from the beginning of the lifecourse, as newborns and 6-month-old infants alike are more attentive to infant-directed singing than non-infant-directed singing (Masataka, 1999; Trainor, 1996). This then suggests that emotional contagion, as Juslin suggests, is a relatively intuitive form of emotional response to music and one which we are primed to both generate and respond to from the earliest moments of life.

Visual Imagery

The notion that music evokes emotion through visual imagery finds a lot of support from developmental literature in that infants tend to respond more positively, and accurately, to music that has an additional visual component. The conditioned head turning and preference procedures used by infant researchers working with music typically depend on visual pairings in order to attract and maintain attention, and it is well established that responses can be obtained earlier and more sensitively from multimodal than unimodal stimuli (Gogate, Walker-Andrews, & Bahrick, 2001). Juslin's original idea was that images could help conjure up emotions while music was being heard, or even in the absence of the musical stimulus itself, and that the pairing strengthened the emotional response. There is no data on emotional responses to audio-visual sequences in infants, although there is evidence that audio-visual pairings can be learned at the age of 3 months (e.g. Fagen et al., 1997). Fagen et al. trained infants to kick their ankle to move an overhead crib mobile while different types of music were played, finding that they were able to remember the contingency between kicking and the mobile moving when the same music was being played a week later, which is perhaps the earliest incidence of music listening affecting learning in a non-musical context (see also effects of music listening in Chapter 8).

Richer environments lead to more learning and earlier rates of development in a general sense. In a review of a wide range of infant research, Bahrick, Lickliter, and Flom (2004) conclude that intersensory redundancy created by the overlap of multimodal stimulation is beneficial, if not essential, for development. Many of their examples, in support of what they propose as the Intersensory Redundancy Hypothesis, refer to the enhanced processing of sounds when accompanied by visual input. For instance, 3-month-old infants were able to discriminate a change of tempo in a toy hammer tapping only when they had both auditory and visual input (Bahrick, Flom, & Lickliter, 2002). Bahrick et al. make reference to Gibson's (1966) ecological theory in support of this principle, drawing on the point that the senses work together to detect stimulation or information that is common across them. In adulthood, musical training plays a role in enhancing the ability to process audio-visual material and detect asynchronies, with typically faster responses seen for trained musicians in judgements about musical sequences (Lee & Noppeney, 2011; Müller, Höfel, Brattico, & Jacobsen, 2007). These findings support the view that experience can shape responses to audio-visual information and that this may be less dependent on general age-related cognitive development, but as yet there is no relevant evidence on this topic with children.

Musical Expectancy

Musical expectancy has been at the core of research on how music evokes emotions in adults (Meyer, 1956; Zatorre & Salimpoor, 2013). Meyer's original notion (1956) was that the structure of music sets patterns of expectation, tension, and release, and this formed the starting point of research in emotional responses to music from an adult perspective. Zatorre and Salimpoor (2013) have provided a clear overview of how the patterns of arousal in the mesolimbic striatal system in the brain mediate the pleasure associated with music listening. They state that like speech, the patterns and emotions evoked by music in the brain depend on pre-existing neural architecture, which implies that patterns of expectancy 'piggyback' on existing brain structures and are thus relatively innate. There is some evidence that different areas of the brain might be activated for basic pitch and melodic processing and for higher-order harmonic processing which would be necessary for understanding expectancy in tonal music. Seger et al. (2013) showed the posterior superior temporal gyrus was dominant in basic processing of pitch and melody, while the right inferior frontal gyrus, anterior superior temporal gyrus, and basal ganglia are all activated in higher-order processing of harmonic expectations in adults; these systems require learning to develop predictions.

Somewhat surprisingly, there is not much research exploring this explicitly with infants or children. As described earlier, most of the research with children has focused on very simple emotional states such as distinguishing happy or sad, but some have explored responses to different patterns of pitch and harmony. Schellenberg, Adachi, Purdy, and McKinnon (2002) explored children's and adults' responses to short melodies, using both perceptual and production tasks. Participants were either asked to rate how well individual tones continued a melodic fragment or to sing continuations to very short two-tone stimuli. The simplest form of expectancy found in this study was that all participants expected the next tone to be close in pitch to the final note of the sequence just heard, irrespective of age. Where developmental change was seen, younger children were less likely to expect a reversal of pitch direction, and Schellenberg et al. conclude that reversal is thus a more complex form of expectation dependent on a degree of enculturation, while proximity is simpler and found at an earlier age. In a further study on harmony, Schellenberg, Bigand, Poulin-Charronat, Garnier, and Stevens (2005) found that children from the age of 6 were able to respond implicitly to the harmony of Western tonal music, being able to judge tonic chords more rapidly and accurately as fitting a tonal sequence than subdominant chords. It is important to note that these studies concern expectancy rather than affect, but they provide some indication of the musical features that might need to be understood (cf. Chapter 3) prior to affect being able to be generated by such features.

Thus, counter to the nativist perspective, as children's sensitivities to aspects of the music of their culture develops gradually (Chapter 3), their ability to predict and then to experience emotion through musical features such as harmonic tension and release also seems develop gradually across childhood to reach adult levels by around the ages of 7 or 8. This is at least partly related to evaluative conditioning (discussed in the following subsection).

Evaluative Conditioning

More specific cultural aspects are embodied in the mechanism of evaluative conditioning, which is useful to explain how infants and children learn through exposure. Responding to intra-musical patterns of expectancy reflects the specificity of a musical style, and thus the influence of the environment. As shown by Plantinga and Trehub (2014), exposure is largely responsible for the preferences and discriminations shown by infants, and as argued by Schubert et al. (2014, see Chapter 2), it may be the ultimate determinant of preference across the lifespan. Schubert et al. suggest that spreading activation may provide a parsimonious explanation for aesthetic experiences of music (see e.g. Schubert, 2012). Spreading activation depends on a mental architecture consisting of a vast network of nodes: when a perception or action occurs, specialised networks representing that perception/action process are activated through the connections of that network. Interestingly, the principle of spreading activation can be found in the work of William James, and in particular in his elementary law of association: 'When two elementary brain-processes have been active together or in succession, one of them, on reoccurring, tends to propagate its excitement into the other' (James, 1890/1950, p. 566). This mechanism is linked in turn with aesthetic preference by Martindale's (1984, 1988) proposal that the process of activation of nodes is in itself pleasurable, provided that the listener is in a disinterested state.

Returning to the earlier notions from experimental aesthetics that exposure leads to enhanced enjoyment through arousal potential (Berlyne, 1971), Schubert et al. propose that as long as the listener is primed for aesthetic experience (cf. DeNora,

2000), exposure to a given kind of music will unconsciously lead to enhanced reception of that music, thereby evoking emotions. Rather than simply focusing at a cognitive level, Schubert et al. propose that listener, response, and situation are all involved in this process of spreading activation, which goes some way to explaining how musical experiences and memories have such depth and richness (see Chapter 2).

The acoustical features of music, to a greater or lesser degree, shape the emotional content perceived in it, and prior experience with these features and their delineations in emotional content is necessary in order to respond appropriately to them. However, as we have seen earlier, this experience need not be extended. By about 2 months, infants seem to prefer consonance over dissonance in Western music (Trainor & Heinmiller, 1998; Trainor, Tsang, & Cheung, 2002; Zentner & Kagan, 1998). By 8 or 9 months, infants seem able to reliably discriminate between music defined by adults and older children from their own culture as happy and sad (Flom, Gentile, & Pick, 2008; Nawrot, 2003), and their performance is more accurate, and their interest greater, when it comes to happy music. For instance, in Nawrot's study, 5- and 9-month-old infants were given paired stimuli of faces and music expressing happiness or sadness. The happy music was a 20-second excerpt from Mozart's Violin Concerto No. 5, while the sad piece was 20 seconds of Bach's Goldberg Variations, as judged happy or sad by children in her study. Infants at both ages looked longer at the happy face when hearing happy music, but while sad music was being played there was no clear face preference. This suggests that there is some discrimination in the responses to the stimuli, and Nawrot also noted that the infants appeared to be less interested overall when the sad music was being played (as was also found by Flom et al., 2008, with 8-month-old infants). However, due to the use of real music, a rich stimulus which varies on a number of features, it is not possible in this study, as for many others, to carefully identify which of those features are responsible for the different response patterns. It is also possible, as Schubert & McPherson have suggested (2016), that the infants were simply more interested in the more dynamic happy visual stimuli.

From this early ability to distinguish emotionally "appropriate" music in infancy, research shows that sensitivity to the nature of the emotions conveyed by the cultural aspects of music develops gradually. The precise age at which happy and sad excerpts can be accurately labelled as such, and the basis on which this is done, are both somewhat contested. As discussed earlier ('Brain stem response'), tempo provides an initial arousal-based focus for this distinction. Dalla Bella, Peretz, Rousseau, and Gosselin (2001) found that 5-year-olds were able to detect happy and sad music based only on tempo, and this study has been much cited to indicate that children younger than 5 are unable to correctly match these emotions to simple musical stimuli (see also Mote, 2011). However, when the materials are rich and the tasks appropriately simple, even 3-year-olds seem able to correctly match happy music (as generated by the use of major mode, fast tempo, and more staccato articulations) with happy facial stimuli or drawings (Franco, Chew & Swaine, 2017; Kastner & Crowder, 1990). The ability to use mode as a distinguishing factor becomes more consistent around the age of 4–5 years. For instance, Cunningham and Sterling (1988) found that 5-year-olds were able to explicitly judge musical excerpts as happy, sad, or angry in a way that reliably matched adults' ratings of the same sequences, based on the musical features of tempo, mode, and pitch. Ziv and Goshen (2006) found 5- to 6-year-olds were able to interpret an emotionally neutral story according to the emotional tone of the music that accompanied it, with sad versions generated by a slow minor melody and upbeat versions by a fast major melody. Morton and Trehub (2007) found 5-year-olds using mode and tempo in the same way as adults to identify positive or negative emotions in singers. Their participants were asked to judge the mood of songs with happy or sad music and incongruent lyrics as well as the same music paired with nonsense syllables. For the nonsense syllables, even 5-year-olds performed near ceiling and all participants (aged 5–10 and adults) judged songs with major mode and fast tempo as happy and those with minor mode and slow tempo as sad. Children were affected more by the incongruent lyrics, however. They judged the emotion of the songs based on their lyrics, in comparison with adults who used the musical cues more in those contexts.

There is a good deal of variation in the ways in which listeners respond to different specific pieces of music which may be explicable in terms of familiarity at a more cultural level. For instance, in Nawrot's (2003) study of children's and adults' responses to pieces carefully selected to represent the basic emotions of happiness, sadness/neutrality, and fear/anger, 3- to 5-year-olds' judgements of certain pieces corresponded neatly with the judgements of the adults, while for other pieces less correspondence was seen. Similarly, Andrade, Vanzella, and Schellenberg (2016) found children aged from 7 to 11 were able to correctly identify emotions in excerpts of Wagner's music as accurately as untrained adults, with better performance from the younger and less experienced participants when considering arousal than valence. This kind of research can tell us more about the complexity of real musical responses than studies using more carefully controlled but less ecologically valid materials. When specially composed materials are used they lose something of the appeal of 'real' music, as Nieminen, Istók, Brattico, and Tervaniemi (2012) found. They carefully composed a major, minor, and free tonal piece in a study of emotional recognition for 6- to 9-year-old children, exploring the effects of age and training on the recognition of tonality, emotions, and aesthetic judgements. Overall the children failed to rate major pieces as representing happiness, with only the older trained children doing so consistently, and their suggestion is that the specially composed materials did not engage the children sufficiently as they also gave them relatively low liking ratings.

Looking at finer musical features, Stachó, Saarikallio, van Zijl, Houtilainen, and Toiviainen (2013) found a gradual developmental improvement in children's abilities to match different emotional performances of the same piece of music. They asked performers to give different renditions of the same piece to communicate the emotions of happy, sad, angry, fearful, or neutral, which allows for a more naturalistic approach to generating stimuli. Careful analysis of the resulting stimuli using the Matlab MIR Toolbox (Lartillot & Toiviainen, 2007) showed that the sad performances were longer and quieter; fearful performances were slightly shorter, quieter, with less attack slope; angry performances were the shortest, loudest, and had the most crisp and direct sound attack; while happy performances were shorter than the fearful ones as well as being relatively loud with a fairly high attack slope. What this results in is highly ecologically valid stimuli but ones which, like many others with young children, provide an ambiguity of auditory cues which is challenging when interpreting results.

Stachó et al. (2013) then asked children to match the performances to visual depictions of the five emotions. Children aged 3–4 were able to correctly match the happy and sad performances better than chance, while 5- to 7-year-olds were also able to match neutral and fearful performances (adults with and without training were able to correctly match all five emotional states). The children typically confused fear and sadness, which has also been found with adults (Terwogt & van Grinsven, 1991) and can be explained by the similarity in dynamics, tone attacks, and timbre. This study confirms that emotional development continues to develop in sophistication throughout childhood and into adolescence.

Some work has also explored how children communicate emotions themselves in their own performances. Adachi and Trehub (1998) asked 4- to 12-year-olds to sing a song familiar to them to an adult with the aim of making her happy or sad, and analysed the resulting versions for a range of musical and general communicative features. They found that tempo and facial expressions, which are ways of communicating emotion in language as well as music, were used most by the children to communicate emotion. Happy performances were faster, louder, and higher in pitch, with smiling and looking straight ahead; conversely, sad performances were slower, quieter, at a lower pitch level, with frowning and looking downwards. Specifically musical features such as articulation and mode were used relatively infrequently. Yamasaki (2004) analysed percussion performances from 5- to 6-year-old children who were asked to match the emotions of joy, sadness, and anger, finding that adults were correctly able to match the performances to the emotions above chance levels. Sad performances were quieter than angry or joyful ones, while angry performances were shorter and had fewer beats than the other two emotions. In this study as in many others children failed to correctly recognise or discriminate the 'fear' response which was originally included, and so this data was omitted. In both these studies results were analysed separately for those children who were more and less skilled at the task at hand, which confirms many findings that musical production skills are more varied within particular age groups in childhood. In these studies they are labelled as 'ordinary' and 'good', and in both cases the emotional communication is more accurate and successful in those more skilled at the task. In some cases, children as young as four do use mode and articulation to express emotions, as shown in Figure 7.1.

In an intriguing performance study, Maes and Leman (2013) showed that 7- to 8-year-old children who danced in a happy or sad style to expressively ambiguous music were more likely to subsequently judge the music as happy or sad. The children were taught different dance routines to match the intended emotional tone: happy

Figure 7.1. Invented 'happy' song from a 4-year-old Canadian child.
Source: From Adachi, M., & Trehub, S. E. (2011). Canadian and Japanese preschoolers' creation of happy and sad songs. *Psychomusicology: Music, Mind & Brain*, 21(1/2), 130–143. American Psychological Association. Figure 2, p. 135, reprinted with permission.

movements included rotating around the vertical axis, upright dancing, fast tempo, and expansive movements, while sadness was expressed through low tension, slow pace, collapsed upper body, and passivity. The music contained elements which point to both happy and sad emotions, including elements such as both minor and major modes and the presence of sad melodic lines combined with upbeat percussion and instrumentation. Children rated the music as happier, more cheerful, energetic, and merry following the happy dance, and as sadder, slower, more lonely, and gloomy following the sad dance. Maes and Leman (2013) cite this as evidence for short-term evaluative conditioning, although it is likely that elements of longer-term conditioning are also playing a role in the children's interpretations of the dances as well as the inherent ambiguity of the musical stimuli. Nonetheless their evidence supports the importance of moving to music and synchronisation not only in generating emotions through entrainment but also by conveying culturally relevant features of emotion.

Episodic Memory

In a more specific manner than evaluative conditioning, episodic memory explains the details of a listener's personal engagement with specific pieces and, by extension, styles and genres (see further in this chapter). The essence and sometimes the ineffability of musical engagement is highly personal. While music may have inherently pleasant characteristics, we do not necessarily like all of it even from the outset. As discussed in Chapter 3, early research (Zentner & Kagan, 1998) suggested that infants might show innate preferences for consonant over dissonant stimuli (consonant melodies having been composed with parallel major and minor thirds, while dissonant melodies consisted of sequences of parallel minor seconds). However, advances in infant research have cast doubt on the notion that innateness explains this preference. For instance, Trainor et al. (2002) found 2- and 4-month-old infants seemed to show a preference for the *first* type of a consonant-dissonant stimulus pair irrespective of the order it was presented, and Plantinga and Trehub (2014) have recently shown that infant preferences for musical sequences, whether consonant or dissonant, are primarily shaped by (short-term) familiarity.

Over longer-term periods, familiar sequences are responded to in different ways than unfamiliar ones. Repeated exposure to complex auditory streams such as speech evokes heart rate changes even in the latter stages of pregnancy (DeCasper, Lecanuet, Maugeais, Granier-Deferre, & Busnel, 1994, Krueger, Holditch-Davis, Quint, & DeCasper, 2004). Exposure during the prenatal period is the reason why infants prefer their mother's voice to that of a stranger (DeCasper & Fifer, 1980; Kisilevsky, Hains, Lee, Xie, Huang et al., 2003), and even at 4 months infants prefer their mother's voice to their father's due to far greater pre-natal exposure (Ward & Cooper, 1999). Peter Hepper's groundbreaking work showed that mothers who watched the Australian TV series *Neighbours* during pregnancy had infants who immediately after birth would show alert concentration to the theme tune, while other infants whose mothers had not watched the programme showed no similar reaction, although this familiarity appeared to be short-lived and had disappeared by 21 days after birth (Shahidullah & Hepper, 1994). Using more controlled materials, three weeks of exposure at the end of pregnancy led 1-month-old infants to show twice as much cardiac deceleration to a familiar version of a simple highly controlled piano melody compared with an unfamiliar version which was identical in amplitude (Granier-Deferre et al., 2011). Some of these musical memories can be long-lasting. Partanen, Kujala, Tervaniemi, and Houtilainen (2013) found that very small within-key changes in *Twinkle Twinkle Little Star* could be detected by both neonates and 4-month-old infants who had been familiarised with the melody in the last trimester of pregnancy, as shown through brain event-related potentials. This shows us how familiarity can begin to shape responses to music even before birth.

Later in life, personal experiences through episodic memories allow us to understand preferences for specific pieces in terms of experience: through highly individual and culturally situated listening experiences, listeners will develop personal likes and dislikes. The distinction between style and piece preference maps neatly on to the distinction between evaluative conditioning and episodic memory. As we have discussed elsewhere (Greasley & Lamont, 2016; Schubert et al., 2014), in the field of music preferences this distinction is often conflated, with one being taken to indicate the other. Furthermore, far less emphasis has been placed on the individual nature of listeners' engagement with specific pieces of music than on the general patterns of preference for styles and traditions of music (see further 'Aesthetic response' and 'Developing style preference' in this chapter). However, considering responses to specific pieces of music, some research has traced biographical narratives through the notion of the record collection (Giles, Pietrzykowski, & Clark, 2007; Greasley, Lamont, & Sloboda, 2013).

Giles et al. first identified the idea of the music collection for young adults as a 'facet of the self' following Csikzentmihalyi and Rochberg-Halton's (1981) notion that material possessions serve a differentiating function. It is generally assumed, based on research on the importance of music to adolescents (Tarrant, North, & Hargreaves, 2001; see section on Social Bonding, Friendship, and Relationships) and young adults (Holbrook & Schindler, 1989), that specific music encountered in these stages in life will remain important throughout life. From a quantitative perspective, Krumhansl and Zupnick (2013) found some evidence of this in their studies of 'reminiscence bumps' in liking for music. They used this term to describe their finding that their 20-year-old participants recognised and liked songs that were at the top of the charts both when they themselves were in adolescence and early adulthood, and when both their parents and grandparents were at the same ages, in comparison to music that was at the top of the charts in the intervening years. Thus they remembered and liked specific songs that were popular between 1980 and 1984 (including *Call Me* by Blondie, *Eye of the Tiger* by Survivor, and *What's Love Got to Do with It* by Tina Turner) more than songs popular in the or the preceding period 1975–1979 (including *Don't Go Breaking My Heart* by Elton John and Kiki Dee, *Night Fever* by the Bee Gees, and *Bad Girls* by Donna Summer) or the next five-year period 1985–1989 (including *Like a Virgin* by Madonna, *Say You, Say Me* by Lionel Richie, and *Need You Tonight* by INXS). There was also a slight bump found in the early 1960s (*Stranger on the Shore* by Acker Bilk, *Sugar Shack* by Jimmy Gilmer and the Fireballs, and *She Loves You* by the Beatles). Krumhansl and Zupnick (2013) argue strongly that the reminiscence 'bumps' for these particular pieces are caused by transmission through generations, although they acknowledge that the 'grandparent' bump might be more to do with the quality of the music at that particular period in time. Evidently all participants would have had different episodic memories in relation to these pieces of music and it is plausible that some of the preference and recognition is based on such memories.

Although not the primary focus of their studies, Greasley and Lamont (2013) were also able to shed some light on listeners' lifespan engagement with specific pieces of music. Looking at a population of adults from 18 to 73, Greasley and Lamont found that people's music collections appeared to grow linearly with age; however, the patterns of listening to specific pieces were found to be highly individualistic, relating to personal circumstances. For example, Rich, aged 25, talked about the album *The Private Press* by DJ Shadow as having reminded him for a long time of a very unhappy point in his life, but that over time those negative memories had subsided: 'I listen in a different way now, I listen to it in a happy kind of way' (Greasley & Lamont, 2013, p. 23). Participants talked about engaging and re-engaging with their own preferred music at different points in time, and regulating their own exposure so that music was constantly kept fresh. One of the older participants, Chrissie (aged 48), had what she described as an epiphany in her mid-forties in relation to the band Hanson (a band normally associated with teenage fans).

'It's [Hanson's music] got a lot of youthfulness about it but it's also got some quite serious underlying themes so you can kind of sit down and feel satisfied by it, it's not just a piece of bubble gum, but also it's light enough to kind of enjoy and just have fun with ... what captured me about it because it was youthful at a time when I suppose I was seeing my youth, well, going, and I was thinking, where do I go from here, all I've got is bloody Cyndi Lauper and Joni Mitchell, you know, and that's not where I want to be forever, and in a sense they [Hanson] kind of kick-started me into loving music in a more youthful exciting sort of way, not being so kind of heavy and serious about it, you know, just saying music's fun and you can just jump about to it and enjoy it, rather than it has to be this really serious encounter with life.' (Greasley & Lamont, 2013, p. 25)

Chrissie rejected the music she had been familiar with and loved in her early adult years in favour of something to recapture her youth, but which also gave her a new lease of life in relation to music preferences and the emotions they can evoke. These trajectories of musical waxing and waning are extremely hard to capture and predict and highly individualised, but music provides a structure to people's autobiographies. Reminiscence also forms a major function of musical engagement in adulthood and into later life, and there is some preliminary evidence that music can serve as a valuable source of reminiscence to help older people in therapeutic situations (Duffey, Somody, & Clifford, 2008). However, it is important to note Subramaniam and Woods' (2012) recommendation that individual reminiscence work must be highly personalised and the memory triggers used should be specifically relevant to the person if such interventions are to be successful, which serves to further highlight the importance of episodic memory and emotion.

Aesthetic Response

Juslin added the final category of aesthetic response later in the development of his framework for understanding the mechanisms of musical emotion (2013), and claims that it is a much more recent addition to the repertoire of human behaviours than the other seven mechanisms. Aesthetic responses, according to Juslin, emerge from an aesthetic stance, and responses are filtered through an individualised set of criteria that may include beauty, skill, novelty, style, message, and expression and emotion. This implies that the seven preceding mechanisms will contribute to this kind of judgement – Juslin suggests that they operate in parallel, to create everyday emotions and then aesthetic emotions – but in a way that is highly individual and tailored to the listener and the context. It can be argued that all responses to music are aesthetic, but Juslin is referring here to the explicitly aesthetic judgement. This relates more to specifically musical emotions, such as wonder, transcendence, tenderness, nostalgia, peacefulness, power, joyful activation, tension, and sadness, as

(a)   (b)

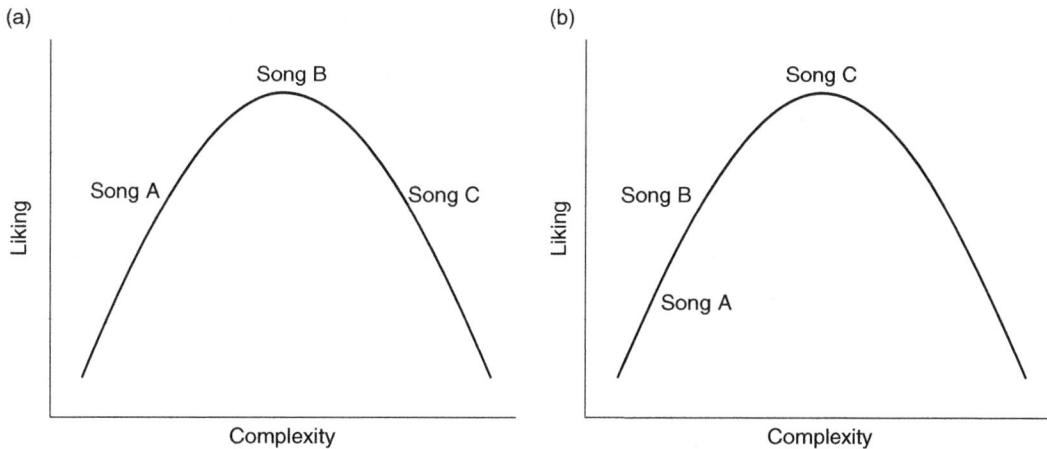

Figure 7.2.   Effect of increasing familiarity over time on the subjective complexity of three songs with different levels of arousal potential.
Source: Redrawn from Figures 16.3a and 16.3b (p. 308) in Hargreaves, D. J., North, A. C., & Tarrant, M. (2016), How and why do musical preferences change during childhood and adolescence? In: G. McPherson (Ed.), *The child as musician: A handbook of musical development* (pp. 303–322). © Oxford University Press. By permission of Oxford University Press.

captured by scales such as the Geneva Emotional Music Scale (Zentner, Grandjean, & Scherer, 2008).

Adult-based theories of experimental aesthetics draw heavily on the work of Berlyne (1971) mentioned earlier (see 'Brain stem response'), and the field of experimental aesthetics has developed to help explain listeners' judgements of music from this point of view. Berlyne proposed that listeners collate the informational properties of music, such as complexity and familiarity, and that liking is principally determined by the effect these collative properties have on the autonomic nervous system. Liking, in Berlyne's account, has an inverted U-shaped relationship with familiarity. Exposure to a given piece or style will lead first to increases and eventually to subsequent decreases in liking as familiarity varies, as shown in Figure 7.2. In the upper panel, we can see liking for three different pop songs at a given moment in time, and in the lower, how preference should change followed repeated exposure. This could be an explanation for the increasing preference for more complex music with age, to which we will return in more detail below: Song B might be moderately arousing for a younger listener but too simplistic for an older one, while Song C might be extremely complex for a younger listener but moderately arousing for an older one. This could explain some aspects of how music preferences within a given culture evolve with age.

A contrasting cognitivist view was proposed by the 'preference for prototypes' approach first championed by Martindale and Moore (1988), who proposed that preference is determined by the extent to which a particular stimulus is typical of its class. From a neural network perspective this approach claims that typical stimuli lead to stronger activation of the salient cognitive categories, allowing the perceiver to make greater sense of the world. Martindale and Moore found only 4 per cent of the variance in participants' preference for classical music themes to be accounted for by complexity, while 51 per cent was ascribed to typicality measures (see also similar evidence in Hekkert & van Wieringen, 1990; Martindale, Moore, & Borkum, 1990), and Martindale, Moore, and West (1988) suggested a rejection of Berlyne's theory on that basis.

In relation to music, we have argued elsewhere (North & Hargreaves, 2000a) that these two theories are perhaps more related than either of their adherents would presume, because the two variables – arousal potential and typicality – co-vary. The arousal potential of a piece of music affects the typicality of the piece of the class from which it is drawn. We have also suggested (Hargreaves, North, & Tarrant, 2016) that the theoretical conflict between these approaches may explain why so little research with children has approached this topic. However there are some studies that have explored musical development explicitly from an experimental aesthetics perspective. North and Hargreaves's (1995) studies of eminence show that listeners seem to develop some kind of prototype of music at a given critical age, following research by Holbrook (1995) that pinpointed a critical period of development in late adolescence or early childhood as having peaks in preferences. In North and Hargreaves' data, participants nominated their most eminent pop musicians as artists who were at the peak of their fame during the participants' own adolescence/early adulthood. We return to this research later when considering how style preferences develop. Neuroaesthetics is a more recent field which may also have the potential to shed light on emotional responses and their development (see Hargreaves et al., 2016), although thus far most of the research has been carried out with adults (see Brattico & Pearce, 2013; Nieminen, Istók, Brattico, Tervaniemi, & Houtilainen, 2011).

In addition to this work looking specifically at aesthetic response, the aesthetic dimension has also been explicitly addressed by other researchers. It is included in Swanwick and Tillman's (1986) model as the pinnacle of the four stages, expected around the age of 15. The final stage of value, in their approach, incorporates a transition from symbolic to systematic expression, with children's understanding of aesthetics becoming more conventional with age. Although this element of Swanwick and Tillman's work was not based on empirical evidence, there is supporting evidence of a similar progression at a younger age from the field of visual art. Rodway, Kirkham, Schepman, Lambert, and Locke (2016) studied children between the ages of 4 and 10 and found more standardisation with age and greater agreement over representational than abstract artworks in the older age ranges. Between the ages of 4 and 8, more references to the artist were found in children's explanations of aesthetic judgements, and it appears that this reflects children's general cognitive development; the more that is understood about the art form, the greater the potential aesthetic appreciation. In a study already mentioned earlier with music, Nieminen et al. (2012) also explored the relevance of aesthetic judgements for school-aged children. In addition to a range of cognitive tasks to do with judging music's tonality and emotions, the children (aged 6–9) were asked to judge the specially composed music for its beauty or ugliness. Each piece was rated by selecting and placing a sticker, with a princess representing beauty and a witch ugliness.

Nieminen et al. (2012) found that the 6- to 7-year-olds made no distinction between the three pieces used (a major piece, a minor piece, and a free tonal piece) in terms of beauty, but 8- to 9-year-olds rated the major piece as the most beautiful (with no difference between the other two). The ugliness ratings were similar (the major piece being rated the least ugly) but far less marked, and not significant. They also found correlations between children's preference and emotion ratings for the pieces and their ratings of beauty and ugliness, with preference and happiness broadly related to beauty and sadness to ugliness. This may suggest that *explicitly* aesthetic judgements are not yet fully developed at this age and are perhaps conflated with emotional responses in a general notion of positive valence.

Looking at music production, which was also the original basis of Swanwick and Tillman's model, Barrett (1996) explored children's compositions for a number of musical features. She concluded that children as young as 5–6 were able to use aesthetic decision-making in their compositions, as illustrated by their use of structure and form. This corresponds to findings from research on invented songs (Davies, 1992) and spontaneous music-making (Pond, 1981) and provides a more positive picture of young children's aesthetic abilities than that implied by Swanwick and Tillman's model. Interestingly, Barrett (1996) found evidence of aesthetic decisions in children both with and without formal music training, suggesting that this develops through experience with a musical culture but does not require explicit training. It has also been argued that aesthetic contexts exist much earlier in musical development, with mother-infant pretend play and babbling being two such (Dissanayake, 2000; Tafuri & Villa, 2002). The notion of aesthetic judgement is returned to later in this chapter ('Developing style preferences').

Explaining Age-Related Developments in Musical Preference

Juslin's proposed emotional mechanisms give us a way of understanding the levels on which music works and some specific concepts to focus upon. Looking at development from this point of view suggests that different mechanisms may underlie different developmental progressions: some (brain stem response, rhythmic entrainment, emotional contagion) are more intuitive and require less learning, while the others depend on experience within a given cultural context and on learning, whether implicit or explicit. Juslin's mechanisms suggest a phylogeny across human evolution, moving from the most primitive brain stem response to music through to the most refined and evolutionarily developed aesthetic response. He claims that sensation and physical coupling processes occur even in very simple organisms, with perception and learning associations being the next features to develop. A capacity for responding empathically is, he suggests, a later development only found in social animals. Imagination, memory, and self-consciousness are all later evolutionary developments for humans, depending on 'newer' regions of the brain such as the medial temporal lobe, Broca's area, and the orbital fronto-lateral cortex.

While it is generally accepted that Haeckel's original claim in the nineteenth century that ontogeny recapitulates phylogeny is erroneous (Gould, 1985), there is some merit in the analogy, and in considering whether individuals experience a similar progression of emotional responses to music across the lifespan. Indeed, Juslin has also suggested an ontological sequence in his mechanisms, with brain stem reflex, rhythmic entrainment, and evaluative conditioning all possibly occurring before birth, contagion being developed during infancy, visual imagery in the preschool years, episodic memory at the age of 3–4, and musical expectancy gradually emerging between the ages of 5 and 11. As noted earlier, aesthetic responses are the last to be added to the evolutionary sequence, and presumably this also applies to the putative ontological sequence he outlines. Aesthetic responses to music may or may not involve emotional responses, but we include them here in order to consider Juslin's framework comprehensively.

In a recent summary, Schubert and McPherson (2016) have considered Juslin's mechanisms in relation to two broad processing styles involving music and emotion: the referentialist (or veridical) and the absolutist (or schematic). Prior theorising suggested that the schematic develops after experience with the veridical. In many aspects of learning through experience this is what happens: for instance, as discussed in Chapter 4, repeated exposure to instances of a particular harmonic pattern or sequence leads young listeners to develop schematic expectations of how future sequences will unfold. In relation to emotional development, Schubert and McPherson argue that schematic connections between musical stimuli and emotional meaning could also be present at birth and enable further emotional development. They give the example of an infant startled by an unexpected *subito forte* loud chord in the midst of an orchestral texture as making a reflex brain stem response. From this perspective they label brain-stem reflexes, evaluative conditioning, emotional contagion, and musical expectancy as related to absolute/schematic processing styles, and visual imagery and episodic memory to referential/veridical processing styles.

Schubert and McPherson (2016) propose a spiral model of the development of emotion perception between the absolutist and referentialist processes, shown in Figure 7.3. Knowledge and connections between music and emotion are held to develop initially dominated by the absolutist processes (birth to 2 years) then referentialist processes (3–7 years), with a further phase of absolutist processes at 8–12 years and a final phase of referentialist processes at 13–18 years. It is important to recognise that they do not claim that only one of these is at play at any given time, but that one dominates in children's understandings of emotion.

This is a potentially useful model, but there are three main challenges that can be raised. The first is that emotional responses to music are often characterised by a large number of mechanisms, as has been illustrated previously, and deciding which one dominates at any given time is a complex and somewhat speculative endeavour. Secondly, evidence shows that many aspects of emotional response and development are further differentiated by aspects of musical experience and/or training which cannot be captured in this model. Finally, and perhaps related to the second point, the model also provides no developmental mechanism or motor, a criticism

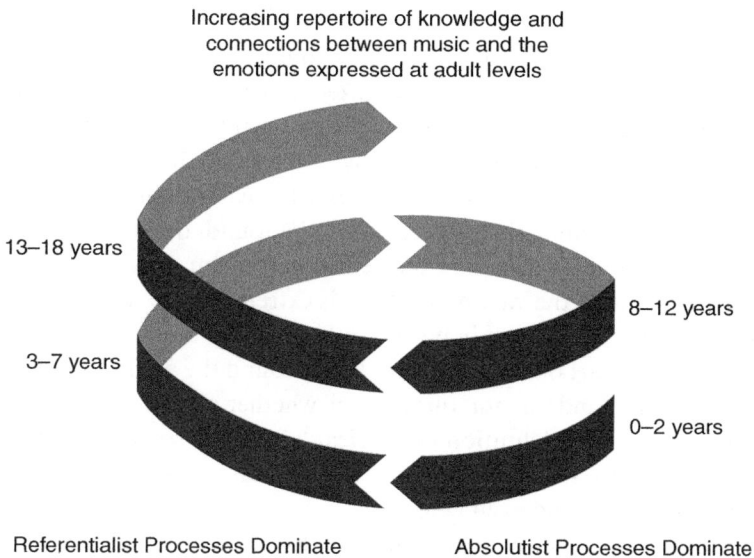

Increasing repertoire of knowledge and
connections between music and the
emotions expressed at adult levels

13–18 years

8–12 years

3–7 years

0–2 years

Referentialist Processes Dominate   Absolutist Processes Dominate

Figure 7.3. Spiral model of the development of emotion perception in music.
Source: Figure 12.2 (p. 231) in Schubert, E., & McPherson, G. E. (2016). Underlying
mechanisms and processes in the development of emotion perception in music. In: G. E.
McPherson (Ed.), *The Child as Musician: A handbook of musical development* (2nd edition)
(pp. 221–237). © Oxford University Press. By permission of Oxford University Press.

we have already levelled at earlier spiral models of perceptual and cognitive development in music (see Chapters 2 and 3). The value of this model in predicting emotional responses is yet to be seen, and may lose something of the sophistication in
Juslin's original mechanisms in reducing them to these two processing types.

Mapping Changes in Age-Related Preference

Preference is an area of music psychology that has received a great deal of research
attention, and much is known about how adults' preferences relate to other individual differences such as personality, gender, levels of musical training, and other
lifestyle correlates (see Greasley & Lamont, 2016 for a summary). In terms of
developmental evidence, a number of different approaches have been adopted to
studying how preferences might change. Cross-sectional experimental studies provide us with evidence on how responses to different types of music might change at
different age levels. Studies have used nomination techniques to generate Top Ten
lists or asked participants to choose pieces from a given selection. More recently,
qualitative research has shed light on how people construct their own musical biog-
raphies and has begun to uncover the factors that influence and shape preference
across the lifespan, with some intriguing social connections being uncovered. As
noted earlier, this research tends to prioritise individuals and their experiences with
music, rather than generic aspects of overall preference.

Developing Interest in Music

Many parents proudly bring their infants to take part in research studies because they feel their infants are particularly 'gifted' when it comes to responding to music. We have covered this issue in more depth in Chapter 5 in relation to more traditional conceptions of musical giftedness in terms of the ability to play a musical instrument. However, even in that context, the early ability to detect fine differences in pitch and timing is often considered a foundation for a successful musical career and something which is expected to vary from child to child. Luckily, the proud parents are in the vast majority: it is extremely rare to find a newborn or an infant who shows no interest in music, and this is why music forms a significant and almost universal part of caregiving routines around the world (Trehub et al., 1997). Returning to the fundamental question of whether all children are 'born musical', and taking the broad definition of musical 'ability' as something all children have the capacity to do, it is hardly surprising that an interest in music and sound is apparent from birth and even before.

The amount of music exposure that children have is considerable. Music forms a vital part of early social experiences, and around two-thirds of parents of 4- to 6-month-olds report singing to and playing music for their infants (Custodero, Britto, & Xin, 2002). Young, Street, and Davies (2006) noted that in addition to singing, recorded music also featured highly in experiences of children under two. As children get older the kind of musical experience shifts from live to recorded: even in the 9 months after birth there is a decline in the amount of singing to infants (Perkins & Fancourt, 2017), and only around 9 per cent of parents sing to preschool children on a daily basis (de Vries, 2009). In the first application of experience sampling methodology to children, Alexandra (Lamont, 2008) mapped 3.5-year-olds' everyday exposure to music. Over the course of a week, the children were reported to have experienced music on or just preceding 81 per cent of the occasions when they were randomly sampled during their waking hours; as a contrast, using the same procedure, adults are found to experience music around 37–53 per cent of the time (Greasley & Lamont, 2011; Juslin, Liljeström, Västfjäll, Barradas, & Silva, 2008; North, Hargreaves, & Hargreaves, 2004; Sloboda, O'Neill, & Ivaldi, 2001). These findings suggest that interest and engagement with music is high throughout childhood, and music listening is widely reported to be one of the most popular activities among young people (North, Hargreaves, & O'Neill, 2000).

While engagement for young adults, as indicated by reported listening times, is generally high, at around 18 hours a week (Papinczak, Dingle, Stoyanov, Hides, & Zelenko, 2015), there is some evidence that an interest in music per se seems to decline with age (Bonneville-Roussy, Rentfrow, Xu, & Potter, 2013; Lonsdale & North, 2011; Schäfer & Sedlmeier, 2010). For instance, Bonneville-Roussy et al. (2013) found 18-year-olds reported listening to the most music at a mean of 25 hours per week, while 58-year-olds reported listening to only 12 hours, and reported ratings of how passionate listeners felt about music also declined from 41 per cent at age 13 to 15 per cent at age 65. Although these results seem to suggest a decline in passion, the overall levels of engagement in their study are relatively high. However, Laukka (2007) reported that adults at retirement age (65 and older) considered that music was more important than any other time in their lives, suggesting that music performs valuable functions for older adults as well as for adolescents (see further 'Mood regulation' later in this chapter). Similarly, Hays and Minichiello (2005) found powerful emotional effects of musical engagement from their older participants, particularly in the realm of transcendence: 'It does take you above yourself. It does me. It's the only that does, actually for something … you know, there are few moments when you hear something that's really, really beautiful. And that does, yes. It does have that effect' (Jane, cited in Hays & Minichiello, 2005, p. 446).

In many of the studies with adults, the number of people who report 'little' or 'no' interest in music is very small (see also Greasley & Lamont, 2011) and so we can conclude that for many, interest and involvement in music continues throughout the lifespan (and may even increase; Saarikallio, 2011). Finer-grained measurements than simple hours of listening are required to capture this appropriately and to enable comparisons to be made across ages; what may change is the time available to engage with music. We also need to know more about how technology impacts on this engagement, given that the potential for music listening across many diverse contexts is now greater than at any previous point in human history.

Developing Style Preferences

Alexandra's review (Lamont, 2006) showed that infants rapidly develop preferences for particular types of music, becoming more sophisticated than non-human animals such as tamarin monkeys, who appear happy to listen to all kinds of tonal sounds whether conventionally 'musical' or not. In the absence of extensive experience, early preferences can be more easily explained in terms of features of the music, which might determine the listener's arousal levels, and its capacity for emotional contagion. The evidence that infants at the age of 6 months seem to prefer low pitch for lullabies and higher pitch for playsongs (Tsang & Conrad, 2010) suggests that emotional contagion is possible before language has developed, as well as indicating that infants have a sense of the appropriateness of a given musical stimuli and their fit with the situation (low arousal music being preferred for preparation for sleep, and high arousal music fitting better with play contexts).

The field of music preferences has proliferated in recent years, with much research devoted to the development of scales to measure preference and studies linking preferences to various other aspects of social life and behaviour (see Greasley & Lamont, 2016 for an overview). Many researchers have developed their own methods of measuring style preference, making comparisons across studies somewhat complex. One very popular scale is the Short Test Of Music Preferences (STOMP) (Rentfrow & Gosling, 2003). Rentfrow and colleagues subsequently revised this into the MUSIC (Mellow, Unpretentious, Sophisticated, Intense, and Contemporary) model, which attempts to bring together commonalities across a range of earlier measures (Rentfrow, Goldberg, & Levitin, 2011; Rentfrow, Goldberg, Stillwell, Kosinski, Gosling, & Levitin, 2012); we first introduced this model in Chapter 6.

However measured, it is apparent that style preferences do change across the lifespan when taking a broad perspective. For instance, North and Hargreaves (2007a) found that younger adults preferred styles such as hip-hop/rap, DJ based music, dance/house, R&B, indie and current chart pop, while older adults preferred classical, sixties pop, musicals and opera. In terms of style knowledge, Hargreaves and North (1999) found more sophisticated knowledge for different styles of music at different ages: while all their participants named common styles such as classical and pop, some were only nominated by particular age groups. For instance, indie and soul were named only by the 16- to 21-year-olds, and ballads, brass bands, folk and choral were only nominated by those aged over 50. Similarly, in a study of musical eminence, in addition to the 'classics' like the Beatles, people nominated artists who were at the height of their fame during the participants' adolescence and early adulthood (North & Hargreaves, 1995). Holbrook and Schindler (1989) proposed the age of 24 as the peak of the critical period for defining music preferences, although a more recent replication of this work by Hemming (2013) suggests that if a peak exists – and he claims the evidence is not convincing statistically, although Holbrook and Schindler (2013) disagree – it might occur at the earlier age of 17.

Using the MUSIC model, Bonneville-Roussy, Rentfrow, Xu, and Potter (2013) also found large scale changes with age in their study of over 254,000 participants aged between 12 and 65. Preference for the Unpretentious and Sophisticated dimensions increased linearly with age, preference for the Mellow dimension showed a peak in early adulthood and a slight decline in later adulthood, and preference for the Intense and Contemporary factors gradually declined across the age range. Bonneville-Roussy et al. ascribe these changing preferences to life stage and age-related processes. Rock and heavy metal was preferred more in adolescence than at other ages, perhaps reflecting adolescents' search for identity and independence. Preference for Mellow music in early adulthood might reflect the intimacy of building lasting social and family relationships, while preference for Unpretentious and Sophisticated music in later adulthood might reflect pressures of family and career life on the one hand and the desire to establish social status on the other. This explanation is appealing in some ways, but is essentially speculative: it highlights the complexity of understanding development and developmental pressures. It is not clear, for instance, why the desire to engage in Unpretentious music should continue to rise between the ages of 40 and 60 when family pressure is presumably relatively stable, nor why the pressure of social status should continually increase in a linear fashion with age. The notion of subjective complexity may be useful here in order to understand the gradual changes found in this data, which may need to be combined with a more social and contextual approach to explaining development.

It is generally acknowledged that people know more about music and more styles of music as they get older and have more experience with it, and also that preference for classical and more complex forms of music increases with age. Why should this be? As discussed earlier, Bonneville-Roussy et al.'s interpretation of the age-related increases in preference for Sophisticated music focuses on the notion that older listeners are attempting to establish themselves further in society, and achieve a higher social status. Differences in social status exist at every age, however, and social class has been often proposed as an explanation for preference for classical and complex music, stemming from the work of Bourdieu (1984; see North & Hargreaves, 2007c). Further evidence to support this comes from qualitative work by Atkinson (2011), who investigated adults' expressed music preferences. Atkinson found that his more privileged participants, even in their twenties and thirties, all included preferences for classical and opera although they might not offer this straight away. For example, one of his participants explained 'I don't dislike [classical] and I would listen to it at home, and again I would go to a classical concert, but it's not what I would put on first really. It depends what kind of mood I'm in' (Atkinson, 2011, p. 174). Closer analysis of this data illustrates that these preferences are rooted in class and often also in early musical performance experiences: Courtney, aged 32, noted that she had played the clarinet until the age of 15 and her sister had played the violin. In certain situations, experience can perhaps be a substitute for class in shaping preference: Elvers, Omigie, Furhmann, and Fischinger (2015) found greater preferences for sophisticated music among musicology students and no additional effects of class.

In-depth explorations of musical preference in adults (Greasley et al., 2013) suggest that many listeners report strong preferences for a wide range of musical styles. Greasley et al. found that more musical styles were nominated as favourites by more engaged listeners (defined as having a greater interest in and spending more time listening to music), and similarly Elvers et al. (2015) found that musicology students engaged more with all types of music, indicating their 'omnivorous' character. Atkinson also challenges the notion of a supposed historical increase in 'omnivore' listeners (from a class perspective) and suggests that while people may report listening to a large number of styles their actual listening habits are likely to be more constrained. Evidence from experience sampling studies has not typically analysed the specific music being heard at any given moment (e.g. Greasley & Lamont, 2011; Juslin et al., 2008), but mapping of music listening behaviours over weeks suggests that there could be some merit in this suggestion at least for less engaged listeners. Lamont and Webb's (2010) 'magpie' young adult listeners were found to have a limited repertoire of constantly changing music to draw on in their daily preferences, and similar findings arise from the replication by Hemming (2013) of Holbrook and Schindler's seminal 1995 study: up to the age of about 37, adults had strong preferences for the newest music available. Hemming points out that towards middle age this relationship changes and older adults show a linear preference for older music, and combining these two patterns in one analysis might have produced an artefactual inverted U-shape in the original research, as illustrated in Figure 7.4 below.

Large-scale age-related changes are apparent in these studies of sensitivity, knowledge, and preference, whatever form they might take. Looking over shorter time periods, the evidence suggests that style preferences are somewhat more consistent. For example, in a cross-sectional study Hargreaves and North (1999) found

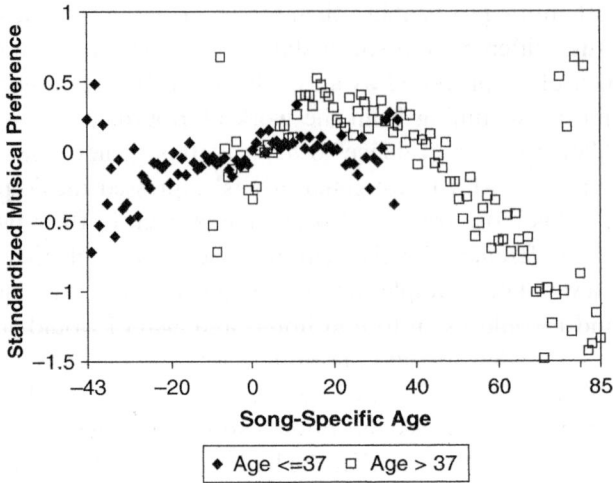

Figure 7.4. Formation of an inverted U-shaped curve (artefactual).
Source: Image republished with the permission of SAGE Publications. Originally published as Figure 8 (p. 303) in Hemming, J. (2013). Is there a peak in popular music preference at a certain song-specific age? A replication of Holbrook & Schindler's 1989 study. *Musicae Scientiae*, 17(3), 293–304.

no difference in children's ability to discriminate either classical (poor) or pop (better) pairings between the ages of 8 and 14. In a longitudinal study with adolescents, Delsing, ter Bogt, Engels, and Meeus (2008) similarly found relatively stable preference dimensions. They used two subsamples aged 12 and 16 at the outset of the study and measured their preferences over three years. The older group was more consistent across the time period, but both groups showed a consistency in their preferences for the four musical style factors (Rock, Elite, Urban, Pop/Dance). Delsing et al. also suggest that their older adolescents have more adventurous music tastes, although they do not report actual preferences in detail for the four styles. Bonneville-Roussy et al. (2013) gathered their large sample across an 8-year period, enabling them to compare preferences from different cohorts between 2003 and 2010 who were at the same age at the time of taking the survey, and found no significant effects at that level, and similarly, Mulder, ter Bogt, Raaijmakers, Nic Gabhainn, and Sikkema (2010) found high levels of consistency in preference for different styles in adolescents and young adults over a 21-month period. These results suggest that within a span of a few years, stylistic preferences are likely to be shared among a particular age group. Mulder et al. (2010) found considerable variation in liking for pieces over that time period, however, which chimes with other work on the need to refresh even among the musically less engaged (Lamont & Webb, 2010).

Modelling Changes in Age-related Preference

David (Hargreaves, 1982) coined the term 'open-earedness' (O-E) to explain the overall pattern of results in a study of children's willingness to listen to and their liking for a wide variety of different styles of music at different ages: the original study investigated 126 children, 42 in each of three mixed ability age groups drawn from two schools in Leicestershire, England. The two younger groups covered the age ranges 7–8 and 9–10 years, and the third group was drawn from pupils in the 14- to 15-year-old range: there were approximately equal numbers of males and females in each group, and approximately the same proportion of pupils with specialised musical training (approximately 20 per cent) in each group. The term O-E was originally used as a shorthand way of conveying the view that younger children were more readily able to listen to and maybe also enjoy unconventional or unusual (e.g., 'avant garde', aleatory, or electronic) musical forms, as they may 'show less evidence of acculturation to normative standards of "good taste" than older children' (Hargreaves, 1982, p. 51). LeBlanc (1991) later adopted the concept more formally, extending its definition to include what he called 'listener tolerance', and operationalising it in terms of music preferences. He also formulated a model of age-related changes in O-E, on the basis of his literature review, which was based on four generalisations: that 'younger children are more open-eared … open-earedness declines as the child enters adolescence … there is a partial rebound of open-earedness as the listener matures from adolescence to young adulthood … open-earedness declines as the listener matures to old age' (pp. 36–38).

Since then, a sizeable body of research has been carried out based on this concept, and on its development across the lifespan: the research literature published in English was reviewed by Hargreaves, North, and Tarrant (2016). With one or two exceptions, LeBlanc's generalisations receive general support. The 'dip' in O-E in later childhood seems to occur at around the age of 10 or 11 years, and this typically shows itself in very strongly expressed preferences for a narrow range of pop styles, and strong general dislike for all other styles, and may well be related to changes in self-identity (see Chapter 6). The 'rebound' of O-E in early adulthood is often a phase in which adults are seeking to acquire music, whether it be recordings or downloads (Greasley, Lamont, & Sloboda, 2013). After this, there seems to be a general decline in liking for popular music styles across the rest of the lifespan, and a corresponding general increase in 'classical' styles – although this does not necessarily seem to apply to more contemporary art music (e.g. Taylor, 1969).

The studies by Holbrook and Schindler (1989), North and Hargreaves (1995), and Hemming (2013) demonstrate a general preference for artists/musicians who were popular during the listeners' late adolescence/early adulthood: the third of these studies also reveals the intriguing finding that some popular artists, Elvis Presley and The Beatles in particular, are consistently rated as eminent by all age groups over the past thirty years or so. Given that the studies vary widely with respect to their theoretical rationales, their participant groups and age ranges, the actual genres and styles under investigation, and the assessment techniques employed, it is perhaps surprising that LeBlanc's generalisations do seem to hold true.

These generalisations about age differences in O-E with respect to 'popular' and 'classical' or 'serious' styles may be valid because they work at a high level of generality: they refer to broad genres rather than to specific styles within those genres, and thus side-step the problems of cohort or historical effects, although Holbrook and Schindler (1989) circumvented this problem by introducing what they called song-specific ages, which is defined as the year of release of the song minus the listener's year of birth. Kopiez and Lehmann (2008) found that the decline in O-E with increasing age in their results disappeared when classical music was excluded from their analyses, which led them to suggest that factors other than O-E may also have influenced their results.

A sizeable German literature has also grown up with its own distinctive characteristics, and some of this is available in English. Gembris and Schellberg (2003), for example, carried out a study of the music preferences of 591 children between ages of 5 and 13, assessing their likes or dislikes for a set of eight short excerpts from four different styles (classical music, pop music, twentieth-century art (avant-garde) music, and ethnic music). There were highly significant age-related declines in liking for all of these styles; pop music was the most preferred, and the younger the children, the more positive were their ratings for classical, avant-garde, and ethnic music, but with increasing age, all the ratings became strongly negative. Busch, Bunte, and Schurig (2016) describe the investigation of a newly established music programme in German primary schools which offers children instrumental tuition. Several joint research projects have been carried out to investigate the effects of this programme on outcomes such as cultural participation, musical preference, co-operation, and transfer, and the SIGrun study is one of these, involving collaboration between the Universities of Bremen and Hamburg and a focus on musical preference.

Busch et al. emphasise the importance of music preferences in teenagers and adults, confirming the idea that this relates to personal identity, and this led them to focus on two determinants of music preferences, namely children's developing musical concepts, and their gender identity. They provide a detailed report on their longitudinal mixed methods study of 735 primary school children over a four-year period, with one set of data collected from the children and their parents in each one of those 4 years. The quantitative measures included a sound questionnaire based on that employed by Kopiez and Lehmann (2008) featuring sixteen 30-second music extracts which included examples of African, Turkish, Russian, and Chinese music as well as popular, classical, and specially composed music, for which children were asked to provide like/dislike ratings on five-point 'smiley face' scales, and also several questionnaires investigating age, gender, migration background, social status, and personality. The study also involved some qualitative data collection from interviews which were designed to throw light on the same questions.

The quantitative data showed that children referred to genre-based musical concepts in indicating their music preferences, even at an early age; that there was a decline in O-E for conventional as well as for unconventional musical styles over this primary school age range; and that gender was the single most important variable in influencing preference ratings. Analysis of the qualitative data using Behne's (1975) approach gave rise to nine distinct superordinate categories of musical concept, namely 'genre', 'gender', 'thematic', 'mood', 'country or language', 'musician', 'up-to-dateness/popularity', 'age', and 'institution', and 'gender' seemed to be the most important factor in describing and explaining the results. The SIGrun group has also published further articles and made other conference presentations which report on different aspects of this basic body of data (e.g. Bunte, 2014, Bunte & Busch, 2015; Schurig, Busch, & Strauss, 2012), which confirm that age and gender seem to be the prime predictors of musical preference in terms of O-E.

Although LeBlanc's generalisations about age-related changes in O-E seem to receive general support in this literature, a recent study and critique by Louven (2016) points out that O-E has been operationalised in terms of musical preference in the vast majority of these studies. He objects to this conceptual imprecision, and suggests a reformulation of O-E in terms of the concepts of *openness, curiosity*, and *tolerance*, which leads to his own operational definition of O-E as *listening time to initially disliked music*. This was tested in a cross-sectional study by Louven and Ritter (2012), which suggested that the well-established age trends in O-E first proposed by LeBlanc were not apparent when it was operationalised in this way: instead, it remained more or less unchanged between the ages of approximately 6–30 years.

Hargreaves and Bonneville-Roussy (2017) responded to Louven's critique, formulating several different conceptual issues involved in the definition of O-E, as well as proposing several alternative approaches to its operationalisation. They also present some empirical data based on Bonneville-Roussy, Stillwell, Kosinski, and Rust's (2017) Musical Genre-Clips Test (MG-CT), in which listeners make preference responses to a series of short musical excerpts as well as associating each excerpt with a musical genre label, thereby gaining more analytic insight into the cognitive and affective bases of music preferences. This ongoing research will be reported in future publications.

What Purposes Does Liking Music Serve across the Lifespan?

It is clear that emotion, preference, and aesthetic responses to music begin very early in life and that there is plenty of scope for future development across the lifespan, into adulthood, and through to the final stages of life. What functions might liking music serve beyond the 'purely' aesthetic? In this final section we consider some of the non-musical benefits that emotional responses to music might serve across the lifespan (others relating to health and wellbeing are considered in Chapter 8).

Social Bonding, Friendship, and Relationships

As shown earlier, engaging through music is one of the earliest ways that social bonds can be made (Dissanayake, 2000). Returning to the notion of rhythmic entrainment as a means of making early social connections, Cirelli, Einarson, & Trainor (2013) found striking early evidence for the importance of interpersonal synchrony. In their study 14-month-old infants were bounced to music – *Twist and Shout* by the Beatles – by one adult either in synchrony or out of synchrony with the experimenter. Those infants in the synchronous conditions were more likely to help the experimenter, and to help more quickly, when she dropped an object after the bouncing had taken place. The regularity of oscillations in timing was the critical factor in this study: infants bounced both in and out of phase with the experimenter were more likely to help than those bounced in an irregular rhythm. Similar evidence is found in 4-year-olds who made music with an adult, as compared with a control condition where the children interacted with the adult socially and linguistically but without music (Kirschner & Tomasello, 2010). These social bonds form the foundation for the large and diverse tradition of music therapy, in which connections can be made with a broad range of clients who may have difficulty expressing emotion verbally.

Beyond the family, self-chosen music also plays a role in the presentation and maintenance of identity, particularly in the critical adolescent period (Tarrant, North, & Hargreaves, 2001). Drawing on the principles of social identity theory, research by Tarrant and colleagues has shown how powerful identity can be in affecting the way adolescents form groups and interact with others (this topic has been covered more fully in Chapters 4 and 6). For instance, even when told in an experimental setting that they shared music preferences with others, adolescents felt more positive towards those others and treated them as an ingroup (Bakagiannis & Tarrant, 2006). Looking at real-life friendships and bonds, adolescents make use of this potentially shared identity and the shared values which accompany it as the basis of friendship. Young adults believe their musical choices reveal key information about their personal qualities, so music is found to be the most popular topic of discussion among strangers (Rentfrow & Gosling, 2006). Selfhout, Branje, ter Bogt, and Meeus (2009) explored similarities in music preferences among best-friend pairs from the age of 13 to 14. At both time points the best friends had moderate but significant levels of similarity in the patterning of their music preferences. Selfhout et al. also showed that shared music preference was a useful predictor of future friendships: pairs with more shared preferences at the start were nearly twice as likely to become friends than pairs who had less shared preferences. Their findings were more marked for what they call 'non-mainstream' forms of music, namely rock, elite, and urban, rather than mainstream preferences for pop/dance music. Similar effects of music in attraction in young adults (average age 18) have been found by Boer, Fischer, Strack, Bond, Lo, and Lam (2011), and Schäfer and Sedlmeier (2009) found that this function of music as communicating information about identity and bonding was the most important factor in understanding strong music preferences. Groarke and Hogan (2016) also highlighted social connections as one of the key functions of music listening for younger adults (aged 18–30), and thus social bonding through music is important from infancy through to adulthood.

Shared preference for different kinds of music thus seems to be very useful in friendship formation and attraction, but Selfhout et al.'s study did not find any effects of shared music preference on friendship stability, and Rentfrow and Gosling found that music dropped down the list of topics of conversation after a few days of interaction once initial connections had been made. As listeners become more open to new styles, and as life events lead them into different social situations, *shared* preference becomes less important as the foundation for social relationships. Young adults at university experience a sudden widening of their social circle and while they may use music stereotypes as a means of getting to know others, they do not necessarily need to share others' music preferences in order to be friends. Greasley (2008) found that many young adults were keen to share their own established music preferences with new friends, and some of the older adults in stable longer-term relationships in her study were found to have very different music preferences, which suggests that beyond the initial stages similarity is not necessary. However, social bonding through engaging with and talking about music of any kind is still important during adulthood (Groarke & Hogan, 2016; Schäfer & Sedlmeier, 2010). Social connections are still being made in later life (Hays & Minichiello, 2005), so music continues to play a social role.

Mood Regulation

From the earliest starting point of building emotional connections with mothers and other caregivers, music serves a primary function of mood regulation. Trevarthen has proposed that intersubjectivity between adult and infant begins from the adult being aware of the self-regulation of physiological state in addition to arousal of voluntary activity and level of attention of the infant (Trevarthen & Aitken, 2001). Matching music to the infant's or child's mood seems to be something that is as intuitive as the process of engaging with music with infants in the first place (Trehub, 2016). As noted earlier ('Brain stem response'), in experimental settings, well-chosen music or sound stimuli can moderate arousal and thus soothe infants, who are as yet unable to regulate their own moods (Shenfield et al., 2003). Trehub, Ghazban, and Corbeil (2015) found that infants who were in a content or neutral state were more likely to sustain attention to lively playsongs than infant- or adult-directed speech, and when infants were fussing, crying, or highly aroused, singing was more effective than maternal speech at calming them.

Outside the laboratory, in a detailed investigation of 2-year-old Beatrice over a 16-month period, Barrett (2011) reported mood regulation as one of the main themes in her analysis of musical behaviours. Beatrice's mother, Barbara, reported many instances of Beatrice's moods being affected and changed by music, whether this be to calm her if she is feeling upset or to divert her. In a large-scale survey, Custodero (2006) uncovered many examples of how parents choose music to soothe their infants and toddlers. One of the mothers in her study, Helena Bucci, gives a clear instance of how self-regulation practices develop and become part of the family's new routine:

'When [Alison] was first born – before she was born, while I was pregnant with her – I had seen the *Tarzan* Disney movie, and the song that Phil Collins sings, 'You'll be in My Heart,' broke my heart, you know, I started crying . . . and I used to always rub my belly. And when she was born, I realized, when she was really acting up, that was the only song I could sing to her that would calm her down. And to this day, I sometimes sing it. And . . . as time as gone

[by] ... I hear her singing it, because she's learning the words, and it makes me feel good. She [says] 'oh, Mommy, that's Tarzan's song' and I ... basically [say] ... 'oh, yes, Tarzan, but it's yours and my song too.' (Custodero, 2006, p. 45)

As Alison learns to sing this song herself, she is taking over responsibility for some of her mood regulation. Through early childhood the active use of music for emotional self-regulation becomes more conscious. Barrett (2011) also identifies examples of 2-year-old Beatrice's use of active singing to enact the emotional state of the music. Beatrice's songs often involve positive emotions, as Barbara notes: 'she went through a phase singing about what she loved ... when she's feeling really happy or something' (Barrett, 2011, p. 419). An example of Beatrice's positive mood song is found in Figure 7.5.

Sole (2017) has mapped how young children use solitary singing for reflection and soothing in the immediate pre-sleep environment in a crib. Music appears to provide a comfort in this solitary situation and eases the transition from consciousness to sleep. Many of these research examples focus on case studies of a small number of children in order to uncover the richness of musical activities which might go unnoticed in the bustle of life with small children; technology and self-report are combined to provide rich data on the minutiae of music in everyday life.

Adults report a range of emotion-related motivations for listening to music including expressing their emotions, to relax, for enjoyment, to energise themselves and to

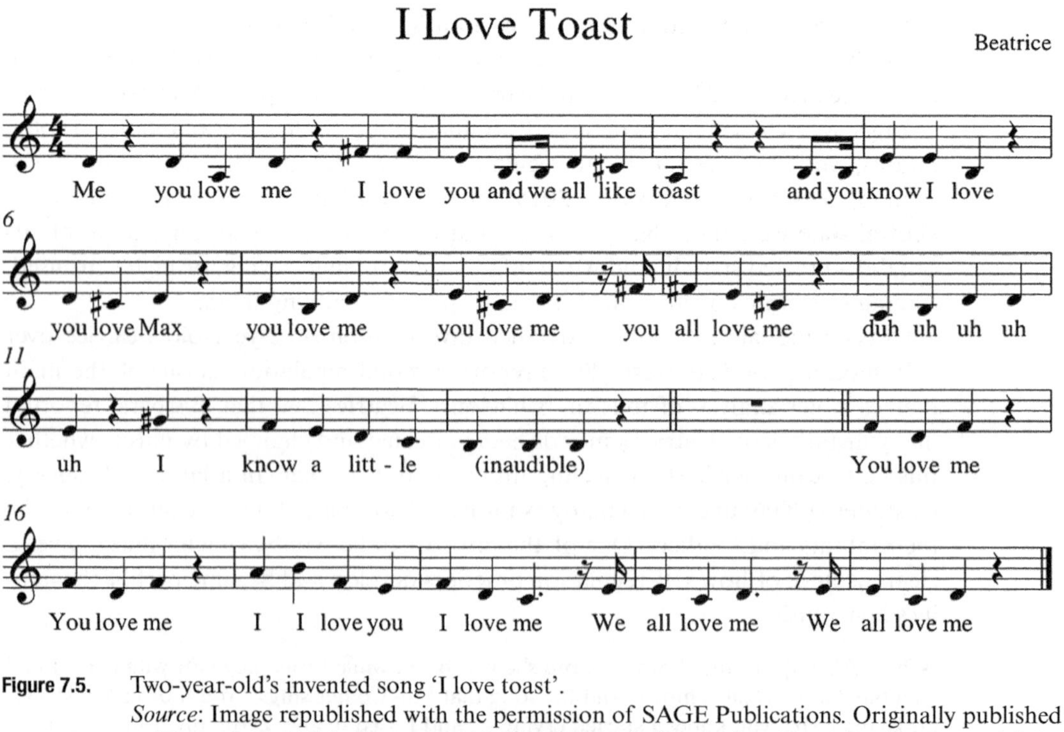

Figure 7.5.   Two-year-old's invented song 'I love toast'.
Source: Image republished with the permission of SAGE Publications. Originally published as Figure 3 (p. 419) in Barrett, M. S. (2011). Musical narratives: A study of a young child's identity work in and through music-making. *Psychology of Music*, 39(4), 403–423.

evoke memories (Juslin & Laukka, 2004; Schäfer & Sedlmeier, 2009). Saarikallio and Erkkilä (2007) set the groundwork for much subsequent research on how music is used for conscious mood regulation, which is clearly both a key emotional purpose and outcome of music listening. Based on a small-scale sample of eight Finnish adolescents aged 14 and 17, Saarikallio and Erkkilä explored how music was chosen for mood regulation through two interviews and experiential responses, studying a week of the adolescents' lives and capturing every time they engaged in a musical activity. Analysis of this data allowed them to generate a model of seven different regulatory strategies that the adolescents used with music: entertainment, revival, strong sensation, diversion, discharge, mental work, and solace. Some of the participants were performers and discussed elements of the strategies through performance, such as strong emotions through the adrenaline created by performance. Discharging emotions through music listening was particularly common in the adolescent sample, with listening to aggressive loud music a particularly good way of venting anger, for example. However, there was considerable sophistication in the adolescents' responses with elements of calm reflection and solace-seeking as well as the more exuberant and outgoing activities of entertainment, revival, and diversion. Saarikallio and Erkkilä also note that the type of music is not necessarily related neatly to the strategy, and not exclusively to one strategy. For example, listening to high arousal dance music could serve the functions of distraction from schoolwork, creating an entertaining atmosphere or generating strong emotional sensations.

Adolescence is a key period for dealing with a range of psychosocial challenges, and ter Bogt, Vieno, Doornwaard, Pastore, and van den Eijnden (2016) have focused in on daily sorrow and stress as one of these. Ter Bogt et al. found that music was used as a source of consolation in a sample of adolescents and young adults (aged 13 to 30), and female respondents and those with greater levels of anxiety and depression sought consolation through music more frequently. They identify the consoling effects as resulting from musical features (sound and texture) and lyrics primarily, with subsidiary influences of connections to the musicians and other fans of the same music.

Saarikallio (2011) has developed her work further with adults (aged 21–70), finding that broadly the same strategies arise as with adolescents (with the addition of 'psyching up') in their use of music for mood regulation. Greasley et al. (2013) found that most adults reported using their own preferred music to regulate mood, with sophisticated and self-aware responses to different kinds of music that reflect the importance of episodic memory as discussed earlier. For instance, a female 26-year-old, Nat, discussed using different parts of the album *A-Ha Shake Heartbreak* by Kings of Leon for different mood purposes:

ALINKA: Do you use different parts of the CD in different ways?

NAT: Definitely, for example, earlier when I was saying if I need to get energised, *Four Kicks* is just the song that just would hype me up no matter what, erm, er, *Milk*, number 5, is more mellow and makes you think and feel a little bit more, I don't know how to describe feel any better for you, sorry, that's not very helpful, erm, *Soft* makes me laugh and *The Bucket* makes me think of my younger sister, 'cause I managed to convert her into this band by making her listen to that over and over again, so yeah, very much so with this album, there's lots of different, sort of, parts to it in my opinion. (Greasley et al., 2013, pp. 415–416)

The functions reported here mirror many identified by Saarikallio, and can occur within a single album. What becomes apparent when talking to people in depth about the functions of their music use is that mood regulation is also something which varies, and the mapping between specific artists or pieces of music and emotion functions is far from stable, as a male 25-year-old explained:

RICH: I listen to different CDs depending on what mood I'm in yeah, I tend to find if I'm feeling like, if I'm feeling happy, I'll just listen to some dance music or some, er, hip-hop or reggae, and if I'm, if I'm not so happy, I, generally I listen to something like Morrissey or Radiohead or something like that, that's a bit darker, although having said that I listened to Morrissey today and I'm not in a bad mood at all, so, you know, it's, it's not exactly all true. (Greasley et al., 2013, p. 416)

Music thus helps achieve the same kinds of emotional goals for adults of all ages. Saarikallio (2011) did find some influence of age in relation to the importance of music, however, thus supporting research by Laukka (2007) which highlighted the importance of music for emotional functions for older listeners, and contradicting other evidence that music's importance declines with age (Bonneville-Roussy et al., 2013). Saarikallio's interpretation is that as we go through adulthood we are likely to have experienced life events that illustrate how music can empower and heal us. One of her participants, Kathleen (aged 53), reported the ability to focus and choose as having increased with age:

'Its meaning has grown, the meaning of music in my life ... It's probably that you listen more, and you allow that to yourself. Previously I listened with a constant hassle around, so you could only hear a short part ... And it's also that now you can select yourself what to listen to'. (Saarikallio, 2011, p. 316)

Age and/or musical experience both seem to bring a greater appreciation of the emotional purposes of music; Saarikallio's adults reported similar levels of self-knowledge and self-care through music as found by Greasley et al.'s 'more engaged' listeners, who were highly self-aware about the purposes that music listening served and the ways in which they could match or choose music for their mood (as illustrated in Rich's aforementioned quote). Getz, Marks, and Roy (2014) uncovered some interesting factors underpinning differences in music uses and preferences, including personality, levels of stress and optimism, and music training. In their sample of young adults (average age 19), those with higher stress levels and also higher optimism levels both used music more frequently for emotional regulation, and those with more music training engaged more cognitively. Whether music was used cognitively or emotionally turned out to be the best predictor of preference types: those who preferred more cognitive engagement with music preferred reflective/complex and intense/rebellious styles, and those preferring emotional engagement also preferred upbeat/conventional styles The suggestion here that music training leads to a more detached response to music is one which is echoed through the developmental literature on the byproducts of music training (see e.g. Bamberger, 1991).

Mood regulation thus appears to be an important emotional benefit of music listening from infancy through to adulthood. More research has been conducted on the younger cohorts and some evidence suggests that mood regulation might tail off in importance for older adults (Groarke & Hogan, 2016) in contrast to personal meaning and therapeutic benefits. Emotional effects are only part of the picture when considering the functions that music listening can achieve, although they are admittedly a substantial one. We elaborate on the functions of music in development for health and wellbeing in more detail in Chapter 8, where we treat the effects of music in a more holistic manner, including some of the concepts of emotional response and development alongside other features of engagement, identity, motivation, and behaviour.

Conclusion

It is apparent that emotional responses to music begin very early in life, and there are certain fundamental elements of these responses which can be seen across many different situations and across the lifespan. Juslin's (2013) more careful definition of these features in the emotional mechanisms in his BRECVEMA framework have enabled us to organise the developmental literature, and also provide a context for focusing on different types of emotional response and understanding their ontogeny. A great deal of the emotional impact of music comes from its inherently social nature and the earliest forms of emotional response are in contexts where an infant is with a caregiver. Music's potential to make social bonds is present throughout the lifespan and helps adolescents find their place in the world, helps adults to form and sustain friendships and relationships, and helps older adults to keep connected to their communities. Although there is considerable development in the finer-grained aspects of emotional development, what is more striking here is the commonality in response across very large age-ranges. Challenging the stereotype that adolescents have more intense and fluctuating emotions which could be enhanced or regulated by listening to music, for instance, there is evidence that the function of emotional discharge remains just as prevalent throughout adulthood. Similarly, it seems likely that interest in music can be maintained throughout the lifespan and while time and resources may diminish, engagement does not.

What is also clear is that experience and knowledge about music changes the nature of our emotional responses to it. Throughout the course of development we have seen the effects of familiarity on emotional response, and the important personal and individual connections that we form with specific pieces of music: the notion of 'open-earedness' provides us with a way of understanding how these connections may wax and wane over the lifespan. In addition, children and adults who have the benefit of musical training seem to have a changed relationship with music. On the one hand they are more explicitly aware of the way music works, and consequently the functions it can serve for them. On the other, they appear to be less 'switched on' to the emotional elements of music and may be more likely to be influenced by cognitive as compared with emotional factors in listening.

Experience also affects the consequences that music listening can have; familiarity, in particular, is important in considering how music can evoke emotions in both a cultural and an individual sense, through the mechanisms of evaluative conditioning and episodic memory. We have moved a long way from explaining preference and aesthetic response to music through mere exposure, as originally proposed by Zajonc (1968). A combination of psychological and social processes is most likely to provide an adequate explanation of the fluctuating nature of musical preference and response across the lifespan.

8   Wellbeing and Health

There has been a proliferation of research over the past two decades looking at the role of music in wellbeing and health from a range of different perspectives (see MacDonald, Kreutz, & Mitchell, 2012a). Some researchers are interested in why people are motivated to engage in music listening and what effects it can have on mood and emotion (as covered in Chapter 7 on mood regulation), while others are more concerned with how to treat health conditions that arise primarily in performing musicians and the crippling performance anxiety that afflicts many, from students through to professionals. There is also a growing body of research looking at the ways in which music can be used to help treat other health conditions. In this final content chapter, we cover the main approaches to music, health, and wellbeing from a developmental point of view, making links to mainstream approaches to adult health and wellbeing and importantly the ways in which these can be changed across the lifespan. The majority of research in this topic area is with adults, but much of it has developmental antecedents or is shaped by early experiences.

Theories of Health and Wellbeing

The World Health Organisation (WHO) defines health as 'a state of complete physical, mental, and social wellbeing and not merely the absence of disease or infirmity'. This gives us a useful starting point for understanding an individual's health and wellbeing, although as MacDonald, Kreutz, and Mitchell (2012b) among others note, it fails to account for the role of economic resources or to highlight cultural resources as particularly important. MacDonald et al. highlight that music is relevant in the field of health and wellbeing because it is ubiquitous, emotional, engaging, distracting, physical, ambiguous, social, and communicative, and because it affects behaviour and identities, thereby having the potential to generate many different kinds of beneficial effects.

Health

Exploring the promotion and maintenance of health, the prevention and treatment of illness, identifying the diagnostic correlates of health illness and related dysfunction, and analysing and improving healthcare systems and policy have been core concerns of health psychology since the founding of the discipline in the 1970s and 80s (Matarazzo, 1982). Medical approaches to health adopt a biomedical model, while health psychology favours the biopsychosocial approach which incorporates the biological and genetic characteristics alongside the study of behavioural factors such as stress, lifestyle, and health beliefs, and social conditions such as family relationships, social support, and cultural influences. Marks (2002) has delineated four main approaches in contemporary health psychology. Clinical health psychology draws on the biopsychosocial model within hospitals and clinics, overlapping with clinical psychology. Public health psychology is concerned with health education and promotion from a psychological perspective, focusing on the social, economic, and political determinants of health. Community health psychology, a part of community health psychology, draws on community research and social action to work on health promotion and prevention of illness in community settings. Finally, critical health psychology is concerned with how power, economics, and wider social processes influence health. Marks argues that many health psychologists will adopt more than one of these stances in their research and practice in order to answer the complex challenges of understanding how people behave in relation to their own health.

Research in health has tended to downplay the role of the individual and autonomy in making good health decisions in favour of social influences, particularly when tackled from a public health perspective. Studies of long term development often pinpoint the effects of early childhood environments on later health outcomes: for example, Non, Román, Gross, and Kubazansky (2016) highlighted how childhood social disadvantage was more likely to lead to smoking, excess alcohol consumption and obesity in middle age by predisposing children to adopt certain unhealthy behaviours. From a developmental perspective, the four different approaches have different concerns, but in emphasising the influence of society on individuals they place responsibility for health at the level of wider communities, healthcare professionals, and society at large. Taken as a whole, approaches to health fit broadly within a sociocultural approach, suggesting that knowledge and understanding about appropriate health behaviour is transmitted and understood in a social context and children and young people will gain relevant knowledge through interactions with others. These interactions might take the form of family relationships, explicit instruction at school, or intentional interventions designed to communicate key health messages (e.g. Woods-Townsend et al., 2015).

Studies of health literacy acknowledge the important role that individuals need to play in gaining relevant knowledge about health behaviours (Nutbeam, 2008), with a particular focus on adolescence as a point when beliefs become established that will affect health behaviours in later life. Knowledge and understanding about health and illness began in the 1980s, with Bibace and Walsh (1980) identifying Piagetian-type stages of what illness means. Three-year-olds were unable to understand the concept at all, where 3- to 7-year-olds believed in simple ideas like phenomenism (the cause of illness is external to the body) and contagion (illness results from physical proximity to a cause), 8- to 10-year olds believed in contamination (direct contact with the cause) and internalisation, 11- to 13-year-olds in internal physiological causes, and the more complex mind-and-body psychophysiological understandings were only found in adolescents. This Piagetian approach dominates a great deal of work on health understandings in childhood in other domains. Counter to this general stage-based approach, however, illness-specific experience has been found to play a large role in children's knowledge (Koopman, Baars, Chaplin, & Zwinderman, 2004), and some studies found intuitive understandings of illness causation and links between stress and illness in children as young as 4–6 years (Goldman, Whitney-Saltiel, Granger, & Rodin, 1991). It seems likely that children's understandings are shaped by both stage theory and a more innate way of understanding illness. Cheetham, Turner-Cobb, and Gamble (2016) found that 6-year-olds responded more quickly to picture pairs depicting stress and illness together than to those depicting stress and wellness or no stress and illness, although the association peaked at around 7–8 years. Cheetham et al. suggest that stage theories may underestimate children's understanding, as has been found in other areas of cognition (Siegler, 1998), and that intuitive understanding also needs to be acknowledged.

Wellbeing

The more positive elements embedded in the WHO's definition of health about wellbeing reflect a general trend over the past twenty-five years to account for the positive aspects of human behaviour and the capacity to not only survive but to flourish. This approach stems from the work of Maslow in the 1940s and 50s, and his motivational hierarchy of human needs (Maslow, 1943). Maslow noted:

It is quite true that man lives by bread alone – when there is no bread. But what happens to man's desires when there *is* plenty of bread and when his belly is chronically filled? *At once other ('higher') needs emerge* and these, rather than physiological hungers, dominate the organism. (Maslow, 1943, p. 375)

Maslow argued that physiological survival needs were fundamental, but then proposed needs for safety, belongingness and love, esteem, and self-actualisation, in ascending order. Self-actualisation, the initial pinnacle of the hierarchy, is described as a desire for self-fulfilment, and may be achieved in many different ways. As recently noted (see Koltko-Rivera, 2006), Maslow later added self-transcendence as the final stage (1969), prompted in part by his work on peak experiences (1968).

Maslow's work set the foundations for positive psychology, a relatively new field begun in the 1990s. Two key figures in this new field, Seligman and Csikszentmihalyi, approached this from their own different perspectives; Seligman had been a leader in the field of stress and learned helplessness research (Garber & Seligman, 1980; Seligman, 1972), while Csikszentmihalyi had developed the concepts of flow and optimal experience (Csikszentmihalyi & Csikszentmihalyi, 1988; Csikszentmihalyi, 1990). Seligman and Csikszentmihalyi (1990) founded the new approach to focus on the flourishing and positive elements of being, drawing together concepts from a range of areas in psychology such as work on self-esteem and motivation, identity, self-determination theory, and subjective wellbeing. Tracing ideas back to ancient Greek philosophy and the work of Aristotle in particular, Seligman identified three types of life in his initial formulation (2002) of authentic happiness. The 'pleasant life' draws on the notion of *hedonism*, simply defined as the presence of positive affect and the absence of negative affect (Kahneman, Diener, & Schwarz, 1999). Experiencing positive emotions has many health and cognitive benefits (e.g. Fredrickson, 2001). Yet Seligman argues that living life in a satisfying way, or *eudaimonia*, is also necessary to achieve a state of balanced wellbeing. Two separate components can be identified here. Firstly the 'good life' or engagement refers to the pursuit of wellbeing through absorption in a task or activity. This incorporates Csikszentmihalyi and Csikszentmihalyi's (1988) concept of flow, drawing on findings that people experiencing high levels of flow are also found to be more motivated and creative in both work and leisure (Csikszentmihalyi & Lefèvre, 1989). Secondly, the 'meaningful life' refers to applying strengths to something larger than oneself, such as voluntary work or religion. This kind of activity has been shown to be among the most highly valued forms of leisure (Argyle, 1996).

On balance, engagement and meaning have been found to contribute more to life satisfaction than the pursuit of pleasure (Seligman, Parks, & Steen, 2005). The eudaimonic side of wellbeing requires input through human agency and autonomy (Ryan, Huta, & Deci, 2008). Seligman argued that all three components of happiness – hedonism, engagement, and meaning – are required in order to achieve a state of subjective wellbeing and authentic happiness (Peterson, Park, & Seligman, 2005) and that a balance between them is required (Sirgy & Wu, 2009). In a more recent formulation, Seligman (2011) has expanded the eudaimonic approach into four different sub-concepts: hedonism is replaced by positive emotions (P); engagement (E) and meaning (M) remain; social relationships (R) are identified separately from meaning; and a final component, achievement (A), is added to account for the importance of goals and goal attainment in contemporary society. The resulting PERMA model of wellbeing is in an early stage of application in terms of research evidence, although Seligman has attempted to apply it within the concept of Positive Psychotherapy (Seligman, Rashid, & Parks, 2006) with indications that it can decrease mild-to-moderate depression and produce higher remission rates in depressed adults.

As Rusk and Waters (2015) point out, however, PERMA does not provide any explanation for the process of development. In attempting to explain intervention programmes, Jayawickreme, Forgeard, and Seligman (2012) proposed an 'engine of wellbeing' systems framework attempting to identify inputs (environmental factors and personality traits), subjective traits (internal beliefs, cognitions, and explanations), and measurable outputs (intrinsically valuable and chosen behaviours reflecting the attainment of wellbeing). A similar approach was put forward by Rusk and Waters (2015) to account for the input of environmental and biological factors to a domain-based system of psychological and social functioning, which can be influenced by wellbeing interventions. Although there are subtle differences in their underlying theories, from a developmental perspective both these models imply a contribution of the environment, which can be changed, and personality traits, which are less modifiable, on overall levels of wellbeing. In considering the malleability of levels of wellbeing, Lyubomirsky, Sheldon, and Schkade (2005) proposed that there are three contributing factors to a person's ongoing happiness: their genetically determined 'set point' (held to be responsible for about 50 per cent of individual differences in happiness), happiness-related circumstantial factors (10 per cent), and happiness-related activities and practices (40 per cent). They argue that this last factor is the only malleable one, and that wellbeing interventions have the potential to affect a substantial amount of overall wellbeing through that route. These views link clearly with self-determination theory as a way of understanding how children and adults take responsibility for their own development (cf. Chapter 6).

General population studies indicate that people with 'naturally' occurring levels of optimism and positive emotions suffer fewer incidences of ill health and live longer (see review by Diener & Chan, 2011). Positive psychology interventions have been applied to a number of different areas of life and to deal with a range of situations and conditions. With normal adult populations, evidence suggests that regular engagement in various positive activities such as counting one's blessings or expressing gratitude leads to increases in wellbeing (Lyubomirsky, Dickerhoof, Boehm, & Sheldon, 2011). In adults, some of the most popular areas of application include mental health conditions such as depression, with findings suggesting moderate effects (e.g. Chancellor, Lyubomirsky, & Wang, 2011; Seligman et al., 2006; Sin & Lyubomirsky, 2009). Other areas of application include encouraging positive psychological states in various kinds of patients including those with cardiovascular disease (Huffman et al., 2011). With children, educational settings have also been a focus for positive psychology interventions (Seligman, Ernst, Gilham, Reivich, & Linkins, 2009). Programmes of positive education have been developed to be both preventative and enabling. For instance, the Penn Resilience Program was developed to teach children seven learnable skills of resilience: how to identify feelings, tolerate ambiguity, develop optimistic explanatory style, how to analyse causes of problems, empathy, self-efficacy, and to try new things (Gillham, Jaycox, Reivich, Seligman, & Silver, 1990). There is some evidence that these interventions can help to prevent as well as alleviate depression and anxiety, improve health behaviours, and improve conduct issues and optimism, again with moderate effects (Seligman, 2011).

The points raised from within positive psychology about the lack of understanding of the precise nature of the engine of change cause a challenge for applying a truly developmental perspective. There is as yet no clear theory of how wellbeing might have the potential to change across the lifespan. The closest developmental theory aligned with this tradition is Erikson's psychosocial model (see also Vaughan & Rodriguez, 2013 and Chapter 6). Stemming from Frankl's work, first published in 1947, on the ability to seek meaning in any given situation (Frankl, 2004), the notion of autonomy is central to the tenets of positive psychology. Following

Table 8.1. Erikson's (1982) stages of identity

Age	Years	Conflict Between		Positive Characteristics
Infancy	0–1.5 yrs.	Trust	Mistrust	Hope
Early childhood	1.5–3 yrs.	Autonomy	Shame and Doubt	Will
Play age	3 to 5	Initiative	Guilt	Purpose
School age	5 to 12	Industry	Inferiority	Competence
Adolescence	12 to 18	Identity	Role Confusion	Fidelity
Young adulthood	18 to 40	Intimacy	Isolation	Love
Adulthood	40 to 65	Generativity	Stagnation	Care
Maturity	65+	Integrity	Despair	Wisdom

Erikson's (1982) stages of psychosocial development, autonomy appears in the second life challenge (see Table 8.1): the conflict between autonomy and shame and doubt is held to be resolved into a positive state of will by the age of 6 years. From this early beginning, autonomy is held to increase gradually across the lifespan, as a result of both social expectations and an intrinsic growth impulse (Erikson, 1968). Older children tend to internalise reasons for tasks (Chandler & Connell, 1987), and older adults express more autonomous reasons for following their own goals than younger adults (Sheldon & Kasser, 2001). Greater autonomy also leads to greater levels of subjective wellbeing (Sheldon, Kasser, Houser-Marko, Jones, & Turban, 2005). The notion of autonomy is also central to self-determination theory (see also Chapter 5) and we will return to look at growth in autonomy through music in the final section of this chapter. The key message from this work is a simple one in developmental terms, however: wellbeing can be changed, and is a function of an interaction between relatively stable components (such as personality) and more adaptable ones (such as self-determination).

Ageing and Lifespan Development

With a rapidly increasing ageing population in many industrialised countries as a consequence of better access to basic levels of healthcare and advances in medical science, a great deal of attention has been focused on how to help adults age well and to focus on health and wellbeing across the lifespan. The field of social gerontology has sprung up alongside this growth in the ageing population, exploring factors that both lead to and could prevent the negative consequences of ageing, such as isolation and loneliness, from a sociological perspective (Bernard, 1995). This research has tended to emphasise the influence of other people in later life, and the importance of connected communities and intergenerational relationships. Research indicates that leisure activities have become more central in older people's lives (Bernard, Phillipson, Phillips, & Ogg, 2001). Bernard et al. note that 96 per cent of older people in three different communities in England reported engaging in a wide variety of activities, including social, sports, hobbies, education, religion, computing, arts, political activism, and 'people watching'.

Engagement in leisure activities in later life provides a potential for a different kind of community than the family relationships that Bernard et al. (2001) note have changed over the decades. The importance of community as a concept is outlined from a sociological perspective by Crow and Allan (1994, p. 1):

> '[M]uch of what we do is engaged in through the interlocking social networks of neighbourhood, kinship and friendship, networks which together make up 'community life' as it is conventionally understood. 'Community' stands as a convenient shorthand term for the broad realm of local social arrangements beyond the private sphere of home and family but more familiar ... than the impersonal institutions of the wider society.'

From a psychological perspective, Murray and Lamont (2012) have emphasised the importance of looking at music's role in and through community as far more than having effects on an individual, with the group simply serving as an enabling context where music might take place. Our analysis of members of a choir for older people in a city centre context has shown how the choir itself becomes the community, and we return to this in the section on music performance in this chapter. The community can be a resource for empowerment as a means of helping its members access resources and importantly, in the case of ageing communities, challenge negative perceptions of them (e.g. Murray & Crummett, 2010). Community here is a far wider term than context, as we have been using it throughout the book to reflect the social settings of musical engagement, and in this penultimate chapter we consider the consequences of musical engagement at this wider level to consider the benefits for the individual in context, community, and society.

In the research on health and wellbeing applications of both music listening and performance there are two distinct types of study. Firstly, research has explored the effects of naturally occurring musical behaviour or preference on health and wellbeing outcomes. This includes studies that group listeners by pre-existing factors such as age, music training, level of engagement, or expressed music preference, for instance, and then explore the different health and wellbeing outcomes that different groups demonstrate. On the performing side, this includes research comparing people engaged in music activity with those involved in other activities or those who choose to do nothing, again looking at group differences in health and wellbeing outcomes. The second kind of research has to do with interventions: studies might involve participants undergoing some kind of additional activity such as structured listening or music training and the effects of these interventions can be measured on a range of health and wellbeing outcomes. The former are easier to conduct, given that they capitalise on naturally occurring social and demographic variables, but have the constant limitation that results are less easy to interpret. For instance, there may be hidden variables underlying apparent influences, such as people who like a given style of music sharing a personality style as well as behavioural outcomes, or people drawn to playing musical instruments having different social backgrounds and personality traits to those who prefer to engage in knitting, for instance. However, intervention studies can be criticised for applying an over-medicalised 'dose-response' model to a cultural and aesthetic phenomenon. Choosing to engage in years of piano playing is a very different kind of activity compared with being randomly allocated to a ten-week singing programme, and so it is not surprising that there are some conflicting results within this body of literature.

Approaches to Health and Wellbeing in Music Listening

It is well established that listening to music activates pleasure and reward systems in the brain and this basic 'feel good' factor is one of the fundamental motivations for engaging with it. From before birth music can be responded to, remembered, and is a source of positive emotions (see Chapters 3 and 7). In Chapter 6 we explored how identities are shaped by musical engagement and how music acts to bring people together and find their place in the world, and in Chapter 7 we considered in detail the way in which preferences for particular styles and pieces of music operate on the emotions at different stages of development. Many studies of emotions with adults show that the more preferred a piece of music is, the greater its emotional impact, and also its potential impact on other non-musical elements (Sloboda, O'Neill, & Ivaldi, 2001). Consequently, studies have illustrated that listening to preferred music or self-chosen music in particular can have wide-ranging effects in a range of domains.

Effects of Music Listening on Physical Health and Wellbeing

As noted earlier, music produces changes in the body which pave the way for its positive effects on various aspects of physical, psychological, and social wellbeing. In a thorough recent review, Fancourt, Ockelford, and Abebech Belai (2014) identified a large number of systematic studies exploring the effects of listening on physiology and hormones in adults. From a range of research studies, listening to music has been found to reduce cortisol, heart rate, epinephrine, norepinephrine, and cytokines and increase oxytocin and immunoglobulins. Some of these effects are more likely to occur with relaxing music listening situations, some of the effects are modulated by whether people have chosen the music or not, and many of the findings have yet to be consistently replicated, but it is clear that music listening has a direct positive physical effect.

Music listening has been theorised to have various effects on people's abilities to engage in physical activity from a range of perspectives: the psychological (how music affects mood, emotion, cognition, and behaviour), the psychophysical (rate of perceived exertion or RPE), the psychophysiological (effects on heart rate, oxygen uptake, and exercise lactate), and the ergogenic (effects of delaying fatigue or increasing work capacity measured through rate of perceived exertion) (Karageorghis, 2016). Music is frequently used by people engaging in exercise

(Hallett & Lamont, 2015), and they report that it helps them concentrate on the exercise or distracts them from the effort required to maintain exercising. Many studies show that music, particularly if found to be motivational, typically results in reduced RPE and enhanced affect (e.g. Karageorghis, Priest, Terry, Chatzisarantis, & Lane, 2006). From a regulation of arousal perspective, faster music helps people during faster exercise situations and slower music is more preferred for slower forms of exercise such as yoga; after engaging in fast exercise slower music is more preferred to moderate arousal back to a resting point (North & Hargreaves, 2000b). As exercise intensity increases, faster tempo in music is more preferred and more effective, although this relationship is not entirely linear. Karageorghis, Jones, Priest, Akers, Clarke, Perry et al. (2011) found that at low exercise intensities, increases in physiological arousal were linearly related to increases in preferred music tempo, and endurance is increased by music listening (Lane, Davis, & Devonport, 2011), but at higher intensities this tailed off. At extremely high exercise intensities exercisers prefer slight reductions in tempo to their state of physiological arousal, and it seems that music is less effective in influencing endurance at very high intensity exercise levels (Doiron, Lehnhard, Butterfield, & Whitesides, 1999). It can, however, still positively influence affective states (Karageorghis & Jones, 2014), and affective valence is greater in music videos than in music alone (Bird, Hall, Arnold, Karageorghis, & Hussein, 2016).

Karageorghis first developed a conceptual model in 1999 to explain what made a motivational piece of music for exercise purposes, including the factors of rhythm response, musicality, cultural impact, and association (Karageorghis, Terry, & Lane, 1999). The first two factors were seen as internal to the music, and the second two as external (how the music was interpreted by the listener). These factors affect the motivational qualities of the music, which then consequently affects control over arousal, reduction in RPE, and improvements in mood, which in turn affect pre-event routines and likelihood of exercise adherence. Alongside this Karageorghis developed the Brunel Music Rating Inventory to try to establish what in the music exercisers found motivational, although he acknowledges that the factors in the inventory – rhythm, style, melody, tempo, instrumentation, and beat – do not fully account for aspects of aesthetic experience like personal meanings or associations (Karageorghis, 2016). However, these are included in the latest iteration of the model of how music affects exercise, which echoes Hargreaves's (2012) reciprocal feedback model, and is similarly organised to include music factors (including intrinsic, e.g. tempo or harmony, and extrinsic, e.g. cultural associations or musical idioms) as antecedents to personal factors (age, personality, gender) and situational factors (location, mode of exercise, synchronicity) which act as moderators to a number of consequences including dissociation, positive affective states, RPE, increased work output, and arousal regulation.

In addition to the positive effects on physical exercise, listening to music has also been found to ameliorate perceptions of pain and distress. Listening to preferred music helped participants undergoing minor surgery to feel less anxious (MacDonald, Mitchell, Dillon, Serpell, Davies, & Ashley, 2003), and similarly, listening to self-chosen music enabled healthy participants to keep their hands in cold water for longer in a cold pressor, in a mimicking of acute pain (Mitchell, MacDonald, & Brodie, 2006). Mitchell, MacDonald and colleagues have thoroughly explored the effects of music on pain to try to explain the underlying mechanisms, and their own and others' findings suggest that emotional and arousal mechanisms are the most potent to distract attention (Mitchell & MacDonald, 2012). Garcia and Hand (2015) also highlight distraction, absorption, and context-dependent memory induction as primary themes when participants are experiencing pain induced by the cold pressor. They also note that self-perceived 'motivational' music was felt to be more effective in such situations than 'relaxing' music (as defined by the participants in their choice of what to listen to).

There are clear similarities between the uses and functions of music for exercise and pain and the developmental needs of early infant caregiving and child-raising in general. Distraction was mentioned by Barbara, Beatrice's mother, as one of the most powerful ways in which music was used in routines (Barrett, 2011, see Chapter 7). Audio-visual integration was found to be a powerful way in which young children learn associations and actions (Chapter 7). Dissociation and distraction are among the most powerful mood regulation strategies in adolescents and adults (Chapter 7). The work is thus underscoring the importance of emotion and affect in explaining the effects of music listening on the body and on physical outcomes. As yet there is very little empirical evidence exploring developmental effects in these fields, although a few researchers have begun to look at children as participants. Preti and Welch (2011), in an interview study with young patients experiencing live music, found the music was felt to help both children and their families to redirect attention on something other than the illness. Longhi, Pickett, and Hargreaves (2015) explored pain and physiological responses in hospitalised children with cardiac and/or respiratory problems, from newborns to 4-year-olds, after being played a live song. As for adults, children showed decreased levels of anxiety and pain after music sessions in comparison with a reading session and a control. Oxygen saturation was also improved (see also Longhi & Pickett, 2008), but only in the youngest infants less than 6 months of age. It seems that live music is effective, and that this involves more than the social interaction it provides, as reading to the child did not produce the same results.

Longhi et al. (2015) suggest that live music works more effectively with young patients because the performer can modify their performance depending on the patient's state. While the musicians in Preti and Welch's (2011) study were not formally trained in music therapy, the type of activity they were undertaking is relatively close to the principles of music therapy: they brought their own instruments, sang, and involved children and their caregivers in musical activities involving percussion instruments, and received training prior to the programme. In Longhi et al.'s study, the sessions were relatively short (10 minutes, compared with 40 minutes in Preti & Welch) but the songs and performance were still modified according to the state of the child, so there is the potential for some of the communicative musicality that mothers and infants use to interact musically in everyday life settings. We return to this more interactive form of music as therapy later in the section on the beneficial effects of music performance.

Effects of Music Listening on Mind and Cognition

Drawing on the arousal-based notions of Berlyne (1971) which were discussed more fully in Chapter 7, it is clear that listening to music can modify mental state. The effects of arousal and preference are currently the best explanation for the short-lived 'Mozart Effect'. After listening to ten minutes of Mozart, adults were found to perform better on spatial-temporal reasoning tasks (Rauscher, Shaw, & Ky, 1993, 1995). Initially this was held to be a result of cross-modal priming, in that the temporal structure of the music activated similar areas of the brain which then resulted in improved performance (Rauscher & Shaw, 1998); the effect is short-lived and did not seem to transfer to other cognitive tasks or work with other kinds of music (Steele, Bass, & Crook, 1999).

The original publications in the 1990s sparked a great deal of media interest and the simplistic message that the media picked up on that 'Mozart could make you smarter' was eagerly embraced by policymakers and educators (see Bangerter & Heath, 2004 for a discussion on how these effects are disseminated and diffused). The original researchers were very careful not to overstate the implications of their findings and the research was very clearly limited to university students undertaking conventional IQ tests which included a spatial-temporal task after listening to Mozart. However, the notion that Mozart could improve intelligence proved extremely popular, and led to numerous collections of Mozart on CD for infants and children, books and websites (www.mozarteffect.com), a registered trademark, and two books explaining how the Mozart Effect works for adults and children (Campbell, 2001, 2009). In 1998 the governor of Georgia, Zell Miller, passed legislation to ensure that mothers of newborns would receive a complimentary classical music CD, and in Florida classical music was mandated for an hour a day in state-funded day-care centres. This was done in the absence of any evidence for beneficial effects on cognition in children.

Subsequent research began to explore the potential of a Mozart Effect in children. McKelvie and Low (2002) compared Mozart with popular dance music by Aqua and relaxation music (Debussy and Gershwin) with 11- to 13-year-old children, and found no differences in spatial task performance depending on the type of music. They did not use a silence condition, so it is possible that the slight improvements they saw between pre- and post-test were simply due to music exposure. Using a more robust design including silence with 10- to 11-year-olds, Črnčec, Wilson, and Prior (2006) found no evidence of a Mozart Effect on spatiotemporal tasks. Using a strict replication of the original studies, they found spatial-temporal scores were the same after listening to Mozart, popular music, or sitting in silence, although they did find that the popular music led to increased levels of mood and arousal. In a slight modification of the original paradigm, Ivanov and Geake (2003) used both prior and concurrent music listening while other tasks were carried out, and found an enhancing effect of Mozart – and also of Bach – on 10- to 12-year-olds' spatial-temporal skills. Unfortunately they did not test any other cognitive tasks so it is not possible to know whether the arousal explanation would have transferred to other skills. Schellenberg and Hallam (2005) applied the original Mozart Effect methodology with children aged 10–11, finding that while listening to Mozart did not lead to any enhancements on cognitive performance, there was a slight 'Blur' effect: the comparison condition of listening to popular music by Blur and others led to improvements on the spatial-temporal task (but not on a pattern completion task). This is supported by findings from Schellenberg, Nakata, Hunter, and Tamoto (2007) that 5-year-olds were more creative, energetic, and proficient in their drawings after listening to familiar children's songs than listening to Mozart or Albinoni.

These results (and a host of others with adults, e.g. Mammarella, Fairfield, & Cornoldi, 2007; Nantais & Schellenberg, 1999; Rideout, Dougherty, & Wernert, 1998) indicate that there is little about Mozart's music specifically that is responsible for the enhanced effects on cognition, and point towards a 'mood and arousal' explanation (Thompson, Schellenberg, & Husain, 2001). This is supported by a more recent meta-analysis by Pietschnig, Voracek, and Formann (2010) that suggests the effects of music are more modest than some of the original publications claimed; that there are no significant differences between Mozart and other types of music in effect size, and thus that arousal can explain almost all of the data.

A slightly different paradigm involves the use of background music during various cognitive tasks. Savan (1999) showed the potential for background music to be used to calm children with behavioural problems in classroom settings, finding remarkable improvements in concentration while Mozart was playing. She attempted to alter the musical stimuli to try to identify what was causing these effects: faster and slower versions and backwards version of the Mozart all had the same physiological effects, although removing either the high or low frequencies seemed to have no effects. Similarly, 11-year-olds were found to concentrate better in a science class when easy-listening music was being played (Davidson & Powell, 1986). The concurrent nature of the music in their study might explain why Ivanov and Geake (2003) were able to find evidence of enhancement on spatial-temporal tasks. Boys aged 7–11 with ADHD were found to concentrate better on arithmetic tasks when their own preferred music was playing, providing a high level of background stimulation (Abikoff, Courtney, Szeibel, & Koplewicz, 1996). Looking at different types of music, Hallam, Price, and Katsarou (2002) found that calming, relaxing music enhanced mathematics, memory, and pro-social behaviour in 10- to 11-year-old children, while arousing, unpleasant music negatively affected memory and pro-social behaviour. Concerning disruption, Anderson and Fuller (2010) found 12- to 14-year-olds were negatively affected by listening to pop music during a reading comprehension task in comparison with silence; interestingly, those students who reported that they normally studied with music were more negatively affected by the background music. This research indicates that in some circumstances background music can be beneficial and in others disruptive.

Adults often choose to listen to music while working, and report that it improves their mood and relieves boredom while also enhancing concentration and blocking out unwanted noise (Haake, 2011; Lesiuk, 2005). There are individual variations in how adults use music for 'brain work' (see Lamont, Greasley, & Sloboda, 2016), and like children under certain circumstances, some adults find music detracts from their performance. Personality is one of the major factors: introverts find music more distracting when trying to concentrate than extraverts, and those scoring higher on neuroticism are similarly negatively affected (see Kämpfe, Sedlmeier, & Renkewitz, 2011). Trained musicians find music distracting in language comprehension tasks, in contrast to untrained adults (Patston & Tippett, 2011), and they also find music played on their own instruments more distracting in cognitive tasks than on other instruments (Yang, McClelland, & Furnham, 2015). Furthermore, some listeners appear to be more distracted by music with lyrics than without (Greasley, Lamont, & Sloboda, 2013). In other situations that require concentration such as driving, music – and particularly drivers' own preferred music – created more errors and aggressive driving, despite putting the drivers in a good mood (Brodsky & Slor, 2013). These negative effects suggest a 'limited capacity' hypothesis (cognitive resources are filled up by the music), in contrast to the enhancing arousal and mood hypothesis proposed by Thompson et al. (2001), as task complexity also plays a role (e.g. Furnham & Bradley, 1997).

Conversely, Bottiroli, Rosi, Russo, Vecchi, and Cavallini (2014) studied older adults aged 60–84 and found evidence directly contradicting the cognitive capacity hypothesis, as processing speed was better following upbeat positive music (Mozart) than white noise, silence, or downbeat negative music (Mahler). Bottiroli et al. also found memory enhancements: episodic memory was better in both music conditions, and semantic memory best with Mozart and better with Mahler than white noise. Evidence is thus mixed for adults as to what effects background music has on performance, with a number of factors including personality, familiarity, task, and experience affecting how distracting it can be. It seems likely that preference and positive emotions also play a role, as suggested in Schellenberg and Hallam's (2005) results (see also Hallam, 2010), and this also corresponds to the literature reviewed earlier on music and exercise and music and pain. In a cognitive context, distraction is perceived as detrimental rather than beneficial, and music's capacity to distract may be responsible for some of the differences in this body of literature. Considering the developmental evidence alongside the considerably larger body of findings with adults, there are few obviously developmental effects. Children seem to be no more or less influenced by background music than adults, but the implication from the adult literature is that if the music proves beneficial it may be useful in maintaining interest and involvement in non-musical tasks.

Effects of Music Listening on Psychological Health and Wellbeing

Psychological wellbeing is also affected by engaging with music and emotional responses to it throughout the lifespan. The benefits of music listening for mood regulation have been discussed extensively in Chapter 7, and despite the prevalence of music listening and self-reported importance of music in adolescence, these appear to be relatively consistent across the lifespan. Laukka (2007) found a great diversity of reasons given by his older sample (aged 65–75) for listening to music, and some positive associations between four listening strategies (agency and identity, mood regulation, relaxation and company, and enjoyment) and a range of wellbeing measures (particularly positive affect, negative affect, environmental mastery, and personal growth). His participants' wellbeing was primarily affected by health status and personality, but adding music into the regression model increased the amount of variance explained, meaning music adds something to the more straightforward predictors of wellbeing. The factors of agency and identity and of mood regulation were the most important here (see also Chapters 6 and 7).

Reflecting the importance of music for social bonding and the importance of emotional memories from across the lifespan, there is a small body of work looking at the efficacy of music interventions in couples counselling. Duffey, Somody, and Eckstein (2009) have applied the notion of the musical chronology from their therapeutic work on family relationships to couples counselling, focusing on the notion of music as a metaphor to express emotion. Their treatment plan includes a seven-step chronology for couples to work through, including making lists of music from different points across their relationship and then identifying songs associated with loving memories, individual pain and hurt, and contributions to the relationship. These music selections are then shared, put together in playlists, and experienced as part of the therapy. Duba and Roseman (2012) extend this beyond the realm of song metaphors and their meanings to the couple to include active music-making, composing short songs, drumming and communicating with simple instruments, and using the body to communicate emotions to the partner. Evidence is yet to be gathered on the efficacy of these techniques but they seem promising given that they draw on the emotional functions and effects of music from infancy through adulthood, emphasising rhythmic entrainment and episodic memory as a way of connecting.

When physical or mental health declines, music can also be used to affect the emotions, as a means of social support, maintaining or rediscovering identity, and for mood regulation purposes. In the Music and Health Promotion project, Batt-Rawden and DeNora (2005) worked with a population of adults aged 34–65 years old with chronic illness over a year. They began by choosing music that was important for the primary researcher (Batt-Rawden), asking the participants to engage with this in terms of their emotions and feelings. Participants then moved on to generate their own compilations of music that was emotionally significant for them, and these were shared among the other participants (self-labelled CD titles included My Mood, Feeling At Your Best, and All Time Best). This project uncovered the ways in which the participants used music in general, but importantly served as an intervention for them to connect or reconnect with music to help with their chronic illness. The CDs highlighted participants' awareness of the potential of music listening, as one participant (male, aged 50 and recovering from a burnout) recounted:

'I am much more conscious as to how I use music to reinforce my health and quality of life. By the way, I was also certified sick the whole of January, feeling awful, and then I thought I had to lay down and listen to music, so I put on Schubert, Mozart and Brahms and then I noticed I managed to get in touch with some hurtful emotions and I felt that my humour improved. I think it has to do with viewing things in perspective ... so, through this project I have been gradually much more aware of how much I miss music (referring to his bachelor life when he used to spend hours listening to music), so now I want to create my own private room where I can do my music, I know it can be a bit hard economically, since I have to throw out my lodger, but, it has to do with the importance of getting in touch with the energy, joy, and quality of life'. (Batt-Rawden & DeNora, 2005, p. 295)

In Batt-Rawden and DeNora's study, participants created their own music and also shared music with others virtually, thus fulfilling some sense of creating a community. What was important throughout this project was the personal nature of the music used, whether it belonged to the researcher, the participant, or other participants. As noted earlier there are some suggestions that personalised and tailored use of music for older people with symptoms of dementia may be effective in both evoking emotions and reducing anxiety (Duffey, Somody, & Clifford, 2008; El Haj, Postal, & Allain, 2012; Sung, Chang, & Lee, 2010). Much more work needs to be done in this area to support these indications, as large-scale randomised controlled trials do not always confirm these effects. Raglio et al. (2015), working across nine different institutions, found that ten weeks of music therapy was more effective than a similar period of music listening interventions in older people with moderate to severe dementia, but neither differed significantly from standard care in its effects. However, Särkamö, Laitinen, Numminen, Kurki, Johnson, and Rantanen (2016a) found improvements from a ten-week period of preferred music listening on general cognition, working memory, and quality of life with participants with moderate non-Alzheimer's dementia. The findings from Vanstone and Cuddy (2010) that AD participants show a very large range of musical memory capacity may be useful here. In their study of twelve patients with moderate or severe AD, five performed within the control group range on musical memory tasks while three had near complete loss of musical memory. It may be important to assess the degree of musical decline as well as cognitive decline in future studies with these populations.

The tailored nature of the interventions is also essential for their success. Using pieces that participants are familiar with rather than choosing styles from eras they might have known is important for the success of interventions. This recapitulates the difference between style and piece preferences discussed earlier: while music popular in the 1950s might be expected to be familiar to a population in their eighties, if one particular listener has not had the in-depth experience and emotional connection to one particular piece being used, then it is unsurprising that this may have little effect. In similar fashion to the 'reminiscence bump' data from Krumhansl and Zupnick (2013) it is possible but by no means certain that certain songs from given time periods will be better recalled and more familiar after substantial time has elapsed, and so the life experience and listening histories of the individuals need to be taken into account.

Effects of Music Listening on Social Health and Wellbeing

As discussed extensively in Chapter 7, music provides one of the earliest mechanisms for social communication and bonding, and shared music preference is also a way of becoming accepted and establishing identity in the crucial adolescent phase (Chapter 6). Music listening also has direct effects on social behaviour. While adolescents listen to most music alone (North, Hargreaves, & O'Neill, 2000), they still share a great deal of their music (Brown & Sellen, 2006). By early adulthood many experiences of music listening are shared with others (Juslin, Liljeström, Västfjäll, Barradas, & Silva, 2008; North et al., 2004), and as discussed earlier in relation to psychological benefits, music provides an important channel of communication in new social settings (Rentfrow & Gosling, 2006). The social dimension of music listening might thus provide a way into a collective musical experience which fulfils the requirements of meaning by allowing the listener to go beyond him or herself as an individual (see also Konečni, 1982 ; Sloboda, 2002). As discussed earlier, Batt-Rawden and DeNora's (2005) adults with chronic illness formed a virtual community through the sharing of music preferences, Chrissie, in Greasley and Lamont's study (2013), reported her experience of getting to know the band Hanson as a way into a new community of friends, and Laukka (2007) reports music as providing a way for older adults to maintain or regain community.

As well as considering the positive effects of music listening for health and wellbeing, there are also potential negative effects. Following on from the work on music preferences and personality, a considerable body of work has shown that 'problem' music can sometimes be associated with problem behaviours (see North & Hargreaves, 2008, for a much more detailed discussion). Correlational studies show that fans of rebellious music styles such as heavy metal and rap have particular personality characteristics: they often score more highly in pessimism, psychoticism, and rebelliousness, and demonstrate greater incidences of antisocial behaviour, delinquency, and drug use. These correlations are found with both adolescents (Miranda & Claes, 2004; Schwartz & Fouts, 2003) and young adults (Hansen & Hansen, 1991; North, Desborough, & Skarstein, 2005), with no apparent developmental trend. However, this evidence is by no means conclusive, and there are instances of fans of rap and heavy metal scoring equivalently or sometimes higher than fans of more conventional musical styles on positive behaviours (North & Hargreaves, 2007a). North and Hargreaves (2008) suggest that certain personality variables, such as high psychoticism and sensation seeking, membership of a minority ethnic or social group, and poor family relationships all affect the relationship between music style and delinquency or problem behaviour, and point out that cause and effect cannot be determined from such evidence. Research with adults by Bodner and Bensimon (2015) found fans of problem music (defined to include heavy metal and rap and also dance music) reported having more tattoos (perhaps associated with 'problem' behaviour), but also using music more frequently to regulate mood (see also Schwartz & Fouts, 2003). Finally, Neguţ and Sârbescu (2014) have shown that negative associations with particular types of music, notably rock and hip-hop, result from stereotypes associated with them rather than anything to do with the music itself. This combines to suggest that 'problem music' may in fact be an expression of personality for certain adolescents and adults, and while it may be associated with problematic outcomes it is not the cause of these. Indeed, there is some preliminary evidence that music listening for children with autism spectrum disorders can result in a reduction in socially reinforced problem behaviours (Lanovaz & Huxley, 2017).

Approaches to Wellbeing in Making Music

Active involvement in creating and playing music also has many well-documented transfer effects. There is a far greater weight of evidence to support the influence of specialised music training in particular and also of engagement with musical activities in a broader sense on many different aspects of psychological health and wellbeing. Being actively involved seems to have more potential influence than 'passive' listening, however engaged and intense that might be; similar findings come from research on leisure activities (Argyle, 1996) that suggests the more active, the better. However, the field is somewhat clogged with research 'evidence' that turns out to be poorly substantiated (cf. Clift, 2012), and we focus here on well-supported evidence for health claims.

In terms of developmental trajectories, it is clear that many children engage in practical music-making and music training and that this declines as children get older and into adulthood. Estimates are that around a third of school-aged children in industrialised societies will have additional extra-curricular music lessons (Lamont, Hargreaves, Marshall, & Tarrant, 2003), with a further third expressing an interest in doing so. However, our data suggests that the patterns of engagement may not be consistent, as children start and stop frequently: while a third of the school population might be having music lessons at any time, the actual children engaging may be different. This is supported by longitudinal research on participation in music which suggests drop-out at various points in children's schooling, including transition from primary to secondary school (Sloboda, 2001). Learning an instrument in childhood is a strong predictor of later involvement in music (Elpus, 2017), although not an essential component: Pitts (2009) identifies parental musical activities and support, singing at school and inspiring teaching as other factors that help children maintain interest in later life. However, the opportunity to learn technical skills in music is one that many adults note they would have appreciated during childhood, as it enables and supports many kinds of engagement in adulthood (Lamont, 2011b).

Looking at population studies, Theorell and Kreutz (2012) cite data from Sweden that illustrates a decline with age in the percentages of adults playing a musical instrument, at around 33 per cent at age 16–19, 25 per cent at age 20–29 and 9 per cent at age 75–84. This data is useful as it shows the effects of cohort as well as age with data collected in 1982–1983, 1990–1991, 1998–1999 and 2006. Proportions of adults playing instruments remained consistent across most age groups over time except the youngest, 16–19, where proportions playing declined from 33 per cent to 21 per cent over the time period studied. Proportions of adults singing in a choir also declines with age from around 12 per cent at 16–19 to 2.4 per cent at 75–84, but as Theorell and Kreutz note, in 2006 that proportion of older participants had risen to 7.5 per cent due to the increasing popularity of singing for older participants. Some of the effects of music-making and singing on various aspects of wellbeing may motivate older participants to maintain or take up activities, and we consider these in the following section.

Effects of Making Music on Physical Health and Wellbeing

Singing in particular has been found to have powerful positive physical effects on adults, including reducing tense arousal and increasing energetic arousal, positive hedonic tone, and heart rate (Valentine & Evans, 2001), and seems to boost the immune system (Beck, Cesario, Yousefi, & Enamoto, 2000; Beck, Gottfried, Hall, Cisler, & Boseman, 2006; Fancourt et al., 2016; Kreutz et al., 2004). Physical health can clearly be improved by participating in singing, as found by a careful comparison study matching singers with other older adults by Johnson, Louhivuori, and Siljander (2016). Supporting evidence comes from two studies of adults engaging in choirs. Teater and Baldwin's (2014) investigation of Golden Oldies, a singing community-arts programme, found participants showed a significant increase in self-reported health after joining the programme. Similarly, Vaag, Saksvik, Milch, Theorell, and Bjerkeset (2014) found improvements in self-perceived health in employees who chose to join a workplace music programme, 'Sound of Well-being', while those employees who chose not to engage showed a decline over the same period.

There are also indications that singing can be beneficial for those suffering from various health conditions such as Parkinson's disease (Di Benedetto et al., 2009; Stegemöller, Radig, Hibbing, Wingate, & Sapienza, 2017), chronic obstructive pulmonary disease (COPD; Morrison et al., 2013), irritable bowel syndrome (Grape, Wikström, Ekman, Hasson, & Theorell, 2010), cancer (Fancourt et al., 2016), or pain (Hopper, Curtis, Hodge, & Simm, 2016). In a recent review, Clift (2012) challenges many of the other studies that report small improvements from singing on other physical outcomes such as lung function and other medical problems, concluding that caution must be applied in considering whether and how benefits might transfer (see also Clift, Hancox, Morrison, Hess, Kreutz, & Stewart, 2010). Similar findings come from a systematic review by Reagon, Gale, Enright, Mann, and van Deursen (2016), looking at singing interventions with participants suffering from a range of health conditions including chronic pain and COPD, who conclude that there is only weak evidence for using singing for chronic health problems on physical health. Nonetheless, participants in many qualitative studies mention the physical benefits of singing in particular, including its energizing capacity and benefits for breathing, posture, voice quality, and lung capacity (e.g. Bailey & Davidson,

2005; Clift & Hancox, 2001; Clift, Nicol, Raisbeck, Whitmore, & Morrison, 2010; Lamont, Murray, Hale, & Wright-Bevans, 2017). For instance, older participants in Lamont et al.'s study noted that physicality in their choir rehearsals was central: 'We don't need exercise, do we, when we're going to sing "Siyahamba". It keeps us all uplifted'. Similarly, participants from a pain clinic reported how singing reduced their reliance on painkillers: 'I don't take my pills on a Friday because when I get there and start singing it sort of lifts you for the day' (Paige, in Hopper et al., 2016, p. 5).

Aside from singing, playing musical instruments or music performance in a more general sense has rarely been studied for its physical benefits, but there is a large body of research exploring the negative physical effects of performance in terms of music performance anxiety (MPA: Kenny, 2004; Wilson, 2002). Performance anxiety includes a range of physical symptoms (as well as cognitive ones) created by the autonomic nervous system's response to perceived threat, including increased heart rate/pounding chest, excessive sweating, dry mouth, nausea, and trembling hands. A range of treatments have been proposed for this which do not involve performing music, but rather focusing on medication, biofeedback training, relaxation techniques, psychological therapy for the performer, and modifying the context of performance itself (Kenny, 2006; Lehmann, Sloboda, & Woody, 2007). From a developmental perspective, some of the antecedents of performance anxiety appear to come from parental expectations. Hruska, Hargreaves, and Ockelford (submitted) found that perfectionism, which is strongly associated with performance anxiety, was linked to high expectations from parents. One participant, a female cellist, reported how these expectations ended up being unhelpful:

'My mum always pushed me; she always compared me to other people and other kids. She'd ask things like "why this child is doing this and you are not?" She'd make me feel bad if I hadn't achieved something that other kids had. And this probably made me work harder in the short term, but in the long term it damaged me in terms of my self-esteem'. (Hruska et al., submitted)

Performance anxiety can begin early in children's musical careers (Kenny & Osborne, 2006). Ryan (2004) found that children's anxiety symptoms were very similar to those of adults. She studied children aged 8–12 who were learning instruments at two time points: a normal school day, and the day of a major school concert, finding that state anxiety was significantly higher on the concert day. Studies with adolescents (Kenny & Osborne, 2006) show that anxiety increased with age throughout adolescence, and that students who had career aspirations in music reported lower levels of MPA than those who were unsure or not interested in a music career. Osborne and Kenny (2008) also found that significant negative experiences of performing predicted future levels of anxiety, which highlights the importance of early experiences in setting the groundwork for lifelong involvement with music.

In addition to MPA, performing music carries a number of physical health challenges for both amateurs and professionals (Altenmüller & Jabusch, 2010; Wynn Parry, 2004), many of which appear to be related to the challenges of ageing in general and thus far less relevant earlier in development. For instance, Kopiez,

Lehmann, and Klassen (2009) illustrated how Clara Schumann altered and then finally halted her performance career due to the onset of rheumatism in her mid-fifties and hearing problems in her seventies. As Gembris (2012) notes, many other performers go through similar kinds of age- and development-related changes in their careers. While there is no straightforward trajectory, the performing musician is likely to experience health problems and challenges at different points in his or her career, which are highly likely given the length and physical and mental challenge of the career (in contrast to sportspeople, for instance, musicians sustain a longer career). On the more positive side, older amateur musicians cite 'provides vitality' and 'keeps me fit' among the benefits of music-making, and the secondary activities of having to go out to rehearsals, carry instruments, and negotiate with others helps to maintain physical mobility in older age (Gembris, 2012).

There has been very little research on the physical effects of music-making in children, but a few researchers have begun to consider how the problems that affect adults might also affect children. Ranelli, Smith, and Straker (2011) studied child instrumentalists from age 7 to 17, exploring physical health outcomes. It is of some concern that 67 per cent of their participants, and more girls than boys, reported symptoms of playing-related musculoskeletal problems, and that 30 per cent reported being unable to play as usual as a result of these problems. Practice time was associated with physical problems, and children learning upper and lower strings and woodwind and brass instruments were more likely to have problems than those learning the piano, with cello, bass, saxophone, and trumpet the worst contenders. This suggests that physical challenges can be present in childhood as well as adulthood, although the implication from most of the research is that physical health should not be affected by music performing in children, since the health challenges are largely age- or ageing-related.

Effects of Making Music on Mind and Cognition

Music training has been shown to improve a very wide range of cognitive skills in children, and there is a large body of research exploring its effects on different kinds of cognition (see Hallam, 2015 for a more detailed summary). The key areas studied include language (which also requires auditory processing), general IQ, executive function, spatial and spatial-temporal abilities, mathematics, reading, and school achievement (as well as social development, which we consider later in this chapter). The patterns of results tend to be different in each study and depend on the methodology: in particular the design, the age of the children, the type and length of music training, and the precise nature of skills tested.

Looking at transfer to other auditory-related skills such as language and memory, the developmental explanation tends to be that music training improves auditory processing, and thus alters the structures of the brain in such a way to transfer to other domains (Kraus, Hornickel, Strait, Slater, & Thompson, 2014). A study with 9-month-old infants found that 12 sessions of music training (targeting temporal structures and incorporating multimodal, social, and repetitive elements of musical play) led to enhanced processing of temporal structure both in music and also in speech (Zhao & Kuhl, 2016). From this early beginning, research has found improvements in young children with music training compared to those without on the development of syntactic abilities and word memory (e.g. Marin, 2009), semantic memory (e.g. Koelsch, Fritz, Schultze, Alsop, & Schlaug, 2005), phonological awareness and speech segmentation (e.g. Anvari, Trainor, Woodside, & Levy, 2002; Herrera, Lorenzo, Defior, Fernandez-Smith & Costa-Giomi, 2011), and category fluency and sentence judgement (Janus, Lee, Moreno, & Bialystok, 2016). All of these abilities are closely involved in the development of early reading ability, and so it follows that early musical training is also associated with improvements in the development of reading.

Many early studies compared children who were specifically given periods of music training for the purposes of research with control groups who did not engage in any additional activities. For instance, Costa-Giomi (1999) studied the effects of three years of piano lessons on a sample of 117 9-year olds in Montreal. Children in the experimental group (n= 63) were given an acoustic piano at no cost to their families, and received weekly individual piano lessons for three years, whereas those in the control group (n= 54) did not receive any formal music training. A range of tests were undertaken at the start, during, and end of the three years. Spatial abilities improved in the music group after the first and second years, but by the third year there were no differences between groups. Similar results were found in a study of younger children by Rauscher and Zupan (2000), in which 5- to 6-year-olds were given 8 months of group keyboard lessons. At both 4 and 8 months after the start of the study, the music group scored more highly on spatial-temporal tasks, although no effects were found on a memory task. Bilhartz, Bruhn, and Olson (1999) gave 4- to 6-year-olds 30 weeks of music training and found that trained children were better at subtests of the Stanford-Binet intelligence scale involving attention and spatial-temporal abilities, although in this study no effects were found on subtests involving verbal measures. Similarly specific effects were found by Roden, Kreutz, and Bongard (2012) with 7-year-olds who had music lessons for 12–18 months, with verbal memory but not visual memory being enhanced for those children.

In a more controlled study Gardiner, Fox, Knowles, and Jeffrey (1996) divided a sample of 96 5- to 7-year-olds into groups who received music training, visual arts training, and controls (no training), and found that the two training groups outperformed controls on measures of reading and mathematics attainment. Some of the children had previously obtained scores on the First-Grade Metropolitan Achievement Test: Gardiner et al. found that those in the two arts training groups started behind the controls in these scores, but that after seven months of training they had caught up on reading and were ahead on learning mathematics. Despite the inclusion of the comparison group there are no specific findings relating to music in Gardiner et al.'s study, and their conclusion that benefits were down to 'the pleasure of the arts' (p. 284) points to a general mood and arousal explanation strengthened by extra input through the music or arts activities.

One of the challenges in interpreting findings about positive effects of music is that it is hard to know what exactly it is about the music training that causes improvements. As Gardiner et al.'s results indicate, any structured additional activity can have positive effects on children's cognitive development and motivation (cf. Schellenberg, 2006). What is needed is data that explores differences between music and other similar activities. For example, Schellenberg (2004) compared the effects of 36 weeks of keyboard, voice, or drama training on 6-year-old children's IQ, finding modest improvements for both the music groups in comparison to drama or control groups. Moreno, Marques, Santos, Santos, Castro, and Besson (2009) studied a sample of 32 8-year-old children before and after 6 months of music or painting training, recording event-related brain potentials while they performed tasks involving reading and pitch discrimination. The children in the music group improved their levels of reading and pitch discrimination abilities in speech, whereas the painting group did not.

Moreno et al. concluded that musical training influenced neural development, with a positive transfer from music to speech, and this is supported by evidence for enhanced auditory processing resulting from intensive and extended music training programmes (Chobart, François, Velay, & Besson, 2014; Habibi, Cahn, Damasio, & Damasio, 2016). Moreno et al.'s findings show brain plasticity in response to a relatively short period of music training, and in follow-up work, Moreno, Bialystok, Barac, Schellenberg, Cepeda, and Chau (2011) found that only twenty days of intensive training was enough for preschool children to show enhanced performance in both verbal intelligence and functional brain plasticity in an executive-function task. However, Janus et al. (2016) had more mixed findings in relation to music training compared with French language training. They explored the effects of music training and second language learning on non-verbal executive control tasks with children aged 4–6. The children were randomly assigned to twenty days of training in either music education or French language, and tested on a range of cognitive abilities. While some skills (English vocabulary, cognitive levels, and spatial spans) showed no change or effects of training, others involving executive control (category fluency, sentence judgement, and visual search) showed consistent improvements after both music and French. These results are similar to Gardiner et al.'s (1996) earlier study, in that no differences were found between music and 'comparison' (in their case art, in this case language) groups, but the explanation is different. Training in a second language is likely to share many features with training in music, including a focus on fine-grained auditory processing.

Moreno et al.'s demonstration that relatively short-term musical training increases verbal intelligence and executive function is striking, as these general cognitive abilities had traditionally been thought of as fairly stable features, or traits, of individuals. Similarly, effects on general IQ and on a number of IQ subtests have been found, as shown earlier (see also Schellenberg, 2016). These powerful findings show that giving children music lessons can influence cognitive abilities at a fairly profound level, presumably making them very attractive to parents and teachers. Furthermore, there is also evidence that music training can improve children's performance on various areas of school achievement and performance. Findings are not consistent across domains and areas of study, however. Costa-Giomi's (2004) participants, undergoing three years of piano training, also took tests of academic achievement, musical abilities, and motor proficiency at the beginning and end of the three years of the project. The results showed that piano training did not affect the children's academic achievement in maths and language as measured by standardized tests and school report cards, although it did have a positive effect on children's school music marks. Spychiger, Patry, Zimmerman, and Weber (1995) found that when reading and mathematics lessons were replaced by music, the children's reading improved more, but their achievement in mathematics was unaffected. A recent meta-analysis by Sala and Gobet (2016) suggests that while effects vary from study to study, the most substantial effects of music training are on IQ and memory.

The early indications that music training could help accelerate other cognitive skills have been used in a range of contexts with children from disadvantaged backgrounds to try to boost their academic achievement. Rauscher and Hinton (2011) found that children from economically disadvantaged backgrounds performed better on arithmetic and spatial-temporal tasks after three years of keyboard lessons. These findings echo the principles of the intensive music training programme El Sistema, developed in 1975 by José Abreu in Venezuela to help at-risk children (Baker, 2014). Following tours of the USA and Europe, and dissemination of the original El Sistema principles worldwide by a number of Abreu Fellows, similar programmes have been set up and researched for their impact on children's social development (discussed later in this chapter) and academic achievement. Osborne, McPherson, Faulkner, Davidson, and Barrett (2016) have explored two programmes in primary schools in Australia, finding an improvement in literacy, non-verbal reasoning, and a weaker effect of mathematical problem solving in one of the schools where the programme had been running for 42 months as compared to the other where the programme began only 25 months prior to testing. This supports Rauscher and Hinton's findings that a certain amount of time is perhaps necessary for effects to be seen, particularly among those children for whom formal learning may be more challenging. Evaluation of six similar government-funded In Harmony programmes in the UK is currently under way (Lord, Sharp, Mehta, & Featherstone, 2015), with indications of improved engagement with school among a host of other social outcomes discussed in this chapter.

One final area in terms of the effects of music on brain function concerns older people suffering from dementia and general cognitive decline. Music cannot provide a panacea for all age-related health issues (see e.g. Vink, Bruinsma, & Scholten, 2003). However, there is some evidence that active participation in music can delay the early stages of age-related cognitive decline (Verghese et al., 2003), and other evidence that participation can help people with dementia relieve stress and promote engagement during sessions (Bannan & Montgomery-Smith, 2008; Davidson & Fedele, 2011). Davidson and Fedele, for instance, found that participants undergoing six weeks of singing showed small increases in lucidity during the singing sessions and improved carry-over memory and recall from one week to the next. Särkamö et al. (2016a) found singing to be beneficial for improving working memory for those with mild dementia, and for maintaining executive function and orientation in younger participants with dementia.

Although our coverage of studies of the early effects of musical training has been necessarily selective in terms of choosing examples from the substantial and rapidly expanding range of literature available in this field, we have nevertheless considered it worthwhile to provide fairly detailed accounts of the studies because of their obvious importance in study of musical development. What constitutes 'musical training' differs from study to study, and so a number of different features and will inevitably have been conflated in drawing general conclusions. The underlying explanations for cognitive improvements in childhood and in later life are still not fully understood. Some explanations focus on the notion that by experiencing and processing sound, certain pathways and close domains are similarly activated. Conway, Pisoni, and Kronenberger (2009) have proposed the auditory scaffolding hypothesis to explain this kind of cognitive benefit. They suggest that the temporal and sequential nature of auditory input scaffolds advancements in general cognitive abilities that depend on these, potentially mediated by the neural connections between temporal and frontal lobes, and this provides a good explanation for findings showing similarities in training in language and in music (e.g. Janus et al., 2016). However, this cannot be responsible for all the benefits seen as there are also 'far' transfer effects from music training to domains that require different cognitive skills such as executive function (Moreno et al., 2011). More complex explanations propose that co-ordination between perceptual and executive functions and the particular combination of auditory, visual, motor, and memory-related processes that music demands may be responsible for the benefits to a wide range of areas of cognition (Moreno & Bidelman, 2013). Effects in older populations are less well studied but centre on memory as a potential key to unlocking conditions like dementia (Peck, Girard, Russo, & Fiocco, 2016). There can be no doubt, however, that a great deal more will emerge from the neuroscientific approach in this area, and that its influence on the study of musical development is likely to increase.

Effects of Making Music on Psychological Health and Wellbeing

Most of the research on the psychological benefits of making music has focused on adulthood and later life (and the same also applies to the social benefits, as shown in our final section), although there are also a few studies with children. In a preliminary study, Rose, Heaton, and Jones-Bartoli (2015) explored well-being among beginner instrumentalists aged 7 years, finding that nine months of learning to play an instrument led to improvements in emotional and behavioural well being (as assessed by teachers and parents), particularly among those children who had more than an hour of lessons and a mixture of instruments each week. Considering the characteristics of eudaimonia discussed earlier, the sense of flow is one which has been studied across the lifespan in relation to music performance.

Custodero (2005) found instances of challenge-seeking and challenge-monitoring indicators in the music-making of infants and children, which she identifies as part of the flow experience. For instance, the young children engaged in self-assignment, a challenge-seeking behaviour, which shows that they have a sense of self-as-agent and control over their activity. Infants and children would initiate a range of musical activities, such as reaching for a maraca or scarf to initiate familiar songs and dances. Similarly they extended the activities beyond the formal element, indicating their retained interest (an example of challenge monitoring). This could be seen in increased vocalising after the music activities, or delayed imitation of actions or gestures from the activities. Custodero also identified different trajectories of development from infancy to school age, with many flow indicators developing from infancy to preschool age and some showing a decline once school began (children aged 6–8 years). This 'decline' in flow may be perhaps due to the more constrained nature of the music activities which were more teacher-led, preventing sufficient space for the exploration of creativity and intuition which are more traditionally associated with flow; thus, rather than a developmental trajectory, this reflects the influence of the external environment on children's behaviour.

It is possible that flow experiences in childhood are influential and perhaps essential for sustaining engagement with performance into adulthood. Sloboda (1991) found that adults who described having had peak experiences with music before the age of about 10 were more likely to pursue involvement with music later in life. Flow could be a predictor of long-term motivation and achievement in performance. In a sample of adolescent musicians, O'Neill (1999) found that higher achieving children reported significantly more flow experiences with music than lower achievers (see also Fritz & Avsec, 2007). Older adults returning to or taking up instrumental music report self-fulfilment as one of the main goals (Lamont, 2011b; Taylor, 2010). In Gabrielsson's (2010, 2011) strong emotional experiences of music project, many of the performing memories contained a strong element of flow. For instance, a middle-aged man recalling an experience from student days described a particular moment working on Schumann's *Mondnacht*:

'We had been working quite a lot with the song, really slogging away at it, you might say. And neither she nor I was satisfied. But we decided to do it all the way through anyway – even though we were a bit tired and grumpy.

Technically it is a very difficult song, because it has to be so restrained, piano nuances in quite a high register. It so easily ends up entirely without feeling and intensity. Or it gets too loud and too tense. The lyrics describe a scene from nature. The moon is shining over the silent fields ...

Anyhow, we started the song ... and very suddenly – from the first note – I was 'inside' the song. It was almost like a mystical experience. It felt as if the ceiling in the practice room disintegrated, and I was standing there under the stars in the moonlight and living in the song – not singing it. And every note meant something very special, and I understood what every note meant. And she and I were not singer and pianist, but had some sort of joint revelation. It was like an enchantment. And I can still see that particular star-filled sky and the moonlight and feel the nameless insight when I think back to it'. (Gabrielsson, 2011, p. 223–224)

In addition to flow, performers' accounts of their memorable experiences with music typically contain other elements of balanced wellbeing (Lamont, 2012). In accounts from young adults of their strongest and most intense experiences of music performing, which typically occurred in late adolescence or early adulthood, four types of response were found. The first two focused on a mixture of positive and negative emotions combined with either personal challenge or relationships with others; anxiety featured in the descriptions of pre-performance settings but typically was soon replaced with positive emotions. The second two emphasised overwhelmingly positive emotions either in less critical and more relaxed musical situations (e.g. a concert rather than an examination) where relationships with others took centre stage, or in more challenging situations where all the features of wellbeing were seen (positive emotions, engagement, meaning, social relationships, and achievement: PERMA). The intrinsic enjoyment of performance which results from this balance of aspects of wellbeing seen in the last group of performers may, as we suggested, be responsible for continued motivation to engage with music into adulthood (cf. Persson, 2001). Exploring the PERMA concepts with professional musicians, Ascenso, Williamon, and Perkins (2017) found evidence of all five components in the discourse used by the musicians, with emphasis on self-concept and identity, positive emotions and engagement, social relationships and the successful negotiation of transitions (particularly from student to professional) as a way of engendering a sense of accomplishment (see also Croom, 2015). Achievement and accomplishment is also at the centre of passion, a concept which has been linked to the use of mastery goals in reaching exceptional levels of music performance achievement (Bonneville-Roussy, Lavigne, & Vallerand, 2011).

A broad measure used in many studies of arts as well as other kinds of intervention is quality of life (QoL), and the World Health Organisation have developed their own measure for QoL which covers physical, psychological, environmental, and social wellbeing. The WHOQoL (BREF) (brief form) includes questions tapping psychological health and wellbeing such as 'how much do you enjoy life?', 'how satisfied are you with yourself?', and 'to what extent do you feel your life to be meaningful?' alongside more physical aspects such as 'to what extent do you feel that physical pain prevents you from doing what you need to do?', environmental aspects such as 'have you enough money to meet your needs?', and social aspects such as 'how satisfied are you with the support you get from your friends?'. The phrase is also used more generally to encapsulate a wide range of measures of psychological wellbeing such as depression and anxiety. Those older adults who regularly engage in musical activities tend to score more highly on QoL. For instance, Pérez-Aldeguer and Leganés (2014) found that adults aged 64–78 who were in a choir had higher overall levels of psychological wellbeing and particularly higher personal growth, environmental management and positive relationships than a similar group who did not sing. Hallam and Creech (2016) compared older adults engaged in musical activities with those in language, arts, and yoga classes, finding consistently higher levels of QoL and wellbeing, although their results suggest that those choosing music already had a more positive outlook on life. Comparing wellbeing in different groups, Stewart and Lonsdale (2016) found choral singing to be more beneficial than solo singing on psychological wellbeing, although group singing was no more effective than team sports, suggesting that the group influence might be the most important in this case. The extent of engagement may also be important: Johnson, Louhivuori, Stewart, Tolvanen, Ross, and Era (2013) found significant correlations between the perceived benefit of singing and psychological, environmental, and social relationship aspects of QoL. Those singers who felt they were gaining most showed the most psychological benefits, along with fewer symptoms of depression and better satisfaction with their own health.

In addition to group comparisons of singers/performing musicians with controls, evidence shows that even short intervention studies using active music performance can improve subjective wellbeing or QoL. This is particularly effective for people suffering various health conditions. For instance, Stegemöller et al. (2017) found that an eight-week singing intervention helped both voice and overall health quality of life in people with Parkinson's disease, whether the singing was once or twice a week. Singing was also found to lead to improvements in energy and reductions in other physical signs of depression (Särkamö, Laitinen, Numminen, Kurki, Johnson, & Rantanen, 2016b). These effects did not last beyond the end of the trial; six months later, no differences were found in their groups. Similar short-lived results were found in a study by Myskyja and Nord (2008), where a leave of absence by the music therapist led to an increase in depression among residents. Myskyja and Nord found significant reductions in depression over a two-month period of reintroducing twice-weekly singing, with more improvements seen in the participants who engaged the most with the singing activities. With a general older population, Coulton, Clift, Skingley, and Rodriguez (2015) found a three-month singing intervention led to a significant decrease in levels of anxiety and depression, but these effects had disappeared after a further three months. The quantitative evidence for psychological benefits is thus not universal, and as both Coulton et al. and Särkamö et al. indicate, may not last beyond the duration of the programme.

Perhaps due to the difficulties in demonstrating effects in randomised controlled trials (cf. Reagon et al., 2016), qualitative enquiries are common in this area, and there are also many studies looking at the benefits reported and demonstrated over time from those involved in music-making. Findings tend to demonstrate many perceived psychological benefits from adults actively making music. For instance, Judd and Pooley (2014), exploring the psychological benefits of singing in a choir for adults, identified sub-themes within the individual benefits including psychological, musical, and physical. (Group factors were also identified which are discussed in the social health and wellbeing section in this chapter). The primary psychological outcomes they found for choral singers were positive emotions (love of singing, joy, and enthusiasm) and decreased feelings of stress. Bailey and Davidson (2005) found similar perceived benefits from choirs in middle-class affluent communities and those from marginalised backgrounds (homeless and disadvantaged communities): members talked about the emotional effects of singing (energy, relaxation, emotional release, and joy) as well as the importance of group participation (see later in this chapter). Older adults can regain a sense of musical identity and enhanced subjective wellbeing through music participation (Creech, Hallam, Varvarigou, & McQueen, 2014). In a study of people undergoing adverse life events, von Lob, Camic, and Clift (2010) also identified within their intrapersonal mechanisms the areas of competence, purposefulness, managing emotions, and creating a meaningful life as the different ways in which music helped. These map closely on to Seligman's pillars of wellbeing (2011). Like the other studies, von Lob et al. also identified interpersonal mechanisms, which are discussed next.

Effects of Making Music on Social Health and Wellbeing

This leads us to the final area of research on the effects of making music on development: namely on social, personal, and emotional development towards health and wellbeing. While research on cognitive and academic benefits has been more mixed, the findings on the social benefits of music-making in childhood are much clearer. All the childhood developmental evidence here comes from studies where music interventions of some kind are delivered either through school or as part of an extra-curricular programme, while the evidence for lifespan influences comes largely from qualitative research with older singers.

For children, positive effects of music training have been found on the communication and recognition of emotion, on social inclusion and empathy, and on social competence and self-esteem. For example, Rickard, Appelman, James, Murphy, Gill, & Bambrick (2013) allocated 359 children from the first and third grades in Australian schools (aged 6–7 and 8–9) either to a music education condition, in which they followed either Kodály music classes or additional strings-based instrumental classes, or to a control condition in which they continued to receive their usual curriculum. The results showed whereas the control group's global, general, and academic self-esteem declined, that of the children in the music education groups did not. As seen earlier, Gerry, Unrau, and Trainor (2012) were able to show that 6 months of active participatory music classes starting at the age of 6 months enhanced prelinguistic communication and social behaviour as well as musical tonal knowledge in infants, and Passanisi, Di Nuovo, Urgese, and Pirrone (2015) found 9-year-olds improved their interpersonal relationships with their peers after 6 months of music education games focusing on listening and creating music. Costa-Giomi (2004) found improvements in self-esteem in her participants over the 3 years of her study of piano training, when considering those who managed to maintain engagement with the programme (as compared to those who dropped out).

Considering children from disadvantaged backgrounds, in Australia, Osborne et al. (2016) found striking benefits in psychosocial variables from those children experiencing the El Sistema-like intensive music programme. Those children scored higher on wellbeing, happiness, purpose in life, sense of belonging, and social relationships, and these findings were more marked in the school that had been undergoing the programme for longer. As discussed in Chapter 4, Zapata Restrepo and Hargreaves (2017) studied the effects of an 18-week music intervention on displaced

6- to 8-year old children in Colombia. The children participated in two hours of music each week including singing, musical games, and improvisations, and showed significantly higher self-esteem scores after the programme compared with a control group. Similarly, in the UK, Lord et al. (2013) found evidence for many social and emotional benefits for children from disadvantaged communities experiencing the intensive In Harmony programmes, although a subsequent evaluation two years later by Lord et al. (2015) found less marked effects. Harkins, Garnham, Campbell, and Tannahill (2016) have gathered preliminary qualitative evidence for enhancements in mental and emotional wellbeing from participants in Sistema Scotland's Big Noise programme. A fuller evaluation is forthcoming, but their participants reported a range of positive effects including happiness and enjoyment from the sessions; growth in security, belonging, and relationships; and pride, confidence, and self-esteem. One of the adolescent participants gives a different perspective on music to the pressure experienced by many training for professional careers:

'Coming to Big Noise is not necessarily fun by other people's standards, but it's to build up your confidence, build up your communication skills, show your talent that you have to express your feelings, or something like that. Usually when, for example, your parents say "go for it, go for it", that's your parents pushing you to do something that's giving you, I don't know how to put it, giving you more confidence. But in Big Noise it's different, you come to Big Noise, what's pushing you is music, music's pushing you to build up your confidence'. (Big Noise Raploch participant, age 14, in Harkins et al., 2016, p. 33)

There is thus growing evidence that active music-making has promise in helping children cope with difficult and challenging circumstances. Similar evidence is found for adolescents: for instance, Cheong-Clinch (2009) found a 10-week music programme had positive effects on adolescent African refugee students (15 to 17 years old) in terms of their self-esteem, communication, social and cognitive functioning. As noted in Chapter 4, children and young people with autism can also benefit from musical activities, and Lindblom (2017) provides fascinating insight into how music helped two young First Nations people living in Canada manage the twin challenges of autism and coming from an ethnic minority. Lindblom showed, for example, how 16-year-old Debbie's talent for learning lyrics and singing popular songs helped her make friendships. Similar effects of music-making in building identity have already been discussed in Chapter 6.

Rabinowitch, Cross, and Burnard (2013) investigated the effects of one year of musical group interaction (MGI) on emotional empathy – what they describe as 'the ability to predict another's emotional state' – in 8- to 10-year-olds by running an MGI programme of musical games which were designed to promote empathy over a whole school year. Their rationale for music developing empathy emphasises the joint contribution of imitation and entrainment. Twenty-three children participated in the MGI group, with a small comparison group of 8 children undergoing a structured additional programme of games and a control group of 21 children who did not undertake anything additional. Measuring empathy on a range of existing and new measures, Rabinowitch et al. found increases in emotional empathy from the MGI group at the end of the year and significantly higher scores than the control group on two out of three of the measures used. These effects are mild, but more convincing evidence comes from Choi, Lee, and Lee (2010) who gave 24 11-year-old children with highly aggressive behaviour 15 weeks of bi-weekly musical activities (50 minutes each session, organised into four therapeutic phases designed to treat anger). Compared to a control group, those in the music group showed significantly lower levels of aggression and higher self-esteem at the end of the intervention. By its focus on a population with challenging behaviours this study is far more aligned to music therapy than mainstream music psychology, and the structured and therapeutic nature of the intervention is likely to be responsible for some of the positive effects seen, but it provides powerful evidence for benefits of training under such conditions.

In addition to the many psychological benefits reported from those adults involved in choirs, there are also many social benefits found in adulthood. The social identity perspective assumes that the group aspect of music is responsible for any effects seen, and Stewart and Lonsdale's (2016) survey of group singers, solo singers, and team sports players found evidence to support this as solo singers did not show any of the benefits found in the other two groups. A neurological explanation for this is provided by Keeler et al. (2015), who found decreases in adrenocorticotropic hormone after singing pre-composed and improvised music. This hormonal change indicates reduced stress and arousal and increased social flow. In addition, there were higher levels of plasma oxytocin (associated with bonding) after improvised, but not pre-composed, singing. Qualitative research also tends to emphasise social benefits. Judd and Pooley (2014) identified two elements within their 'group' theme: firstly the ethos of the choir in creating its particular social network (which could vary: some choirs welcome all-comers while others audition to provide a sense of commitment and effort), and secondly the group dynamic within the choir. The nature of collective community experience is emphasised by many studies (e.g. von Lob et al., 2010). In terms of ethos, one participant, June, in Lamont et al. (2017), described how stronger singers could support weaker ones through music in choir rehearsals:

'what I do is sort of lean and Gwen will tell you, I'll tell her "I'll lean on you" because I think she can read a bit of music where I can't and I'll lean on her, not physically, but I'm listening to her voice and as soon as I know she's going up and I can read a bit of the music and the chords, I'll go up as well. But it is a little difficult if you don't read music but it doesn't stop you, it doesn't stop you because you lean and listen.' (Lamont et al., 2017)

In addition to the social networks formed in and through the music-making itself, choir members frequently discussed group dynamics and friendship groups. Judd and Pooley (2014) reported one participant's discussion of the strong bonds in her choir:

'The success of Yellow lies in the strong bond we forge each week as we sing our cares away. We care for one another in a way that rarely exists in choral groups. We truly are a choir with heart'. (Beth, in Judd & Pooley, 2014, p. 277)

Beth's experience is not rare, however, but seems fairly typical of those making music together, particularly in choirs. Faulkner and Davidson (2004) described how members of a male choir valued the role of singing to connect with other people in and beyond the choir. Social impact and connectedness was a major theme from Dingle, Brander, Ballantyne, and Baker's (2013) study of adults with mental health challenges, and in Lamont et al.'s study, many choir members took the initiative in looking out for each other and socialising in between rehearsals. Choirs are typically made up of a broad range of people, from different backgrounds, and members talked about the personal benefits they gained from working with and supporting others (Judd & Pooley, 2014). Members cited the fundamentally social nature of music-making as responsible for these effects, as Joan explained:

'You get to know more people obviously and also different people you know, people from different walks of life, erm, and then there's, I suppose, it's a sort of team thing isn't it, you know. Because you've got to work as a team, you know, you can't be going off and doing your own thing.' (Lamont et al., 2017)

Social identity is a key element of this group dynamic (see Chapter 6). A lack of musical self-concept or musical identity leads many people to disengage from musical activities (e.g. Ruddock & Leong, 2005; Wise & Sloboda, 2008), and managing transitions while retaining a positive identity is important for long-term success in a musical career (Juuti & Littleton, 2010). A lack of such positive social contact through music is one reason performers drop out later in their careers (Moore, Burland, & Davidson, 2003), so social support is important for maintaining motivation as well as being a positive outcome of group engagement. There is even some recent evidence that singing can help make more rapid social bonds compared with other forms of creative activity (creative writing and crafts) (Pearce, Launay, MacCarron, & Dunbar, 2017), which may explain its popularity and efficacy.

Comparisons between Active and Passive Musical Engagement

In this chapter we have organised the literature on development into two separate accounts, one of listening behaviour and one of formal training or musical activities. This is partly inspired by Rauscher and Hinton's (2008) argument that exposure and training are very different 'inputs' and should be carefully separated and studied. While this has been a useful way of reviewing and organising a wealth of evidence, there is also a need to compare the effects of 'active' and 'passive' musical experiences.

A few studies have undertaken explicit comparisons. Gerry, Unrau, and Trainor (2012) compared responses from 12-month-old infants at the end of six months of music learning sessions (begun at the age of 6 months). The infants who attended music learning sessions recognized Western tonality earlier, but more interestingly they developed better prelinguistic communicative gestures and social behaviour than a comparison group of those who passively listened to music. The authors conclude that '(1) infants can engage in meaningful musical training when appropriate pedagogical approaches are used, (2) active musical participation in infancy enhances culture-specific musical acquisition, and (3) active musical participation in infancy impacts social and communication development' (p. 398).

Considering adulthood and older age, Raglio et al. (2015) found across nine different institutions that 10 weeks of music therapy was more effective than a similar period of music listening interventions in older people with moderate to severe dementia, but neither differed from standard care in its effects. This suggests that the active nature of therapy could be more beneficial, although this is not a great surprise. Studies that target particular conditions or populations in a sensitive manner are likely to have wider-reaching effects, such as the effects on aggressive children found by Choi et al. (2010) discussed earlier. Särkamö et al. (2016b) noted that the differences they found in their study of dementia patients between music listening and singing are most probably due to the nature of the activity. Listening to music, they suggested, focuses more on reminiscence and is thus more calming and relaxing, while the singing activity is more energizing and stress-reducing. This distinction is critical as different physiological and hormonal effects have been seen from exposure to different kinds of music (Fancourt et al., 2014), and mood and arousal levels seem critical in determining *how* exactly music benefits us.

Looking across the range of studies we have reviewed, there are clearly more demonstrable and longer-lasting benefits seen in music making than in listening to music. However, even when an activity is undertaken for several years its effects can and do wear off. The children in Costa-Giomi's (2004) study and the older adults in Särkamö et al.'s (2016a) research did not continue to experience lasting gains from their musical activities, and Grape et al. (2010) found hormonal enhancements only for the first 6 months of their singing project. The evaluation of El Sistema programmes by Osborne et al. (2016) explicitly mentions 'dose-response' factors as likely to be involved in the effectiveness of the programme: continued input is necessary to maintain the positive outcomes. In qualitative research many older participants talk about the need to continue engaging in order to continue receiving benefits, and Lamont et al. (2017) noted the importance for many choir members of continuing to be able to access the choir to continue benefitting. As a health-care intervention, music (whether it be listening or performing) seems to require constant input of some kind in order to sustain beneficial effects. What is also interesting is that the social benefits of music are common to listening and performing: while one might assume that listening is a relatively solitary activity it turns out to be highly social and to have many social benefits, from toddlers sharing songs with their caregivers through to adolescents and adults defining their identities and friendship groups through shared music preferences.

Conclusion

This chapter has reviewed a range of research which covers diverse topics and spans the entire age-range but which share many features of design and problems of demonstration. Music, whether listening or performing, undoubtedly brings many benefits across the lifespan for physical, cognitive, psychological, and social health and wellbeing. Most of the research has been with adults and older adults, but a great deal of this pinpoints earlier stages in development as being critical for later involvement. In each of the areas surveyed there is a tension between studies that capitalise on naturally occurring contexts (such as comparisons of people involved in music groups and those who are not) and those which are deliberately set up for research (such as eight-week programmes of singing). In many of the areas, mood and arousal are found to be central for benefits perceived, and from a health perspective it is interesting that evidence shows that people who think there are benefits to music are often those who show the greatest benefit (e.g. Johnson et al., 2013).

Many different explanations have been proposed for the beneficial effects of music on other aspects of human functioning, including near 'priming' effects, further 'transfer' effects, and generalised mood and arousal effects. With the burgeoning of evidence there are almost as many theories as there are research studies: this topic area has seen a flurry of research in the past few years and we suspect it will take a good few years of further dedicated effort for a coherent theory of musical benefits to be developed. In this chapter which brings together many themes from earlier in the book we have seen how cognition, motivation, identity, and emotion all work together to make music an enriching and rewarding experience for those who choose to engage, as listeners or as performers. What is clear here is that the trajectories are complex (cf. Pitts, 2009) and there is no one ideal 'route' into being a lifelong healthy and happy musician. Musical engagement, as we have shown throughout this book, is highly context-dependent.

9 Afterword

In this book we have provided a broad and theoretically informed overview of the range of fields that relate to musical development across the lifespan. We have organized our review of this wide-ranging and multifaceted area of study according to the current trends and priorities of these fields, which include an emphasis on the sociocultural and an increasing recognition of the importance of social interaction in shaping musical engagement from listening to improvisation, and a growing recognition of the importance of the neuropsychological research that is beginning to shed light on aspects of musical processing, thinking, and understanding. What we offer in this final chapter are some thoughts on five key themes that can be identified, and how these might develop in the coming years.

The first of these concerns the social nature of musical development. We have shown that right from before birth, music is shared: even during the foetal period, music is part of the auditory environment and memories are being formed. We have drawn extensively on Trevarthen and Malloch's (2017) concept of communicative musicality, which they propose as a way of bringing together aspects of sociocultural theory and other areas of developmental psychology, as well as 'applied' areas of music psychology, in particular music education and music therapy, in an ambitious attempt to integrate all these different aspects of human development into a broad theory of 'communicative musicality as the human way of life': this is discussed at length in Chapter 6. Their fundamental message is that the basic template of infant development is a musical one: the origins and complexities of infant–caretaker interaction are best described in musical terms. This is a profound reconceptualisation which clearly raises the status of musical development within developmental psychology as a whole.

Second, technology has dramatically altered the fundamental subject matter of musical development. As we pointed out in Chapter 1, the basic content and nature of music itself has changed, and perhaps even more significantly, developments in digital technology have meant that the ways in which we engage with music, and use it in society, have also changed radically. Research is beginning to catch up with the pace of technological change, and children and young people are more enthusiastically embracing the opportunities that new technology affords, and can therefore be willing participants in studies using new technology to capture data as well as to present music. Randall and Rickard (2013) describe the development and trial of a smartphone app that is applied to people's real-life music listening in this way, which enables a much higher degree of ecological validity and of real-time data sampling, and which also minimizes the disruption of the listener's everyday activities. In Chapter 6 we described how Randall, Rickard, and Vella-Brodrick (2014) used this technique to study young people's regulation of their emotional states, and there are clearly many more potential applications.

In Chapter 1 we introduced Andrew Brown's (2016) model of the ways in which children and adults engage with music as part of the 'technoculture' – his three-dimensional framework leads to a much broader conception of musicianship than in the past, and a similar broadening of the concept of musicianship has been suggested by Rickard and Chin (2017). Brown's model provides a valuable overall perspective on the ways in which people's engagement with music has changed as we have entered the digital age. Unfortunately, as with other groundbreaking technological innovations, digital developments can have negative as well as positive effects – this depends on the ways in which they are used and the uses to which they are put. In the case of music listening, it has become much easier for listeners, or 'music consumers', to download and copy commercially released digital music files without paying for them: the practices of illegal downloading or filesharing have collectively become known as 'music piracy'.

Steven Caldwell Brown (2014, 2015) has written a wide-ranging and multidisciplinary account of music piracy, which originated with the home taping of radio programmes and vinyl recordings using tape cassettes in the 1960s. With the onset of digitization, this practice gave way to rise to internet filesharing, which was made available by companies including Napster and Kazaa, whose legal status in relation to the music publishers was somewhat unclear. Brown also describes further developments which included the sharing of segments of files by BitTorrent, the development of 'cyberlockers' such as Pirate Bay which involved cloud storage of music files, which ultimately led onto the use of digital streaming as it exists today via companies like Spotify and Apple Music, who charge a monthly subscription for the use of some of their services. These provide a legal and acceptable means of downloading for many, though music piracy still takes place: and trying to explain why raises some difficult moral as well as practical questions about both the positive and negative effects of music piracy for different artists, and about the motivations, personalities, and attitudes of people who still engage in it.

Our third key theme is the adoption of the lifespan approach to musical development. The rapid increase in research on the ageing population, and in researchers' willingness to embrace a lifespan perspective, has meant that we have been able to devote much more attention to adolescence, adulthood, and old age in the present book. One clear manifestation of this is to be found in our account of the Sydney longitudinal study in Chapter 5: this large-scale, long-term study of 157 Australian children between the ages of 7 and 22 is particularly valuable and significant given the general paucity of similar longitudinal studies. With respect to older age, one significant part of the development of research on music, wellbeing, and health has been the investigation of the beneficial effects of music listening on older people, in particular those who are afflicted by dementia: a number of empirical studies have been able to show that music can alleviate the 'unholy trinity' of pain, anxiety, and depression in these cases.

What we see from a range of studies looking at the lifespan, in listening, creativity, and performance, is an inverted backwards J-shaped curve. Musical development seems to proceed in a rather rapid upwards curve in terms of rate, pace, and sophistication. Where we position this curve depends on the field of study: in some areas, such as the development of pitch perception, the initial peak occurs in the first year of life, whereas in other more complex domains such as collaborative composition, this occurs during the school years. The start of the upward curve may reflect the existence and position of critical periods: for pitch and metre perception, this appears to be before the age of 12 months, while for absolute pitch a period of around 3–6 years of age seems to be more relevant. For the effect of instrumental lessons on cognitive development, the period before age 7 seems to be critical, and we have even seen that the early twenties can been seen as a critical period in the longer-term development of music preferences..

Engagement with music, itself a relatively new concept which is growing in popularity, seems to continue at a relatively high level throughout most of adulthood. This counters the earlier supposition that interest in and involvement with music declines after young adulthood; this earlier assumption may arise from cohort effects, since today's 'middle youth' population seem to be just as engaged with technology and new forms of music as their teenage children. Due to the growing ageing population there are also many more opportunities provided for older adults to engage in musical activities, as these are widely recognised as an antidote to the challenges posed by ageing such as cognitive decline and loneliness. Longitudinal research will provide more definitive answers to questions about long-term influences on musical involvement.

After this rapid rise in the curve, evidence from several domains suggests a slight tailing off in abilities and in musical interest in later old age, representing the last part of the inverted backwards J-shaped curve. Again, this counters the assumption that older age is a time of rapid decline, as there is plenty of evidence that shows how adults positively respond to musical opportunities, in both listening and performing, and it is encouraging to note that in most cases the decline is mild. With increased life expectancy and the accompanying rise in conditions such as dementia it will be important to establish whether this decline continues in the oldest old, and to explore how to support older adults in their continued involvement with music.

Our fourth key theme is the new emphasis on the importance of the self, and we have approached this from two different perspectives. In Chapter 2 we reviewed social cognitive approaches to the explanation of musical development, looking in particular at research on self-regulation and metacognition. There are many different formal definitions of self-regulation and self-regulated learning, seventeen of which were collated by Robson (2014): a representative one of these, by Schunk and Zimmerman (1994), is 'the process whereby students activate and sustain cognitions, behaviors, and affects which are systematically oriented towards attainment of their goals' (p. 309). These ideas have been very influential in research on self-regulated learning, and especially on the development of self-regulation in children. The second broad area of research on the self is that which is based on the concept of identity: along with the more specific concept of musical identity, this has become a huge and burgeoning field of study, to which we devoted the whole of Chapter 6. We have emphasised the active, constructive, and fluid nature of musical identities as both social and performative, and explored the many influences on their development.

The study of musical development has many practical applications, and this is our fifth and final key theme. In characterising the discipline of music psychology in Chapter 1, we drew attention to an emerging field which might be called applied music psychology, in which the findings of the discipline are applied in the areas such as education, broadcasting and the media, health and wellbeing, consumer behaviour, social inclusion, and musicianship itself. This is an encouraging development at a time when research is increasingly required to demonstrate external 'impact'. The first, education, is likely to benefit most directly from the increase in our knowledge about and understanding of musical development, and to bear directly on some key questions in music education. A range of innovative and ingenious research is being conducted with children of all ages, often in collaboration with teachers and schools, and this kind of applied approach will be vital in helping ensure that clear messages can be given to policymakers and practitioners about how best to support children's musical development. These include arguments we made earlier in Chapters 5 and 6 about the need to consider more than just performance skills when thinking about developing children's musicality and musicianship (and in particular to incorporate creativity and imagination when thinking about musical development), to acknowledge the importance of different cultures, traditions, and processes of music teaching and learning, and to address how children and adults develop and sustain their musical identities and how this shapes their engagement with music across the lifespan.

Another important area of application which we described in Chapter 2 is that which brings together music psychology and music theory. Our colleague Adam Ockelford (2016) has written an entertaining account of the debate which occurred in the 1980s and 1990s between music psychologists and those musicologists known as music theorists in North America, and as music analysts in the UK. Clarke (1989), for example, in a widely quoted article entitled 'Mind the gap', suggested that the emphasis of composers and musicologists was on constructing accounts of the structural relationships within and between different musical works, whereas music psychologists were more interested in developing theories of the mental processing of musical events, and in investigating the relationships between composers, performers, listeners, and their musical environments.

Ockelford himself starts from the point of view that a great deal of research on music, including that by music psychologists, uses indirect measures of musical behaviour such as people's answers to interviews, patterns of ticks in boxes on questionnaires, responses to isolated tones, and so on. In doing so they fail to access the most direct source of data, namely what is going on in the music itself – which can be accessed through recordings and transcriptions of real-life musical outputs and interactions. He has developed *zygonic theory*, which we described in Chapter 2, and this is the core around which he has been able to build a whole new interdisciplinary approach which he calls *applied musicology* (Ockelford, 2013). This applies analytical methods derived from zygonic theory to real-life musical interactions, such as those occurring in teacher–learner and therapist–client pairs. This has the potential to enable researchers to investigate phenomena such as musicians' mutual influences upon each other in performance, or the therapeutic processes taking place in therapist–client interactions, via the structure of their real musical interactions.

Finally, we look forward to the future: the pace of change in musical development and its investigation seems likely to increase still further in the years to come. Although it is unwise to attempt specific predictions as to what might happen, at the very least we can try to guess what kinds of changes are likely to take place, and three of these emerge from our earlier comments in this Afterword.

The first is that the development of digital technology is likely to accelerate even further, and that this will continue to exert a profound impact on musical behaviour, experience, and development. At the time of writing, the main changes on the horizon seem to be in the rapid take-up of social networking, which seems to have the potential to take over from email communication: in the recent advances in virtual reality equipment: and in the increasing miniaturisation and falling cost of portable tablet computers and music hardware and software, to the extent that young children are computer-literate at earlier and earlier ages.

The second change is likely to be in further interdisciplinary developments, and in particular in those arising from the neurosciences. The speed of progress in neuroscientific music research is very rapid, such that the history and research agenda of a new interdisciplinary field of study, psychoneuroimmunology, was recently set out by Fancourt (2016), as we mentioned in Chapter 2. It also seems likely that the increasing interest in self-regulation, and increasing sophistication of psychological and social understandings of the self could well have powerful implications for our understanding of musical identity, and people's musical self-concept and self-esteem.

Finally, we expect the applications of music psychology to expand and to develop rapidly, and to have their impact on more and more areas of everyday life. At the time of writing, the most promising areas of applied music psychology seem to be the effects of music training in the early years; the applications of music to issues in wellbeing and health, including the relief of stress, pain, anxiety, and depression, and of course in music therapy; in increasing social inclusion among disenfranchised members of society, for whom the media and the internet may play a critical role; in changing the nature and aims of music education, which is already beginning to happen; and in helping and alleviating the problems of musicians themselves, which is beginning to occur in the research departments which are now established in many music conservatoires.

It is clear that the study of musical development, and its application to real-life practical problems, is currently in a very healthy state: but we should temper our enthusiasm with a sense of humility, as it is impossible to predict the state of the discipline another thirty years hence. This view is eloquently expressed by the Bard, and so we finish, as we started, with the words of Shakespeare:

Horatio:
O day and night, but this is wondrous strange!

Hamlet:
And therefore as a stranger give it welcome.
There are more things in heaven and earth, Horatio,
Than are dreamt of in your philosophy.

Hamlet Act 1, scene 5, 159–167

References

Abbott, A., & Collins, D. (2004). Eliminating the dichotomy between theory and practice in talent identification and development: Considering the role of psychology. *Journal of Sport Science*, 22(5), 395–408.

Abikoff, H., Courtney, M. E., Szeibel, P. J., & Koplewicz, H. S. (1996). The effects of auditory stimulation on the arithmetic performance of children with ADHD and nondisabled children. *Journal of Learning Disabilities*, 29(3), 238–246.

Abrahams, F., & Abrahams, D. (2016). Child as musical apprentice. In G. E. McPherson (Ed.), *The child as musician: A handbook of musical development* (2nd edition, pp. 538–555). Oxford: Oxford University Press.

Adachi, M. (1994). The role of the adult in the child's early musical socialization: A Vygotskian perspective. *Quarterly Journal of Music Teaching and Learning*, 5, 26–35.

Adachi, M., & Trehub, S. E. (1998). Children's expression of emotion in song. *Psychology of Music*, 26, 133–153.

Adachi, M., & Trehub, S. E. (2011). Canadian and Japanese preschoolers' creation of happy and sad songs. *Psychomusicology: Music, Mind & Brain*, 21(1/2), 130–143.

Adams, G., & Markus, H. R. (2004). Toward a conception of culture suitable for a social psychology of culture. In M. Schaller & C. S. Crandall (Eds.), *The psychological foundations of culture* (pp. 335–360). Mahwah, NJ: Lawrence Erlbaum Associates.

Addessi, A. R., Baroni, M., Luzzi, C., & Tafuri, J. (1995). The development of musical stylistic competence in children. *Council for Research in Music Education (CRME) Bulletin*, 127, 8–15.

Adorno, T. W. (1941). On popular music. *Zeitschrift für Sozialforschung*, 9, 17–49.

Adorno, T. W. (1976). *Introduction to the sociology of music*. Stanford, CA: Stanford University Press.

Alexander, R. J. (2001). *Culture and pedagogy: International comparisons in primary education*. Oxford: Blackwell Publishing.

Alexander, R. J. (2008). *Towards dialogic teaching* (4th edition). York: Dialogos.

Alluri, V., Toiviainen, P., Jääskeläinen, I. P., Glerean, E., Sams, M., & Brattico, E. (2012). Large-scale brain networks emerge from dynamic processing of musical timbre, key and rhythm. *NeuroImage*, 59(4), 3677–3689.

Altenmüller, E., & Jabusch, H. C. (2010). Focal dystonia in musicians: Phenomenology, pathophysiology, triggering factors, and treatment. *Medical Problems of Performing Artists*, 25(1), 3–9.

Amabile, T. M. (1983). The social psychology of creativity: A componential conceptualization. *Journal of Personality and Social Psychology*, 45(2), 357–377.

Amabile, T. M. (1996). *Creativity in context*. Boulder, CO: Westview Press.

Ammirante, P., Patel, A. D., & Russo, F. A. (2016). Synchronizing to auditory and tactile metronomes: A test of the auditory-motor enhancement hypothesis. *Psychonomic Bulletin & Review*, 23(6), 1882–1890.

Anderson, S. A., & Fuller, G. B. (2010). Effect of music on reading comprehension of junior high school students. *School Psychology Quarterly*, 25(3), 178–187.

Ando, Y., & Hattori, H. (1970). Effects of intense noise during fetal life upon postnatal adaptability (statistical study of the reactions of babies to aircraft noise). *Journal of the Acoustical Society of America*, 47, 1128.

Andrade, P. E., Vanzella, P., Andrade, O. V. C. A., & Schellenberg, E. G. (2016). Associating emotions with Wagner's music: A developmental perspective. *Psychology of Music*, Online First, DOI: 10.1177/0305735616678056.

Anvari, S. H., Trainor, L. J., Woodside, J., & Levy, B. A. (2002). Relations among musical skills, phonological processing, and early reading ability in preschool children. *Journal of Experimental Child Psychology*, 83(2), 111–113.

Araújo, M. V. (2016). Measuring self-regulated practice behaviours in highly skilled musicians. *Psychology of Music*, 44(2), 278–292.

Argyle, M. (1996). *The social psychology of leisure*. Harmondsworth: Penguin.

Ascenso, S., Williamon, A., & Perkins, R. (2017). Understanding the wellbeing of professional musicians through the lens of positive psychology. *Psychology of Music*, 45(1), 65–81.

Atkinson, W. (2011). The context and genesis of musical tastes: Omnivorousness debunked, Bourdieu buttressed. *Poetics*, 39, 169–186.

Auh, M.-S., & Walker, R. (2017). Musical identities in Australia and South Korea and new identities emerging through social media and digital technology. In R. A. R. MacDonald, D. J. Hargreaves, & D. E. Miell (Eds.), *Handbook of musical identities* (pp. 789–805). Oxford: Oxford University Press.

Austin, J., Renwick, J., & McPherson, G. E. (2006). Developing motivation. In G. E. McPherson (Ed.), *The child as musician: A handbook of musical development* (pp. 213–238). Oxford: Oxford University Press.

Azzara, C. D. (1993). Audiation-based improvisation techniques and elementary instrumental students' music achievement. *Journal of Research in Music Education*, 41(4), 328–342.

Bacher L. F., & Robertson S. S. (2001). Stability of coupled fluctuations in movement and visual attention in infants. *Developmental Psychobiology*, 39, 99–106.

Bahrick, L., Flom, R., & Lickliter, R. (2002). Intersensory redundancy facilitates discrimination of tempo in 3-month-old infants. *Developmental Psychobiology*, 41, 352–363.

Bahrick, L., Lickliter, R., & Flom, R. (2004). Intersensory redundancy guides the development of selective attention, perception, and cognition in infancy. *Current Directions in Psychological Science*, 13(3), 99–102.

Bailey, B., & Davidson, J. W. (2005). Effects of group singing and performance for marginalized and middle-class singers. *Psychology of Music*, 33, 269–303.

Bakagiannis, S., & Tarrant, M. (2006). Can music bring people together? Effects of shared musical preference on intergroup bias in adolescence. *Scandinavian Journal of Psychology*, 47(2), 129–136.

Baker, G. (2014). *El Sistema: Orchestrating Venezuela's youth*. New York: Oxford University Press.

Baltes, P. (1987). Theoretical propositions of life-span developmental psychology: On the dynamics between growth and decline. *Developmental Psychology*, 23(5), 611–626.

Balzano, G. J. (1982). The pitch set as a level of description for studying musical pitch perception. In M. Clynes (Ed.), *Music, mind and brain* (pp. 321–351). New York: Plenum.

Bamberger, J. (1982). Revisiting children's drawings of simple rhythms: A function for reflection-in-action. In S. Strauss & R. Stavy (Eds.), *U-shaped behavioral growth* (pp. 191–226). New York: Academic Press.

Bamberger, J. (1986). Cognitive issues in the development of musically gifted children. In R. J. Sternberg & J. E. Davidson (Eds.), *Conceptions of giftedness* (pp. 388–413). Cambridge: Cambridge University Press.

Bamberger, J. (1991). *The mind behind the musical ear.* Cambridge, MA: Harvard University Press.

Bamberger, J. (2006). What develops in musical development? In G. E. McPherson (Ed.), *The child as musician: A handbook of musical development* (pp. 69–91). Oxford: Oxford University Press.

Bamberger, J. (2013). *Discovering the musical mind: A view of creativity as learning.* Oxford: Oxford University Press.

Bandura, A. (1969). Social-learning theory of identificatory processes. In D. A. Goslin (Ed.), *Handbook of socialization theory and research* (pp. 213–262). Chicago, IL: Rand-McNally.

Bandura, A. (1977). *Social learning theory.* Englewood Cliffs, NJ: Prentice-Hall.

Bandura, A. (1986). *Social foundations of thought and action: A social cognitive theory.* Englewood Cliffs, NJ: Prentice-Hall.

Bandura, A. (1997). *Self-efficacy: The exercise of control.* New York: W. H. Freeman.

Bandura, A. (2000) Exercise of human agency through collective efficacy. *Current Directions in Psychological Science*, 9(3), 75–78.

Bangerter, A., & Heath, C. (2004). The Mozart effect: Tracking the evolution of a scientific legend. *British Journal of Social Psychology*, 43(40), 605–623.

Bannan, N., & Montgomery-Smith, C. (2008). 'Singing for the brain': Reflections on the human capacity for music arising from a pilot study of group singing with Alzheimer's patients. *Journal for the Royal Society for the Promotion of Health*, 128(2), 73–78.

Bannan, N., & Woodward, S. (2009). Spontaneity in the musicality and music learning of children. In S. Malloch and C. Trevarthen (Eds.), *Communicative musicality: Exploring the basis of human companionship* (pp. 465–494). Oxford: Oxford University Press.

Barbot, B., & Lubart, T. (2012). Creative thinking in music: Its nature and assessment through musical exploratory behaviors. *Psychology of Aesthetics, Creativity, and the Arts*, 6(3), 231–242.

Barlow, H., & Morgenstern, S. (1948). *A dictionary of musical themes.* New York: Crown.

Barlow, H., & Morgenstern, S. (1976). *A dictionary of opera and song themes* (revised edition). New York: Crown.

Baron-Cohen, S., Leslie, A. M., & Frith, U. (1985). Does the autistic child have a 'theory of mind'? *Cognition*, 21(1), 37–46.

Barrett, M. (2007). *Children's knowledge, beliefs and feelings about nations and national groups.* Hove, UK: Psychology Press.

Barrett, M. S. (1996). Children's aesthetic decision-making: An analysis of children's musical discourse as composers. *International Journal of Music Education*, 28, 37–62.

Barrett, M. S. (1997). Invented notations: A view of young children's musical thinking. *Research Studies in Music Education*, 8, 2–14.

Barrett, M. S. (2010). *A cultural psychology of music education.* Oxford: Oxford University Press.

Barrett, M. S. (2011). Musical narratives: A study of a young child's identity work in and through music-making. *Psychology of Music*, 39(4), 403–423.

Barrett, M. S., & Tafuri, J. (2012). Creative meaning-making in infants' and young children's musical cultures. In G. E. McPherson & G. F. Welch (Eds.), *Oxford handbook of music education* (pp. 296–331). New York, NY: Oxford University Press.

Barry, N. H., & Hallam, S. (2002). Practice. In R. Parncutt & G. E. McPherson (Eds.), *The science and psychology of music performance* (pp. 151–165). Oxford: Oxford University Press.

Baruch, C., & Drake, C. (1997). Tempo discrimination in infants. *Infant Behavior and Development*, 20, 573–577.

Baruch, C., Panissal-Vieu, N., & Drake, C. (2004). Preferred perceptual tempo for sound sequences: Comparison of adults, children and infants. *Perceptual & Motor Skills*, 98, 325–339.

Bashwiner, D. M., Wertz. C. J., Flores, R. A., & Jung, R. E. (2016). Musical creativity 'revealed' in brain structure: Interplay between motor, default mode, and limbic networks. *Scientific Reports*, 6:20482, DOI: 10.1038/srep20482.

Batt-Rawden, K., & DeNora, T. (2005). Music and informal learning in everyday life. *Music Education Research*, 7(3), 289–304.

Beaty, R. E. (2015). The neuroscience of musical improvisation. *Neuroscience and Biobehavioral Reviews*, 51, 108–117.

Beck, R. J., Cesario, C., Yousefi, A., & Enamoto, H. (2000). Choral singing, performance perception, and immune system changes in salivary immunoglobulin A and cortisol. *Music Perception*, 18(1), 87–106.

Beck, R. J., Gottfried, T. L., Hall, D. J., Cisler, C. A., & Bozeman, K. W. (2006). Supporting the health of college solo singers: The relationship of positive emotions and stress to changes in salivary IgA and cortisol during singing. *Journal of Learning through the Arts: A Research Journal on Arts Integration in Schools and Communities*, 2(1), article 19.

Beck, U. (1992). *Risk society: Towards a new modernity*. London and Thousand Oaks: Sage Publications.

Behne, K.-E. (1975). Musikalische Konzepte: Zur Schicht- und Altersspezifität musikalischer Präferenzen. In E. Kraus (Ed.), *Forschung in der Musikerziehung* (pp. 35–61). Mainz: Schott.

Bennett, M., Lyons, E., Sani, F., & Barrett, M. (1998). Children's subjective identification with the group and ingroup favoritism. *Developmental Psychology*, 34, 902–909.

Bergeson, T. R., & Trehub, S. E. (2006). Infants' perception of rhythmic patterns. *Music Perception*, 23(4), 345–360.

Berliner, P. F. (1994). *Thinking in jazz: The infinite art of improvisation*. Chicago, IL: University of Chicago Press.

Berlyne, D. E. (1971). *Aesthetics and psychobiology*. New York: Appleton-Century-Crofts.

Bernard, M. (1995). Social forces and aging: An introduction to social gerontology. *Ageing and Society*, 15, 566–569.

Bernard, M., Phillipson, C., Phillips, J., & Ogg, J. (2001). Continuity and change in the family and community life of older people. *Journal of Applied Gerontology*, 20(3), 259–278.

Berzonsky, M. D. (1989). Identity style: Conceptualization and measurement. *Journal of Adolescent Research*, 4, 268–282.

Berzonsky, M. D. (1990). Self-construction over the lifespan: A process perspective on identity formation. In G. J. Neimeyer & R. A. Neimeyer (Eds.), *Advances in personal construct theory* (vol. 1, pp. 155–186). Greenwich, CT: JAI Press.

Bharucha, J. J. (1984). Event hierarchies, tonal hierarchies, and assimilation: A reply to Deutsch and Dowling. *Journal of Experimental Psychology: Human Perception and Performance*, 6, 501–515.

Bibace, R., & Walsh, M. E. (1980). Development of children's concepts of illness. *Pediatrics*, 66, 912–917.

Bigand, E., Delbé, C., Poulin-Charronnat, B., Leman, M., & Tillmann, B. (2014). Empirical evidence for musical syntax processing? Computer simulations reveal the contribution of auditory short-term memory. *Frontiers in Systems Neuroscience*, DOI: 10.3389/fnsys.2014.00094.

Bilhartz, T. D., Bruhn, R. A., & Olson, J. E. (1999). The effect of early music training on child cognitive development. *Journal of Applied Developmental Psychology*, 20, 615–636.

Billig, M., & Tajfel, H. (1973). Social categorization and similarity of intergroup behaviour. *European Journal of Social Psychology*, 3, 27–52.

Bird, J. M., Hall, J., Arnold. R., Karageorghis, C. I., & Hussein, A. (2016). Effects of music and music-video on core affect during exercise at the lactate threshold. *Psychology of Music*, 44(6), 1471–1487.

Birns, B. (1965). Individual differences in human neonates' responses to stimulation. *Child Development*, 36(1), 249–256.

Birns, B., Blank, M., Bridger, W. H., & Escalona, S.K. (1965). Behavioral inhibition in neonates produced by auditory stimuli. *Child Development*, 36(3), 639–645.

Bjurström, E., & Wennhall, J. (1991). Ungdomar och music. In *Statens Ungdomsråds Årsbok om ungdom* (pp. 82–88). Stockholm: Statens ungdomsråd.

Blacking, J. (1973). *How musical is man?* Seattle: University of Washington Press.

Blair, C., & Razza, R. P. (2007) Relating effortful control, executive function, and false belief understanding to emerging math and literacy ability in kindergarten. *Child Development*, 78(2), 647–663.

Blakemore, S.-J. (2010). The developing social brain: Implications for education. *Neuron*, 65, 744–747.

Blood, A. J., & Zatorre, R. J. (2001). Intensely pleasurable responses to music correlate with activity in brain regions implicated in reward and emotion. *Proceedings of National Academy of Sciences*, 98, 11818–11823.

Boal-Palheiros, G. M., & Hargreaves, D. J. (2001). Listening to music at home and at school. *British Journal of Music Education*, 18, 103–118.

Boden, M. (1994). *Dimensions of creativity*. Cambridge, MA: MIT Press.

Boden, M. (1999). Computer models of creativity. In R. J. Sternberg (Ed.), *Handbook of creativity* (pp. 351–372). Cambridge: Cambridge University Press.

Bodner, E., & Bensimon, M. (2015). Problem music and its different shades over its fans. *Psychology of Music*, 43(5), 641–660.

Boer, D., Fischer, R., Strack, M., Bond, M. H., Lo, E., & Lam, J. (2011). How shared preferences in music create bonds between people. *Personality and Social Psychology Bulletin*, 37(9), 1159–1171.

Bonneville-Roussy, A., & Bouffard T. (2015). When quantity is not enough: Disentangling the roles of practice time, deliberate practice and self-regulation in musical achievement. *Psychology of Music*, 43(5), 686–704.

Bonneville-Roussy, A., Lavigne, G. L., & Vallerand, R. J. (2011). When passion leads to excellence: The case of musicians. *Psychology of Music*, 39(1), 123–138.

Bonneville-Roussy, A., Rentfrow, P. J., Xu, M. K., & Potter, J. (2013). Music through the ages: Trends in musical engagement and preferences from adolescence through middle adulthood. *Journal of Personality and Social Psychology*, 105(4), 703–717.

Bonneville-Roussy, A., Stillwell, D., Kosinski, M., & Rust, J. (2016). Age trends in musical preferences in adulthood 1: Conceptualization and empirical investigation. *Musicae Scientiae.* Online First, DOI: 10.1177/1029864917691571.

Boone, R. T., & Cunningham, J. G. (2001). Children's expression of emotional meaning in music through expressive body movement. *Journal of Nonverbal Behavior*, 25(1), 21–41.

Bottiroli, S., Rosi, A., Russo, R., Vecchi, T., & Cavallini, E. (2014). The cognitive effects of listening to background music on older adults: Processing speed improves with upbeat music, while memory seems to benefit from both upbeat and downbeat music. *Frontiers in Aging Neuroscience*, 6(284), 1–7, DOI: 10.3389/fnagi.2014.00284.

Bourdieu, P. (1971). Intellectual field and creative project. In M. F. D. Young (Ed.), *Knowledge and control* (pp. 161–188). London: Collier-Macmillan.

Bourdieu, P. (1984). *Distinction: A social critique of the judgement of taste*. London: Routledge.

Boysson-Bardies, B. de (1999). *How language comes to children: From birth to two years.* Cambridge, MA: The MIT Press.

Brace, G. (1968). *The story of music.* London: Ladybird Books.

Bradley, B. S. (2009). Early trios: Patterns of sound and movement in the genesis of meaning between infants. In S. Malloch and C. Trevarthen (Eds.), *Communicative musicality: Exploring the basis of human companionship* (pp. 263–280). Oxford: Oxford University Press.

Brand, E. (2000). Children's mental musical organisations as highlighted by their singing errors. *Psychology of Music*, 28(1), 62–80.

Brattico, E., & Pearce, M. (2013). The neuroaesthetics of music. *Psychology of Aesthetics, Creativity, and the Arts*, 7(1), 48.

Braun Janzen, T., Thompson, W. F., & Ranvaud, R. (2014). A developmental study of the effect of music training on timed movements. *Frontiers in Human Neuroscience*, 8, 801, DOI: 10.3389/fnhum.2014.00801.

Brodsky, W., & Slor, Z. (2013). Background music as a risk factor for distraction among young-novice drivers. *Accident Analysis & Prevention*, 59, 382–393.

Bronfenbrenner, U. (1979). *The ecology of human development.* Cambridge, MA: Harvard University Press.

Bronfenbrenner, U. (1986). Ecology of the family as a context for human development: Research perspectives. *Developmental Psychology*, 22(6), 723–742.

Bronfenbrenner, U. (2001). Human development, bioecological theory of. In N. J. Smelser & B. Baltes (Eds.), *International encyclopedia of the social and behavioral sciences*. 10–6963.

Bronfenbrenner, U. (2005). *Making human beings human: Bioecological perspectives on human development.* Thousand Oaks, CA: Sage Publications.

Brophy, T. S. (2005). A longitudinal study of selected characteristics of children's melodic improvisations. *Journal of Research in Music Education*, 53(2), 120–133.

Brown, A. R. (2016). Engaging in a sound musicianship. In G. E McPherson (Ed.), *The child as musician: A handbook of musical development* (2nd edition, pp. 208–220). Oxford: Oxford University Press.

Brown, B., & Sellen, A. (2006). Sharing and listening to music. In K. O'Hara & B. Brown (Eds.), *Consuming music together: Social and collaborative aspects of music consumption technologies* (pp. 37–56). London: Springer.

Brown, H., Butler, D., & Jones, M. R. (1994). Musical and temporal influences on key discovery. *Music Perception*, 11, 371–407.

Brown, S. C. (2014). Approaches to digital piracy research: A call for innovation. *Convergence: The International Journal of Research in New Music Technologies*, 20(2), 129–139.

Brown, S. C. (2015). *The psychology of music piracy*. Unpublished Ph.D. thesis, Glasgow Caledonian University.

Brown, W. A., Cammuso, K., Sachs, H., Winklosky, B., Mullane, J., Bernier, R., Svenson, S., Arin, D., Rosen-Sheidley, B., & Folstein, S. E. (2003). Autism-related language, personality, and cognition in people with absolute pitch: Results of a preliminary study. *Journal of Autism and Developmental Disorders*, 33, 163–167.

Bruner, J. S. (1960). *The process of education*. Cambridge, MA: Harvard University Press.

Bruner, J. S. (1966). *Toward a theory of instruction*. Cambridge, MA: Belknapp Press.

Bruner, J. S. (1986). *Actual minds, possible worlds*. Cambridge. MA: Harvard University Press.

Bruner, J. S. (1990). *Acts of meaning*. Cambridge. MA: Harvard University Press.

Bunte, N. (2014). Musical concepts as explanation for children's musical preference in primary school age. In K. Jakubowski, N. Farrugia, G. A. Floridou, & J. Gagen (Eds.), *Proceedings of the 7th International Conference of Students of Systematic Musicology* (SysMus14). London, UK, 18–20 September 2014. www.musicmindbrain.com/#!sysmus-2014/cf, accessed 8 April 2017.

Bunte, N., & Busch, V. (2015). Exploring musical concepts for their relevance to children's music preferences. In J. Ginsborg, A. Lamont, M. Phillips, & S. Bramley (Eds.), *Proceedings of the Ninth Triennial Conference of the European Society for the Cognitive Sciences of Music*, 17–22 August 2015, Manchester, UK.

Bunting, R. (1977). The common language of music, music in the secondary school curriculum. *Working Paper 6*.

Burnard, P. (2006). Children's meaning-making as composers. In I. Deliège & G. A. Wiggins (Eds.), *Musical creativity: Multidisciplinary research in theory and practice* (pp. 111–133). Hove: Psychology Press.

Burnard, P., & Kuo, H.-C. (2016). The individual and social worlds of children's musical creativities. In G. E. McPherson (Ed.), *The child as musician: A handbook of musical development* (pp. 485–499). Oxford: Oxford University Press.

Burnard, P., & Younker, B.A. (2008). Investigating children's musical interactions within the activities systems of group composing and arranging: An application of Engeström's activity theory. *International Journal of Educational Research*, 47(1), 11–26.

Busch, V., Bunte, N., & Schurig, M. (2016). Open-earedness, musical concepts, and gender identity. In O. Krämer & I. Malmberg (Eds.), *European perspectives on music education VI: Open ears – open minds. Listening and understanding music* (pp. 151–165). Innsbruck, Esslingen, Bern-Belp: Helbling.

Byrne, C., MacDonald, R., & Carlton, L. (2003). Assessing creativity in musical compositions: Flow as an assessment tool. *British Journal of Music Education*, 20(3), 277–290.

Campbell, D. (2001). *The Mozart Effect: Tapping the power of music to heal the body, strengthen the mind, and unlock the creative spirit*. London: HarperCollins.

Campbell, D. (2009). *The Mozart Effect for children: Awakening your child's mind, health, and creativity with music*. London: HarperCollins.

Campbell, J. D., Trapnell, P. D., Heine, S. J., Katz, I. M., Lavalle, L. F., & Lehman, D. R. (1996). Self-concept clarity: Measurement, personality correlates, and cultural boundaries. *Journal of Personality and Social Psychology*, 70, 141–156.

Campbell, P. S. (1991). *Lessons from the world: A cross-cultural guide to teaching and learning.* New York; Schirmer.

Campbell, P. S. (2010). *Songs in their heads: Music and its meaning in children's lives* (2nd edition). Oxford: Oxford University Press.

Campbell, P. S. (2011). Musical enculturation: Sociocultural influences and meanings of children's experiences in and through music. In M. S. Barrett (Ed.), *A cultural psychology of music education* (pp. 61–81). Oxford: Oxford University Press.

Campbell, P. S. (2016). Global practices. In G. E. McPherson (Ed.), *The child as musician: A handbook of musical development* (2nd edition, pp. 556–576). Oxford: Oxford University Press.

Capra, F. (1996). *The web of life: A new scientific understanding of living systems.* New York: HarperCollins.

Castano, E., Paladino, M. P., Coull, A., & Yzerbyt, V. Y. (2002). Protecting the ingroup stereotype: Ingroup identification and the management of deviant ingroup members. *British Journal of Social Psychology*, 41, 365–385.

Castell, K. C. (1982). Children's sensitivity to stylistic differences in 'classical' and 'popular' music. *Psychology of Music, Special issue*, 22–25.

Castellano, M. A., Bharucha, J. J., & Krumhansl, C. L. (1984). Tonal hierarchies in the music of North India. *Journal of Experimental Psychology: General*, 113, 394–412.

Chaffin, R., Imreh, G., & Crawford, M. (2002). *Practicing perfection: Memory and piano performance.* New York: Psychology Press.

Chan, T., & Goldthorpe, J. H. (2007). The social stratification of cultural consumption: Some policy implications of a research project. *Cultural Trends*, 16(4), 373–384.

Chancellor, J., Lyubomirsky, S., & Wang, L. (2011). Delivering happiness: Translating positive psychology intervention research for treating major and minor depressive disorders. *Journal of Alternative and Complementary Medicine*, 17(8), 1–9.

Chandler, C. L., & Connell, J. P. (1987). Children's intrinsic, extrinsic and internalized motivation: A developmental study of children's reasons for liked and disliked behaviours. *British Journal of Developmental Psychology*, 5, 357–365.

Chang, H. W., & Trehub, S. E. (1977). Infants' perception of temporal grouping in auditory patterns. *Child Development*, 48, 1666–1670.

Chappell, T. (2011). On the very idea of criteria for personhood. *Southern Journal of Philosophy*, 49(1), 1–27.

Cheetham, T. J., Turner-Cobb, J. M., & Gamble, T. (2016). Children's implicit understanding of the stress-illness link: Testing development of health cognitions. *British Journal of Health Psychology*, 21(4), 781–795.

Chelli, D., & Chanoufi, B. (2008). Audition foetale: Mythe ou réalité? *Journal de Gynécologie Obstétrique et Biologie de la Reproduction*, 37(6), 554–558.

Cheong-Clinch, C. (2009). Music for engaging young people in education. *Youth Studies Australia*, 28(2), 29–57.

Chobart, J., François, C., Velay, J. L., & Besson, M. (2014). Twelve months of active musical training in 8- to 10-year-old children enhances the preattentive processing of syllabic duration and voice onset time. *Cerebral Cortex*, 24, 956–967.

Choi, A.-N., Lee, M. S., & Lee, J.-S. (2010). Group music intervention reduces aggression and improves self-esteem in children with highly aggressive behavior: A pilot controlled trial. *eCAM*, 7(2), 213–217.

Cirelli, L. K., Bosnyak, D., Manning, F. C., Spinelli, C., Marie, C., Fujioka, T., Ghahremani, A., & Trainor, L. J. (2014). Beat-induced fluctuations in auditory cortical beta-band activity: Using EEG to measure age-related changes. *Frontiers in Psychology*, 5(742), DOI: 10.3389/fpsych.2014.00742.

Cirelli, L. K., Einarson, K. M., & Trainor, L. J. (2013). Interpersonal synchrony increases prosocial behavior in infants. *Developmental Science*, 16(6), 1003–1011.

Cirelli, L. K., Spinelli, C., Nozaradan, S., & Trainor, L. J. (2016). Measuring neural entrainment to beat and meter in infants: Effects of musical background. *Frontiers in Neuroscience*, DOI: 10.3389/fnins.2016.00229.

Clarke, E. (1988). Generative principles in music performance. In J. A. Sloboda (Ed.), *Generative processes in music* (pp. 1–26). Oxford: Clarendon Press.

Clarke, E. (1989). Mind the gap: formal structures and psychological processes in music. *Contemporary Music Review*, 3, 1–13.

Clarke, E. (2004). Empirical methods in the study of performance. In E. Clarke & N. Cook (Eds.), *Empirical musicology: Aims, methods, prospects* (pp. 77–102). Oxford: Oxford University Press.

Clarke, E. (2005). *Ways of listening: An ecological approach to the perception of musical meaning.* Oxford: Oxford University Press.

Clarke, E. (2012). Creativity in performance. In D. J. Hargreaves, D. E. Miell, & R. A. R. MacDonald (Eds.), *Musical Imaginations: Multidisciplinary perspectives on creativity, performance and perception* (pp. 17–30). Oxford: Oxford University Press.

Clarke, E., & Cook, N. (Eds.) (2004). *Empirical musicology: Aims, methods, prospects.* Oxford: Oxford University Press.

Clift, S. (2012). Singing, wellbeing, and health. In R. A. R. MacDonald, G. Kreutz, & L. Mitchell (Eds.), *Music, health, & wellbeing* (pp. 113–124). Oxford: Oxford University Press.

Clift, S., & Hancox, G. (2001). The perceived benefits of singing: Findings from preliminary surveys of a university college choral society. *Journal of the Royal Society for the Promotion of Health*, 121(4), 248–256.

Clift, S., Hancox, G., Morrison, I., Hess, B., Kreutz, G., & Stewart, D. (2010). Choral singing and psychological wellbeing: Quantitative and qualitative findings from English choirs in a cross-national survey. *Journal of Applied Arts and Health*, 1(1), 19–34.

Clift, S., Nicol, J., Raisbeck, M., Whitmore, C., & Morrison, I. (2010). *Group singing, wellbeing and health: A systematic mapping of research evidence.* Kent: Sidney De Haan Research Centre for Arts and Health, Canterbury Christ Church University.

Cole, M. (1996). *Cultural psychology: A once and future discipline.* Cambridge, MA: Harvard University Press.

Coleman, J. C., & Hagell, A. (Eds.) (2007). *Adolescence: Risk and resilience.* Chichester: John Wiley.

Coleman, J. C., & Hendry, L. B. (1999). *The nature of adolescence* (3rd edition). London: Routledge.

Colwell, R., & Abrahams, F. (1991). Edwin Gordon's contribution: An appraisal. *The Quarterly Journal of Music Teaching and Learning*, 2(1/2), 19–36.

Connell, J. P. (1990). Context, self, and action: A motivational analysis of self-system processes across the life span. In D. Cicchetti (Ed.), *The self in transition: Infancy to adulthood* (pp. 61–97). Chicago, IL: University of Chicago Press.

Conrad, N. J., Walsh, J., Allen, J. M., & Tsang, C. D. (2011). Examining infants' preferences for tempo in lullabies and playsongs. *Canadian Journal of Experimental Psychology*, 65(3), 168–172.

Conway, C. M., Pisoni, D. B., & Kronenberger, W. G. (2009). The importance of sound for cognitive sequencing abilities: The auditory scaffolding hypothesis. *Current Directions in Psychological Science*, 18(5), 275–279.

Cook, N. (1987). The perception of large-scale tonal closure. *Music Perception*, 5(2), 197–206.

Cook, N. (1998). *Music: A very short introduction*. Oxford: Oxford University Press.

Cooper, R. P., & Aslin, R.N. (1990). Preference for infant-directed speech in the first month after birth. *Child Development*, 61, 1584–1595.

Corrigall, K. A., & Trainor, L. J. (2009). Effects of musical training on key and harmony perception. *The Neurosciences and Music III: Disorders and Plasticity: Annals of the New York Academy of Sciences*, 1169, 164–168.

Corrigall, K. A., & Trainor, L. J. (2010). Musical enculturation in preschool children: Acquisition of key and harmonic knowledge. *Music Perception*, 28(2), 195–200.

Corrigall, K. A., & Trainor, L. J. (2014). Enculturation to musical pitch structure in young children: Evidence from behavioural and electrophysiological methods. *Developmental Science*, 17(1), 142–158.

Costa, P. T. Jr., & McCrae, R. R. (1985). *The NEO Personality Inventory*. Odessa, FL: Psychological Assessment Resources.

Costa-Giomi, E. (1999). The effects of three years of piano instruction on children's cognitive development. *Journal of Research in Music Education*, 47, 198–212.

Costa-Giomi, E. (2004). Effects of three years of piano instruction on children's academic achievement, school performance and self-esteem. *Psychology of Music*, 32(2), 139–152.

Costa-Giomi, E., & Descombes, V. (1996). Pitch labels with single and multiple meanings: A study with French-speaking children. *Journal of Research in Music Education*, 44(3), 204–214.

Costa-Giomi, E., & Ilari, B. (2014). Infants' preferential attention to sung and spoken stimuli. *Journal of Research in Music Education*, 62(2), 188–194.

Coulton, S., Clift, S., Skingley, A., & Rodriguez, J. (2015). Effectiveness and cost-effectiveness of community singing on mental health-related quality of life of older people: Randomised controlled trial. *The British Journal of Psychiatry*, 206, 1–6.

Cox, G., Crickmore, L., Plummeridge, C., & Sergeant, D. (2012). SEMPRE: Forty years on. *Psychology of Music*, 40(5), 523–538.

Crafts, S. D., Cavicchi, D., Keil, C., and the Music in Daily Life Project (1993). *My Music*. Hanover, NH: Wesleyan University Press /University Press of New England.

Creech, A., & Hallam, S. (2003). Parent-teacher-pupil interactions in instrumental music tuition: A literature review. *British Journal of Music Education*, 20, 29–44.

Creech, A., Hallam, S., Varvarigou, M., & McQueen, H. (2014a). *Active ageing with music: Supporting wellbeing in the third and fourth ages*. Institute of Education, London.

Creech, A., Hallam, S., Varvarigou, M., Gaunt, H., McQueen, H., & Pincas, A. (2014b). The role of musical possible selves in supporting subjective well-being in later life. *Music Education Research*, 16, 32–49.

Creel, S. C. (2016). Ups and downs in auditory development: Preschoolers' sensitivity to pitch contour and timbre. *Cognitive Science*, 40(2), 373–403.

Crisp, R. J., Stone, C. H., & Hall, N. R. (2006). Recategorization and subgroup identification: Predicting and preventing threats from common ingroups. *Personality and Social Psychology Bulletin*, 32(2), 230–243.

Črnčec, R., Wilson, S. J., & Prior, M. (2006). No evidence for the Mozart effect in children. *Music Perception*, 23(4), 305–317.

Croom, A. M. (2015). Music practice and participation for psychological well-being: A review of how music influences positive emotion, engagement, relationships, meaning, and accomplishment. *Musicae Scientiae*, 19(1), 44–64.

Crow, G., & Allan, G. (1994). *Community life*. Hemel Hempstead: Harvester Wheatsheaf.

Crowne, D. P., & Marlowe, D. (1960). A new scale of social desirability independent of psychopathology. *Journal of Consulting Psychology*, 24, 349–354.

Crozier, J. (1997). Absolute pitch: Practice makes perfect, the earlier the better. *Psychology of Music*, 25(2), 110–119.

Csikszentmihalyi, M. (1990). *Flow: The psychology of optimal experience*. New York: Harper and Row.

Csikszentmihalyi, M. (2002). *Flow: The classic work on how to achieve happiness*. London: Rider.

Csikszentmihalyi, M., & Csikszentmihalyi, I. S. (1988). *Optimal experience*. Cambridge: Cambridge University Press.

Csikszentmihalyi, M., & Lefèvre, J. (1989). Optimal experience in work and leisure. *Journal of Personality and Social Psychology*, 56(5), 815–822.

Csikszentmihalyi, M., & Rochberg-Halton, E. (1981). *The meaning of things: Domestic symbols and the self*. Cambridge: Cambridge University Press.

Cuddy, L. L., & Badertscher, B. D. (1987). Recovery of the tonal hierarchy: Some comparisons across age and levels of musical experience. *Perception and Psychophysics*, 41, 609–620.

Cunningham, J. G., & Sterling, R. S. (1988). Developmental change in the understanding of affective meaning in music. *Motivation and Emotion*, 12, 399–413.

Custodero, L. A. (2005). Observable indicators of flow experience: A developmental perspective on musical engagement in young children from infancy to school age. *Music Education Research*, 7(2), 185–209.

Custodero, L. A. (2006). Singing practices in 10 families with young children. *Journal of Research in Music Education*, 54(1), 37–56.

Custodero, L. A., Britto, P. R., & Xin, T. (2002). From Mozart to Motown, lullabies to love songs: A preliminary report on the Parents' Use of Music with Infants Survey (PUMIS). *Zero to Three*, 23(1), 41–46.

Custodero, L. A., Calì, C., & Diaz-Donoso, A. (2016). Music as transitional object and practice: Children's spontaneous musical behaviors in the subway. *Research Studies in Music Education*, 38(1), 55–74.

Dalla Bella, S., Peretz, I., Rousseau, L., & Gosselin, N. (2001). A developmental study of the affective value of tempo and mode in music. *Cognition*, 80(3), B1–B10.

Davidson, C. W., & Powell, L. A. (1986). The effects of easy-listening background music on the on-task-performance of fifth-grade children. *The Journal of Educational Research*, 80(1), 29–33.

Davidson, J. W. (2004). Music as social behavior. In E. Clarke & N. Cook (Eds.), *Empirical musicology: Aims, methods, prospects* (pp. 57–75). Oxford: Oxford University Press.

Davidson, J. W. (2011). Musical participation: Expectations, experiences, and outcomes. In I. Deliège & J. W. Davidson (Eds.), *Music and the mind: Essays in honour of John Sloboda* (pp. 65–87). Oxford: Oxford University Press.

Davidson, J. W., & Burland, K. (2006). Musician identity formation. In G. E. McPherson (Ed.), *The child as musician: A handbook of musical development* (pp. 475–490). Oxford: Oxford University Press.

Davidson, J. W., & Faulkner, R. (2013). Music in our lives. In S. B. Kaufmann (Ed.), *Beyond 'talent or practice?': The multiple determinants of greatness* (pp. 367–390). Oxford: Oxford University Press.

Davidson, J. W., & Fedele, J. (2011). Investigating group singing activity with people with dementia and their caregivers: Problems and positive prospects. *Musicae Scientiae*, 15(3), 402–422.

Davidson, J. W., Howe, M. J. A., Moore, D. M., & Sloboda, J. A. (1996). The role of parental influences in the development of musical ability. *British Journal of Developmental Psychology*, 14, 399–412.

Davidson, J. W., Moore, D. G., Howe, M. J. A., & Sloboda, J. A. (1998). Characteristics of music teachers and the progress of young instrumentalists. *Journal of Research in Music Education*, 46,141–160.

Davidson, L. (1985). Tonal structures of children's early songs. *Music Perception*, 2(3), 361–373.

Davidson, L. (1994). Songsinging by young and old: A developmental approach to music. In R. Aiello with J. A. Sloboda (Eds.), *Musical perceptions*, pp. 99–130. Oxford: Oxford University Press.

Davidson, L., & Scripp, L. (1988). Young children's musical representations: Windows on music cognition. In J. A. Sloboda (Ed.), *Generative processes in music: The psychology of performance, improvisation, and composition* (pp. 195–230). Oxford: Clarendon Press.

Davidson, L., & Scripp. L. (1989). Education and developmental in music from a cognitive perspective. In D. J. Hargreaves (Ed.), *Children and the arts* (pp. 59–86). Milton Keynes: Open University Press.

Davidson, L., McKernon, P., & Gardner, H. (1981). The acquisition of song: A developmental approach. In *Documentary report of the Ann Arbor symposium on the applications of psychology to the teaching and learning of music* (pp. 301–315). Reston, VA: Music Educators National Council (MENC).

Davies, C. (1992). Listen to my song: A study of songs invented by children aged 5 to 7 years. *British Journal of Music Education*, 9(1), 19–48.

Davies, J. B. (1978). *The psychology of music*. London: Hutchinson.

Davies, J. B. (1994). Seeds of a false consciousness. In Peer Commentary Issue: Is everyone musical? *The Psychologist*, 7(8), 355–356.

Davis, J., & Gardner, H. (1992). The cognitive revolution: Consequences for the understanding and education of the child as artist. In B. Reimer & R. A. Smith (Eds.), *The arts, education, and aesthetic knowing* (vol. 2, pp. 92–123). Chicago, IL: The National Society for the Study of Education.

Davis, S. (2016). Children, popular music, and identity. In G. E. McPherson (Ed.), *The child as musician: A handbook of musical development* (2nd edition, pp. 265–283). Oxford: Oxford University Press.

De Boise, S. (2016). Post-Bourdieusian moments and methods in music sociology: Toward a critical, practice-based approach. *Cultural Sociology*, 10(2), 178–194.

De Vries, P. (2009). Music at home with the under fives: What is happening? *Early Child Development and Care*, 179(4), 395–405.

DeCasper, A. J., & Fifer, W. P. (1980). Of human bonding: Newborns prefer their mother's voice. *Science*, 208, 1174–1176.

DeCasper, A. J., Granier-Deferre, C., Fifer, W. P., & Moon, C. M. (2011). Measuring fetal cognitive development: When methods and conclusions don't match. *Developmental Science*, 14(2), 224–225.

DeCasper, A. J., Lecanuet, J.-P., Maugeais, R., Granier-Deferre, C., & Busnel, M.-C. (1994). Fetal reactions to recurrent maternal speech. *Infant Behavior & Development*, 17, 159–164.

Deci, E. L., & Ryan, R. M. (2002). *Handbook of self-determination research*. Rochester: University of Rochester Press.

Deffler, S. A., & Halpern, A. R. (2011). Contextual information and memory for unfamiliar tunes in older and younger adults. *Psychology and Aging*, 26(4), 900–904.

Delalande, F. (Ed.) (2009). *La nascita della musica. Esplorazioni sonore nella prima infanzia.* Milano: Franco Angeli.

Delsing, M. J. M. H., ter Bogt, T. F. M., Engels, R. C. M. E., & Meeus, W. H. J. (2008). Adolescents' music preferences and personality characteristics. *European Journal of Personality*, 22, 109–130.

Demorest, S. M., & Pfordresher, P. Q. (2015). Singing accuracy development from K–adult: A comparative study. *Music Perception*, 32(3), 293–302.

Dennis, M. (1980). Capacity and strategy for syntactic comprehension after left or right hemidecortication. *Brain and Language*, 10, 287–317.

DeNora, T. (2000). *Music in everyday life.* Cambridge: Cambridge University Press.

DeNora, T. (2001). Aesthetic agency and musical practice: New directions in the sociology of music. In P. N. Juslin & J. A. Sloboda (Eds.), *Music and emotion: Theory and research* (pp. 161–180). Oxford: Oxford University Press.

DeNora, T. (2017). Music-ecology and everyday action: Creating, changing and contesting identities. In R. A. R. MacDonald, D. J. Hargreaves, & D. E. Miell (Eds.), *Handbook of musical identities* (pp. 46–62). Oxford: Oxford University Press.

Department for Education (DfE) (2011). *The importance of music: A national plan for music education.* London: DfE.

Department for Education and Science (DfES) (2004). *The music manifesto.* www.music-manifesto.co.uk/

Deutsch, D. (Ed.). (1982). *The psychology of music.* New York: Academic Press.

Deutsch, D. (Ed.). (1999). *The psychology of music* (2nd edition). New York: Academic Press.

Deutsch, D. (Ed.). (2013). *The psychology of music* (3rd edition). New York: Academic Press.

Deutsch, D., & Dooley, K. (2013). Absolute pitch is associated with a large auditory digit span: A clue to its genesis (L). *Journal of the Acoustical Society of America*, 133(4), 1859–1891.

Di Benedetto, P., Cavazzon, M., Mondolo, F., Rugiu, G., Peratoner, A., & Biasutti, E. (2009). Voice and choral singing treatment: A new approach for speech and voice disorders in Parkinson's disease. *European Journal of Physical and Rehabilitation Medicine*, 45(1), 13–19.

Diener, E., & Chan, M. (2011). Happy people live longer: Subjective well-being contributes to health and longevity. *Applied Psychology: Health and Wellbeing*, 3(1), 1–43.

DiMaggio, P., & Useem, M. (1978). Social class and arts consumption: The origins and consequences of class differences in exposure to the arts in America. *Theory and Society*, 5, 141–161.

Dingle, G. A., Brander, C., Ballantyne, J., & Baker, F. A. (2013). 'To be heard': The social and mental health benefits of choir singing for disadvantaged adults. *Psychology of Music*, 41(4), 405–421.

Dissanayake, E. (2000). Antecedents of the temporal arts in early mother-infant interaction. In N. K. Wallin, B. Merker, & S. Brown (Eds.), *The origins of music* (pp. 389–410). Cambridge, MA: MIT Press.

Doiron, B. A. H., Lehnhard, R. A., Butterfield, S. A., & Whitesides, J. F. (1999). Betaendorphin response to high intensity exercise and music in college-age women. *Journal of Strength and Conditioning Research*, 13, 24–28.

Dowling, W. J., Bartlett, J. C., Halpern, A. R., & Andrews, M. W. (2008). Melody recognition at fast and slow tempos: Effects of age, experience, and familiarity. *Perception & Psychophysics*, 70(3), 496–502.

Drake, C. (1993). Influence of age and experience on timing and intensity variations in the reproduction of short musical rhythms. *Psychological Belgica*, 33, 217–228.

Drake, C., Jones, M. R., & Baruch, C. (2000). The development of rhythmic attending in auditory sequences: attunement, reference period, focal attending. *Cognition*, 77, 251–288.

Drayton, S., Turley-Ames, K. J., & Guajardo, N. R. (2011). Counterfactual thinking and false belief: The role of executive function. *Journal of Experimental Child Psychology*, 108(3), 523–548.

Duba, J. D., & Roseman, C. (2012). Musical 'Tune-Ups' for couples: Brief treatment interventions. *The Family Journal: Counseling and Therapy for Couples and Families*, 20(3), 322–326.

Duffey, T., Somody, C., & Clifford, S. (2008). Conversations with my father: Adapting *A Musical Chronology* and *The Emerging Life Song* with older adults. *Journal of Creativity in Mental Health*, 2(4), 45–63.

Duffey, T., Somody, C., & Eckstein, D. (2009). Musical relationship metaphors: Using *A Musical Chronology* and *The Emerging Life Song* with couples. *The Family Journal: Counseling and Therapy for Couples and Families*, 17(2), 151–155.

Dunn, K., Reissland, N., & Reid, V. M. (2015). The functional foetal brain: A systematic preview of methodological factors in reporting foetal visual and auditory capacity. *Developmental Cognitive Neuroscience*, 13, 43–52.

Dweck, C. S. (2000). *Self-theories: Their role in motivation, personality and development*. Philadelphia, PA: Psychology Press.

Dys, S. P., Schellenberg, E. G., & McLean, K. C. (2017). Musical identities, music preferences, and individual differences. In R. A. R. MacDonald, D. J. Hargreaves, & D. E. Miell (Eds.), *Handbook of musical identities* (pp. 247–266). Oxford: Oxford University Press.

Eccles, J. S., Wigfield, A., & Schiefele, U. (1998). Motivation to succeed. In N. Eisenberg (Ed.), *Handbook of child psychology: Volume 3. Social, emotional and personality development* (5th edition) (pp. 1017–1095). New York: Wiley.

Eccles, J., Adler, T. F., Futterman, R., Goff, S. B., Kaczala, C. M., Meece, J. L., & Midgley, C. (1983). Expectancy, values, and academic behaviours. In J. T. Spence (Ed.), *Achievement and achievement motives: Psychological and sociological motives* (pp. 75–146). San Francisco: Freeman.

Einarson, K. M., & Trainor, L. J. (2015). The effect of visual information on young children's perceptual sensitivity to musical beat alignment. *Timing & Time Perception*, 3(1–2), 88–101.

Einarson, K. M., & Trainor, L. J. (2016). Hearing the beat: Young children's perceptual sensitivity to beat alignment varies according to metric structure. *Music Perception*, 34(1), 56–70.

Eitan, Z., & Timmers, R. (2010). Beethoven's last piano sonata and those who follow crocodiles: Cross-domain mappings of auditory pitch in a musical context. *Cognition*, 114, 405–422.

El Haj, M., Postal, V., & Allain, P. (2012). Music enhances autobiographical memory in mild Alzheimer's disease. *Educational Gerontology*, 38, 30–41.

Elder, G. H., & Giele, J. Z. (2009). *The craft of life course research*. New York: Guilford Press.

Elliott, D. J., & Silverman, M. (2015). *Music matters: A philosophy of music education* (2nd edition). New York: Oxford University Press.

Elliott, D. J., & Silverman, M. (2017). Identities and musics: Reclaiming personhood. In R. A. R. MacDonald, D. J. Hargreaves, & D. E. Miell (Eds.), *Handbook of musical identities* (pp. 27–45). Oxford: Oxford University Press.

Elpus, K. (2017). Music education promotes lifelong engagement with the arts. *Psychology of Music*. Online First, DOI: 10.1177/0305735617697508.

Elvers, P., Omigie, D., Fuhrmann, W., & Fischinger, T. (2015). Exploring the musical taste of expert listeners: musicology students reveal tendency toward omnivorous taste. *Frontiers in Psychology*, 6. DOI: 10.3389/fpsyg.2015.01252.

Engeström, Y. (1987). *Learning by expanding: An activity theoretical approach to developmental research*. Helsinki: Orienta-Konsultit Oy.

Engeström, Y. (2001). Expansive learning at work: Toward an activity theory reconceptualisation. *Journal of Education and Work*, 14, 133–161.

Engeström, Y., & Miettinen, R. (1999). Introduction, and activity theory and individual and social transformation. In Y. Engeström, R. Miettinen, & R. L. Punamäki (Eds.), *Perspectives on activity theory*. Cambridge: Cambridge University Press.

Ericsson, K. A., & Smith, J. (Eds.) (1991). *Toward a general theory of expertise: Prospects and limits*. New York: Cambridge University Press.

Ericsson, K. A., Krampe, R., & Tesch-Römer, C. (1993). The role of deliberate practice in the acquisition of expert performance. *Psychological Review*, 100, 363–406.

Erikson, E. H. (1950). *Childhood and society*. New York: Norton.

Erikson, E. H. (1968). *Identity, youth, and crisis*. New York: Norton.

Erikson, E. H. (1982). *The life cycle completed: A review*. New York: W. W. Norton & Company, Inc.

Eriksson, H., Harmat, L., Theorell, T., & Ullén, F. (2016). Similar but different: Interviewing monozygotic twins discordant for musical practice. *Musicae Scientiae*, Online First, DOI: 10.1177/1029864916649791.

Evans, P. (2015). Self-determination theory: An approach to motivation in music education. *Musicae Scientiae*, 19(1), 65–83.

Evans, P. (2016). Motivation. In G. E McPherson (Ed.), *The child as musician: A handbook of musical development* (2nd edition, pp. 325–339). Oxford: Oxford University Press.

Evans, P., & Bonneville-Roussy, A. (2016). Self-determined motivation for practice in university music students. *Psychology of Music*, 44(5), 1095–1110.

Evans, P., & McPherson, G. E. (2017). Processes of musical identity consolidation during adolescence. In R. A. R. MacDonald, D. J. Hargreaves, & D. E. Miell (Eds.), *Handbook of musical identities* (pp. 213–231). Oxford: Oxford University Press.

Evans, P., McPherson, G. E., & Davidson, J. W. (2013). The role of psychological needs in ceasing music and music learning activities. *Psychology of Music*, 41(5), 598–617.

Everett, W. (2001). *The Beatles as musicians: The quarry men through rubber soul*. New York: Oxford University Press.

Eysenck, M. W. (Ed.) (1998). *Psychology: An integrated approach*. Harlow, Essex: Addison-Wesley-Longman.

Fagen, J., Prigot, J., Carroll, M., Pioli, L., Stein, A., & Franco, A. (1997). Auditory context and memory retrieval in young infants. *Child Development*, 68(6), 1057–1066.

Fancourt, D. (2016). An introduction to the psychoneuroimmunology of music: History, future collaboration and a research agenda. *Psychology of Music*, 44(2), 168–182.

Fancourt, D., Ockelford, A., & Abebech Belai, A. (2014). The psychoneuroimmunological effects of music: A systematic review and a new model. *Brain, Behavior and Immunity*, 36, 15–26.

Fancourt, D., Williamon, A., Carvalho, L. A., Steptoe, A., Dow, R., & Lewis, I. (2016). Singing modulates mood, stress, cortisol, cytokine and neuropeptide activity in cancer patients and carers. *eCancer*, 10, 631, DOI: 10.3332/ecancer.2016.631.

Farnsworth, P. R. (1954). *The social psychology of music*. Ames: Iowa State University Press.

Farnsworth, P. R. (1969). *The social psychology of music* (2nd edition). Ames: Iowa State University Press.

Farrell, G. (2001). India. In D. J. Hargreaves & A. C. North (Eds.), *Musical development and learning: The international perspective* (pp. 56–72). London: Continuum.

Faulkner, R., & Davidson, J. W. (2004). Men's vocal behaviour and the construction of self. *Musicae Scientiae*, 8(2), 231–255.

Feldman, D. H. with Goldsmith, L. T. (1986). *Nature's gambit: Child prodigies and the development of human potential*. New York: Basic Books.

Fenigstein, A., Scheier, M. F., & Buss, A. H. (1975). Public and private self-consciousness: Assessment and theory. *Journal of Consulting and Clinical Psychology*, 43, 522–527.

Finnegan, R. (1989). *The hidden musicians: Music-making in an English town*. Cambridge: Cambridge University Press.

Fishbein, M., & Ajzen, I. (1975). *Belief, attitude, intention, and behavior: An introduction to theory and research*. Reading: Addison-Wesley.

Flavell, J. H. (1977). *Cognitive development*. Englewood Cliffs, NJ: Prentice-Hall.

Flavell, J. H. (1979). Metacognition and cognitive monitoring. *American Psychologist*, 34(10), 906–911.

Flecha, R. (2000). *Sharing words: Theory and practice of dialogic learning*. Lanham, MD: Rowman & Littlefield.

Flohr, J. (1985). Young children's improvisations: Emerging creative thought. *Creative Child and Adult Quarterly*, 10, 79–85.

Flom, R., Gentile, D. A., & Pick, A. D. (2008). Infants' discrimination of happy and sad music. *Infant Behavior and Development*, 31, 716–728.

Folkestad, G. (2002). National identity and music. In R. A. R. MacDonald, D. J. Hargreaves, & D. Miell (Eds.), *Musical identities* (pp. 151–162). Oxford: Oxford University Press.

Folkestad, G. (2005). Here, there and everywhere: Music education research in a globalised world. *Music Education Research*, 7, 279–287.

Folkestad, G. (2006). Formal and informal learning situations or practices vs. formal and informal ways of learning. *British Journal of Music Education*, 23, 135–145.

Folkestad, G. (2012). Digital tools and discourse in music: The ecology of composition. In D. J. Hargreaves, D. E Miell, & R. A. R. MacDonald (Eds.), *Musical imaginations* (pp. 193–205). Oxford: Oxford University Press.

Folkestad, G., Lindström, B., & Hargreaves, D. J. (1997). Young people's music in the digital age. *Research Studies in Music Education*, 9, 1–12.

Folkestad, G., Hargreaves, D. J., & Lindström, B. (1998). Compositional strategies in computer-based music-making. *British Journal of Music Education*, 15(1), 83–98.

Fox, W. S., & Wince, M. H. (1975). Musical taste cultures and taste publics. *Youth and Society*, 7, 198–224.

Franco, F., Chew, M., & Swaine, J. (2017). Preschoolers' attribution of affect to music: A comparison between vocal and instrumental performance. *Psychology of Music*, 45(1), 131–149.

Frankl, V. E. (2004). *Man's search for meaning: The classic tribute to hope from the Holocaust*. New York: Rider.

Fredrickson, B. L. (2001). The role of positive emotions in positive psychology: The broaden and build theory of positive emotions. *American Psychologist*, 56(3), 218–226.

Freeston, M. H., Rhéaume, J., Letarte, H., Dugas, M. J., & Ladouceur, R. (1994). Why do people worry? *Journal of Personality and Individual Differences*, 17, 791–802.

Freire, P. (1973). *Education for critical consciousness*. New York: Continuum.

Frith, S. (1978). *The sociology of rock*. London: Constable.

Frith, S. (1981). *Sound effects: Youth, leisure, and the politics of rock 'n' roll*. New York: Pantheon.

Frith, S. (1990). *Facing the music: Essays on pop, rock and culture*. London: Mandarin.

Frith, S. (1996). *Performing rites*. Oxford: Oxford University Press.

Fritz, B. S., & Avsec, A. (2007). The experience of flow and subjective well-being of music students. *Horizons of Psychology*, 16, 5–17.

Fung, C. V., & Gromko, J. E. (2001). Effects of active *versus* passive listening on the quality of children's invented notations and preferences for two pieces from an unfamiliar culture. *Psychology of Music*, 29(2), 128–138.

Furnham, A., & Bradley, A. (1997). Music while you work: The differential distraction of background music on the cognitive test performance of introverts and extraverts. *Applied Cognitive Psychology*, 11, 445–455.

Gabrielsson, A. (2010). Strong experiences with music. In P. N. Juslin & J. A. Sloboda (Eds.), *Handbook of music and emotion: Theory, research, applications* (pp. 547–574). Oxford: Oxford University Press.

Gabrielsson, A. (2011). *Strong experiences with music: Music is much more than just music*. Oxford: Oxford University Press (translation of Gabrielsson, A., 2008, *Starka musikupplevelser – Musik är mycket mer än bara music*, Hedemora: Gidlunds).

Gaertner, S. L., Dovidio, J. F., Anastasio, P. A., Bachman, B. A., & Rust, M. C. (1993). The common ingroup identity model: Recategorization and the reduction of intergroup bias. In W. Stroebe & M. Hewstone (Eds.), *The European Review of Social Psychology* (vol. 4, pp. 1–26). Chichester: Wiley.

Gagné, F. (2009). Building gifts into talents: Detailed overview of the DMGT 2.0. In B. MacFarlane & T. Stambaugh (Eds.), *Leading change in gifted education: The Festschrift of Dr Joyce Van Tassel–Basca* (pp. 61–80). Waco, TX: Prufrock Press.

Gall, M., & Breeze, N. (2008). Music and eJay: An opportunity for creative collaborations in the classroom. *International Journal of Educational Research*, 47(1), 27–40.

Galvin III, J. J., Fu, Q.-J., & Oba, S. (2008). Effect of instrument timbre on melodic contour identification by cochlear implant users. *Journal of the Acoustical Society of America*, 124(4), EL189–EL195.

Gans, H. J. (1974). *Popular culture and high culture: An analysis and evaluation of taste*. New York: Basic Books.

Garber, J., & Seligman, M. E. P. (1980). *Human helpnessness: Theory and applications*. Cambridge: Cambridge University Press.

Garcia, R. L., & Hand, C. J. (2016). Analgesic effects of self-chosen music type on cold pressor-induced pain: Motivating vs. relaxing music. *Psychology of Music*, 44(5), 967–983.

Gardiner, M. F., Fox, A., Knowles, F., & Jeffrey, D. (1996). Learning improved by arts training. *Nature*, 381(6580), 284.

Gardner, H. (1970). Children's sensitivity to painting styles. *Child Development*, 41, 813–821.

Gardner, H. (1973a). Children's sensitivity to musical styles. *Merrill-Palmer Quarterly*, 19, 67–77.

Gardner, H. (1973b). *The arts and human development*. New York: John Wiley.

Gardner, H. (1979). Development psychology after Piaget: An approach in terms of symbolisation. *Human Development*, 22, 73–88.

Gardner, H. (1983). *Frames of mind: The theory of multiple intelligences*. New York: Basic Books.

Gardner, H. (1987). *The mind's new science: A history of the cognitive revolution*. New York: Basic Books.

Gardner, H. (1989). Zero-based arts education: An introduction to Arts Propel. *Studies in Art Education*, 30, 71–83.

Gardner, H. (1993). *Multiple intelligences: The theory in practice*. New York: Basic Books.

Gardner, H. (1999). *Intelligence reframed: Multiple intelligences for the 21st century.* New York: Basic Books.

Gardner, H. (2003). *MI after 20 years.* Paper presented at the American Educational Research Association, Chicago.

Gardner. H., & Gardner, J. (1971). Children's literary skills. *Journal of Experimental Education,* 39, 42–46.

Gaser, C., & Schlaug, G. (2003). Brain structures differ between musicians and non-musicians. *The Journal of Neuroscience,* 23(27), 9240–9245.

Gaunt, H., & Westerlund, H. (Eds.) (2013). *Collaborative learning in higher music education.* Abingdon: Ashgate.

Gembris, H. (2012). Music-making as a lifelong development and resource for health. In R. A. R. MacDonald, G. Kreutz, & L. Mitchell (Eds.), *Music, health, and wellbeing* (pp. 367–382). Oxford: Oxford University Press.

Gembris, H., & Schellberg, G. (2003). *Musical preferences of elementary school children* (p. 324). Abstracts of the 5th ESCOM conference, University of Hanover, Germany.

Gentile, D. (1998). *Infants' discrimination of musical affective expressiveness.* Unpublished doctoral dissertation. University of Minnesota.

Gergen, K. J., & Davis, K. E. (1985). *The social construction of the person.* New York: Springer-Verlag.

Gerry, D. W., Faux, A. L., & Trainor, L. J. (2010). Effects of Kindermusik training on infants' rhythmic enculturation. *Developmental Science,* 13(3), 545–551.

Gerry, D. W., Unrau, A., & Trainor, L. J. (2012). Active music classes in infancy enhance musical, communicative and social development. *Developmental Science,* 15(3), 398–407.

Gerson, S. A., Schiavio, A., Timmers, R., & Hunnius, S. (2015). Active drumming experience increases infants' sensitivity to audiovisual synchrony during observed drumming actions. *PLoS One,* 10(6), e0130960, DOI: 10.1371/journal.pone.0130960.

Getz, L., Marks, S., & Roy, M. (2014). The influence of stress, optimism, and music training on music uses and preferences. *Psychology of Music,* 42(1), 71–85.

Ghiselin, B. (Ed.) (1952). *The creative process.* Cambridge: Cambridge University Press.

Gibson, E. J. (1969). *Principles of perceptual learning and development.* New York: Appleton-Century-Crofts.

Gibson, J. J. (1966). *The senses considered as perceptual systems.* Boston: Houghton Mifflin.

Gibson, J. J. (1979/2015). *The ecological approach to visual perception.* New York: Psychology Press.

Giddens, A. (1991). *Modernity and self-identity: Self and society in the late modern age.* Cambridge: Polity Press.

Gilder, E., & Port, J. G. (1978). *The dictionary of composers and their music.* New York: Ballantine.

Giles, D. C., Pietrzykowski, S., & Clark, K. E. (2007). The psychological meaning of personal record collections and the impact of changing technological forms. *Journal of Economic Psychology,* 28, 429–443.

Gillham, J. E., Jaycox, L. H., Reivich, K. J., Seligman, M. E. P., & Silver, T. (1990). *The Penn Resiliency Program.* Philadelphia, PA: University of Pennsylvania.

Glover, J. (2000). *Children composing 4–14.* London: Routledge.

Gogate, L. J., Walker-Andrews, A. S., & Bahrick, L. E. (2001). The intersensory origins of word comprehension: An ecological-dynamic systems view. *Developmental Science,* 4, 1–18.

Goldman, S. L., Whitney-Saltiel, D., Granger, J., & Rodin, J. (1991). Children's representations of 'everyday' aspects of health and illness. *Journal of Pediatric Psychology,* 16, 747–766.

Gordon, E. E. (1965). *Musical aptitude profile*. Boston, MA: Houghton Mifflin.

Gordon, E. E. (1976). *Learning sequence and patterns in music*. Buffalo, NY: Tometic Associates Ltd.

Gordon, E. E. (1997). *A music learning theory for newborn and young children*. Chicago, IL: GIA Publications, Inc.

Gordon, E. E. (2007). *Learning sequences in music: A contemporary music learning theory, 2007 edition*. Chicago, IL: GIA publications, Inc.

Goswami, U. (2008). *Cognitive development: The learning brain*. Hove: Psychology Press.

Goswami, U., & Bryant, P. E. (2010). Children's cognitive development and learning. In R. J. Alexander, C. Doddington, J. Gray, L. Hargreaves, & R. Kershner (Eds.), *The Cambridge primary review research surveys* (pp. 141–169). London: Routledge.

Gould, S. J. (1985). *Ontogeny and phylogeny*. Boston, MA: Belknap Press.

Granier-Deferre, C., Bassereau, S., Ribeiro, A., Jacquet, A. -Y., & DeCasper, A. J. (2011) A melodic contour repeatedly experienced by human near-term fetuses elicits a profound cardiac reaction one month after birth. *PLoS ONE*, 6(2): e17304, DOI: 10.1371/journal.pone.0017304.

Grape, C., Wikström, B.-M., Ekman, R., Hasson, D., & Theorell, T. (2010). Comparison between choir singing and group discussion in irritable bowel syndrome patients over one year: Saliva testosterone increases in new choir singers. *Psychotherapy and Psychosomatics*, 79, 196–198.

Greasley, A. E. (2008). *Engagement with music in everyday life: An in-depth study of adults' musical preferences and listening behaviours*. Unpublished PhD thesis, Keele University.

Greasley, A. E., & Lamont, A. (2011). Exploring engagement with music in everyday life using experience sampling methodology, *Musicae Scientiae*, 15(1), 45–71.

Greasley, A. E., & Lamont, A. (2013). Keeping it fresh: How listeners regulate their own exposure to familiar music. In E. King & H. Prior (Eds.), *Music and familiarity: Listening, musicology and performance* (pp. 13–31). Basingstoke: Ashgate.

Greasley, A. E., & Lamont, A. (2016). Musical preferences. In S. Hallam, I. Cross, & M. Thaut (Eds.), *The Oxford handbook of music psychology* (2nd edition, pp. 263–281). Oxford: Oxford University Press.

Greasley, A. E., Lamont, A., & Sloboda, J. A. (2013). Exploring musical preferences: An in-depth study of adults' liking for music in their personal collections. *Qualitative Research in Psychology*, 10(4), 402–427.

Green, L. (2002). *How popular musicians learn: A way ahead for music education*. Aldershot: Ashgate.

Green, L. (2005). *Meaning, autonomy and authenticity in the music classroom: Professorial lecture*. Institute of Education, University of London.

Green, L. (2008). *Music, informal learning and the school: A new classroom pedagogy*. Aldershot: Ashgate.

Greenberg, D. M., & Rentfrow, P. J. (2017). The psychological underpinnings and manifestations of musical identities. In R. A. R. MacDonald, D. J. Hargreaves, & D. E. Miell (Eds.), *Handbook of musical identities* (pp. 304–321). Oxford: Oxford University Press.

Gregory, A. H. (1997). The roles of music in society: The ethnomusicological perspective. In D. J. Hargreaves & A. C. North (Eds.), *The social psychology of music* (pp. 123–140). Oxford: Oxford University Press.

Groarke, J. M., & Hogan, M. J. (2016). Enhancing wellbeing: An emerging model of the adaptive functions of music listening. *Psychology of Music*, 44(4), 769–791.

Gudmundsdottir, H. (1999). Children's auditory discrimination of simultaneous melodies. *Journal of Research in Music Education*, 47(2), 101–110.

Haake, A. B. (2011). Individual music listening in workplace settings: An exploratory survey of offices in the UK. *Musicae Scientiae*, 15(1), 107–129.

Habermas, J. (1987). *The theory of communicative action. Vols. 1 and 2.* Boston, MA: Beacon.

Habibi, A., Cahn, B. R., Damasio, A., & Damasio, H. (2016). Neural correlates of accelerated auditory processing in children engaged in music training. *Developmental Cognitive Neuroscience*, 21, 1–14.

Hadwin, A. F., Järvelä, S., & Miller, M. (2011). Self-regulated, co-regulated and socially shared regulation of learning. In B. J. Zimmerman & D. H. Schunk (Eds.), *Handbook of self-regulation of learning and performance*. Abingdon: Routledge.

Hallam, S. (1997). What do we know about practising? Towards a model synthesizing the research literature. In H. Jørgensen & A. Lehmann (Eds.), *Does practice make perfect?* (pp. 179–231). Oslo: Norges Musikkhøgskole.

Hallam, S. (2002). Musical motivation: Towards a model synthesising the research. *Music Education Research*, 4, 225–244.

Hallam, S. (2010). The power of music: Its impact on the intellectual, social and personal development of children and young people. *International Journal of Music Education*, 28(3), 269–289.

Hallam, S. (2015). *The power of music: A research synthesis of the impact of actively making music on the intellectual, social and personal development of children and young people.* London: Music Education Council, retrieved from www.mec.org.uk.

Hallam, S. (2016). Musicality. In G. E McPherson (Ed.), *The child as musician: A handbook of musical development* (2nd edition, pp. 67–80). Oxford: Oxford University Press.

Hallam, S., & Creech, A. (2016). Can active music making promote health and well-being in older citizens? Findings of the Music for Life Project, *London Journal of Primary Care*, DOI: 10.1080/17571472.2016.1152099.

Hallam, S., Price, J., & Katsarou, G. (2002). The effects of background music on primary school pupils' task performance. *Educational Studies*, 28(2), 111–122.

Hallam, S., Creech, A., Sandford, C., Rinta, T., & Shave, K. (2008). *Survey of Musical Futures: A report from Institute of Education University of London*, http://eprints.ioe.ac.uk/2301/1/Hallam2008_Musical_Futures_report_final_version.pdf

Hallett, R., & Lamont, A. (2015). How do gym members engage with music during exercise? *Qualitative Research in Sport, Exercise and Health*, 7, 411–427.

Halpern, A. R., & Bartlett, J. C. (2002). Aging and memory for music: A review. *Psychomusicology*, 18, 10–27.

Halpern, A. R., & Zatorre, R. J. (1999). When that tune runs through your head: A PET investigation of auditory imagery for familiar melodies. *Cerebral Cortex*, 9, 697–704.

Halpern, A. R., Bartlett, J. C., & Dowling, W. J. (1995). Aging and experience in the recognition of musical transpositions. *Psychology and Aging*, 10(3), 325–342.

Halpern, A. R., Kwak, S-Y., Bartlett, J. C., & Dowling, W. J. (1996). Effects of aging and musical experience on the representation of tonal hierarchies. *Psychology and Aging*, 11(2), 235–246.

Hambrick, D. Z., Oswald, F. L., Altmann, E. M., Meinz, E. J., Gobet, F., & Campitelli, G. (2014). Deliberate practice: Is that all it takes to become an expert? *Intelligence*, 45, 34–45.

Hannon, E. E., & Trehub, S. E. (2005a). Metrical categories in infancy and adulthood. *Psychological Science*, 16, 48–55.

Hannon, E. E., & Trehub, S.E. (2005b). Tuning in to musical rhythms: Infants learn more readily than adults. *Proceedings of the National Academy of Sciences*, 102(35), 12639–12643

Hansen, C. H., & Hansen, R. D. (1991). Constructing personality and social reality through music: Individual differences among fans of punk and heavy metal music. *Journal of Broadcasting and Electronic Media*, 35, 355–350.

Hargreaves, D. J. (1982). The development of aesthetic reactions to music. *Psychology of Music, Special Issue*, 51–54.

Hargreaves, D. J. (1986a). *The developmental psychology of music*. Cambridge: Cambridge University Press.

Hargreaves, D. J. (1986b). Developmental psychology and music education. *Psychology of Music*, 14, 83–96.

Hargreaves, D. J. (Ed.) (1989). *Children and the arts*. Milton Keynes: Open University Press.

Hargreaves, D. J. (1994). Musical education for all: Open peer commentary on 'Is everyone musical?', by J. A. Sloboda, J. W. Davidson, & M. J. A. Howe. *The Psychologist*, 7(8), 357–358.

Hargreaves, D. J. (1996). The development of musical and artistic competence. In I. Deliège & J. A. Sloboda (Eds.), *Musical beginnings: Origins and development of musical competence* (pp. 145–170). Oxford: Oxford University Press.

Hargreaves, D. J. (2008). Commentary. Special issue of the *International Journal of Educational Research*. In D. Miell, K. Littleton, & S. Rojas-Drummond (Eds.), *Music education: A site for collaborative creativity*, 47, 75–77.

Hargreaves, D. J. (2012). Musical imagination: Perception and production, beauty and creativity. *Psychology of Music*, 40(5), 539–57.

Hargreaves, D. J., & Bonneville-Roussy, A. (2017). What is 'open-earedness', and how can it be measured? *Musicae Scientiae*. Online First, DOI: 10.1177/1029864917697783.

Hargreaves, D. J., & Galton, M. (1992). Aesthetic learning: Psychological theory and educational practice. In B. Reimer & R. A. Smith (Eds.), *National Society for the Study of Education yearbook on the arts in education* (pp. 124–150). Chicago, IL: NSSE.

Hargreaves, D. J., & Marshall, N. A. (2003). Developing identities in music education. *Music Education Research*, 5(3), 263–273.

Hargreaves, D. J., & North, A. C. (Eds.) (1997). *The social psychology of music*. Oxford: Oxford University Press.

Hargreaves, D. J., & North, A. C. (1999). Developing concepts of musical style. *Musicae Scientiae*, 3(2), 193–216.

Hargreaves, D. J., & North, A. C. (Eds.) (2001). *Musical development and learning: The international perspective*. London & New York: Continuum.

Hargreaves, D. J., & Zimmerman, M. (1992). Developmental theories of music learning. In R. Colwell (Ed.), *Handbook for research in music teaching and learning* (pp. 377–391). New York: Schirmer / Macmillan.

Hargreaves, D. J., Comber, C. J. F., & Colley, A. M. (1995). Effects of age, gender, and training on the musical preferences of British secondary school students. *Journal of Research in Music Education*, 43(3), 242–250.

Hargreaves, D. J., Cork, C. A., & Setton, T. (1991). Cognitive strategies in jazz improvisation: An exploratory study. *Canadian Music Educators Journal*, 33, 47–54.

Hargreaves, D. J., Galton, M., & Robinson, S. (1996). Teachers' assessments of primary children's classroom work in the creative arts. *Educational Research*, 38, 199–211.

Hargreaves, D. J., Hargreaves, J. J., & North, A. C. (2012). Imagination and creativity in music listening. In D. J. Hargreaves, D. E. Miell, & R. A. R. MacDonald (Eds.), *Musical imaginations* (pp. 156–72). Oxford: Oxford University Press.

Hargreaves, D. J., Jones, P., & Martin, D. (1981). The air gap phenomenon in children's landscape drawings. *Journal of Experimental Child Psychology*, 32, 11–20.

Hargreaves, D. J., MacDonald, R. A. R., & Miell, D. E. (2002). What are musical identities, and why are they important? In R. A. R. MacDonald, D. J. Hargreaves, & D. E. Miell (Eds.), *Musical identities* (pp. 1–20). Oxford: Oxford University Press.

Hargreaves, D. J., MacDonald, R. A. R., & Miell, D. E. (2005). How do people communicate using music? In D. E. Miell, R. A. R. MacDonald, & D. J. Hargreaves (Eds.), *Musical communication* (pp. 1–25). Oxford: Oxford University Press.

Hargreaves, D. J., MacDonald, R. A. R., & Miell, D.E (2012a). Musical identities mediate musical development. In G. McPherson and G. Welch (Eds.), *The Oxford handbook of music education* (pp. 125–142). Oxford: Oxford University Press.

Hargreaves, D. J., MacDonald, R. A. R., & Miell, D. E. (2012b). Explaining musical imaginations: Creativity, performance and perception. In D. J. Hargreaves, D. E. Miell, & R. A. R. MacDonald (Eds.), *Musical imaginations* (pp. 1–14). Oxford: Oxford University Press.

Hargreaves, D. J., MacDonald, R. A. R., & Miell, D. E. (2017). The changing identity of musical identities. In R. A. R. MacDonald, D. J. Hargreaves, & D. E. Miell (Eds.), *Handbook of musical identities* (pp. 3–23). Oxford: Oxford University Press.

Hargreaves, D. J., Marshall, N., & North, A. C. (2003). Music education in the 21st century: A psychological perspective. *British Journal of Music Education*, 20(2), 147–163.

Hargreaves, D. J., North, A. C., & Tarrant, M. (2016). How and why do musical preferences change during childhood and adolescence? In G. McPherson (Ed.), *The child as musician: A handbook of musical development* (pp. 303–322). Oxford: Oxford University Press.

Hargreaves, D. J., Purves, R. M., Welch, G. F., & Marshall, N. A. (2007). Developing identities and attitudes in musicians and music teachers. *British Journal of Educational Psychology*, 77(3), 665–682.

Hargreaves, D. J., Welch, G. F., Purves, R., & Marshall, N. (2003). Effective teaching in secondary school music: teacher and pupil identities. *End of Award Report, ESRC award R000223751.*

Harkins, C., Garnham, L., Campbell, A., & Tannahill, C. (2016). Hitting the right note for child and adolescent mental and emotional wellbeing: A formative qualitative evaluation of Sistema Scotland's "Big Noise" orchestral programme. *Journal of Public Mental Health*, 15(1), 25–36.

Harland, J., Kinder, K., Lord, P., Stott, A., Schagen, I., Haynes, J., Cusworth, L., White, R., & Paola, R. (2000). *Arts education in secondary schools: Effects and effectiveness*. Slough: NFER.

Harris, K. C., Mills, J. H., He, N.-J., & Dubno, J. R. (2008). Age-related differences in sensitivity to small changes in frequency assessed with cortical evoked potentials. *Hearing Research*, 243, 47–56.

Harris, P. L. (1989). *Children and emotion: The development of psychological understanding*. Oxford: Basil Blackwell.

Harter, S. (1999). *The construction of the self: A developmental perspective*. New York: Guilford Press.

Hayes, J. R. (1989). *The complete problem solver* (2nd edition). Hillsdale, NJ: Erlbaum.

Hays, T., & Minichiello, V. (2005). The meaning of music in the lives of older people: A qualitative study. *Psychology of Music*, 33(4), 437–451.

He, C., Hotson, L., & Trainor, L. J. (2007). Mismatch responses to pitch changes in early infancy. *Journal of Cognitive Neuroscience*, 19, 878–892.

He, C., Hotson, L., & Trainor, L. J. (2009). Maturation of cortical mismatch responses to occasional pitch change in early infancy: Effects of presentation rate and magnitude of change. *Neuropsychologia*, 47, 218–229.

He, N.-J., Mills, J. H., & Dubno, J. R. (2007). Frequency modulation detection: Effects of age, psychophysical method, and modulation waveform. *Journal of the Acoustical Society of America*, 122(1), 467–477.

Heath, S. B. (2001). Three's not a crowd: Plans, roles and focus in the arts. *Educational Researcher*, 30, 10–17.

Heaton, P. (2009). Assessing musical skills in autistic children who are not savants. *Philosophical Transactions of the Royal Society B*, 364, 1443–1447.

Heaton, P., Hermelin, B., & Pring, L. (1998). Autism and pitch processing: A precursor for savant musical ability. *Music Perception*, 15, 291–305.

Heider, F. (1958). *The psychology of interpersonal relationships*. New York: Wiley.

Hekkert, P., & van Wieringen, P. C. W. (1990). Complexity and prototypicality as determinants of the appraisal of cubist paintings. *British Journal of Psychology*, 81(4), 483–495.

Hemming, J. (2013). Is there a peak in popular music preference at a certain song-specific age? A replication of Holbrook & Schindler's 1989 study. *Musicae Scientiae*, 17(3), 293–304.

Henley, D. (2011). *Music education in England: A review by Darren Henley for the Department of Education and the Department for Culture, Media and Sport*. www.educationengland.org.uk/documents/pdfs/2011–music–henley–review.pdf

Hentschke, L., & Del Ben, L. (1999). The assessment of audience-listening: Testing a model in the educational setting of Brazil. *Music Education Research*, 1(2), 127–146.

Hepper, P. G. (1991). An examination of fetal learning before and after birth. *Irish Journal of Psychology*, 12, 95–107

Hepper, P. G. (1996). Fetal memory: Does it exist? What does it do? *Acta Paediatrica Supplement*, 416, 16–20.

Herholz, S. C., Halpern, A. R., & Zatorre, R. J. (2012). Neuronal correlates of perception, imagery, and memory for familiar tunes. *Journal of Cognitive Neuroscience*, 24(6), 1382–1397.

Herrera, L., Lorenzo, O., Defior, S., Fernandez-Smith, G., & Costa-Giomi, E. (2011). Effects of phonological and musical training on the reading readiness of native- and foreign-Spanish-speaking children. *Psychology of Music*, 39(1), 68–81.

Hetland, L., & Winner, E. (2000). The arts and academic achievement: What the evidence shows. *The Journal of Aesthetic Education*, 34(3/4), 3–10.

Hewitt, A. (2008). Children's creative collaboration during a computer-based music task. *International Journal of Educational Research*, 47 (1), 11–26.

Hickey, M. (2001). An application of Amabile's consensual assessment technique for rating the creativity of children's musical compositions. *Journal of Research in Music Education*, 49(3), 234–244.

Hickey, M., & Lipscomb, S. D. (2006). How different is good? How good is different? The assessment of children's creative musical thinking. *Musical Creativity: Multidisciplinary Research in Theory and Practice*, 97–110.

Holahan, J., (1986). Teaching music through music learning theory: The contribution of Edwin E. Gordon. In M. Mark (Ed.), *Contemporary music education* (pp. 152–172). New York: Schirmer.

Holbrook, M. B. (1995). An empirical approach to representing patterns of consumer tastes, nostalgia, and hierarchy in the market for cultural products. *Empirical Studies of the Arts*, 13(1), 55–71.

Holbrook, M. B., & Schindler, R. M. (1989). Some exploratory findings on the development of musical tastes. *Journal of Consumer Research*, 16(6), 119–124.

Holbrook, M. B., & Schindler, R. M. (2013). Commentary on 'Is there a peak in popular music preference at a certain song-specific age? A replication of Holbrook & Schindler's 1989 study'. *Musicae Scientiae*, 17(3), 305–308.

Honing, H. (2004). The comeback of systematic musicology: New empiricism and the cognitive revolution. *Tijdschrift voor Muziektheorie [Dutch Journal of Music Theory]*, 9(3), 241–244.

Hopper, M. J., Curtis, S., Hodge, S., & Simm, R. (2016). A qualitative study exploring the effects of attending a community pain service choir on wellbeing in people who experience chronic pain. *British Journal of Pain*, 10(3), 124–134.

Howe, C., & Abedin, M. (2013). Classroom dialogue: A systematic review across four decades of research. *Cambridge Journal of Education*, 43(3), 325–356.

Howe, M. J. A., Davidson, J. W., & Sloboda, J. A. (1998). Innate gifts and talents: Reality or myth? *Behavioural and Brain Sciences*, 21, 399–407.

Howe, M. J. A., Davidson, J. W., Moore, D. M., & Sloboda, J. A. (1995). Are there early signs of musical excellence? *Psychology of Music*, 23, 162–176.

Hruska, E., Hargreaves, D. J., & Ockelford, A. (submitted). Exploring parental and educational influences on the development of performance anxiety and perfectionism in classical musicians.

Huffman, J. C., Mastromauro, C. A., Boehm, J. K., Seabrook, R., Fricchione, G. L., Denninger, J. W., & Lyubomirsky, S. (2011). Development of a positive psychology intervention for patients with acute cardiovascular disease. *Heart International*, 6:e14, 47–54.

Hunter, P. G., Schellenberg, E. G., & Stalinski, S. (2011). Liking and identifying emotionally expressive music: Age and gender differences. *Journal of Experimental Child Psychology*, 110, 80–93.

Huron, D. (1990). Review of *Music as cognition*, by M. L. Serafine. *Psychology of Music*, 18, 99–103.

Husserl, E. (1936/1970). *The crises of the European sciences and transcendental phenomenology*. D. Carr (Trans.). Evanston, IL: Northwestern University Press.

Hutchinson, J. C., Karageorghis, C. I., & Jones, L. (2015). See hear: Psychological effects of music and music-video during treadmill running. *Annals of Behavioral Medicine*, 49, 199–211.

Hutka, S., Bidelman, G. M., & Moreno, S. (2015). Pitch expertise is not created equal: Cross-domain effects of musicianship and tone language experience on neural and behavioural discrimination of speech and music. *Neuropsychologia*, 71, 52–63.

Hyde, K. L., & Peretz, I. (2004). Brains that are out of tune but in time. *Psychological Science*, 15(5), 356–360.

Hyde, K. L., Lerch, J., Norton, A., Forgeard, M., Winner, E., Evans, A. C., & Schlaug, G. (2009). Musical training shapes structural brain development. *The Journal of Neuroscience*, 29(10), 3019–3025.

Ilari, B. (2016). Music in the early years: Pathways into the social world. *Research Studies in Music Education*, 38(1), 23–39.

Ilari, B. (2017). Children's ethnic identity, cultural diversity, and music education. In R. A. R. MacDonald, D. J. Hargreaves, & D. E. Miell (Eds.), *Handbook of musical identities* (pp. 527–542). Oxford: Oxford University Press.

Ilari, B., & Polka, I. (2006). Music cognition in early infancy: Infants' preferences and long-term memory for Ravel. *International Journal of Music Education*, 24, 7–20.

Ilari, B., & Sundara, M. (2009). Music listening preferences in early life: Infants' responses to accompanied versus unaccompanied listening. *Journal of Research in Music Education*, 56(4), 357–369.

Ilari, B., & Young, S. (Eds.) (2016). *Children's home musical experiences across the world*. Bloomington and Indianapolis: Indiana University Press.

Ivanov, V. K., & Geake, J. G. (2003). The Mozart Effect and primary school children. *Psychology of Music*, 31(4), 405–413.

Jakubowski, K., Müllensiefen, D., & Stewart, L. (2017). A developmental study of latent absolute pitch memory. *The Quarterly Journal of Experimental Psychology*, 70(3), 434–443.

James, W. (1890/1950). *The principles of psychology, vol.1*. New York: Holt.

Janus, M., Lee, Y., Moreno, S., & Bialystok, E. (2016). Effects of short-term music and second-language training on executive control. *Journal of Experimental Child Psychology*, 144, 84–97.

Jayawickreme, E., Forgeard, M. J. C., & Seligman, M. E. P. (2012). The engine of well-being. *Review of General Psychology*, 16(4), 327–342.

Jentschke, S., & Koelsch, S. (2009). Musical training modulates the development of syntax processing in children. *NeuroImage*, 47, 735–744.

Jentschke, S., Friederici, A. D., & Koelsch, S. (2014). Neural correlates of music-syntactic processing in two-year old children. *Developmental Cognitive Neuroscience*, 9, 200–208.

Johansson, K. (2012). Organ improvisation: Edition, extemporisation, expansion and instant composition. In D. J. Hargreaves, D. E Miell, & R. A. R. MacDonald (Eds.), *Musical imaginations* (pp. 220–232). Oxford: Oxford University Press.

John, O. P., & Srivastava, S. (1999). The Big Five trait taxonomy: History, measurement, and theoretical perspectives. *Handbook of personality: Theory and research*, 2, 102–138.

John-Steiner, V. (2000). *Creative collaboration*. New York: Oxford University Press.

Johnson, J. K., Louhivuori, J., & Siljander, E. (2016). Comparison of well-being of older adult choir singers and the general population in Finland: A case-control study. *Musicae Scientiae*, DOI: 10.1177/1029864916644486.

Johnson, J. K., Louhivuori, J., Stewart, A. L., Tolvanen, A., Ross, L., & Era, P. (2013). Quality of Life (QOL) of older adult community choral singers in Finland. *International Psychogeriatrics*, 25(7), 1055–1064.

Johnson-Laird, P. N. (1988a). Freedom and constraint in creativity. In: R. J. Sternberg (ed.), *The nature of creativity* (pp. 202–219). Cambridge: Cambridge University Press.

Johnson-Laird, P. N. (1988b). The computer and the mind: An introduction to cognitive science. Harvard University Press.

Jørgensen, H., & Lehmann, A. C. (Eds.) (1997). *Does practice make perfect?: Current theory and research on instrumental music practice*. Norges musikkhøgskole.

Joseph, R. (2000). Fetal brain behavior and cognitive development. *Developmental Review*, 20, 81–98.

Jourdan, K., & Holloway, R. (2017). Sistema Scotland: Emerging musical identities in Raploch. In R. A. R. MacDonald, D. J. Hargreaves, & D. E. Miell (Eds.), *Handbook of musical identities* (pp. 768–788). Oxford: Oxford University Press.

Judd, M., & Pooley, J. A. (2014). The psychological benefits of participating in group singing for members of the general public. *Psychology of Music*, 42(2), 269–283.

Juslin, P. N. (2013). From everyday emotions to aesthetic emotions: Toward a unified theory of musical emotions. *Physics of Life Reviews*, 10(3), 235–266.

Juslin, P. N., & Laukka, P. (2004). Expression, perception, and induction of musical emotions: A review and a questionnaire study of everyday listening. *New Music Research*, 33(3), 217–238.

Juslin, P. N., Liljeström, S., Västfjäll, D., Barradas, G., & Silva, A. (2008). An experience sampling study of emotional reactions to music: Listener, music, and situation. *Emotion*, 8(5), 668–683.

Juuti, S., & Littleton, K. (2010). Musical identities in transition: Solo-piano students' accounts of entering the academy. *Psychology of Music*, 38(4), 481–497.

Kahneman, D., Diener, E., & Schwarz, N. (Eds.) (1999). *Well-being: The foundations of hedonic psychology*. New York: Russell Sage Foundation.

Kämpfe, J., Sedlmeier, P., & Renkewitz, F. (2011). The impact of background music on adult listeners: A meta-analysis. *Psychology of Music*, 39(4), 424–448.

Karageorghis, C. I. (2016). The scientific application of music in exercise and sport: Towards a new theoretical model. In A. M. Lane (Ed.), *Sport and exercise psychology* (2nd edition, pp. 276–322). London, UK: Routledge.

Karageorghis, C. I., & Jones, L. (2014). On the stability and relevance of the exercise heart rate–music-tempo preference relationship. *Psychology of Sport and Exercise*, 15, 299–310.

Karageorghis, C. I., Terry, P. C., & Lane, A. M. (1999). Development and initial validation of an instrument to assess the motivational qualities of music in exercise and sport: The Brunel Music Rating Inventory. *Journal of Sports Sciences*, 17, 713–724.

Karageorghis, C. I., Jones, L., Priest, D. L., Akers, R. I., Clarke, A., Perry, J. M., et al. (2011). Revisiting the exercise heart rate-music tempo preference relationship. *Research Quarterly for Exercise and Sport*, 82, 274e284.

Karageorghis, C. I., Priest, D. L., Terry, P. C., Chatzisarantis, N. D., & Lane, A. M. (2006). Redesign and initial validation of an instrument to assess the motivational qualities of music in exercise: The Brunel Music Rating Inventory-2. *Journal of Sports Sciences*, 24, 899–909.

Karlsen, S. (2011). Using musical agency as a lens: Researching music education from the angle of experience. *Research Studies in Music Education*, 33(2), 107–121.

Kastner, M. P., & Crowder, R. G. (1990). Perception of the major/minor distinction: IV. Emotional connotations in young children. *Music Perception*, 8, 189–202.

Kaufman, J. C., & Sternberg, R. J. (Eds.) (2006). *The international handbook of creativity*. Cambridge University Press.

Keeler, J. R., Roth, E. A., Neuser, B. L., Spitsbergen, J. M., Waters, D. J. M., & Vianney, J.-M. (2015). The neurochemistry and social flow of singing: Bonding and oxytocin. *Frontiers in Human Neuroscience*, 9, 518, DOI: 10.3389/fnhum.2015.00518.

Kelley, H. H. (1973). The processes of causal attribution. *American Psychologist*, 28, 107–128.

Kemp, A. E. (1981a). The personality structure of the musician: I. Identifying a profile of traits for the performer. *Psychology of Music*, 9, 3–14.

Kemp, A. E. (1981b). Personality differences between the players of string, woodwind, brass and keyboard instruments, and singers. *Council for Research in Music Education Bulletin*, 66, 33–8.

Kemp, A. E. (1982). Personality traits of successful student music teachers. *Psychology of Music, Special Issue*, 72–75.

Kemp, A. E. (1996). *The musical temperament: Psychology and personality of musicians.* Oxford: Oxford University Press.

Kenny, D. T. (2004). Music performance anxiety: Is it the music, the performance or the anxiety? *Music Forum*, 10(4), 38–43.

Kenny, D. T. (2006). A systematic review of treatments for music performance anxiety. *Anxiety, Stress & Coping: An International Journal*, 18(3), 183–208.

Kenny, D. T. (2011). *The psychology of music performance anxiety.* New York: Oxford University Press.

Kenny, D. T., & Osborne, M. S. (2006). Music performance anxiety: New insights from young musicians. *Advances in Cognitive Psychology*, 2(2–3), 103–112.

Kirschner, S., & Tomasello, M. (2009). Joint drumming: Social context facilitates synchronization in preschool children. *Journal of Experimental Child Psychology*, 102, 299–314.

Kirschner, S., & Tomasello, M. (2010). Joint music making promotes prosocial behavior in 4-year-old children. *Evolution and Human Behavior*, 31(5), 354–364.

Kisilevsky, B. S., Hains, S. M., Jacquet, A.-Y., Granier-Deferre, C., & Lecanuet, J. P. (2004). Maturation of fetal responses to music. *Developmental Science*, 7, 550–559.

Kisilevsky, B. S., Hains, S. M., Lee, K., Xie, X., Huang, H., et al. (2003). Effects of experience on fetal voice recognition. *Psychological Science*, 4, 220–224.

Koelsch, S., Fritz, T., Schulze, K., Alsop, D., & Schlaug, G. (2005). Adults and children processing music: an fMRI study. *Neuroimage*, 25(4), 1068–1076.

Koelsch, S., Gunter, T. C., Friederici, A. D., & Schröger, E. (2000). Brain indices of music processing: 'nonmusicians' are musical. *Journal of Cognitive Neuroscience*, 12, 520–541.

Koelsch, S., Grossman, T., Gunter, T. C., Hahne, A., Schröger, E., & Friederici, A. D. (2003). Children processing music: Electrical brain responses reveal musical competence and gender differences. *Journal of Cognitive Neuroscience*, 15(5), 683–693.

Koelsch, S., Gunter, T. C., Schröger, E., & Friederici, A. D. (2003). Processing tonal modulations: An ERP study. *Journal of Cognitive Neuroscience*, 15(8), 1149–1159.

Kohn, D., & Eitan, Z. (2016). Moving music: Correspondences of musical parameters and movement dimensions in children's motion and verbal responses. *Music Perception*, 34(1), 40–55.

Koltko-Rivera, M. E. (2006). Rediscovering the later version of Maslow's hierarchy of needs: Self-transcendence and opportunities for theory, research, and unification. *Review of General Psychology*, 10(4), 302–317.

Konečni, V. J. (1982). Social interaction and music preference. In D. Deutsch (Ed.), *The psychology of music* (1st edition, pp. 497–516). New York: Academic Press.

Koniari, D., Predazzer, S., & Mélen, M. (2001). Categorization and schematization processes used in music perception by 10- to 11-year old children. *Music Perception*, 18(3), 297–324.

Koopman, H. M., Baars, R. M., Chaplin, J., & Zwinderman, K. H. (2004). Illness through the eyes of the child: The development of children's understanding of the causes of illness. *Patient Education and Counseling*, 55, 363–370.

Kopiez, R., & Lehmann, M. (2008). The 'open-earedness' hypothesis and the development of age-related reactions to music in elementary school children. *British Journal of Music Education*, 25(2), 121–138.

Kopiez, R., Lehmann, A. C., & Klassen, J. (2009). Clara Schumann's collection of program leaflets: A historiometric analysis of life-span development, mobility, and repertoire canonization. *Poetics*, 37(1), 50–73.

Kopp, C. B. (1982). Antecedents of self-regulation: A developmental perspective. *Developmental Psychology*, 18(2), 199–214.

Koutsoupidou, T., & Hargreaves, D. J. (2009). An experimental study of the effects of improvisation on the development of creative thinking in music. *Psychology of Music*, 37(3), 251–278.

Kratus, J. (1994). Relationships among children's music audiation and their compositional processes and products. *Journal of Research in Music Education*, 42(2), 115–130.

Kraus, N., Hornickel, J., Strait, D. L., Slater, J., & Thompson, E. (2014). Engagement in community music classes sparks neuroplasticity and language development in children from disadvantaged backgrounds. *Frontiers in Psychology*, 5, DOI: 10.3389/fpsyg.2014.01403.

Krause, A. E., & Hargreaves, D. J. (2013). myTunes: Digital music library users and their self-images. *Psychology of Music*, 41(5), 531–544.

Krause, A. E., North, A. C., & Hewitt, L. Y. (2014). Music selection behaviors in everyday listening. *Electronic Media*, 58(2), 306–323.

Krause, A. E., North, A. C., & Hewitt, L. Y. (2015). Music-listening in everyday life: Devices and choice. *Psychology of Music*, 43(2), 155–270.

Krause, A. E., North, A. C., & Hewitt, L. Y. (2016). The role of location in everyday experiences of music. *Psychology of Popular Media Culture*, 5(3), 232–257.

Kreutz, G., Bongard, S., Rohrmann, S., Grebe, D., Bastian, H. G., & Hodapp, V. (2004). Effects of choir singing or listening on secretory immunoglobulin: A, cortisol and emotional state. *Journal of Behavioral Medicine*, 27(6), 623–635.

Krueger, C., Holditch-Davis, D., Quint, S., & DeCasper, A. J. (2004). Recurring auditory experience in the 28– to 34–week old fetus. *Infant Behavior & Development*, 27, 537–543.

Krumhansl, C. L. (2010). Plink: "Thin slices" of music. *Music Perception*, 27(5), 337–354.

Krumhansl, C. L., & Jusczyk, P. W. (1990). Infants' perception of phrase structure in music. *Psychological Science*, 1(1), 70–73.

Krumhansl, C. L., & Keil. F. C. (1982). Acquisition of the hierarchy of tonal functions in music. *Memory and Cognition*, 10, 243–251.

Krumhansl, C. L., & Zupnick, J. A. (2013). Cascading reminiscence bumps in popular music. *Psychological Science*, 24, 2057–2068.

Kuhl, P. K., Tsao, F.-M., & Liu, H.-M. (2003). Foreign-language experience in infancy: Effects of short-term exposure and social interaction on phonetic learning. *Proceedings of the National Academy of Sciences*, 100(15), 9096–9101.

Labbé, C., & Grandjean, D. (2014). Musical emotions predicted by feelings of entrainment. *Music Perception*, 32(2), 170–185.

Lamont, A. (1998). Music, education, and the development of pitch perception: The role of context, age, and musical experience. *Psychology of Music*, 26(1), 7–25.

Lamont. A. (1999). *A contextual account of developing representations of music*. Paper presented at the International Conference on Research in Music Education, Exeter University, UK.

Lamont, A. (2002). Musical identities and the school environment. In R. A. R. MacDonald, D. J. Hargreaves, & D. E. Miell (Eds.), *Musical identities* (pp. 41–59). Oxford: Oxford University Press.

Lamont, A. (2006). What do monkeys' music choices mean? *Trends in Cognitive Science*, 9(8), 359–361.

Lamont, A. (2008). Young children's musical worlds: Musical engagement in three-year-olds. *Journal of Early Childhood Research*. 6(3), 247–261.

Lamont, A. (2011a). University students' strong experiences of music: Pleasure, engagement and meaning. *Musicae Scientiae*, 15(2), 229–249.

Lamont, A. (2011b). The beat goes on: Music education, identity and lifelong learning. *Music Education Research*, 13(4), 369–388.

Lamont, A. (2012). Emotion, engagement and meaning in strong experiences of music performance. *Psychology of Music*, 40(5), 574–594.

Lamont, A. (2016). Musical development from the early years onwards. In S. Hallam, I. Cross, & M. Thaut (Eds.), *The Oxford handbook of music psychology* (2nd edition, pp. 399–414). Oxford: Oxford University Press.

Lamont, A. (2017). Musical identity, interest, and involvement. In R. A. R. MacDonald, D. J. Hargreaves, & D. E. Miell (Eds.), *Handbook of musical identities* (pp. 176–196). Oxford: Oxford University Press.

Lamont, A., & Cross, I. (1994). Children's cognitive representations of musical pitch. *Music Perception*, 12, 27–55.

Lamont, A., & Maton, K. (2008). Choosing music: Exploratory studies into the low uptake of music GCSE. *British Journal of Music Education*, 25(3), 267–282.

Lamont, A., & Maton, K. (2010). Unpopular music: Beliefs and behaviours towards music in education. In R. Wright (Ed.), *Sociology and music education* (pp. 63–80). Basingstoke: Ashgate.

Lamont, A., & Webb, R. J. (2010). Short- and long-term musical preferences: What makes a favourite piece of music? *Psychology of Music*, 38(2), 222–241.

Lamont, A., Greasley, A. E., & Sloboda, J. A. (2016). Choosing to hear music: motivation, process and effect. In S. Hallam, I. Cross, & M. Thaut (Eds.), *The Oxford handbook of music psychology* (2nd edition, pp. 711–724), Oxford: Oxford University Press.

Lamont, A., Hargreaves, D. J., Marshall, N. A., & Tarrant, M. (2003). Young people's music in and out of school. *British Journal of Music Education*, 20(3), 229–241.

Lamont, A., Murray, M., Hale, R., & Wright-Bevans, K. (2017). Singing in later life: The anatomy of a choir. *Psychology of Music*, Online First, DOI: 10.1177/0305735617715514.

Lane, A. M., Davis, P. A., & Devonport, T. J. (2011). Effects of music interventions on emotional states and running performance. *Journal of Sports Science and Medicine*, 10, 400–407.

Lanovaz, M. J., & Huxley, S. C. (2017). Effects of background music on socially reinforced problem behaviors in children with autism spectrum disorders. *Psychology of Music*, 45(3), 450–456.

Lartillot, O., & Toiviainen, P. (2007). MIR in Matlab (II): A toolbox for musical feature extraction from audio. In S. Dixon, D. Bainbridge, & R. Typke (Eds.), *Proceedings of the 8th International Conference on Music Information Retrieval* (pp. 237–244). Vienna, Austria: Osterreichische Computer Gesellschaft.

Laukka, P. (2007). Uses of music and psychological well-being among the elderly. *Journal of Happiness Studies*, 8, 215–241.

Lave, J., & Wenger, E. (1991). *Situated learning: Legitimate peripheral participation.* Cambridge: Cambridge University Press.

Layard, R., & Dunn, J. (2009). *A good childhood – Searching for values in a competitive age.* London: Penguin Books.

LeBlanc, A. (1991). *Effect of maturation/aging on music listening preference: A review of the literature.* Paper presented at the Ninth National Symposium on Research in Music Behavior, Cannon Beach, Oregon, USA, 7–9 March 1991.

Lee, H. L., & Noppeney, U. (2011). Long-term music training tunes how the brain temporally binds signals from multiple senses. *Proceedings of the National Academy of Sciences*, 108(51), 20295–20296.

Lehman, H. C. (1953). *Age and achievement*. Princeton, NJ: Princeton University Press.

Lehmann, A. C. (1997). Acquired mental representations in music performance: Anecdotal and preliminary empirical evidence. In H. Jørgensen & A. Lehmann (Eds.), *Does practice make perfect?* (pp. 141–164). Oslo: Norges Musikkhøgskole.

Lehmann, A. C., & Davidson, J. W. (2002). Taking an acquired skills perspective on music performance. In R. Colwell & C. Richardson (Eds.), *Second handbook on music teaching and learning* (pp. 542–562). Oxford: Oxford University Press.

Lehmann, A. C., Sloboda, J. A., & Woody, R. H. (2007). *Psychology for musicians: Understanding and acquiring the skills*. Oxford: Oxford University Press.

Leighton, G. L., & Lamont, A. (2006). Exploring children's singing development: Do experiences in early schooling help or hinder? *Music Education Research*, 8(3), 311–330.

Leont'ev, A.N. (1981). *Problems of the development of mind*. Moscow: Progress Publishers.

Lesiuk, T. (2005). The effect of music listening on work performance. *Psychology of Music*, 33(2), 173–191.

Levitin, D. (1994). Absolute memory for musical pitch: Evidence from the production of learned melodies. *Perception & Psychophysics*, 52, 599–608.

Lewis, K. (2011). *In Harmony Lambeth – An evaluation*. www.ihsc.org.uk/evaluation–Lambeth–2011.

Limb, C. J., & Braun, A. R. (2008). Neural substrates of spontaneous musical performance: An FMRI study of jazz improvisation. *PLoS ONE, I*, e1679.

Lindblom, A. (2017). 'It gives them a place to be proud' – Music and social inclusion. Two diverse cases of young First Nations people diagnosed with autism in British Columbia, Canada. *Psychology of Music*, 45(2), 268–282.

Littleton, K., & Mercer, N. (2012). Communication, collaboration, and creativity: How musicians negotiate a collective 'sound'. In D. J. Hargreaves, D. E. Miell, & R. A. R. MacDonald (Eds.), *Musical imaginations* (pp. 233–241). Oxford: Oxford University Press.

London, J. (2004). *Hearing in time: Psychological aspects of musical meter*. Oxford: Oxford University Press.

Longhi, E., & Pickett, N. (2008). Music and well-being in long-term hospitalized children. *Psychology of Music*, 36(2), 247–256.

Longhi, E., Pickett, N., & Hargreaves, D. J. (2015). Wellbeing and hospitalized children: Can music help? *Psychology of Music*, 43(2), 188–196.

Lonsdale, A. J., & North, A. C. (2011). Why do we listen to music? A uses and gratifications analysis. *British Journal of Psychology*, 102, 108–134.

Lord, P., Sharp, C., Dawson, A., Mehta, P., White, R., & Jeffes, J. (2013). *Evaluation of In Harmony: Year 1 Interim Report*. Slough: National Foundation for Educational Research. www.nfer.ac.uk/publications/ACII01/ACII01.pdf

Lord, P., Sharp, C., Mehta, P., & Featherstone, G. (2015). *Evaluation of In Harmony: Year 2 Interim Report*. Slough: National Foundation for Educational Research. www.nfer.ac.uk/publications/ACII02/ACII02.pdf

Loui, P., Alsop, D., & Schlaug, G. (2009). Tone deafness: A new disconnection syndrome. *Journal of Neuroscience*, 29, 10215–10220.

Louven, C. (2016). Hargreaves' 'open-earedness': A critical discussion and new approach on the concept of musical tolerance and curiosity. *Musicae Scientiae*, 20(2), 235–247.

Louven, C., & Ritter, A. (2012). Hargreaves' "Offenohrigkeit" - Ein neues, softwarebasiertes Forschungsdesign. In J. Knigge & A. Niessen (Eds.), *Musikpädagogisches Handeln. Begriffe, Erscheinungsformen, politische Dimensionen* (pp. 275–299). Essen: Die Blaue Eule.

Lowther, D. (2004). An investigation of young children's timbral sensitivity. *British Journal of Music Education*, 21(1), 63–80.

Luhtanen, R., & Crocker, J. (1992). A collective self-esteem scale: Self-evaluation of one's social identity. *Personality and Social Psychology Bulletin*, 18, 302–318.

Lundin, R. W. (1967). *An objective psychology of music* (2nd edition). New York: Ronald.

Lynch, M. P., & Eilers, R. E. (1992). A study of perceptual development for musical tuning. *Perception & Psychophysics*, 52(6), 599–608.

Lynch, M. P., Eilers, R. E., Oller, D. K., & Urbano, R. C. (1990). Innateness, experience, and music perception. *Psychological Science*, 1, 272–276.

Lyubomirsky, S., Sheldon, K. M., & Schkade, D. (2005). Pursuing happiness: The architecture of sustainable change. *Review of General Psychology*, 9, 111–131.

Lyubomirsky, S., Dickerhoof, R., Boehm, J. K., & Sheldon, K. M. (2011). Becoming happier takes both a will and a proper way: An experimental longitudinal intervention to boost well-being. *Emotion*, 11(2), 391–402.

MacDonald, R. A. R. (2008). The universality of musical communication. In M. Suzanne Zeedyk (Ed.), *Promoting social interaction with individuals with communication impairments* (pp. 39–51). London: Jessica Kingsley.

MacDonald, R., Byrne, C., & Carlton, L. (2006). Creativity and flow in musical composition: An empirical investigation. *Psychology of Music*, 34(3), 292–306.

MacDonald, R. A. R., & Miell, D. E. (2002). Music for individuals with special needs: A catalyst for developments in identity, communication and musical ability. In R. A. R. MacDonald, D. J. Hargreaves, & D. E. Miell (Eds.), *Musical identities* (pp. 163–179). Oxford: Oxford University Press.

MacDonald, R. A. R., Davies, J. B., & O'Donnell, P. J. (1999). Structured music workshops for individuals with learning difficulty: an empirical investigation. *Journal of Applied Research in Intellectual Disabilities*, 12(3), 225–241.

MacDonald, R. A. R., Hargreaves, D. J., & Miell, D. E. (Eds.) (2002). *Musical identities*. Oxford: Oxford University Press.

MacDonald, R. A. R., Hargreaves, D. J., & Miell, D. E. (2009). Musical identities. In S. Hallam, I. Cross, & M. Thaut (Eds.), *The Oxford handbook of music psychology* (pp. 462–470). Oxford: Oxford University Press.

MacDonald, R. A. R., Hargreaves, D. J., & Miell, D. E. (Eds.) (2017). *Handbook of musical identities*. Oxford: Oxford University Press.

MacDonald, R. A. R., Kreutz, G., & Mitchell, L. (Eds.) (2012a). *Music, health, and wellbeing*. Oxford: Oxford University Press.

MacDonald, R. A. R., Kreutz, G., & Mitchell, L. (2012b). What is *music, health, and wellbeing* and why is it important? In R. A. R. MacDonald, G. Kreutz, & L. Mitchell (Eds.), *Music, health, and wellbeing* (pp. 3–11). Oxford: Oxford University Press.

MacDonald, R. A. R., Mitchell, L. A., Dillon, T., Serpell, M. G., Davies, J. B., & Ashley, E. A. (2003). An empirical investigation of the anxiolytic and pain reducing effects of music. *Psychology of Music*, 31(2), 187–203.

MacDonald, R. A. R., Wilson, G., & Miell, D. (2012). Improvisation as a creative process within contemporary music. In D. J. Hargreaves, D. E Miell, & R. A. R. MacDonald (Eds.), *Musical imaginations* (pp. 242–256). Oxford: Oxford University Press.

MacKinlay, A., & McVittie, C. (2017). 'Will the real Slim Shady please stand up?' Identity in popular music. In R. A. R. MacDonald, D. J. Hargreaves, & D. E. Miell (Eds.), *Handbook of musical identities* (pp. 137–151). Oxford: Oxford University Press.

MacKinnon, D. W. (1962). The nature and nurture of creative talent. *American Psychologist*, 17, 484–495.

Macnamara, B. N., Hambrick, D. Z., & Oswald, F. L. (2014). Deliberate practice and performance in music, games, sports, education, and professions: A meta-analysis. *Psychological Science*, 25(8), 1608–1618.

Maes, P.- J., & Leman, M. (2013). The influence of body movements on children's perception of music with an ambiguous expressive character. *PLoS ONE*, 8(1): e54682, DOI: 10.1371/journal.pone.0054682.

Malloch, S. (1999). Mothers and infants and communicative musicality. *Musicae Scientiae (Special Issue 1999–2000)*, 29–57.

Malloch, S., & Trevarthen, C. (2009). *Communicative musicality: Exploring the basis of human companionship*. Oxford: Oxford University Press.

Mammarella, N., Fairfield, B., & Cornoldi, C. (2007). Does music enhance cognitive performance in healthy older adults? The Vivaldi effect. *Aging Clinical and Experimental Research*, 19(5), 394–399.

Marcia, J. E. (1980). Identity in adolescence. In J. Adelson (Ed.), *Handbook of adolescent psychology* (pp. 159–187). New York: Wiley.

Margulis, E. H. (2005). A model of melodic expectation. *Music Perception*, 22(4), 663–714.

Marin, M. M. (2009). Effects of early music training on musical and linguistic syntactic abilities. *Annals of the New York Academy of Sciences*, 1169(1), 187–190.

Marks, D. F. (2002). Introduction. In D. F. Marks (Ed.), *The health psychology reader* (pp. 1–7). London: Sage Publications.

Marques, J. M., Yzerbyt, V. Y., & Leyens, J.-P. (1988). The black sheep effect: Judgmental extremity towards ingroup members as a function of ingroup identification. *European Journal of Social Psychology*, 18, 1–16.

Marsh, K. (1995). Children's singing games: Composition in the playground? *Research Studies in Music Education*, 4, 2–11.

Marsh, K. (1999). Mediated orality: The role of popular music in the changing tradition of children's musical play. *Research Studies in Music Education*, 13, 2–12.

Marsh, K. (2008). *The musical playground: Global tradition and change in children's songs and games*. New York: Oxford University Press.

Marsh, K. (2011). Meaning-making through musical play: Cultural psychology of the playground. In M. S. Barrett (Ed.), *A cultural psychology of music education* (pp. 41–60). Oxford: Oxford University Press.

Marsh, K., & Young, S. (2016). Musical play. In G. E. McPherson (Ed.), *The child as musician: A handbook of musical development* (2nd edition, pp. 462–484). Oxford: Oxford University Press.

Marshall, N., & Hargreaves, D. J. (2007). Musical style discrimination in the early years. *Journal of Early Childhood Research*, 5(1), 35–49.

Marshall, N., & Shibazaki, K. (2011). Two studies of musical style sensitivity with children in early years. *Music Education Research*, 13(2), 227–240.

Martin, A. J. (2007). Examining a multidimensional model of student motivation and engagement using a construct validation approach. *British Journal of Educational Psychology*, 77(2), 413–440.

Martindale, C. (1984). The pleasures of thought: a theory of cognitive hedonics. *Journal of Mind and Behavior*, 5, 49–80.

Martindale, C. (1988). Aesthetics, psychobiology, and cognition. In F. H. Farley & R. W. Neperud (Eds.), *The foundations of aesthetics, art, & art education* (pp. 7–42). New York: Praeger Publisher.

Martindale, C., & Moore, K. (1988). Priming, prototypicality, and preference. *Journal of Experimental Psychology: Human Perception and Performance*, 14(4), 661–670.

Martindale, C., Moore, K., & Borkum, J. (1990). Aesthetic preference: Anomalous findings for Berlyne's psychobiological theory. *American Journal of Psychology*, 103(1), 53–80.

Martindale, C., Moore, K., & West, A. (1988). Relationship of preference judgements to typicality, novelty, and mere exposure. *Empirical Studies of the Arts*, 6, 79–96.

Masataka, N. (1999). Preference for infant-directed singing in 2-day-old hearing infants of deaf parents. *Developmental Psychology*, 35, 1001–1005.

Masataka, N. (2006). Preference for consonance over dissonance by hearing newborns of deaf parents and of hearing parents. *Developmental Science*, 9(1), 46–50.

Maslow, A. H. (1943). A theory of human motivation. *Psychological Review*, 50, 370–396.

Maslow, A. H. (1968). *Toward a psychology of being* (2nd edition). New York: Van Nostrand Reinhold.

Maslow, A. H. (1969). The farther reaches of human nature. *Journal of Transpersonal Psychology*, 1(1), 1–9.

Matarazzo, J. D. (1982). Behavioral health's challenge to academic, scientific, and professional psychology. *American Psychologist*, 37(1), 1–14.

Mawbey, W. E. (1973). Wastage from instrumental classes in schools. *Psychology of Music*, 1(1), 33–43.

McAuley, J. D., Jones, M. R., Holub, S., Johnston, H. M., & Miller, N. S. (2006). The time of our lives: Life span development of timing and event tracking. *Journal of Experimental Psychology: General*, 135(3), 348–367.

McKelvie, P., & Low, J. (2002). Listening to Mozart does not improve children's spatial ability: Final curtains for the Mozart effect. *British Journal of Developmental Psychology*, 20, 241–258.

McPherson, G. E. (1993). *Factors and abilities influencing the development of visual, aural, and creative performance skills in music and their educational implications.* Unpublished doctoral thesis, University of Sydney.

McPherson, G. E. (1995a). The assessment of musical performance: Development and validation of five new measures. *Psychology of Music*, 23(2), 142–161.

McPherson, G. E. (1995b). Redefining the teaching of musical performance. *The Quarterly Journal of Music Teaching and Learning*, 1(2), 56–64.

McPherson, G. E. (2000a). Commitment and practice: Key ingredients for achievement during the early stages of learning a musical instrument. *Bulletin of the Council for Research in Music Education*, 147, 122–127.

McPherson, G. E. (2000b). Commitment and practice: Key ingredients for achievement needs in ceasing music and music learning activities. *Psychology of Music*, 41(5), 598–617.

McPherson, G. E. (2005). From child to musician: Skill development during the beginning stages of learning an instrument. *Psychology of Music*, 33(1), 5–35.

McPherson, G. E. (Ed.). (2016). *Musical prodigies: Interpretations from psychology, education, musicology, and ethnomusicology.* Oxford: Oxford University Press.

McPherson, G. E., & Davidson, J. W. (2006). Playing an instrument. In G. E. McPherson (Ed.), *The child as musician: A handbook of musical development* (pp. 331–351). Oxford: Oxford University Press.

McPherson, G. E., & Gagné, F. (2016). Analysing musical prodigiousness using Gagné's integrative model of talent development. In G. E. McPherson (Ed.), *Musical prodigies: Interpretations from psychology, education, musicology, and ethnomusicology* (pp. 3–114). Oxford: Oxford University Press.

McPherson, G. E., & McCormick, J. (2006). Self-efficacy and performing music. *Psychology of Music*, 34(3), 321–336.

McPherson, G. E., & O'Neill, S. A. (2010). Students' motivation to study music as compared to other school subjects: A comparison of eight countries. *Research Studies in Music Education*, 32, 101–137.

McPherson, G. E., & Renwick, J. M. (2001). A longitudinal study of self-regulation in children's musical practice. *Music Education Research*, 3, 169–186.

McPherson, G. E., & Renwick, J. M. (2011). Self-regulation and mastery of musical skills. In B. J. Zimmerman & D. Schunk (Eds.), *Handbook of self regulation of learning and performance* (pp. 234–248). New York: Routledge.

McPherson, G. E., & Williamon, A. (2016). Building gifts into musical talents. In G. E. McPherson (Ed.), *The child as musician: A handbook of musical development* (2nd edition, pp. 340–360). Oxford: Oxford University Press.

McPherson, G. E., Davidson, J. W., & Faulkner, R. (2012). *Music in our lives*. Oxford: Oxford University Press.

Mehrabian, A., & Russell, J. A. (1974). *An approach to environmental psychology*. Cambridge: MIT Press.

Mellor, L. (2008). Creativity, originality, identity: Investigating computer-based composition in the secondary school. *Music Education Research*, 10(4), 451–472.

Menon, V., & Levitin, D. J. (2005). The rewards of music listening: Response and physiological connectivity of the mesolimbic system. *NeuroImage*, 28, 175–184.

Mercer, N. (1995). *The guided construction of knowledge: Talk amongst teachers and learners*. Clevedon: Multilingual Matters Ltd.

Mercer, N. (2000). *Words and minds*. London: Routledge.

Merleau-Ponty, M. (1962). *Phenomenology of perception* (First English edition, transl. C. Smith). London: Routledge and Kegan Paul.

Merriam, A. P. (1997). *The anthropology of music*. Chicago, IL: Northwestern University Press.

Messenger, J. J. (1958). Aesthetic talent. *Basic College Quarterly*, 4, 20–24.

Meyer, L. B. (1956). *Emotion and meaning in music*. Chicago, IL: Chicago University Press.

Miell, D., & Littleton, K. (2004) (Eds.). *Collaborative creativity: Contemporary perspectives*. London: Free Association Books.

Miell, D., & Littleton, K. (2008). Musical collaboration outside school: Processes of negotiation in band rehearsals. *International Journal of Educational Research*, 47(1), 11–26.

Miell, D., & MacDonald, R. A. R. (2000). Children's creative collaborations: The importance of friendship when working together on a musical composition. *Social Development*, 9(3), 348–364.

Miell, D., Littleton, K., & Rojas-Drummond, S. (Eds.) (2008). Music education: A site for collaborative creativity. *Special issue of the International Journal of Educational Research*, 47(1), 1–77.

Miranda, D., & Claes, M. (2004). Rap music genres and deviant behaviors in French-Canadian adolescents. *Journal of Youth and Adolescence*, 33, 113–122.

Miranda, D., & Claes, M. (2008). Personality traits, music preferences and depression in adolescence. *International Journal of Adolescence and Youth*, 14(3), 277–298.

Miranda, D., & Overy, K. (2009). Preface: The neuroscience of music. *Contemporary Music Review*, 28(3), 247–250.

Miranda, D., Blaise-Rochette, C., Vaugon, K., Osman, M., & Arias-Velanzuela, M. (2015). Towards a cultural–developmental psychology of music in adolescence. *Psychology of Music*, 43(2), 197–218.

Mitchell, L. A., & MacDonald, R. A. R. (2012). Music and pain: Evidence from experimental perspectives. In R. MacDonald, G. Kreutz, & L. Mitchell (Eds.), *Music, health, & wellbeing* (pp. 230–238). Oxford: Oxford University Press.

Mitchell, L., MacDonald, R. A. R., & Brodie, E. (2006). A comparison of the effects of preferred music, arithmetic and humor on cold pressor pain. *European Journal of Pain*, 10, 343–351.

Mito, H. (2004). Role of daily musical activity in acquisition of musical skill: Comparisons between young musicians and nonmusicians. *Bulletin of the Council for Research in Music Education*, 161/2, 1–8.

Mito, H. (2007). *Learning musical skills through everyday listening.* Unpublished PhD thesis, Roehampton University, London.

Miyazaki, K. (1988). Musical pitch identification by absolute pitch possessors. *Perception and Psychophysics*, 44, 501–512.

Miyazaki, K. (1990). The speed of musical pitch identification by absolute pitch possessors. *Music Perception*, 8, 177–188.

Molnar-Szakacs, I., Assuied, V. G., & Overy, K (2012). Shared affective motion experience (SAME) and creative, interactive music therapy. In D. J. Hargreaves, D. E. Miell, & R. A. R. MacDonald (Eds.), *Musical imaginations* (pp. 313–331). Oxford: Oxford University Press.

Monson, I. (1996). *Saying something: Jazz improvisation and interaction.* Chicago, IL: University of Chicago Press.

Moog, H. (1976). *The musical experience of the pre-school child.* (Translated by C. Clarke). London: Schott.

Moon, C., Zernzach, R. C., & Kuhl, P. K. (2015). Mothers say 'baby' and their newborns do not choose to listen: A behavioral preference study to compare with ERP results. *Frontiers in Human Neuroscience*, 9, 153, DOI: 10.3389/fnhum.2015.00153.

Moore, D. G., Davidson, J. W., & Burland, K. (2003). The social context of musical success. *British Journal of Psychology*, 94, 529–549.

Moorhead, G. E., & Pond, D. (1978). *Music of young children.* Santa Barbara, CA: Pillsbury Foundation.

Moreno, S., & Bidelman, G. M. (2013). Examining neural plasticity and cognitive benefit through the unique lens of musical training. *Hearing Research*, 308, 84–97.

Moreno, S., Bialystok, E., Barac, R., Schellenberg, E. G., Cepeda, N. J., & Chau, T. (2011). Short-term music training enhances verbal intelligence and executive function. *Psychological Science*, 22, 1425–1433.

Moreno, S., Marques, C., Santos, A., Santos, M., Castro, S. L., & Besson, M. (2009). Musical training influences linguistic abilities in 8-year-old children: More evidence for brain plasticity. *Cerebral Cortex*, 19, 712–723.

Morison, P., & Gardner, H. (1978). Dragons and dinosaurs: The child's capacity to differentiate fantasy from reality. *Child Development*, 49, 642–648.

Morrison, I., Clift, S., Page, S., Salisbury, I., Shipton, M., Skingley, A., & Vella Burrows, T. (2013). A UK feasibility study on the value of singing for people with Chronic Obstructive Pulmonary Disease (COPD). *UNESCO-Observatory Multi-Disciplinary Journal in the Arts: International perspectives on the development of research-guided practice in community-based arts in health*, 3(3), 1–19.

Morrongiello, B. A., Roes, C. L., & Donnelly, F. (1989). Children's perception of musical patterns: Effects of music instruction. *Music Perception*, 6, pp. 447–462.

Morton, J. B., & Trehub, S. E. (2007). Children's judgements of emotion in song. *Psychology of Music*, 35, 629–639.

Moscardini, L., Barron, D. S., & Wilson, A. (2013). Who gets to play? Investigating equity in musical instrument instruction in Scottish primary schools. *International Journal of Inclusive Education*, 17(6), 646–662.

Mosing, M. A., & Ullén, F. (2016). Genetic influences on musical giftedness, talent, and practice. In G. E. McPherson (Ed.), *Musical prodigies: Interpretations from psychology, education, musicology, and ethnomusicology* (pp. 156–167). Oxford: Oxford University Press.

Mote, J. (2011). The effects of tempo and familiarity on children's affective interpretation of music. *Emotion*, 11, 618–622.

Mulder, J., ter Bogt, T. F. M., Raaijmakers, Q. A. W., Nic Gabhainn, S., & Sikkema, P. (2010). From death metal to R&B? Consistency of music preferences among Dutch adolescents and young adults. *Psychology of Music*, 38, 67–83.

Müller, M., Höfel, L., Brattico, E., & Jacobsen, T. (2009). Electrophysiological correlates of aesthetic music processing: Comparing experts with laypersons. *Annals of the New York Academy of Sciences. Neuroscience and Music III – Disorders and Plasticity*, 1169 (July), 355–358.

Murray, M., & Crummett, A. (2010). 'I don't think they knew we could do these sorts of things': Social representations of community and participation in community arts by older people. *Journal of Health Psychology*, 15(5), 777–785.

Myskyja, A., & Nord, P. G. (2008). 'The day the music died': A pilot study on music and depression in a nursing home. *Nordic Journal of Music Therapy*, 17(1), 30–40.

Nakata, T., & Trehub, S. E. (2004). Infants' responsiveness to maternal speech and singing. *Infant Behavior & Development*, 27, 455–464.

Nantais, K. M., & Schellenberg, E. G. (1999). The Mozart effect: An artifact of preference. *Psychological Science*, 10(4), 370–373.

Narmour, E. (1990). *The analysis and cognition of basic melodic structures*. Chicago: University of Chicago Press.

Nawrot, E. S. (2003). The perception of emotional expression in music: Evidence from infants, children, and adults. *Psychology of Music*, 31(1), 75–92.

Neguţ, A., & Sârbescu, P. (2014). Problem music or problem stereotypes? The dynamics of stereotype activation in rock and hip-hop music. *Musicae Scientiae*, 18(1), 3–16.

Nelson, T. O., & Narens, L. (1994) Why investigate metacognition? In J. Metcalfe & A.P. Shimaura (Eds.), *Metacognition: Knowing about knowing* (pp. 1–25). Cambridge, MA: MIT Press.

Nesdale, D., Maas, A., Griffiths, J., & Durkin, K. (2003). Effects of ingroup and outgroup ethnicity on children's attitudes towards members of the ingroup and outgroup. *British Journal of Developmental Psychology*, 21, 177–192.

Nesselroade, J. R., & Baltes, P. B. (1974). Adolescent personality development and historical change: 1970–1972. *Monographs of the Society for Research in Child Development*, 39(1) 1–80.

Nettl, B. (2012). Some contributions of ethnomusicology. In G. McPherson & G. Welch (Eds.), *The Oxford handbook of music education*, 1 (pp. 105–124). Oxford: Oxford University Press.

Nieminen, S., Istók, E., Brattico, E., & Tervaniemi, M. (2012). The development of the aesthetic experience of music: Preference, emotions, and beauty. *Musicae Scientiae*, 16(3), 372–391.

Nieminen, S., Istók, E., Brattico, E., Tervaniemi, M., & Huotilainen, M. (2011). The development of aesthetic responses to music. *Cortex*, 47(9), 1138–1146.

Non, A. L., Román, J. C., Gross, C. L., & Kubazansky, L. D. (2016). Early childhood social disadvantage is associated with poor health behaviours in adulthood. *Annals of Human Biology*, 43(2), 1–42.

North, A. C., & Hargreaves, D. J. (1995). Eminence in pop music. *Popular Music and Society*, 19(4), 41–66.

North, A. C., & Hargreaves, D. J. (1999). Music and adolescent identity. *Music Education Research*, 1(1), 75–92.

North, A. C., & Hargreaves, D. J. (2000a). Collative variables versus prototypicality. *Empirical Studies of the Arts*, 18(1), 13–17.

North, A. C., & Hargreaves, D. J. (2000b). Musical preferences during and after relaxation and exercise. *American Journal of Psychology*, 113(1), 43–67.

North, A. C., & Hargreaves, D. J. (2007a). Lifestyle correlates of musical preference: 1. Relationships, living arrangements, beliefs, and crime. *Psychology of Music*, 35(1), 58–87.

North, A. C., & Hargreaves, D. J. (2007b). Lifestyle correlates of musical preference: 2. Media, leisure time and music. *Psychology of Music*, 35(2), 179–200.

North, A. C., & Hargreaves, D. J. (2007c). Lifestyle correlates of musical preference: 3. Media, leisure time and music. *Psychology of Music*, 35(3), 473–497.

North, A. C., & Hargreaves, D. J. (2008). *The social and applied psychology of music*. Oxford: Oxford University Press.

North, A. C., Desborough, L., & Skarstein, L. (2005). Musical preference, deviance, and attitudes towards celebrities. *Personality and Individual Differences*, 383, 1903–1914.

North, A. C., Hargreaves, D. J., & Hargreaves, J. J. (2004). Uses of music in everyday life. *Music Perception*, 22(1), 41–77.

North, A. C., Hargreaves, D. J., & O'Neill, S. A. (2000). The importance of music to adolescents. *British Journal of Educational Psychology*, 70(2), 255–272.

Nutbeam, D. (2008). The evolving concept of health literacy. *Social Science & Medicine*, 67, 2072–2078.

O'Neill, C. T., Trainor, L. J., & Trehub, S. E. (2001). Infants' responsiveness to fathers' singing. *Music Perception*, 18(4), 409–425.

O'Neill, S. A. (1997). The role of practice in children's early musical performance achievement. In H. Jørgensen & A. C. Lehmann (Eds.), *Does practice make perfect? Current theory and research on instrumental practice* (pp. 53–70). Oslo: Nordes Musikhøgskole.

O'Neill, S. A. (1999). Flow theory and the development of musical performance skills. *Bulletin of the Council for Research in Music Education*, 141, 129–134.

O'Neill, S. A. (2017) Young people's musical lives: Identities, learning ecologies and connectedness. In R. A. R. MacDonald, D. J. Hargreaves, & D. E. Miell (Eds.), *Handbook of musical identities* (pp. 79–104). Oxford: Oxford University Press.

O'Neill, S. A., & McPherson, G. E. (2002). Motivation. In R. Parncutt & G. E. McPherson (Eds.), *The science and psychology of music performance* (pp. 31–46). Oxford: Oxford University Press.

Ockelford, A. (2006). Implication and expectation in music: A zygonic model. *Psychology of Music*, 34(1), 81–142.

Ockelford, A. (2008). *Music for children and young people with complex needs*. Oxford: Oxford University Press

Ockelford, A. (2012). Imagination feeds memory: Exploring evidence from a musical savant using zygonic theory. In D. J. Hargreaves, D. E Miell, & R. A. R. MacDonald (Eds.), *Musical imaginations* (pp. 31–61). Oxford: Oxford University Press.

Ockelford, A. (2013). *Applied musicology: Using zygonic theory to inform music education, therapy, and psychology research.* Oxford: Oxford University Press.

Ockelford, A. (2016). The potential impact of autism on musical development. In G. McPherson (Ed.) *The child as musician: A handbook of musical development* (2nd edition, pp. 122–145). Oxford: Oxford University Press.

Ockelford, A., & Voyajolu, A. (2017). The development of music-structural cognition in the early years: A new study offering a perspective from zygonic theory. In *New approaches to analysis in music psychology and music education research using zygonic theory,* London: Routledge.

Ockelford, A., Welch, G., Jewell-Gore, L., Cheng, E., Vogiatzoglou, A., & Himonides, E. (2011). Sounds of Intent, Phase 2: Approaches to the quantification of music-developmental data pertaining to children with complex needs. *European Journal of Special Needs Education,* 26(2), 177–199.

Odena, O., & Welch, G. (2009). A generative model of teachers' thinking on musical creativity. *Psychology of Music,* 37(4), 416–442.

Olivetti Belardinelli, M. (2006). Beyond global and local theories of musical creativity: Looking for specific indicators of mental activity during music processing. In I. Deliège & G. A. Wiggins (Eds.), *Musical creativity: Multidisciplinary research in theory and practice* (pp. 322–344). Hove: Psychology Press.

Olivetti Belardinelli, M., Di Matteo, R., Del Gratta, G., De Nicola, A., Ferreti, A., Tartaro, A., Bonomo, L., & Romani, G. L. (2004). Intermodal sensory image generation: An fMRI analysis. *European Journal of Cognitive Psychology,* 16, 729–752.

Onishi, K. H., & Baillargeon, R. (2005). Do 15-month-old infants understand false beliefs? *Science,* 308, 255–258.

Osborne, M. S., & Kenny, D. T. (2008). The role of sensitizing experiences in music performance anxiety in adolescent musicians. *Psychology of Music,* 36(4), 447–462.

Osborne, M. S., McPherson, G. E., Faulkner, R., Davidson, J. W., & Barrett, M. S. (2016). Exploring the academic and psychosocial impact of El Sistema-inspired music programs within two low socio-economic schools. *Music Education Research,* 18(2), 156–175.

Oura, Y., & Hatano, G. (1988). Memory for melodies among subjects differing in age and experience in music. *Psychology of Music,* 16, 91–109.

Paananen, P. A. (2006). Harmonizing a tonal melody at the age of 6–15 years. In M. Baroni, A. R. Addessi, R. Caterina, & M. Costa (Eds.), *Proceedings of the 9th International Conference on Music Perception and Cognition* (pp. 484–488). Bologna, Italy: University of Bologna.

Paananen, P. A. (2007). Melodic improvisation at the age of 6–11 years: Development of pitch and rhythm. *Musicae Scientiae,* 11(1), 89–119.

Pachet, F. (2006). Enhancing individual creativity with interactive musical reflexive systems. *Musical Creativity,* 359.

Pantev, C., Oostenveld, R., Engelien, A., Ross, B., Roberts, L. E., & Hoke, M. (1998). Increased auditory cortical representation in musicians. *Nature,* 392, 811–814.

Papinczak, Z., Dingle, G. A., Stoyanov, S. R., Hides, L., & Zelenko, O. (2015). Young people's use of music for wellbeing. *Journal of Youth Studies,* 18(9), 1119–1134.

Papoušek, M. (1992). Early ontogeny of vocal communication in parent-infant interactions. In H. Papoušek, U. Urgens, & M. Papoušek (Eds.), *Nonverbal vocal communication: Comparative and developmental approaches* (pp. 230–261). Cambridge: Cambridge University Press.

Papoušek, M., & Papoušek, H. (1981). Musical elements in the infant's vocalization: Their significance for communication, cogntion, and creativity. In L. P. Lipsitt & C. K. Rovee-Collier (Eds.), *Advances in Infancy Research, 1* (pp. 163–224). Norwood, NJ: Ablex.

Parncutt, R. (2016a). Prenatal development and the phylogeny and ontogeny of musical behavior. In S. Hallam, I. Cross, & M. Thaut (Eds.), *The Oxford handbook of music psychology* (2nd edition, pp. 371–386). Oxford: Oxford University Press.

Parncutt, R. (2016b). Prenatal development. In G. E. McPherson (Ed.), *The child as musician: A handbook of musical development* (pp. 3–30). Oxford: Oxford University Press.

Parncutt, R., & McPherson, G. E. (Eds.) (2002). *The science and psychology of music performance.* Oxford: Oxford University Press.

Parsons, M. (1987). *How we understand art.* Cambridge: Cambridge University Press.

Partanen, E., Kujala, T., Tervaniemi, M., & Houtilainen, M. (2013). Prenatal music exposure induces long-term neural effects. *PLOS One,* 8(10), e78946.

Parzer, M. (2013). Cultural variety as a resource? Musical taste and social distinction in contemporary cultural sociology. In S. Gies & F. Hess (Eds.), *Kulturelle Identität und soziale Distinktion* (pp. 59–71). Innsbruck: Helbling.

Passanisi, A., Di Nuovo, S., Urgese, L., & Pirrone, C. (2015). The influence of musical expression on creativity and interpersonal relationships in children. *Procedia – Social and Behavioral Sciences,* 191, 2476–2480.

Patston, L. L., & Tippett, L. J. (2011). The effect of background music on cognitive performance in musicians and nonmusicians. *Music Perception,* 29, 173–183.

Pearce, E., Launay, J., MacCarron, P., & Dunbar, R. I. M. (2017). Tuning in to others: Exploring relational and collective bonding in singing and non-singing groups over time. *Psychology of Music,* 45(4), 496–512.

Peck, K. J., Girard, T. A., Russo, F. A., & Fiocco, A. J. (2016). Music and memory in Alzheimer's disease and the potential underlying mechanisms. *Journal of Alzheimer's Disease,* 51(4), 949–959.

Pegg, J. E., Werker, J. F., & McLeod, P. J. (1992). Preference for infant-directed over adult-directed speech: Evidence from 7-week-old infants. *Infant Behavior and Development,* 15, 325–345.

Peretz, I., Gosselin, N., Tillmann, B., Cuddy, L. L., Gagnon, B., Trimmer, C. G., et al. (2008). Online identification of congenital amusia. *Music Perception,* 25(4), 331–343.

Peretz, I., Gosselin, N., Caron-Caplette, E., Trehub, S. E., & Béland, R. (2013). A novel tool for evaluating children's musical abilities across age and culture. *Frontiers in Systems Neuroscience,* DOI: 10.3389/fnsys.2013.00030.

Pérez-Aldeguer, S., & Leganés, E.-N. (2014). Differences in psychological well-being between choristers and non-choristers in older adults. *International Journal of Community Music,* 7(3), 397–407.

Perkins, R., & Fancourt, D. (2017). Maternal engagement with music up to nine months post-birth: Findings from a cross-sectional study in England. *Psychology of Music,* DOI: 10.1177/0305735617705720.

Persson, R. (2001). The subjective world of the performer. In P. N. Juslin & J. A. Sloboda (Eds.), *Music and emotion: Theory and research* (pp. 275–289). Oxford: Oxford University Press.

Peterson, C., Park, N., & Seligman, M. E. P. (2005). Orientations to happiness and life satisfaction: The full life versus the empty life. *Journal of Happiness Studies,* 6, 24–41.

Phillips-Silver, J., & Trainor, L. J. (2005). Feeling the beat: Movement influences infant rhythm perception. *Science,* 308, 1430.

Piaget. J. (1951). *Play, dreams and imitation in childhood.* London: Routledge & Kegan Paul.

Piaget, J. (1953). *The origins of intelligence in children.* London: Routledge & Kegan Paul.

Piaget, J., & Inhelder, B. (1969). *The psychology of the child*. London: Routledge & Kegan Paul.

Pietschnig, J., Voracek, M., & Formann, A. K. (2010). Mozart effect-Schmozart effect: A meta-analysis. *Intelligence*, 38(3), 314–323.

Pintrich, P. R., & Schunk, D. H. (2002). *Motivation in education: Theory, research, and applications* (2nd edition). Columbus, OH: Merrill Prentice Hall.

Pitts, S. E. (2009). Roots and routes in adult music participation: Investigating the impact of home and school on lifelong musical interest and involvement. *British Journal of Music Education*, 26(3), 241–256.

Plantinga, J., & Trainor, L. J. (2005). Memory for melody: infants use a relative pitch code. *Cognition*, 98, 1–11.

Plantinga, J., & Trainor, L. J. (2009). Melody recognition by two-month-old infants. *Journal of the Acoustical Society of America*, 125(2), EL58–62.

Plantinga, J., & Trehub, S. E. (2014). Revisiting the innate preference for consonance. *Journal of Experimental Psychology: Human Perception and Performance*, 40(1), 40–49.

Pond, D. (1981). A composer's study of young children's innate musicality. *Bulletin of the Council for Research in Music Education*, 68, 1–12.

Pressing, J. (1988). Improvisation: Methods and models. In J. A. Sloboda (Ed.), *Generative processes in music: The psychology of performance, improvisation and composition* (pp. 129–178). Oxford: Oxford University Press.

Preti, C., & Welch, G. F. (2011). Music in a hospital: The impact of a live music program on pediatric patients and their caregivers. *Music and Medicine*, 3(4), 213–223.

Primos, K. (2001). South Africa. In D. J. Hargreaves & A. C. North (Eds.), *Musical development and learning: The international perspective* (pp. 56–72). London: Continuum.

Provasi, J., & Bobin-Bègue, A. (2003). Spontaneous motor tempo and rhythmical synchronisation in 2½- and 4-year-old children. *International Journal of Behavioral Development*, 27(3), 220–231.

QCA (2002). *Developing new models for music education*. Paper presented to the National Music Education Forum, 17 June 2002.

Rabinowitch, T. C., Cross, I., & Burnard, P. (2013). Long-term musical group interaction has a positive influence on empathy in children. *Psychology of Music*, 41(4), 484–498.

Radford, J. (1994). Variations on a musical theme. Open peer commentary on 'Is everyone musical?', by J. A. Sloboda, J. W. Davidson, & M. J. A. Howe. *The Psychologist*, 7(8), 359–360.

Raglio, A., Bellandi, D., Baiardi, P., Gianotti, M., Ubezio, M. C., Zanacchi, E., Granieri, E., Imbriani, M., & Stramba-Badiale, M. (2015). Effect of active music therapy and individualized listening to music on dementia: A multicenter randomized controlled trial. *Journal of the American Geriatrics Society*, 6(3), 1534–1539.

Randall, W. M., & Rickard, N. S. (2013). Development and trial of a mobile experience sampling method (m-ESM) for personal music listening. *Music Perception*, 31(2), 157–170.

Randall, W. M., Rickard, N. S., & Vella-Brodrick, D. A. (2014). Emotional outcomes of regulation strategies used during personal music listening: A mobile experience sampling study. *Musicae Scientiae*, 18(3), 275–291.

Ranelli, S., Smith, A., & Straker, L. (2011). Playing-related musculoskeletal problems in child instrumentalists: The influence of gender, age and instrument exposure. *International Journal of Music Education*, 29(1), 28–44.

Ratterman, M., & Gentner, D. (1988). More evidence for a relational shift in the development of analogy: Children's performance on a causal mapping task. *Cognitive Development*, 13, 453–478.

Rauscher, F. H., & Hinton, S. C. (2008). The Mozart Effect: Music listening is not music instruction. *Educational Psychologist*, 41(4), 233–238.

Rauscher, F. H., & Hinton, S. C. (2011). Music instruction and its diverse extra-musical benefits. *Music Perception*, 29(2), 215–226.

Rauscher, F. H., & Shaw, G. L. (1998). Key components of the Mozart effect. *Perceptual and Motor Skills*, 86(3, Part 1), 835–841.

Rauscher, F. H., & Zupan, M. A. (2000). Classroom keyboard instruction improves kindergarten children's spatial-temporal performance: A field experiment. *Early Childhood Research Quarterly*, 15(2), 215–228.

Rauscher, F. H., Shaw, G. L., & Ky, K. N. (1993). Music and spatial task performance. *Nature*, 365(6447), 611.

Rauscher, F. H., Shaw, G. L., & Ky, K. N. (1995). Listening to Mozart enhances spatial-temporal reasoning: Towards a neurophysiological basis. *Neuroscience Letters*, 185(1), 44–47.

Reagon, C., Gale, N., Enright, S., Mann, M., & van Deursen, R. (2016). A mixed-method systematic review to investigate the effect of group singing on health related quality of life. *Complementary Therapies in Medicine*, 27, 1–11.

Rentfrow, P. J., & Gosling, S. D. (2003). The do re mi's of everyday life: Examining the structure and personality correlates of music preferences. *Journal of Personality and Social Psychology*, 84(6), 1236–1256.

Rentfrow, P. J., & Gosling, S. D. (2006). Message in a ballad: The role of musical preferences in interpersonal perception. *Psychological Science*, 17(3), 236–242.

Rentfrow, P. J., & Gosling, S. D. (2007). The content and validity of music-genre stereotypes among college students. *Psychology of Music*, 35(2), 306–326.

Rentfrow, P. J., Goldberg, L. R., & Levitin, D. J. (2011). The structure of musical preferences: A five-factor model. *Journal of Personality and Social Psychology*, 100(6), 1139–1157.

Rentfrow, P. J., McDonald, J. A., & Oldmeadow, J. A. (2009). You are what you listen to: Young people's stereotypes about music fans. *Group Processes and Intergroup Relations*, 12(3), 329–344.

Rentfrow, P. J., Goldberg, L. R., Stillwell, D. J., Kosinski, M., Gosling, S. D., & Levitin, D. J. (2012). The song remains the same: A replication and extension of the MUSIC model. *Music Perception*, 30(2), 161–185.

Renwick, J., & Reeve, J. (2012). Supporting motivation in music education. In G. McPherson & G. Welch (Eds.), *The Oxford handbook of music education, 1*, (pp. 143–162). Oxford: Oxford University Press.

Repp, B. H., & Penel, A. (2004). Rhythmic movement is attracted more strongly to auditory than to visual rhythms. *Psychological Research*, 68, 252–270.

Reyna, C., Brandt, M., & Viki, G. D. (2009). Blame it on hip-hop: Anti-rap attitudes as a proxy for prejudice. *Group Processes and Intergroup Relations*, 12(3), 361–380.

Richards, R. (2010). Everyday creativity: Process and way of life – four key issues. In J. C. Kaufman & R. J. Sternberg (Eds.), *The Cambridge Handbook of Creativity* (pp. 189–215). New York: Cambridge University Press.

Rickard, N. S., & Chin, T. (2017). Defining the musical identity of 'non-musicians'. In R. A. R. MacDonald, D. J. Hargreaves, & D. E. Miell (Eds.), *Handbook of musical identities* (pp. 288–303). Oxford: Oxford University Press.

Rickard, N. S., Appelman, P., James, R., Murphy, F., Gill, A., & Bambrick, C. (2012). Orchestrating life skills: The effect of increased school-based music classes on children's social competence and self-esteem. *International Journal of Music Education*, 31(3), 292–309.

Rideout, B. E., Dougherty, S., & Wernert, L. (1998). Effect of music on spatial performance: A test of generality. *Perceptual and Motor Skills*, 86(2), 512–514.

Rizzolati, G., & Craighero, L. (2004). The mirror neuron system. *Annual Review of Neuroscience*, 27, 169–192.

Robins, R. W., Hendin, H. M., & Trzesniewski, K. H. (2001). Measuring global self-esteem: Construct validation of a single-item measure and the Rosenberg Self-Esteem Scale. *Personality and Social Psychology Bulletin*, 27(2), 151–161.

Robinson, K., Minkin, L., Bolton, E., French, D., Fryer, L., Greenfield, S., & Green, L. (1999). *All our futures: Creativity*. London: HMSO.

Robson, S. (2014). *The relationship between responsibility for children's choice of activity and evidence of self-regulation and metacognition*. Unpublished PhD thesis. University of Roehampton.

Roden, I., Kreutz, G., & Bongard, S. (2012). Effects of a school-based instrumental music program on verbal and visual memory in primary school children: A longitudinal study. *Frontiers in Psychology*, 3, 572.

Rodway, P., Kirkham, J., Schepman, A., Lambert, J., & Locke, A. (2016). The development of shared liking of representational but not abstract art in primary school children and their justifications for liking. *Frontiers in Human Neuroscience*, 10, 21, DOI: 10.3389/fnhum.2016.00021.

Roe, A. (1953). A psychological study of eminent psychologists and anthropologists and a comparison with biological and physical scientists. *Psychological Monographs*, 67, no, 2.

Rogoff, B. (1990). *Apprenticeship in thinking: Cognitive development in social context*. New York: Oxford University Press.

Rogoff, B. (2003). *The cultural nature of human development*. New York: Oxford University Press.

Romaniuk, J. G., & Romaniuk, M. (1981). Creativity across the life span: A measurement perspective. *Human Development*, 24, 366–381.

Rose, D., Heaton, P., & Jones-Bartoli, A. (2015). Changes in the well-being of children starting to play musical instruments. *Assessment & Development Matters*, 7(1), 26–30.

Rosenberg, M. (1965). *Society and the adolescent self-image*. Princeton, NJ: Princeton University Press.

Ross, M. (Ed.) (1984). *The aesthetic impulse*. Oxford: Pergamon Press.

Ross, M. (Ed.) (1986). *The aesthetic in education*. Oxford: Pergamon Press.

Ruddock, E., & Leong, S. (2005). 'I am unmusical!': The verdict of self-judgement. *International Journal of Music Education*, 23(1), 9–22.

Runfola, M., & Swanwick, K. (2002). Developmental characteristics of music learners. In R. Colwell & C. Richardson (Eds.), *New handbook of research on music teaching and learning* (pp. 373–397). Oxford: Oxford University Press.

Rusk, R. D., & Waters, L. (2015). A psycho-social system approach to well-being: Empirically deriving the five domains of positive functioning. *The Journal of Positive Psychology*, 10(2), 141–152.

Rutkowski, J. (2015). The relationship between children's use of singing voice and singing accuracy. *Music Perception*, 32(3), 283–292.

Ryan, K. J., Boulton, M. J., O'Neill, S., & Sloboda, J. A. (2000). Perceived social support and children's participation in music. In C. Woods, G. Luck, R. Brochard, F. Seddon, & J. A. Sloboda (Eds.), *Science, music & society: 6th International Conference on Music Perception and Cognition*. Newcastle; Staffordshire: Keele University.

Ryan, R. M., & Deci, E. L. (2000). Self-determination theory and the facilitation of intrinsic motivation, social development, and well-being. *American Psychologist*, 55(1), 68–78.

Ryan, R. M., Huta, V., & Deci, E. L. (2008). Living well: A self-determination theory perspective on eudaimonia. *Journal of Happiness Studies*, 9, 139–170.

Saarikallio, S. (2011). Music as emotional self-regulation throughout adulthood. *Psychology of Music*, 39(3), 307–327.

Saarikallio, S., & Erkkilä, J. (2007). The role of music in adolescents' mood regulation. *Psychology of Music*, 35, 88–109.

Saffran, J. R., & Griepentrog, G. J. (2001). Absolute pitch in infant auditory learning: Evidence for developmental reorganization. *Developmental Psychology*, 37(1), 74–85.

Saffran, J. R., Aslin, R. A., & Newport, E. L. (1996). Statistical learning by 8-month-old infants. *Science*, 274, 1926–1928.

Saffran, J. R., Loman, M. M., & Robertson, R. R. W. (2000). Infant memory for musical experiences. *Cognition*, 77, B15–B23.

Sala, G., & Gobet, F. (2016). When the music's over: Does music skill transfer to children's and young adolescents' cognitive and academic skills? A meta-analysis. *Educational Research Review*, 20, 55–67.

Sameroff, A. (2000). Developmental systems and psychopathology. *Development and Psychopathology*, 12(3), 297–312.

Sameroff, A. (2009). The transactional model. In A. Sameroff (Ed.), *The transactional model of development: How children and contexts shape each other* (pp. 3–21). Washington, DC: American Psychological Association.

Sameroff, A. (2010). A unified theory of development; A dialectic integration of nature and nurture. *Child Development*, 81(1), 6–22.

Sameroff, A., & Fiese, B. (Eds.) (2000). *Transactional regulation: The developmental ecology of early intervention.* Cambridge: Cambridge University Press.

Santrock, J. W. (2010). *A topical approach to life-span development.* New York: McGraw-Hill.

Särkamö, T., Laitinen, S., Numminen, A., Kurki, M., Johnson, J. K., & Rantanen, P. (2016a). Clinical and demographic factors associated with the cognitive and emotional efficacy of regular musical activities in dementia. *Journal of Alzheimer's Disease*, 49(3), 767–781.

Särkamö, T., Laitinen, S., Numminen, A., Kurki, M., Johnson, J. K., & Rantanen, P. (2016b). Pattern of emotional benefits induced by regular singing and music listening in dementia. *Journal of the American Gerontological Society*, Letters to the Editor, 64(2), 439–440.

Savan, A., (1999). The effect of background music on learning. *Psychology of Music*, 27(2), 138–146.

Sawyer, R. K. (2003). *Group creativity: Music, theater, collaboration.* Mahwah, NJ: Lawrence Erlbaum Associates.

Sawyer, R. K. (2008). Learning music from collaboration. *International Journal of Educational Research*, 47(1), 50–59.

Schäfer, T., & Sedlmeier, P. (2009). From the functions of music to music preference. *Psychology of Music*, 37, 279–300.

Schäfer, T., & Sedlmeier, P. (2010). What makes us like music? Determinants of music preference. *Psychology of Aesthetics, Creativity, and the Arts*, 4, 223–234.

Schaie, K. W. (1965). A general model for the study of developmental problems. *Psychological Bulletin*, 64, 92–107.

Schaie, K. W. (Ed.). (1983). *Longitudinal studies of adult psychological development*. New York: Guilford Press.

Schaie, K. W. (1996). *Intellectual development in adulthood: The Seattle longitudinal study*. Cambridge: Cambridge University Press.

Schellenberg, E. G. (1997). Simplifying the implication-realization model of melodic expectancy. *Music Perception*, 14, 295–318.

Schellenberg, E. G. (2004). Music lessons enhance IQ. *Psychological Science*, 15(8), 511–514.

Schellenberg, E. G. (2006). Exposure to music: The truth about the consequences. In G. E. McPherson (Ed.), *The child as musician* (pp. 111–134). Oxford: Oxford University Press.

Schellenberg, E. G. (2016). Music and non-musical abilities. In G. E. McPherson (Ed.), *The Child as musician: A handbook of musical development* (pp. 149–176). Oxford: Oxford University Press.

Schellenberg, E. G., & Hallam, S. (2005). Music listening and cognitive abilities in 10- and 11-year-olds: The Blur effect. *Annals of the New York Academy of Sciences*, 1060, 202–209.

Schellenberg, E. G., & McKinnon, M. C. (1996). Melodic expectancy: A comparison of adults and children. In: *Proceedings of the Fourth International Conference on Music Perception and Cognition*, McGill University, Montreal, 301–304.

Schellenberg, E. G., & Trehub, S. E. (1996). Natural musical intervals: Evidence from infant listeners. *Psychological Science*, 7(5), 272–277.

Schellenberg, E. G., & Trehub, S. E. (2003). Good pitch memory is widespread. *Psychological Science*, 14, 262–266.

Schellenberg, E. G., Adachi, M., Purdy, K. T., & McKinnon, M. C. (2002). Expectancy in melody: Tests of children and adults. *Journal of Experimental Psychology: General*, 131(4), 511–537.

Schellenberg, E. G., Nakata, T., Hunter, P. G., & Tamoto, S. (2007). Exposure to music and cognitive performance: tests of children and adults. *Psychology of Music*, 35(1), 5–19.

Schellenberg, E. G., Bigand, E., Poulin-Charronat, B., Garnier, C., & Stevens, C. (2005). Children's implicit knowledge of harmony in Western music. *Developmental Science*, 8(6), 551–566.

Schlaug, G., Jancke, L., Huang, Y., Staiger, J. F., & Steinmetz, H. (1995). Increased corpus callosum size in musicians. *Neuropsychologia*, 33(8), 1047–1055.

Schubert, E. (2012). Spreading activation and dissociation: a cognitive mechanism for creative processing in music. In D. J. Hargreaves, D. E. Miell, & R. A. R. MacDonald (Eds.), *Musical imaginations: Multidisciplinary perspectives on creativity, performance, and perception* (pp. 124–140). Oxford: Oxford University Press.

Schubert, E., & McPherson, G. E. (2016). Underlying mechanisms and processes in the development of emotion perception in music. In G. E. McPherson (Ed.), *The Child as musician: A handbook of musical development* (2nd edition, pp. 221–237). Oxford: Oxford University Press.

Schubert, E., Hargreaves, D. J., & North, A. C. (2014). A dynamically minimalist cognitive explanation of musical preference: Is familiarity everything? *Frontiers in Psychology*, 5, 1–8.

Schunk D. H., & Zimmerman, B. J. (Eds.) (1994). *Self-regulation of learning and performance: Issues and educational implications*. Hillsdale, NJ: Lawrence Erlbaum Associates.

Schunk, D. H., Meece, J. L., & Pintrich, P. R. (2014). *Motivation in education: Theory, research, and applications* (4th edition). Englewood Cliffs, NJ: Prentice-Hall.

Schurig, M., Busch, V., & Strauss, J. (2012). Effects of structural and personal variables on children's development of music preference. In E. Cambouropoulos et al. (Eds.),

Proceedings of the 12th International Conference on Music Perception and Cognition and the 8th Triennial Conference of the European Society for the Cognitive Sciences of Music, pp. 897–902. Thessaloniki, 2012.

Schwartz, K. D., & Fouts, G. T. (2003). Music preferences, personality style, and developmental issues of adolescents. *Journal of Youth and Adolescence, 323,* 205–213.

Schwarzer, G. (1997). Analytic and holistic modes in the development of melody perception. *Psychology of Music,* 25(1), 35–56.

Seashore, C. (1938). *Psychology of music.* New York: McGraw–Hill.

Seddon, F. A. (2005). Modes of communication during jazz improvisation. *British Journal of Music Education,* 22(1), 47–61.

Seesjärvi, E., Särkämo, T., Vuoksimaa, E., Tervaniemi, M., Peretz, I., & Kaprio, J. (2016). The nature and nurture of melody: A twin study of musical pitch and rhythm perception. *Behavioural Genetics,* 46(4), 506–515.

Seger, C. A., Spiering, B. J., Sares, A. G., Quraini, S. I., Alpeter, C., David, J., & Thaut, M. H. (2013). Corticostriatal contributions to musical expectancy perception. *Journal of Cognitive Neuroscience,* 25(7), 1062–1077.

Selfhout, M. H. W., Branje, S. J. T., ter Bogt, T. F. M., & Meeus, W. H. J. (2009). The role of music preferences in early adolescents' friendship formation and stability. *Journal of Adolescence,* 32(1), 95–107.

Seligman, M. E. P. (1972). Learned helplessness. *Annual Review of Medicine,* 23, 407–412.

Seligman, M. E. P. (2002). *Authentic happiness: Using the new positive psychology to realize your potential for lasting fulfillment.* New York: Free Press.

Seligman, M. E. P. (2011). *Flourish: A new understanding of happiness and well-being – and how to achieve them.* London: Nicholas Brealey Publishing.

Seligman, M. E. P., & Csikszentmihalyi, M. (2000). Positive psychology: An introduction. *American Psychologist,* 55, 5–14.

Seligman, M. E. P., Parks, A. C., & Steen, T. (2005). A balanced psychology and a full life. In F. A. Huppert, N. Baylis. & B. Keverne (Eds.), *The science of well-being* (pp. 275–304). Oxford: Oxford University Press.

Seligman, M. E. P., Rashid, T., & Parks, A. C. (2006). Positive psychotherapy. *American Psychologist,* 61(8), 774–788.

Seligman, M. E. P., Ernst, R. M., Gilham, J., Reivich, K., & Linkins, M. (2009). Positive education: Positive psychology and classroom interventions. *Oxford Review of Education,* 35(3), 293–311.

Serafine, M. L. (1988). *Music as cognition: The development of thought in sound.* New York: Columbia University Press.

Sergeant, D., & Boyle, J. D. (1980). Contextual influences on pitch judgement. *Psychology of Music,* 8(2), 3–15.

Shaffer, L. H. (1981). Performances of Chopin, Bach, and Bartok: Studies in motor programming. *Cognitive Psychology,* 13(3), 326–376.

Shahidullah, S., & Hepper, P. (1994). Frequency discrimination by the fetus. *Early Human Development,* 36, 365–394.

Shahin, A., Roberts, L. E., & Trainor L. J. (2004). Enhancement of auditory cortical development by musical experience in children. *NeuroReport: Auditory and Vestibular Systems,* 15(12), 1917–1921.

Sheldon, K. M., & Kasser, T. (2001). Getting older, getting better? Personal strivings and psychological maturity across the lifespan. *Developmental Psychology,* 37, 491–501.

Sheldon, K. M., Kasser, T., Houser-Marko, L., Jones, T., & Turban, D. (2005). Doing one's duty: Chronological age, felt autonomy, and subjective well-being. *European Journal of Personality*, 19, 97–115.

Shenfield, T., Trehub, S., & Nakata, T. (2003). Maternal singing modulates infant arousal. *Psychology of Music*, 31, 365–375.

Shepherd, J. (2003). Music and social categories. In M. Clayton, T. Herbert, & R. Middleton (Eds.), *The cultural study of music: A critical introduction* (pp. 69–79). London: Routledge.

Shotwell, J. (1979). Counting steps. *New Directions for Child and Adolescent Development*, 3, 85–96.

Shuter-Dyson, R. (1999). Musical ability. In D. Deutsch (Ed.), The psychology of music (2nd edition, pp. 627–651). New York: Academic Press.

Shuter-Dyson, R. (1968). *The psychology of musical ability.* London: Methuen.

Shuter-Dyson, R., & Gabriel, C. (1981). *The psychology of musical ability*. London: Methuen.

Shweder, R. A. (1990). Cultural psychology: What is it? In J. Stigler, R. A. Shweder, & G. Herdt (Eds.), *Cultural psychology: Essays on comparative human development*. New York: Cambridge University Press.

Siegler, R. S. (1998). *Emerging minds: The process of change in children's thinking.* Oxford: Oxford University Press.

Simonton, D. K. (1980a). Thematic fame and melodic originality: A multivariate computer-content analysis. *Journal of Personality*, 48, 206–219.

Simonton, D. K. (1980b). Thematic fame, melodic originality, and musical zeitgeist: A biographical and transhistorical content analysis. *Journal of Personality and Social Psychology*, 39, 972–983.

Simonton, D. K. (1984). Genius, creativity, and leadership. Cambridge, MA: Harvard University Press.

Simonton, D. K. (1991). Emergence and realisation of genius: The lives and works of 120 classical composers. *Journal of Personality and Social Psychology*, 61, 829–840.

Simonton, D. K. (2016). Early and late bloomers among 120 classical composers: Were the greatest geniuses also prodigies? In G. E. McPherson (Ed.), *Musical prodigies: Interpretations from psychology, education, musicology, and ethnomusicology* (pp. 185–197). Oxford: Oxford University Press.

Sin, N. L., & Lyubomirsky, S. (2009). Enhancing well-being and alleviating depressive symptoms with positive psychology interventions: A practice-friendly meta-analysis. *Journal of Clinical Psychology*, 65, 467–487.

Sing Up (2012). *All together now: An in-depth guide to the benefits of accessible Learning networks.* www.singup.org/fileadmin/singupfiles/previous_uploads/AcLe_3MB.pdf

Sirgy, M. J., & Wu, J. (2009). The pleasant life, the engaged life, and the meaningful life: What about the balanced life? *Journal of Happiness Studies*, 10(2), 183–196.

Slater, J., Tierney, A., & Kraus, N. (2014). At-risk elementary school children with one year of classroom music instruction are better at keeping a beat. *PLoS ONE*, 8(10): e77250.

Sloboda, J. A. (1985). *The musical mind: The cognitive psychology of music.* Oxford: Clarendon Press.

Sloboda, J. A. (1986). Open letter: Achieving our aims in music education. *Psychology of Music*, 14(2), 144–145.

Sloboda, J. A. (1991). Music structure and emotional response: Some empirical findings. *Psychology of Music*, 19, 110–120.

Sloboda, J. A. (1994). Music performance: Expression and the development of excellence. In R. Aiello & J. A. Sloboda (Eds.), *Musical perceptions*. New York: Oxford University Press.

Sloboda, J. A. (2001). Emotion, functionality and the everyday experience of music: Where does music education fit? *Music Education Research*, 3(2), 243–253.

Sloboda, J. A. (2002). Music and worship: A psychologist's perspective. In T. Hone, M. Savage, & J. Astley (Eds.), *Creative chords: Studies in music, theology and Christian formation* (pp. 110–125). Leominster: Gracewing.

Sloboda, J. A. (2005). *Exploring the musical mind: Cognition, emotion, ability, function.* Oxford: Oxford University Press.

Sloboda, J. A., & Davidson, J. W. (1996). The young performing musician. In I. Deliège & J. A. Sloboda (Eds.), *Musical beginnings: Origins and development of musical competence* (pp. 171–190). New York: Oxford University Press.

Sloboda, J. A., & Howe, M. J. A. (1991). Biographical precursors of musical excellence: An interview study. *Psychology of Music*, 19, 3–21.

Sloboda, J. A., Davidson, J. W., & Howe, M. J. A. (1994). Is everyone musical? *The Psychologist*, 7, 349–354.

Sloboda, J. A., O'Neill, S. A., & Ivaldi, A. (2001). Functions of music in everyday life: An exploratory study using the Experience Sampling Method. *Musicae Scientiae*, 5(1), 9–32.

Sloboda, J. A., Davidson J. W., Howe, M. J. A., & Moore D. M. (1996). The role of practice in the development of expert musical performance. *British Journal of Psychology*, 87, 287–309.

Smith, K. C., Cuddy, L. L., & Upitis, R. (1994). Figural and metric understanding of rhythm. *Psychology of Music*, 22, 117–135.

Snyder, M. (1974). Self-monitoring of expressive behavior. *Journal of Personality and Social Psychology*, 30, 526–537.

Soderquist, D. R., & Moore, M. J. (1970). Effect of training on frequency discrimination in primary school children. *Journal of Auditory Research*, 10, 185–192.

Sole, M. (2017). Crib song: Insights into developmental functions of toddlers' private spontaneous singing. *Psychology of Music*, 45(2), 172–192.

Sosniak, L. A. (1985). Learning to be a concert pianist. In B. S. Bloom (Ed.), *Developing talent in young people* (pp. 19–67). New York: Ballantine.

Sosniak, L. A. (1990). The tortoise, the hare, and the development of talent. In M. J. A. Howe (Ed.), *Encouraging the development of exceptional skills and talents* (pp. 149–164). Leicester: British Psychological Society.

Spychiger, M., Patry, J. L. G., Zimmerman, E., & Weber, E. (1995). Does more music teaching lead to a better social climate? In R. Olechowski & G. Svik (Eds.), *Experimental research in teaching and learning* (pp. 322–336). Bern: Peter Lang.

Stachó, L., Saarikallio, S., van Zijl, A., Houtilainen, M., & Toiviainen, P. (2013). Perception of emotional content in musical performances by 3- to 7-year-old children. *Musicae Scientiae*, 17(4), 495–512.

Stakelum, M. (2013). John Finney, Music education in England, 1950–2010: The child-centred progressive tradition (2011). *Journal of the Society for Musicology in Ireland*, 8, 105–108.

Stalinski, S. M., & Schellenberg, E. G. (2010). Shifting perceptions: Developmental changes in judgments of melodic similarity. *Developmental Psychology*, 46, 799–1803.

Stalinski, S. M., Schellenberg, E. G., & Trehub, S. E. (2008). Developmental changes in the perception of pitch contour: Distinguishing up from down. *Journal of the Acoustical Society of America*, 124, 1759–1763.

Steele, K. M., Bass, K. E., & Crook, M. D. (1999). The mystery of the Mozart Effect: Failure to replicate. *Psychological Science*, 10(4), 366–369.

Stegemöller, E. L., Radig, H., Hibbing, P., Wingate, J., & Sapienza, C. (2017). Effects of singing on voice, respiratory control and quality of life in persons with Parkinson's disease. *Disability and Rehabilitation*, 39(6), 594–600.

Stevens, C., & Gallagher, M. (2004). The development of mental models for auditory events: Relational complexity and discrimination of pitch and duration. *British Journal of Developmental Psychology*, 22, 569–583.

Stewart, N. A. J., & Lonsdale, A. J. (2016). It's better together: The psychological benefits of singing in a choir. *Psychology of Music*, 44(6), 1240–1254.

Street, A., Young, S., Tafuri, J., & Ilari, B. (2003). Mothers' attitudes to singing to their infants. In R. Kopiez, A. C. Lehmann, I. Wolther, and C. Wolf (Eds.), *Proceedings of the 5th Triennial ESCOM Conference*, Hanover, pp. 628–631.

Subramaniam, P., & Woods, B. (2012). The impact of individual reminiscence therapy for people with dementia: Systematic review. *Expert Review of Neurotherapeutics*, 12(5), 545–555.

Sudnow, D. (2001). *Ways of the hand: A rewritten account*. Cambridge, MA: MIT Press.

Sundin, B. (1998). Musical creativity in childhood: A research project in retrospect. *Research Studies in Music Education*, 9(1), 48–57.

Sung, H. C., Chang, A. M., & Lee, W. L. (2010). A preferred music listening intervention to reduce anxiety in older adults with dementia in nursing homes. *Journal of Clinical Nursing*, 19(7–8), 1056–1064.

Sutton-Smith , B. S. (1997). *The ambiguity of play*. Boston, MA: Harvard University Press.

Swanwick, K. (1998). *Music, mind, and education*. London: Routledge.

Swanwick, K., & Runfola, M. (2002). Developmental characteristics of learners. In R. Colwell & C. P. Richardson (Eds.), *New handbook of research on music teaching and learning* (pp. 373–397). Oxford: Oxford University Press.

Swanwick, K., & Tillman, J. (1986). The sequence of musical development: A study of children's composition. *British Journal of Music Education*, 6, 305–339.

Tafuri, J. (2008). *Infant musicality: New research for educators and parents*. Farnham, Surrey: Ashgate Publishing Limited.

Tafuri, J. (2017). Building musical self-identity in early infancy. In R. A. R. MacDonald, D. J. Hargreaves, & D. E. Miell (Eds.), *Handbook of musical identities* (pp. 197–212). Oxford: Oxford University Press.

Tafuri, J., & Villa, D. (2002). Musical elements in the vocalisations of infants aged 2–8 months. *British Journal of Music Education*, 19(1), 73–88.

Tajfel, H. (Ed.) (1978). *Differentiation between social groups: Studies in the social psychology of intergroup relations*. London: Academic Press.

Tajfel, H., & Turner, J. C. (1986). An integrative theory of intergroup conflict. In S. Worchel & W. G. Austin (Eds.), *Social psychology of intergroup relations* (pp. 2–24). Chicago, IL: Nelson-Hall.

Tajfel, H., Billig, M. G., Bundy, R. P., & Flament, C. (1971). Social categorization and intergroup behaviour. *European Journal of Social Psychology*, 1(2), 149–178.

Takeuchi, A. H., & Hulse, S. H. (1993). Absolute pitch. *Psychological Bulletin*, 113(2), 345–361.

Tarrant, M., Calitri, R., & Weston, D. (2012). Social identification structures the effects of perspective taking. *Psychological Science*, 23(9), 973–978.

Tarrant, M., North, A. C., & Hargreaves, D. J. (2000). English and American adolescents' reasons for listening to music. *Psychology of Music*, 28, 166–173.

Tarrant, M., North, A. C., & Hargreaves, D. J. (2001). Social categorization, self-esteem, and the estimated musical preferences of male adolescents. *Journal of Social Psychology*, 141(5), 565–581.

Tarrant, M., North, A. C., & Hargreaves, D. J. (2002). Youth identity and music. In R. A. R. MacDonald, D. J. Hargreaves, & D. E. Miell (Eds.), *Musical identities* (pp. 134–151). Oxford: Oxford University Press.

Tarrant, M., North, A. C., Edridge, M. D., Kirk, L. E., Smith, E. A., & Turner, R. E. (2001). Social identity in adolescence. *Journal of Adolescence*, 24(5), 597–609.

Taylor, A. (2010). Older amateur keyboard players learning for self-fulfilment. *Psychology of Music*, 39(3), 345–363.

Taylor, S. (1969). Development of children aged seven to eleven. *Journal of Research in Music Education*, 17(1), 100–107.

Teater, B., & Baldwin, M. (2012). Singing for successful ageing: The perceived benefits of participating in the Golden Oldies Community-Arts Programme. *British Journal of Social Work*, 44(1), 81–99.

Temperley, D. (2003). End-accented phrases: An analytical exploration. *Journal of Music Theory*, 47(1), 125–154.

Ter Bogt, T. F. M., Vieno, A., Doornwaard, S. M., Pastore, M., & van den Eijnden, J. J. M. (2016). 'You're not alone': Music as a source of consolation among adolescents and young adults. *Psychology of Music*, 45(2), 155–171.

Terhardt, E. (1984). The concept of musical consonance: A link between music and psycho-acoustics. *Music Perception*, 1, 276–295.

Terwogt, M. M., & van Grinsven, F. (1991). Musical expression of moodstates. *Psychology of Music*, 19, 99–109.

Tew, S., Fujioka, T., He, C., & Trainor, L. (2009). Neural representation of transposed melody in infants at 6 months of age. *Annals of the New York Academy of Sciences, The Neurosciences and Music III: Disorders and Plasticity*, 1169, 287–290.

Tharp, R., & Gallimore, R. (1991). A theory of teaching as assisted performance. In P. Light, S. Sheldon, & M. Woodhead (Eds.), *Learning to think*, (pp. 42–62). London: Routledge, in association with the Open University.

Theorell, T., & Kreutz, G. (2012). Epidemiological studies of the relationship between musical experiences and public health. In R. A. R. MacDonald, G. Kreutz, & L. Mitchell (Eds.), *Music, health, & wellbeing* (pp. 424–435). Oxford: Oxford University Press.

Thompson, E. C., White-Schwoch, T., Tierney, A., & Kraus, N. (2015). Beat synchronization across the lifespan: Intersection of development and musical experience. *PLoS ONE*, 10(6): e0128839, DOI: 10.1371/journal.pone.0128839.

Thompson, W. F., Schellenberg, E. G., & Husain, G. (2001). Arousal, mood, and the Mozart Effect. *Psychological Science*, 12(3), 248–251.

Thorpe, L. A., & Trehub, S. E. (1989). The duration illusion and auditory grouping in infancy. *Developmental Psychology*, 25, 122–127.

Torff, B., & Winner, E. (1994). Don't throw out the baby with the bathwater. Open peer commentary on 'Is everyone musical?', by J. A. Sloboda, J. W. Davidson, & M. J. A. Howe. *The Psychologist*, 7(8), 361–362.

Torrance, E. P. (1967). *Understanding the fourth grade slump in creative thinking.* US Office of Education Report.

Torrance, E. P. (1974). *The Torrance tests of creative thinking: Technical-norms manual.* Bensenville, IL.: Scholastic Testing Services.

Trainor, L. J. (1996). Infant preferences for infant-directed versus noninfant-directed play-songs and lullabies. *Infant Behavior and Development,* 19, 83–92.

Trainor, L. J. (2005). Are there critical periods for musical development? *Developmental Psychobiology,* 46, 262–278.

Trainor, L. J., & Heinmiller, B. M. (1998). The development of evaluative responses to music: Infants prefer to listen to consonance over dissonance. *Infant Behavior and Development,* 21(1), 77–88.

Trainor, L. J., & Trehub, S. E. (1992). A comparison of infants' and adults' sensitivity to Western musical structures. *Journal of Experimental Psychology: Human Perception and Performance,* 18(2), 394–402.

Trainor, L. J., & Trehub, S. E. (1994). Key membership and implied harmony in Western tonal music: Developmental perspectives. *Perception and Psychophysics,* 56, 125–132.

Trainor, L. J., & Zacharias, C. A. (1998). Infants prefer higher-pitched singing. *Infant Behavior and Development,* 21, 799–805.

Trainor, L. J., Clark, E. D., Huntley, A., & Adams, B. A. (1997). The acoustic basis of preferences for infant-directed singing. *Infant Behavior and Development,* 20(3), 383–396.

Trainor, L. J., Tsang, C. D., & Cheung, V. H. W. (2002). Preference for sensory consonance in 2- and 4-month-old infants. *Music Perception,* 20, 187–194.

Trainor, L. J., Wu, L., & Tsang, C. D. (2004). Long-term memory for music: Infants remember tempo and timbre. *Developmental Science,* 7(3), 289–296.

Trautwein, U., Kastens, C., & Köller, O. (2006a) Effort on homework in grades 5–9: Development, motivational antecedents, and the association with effort on classwork. *Child Development,* 77(4), 1094–1111.

Trautwein, U., Ludtke, O., Schnyder, I., & Niggli, A. (2006b). Predicting homework effort: Support for a domain-specific, multilevel homework model. *Journal of Educational Psychology,* 98(2), 438–456.

Trehub, S. E. (1990). The perception of musical patterns by human infants: The provision of similar patterns by their parents. In M. A. Berkley & W. C. Stebbins (Eds.), *Comparative perception, vol. 1, Basic mechanisms* (pp. 429–459). New York: Wiley.

Trehub, S. E. (2012). Behavioral methods in infancy: Pitfalls of single measures. *Annals of the New York Academy of Sciences, Issue: The Neurosciences and Music IV: Learning and Memory,* 1252, 37–42.

Trehub, S. E. (2016). Infant musicality. In S. Hallam, I. Cross, & M. Thaut (Eds.), *The Oxford handbook of music psychology,* 2nd ed. (pp. 387–397). Oxford: Oxford University Press.

Trehub, S. E. & Degé, F. (2016). Reflections on infants as musical connoisseurs. In G. McPherson (Ed.), *The child as musician: A handbook of musical development.* Oxford: Oxford University Press.

Trehub, S. E., & Hannon, E. E. (2009). Conventional rhythms enhance infants' and adults' perceptions of musical patterns. *Cortex,* 45, 110–118.

Trehub, S. E., Cohen, A. J., Thorpe, L. A., & Morrongiello, B. A. (1986). Development of the perception of musical relations: Semitone and diatonic structure. *Journal of Experimental Psychology: Human Perception and Performance,* 12, 295–301.

Trehub, S. E., Ghazban, N., & Corbeil, M. (2015). Musical affect regulation in infancy. *Annals of the New York Academy of Sciences,* 1337, 186–192.

Trehub, S. E., Schellenberg, E. G., & Kamenetsky, S. B. (1999). Infants' and adults' perception of scale structure. *Journal of Experimental Psychology: Human Perception & Performance*, 25, 965–975.

Trehub, S. E., Schellenberg, E. G., & Nakata, T. (2008). Cross-cultural perspectives on pitch memory. *Journal of Experimental Child Psychology*, 100(1), 40–52.

Trehub, S. E., Schneider, B. A., & Henderson, J. L. (1995). Gap detection in infants, children, and adults. *Journal of the Acoustical Society of America*, 98(5), 2532–2541.

Trehub, S. E., Thorpe, L. A., & Morrongiello, B. A., (1985). Infants' perception of melodies: Changes in a single tone. *Infant Behavior and Development*, 8, 213–223.

Trehub, S. E., Thorpe, L. A., & Morrongiello, B. A., (1987). Organizational processes in infants' perception of auditory patterns. *Child Development*, 58, 741–749.

Trehub, S. E., Thorpe, L. A., & Trainor, L. J. (1990). Infants' perception of *good* and *bad* melodies. *Psychomusicology*, 9(1), 5–19.

Trehub, S. E., Unyk, A. M., Kamenetsky, S. B., Hill, D. S., Trainor, L. J., Henderson, J. L., et al. (1997). Mothers' and fathers' singing to infants. *Developmental Psychology*, 33, 500–507.

Trevarthen, C. (1999). Musicality and the intrinsic motive pulse: Evidence from human psychobiology and infant communication. *Musicae Scientiae, Special Issue (1999–2000)*, 155–215.

Trevarthen, C. (2002). Origins of musical identity: Evidence from infancy for musical social awareness. In R. A. R. MacDonald, D. J. Hargreaves, & D. E. Miell (Eds.), *Musical identities* (pp. 21–38). Oxford: Oxford University Press.

Trevarthen, C. (2012) Communicative musicality: The human impulse to create and share music. In D. J. Hargreaves, D. E. Miell, & R. MacDonald (Eds.), *Musical imaginations* (pp. 259–284). Oxford: Oxford University Press.

Trevarthen, C., & Aitken, K. J. (2001). Infant intersubjectivity: Research, theory and clinical applications. *Annual Research Review, Journal of Child Psychology and Psychiatry*, 42(1), 3–48.

Trevarthen, C., & Malloch, S. (2017). The musical self: Affections for life in a community of sound. In R. A. R. MacDonald, D. J. Hargreaves, & D. E. Miell (Eds.), *Handbook of musical identities* (pp. 155–175). Oxford: Oxford University Press.

Tsang, C. D., & Conrad, N. J. (2010). Does the message matter? The effect of song type on infants' pitch preferences for lullabies sand playsongs. *Infant Behavior and Development*, 33, 96–100.

UNICEF (2007). *Child poverty in perspective: An overview of child well-being in rich countries: A comprehensive assessment of the lives and well-being of children and adolescents in the economically advanced nations.* Innocenti Report Card, Vol. 7. Florence, Italy: UNICEF Innocenti Research Centre.

Vaag, J., Saksvik, P. Ø., Milch, V., Theorell, T., & Bjerkeset, O. (2014). 'Sound of Well-being' revisited: Choir singing and well-being among Norwegian municipal employees. *Journal of Applied Arts & Health*, 5(1), 51–63.

Valentine, E., & Evans, C. (2001). The effects of solo singing, choral singing and swimming on mood and physiological indices. *British Journal of Medical Psychology*, 74, 115–120.

Vallerand, R. J. (1997). Toward a hierarchical model of intrinsic and extrinsic motivation. *Advances in experimental social psychology*, 29, 271–360.

Vallerand, R. J., & Ratelle, C. F. (2002). Intrinsic and extrinsic motivation: A hierarchical model. *Handbook of self-determination research*, 128, 37–63.

Van Hedger, S. C., Heald, S. L. M., Koch, R., & Nusbaum, H. C. (2015). Auditory working memory predicts individual differences in absolute pitch learning. *Cognition*, 140, 95–110.

Van Noorden, L. (2014). Auto-correlation and entrainment in the synchronous reproduction of musical pulse: Developments in childhood. *Procedia – Social and Behavioral Sciences*, 126, 117–118.

Vandervert, L. (2016a). Working memory in musical prodigies: A 10,000-year-old story, one million years in the making. In G. E. McPherson (Ed.), *Musical prodigies: Interpretations from psychology, education, musicology, and ethnomusicology* (pp. 223–244). Oxford: Oxford University Press.

Vandervert, L. (2016b). The brain's rapid encoding of rule-governed domains of knowledge: A case analysis of a musical prodigy. In G. E. McPherson (Ed.), *Musical prodigies: Interpretations from psychology, education, musicology, and ethnomusicology* (pp. 245–257). Oxford: Oxford University Press.

Vanstone, A. D., & Cuddy, L. L. (2010). Musical memory in Alzheimer disease. *Aging, neuropsychology and cognition: A Journal on Normal and Dysfunctional Development*, 17(1), 108–128.

Varela, W., Abrami, P. C., & Upitis, R. (2016). Self-regulation and music learning: A systematic review. *Psychology of Music*, *44*(1), 55–74.

Vaughan, M. M. (1977). Musical creativity: Its cultivation and measurement. *Bulletin of the Council for Research in Music Education*, 50, 72–77.

Vaughan, M. D., & Rodriguez, E. M. (2013). The influence of Erik Erikson on positive psychology theory and research. In J. D. Sinnott (Ed.), *Positive psychology: Advances in understanding adult motivation* (pp. 231–245). New York: Springer.

Verghese, J., Upton, R. B., Katz, M. J., Hall, C. B., Derby, C. A., Kuslansky, G., et al. (2003). Leisure activities and the risk of dementia in the elderly. *The New England Journal of Medicine*, 348(25), 2508–2516.

Vink, A. C., Bruinsma, M. S., & Scholtern, R. J. P. M. (2003). Music therapy for people with dementia. *Cochrane Database of Systematic Reviews*, 4. DOI: 10.1002/14651858.D003477.pub2.

Volkova, A., Trehub, S. E., Schellenberg, E. G., Papsin, B. C., & Gordon, K. A. (2014). Children's identification of familiar songs from pitch and timing cues. *Frontiers in Psychology*, 5, 863, DOI: 10.3389/fpsyg.2014.00863.

Von Lob, G., Camic, P., & Clift, S. (2010). The use of singing in a group as a response to adverse life events. *International Journal of Mental Health Promotion*, 12(3), 45–53.

Vongpaisal, T., Trehub, S. E., & Schellenberg, E. G. (2009). Identification of TV tunes by children with cochlear implants. *Music Perception*, 27(1), 17–24.

Vygotsky, L. S. (1956). *Selected psychological investigations*. Moscow: Izdatel'stvo Akademii Pedagogicheskikh Nauk.

Vygotsky, L. S. (1966). Genesis of the higher mental functions (abridged translation). In P. H. Light, S. Sheldon, & M. Woodhead (1991). *Learning to think* (pp. 32–41). London: Routledge and Open University Press.

Vygotsky, L. S. (1978). *Mind in society: The development of higher psychological processes*. London: Harvard University Press.

Walker, R. (2006). Cultural traditions. In G. E. McPherson (Ed.), *The child as musician* (pp. 439–460). Oxford: Oxford University Press.

Wan, C. Y., & Schlaug, G. (2010). Music-making as a tool for promoting brain plasticity across the lifespan. *The Neuroscientist*, 16(5), 566–577.

Ward, C. D., & Cooper, R. P. (1999). A lack of evidence in 4-month-old human infants for paternal voice preference. *Developmental Psychobiology*, 35(1), 49–59.

Webster, P. R. (1979). Relationship between creative behavior in music and selected variables as measured in high school students. *Journal of Research in Music Education*, 27, 227–242.

Webster, P. R. (1987). Conceptual bases for creative thinking in music. In *Music and child development* (pp. 158–174). New York: Springer.

Webster, P. R. (1994). *Measure of Creative Thinking in Music (MCTM): Administrative Guidelines*. Peter Webster.

Webster, P. R., & Hickey, M. (1995). Rating scales and their use in assessing children's music compositions. *Quarterly Journal of Music Teaching and Learning*, 6, 28–44.

Weiner, B. (1985). An attributional theory of achievement motivation and emotion. *Psychological Review*, 92(4), 548–573.

Weiner, B. (1992). *Human motivation: Metaphors, theories, and research*. Thousand Oaks: Sage Publications.

Weinstein, D. (1991). *Heavy metal: A cultural sociology*. New York: Lexington.

Weisberg, R. W. (1993). *Creativity: Beyond the myth of genius*. New York: W.H. Freeman.

Welch, G. F. (2005). We are musical. *International Journal of Music Education*, 23(2), 117–120.

Welch, G. F. (2012). Musical creativity, biography, genre and learning. In D. J. Hargreaves, D. E Miell, & R. A. R. MacDonald (Eds.), *Musical imaginations* (pp. 385–398). Oxford: Oxford University Press.

Welch, G., & Ockelford, A. (2016). The role of the institution and teachers in supporting learning. In S. Hallam, I. Cross, & M. Thaut (Eds.), *The Oxford handbook of music psychology* (2nd edition, pp. 509–526). Oxford: Oxford University Press.

Wenger, E. (1998). *Communities of practice: Learning, meaning and identity*. New York: Cambridge University Press.

Wenger, E., McDermott, R., & Snyder, W. M. (2002). *Cultivating communities of practice*. Boston, MA: Harvard Business School Press.

Werker, J. F., & Lalonde, C. E. (1988). Cross-language speech perception: Initial capabilities and developmental change. *Developmental Psychology*, 24, 672–683.

Wertsch, J. V. (1997). *Mind as action*. Oxford: Oxford University Press.

West Marvin, E., & Brinkman, A. (1999). The effect of modulation and formal manipulation on perception of tonic closure by expert listeners. *Music Perception*, 16(4), 389–408.

Westerlund, H., Partti, H., & Karlsen, S. (2017). Identity formation and agency in the diverse music classroom. In R. A. R. MacDonald, D. J. Hargreaves, & D. E. Miell (Eds.), *Handbook of musical identities* (pp. 493–509). Oxford: Oxford University Press.

Wexler-Sherman, C., Gardner, H., & Feldman, D. H. (1988). A pluralistic view of early assessment: The Project Spectrum approach. *Theory into Practice*, 27, 77–83.

Whitebread, D. (2013). Self-regulation in young children: Its characteristics and the role of communication and language in its early development. *Self-regulation and dialogue in primary classrooms. British Journal of Educational Psychology Monograph series II: Psychological aspects of education–current trends*, (10), 25–44.

Whitebread, D., Coltman, P., Pasternak, D. P., Sangster, C., Grau, V., Bingham, S. I., Almeqdad, Q., & Demetriou, D. (2009). The development of two observational tools for assessing metacognition and self-regulated learning in young children. *Metacognition & Learning*, 4, 63–85.

Wiggins, J. (2016). Musical agency. In G. E McPherson (Ed.), *The child as musician: A handbook of musical development* (2nd edition, pp. 102–121). Oxford: Oxford University Press.

Williamon, A. (Ed.) (2004). *Musical excellence: Strategies and techniques to enhance performance.* Oxford: Oxford University Press.

Williams, F. E. (1976). Rediscovering the fourth-grade slump in a study of children's self-concept. *Journal of Creative Behavior*, 10, 15–28.

Wilson, G. D. (2002). *Psychology for performing artists* (2nd edition). London: Whurr.

Winkler, I., Háden, G. P., Ladinig, O., Sziller, I., & Honing, H. (2009). Newborn infants detect the beat in music. *Proceedings of the National Academy of Sciences, U.S.A.*,106, 2468–2471, DOI: 10.1073/pnas.0809035106.

Winner, E. (1997). *Gifted children: Myths and realities.* New York: Basic Books.

Winner, E, Rosenstiel, A. & Gardner, H. (1976). The development of metaphor understanding. *Developmental Psychology*, 12, 289–297.

Winner, E., Rosenblatt, E., Windmueller, G., Davidson, L., & Gardner, H. (1986). Children's perception of 'aesthetic' properties of the arts: Domain-specific or pan–artistic? *British Journal of Developmental Psychology*, 4, 149–160.

Winstone, N., & Witherspoon, K. (2016). 'It's all about our great Queen': The British national anthem and national identity in 8–10 year-old children. *Psychology of Music*, 44(2), 263–277.

Wise, K. J., & Sloboda, J. A. (2008). Establishing an empirical profile of self-defined 'tone deafness': Perception, singing performance and self-assessment. *Musicae Scientiae*, 12, 3–23.

Wolf, D. P., & Gardner, H. (1981). On the structure of early symbolisation. In R. Schiefelbusch & D. Bricker (Eds.), *Early language intervention* (pp. 287–329). Baltimore, MD: University Park Press.

Wolf, D. P. (1998a). Artistic learning: what and where is it? *Journal of Aesthetic Education*, 22, 143–155.

Wolf, D. P. (1998b). Opening up assessment: ideas from the arts. *Educational Leadership*, 45, 24–29.

Wood, D. J., Bruner, J., & Ross, G. (1976). The role of tutoring in problem solving. *Journal of Child Psychology and Psychiatry*, 17, 89–100.

Woods-Townsend, K., Bagust, L., Barker, M., Chrisodoulou, A., Davey, H., Godfrey, K., Grace, M., Griffiths, J., Hanson, M., & Inskip, H. (2015). Engaging teenagers in improving their health behaviours and increasing their interest in science (Evaluation of LifeLab Southampton): Study protocol for a cluster randomized controlled trial. *Trials*, 16, 372.

Wynn Parry, C. (2004). Managing the physical demands of musical performance. In A. Williamon (Ed.), *Musical excellence: Strategies and techniques to enhance performance* (pp. 41–60). Oxford: Oxford University Press.

Yamasaki, T. (2004). Emotional communication through music performance played by young children. In S. D. Lipscomb, R. Ashley, R. O. Gjerdingen, & P. Webster (Eds.), *Proceedings of the 8th International Conference on Music Perception and Cognition* (pp. 204–206), Evanston, IL, USA.

Yang, J., McClelland, A., & Furnham, A. (2016). The effect of background music on the cognitive performance of musicians: A pilot study. *Psychology of Music*, 44(5), 1202–1208.

York, N. (2000). *Valuing school music: A report on school music.* London: University of Westminster and RockSchool Ltd.

Young. S. (2005). Musical communication between adults and young children. In D. E. Miell, R. A. R. MacDonald, & D. J. Hargreaves (Eds.), *Musical communication* (pp. 281–299). Oxford: Oxford University Press.

Young, S. (2008). Collaboration between 3- and 4-year-olds in self-initiated play on instruments. *International Journal of Educational Research*, 47(1), 3–10.

Young, S. (2012). Theorizing musical childhoods with illustrations from a study of girls' karaoke use at home. *Research Studies in Music Education*, 34(2), 113–127.

Young, S. (2016). Early childhood music education research: A review. *Research Studies in Music Education*, 38(1), 9–21.

Young, S., & Rowe, V. (2012). Young children's improvisations on a keyboard: How might reflexive technologies support the process of learning to improvise? In E. Cambouropoulos, C. Tsougras, P. Mavromatis, & K. Pastiadis (Eds.), *Proceedings of the 12th international Conference on Music Perception and Cognition and the 8th Triennial Conference of the European Society for the Cognitive Sciences of Music* (pp. 1162–1163). Thessaloniki: University of Thessaloniki.

Young, S., Street, A., & Davies, E. (2006). *The Music One2One Project: Final report.* University of Exeter, available online at http://education.exeter.ac.uk/music-one2one/, accessed 30 September 2006.

Zachariou, A. (2014). *An exploration of 6- and 8-year-old children's self-regulatory behaviours during musical play sessions in Cypriot primary schools.* Unpublished PhD. Thesis, University of Cambridge.

Zajonc, R. B. (1968). Attitudinal effects of mere exposure. *Journal of Personality and Social Psychology*, 9, Monograph Supplement 2, 1–21.

Zapata Restrepo, G. P., & Hargreaves, D. J. (2017). Musical identities, resilience and wellbeing: The effects of music on displaced children in Colombia. In D. J. Hargreaves, R. A. R. MacDonald, & D. E. Miell (Eds.), *Handbook of musical identities* (pp. 736–750). Oxford: Oxford University Press.

Zatorre, R. J., & Baum, S. R. (2012). Musical melody and speech intonation: Singing a different tune? *PLoS Biology*, 10(7), e1001372, DOI: 10.1371/journal.pbio.1001372.

Zatorre., R. J., & Halpern, A. R. (2005). Mental concerts: Musical imagery and auditory cortex. *Neuron*, 47(1), 9–12.

Zatorre, R. J., & Salimpoor, V. N. (2013). From perception to pleasure: Music and its neural substrates. *Proceedings of the National Academy of Sciences*, 110 (suppl.2), 10430–10437.

Zentner, M. R., & Kagan, J. (1998). Infants' perception of consonance and dissonance in music. *Infant Behavior & Development*, 21(3), 483–492.

Zentner, M. R., Grandjean, D., & Scherer, K. R. (2008). Emotions evoked by the sound of music: Characterization, classification, and measurement. *Emotion*, 8, 494–521.

Zentner, M., & Eerola, T. (2010). Self-report measures and models. In P. N. Juslin & J. A. Sloboda (Eds.), *Handbook of music and emotion: Theory, research, applications* (pp. 187–221). Oxford: Oxford University Press.

Zeserson, K, Welch, G., Burn, S., Saunders, J., & Himonides, E. (2014). *Inspiring music for all: Next steps in innovation, improvement and integration.* London: Paul Hamlyn Foundation.

Zhao, T. C., & Kuhl, P. K. (2016). Musical intervention enhances infants' neural processing of temporal structure in music and speech. *Proceedings of the National Academy of Sciences*, 113 (19), 5212–5217, DOI: 10.1073/pnas.1603984113.

Zimmerman, B. J. (2000). Attaining self-regulation: A social cognitive perspective. In M. Boekaerts, P. R. Pintrich, & M. Zeidner (Eds.), *Handbook of self-regulation* (pp. 13–39). San Diego, CA: Academic Press.

Ziv, N., & Goshen, M. (2006). The effect of 'sad' and 'happy' background music on the interpretation of a story in 5 to 6-year-old children. *British Journal of Music Education*, 23(3), 303–314.

Index